Data Structures, Algorithms, and Program Style

James F. Korsh

Temple University

PWS COMPUTER SCIENCE
Boston

PWS PUBLISHERS

Prindle, Weber & Schmidt · ♣ · Duxbury Press · ♠ · PWS Engineering · ⚠ · Breton Publishers · ⚙
Statler Office Building · 20 Park Plaza · Boston, Massachusetts 02116

PWS Publishers is a division of Wadsworth, Inc.

Library of Congress Cataloging-in-Publication Data
Korsh, James F.
    Data structures, algorithms, and program style.

    Includes index.
    1. Data structures (Computer science) I. Title.
QA76.9.D35K67 1986   005.7′3   85–16873
ISBN 0–87150–936–9

ISBN 0-87150-936-9

Printed in the United States of America
86 87 88 89 90 — 10 9 8 7 6 5 4 3 2 1

Sponsoring Editor: Bob Prior
Signing Representative: Jack Fox
Editorial Assistant: Jane Parker
Developmental Editor: Veronica Dort
Production Editor: Ellie Connolly
Manuscript Editor: Cynthia Insolio Benn
Interior Design: Ellie Connolly
Cover Design: Julie Gecha
Interior Illustration: George Nichols
Typesetting: Beacon Graphics Corporation
Cover Printing: New England Book Components, Inc.
Printing and Binding: Halliday Lithographic

One must learn by doing the thing,
for though you can think you know it
you have no certainty until you try it.

Sophocles

Preface

This text is intended for use in the just revised second programming course, CS2 in the curriculum of the Association for Computing Machinery, as well as data structures courses such as CS7 of the ACM curriculum, and independent study. A knowledge of the Pascal programming language is the only prerequisite. All programs appear in Pascal, although the concepts and methods presented are independent of the language used. The text emphasizes current techniques for the creation and testing of a program. The text stresses writing programs that are general enough to be readily adapted for use in the solution of related problems or more complex problems. This technique of program adaptation is consistently applied. Other basic programming paradigms presented are: the top-down approach, recursion (as a special case of the top-down approach), a search or traversal through the set of all solutions, and the direct construction of a solution. Sophisticated concepts are presented in a clear, informal way, theory always being coupled with concrete practical examples.

In terms of organization, the table of contents speaks for itself, but a few comments may prove helpful.

Chapters 1 to 6 deal with the fundamental concepts of program and data structure. Combined with selected topics from Chapter 7, they provide more than enough subject matter for CS2, the second programming course. Some instructors may wish to include or substitute topics from later chapters.

Chapters 7 to 12 deal with important and illustrative applications of the earlier concepts and introduce advanced data structures. They contain enough material for a solid data structures course. Many of the case studies from earlier chapters might profitably be presented in such a course. Chapters 8 to 12 may be covered in arbitrary order, with the preceding chapters serving as a quick review of the basics.

Considerable care has been taken to include sets of exercises that are graduated in degree of complexity or difficulty. Also included are suggested assignments that incorporate essential concepts of each chapter. You will find that each program is thoroughly discussed. For the most part, however, it is up to the reader to combine structural components to achieve an executable program. Thus a student must understand the program in order to use it.

Several analogies are useful in explaining structured programming. Knowing the grammar of a language does not ensure quality writing. Learning to write well entails internalizing principles of good style and is an advanced task beyond simply learning a language. In the same way, learning to write good programs requires skill in the use of a wide range of tools, and involves much more than acquiring a language. When the master mechanic opens the hood of a well-designed automobile, he doesn't see just a jumble of wires and metal, but essential components properly linked and aligned. The knowledgeable programmer should be able to see at a glance the major components and linkages of a finely crafted program. Such a program consists of many threads carefully interwoven to support the whole. A weak thread can have serious consequences, yet the replacement of a thread must not cause the structure to unravel. Program structure enhances or obscures a program's intelligibility, while efficiency is determined by the details of a program's parts.

This book demonstrates the tools needed to craft fine programs and to solve substantial problems. These tools, although few in number, must be used with care and forethought. The tool kit includes the basic paradigms for problem solving, for structuring programs, and for structuring data. Their proper use involves data abstraction, modularization, and the intelligent choice of data structure. This text stresses the entire process of program development, and will enable you to write a well-designed program and to recognize one when you see it. At the same time, you will develop insight into program analysis, learning how to analyze programs in order to determine their correctness and efficiency.

Many individuals contributed to this book. Pam Bennett typed the manuscript. Colleagues and students deserving special thanks are Frank Friedman, Len Garrett, Mordechai Halpern, Giorgio Ingargiola, Elliot Koffman, Seymour Lipschutz, Alex Pelin, Artur Ramer, Jan Stone, Judy Weiner, Brad Wilson, Sharon Doherty, Dan Joyce, Bob Mulholland, Regis McKenzie, Ken Sall, Judy Stull, and Jane Turk.

The staff of PWS Publishers, including Ellie Connolly, Veronica Dort, Karin Ellison, and Bob Prior, all provided valuable support and guidance. The technical editing of Cynthia Insolio Benn was a particular blessing. It is also a delight to acknowledge the painstaking and helpful work of the reviewers: John Beidler, University of Scranton; Sudesh Bhatia, Middlesex Community College; John Davenport, Georgia Southern College; Michael Donlavey, Boston College; Gary Ford, University of Colorado; William Ford, University of the Pacific; John Herman, Western Michigan University; Clyde Kruskal, University of Illinois; Steven Reiss, Brown University; Richard Schlichting, University of Arizona; Jan Stone and Harold Stone, The Interfactor, Inc.; Helen Takacs, Mississippi State University; Alan Tharp, North Carolina State University; Brad Wilson, Bowling Green State University; and Scott Woodfield, Arizona State University.

Harold Stone was kind enough to contribute the historical notes in Chapter 1 and Roger Webster provided the data for the table of sorting times in Chapter 7.

Finally, without the support of my wife, Nina, and my children, Eric, Aaron, and Joanna, it would have been impossible ever to finish the task of writing this book. Nina is also responsible for numerous improvements in the presentation. Any errors, of course, are due to the devil in us all.

Contents

APPLICATIONS ☐

1 Programming Structure

1.1 Structure: Data and Program

Two programs doing exactly the same task may look entirely different. One may be highly readable, concise, and easily adjusted to carry out related tasks. The other may be impenetrable, lengthy, and difficult to modify. The same two may differ so much in execution time and storage needs that one program executes while the other aborts, having exceeded time or space restrictions. Experience has shown such differences to be traceable to choice of program structure and data structure.

Programs are written to solve real problems. *Program structure* breaks the problem and its solution down into simpler, more easily understood parts. The information to be processed is stored in *data structures* (arrays, records, stacks, lists, trees, and files) provided by the programming language. A data structure groups data. The right data structure for an operation can make it simple and efficient; the wrong one can make the operation cumbersome and inefficient.

Data structures contain information and are operated on during the execution of a program. Programs are said to process information when, in fact, they process data structures. Thus it is not surprising that data and program structure are important and need to be properly related to achieve the goal of successful programming. How this is done is the subject of this book. The story is fascinating and sometimes involved, but it has a happy ending: you master practical programming techniques. These techniques provide the programmer with the means to keep a tight rein on programs so that they remain understandable and efficient even as they grow in size.

There is structure, then, in both the data and the program itself, and both program and data structure must be appropriate to their tasks. This book presents data structures, not as an isolated theoretical subject, but as an essential object of the problem-solving process leading to the creation of a good program. Three main themes are stressed.

1. Data structures and their impact on programs
2. Programming methodology and its impact on programs
3. Consolidation and extension of knowledge of a high-level language

Data structures are important because the way the programmer chooses to represent data significantly affects the clarity, conciseness, speed of execution, and storage requirements of the program. The text shows how to use particular data structures to create correct and efficient programs. You will see that the operations to be performed on the data determine the best data structures to use.

Developing programs is difficult, especially when done without good guidelines. Creating programs entails solving problems. *Top-down programming*, another name for *structured programming*, makes program development easier and leads to well-structured programs. It is the controlled breaking down of a complex task into simpler ones whose individual solutions easily combine to carry out the original task. This process gives structure to the development of programs, hence its name. The top-down, or structured, approach, combined with good programming style, is emphasized in this text. Elements of good programming style include the use of data abstractions and modularization, which significantly enhance the readability and changeability of programs.

Data abstraction treats a collection of data by abstracting its important aspects while ignoring as much detail as possible. A data abstraction reduces data to a collection, and to those processing operations directly allowed on that collection. The effect is as though the collection were in an impenetrable black box, the only access to the contents of the box being through the invocation of one or more of the allowed operations. How the collection is actually stored within the box, and how the operations are actually performed, become irrelevant details. Such details determine the efficiency of a program but do not affect its logic.

Modularization is the use of a special program unit to carry out a task. In FORTRAN such a unit would be a function or subroutine, while in Pascal it would be a function or procedure. These program units, or modules, are used to carry out each of the processing tasks of a data abstraction.

Practice may not make perfect but seems to be the best way to make problem solvers and programmers out of computer science students. As a student you must repeatedly practice creating programs, because it is repetition that facilitates learning. As in learning to dance, draw, or drive, no matter how closely you watch others perform, you can develop skills only by practice.

Finally, whatever high-level programming language you use, studying and understanding the material in this text will enhance your knowledge of that language and your ability to use it effectively. It is assumed the reader of this book is familiar with some high-level computer language. While such languages share many features, each is unique. Although upon occasion we indulge in comparative investigations in this text, all programs are written in Pascal.

1.2   A Look Ahead

A nucleus of commonly used data structures will be introduced. These include arrays and records, which are *static* structures that change only their values; and stacks, lists, trees, and files, which are *dynamic* structures, whose size and shape also change as well as their values. Specific ways to implement each structure will be explained and typical and important operations on them investigated. These operations include selection, traversal, insertion, deletion, searching, and sorting. Although particular methodologies and data structures are important, it is more important to acquire skill in applying a methodology and in determining which data structures are appropriate for a given problem.

Programs are built from data structures. Yet the methodology an expert programmer uses makes the data structures invisible and makes the program structure clear and understandable. Neither good program structure nor good data structure selection alone produces good programs. Both must be done well, but they cannot be done independently. Obtaining a good program requires a well-designed solution, expressed first as an algorithm. The final step is writing the program in a programming language.

Determining what information is required and how to store it for efficient use and processing is perhaps the most crucial aspect of the problem solving that is commonly called computer programming. The aim of this text is to illustrate good algorithm design, data structure selection, and programs.

If you do not know how to solve a given problem, then you cannot magically write a program to do so. In other words, if you don't know where you are going, then it makes no difference how you fail to get there. Moreover, as H. L. Mencken said, "Every complex problem has a simple easy-to-understand wrong answer." So before you begin writing a program you will need to understand the problem and write a step-by-step solution, or *algorithm*.

Unfortunately, there is no algorithm for finding algorithms. There isn't even an algorithm for checking a candidate to see if it really is an algorithm. But there are some useful techniques for developing algorithms. For example, it is useful to recognize when a known algorithm or program can be modified to give a solution to a new problem. One way to enhance this recognition is to solve problems in general or abstract terms. Sometimes a problem requires finding an object stored in computer memory that has certain properties. One technique is to search through the set of all objects until one with the desired properties is found. Alternatively, objects *without* the desired properties may be eliminated. This is the technique used to find a prime number algorithm in Section 1.3. At other times it may be possible to avoid searching altogether by constructing the desired object directly. Thinking up an algorithm is usually more difficult than programming it.

1.3   The Need for Structure

Imagine that you are a census taker charged with visiting all the homes in Spokesville and Squaresville (Figure 1.1). In each town, you must start and finish at home 1, after visiting each home once. All roads are the same length, and there are the same number of homes in each town. Nonetheless, in Spokesville you will travel a total

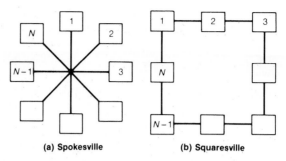

(a) Spokesville   (b) Squaresville

Figure 1.1   A Tale of Two Cities

distance exactly twice the distance required in Squaresville! The difference is due to structure.

It is easy to find the telephone number of a company whose name you know, even in the telephone directory of a large city. But finding the name of a company when you know only its telephone number is a tedious and time-consuming chore. The information in the telephone directory is structured so that one task is easy while the other causes tension headache and eyestrain!

(a) "For Better"

Figure 1.2   Two Maps (Maps courtesy: Hammond Incorporated, Maplewood, NJ 07040.)

Two maps of the continental United States appear in Figure 1.2. One gives a much clearer overall picture, while the other gives a more detailed view. Structure clarifies, and detail obscures. Still, both are needed for a complete picture. Notice that drawing a border around and naming each state, in the absence of other distracting details, makes the composition of the country discernible. It is the plethora of detail and lack of structure that is overwhelming in the other map. The less detailed map is analogous to a modularized program, the other to an unmodularized program.

An algorithm for a given problem specifies a series of operations to be performed that eventually leads to a correct result. Algorithms express solutions step by step. In stating an algorithm, care must be taken to avoid ambiguity and to be sure that it is clear how each step is to be done. When the solution is translated into a programming language for execution by a computer, even more care and attention to detail are needed. But first, the solution is usually expressed in English or flowchart form, before the details required by the programming language are introduced. The next example illustrates the effect of structure in this context.

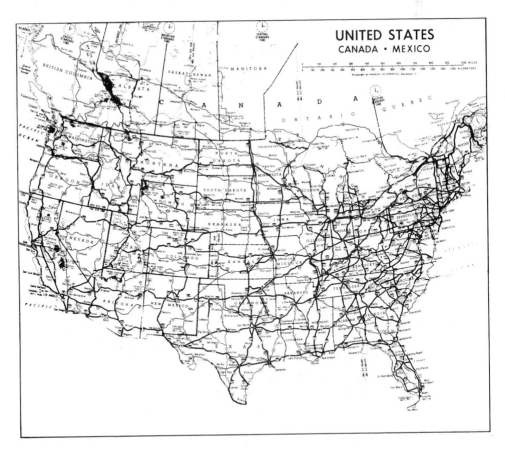

(b) "For Worse"

An integer larger than 1 is a *prime number* if it cannot be written as the product of two integers, each larger than 1. Suppose we must find a way to print all prime numbers between 2 and some integer N. Thus, if N is 12 these primes are 2, 3, 5, 7, and 11. Compare the following two algorithms for accomplishing this task.

<table>
<tr><th>PRIMES(N)</th><th>ANOTHERPRIMES(N)</th></tr>
<tr><td>

1. Create a collection C consisting of all integers from 2 to N.
2. Remove all nonprime integers from C.
3. Print all integers that remain in C.

</td><td>

1. Set $X_1, X_2, \ldots, X_N$ to zero.
2. Set K to 2.
3. If X_K is 1 go to step 7.
4. Print K.
5. Set M to the integer part of N/K.
6. Set $X_K, X_{2K}, \ldots, X_{MK}$ to 1.
7. Set K to K + 1.
8. If $K \leq \sqrt{N}$ go to step 3.
9. If X_K is zero, print K.
10. Set K to K + 1.
11. If $K \leq N$, go to step 9.

</td></tr>
</table>

It is not difficult to see that if each step of the first algorithm can be carried out, the correct result will be printed. It is considerably more difficult to see that the same is also true of the second algorithm. The first is structured to provide clarity, while the second is poorly structured and provides too much detail. These examples indicate why structure is needed in each stage of program design. Structured solutions are easier to understand, expand, and alter, and structured data make the operations of the algorithm easier and faster to perform.

1.3.1 Using Structure

Well-designed, clear programs are based on the explicit underlying methodology called **structured** programming. As problems and their solutions become more sophisticated, the brute-force or ad hoc method of programming becomes much less effective. Compilers, operating systems, business management systems, and word processing systems consist of many thousands of program statements. Just as writing a lengthy book is several magnitudes more difficult than writing a paragraph, so is the process of developing a large programming system much more involved than writing a short program. There must be an overall structure.

An example of a large and complex program is the operating system. Many years ago it was thought that operating systems could not be implemented without errors. The immensity of the task was believed to cause inherent problems that could not be isolated and debugged in advance of system implementation. Hence system failure seemed inevitable and getting the system up and running meant a long trial-and-error period of testing and debugging. A new methodology of system design based on the concept of structured programming has demonstrated, however, that error-free operating systems *are* possible.

Since the programs you see as a student may be relatively trivial, the need for a well-founded methodology of programming may not be evident. However, imagine a large program (twenty pages long, and over a thousand lines of program statements) that you did not write. If you were assigned the task of modifying the program to add a new feature, how or where would you start? Certainly you must have a full understanding of what the program does, how it does it, and how it relates to other programs that use it or are used by it. Anyone who intends to read, write, modify, or correct any programming systems with more than a few dozen statements should use structured programming.

1.3.2 A Prime Example

The example of prime numbers is presented here in more detail to illustrate the process and benefits of structuring. To do this, a program is developed from the prime number algorithm. Consider first a simple procedure.

```
procedure PRIMES(N : integer);
var
    C : collection;
begin
    CREATE(N, C);
    REMOVE(N, C);
    PRINT(N, C);
end;
```

Although the procedure PRIMES is not a program, it resembles one and may be obtained directly from the first of the previous prime number algorithms, PRIMES (N), when CREATE, REMOVE, and PRINT are interpreted as procedures carrying out steps 1, 2, and 3, respectively.

The next step is to refine and verify each procedure of PRIMES. *Refine* means to express or define in more detail; *verify* means to confirm that a refinement does indeed do its job. To refine and verify CREATE and PRINT is straightforward enough, but to refine and verify REMOVE is more difficult. If you want to know more about a state than you see in the first map of Figure 1.2, you may consult another map containing more information on the state's geography. Similarly, if you want to know how to carry out REMOVE, a more detailed description may be available. If not, as is the case here, REMOVE may be treated as a new problem whose solution must be found. One solution is this:

REMOVE(*N*, *C*)

Set FACTOR to the first prime.
While (nonprimes remain in *C*),
    Delete from *C* all integers that are multiples of FACTOR, and
    Increase FACTOR by 1.

It is again easy to see that, as long as each step is done correctly, the desired effect is obtained.

Still, more examination is needed to determine whether "nonprimes remain in *C*." A little thought should convince you that nonprimes remain in *C* only as long as FACTOR is no greater than $\sqrt{N}$. Consequently the condition (nonprimes remain in *C*) may be replaced by the condition (FACTOR $\leq \sqrt{N}$). But doing this will make REMOVE more difficult to understand. It is better to consider the evaluation of the condition as a new task that must be refined. We are now ready to write the procedure for REMOVE and to verify it. The three procedures appear in Figure 1.3, where INSERT adds I to the collection C, NONPRIMES is a function assumed to return the value true when FACTOR $\leq \sqrt{N}$ and false otherwise, DELETE removes all integers from C that are multiples of FACTOR, and BELONGS returns the value true if I is in C and false otherwise.

DELETE is refined next (Figure 1.3). You should verify that this procedure correctly performs its task as long as OMIT takes NEXTMULTIPLE out of C. It may help to simulate the execution of DELETE when N is 40 and FACTOR is 2, and then 3.

Each task of procedure PRIMES has now been defined and is, in fact, a complete Pascal procedure. PRIMES itself is lacking only the declaration for the type of collection. All other tasks, except for INSERT, BELONGS, and OMIT, have also been defined. PRIMES and all other tasks have been written **modularly,** meaning that for each task there is a module (a procedure or function). For example, new modules have been introduced for each of the three tasks of PRIMES: CREATE, REMOVE, and PRINT. Had PRIMES along with REMOVE and DELETE not been modularized, it would appear as follows:

```
procedure PRIMES(N : integer);
const
    FIRSTPRIME = 2;
var
    C : collection;
    I, FACTOR, NEXTMULTIPLE : integer;
begin
    for I := 2 to N do
        INSERT(I, C);
    FACTOR := FIRSTPRIME;
    while (FACTOR <= SQRT(N)) do
        begin
            NEXTMULTIPLE := 2 * FACTOR;
            while (NEXTMULTIPLE <= N) do
                begin
                    OMIT(NEXTMULTIPLE, C);
                    NEXTMULTIPLE := NEXTMULTIPLE + FACTOR
                end;
            FACTOR := FACTOR + 1
        end;
    for I := 2 to N do
        if (BELONGS(I, C)) then
            WRITELN(I)
end;
```

This version is also a refinement of PRIMES, but instead of defining new modules for its three tasks, the tasks have been replaced by *program segments*. Thus there are the two basic ways to refine any task.

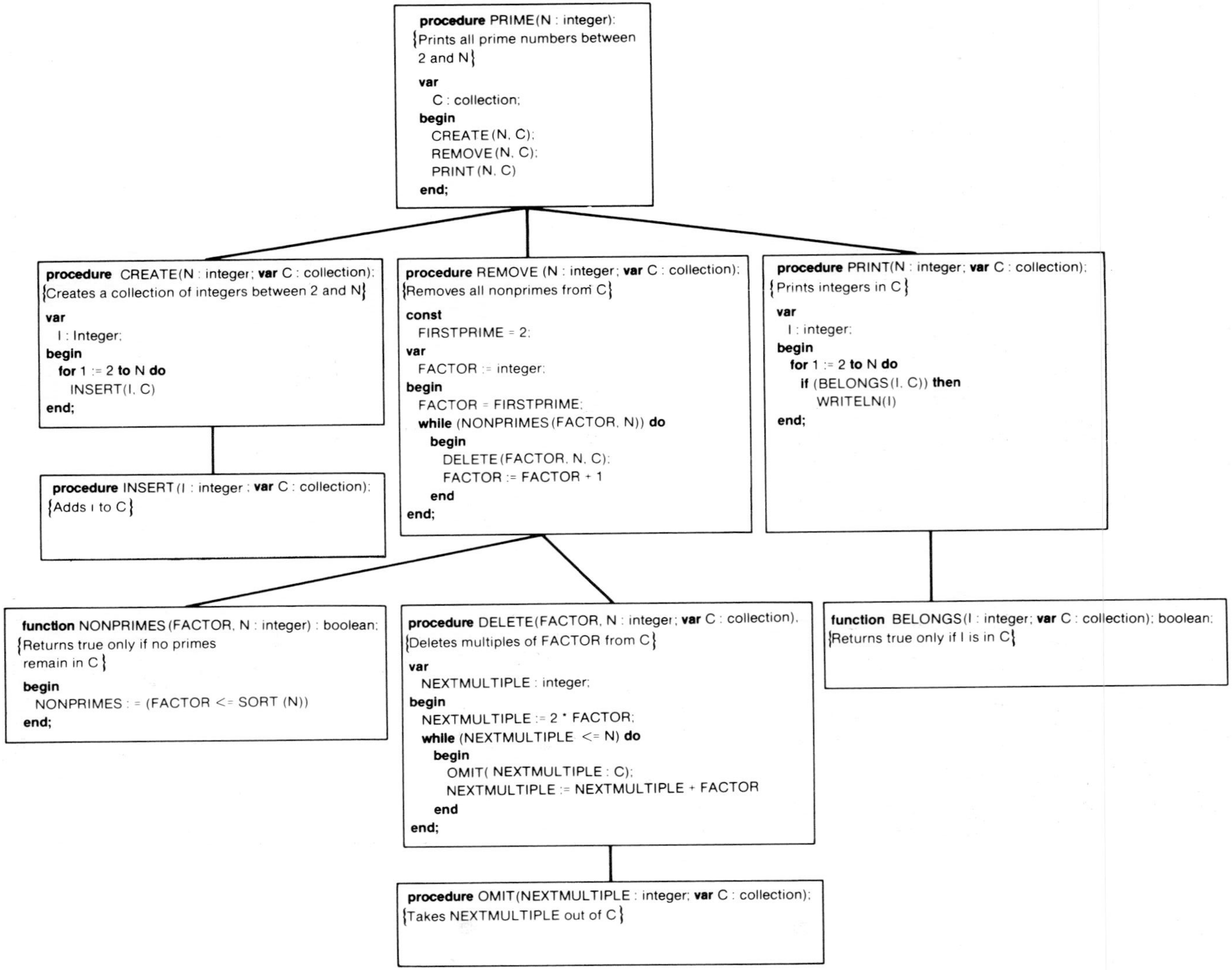
procedure PRIME(N : integer):
{Prints all prime numbers between 2 and N}
var
C : collection;
begin
CREATE(N, C);
REMOVE(N, C);
PRINT(N, C)
end;
procedure CREATE(N : integer; var C : collection):
{Creates a collection of integers between 2 and N}
var
I : Integer;
begin
for 1 := 2 to N do
INSERT(I, C)
end;
procedure REMOVE (N : integer; var C : collection):
{Removes all nonprimes from C}
const
FIRSTPRIME = 2;
var
FACTOR := integer;
begin
FACTOR = FIRSTPRIME;
while (NONPRIMES(FACTOR, N)) do
begin
DELETE(FACTOR, N, C);
FACTOR := FACTOR + 1
end
end;
procedure PRINT(N : integer; var C : collection);
{Prints integers in C}
var
I : integer;
begin
for 1 := 2 to N do
if (BELONGS(I, C)) then
WRITELN(I)
end;
procedure INSERT(I : integer ; var C : collection):
{Adds I to C}
function NONPRIMES(FACTOR, N : integer) : boolean;
{Returns true only if no primes remain in C}
begin
NONPRIMES : = (FACTOR <= SORT (N))
end;
procedure DELETE(FACTOR, N : integer; var C : collection).
{Deletes multiples of FACTOR from C}
var
NEXTMULTIPLE : integer;
begin
NEXTMULTIPLE := 2 * FACTOR;
while (NEXTMULTIPLE <= N) do
begin
OMIT(NEXTMULTIPLE : C);
NEXTMULTIPLE := NEXTMULTIPLE + FACTOR
end
end;
function BELONGS(I : integer; var C : collection); boolean;
{Returns true only if I is in C}
procedure OMIT(NEXTMULTIPLE : integer; var C : collection);
{Takes NEXTMULTIPLE out of C}

Figure 1.3 PRIMES Modularized

1. Define a new module for the task.

or

2. Replace the task directly by its refinement expressed as a program segment in code.

Compare this version with the modularized form, the simple procedure PRIMES given earlier. Notice that modularization suppresses detail.

Deciding how to modularize a program is often a matter of individual taste, but as this text unfolds, the process will become clearer, and you will be able to develop your own style. Modularization is intended to highlight and isolate important tasks. The advantage of using modules may not be apparent with this simple prime number problem but will be striking in more complex problems.

Finally, the low-level tasks INSERT, OMIT, and BELONGS must be coded. To do this requires deciding how to implement C — that is, deciding which data structures of Pascal shall be used to store C and how to write the basic modules that operate on C. Recall that data structures such as C contain information and are operated on during the execution of a program. No matter how C is implemented, none of the procedures or functions already defined need to be changed. They are independent of C's implementation (except for the declaration of collection). As long as INSERT, OMIT, and BELONGS do their tasks correctly, no module invoking them needs to be changed. This is because we have written them treating C as a *data abstraction*. That is, we have assumed that C and the basic operations on it are available via procedures and functions (INSERT, OMIT, and BELONGS), and further, that any other operations on C have been expressed in terms of these procedures and functions. For instance, DELETE uses OMIT, and CREATE uses INSERT. If, instead of calls to INSERT, OMIT, and BELONGS, the code defining them had been used, all procedures containing these codes *would* be dependent on the implementation. Later, if we changed to a better implementation, it would be necessary to hunt through each procedure, find any code that would be affected by the change, and modify that code appropriately. A data abstraction consists of a data structure, to store data, and allowed operations on the data structure, to manipulate it. As a result, wherever one of these operations is invoked in a program, the data structure is being affected. Just as important, the data structure is *not* being affected unless one of these operations is invoked.

The use of data abstraction and modularization not only enhances understanding, but also simplifies *maintaining* a program. Maintenance is the primary focus of most programming. It involves changing a program to do something new, to stop doing something, or to do better what it now does. See Exercises 5 to 8 for examples of required improvements.

Using data abstractions as outlined above hides implementation details and makes the program independent of those details. On the other hand, the program's speed of execution and storage requirements will be greatly influenced by the implementation of the data abstraction. Consequently, the selection of an implementation should be based on the data abstraction's operations. Sometimes the choice that minimizes execution time and storage will be evident. More typically, conflicts arise, and the choice will involve trade-offs between time and storage. How to make this choice properly is a major focus of this text.

Consider two ways to implement the collection C. The set data structure of Pascal might be used to implement C, with INSERT, OMIT, and BELONGS defined in terms of the set operations provided by Pascal. Alternatively, collection could be implemented using a Pascal boolean array with its Ith entry containing the value true, if I is in the collection, and the value false otherwise. The code below defines the operations on C for each possibility.

```
type
    collection = set of 2 .. MAXN;

procedure INSERT(I : integer;
var C : collection);
begin
    C := C + A[I]
end;

procedure OMIT(I : integer;
var C : collection);
begin
    C := C − A[I]
end;

function BELONGS(I : integer;
var C : collection) : boolean;
begin
    BELONGS := (I in C)
end;
```

```
type
    collection = array [2 .. MAXN]
        of boolean;

procedure INSERT(I : integer;
var C : collection);
begin
    C [I] := true
end;

procedure OMIT(I : integer;
var C : collection);
begin
    C [I] := false
end;

function BELONGS(I : integer;
var C : collection) : boolean;
begin
    BELONGS := C [I];
end;
```

Each implementation specifies a data structure for the collection and defines the same three basic operations allowed on C. Each entails some explicit restriction on the size of C. Such restrictions can be avoided by using dynamic data structures to be introduced in later chapters. Also, the set implementation requires an array of sets A, which must be initialized prior to invoking PRIMES. $A[I]$ is a set containing the integer I for I from 2 to MAXN.

Both choices for C allow INSERT, OMIT, and BELONGS to be written so they take constant time to execute. However, the amount of storage required for C will depend directly on N. Other choices for C may increase the execution times of the basic operations on C, but reduce C's storage requirement so it depends directly only on $N/\lg N$.* In general such a choice may be critical, determining whether a program will run to completion or abort because of insufficient time or storage. Section 1.8 discusses the selection of program and data structure in more detail. In any case, once the decision is made, the declaration for collection may be added to PRIMES. The final result is a well-structured program.

Abstraction allows us to focus on concepts rather than concrete details. The architects planning a building assume an elevator as part of the plan. They know the elevator will hold passengers and freight. They know the elevator will convey its

---

*In this text, the symbol lg will be used to denote logarithm with base 2.

contents between floors, respond to call buttons, be warm in winter and cool in summer. The initial building plans can proceed using only these essential conceptions regarding the elevator. Later, the detailed choices necessary to build the elevator will be made. They will determine its size, shape, and structure, as well as its speed, responsiveness, and reliability. Notice that, as long as the elevator is treated as an abstraction, any specific implementation can be substituted for another without requiring changes to the plan.

Data abstraction similarly allows us to focus on what is needed rather than how it will be assembled and packaged. Planning a program, we assume that we have specific means to store and operate on data. Only later must an implementation be selected. The implementation determines how well the job is done, but does not affect its logical design. The longer this choice can be delayed in program development, the more independent our program will be of this specific choice. This is highly desirable, making program change much easier to effect.

1.4 Basic Constructs

The richness and power of a language are related to the variety and ease of expression that the language allows. Thus high-level computer languages provide more expressive power than more limited languages such as assembly languages. However, it is theoretically possible to state *any* algorithm using only three basic constructs and the rules for their combination. In this discussion three basic constructs have been chosen for the sake of conciseness, but others are used freely when appropriate.

The three constructs indicate different types of *flow of control*. Each construct determines the order in which its tasks are processed, and each was chosen for its logic and clarity.

The first is the ***sequence*** construct, in which each task follows the previous one without altering the order of the tasks. Each task is executed once. Notice that PRIMES (Figure 1.4) is based on this construct. The second is the ***decision*** construct, which allows only one of two tasks to be carried out depending on a controlling logical condition. The appropriate task is executed once. It is the true task when the condition is true and the false task when the condition is false. The final construct is the ***loop***, which enables a task to be repeated until a controlling condition no longer holds. Obviously, the loop must at some point end so the next task can be executed. Failure to change the value of the controlling condition in order to end the loop task results in the infamous "infinite loop." Examples of algorithms formulated according to the three basic constructs appear in Figure 1.4 as structured flowcharts along with their structured English equivalents. The corresponding Pascal versions are obvious.

Each construct has exactly one entry and one exit point. The constructs may be combined only by making the exit arrow of one the entrance arrow of another. This results in complex constructs that are sequences of constructs. The only allowed modification of a construct is the replacement of any of its tasks by one of the three basic constructs. This amounts to incorporating the task's refinements into the construct, producing a more complex construct.

There are two different ways to express a solution using these constructs and rules for their combination. One is to start with a basic construct and repeatedly apply modifications to it. Each modification corresponds to the use of a program segment

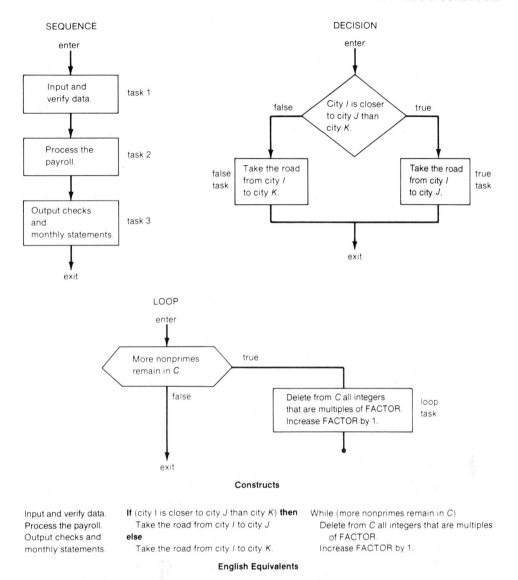

Figure 1.4 The Basic Control Constructs and Their English Equivalents

for its implementation. This results in a final unmodularized flowchart, English equivalent, or program. See the unmodularized version of PRIMES for an example. The second is to start with a basic construct, and, instead of modifying it, express the solution for each of its tasks separately. This amounts to modularizing each task's refinement, with the complete solution consisting of the collection of individual solutions. This results in a final collection of modularized flowcharts, their English equivalents, or program components. Usually a combination of the two is better than using one method only. It is wise to keep each part of a solution to a reasonable size, say one page. This can serve as a guide to whether or not *modularization*, the use of a module, or *modification,* the use of a program segment, is appropriate. But remember: the primary goal is clarity.

1.5 Top-Down Design

The purpose of structured programming is to create programs that are

- ☐ *Understandable,* meaning the logic is readily followed
- ☐ *Reliable,* so the program performs as intended
- ☐ *Adaptable,* so modifications require reasonable effort

Structured programming is a matter of how to approach a problem rather than adherence to a rigid set of rules.

As Dijkstra [1972] observed, the "art of programming is the art of organizing complexity, of mastering multitude and avoiding its bastard chaos as effectively as possible." The essential concept of structured programming is that dealing with complexity requires simplicity.

Basic operations in high-level computer languages are actually simple algorithms. Procedures using these operations or invoking other procedures embody more complex algorithms. This process is analogous to the building of complex data structures out of simpler ones, the writing of complex procedures that invoke simpler procedures, and the creating of complex algorithms by combining simpler ones. The approach is called *bottom-up.* The top-down approach turns such processes around and attempts to decompose a more complex entity into its simpler components. This decomposition is repeated for each component until only the simplest remain.

A note on terminology: The tasks performed by a program solve problems. In this book the words *task* and *problem* are used interchangeably. Each programming task entails defining the input information to be processed, defining the output information to be produced, and stating clearly the precise instructions as to *what,* but not *how,* it is to be done.

Simplicity and clarity are achieved in a complex program by focusing attention on just *one* task at a time. To show *how* the task is done, it is broken down into smaller meaningful subtasks. The combination of smaller tasks to perform the given task is called a *refinement* of that task. The next step is verifying that the refinement is correct—that is, that the refinement indeed accomplishes the task, as long as each of its components does its job. This verification may be done even without knowing *how* each component works. This is important. How the components of a refinement work is irrelevant to verification. The goal is to ensure that, if they work correctly, then the refinement itself works correctly.

Top-down design begins with the original problem and involves a loop, a repeated refining and verifying of the problem and its refinements until only implementable problems remain. *Implementable* means simple enough to be directly coded in a programming language. Review the development of Section 1.3.2 for PRIMES to see that this loop was, in fact, being used. Using this approach the programmer can be sure the final program is correct even though he or she has considered only one manageable piece at a time.

If the total number of tasks needed to complete a detailed solution is proportional to the complexity of the initial problem (as we hope), then the effort to create, understand, and verify a solution to a complex problem will also be proportional to its complexity. This is a very desirable situation. If the cost of a solution increased more drastically with complexity, then the complexity of problems we could solve would be much more severely limited.

Think about building a jigsaw puzzle. You probably use the top-down approach. You break up the picture conceptually into components, say the border and recognizable objects with distinct shapes and colors. Then you build each component and combine them all. Surely the most difficult puzzles are those with no distinguishable objects. They prevent refinement, forcing one to deal with all the complexity at one time. Perhaps this is why all the problems humans solve have structure; they are the only ones we can handle.

Two caveats must be added:

1. At each level of refinement, keep the number of component tasks small and keep them independent. This is critical because human beings can deal well with only a few things at a time, and can do so more readily when they are not intertwined. Psychological studies suggest a "magic number": a maximum of seven tasks plus or minus two. Independence means that how one task is accomplished need not be a consideration in how another task is done. Sometimes independence must be given up for other considerations such as efficiency. These trade-offs should be well considered.

2. Control carefully how tasks of a refinement are combined. Simplicity requires structure that makes the logic of a program easily discernible. Certain combinations or constructs foster such clarity. Some programs present a bewildering panorama of program statements. Instead, programs that appear as a logical sequence of tasks to be executed are needed. Some ways of expressing the order in which tasks are to be executed are more understandable than others. Constructs that are well designed allow anyone working with a program to grasp quickly what is intended. This is the hallmark of the basic constructs—sequence, decision, and loop—introduced in Section 1.4.

1.6 High-Level Languages

High-level languages provide basic data structures and operations and the capability of building, from these, more complex data structures and operations. With some languages, realizing this capability can be hard, while with others it is relatively effortless. In addition, languages vary in idiosyncrasies and subtle shortcomings. In this text, the focus is not on the language but on the more general topics of program structure and data structure selection. Still, whatever background in high-level languages you have may be helpful.

A program written in a high-level language specifies a series of operations to be performed on data structures. Think of a high-level language as having an associated *high-level computer* that carries out those operations and stores those data structures in its memory. Such high-level computers are just conceptual and normally are not built. The conventional computer is neither a Pascal nor a FORTRAN machine. Instead, we rely on compilers to translate programs from high-level languages into the languages of existing computers. The translated version is then executed by the conventional computer. The compiler, in effect, makes the conventional computer appear to be a high-level computer for the high-level language.

To do this translation, the compiler must find a way to represent the program's data structures, using those in the conventional computer's language. It must also apply operations of the conventional computer's language to these representations to simulate the program's operations on its data structures. How this is done, or what the actual computer is, does not affect the correctness of programs written in the high-level language. This is data abstraction par excellence! However, how this is done will influence the storage requirements and execution time of the program. It can also cause problems for the unwary user. As examples, in Pascal, it is necessary to limit the size of sets when we use the SET data structure, pointer variables may not be printed, and local variables are not saved between procedure calls.

1.6.1 Data Types

Programs use *variables* to refer to storage elements in the memory of the high-level computer. Each variable has a *name*, which refers to its storage elements, and a *value*, which is the content of those elements. For example, the Pascal assignment statement

    SUM := SUM + INCREMENT

uses two variables with names SUM and INCREMENT. Individual variables, which correspond to a single storage element, are the simplest type of data structure. More complex structures are built from variables, and operations on the more complex structures are built from operations on the simpler structures. High-level languages differ in the kinds of basic data structures they provide. For example, FORTRAN includes individual variables and dimensioned arrays. Pascal adds records and pointers. Significantly, the Pascal computer allows the definition of new data types and data structures. The Ada language allows new basic operations to be introduced as well.

Each variable must be defined by a declaration that gives its name and data type. The *data type* indicates the actual values that may be assumed by the variable. For example, the Pascal declaration

    var
        SUM, INCREMENT : integer;
              CHECK : boolean;

specifies that SUM and INCREMENT are the names of variables whose values will be integers, and that CHECK is the name of a variable whose values will be true or false.

1.6.2 Data Representation

Data type must be specified. An example will show why. Suppose a compiler represents integer and real variables using seven decimal digits. Then in storage elements of type integer, the value 1230045 represents the integer number 1,230,045. In storage elements of type real, the value 1230045 represents the real number 0.30045×10^{12}. In general, the compiler interprets

$d_1d_2 \ldots d_7$ of type integer as the integer number $d_1d_2 \ldots d_7$

and

$d_1d_2 \ldots d_7$ of type real as the real number $0.d_3d_4 \ldots d_7 \times 10^{d_1d_2}$

Given this situation, suppose the compiler must cause the contents of SUM = 1230045 to be added to the contents of INCREMENT = 1250047, where they are both of type integer. The compiler might apply the usual column-by-column addition algorithm:

```
SUM               1230045
+

INCREMENT   1250047
                  2480092
```

Here, 2480092, when stored in SUM, represents the correct result. If SUM and INCREMENT are of type real, then SUM's content represents the real number 0.30045×10^{12} and INCREMENT's content represents the real number 0.50047×10^{12}. Their sum is 0.80092×10^{12}. However, if the above column-by-column addition algorithm is applied and the result stored in SUM, then its contents will still be 2480092, but this now represents the real number 0.80092×10^{24}. This is incorrect by a factor of 10^{12}. To represent the correct result, SUM should contain 1280092.

The difficulty is, of course, that the same algorithm should *not* be applied for the addition of numbers of both type integer and type real. Two distinct algorithms are needed because two distinct representations are used. In general, the algorithms used must depend on the data types of the variables involved. The compiler can choose the correct algorithm only when it knows the data types.

Thus it is essential to declare the data type of each variable so that the compiler can choose the proper algorithm to achieve the intended result. Type declarations also allow high-level language compilers to build in checks for validity. Such checks may generate error messages during compilation or during execution of the program. Languages with more restrictive rules for the manipulation of different data types, called **strongly typed languages,** allow more checking. For example, Pascal's strong typing prevents the contents of a variable of one type from being copied into a variable of a different type. FORTRAN and COBOL allow this to be done in some cases but not in others.

The Pascal data types **integer, real, char,** and **boolean,** or their equivalents, are now standard in most high-level languages. The values they may assume, and the operations that may be performed on variables of these types, are specified in each language.

1.7 Elements of Style

Individual writers, even whole magazines or journals, have their own writing style. Often a glimpse at a few paragraphs can give clues to the author or the type of publication. Still, there are general rules to follow for acceptable style. Entire books have been devoted to this subject. Style will always be in style.

Dress, carriage, and response are parts of personal style, as are straight teeth, polished shoes, and a fast gait. Program style is determined by overall appearance as well as by implementation details. We want to see the logical structure of a program clearly. Too many details cloud the picture. Data abstraction and modularization are tools for sharpening the picture. Hiding information, so only parts of a program that need it can see it, also provides better focus. People react differently to unexpected situations. Some become erratic, others remain calm, going cheerfully about their business. Programs should react to unexpected data with aplomb, letting us know about errors, but getting on with the job when possible. Details of a program should not affect its logical structure, only its efficiency. Details can make an otherwise stylish program sloppy, slow, and in need of repair, or they can finish the design so it is elegant, sleek, and well-tuned. What we see isn't always what we get, but stylish programs suggest a better thought-out design and product.

Since good programs must be written with style, guidelines are offered here for this purpose. A good program is correct, easy to read, and changeable without unreasonable effort. Whether or not it should be efficient depends on the application. In some cases an efficient program may be written with the same effort as an inefficient one. In other cases it will be necessary to put in more effort to achieve efficiency and so the additional programming may be done only if it means a substantial savings in computation time.

1.7.1 Expressing Purpose

What's in a name? "A rose is a rose is a..." "There's more form than substance." Perhaps these sentiments are true, but in a well-presented program a great deal is in a name. One module is not another module, and understanding of substance is enhanced by form.

Indentation and proper spacing serve to delineate significant components of a program. Choosing names to convey and delineate purpose is also extremely important. Even without the descriptions given for the modules of Figure 1.3, the names of each module, variable, and constant almost provide, by themselves, enough information to see what each does. On the other hand, inappropriate names can be very misleading and distracting.

Reading identifiers to understand what a program does requires reading the entire program. This is too demanding. After all, when selecting a book, no one wants to be forced to read from cover to cover just to see what it is about. The same holds for a program. Program documentation must be provided for this purpose; good name selection is not enough. The main program and each of its modules must start with comments that allow users (including its author) to understand readily what it does and what its inputs, outputs, and parameters are. The main program's documentation then tells immediately *what* it does. No further reading is necessary unless someone wants to know *how* it is done. Similar comments can precede program segments that implement tasks of some complexity. To a great extent, the structure of a module, coupled with the documentation of each of its tasks, explains *how* the module does what it does. In this sense, with proper comments, structured programs are self-documenting. Modularization and data abstraction help to elucidate structure by obscuring detail. Some programmers are free to develop their own style for delineation and documentation; for others it may be specified rigidly. The case study presented later gives a complete program with documentation as a guide for annotating your own programs. As a rule, documentation is not included in programs appearing in this book, since in effect the text itself serves as documentation, discussing completely each program presented. Proper documentation is a prominent aspect of every good program and should become a habit of the programmer. Since the top-down approach requires a description for each task, the documentation for a task may be done as it is introduced, even before it is written.

1.7.2 Communication between Modules

High-level languages allow the definition of three kinds of variables: local, nonlocal, and global. A program consists of components, namely its main program and all procedures and functions of the program. A component of a program may reference

- [ ] *Local* variables, to which it alone has access
- [ ] *Nonlocal* variables, to which it and some other components have access
- [ ] *Global* variables, to which all components have access

A variable is referenced by a component in order to copy, modify, or simply look at its value.

FORTRAN, for example, considers variables to be local to a component unless they appear as formal parameters of that component (in which case they are nonlocal). Variables stored in special common areas of memory are global. Pascal determines whether a variable is local, nonlocal, or global by using scope rules. In Figure 1.3, C is local to PRIMES, FACTOR is local to REMOVE, and NEXTMULTIPLE is local to DELETE, while N is nonlocal or global to each.

Each high-level language has its own rules to give one component access to variables of another component. Merely using the same variable name in two components will not normally allow one component to reference a variable in another. For example, I in CREATE and I in PRINT (Figure 1.3) do not represent the same variable; each is local to its procedure. If this were not so, modules could not be written independently. Once a complex problem has been refined, different individuals or groups should be able to develop components independently. Otherwise, each time a group used a new variable name, it would have to check that no other group used the same name. These access rules apply to module names and other identifiers as well as to variable names.

The issue here is really communication between modules of a program. *Communication between modules* — allowing one module to reference variables also used by another — occurs in two basic ways: using nonlocal or global variables, or using formal parameters in defining components.

When a component changes the value of a variable used by another component, and the variable is not communicated (or passed) between them as a parameter, a *side effect* has occurred. Side effects make it extremely difficult to understand what components do. It is easier to see what a component does when we can be sure that only the parameters and the local variables will be affected by the execution of the component. The communication structure of a program is clearer when information is communicated explicitly by the use of parameters. This shows "who is doing what to whom." For example, in DELETE (Figure 1.3), no side effects can occur, since the only nonlocal variables FACTOR, N, and C all appear as parameters. Thus the only variables not local to DELETE that it can reference are FACTOR, N, and C.

At one extreme, it is possible to make all variables global. Every module may then reference any variable. Making all variables global requires extremely careful adherence to the use of variable names, and makes side effects inevitable. In COBOL, programs are typically written this way. However, such programs deal with high-volume input and output and use relatively simple algorithms, so this method may not cause difficulty.

The other extreme is to use only parameters between modules. This may not always be possible. For example, storage considerations may intrude, as we see next.

Communication between modules by using parameters may be a one-way or a two-way street. In some high-level languages, like FORTRAN, any change in the value of a parameter in a called module is passed or reflected back to the calling module. Other languages, such as Pascal, allow this to occur, but also allow one component to communicate information to another as a parameter, yet never reflect changes made to the parameter's value. Upon return, the parameter's value is the same as prior to the call. Also, upon return from a call, different languages treat local variables of modules differently. Some preserve their values between calls; others do not. In FORTRAN, it is possible to have local variables retain their values between invocations of a module; in Pascal it is not. Whenever a non-**var** variable, such as an array, is used as a parameter in Pascal, storage will be allocated for a copy of that variable. When large structures are passed in this way, large amounts of storage may be quickly consumed.

1.7.3 Ensuring against Data Errors: Defensive Programming

Modules receive and output data. In our PRIMES program, what happens if N is negative or so large that it exceeds the storage capacity allocated to the data structure implementing the collection C? Think how upset a company's personnel would be if no one received paychecks because the input data for one employee was not valid. Or suppose each employee received an output check equal to the entire payroll. Defensive programming is ensuring that your programs guard against such outcomes by checking for invalid data, incoming or outgoing, and doing something reasonable when such data are discovered. What is reasonable can vary from signaling an error and stopping further processing to simply outputting an error message, ignoring the invalid data, and continuing processing. Sometimes the correct data may be inferred from the invalid data, but this approach must be taken with great caution. The important point is to ensure that errors are discovered. It is safer to have no output than output that is in error but thought to be correct. Invalid data is a very serious problem whether it is due to design or to happenstance. Validation modules for input and output should be used, even though it is not always easy to see how to guard against all possible errors. This text does not have space to dwell on the issue of data validation, but it should always be in your mind. Chapter 9 discusses, for a specific nontrivial example, how to guard against invalid data.

1.7.4 Changing Programs

Consider a new problem: count the number of primes that are no greater than N. Instead of immediately attempting a solution, can you think of a program that already solves a related problem? You've already seen one: PRIMES. Perhaps it can be changed to help with the solution. Looking at PRIMES's refinement (Figure 1.3), you can see that replacing the PRINT module by a COUNT module that returns the proper count does the trick. The solution COUNTPRIMES, using the changed PRIMES and a COUNT module, is

```
procedure COUNTPRIMES(N : integer; var COUNTER : integer);
var
    C : collection;
begin
    CREATE(N, C);
    REMOVE(N, C);
    COUNT(N, C, COUNTER)
end

procedure COUNT(N : integer; C : collection; var COUNTER : integer);
var
    I : integer;
begin
    COUNTER := 0;
    for I := 2 to N do
        if (BELONGS(I, C)) then
            COUNTER := COUNTER + 1
end;
```

Solutions are rarely obtained so easily. Yet this example teaches us something. Programs that have been designed wisely, with an eye to generality, may often be used as tools in the solution of related problems. When beginning the development of a solution to a problem, see first if a program for a related problem is already known, and whether or not it may be adapted. This can save significant time, effort, and money compared to writing a new program or program module.

It was easy to see what to change and how to change it in our example, because PRIMES is modular, with narrowly defined tasks and independent modules. Changes are rarely as straightforward as this; for contrast, consider changing the algorithm ANOTHERPRIMES to a program for COUNTPRIMES. In general, though, isolating functions in modules that carry out a single narrowly defined task tends to generate lower level modules that are clear, simple, and of moderate size. At higher levels, such single-task modules need not be simple. For example, the module "Select the best next chess move" is such a module, but it is not simple. The lower the level of a module that needs changing, the less the effort required. However, the higher the level of the task for which one can adapt a known program, the greater the savings, since much refinement is avoided. An enviable situation is when changes require little effort and benefits are great.

Often a programmer's assignment or goal is to increase the efficiency of a program, and this will involve changing the way data are stored. If the program has been written using data abstractions, it is much easier to see exactly which modules need changing. For example, in PRIMES, to change the implementation of collection involves changing only its declaration and INSERT, OMIT, and BELONGS.

1.7.5 Verification and Debugging

Verifying a solution means checking that program segments and modules do their tasks correctly. It is difficult to verify programs, although some formal methods are known. This text will illustrate how a program can be verified informally, but rigorously, for appropriate examples. For most of the small examples, verification is left to the reader.

Although only proper verification can ensure the correctness of a program, debugging can help in locating mistakes. Your goal should be not to run or even code programs until you are sure the algorithm is correct. Even if you are sure of the algorithm, debugging tools should be employed. Then, when your program fails to work correctly (as you know by now it will), you can track down the cause without Holmes' or Watson's help.

In addition to debugging aids provided by your computer system and compiler, programming techniques aid debugging. For example, it is important to learn to display appropriate error messages and information. The top-down approach includes debugging individual modules or program segments as they are refined, so that debugging proceeds as the program is developed. Verification, debugging, and documenting all require basic understanding of the program and much the same information. To a large extent, then, they should be done concurrently with program development. During development you have the concepts and information fresh in your mind.

The main program and the other components may each be debugged independently, just as they may be verified and documented independently. This requires stubs and drivers.

A *stub* takes the place of a component. It should have the same name and parameters as the component, and, when called, should output a message indicating it was called. For example,

```
procedure REMOVE(N : integer; var C : collection);
{This is a stub for REMOVE.}
begin
    WRITELN('REMOVE was called.')
end;
```

A *driver* plays the role of a component that calls another component, and is used to debug the called component. The driver should set up test values for the parameters used by the component it calls, output those values, call the component, and output the returned values. For example,

```
procedure REMOVE DRIVER;
{This is a driver for REMOVE.}
const
    SENTINELVALUE = -1;
var
    N : integer;
    C : collection;
begin
    READLN(N);
    while (N < > SENTINELVALUE) do
        begin
            WRITELN('REMOVE is called with N = ', N);
            CREATE(N, C);
            WRITELN('and with C : ');
            PRINT(N, C);
            REMOVE(N, C);
            WRITELN('REMOVE returns N = ', N);
            WRITELN('and C : ');
            PRINT(N, C);
            READLN(N)
        end
end;
```

Using drivers and stubs allows any individual component to be tested and debugged even though components that call it and are called by it have not yet been written. Within the component, program segments that correspond to algorithmic tasks can be isolated. A statement can be inserted before and after each of these segments to output a message indicating that the segment was reached during execution, giving the values of variables worked on by the segment, specifying that the segment was exited during execution, and giving the modified values of the variables.

In this way, you can see the progress of a program during its execution by studying the output of the drivers, stubs, and component being tested. With this approach, you never find yourself with a program that has not run correctly and for which you have no output, or output that gives no clue as to what went wrong or where!

Suppose module M has just been refined and it is to be tested and debugged. Its refinement may include calls to other modules not yet written or debugged. To test and debug M you must

1. Write a driver to call M and feed it test data to work on
2. Replace each module of M's refinement by its own stub

For example, to test and debug REMOVE (Figure 1.3) requires

1. A driver to call REMOVE and feed it test values for N and C
2. Replacing NONPRIMES and DELETE by their individual stubs

This assumes that PRIMES (which calls REMOVE) and NONPRIMES and DELETE (which REMOVE calls) have not yet been verified or even written.

Instead, suppose PRIMES has already been debugged. PRIMES, in conjunction with the driver used to debug it, could then be taken as the basis for REMOVE's driver. Next, this driver plus REMOVE could be used as the basis for DELETE's driver. This way of proceeding parallels the top-down development of the program. It amounts to inserting one new module at a time into an already debugged program.

To illustrate the proper way to use debugging statements, a complete listing and output is given for an execution of the case study program later in the chapter.

1.7.6 In a Nutshell

The discussion of good programming style may be summarized with the following guidelines.

1. Take care to present programs well.
    Don't choose a name without a purpose.
    Don't leave a component's purpose unspecified.
    Descriptions should be simple even if tasks are not.
2. Communicate well.
    Store data only where it is needed (use local variables).
    Pass information explicitly when needed elsewhere (use parameters).
    Avoid side effects.
3. Use data abstraction.
    This is the basic way to make programs independent of data implementation and it makes implementation changes easier and more reliable.
4. Modularize programs.
    Modules should execute a simple, narrowly defined task.
    It should be possible to determine what a module does by looking only at it.
    Changes to a module should not necessitate changes in other modules.
    Prevent unreasonable input and output data by defensive programming.
5. Use debugging aids.
    Also verify your programs.

Strict adherence to rules may not always be possible, of course, or even yield the best results. Knowing how or to what extent to apply programming rules comes only from experience in using them and in studying their effects.

1.8 Time and Storage Requirements

Sometimes the time of execution or the storage required by a program, or both, are limited. Analysis helps pinpoint parts of a program whose efficiency may be worth trying to improve, because they are executed frequently or require large amounts of storage. Such analysis can be very difficult, and simulation of the program may be needed for estimates. *Simulation* means the program is executed repeatedly for appropriately chosen data, and the results averaged or otherwise statistically analyzed. Sometimes it is possible to analyze how these requirements increase as the amount or size of the data increases, even though we cannot say what happens exactly for smaller amounts or sizes. This is called *asymptotic analysis.* When exact analysis cannot be done, we settle for bounds on the time and storage required.

1.8.1 Analyzing the Prime Example

The nonmathematically inclined reader may want to skip the following analysis of PRIMES (Figure 1.3), which demonstrates how to go about informally analyzing a program and shows how trade-offs arise. Even such simple programs do not necessarily have simple analyses.

When a statement is said to take *constant time,* it means that the statement is always executed in the same amount of time, whatever the current values of the variables it processes. Clearly, the execution time of PRIMES is given by the sum of the execution times of its three modules. In what follows it is assumed that INSERT, BELONGS, and OMIT all take constant time (notice that for the array implementation for the collection C of Section 1.3.2, Prime Example, this will be true).

CREATE executes INSERT exactly $N - 1$ times. Similarly PRINT executes its *if* statement $N - 1$ times. The amount of time the *if* statement takes depends on whether BELONGS is true or false but requires, at most, the time for BELONGS plus the time for WRITELN.

REMOVE is more complex. Its initial assignment statement takes constant time, to which must be added the loop time. The loop is executed $\sqrt{N} - 1$ times, so the loop condition is evaluated $\sqrt{N}$ times. Assuming, for simplicity, that SQRT(N) takes constant time C, then $C \times \sqrt{N}$ is the *total* time for the evaluation of the condition. If the loop task took constant time, then the *total* loop time would be the product of this constant and $(\sqrt{N} - 1)$. Unfortunately DELETE's time varies, depending on the value of FACTOR. Nonetheless, the *total* time for DELETE can still be derived.

DELETE's own loop is executed for each multiple of FACTOR between $2 \times$ FACTOR and $M \times$ FACTOR, where M is the largest number of times that FACTOR divides into N. M is the integer part of $N/$FACTOR denoted by $\lfloor N/$FACTOR$\rfloor$. Hence DELETE's loop is executed $\lfloor N/$FACTOR$\rfloor$ times for this value of FACTOR. Since FACTOR takes on values $2, 3, 4, \ldots, \sqrt{N}$, the total number of DELETE's loop executions is

$$N/2 + N/3 + N/4 + \cdots + N/\lfloor\sqrt{N}\rfloor \quad \text{or} \quad N \times [1/2 + 1/3 + \cdots + 1/\lfloor\sqrt{N}\rfloor]$$

But $1/2 + 1/3 + \cdots + 1/N$ is roughly the natural logarithm of N, denoted by $\ln N$. Thus the *entire* time for the loop of DELETE is a constant (for OMIT and the assignment statement) times $N \ln \lfloor\sqrt{N}\rfloor$. The condition of this loop contributes roughly its own constant times $N \ln \lfloor\sqrt{N}\rfloor$. The initialization of NEXTMULTIPLE in DELETE contributes its constant times $\sqrt{N}$.

Adding everything, we get a good execution time estimate of

$$C_1 + C_2\sqrt{N} + C_3N + C_4N \ln N$$

where C_1, C_2, C_3, and C_4 come from the times for condition evaluation, assignment statement execution, and INSERT, OMIT, and BELONGS.

For large N, this expression is dominated by the term $C_4 N \ln N$. In fact, for large enough values of N, the expression will be no greater than $CN \ln N$ for an appropriate value of C. We describe this concisely by saying the expression is $O(N \ln N)$, read "order $N \ln N$"; this notation will be used throughout the text.

By the storage requirements of PRIMES is meant the total storage required for its data structures. Except for a few variables, the storage is required primarily for the collection C and will be determined by its implementation.

The analysis reveals that the bulk of the execution time for PRIMES is spent executing the loop in DELETE. Consequently, to improve its time we speed up the time of the loop itself, or reduce the number of times it needs to be executed. For the array implementation, the storage required will be proportional to N, and this is where the bulk of the storage required is needed.

PRIMES can be improved in a number of obvious ways. Except for 2, no primes are even. Hence all other even numbers can be eliminated from consideration. This means that FACTOR need never take on even values, so it can be increased by 2 instead of 1 in REMOVE and can also be initialized to 3. DELETE can be changed so that NEXTMULTIPLE takes on only odd multiples of FACTOR. With a little more work, C can be cut to roughly half its size by eliminating even integers. This will necessitate changes to INSERT, OMIT, and BELONGS, as well as changes to the FOR loops in CREATE and PRINT, but it reduces the storage needed by about one-half and the time by more than one-half.

Perhaps a less obvious improvement is to modify the increase of FACTOR in REMOVE so instead of increasing by 1 (or 2), FACTOR increases to the value of the next prime in C (see Exercise 8). To realize fully this saving requires a new data structure, the list or the balanced binary tree, for the collection. Lists are discussed in Chapter 3, balanced binary trees in Chapter 7. These would save not only time but storage as well. Borrowing a result from mathematics about the distribution of prime numbers, we can state that any version of PRIMES which stores all the primes from 2 to N in a collection will need $N/\ln N$ storage locations, since there are about that many such primes. Thus we will run out of storage before we run out of time!

PRIMES may be written so that its execution time increases, but its storage needs decrease or vice versa. Thus time is traded for storage, as is often done. PRIMES represents one extreme where all the primes are saved. A version of PRIMES in which no primes are saved is at the other extreme (Exercise 10). This version would require significantly more time.

1.8.2 Limits on Time and Storage

Programs carry out certain basic operations. For example, PRIMES executes assignment statements, evaluates conditions, and executes INSERT, OMIT, and BELONGS. In fact, its total execution time equals the number of times each of the operations is executed multiplied by the time taken by that operation. Determining the number of basic operations performed by a program to solve a problem allows evaluation of its practicality. For illustration, suppose that one million (10^6) basic operations can be carried out in 1 second by a computer. Then the number of basic operations that it can carry out in one year is

10^6 basic operations/second $\times$ 60 seconds/minute $\times$ 60 minutes/hour

$\times$ 24 hours/day $\times$ 365 days/year

This is fewer than 10^{13} basic operations/year. And this is assuming that the computer is available for the exclusive use of the program and that it will never fail during the year. Thus 10^{13} can be taken as a benchmark figure—any program that requires a number of operations on this order to solve a problem is not feasible!

How much storage is available is determined by your computer system. The amount needed is surely not feasible when your program aborts during execution with a message indicating insufficient storage, or when the compiler tells you there is insufficient storage. If you run out of time or storage, you must then abandon the problem (and perhaps your job), find a more efficient program, or trade time for storage.

1.9 Case Study: Bowling Scores

This section illustrates the way a flowchart and program are developed for a problem connected with the game of bowling. The way in which the spirit of the structured programming philosophy is adhered to is more important than the particular development.

Bowling, as you may know, consists of ten *frames*. In each frame, there is a chance to knock down ten pins by throwing one or two balls down the bowling alley. To start, you roll the first ball of a given frame. If all ten pins are knocked down, a *strike* is achieved for that frame and a frame score of 10 plus the total number of pins knocked down on the next two rolls is earned. If any pins remain standing, you roll a second ball for the frame. After this roll, if all pins are down, you have a *spare*, and a frame score of 10 plus the number of pins knocked down on the next roll. If any pins remain standing after the second roll, then the result is an *open frame*, and the frame score obtained is given by the total number of pins knocked down on the two rolls of the frame. A strike or spare occurring on the last (the tenth), results in, respectively, two or one additional rolls. The total score for a game is the sum of all the individual frame scores.

Getting twelve strikes in a row results in the maximum attainable score of 300. In this case, twelve rolls are made. The least number of rolls possible is eleven and the greatest is twenty-one. In fact there is a correlation between the number of rolls in a game and the game score. Many rolls correspond to low scores and few rolls to high scores. The better a bowler you are, the fewer rolls you get!

Example 1.1 The problem is to print the total score for each of a series of games as well as the minimum, average, and maximum scores. Assume the input is given as a series of roll scores for each game. □

1.9.1 Algorithm

An initial flowchart might be as shown in Figure 1.5(a). This initial flowchart is a sequence structure. If the three tasks can be carried out correctly, in the sequence indicated, then the problem is solved. The flowchart decomposes the original problem into three smaller problems. Obtaining their solutions and sequencing them correctly provides the solution to the original problem. This is the top-down approach to problem solving. It is applied next to each of the three problems.

Problem 1 is transparent enough. Problem 3 is clearly solved by the expanded or refined flowchart shown in Figure 1.5(b).

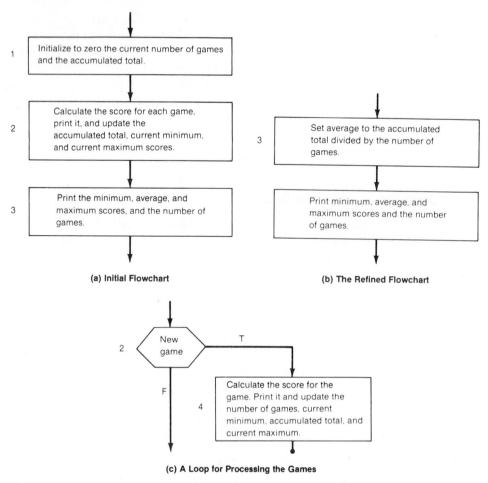

(a) Initial Flowchart   (b) The Refined Flowchart

(c) A Loop for Processing the Games

Figure 1.5   Flowcharts of the Bowling Scores Algorithm

Problem 2 needs to be refined. It seems clear that the basic structure for its solution is a loop. Within the loop, each game is processed. When all games have been processed, the loop should be exited. (See Figure 1.5(c).)

The new problem introduced as task 4 must be solved next. The input for this new problem will be the roll scores that must be processed for the new game. A basic looping structure can accomplish the task. The loop task will be executed ten times, once for each frame. Each execution calculates the score for the current frame and updates the game score and a frame counter, FRAME. Prior to entering the loop, FRAME must be initialized to 1, and GAMESCORE, to 0. Other initialization may be required. After the loop is exited, the game score must be printed, and proper updating must occur. This refinement is shown in Figure 1.6.

Suppose that each time the programmer expands a task, the expanded version of the task does in fact solve the problem introduced by that task. Then the pro-

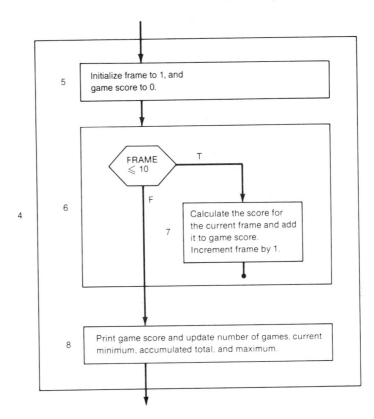

Figure 1.6   Refinement of Task 4

grammer knows that, whatever the current structured flowchart, it must represent a solution to the original problem as long as each of its tasks can be correctly carried out. The detailed structured flowchart of Figure 1.7 is thus a solution to the problem, as long as each of its tasks can correctly be carried out. It is detailed enough so that we know how to carry out (or program) each of its tasks except for 5, 6, 7, and 8. However, if the high-level language chosen for the program allows direct implementation of those tasks, then no more detail is needed to complete the solution.

Instead of increasing the complexity of the flowchart of Figure 1.7, tasks 5–8 can be modularized.

Modules for tasks 7 and 8 appear in Figures 1.8 and 1.9. The solution to the original problem will then consist of Figure 1.8 plus the modules for tasks 5–8. This illustrates the application of structured programming to a relatively simple problem. Note again the importance of choosing variable names that convey information about the meaning and use of the variables. Good names make the algorithm clearer.

When task 7 is entered, the variables ROLLSCORE and R1 must contain, respectively, the first roll score of the current frame and the next roll score. Consequently, before entering task 6, the first two roll scores of the game must be read into ROLLSCORE and R1. This is the "other initialization" required of task 5.

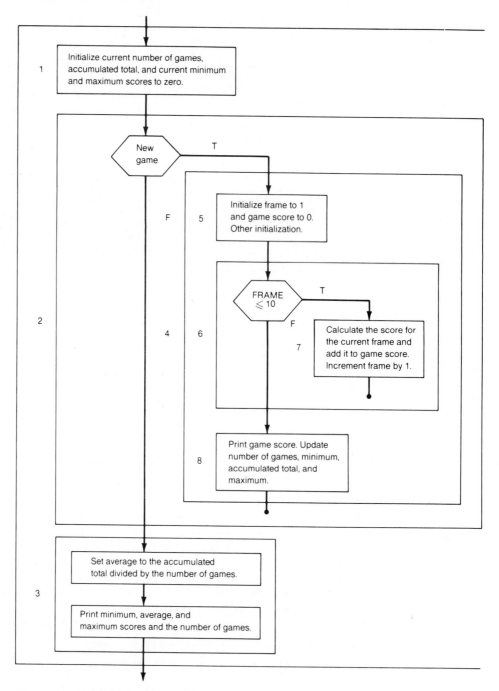

Figure 1.7   Refinement of Initial Flowchart

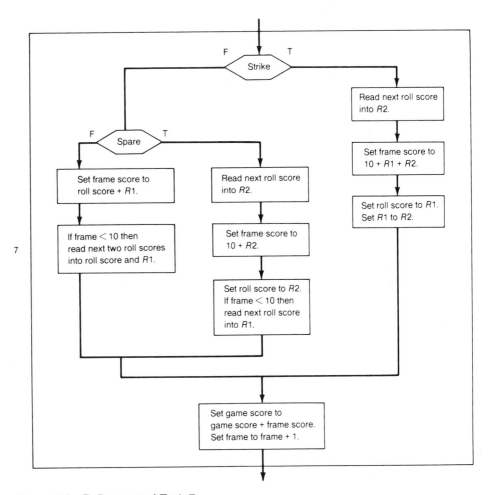

Figure 1.8 Refinement of Task 7

The conditions "strike" and "spare" (Figure 1.8) are actually implemented as "ROLLSCORE equals 10" and "(ROLLSCORE + R1) equal 10," respectively. To emphasize that complexity in a flowchart should be limited, Figure 1.10 (p. 35) is the complete detailed flowchart for the solution as it could appear without modularization. Descriptions do not appear; the chart simply indicates the structure of the solution. The flowchart can be derived by adding the detailed expansions of tasks 5–8 to Figure 1.6.

1.9.2 Program

The program now follows directly from the flowcharts. Notice that its structure parallels the flowcharts', that we have attempted to minimize side effects by passing information between components explicitly as parameters, and that information needed only by a component is kept local to that component.

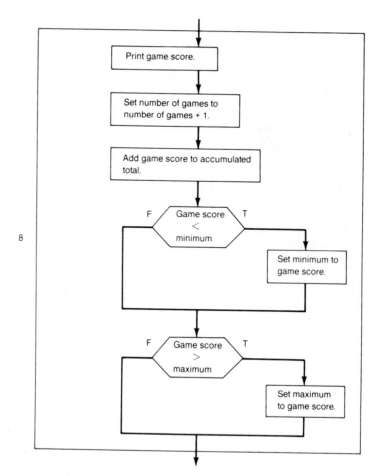

Figure 1.9   Refinement of Task 8

program BOWLINGSCORES(input, output);

    {Calculates and prints out the game scores for a series of bowling games. Also prints out the number of games bowled, and the minimum, average, and maximum of all the game scores. The input consists, for each game, of a sequence of roll scores. Each roll score represents the number of pins knocked down on the corresponding roll.

    Main variables:

AVERAGE	— average of all game scores
GAMESCORE	— score for current game
MAX	— current maximum game score
MIN	— current minimum game score
NUMBER	— current number of games played
TOTAL	— accumulated total of all game scores

                                                                                                         }

```
Var
    GAMESCORE, NUMBER, MIN, TOTAL, MAX : integer;
    AVERAGE : real;

procedure FRAMECALC(var GAMESCORE, FRAME, ROLLSCORE, R1 : integer);
    {Calculates the FRAMESCORE for the current game, adds it to GAMESCORE, increases FRAME
    by 1, and updates ROLLSCORE and R1.

    Main variables:
        FRAME          —current frame
        FRAMESCORE—score for current frame
        GAMESCORE  —score for current game
        ROLLSCORE  —first roll score of current frame
        R1, R2             —succeeding roll scores after ROLLSCORE               }
var
    FRAMESCORE, R2 : integer;
begin {procedure FRAMECALC}
    if (ROLLSCORE = 10) then                                          {strike}
        begin
            READLN(R2);
            FRAMESCORE := 10 + R1 + R2;
            ROLLSCORE := R1;
            R1 := R2
        end
    else
        begin
            if (ROLLSCORE + R1 = 10) then                             {spare}
                begin
                    READLN(R2);
                    FRAMESCORE := 10 + R2;
                    ROLLSCORE := R2;
                    if FRAME < 10 then
                        READLN(R1)
                end
            else
                begin                                                 {open frame}
                    FRAMESCORE := ROLLSCORE + R1;
                    if FRAME < 10 then
                        begin
                            READLN(ROLLSCORE);
                            READLN(R1)
                        end
                end
        end;
    GAMESCORE := GAMESCORE + FRAMESCORE;
    FRAME :=FRAME + 1
end; {procedure FRAMECALC}

procedure GAMECALC(var GAMESCORE : integer);
    {Calculates GAMESCORE for the current game.
```

```
        Main variables:
            FRAME        — current frame
            GAMESCORE — score for the current game
            ROLLSCORE  — first roll score of current frame
            R1              — succeeding roll score after ROLLSCORE          }
    var
        FRAME, ROLLSCORE, R1 : integer;
    begin {procedure GAMECALC}
        GAMESCORE := 0;
        FRAME := 1;
        READLN(ROLLSCORE);
        READLN(R1);
        while FRAME <= 10 do
            FRAMECALC(GAMESCORE, FRAME, ROLLSCORE, R1)
    end; {procedure GAMECALC}

    procedure UPDATE(GAMESCORE : integer; var NUMBER, MIN, MAX, TOTAL : integer);
        {Prints GAMESCORE, and updates NUMBER, MIN, MAX, and TOTAL to reflect GAMESCORE.
        Main variables:
            GAMESCORE — score for the current game
            MAX           — current maximum game score
            MIN            — current minimum game score
            NUMBER     — current number of games
            TOTAL         — accumulated total of all game scores                }
    begin {procedure UPDATE}
        NUMBER := NUMBER + 1;
        TOTAL := TOTAL + GAMESCORE;
        if GAMESCORE < MIN then
            MIN := GAMESCORE;
        if GAMESCORE > MAX then
            MAX := GAMESCORE
    end; {procedure UPDATE}

    begin {BOWLINGSCORES}
        NUMBER := 0;
        MIN := 300;
        MAX := 0;
        TOTAL := 0;
        while not EOF do
            begin
                GAMECALC(GAMESCORE);
                UPDATE(GAMESCORE, NUMBER, MIN, MAX, TOTAL)
            end;
        AVERAGE := TOTAL/NUMBER;
        WRITELN('MINIMUM GAME', MIN);
        WRITELN('AVERAGE GAME', AVERAGE);
        WRITELN('MAXIMUM GAME', MAX);
        WRITELN('NUMBER OF GAMES', NUMBER)
    end. {BOWLINGSCORES}
```

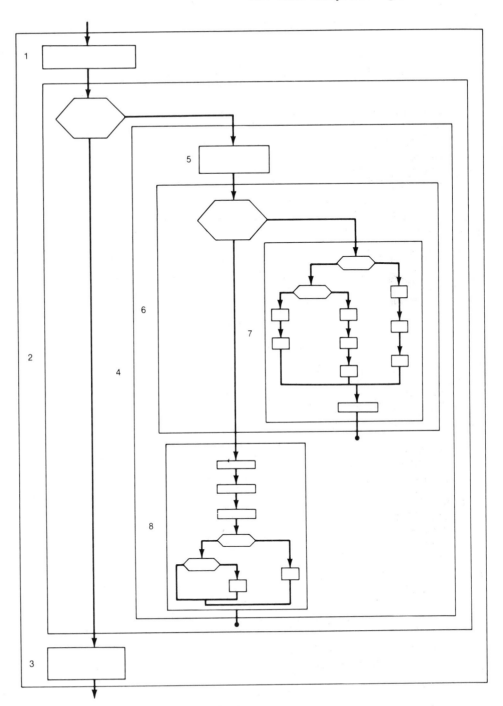

Figure 1.10 Too Detailed a Refinement

1.9.3 Debugging

The following is a complete listing and output of a version of BOWLINGSCORES program that contains statements used as debugging aids (the boxed lines). This listing demonstrates how to use such statements and what they can tell us as we peruse the output. The roll scores of the two games that served as input are 5, 4, 6, 4, 2, 4, 1, 4, 3, 4, 8, 1, 9, 0, 10, 10, 9, 0, 9, 1, 10, 7, 3, 9, 0, 10, 10, 5, 4, 6, 4, 10, 10, 8.

```
program BOWLINGSCORES(input, output);
    {Calculates and prints the game scores for a series of bowling games. Also prints the number of
    games bowled, and the minimum, average, and maximum of all the game scores. The input
    consists, for each game, of a sequence of roll scores. Each roll score represents the number of
    pins knocked down on the corresponding roll.
    Main variables:
        AVERAGE       —average of all game scores
        GAMESCORE —score for current game
        MAX             —current maximum game score
        MIN             —current minimum game score
        NUMBER        —current number of games played
        TOTAL           —accumulated total of all game scores                                  }
const
    B = ' ';                                              {Blank used for formatting purposes}
var
    GAMESCORE, NUMBER, MIN, TOTAL, MAX : integer;
    AVERAGE : real;

procedure FRAMECALC(var GAMESCORE, FRAME, ROLLSCORE, R1 : integer);
    {Calculates the FRAMESCORE for the current game, adds it to GAMESCORE, increases FRAME
    by 1, and updates ROLLSCORE and R1.
    Main variables:
        FRAME             —current frame
        FRAMESCORE —score for the current frame
        GAMESCORE   —score for the current game
        ROLLSCORE    —first roll score of current frame
        R1, R2             —succeeding roll scores after ROLLSCORE                            }
var
    FRAMESCORE, R2 : integer;
begin {procedure FRAMECALC}

    ┌──────────────────────────────────────────────────────────────────────────┐
    │   WRITE(B : 3, 'STARTING FRAMECALC WITH :');                               │
    │   WRITELN(B : 3, 'GAMESCORE FRAME ROLLSCORE R1');                          │
    │   WRITELN(B : 33, GAMESCORE : 3, B : 4, FRAME : 4, B : 4,                  │
    │                ROLLSCORE : 5, B : 6, R1 : 2);                              │
    └──────────────────────────────────────────────────────────────────────────┘

    if (ROLLSCORE = 10) then
        begin                                                        {strike}
            READLN(R2);
            FRAMESCORE := 10 + R1 + R2;
```

```
              ROLLSCORE := R1;
              R1 := R2;
```

```
              WRITELN(B : 3, 'AFTER STRIKE, FRAMESCORE =', FRAMESCORE : 2)
```

```
        end
    else
      begin
        if (ROLLSCORE + R1 = 10) then                              {spare}
            begin
               READLN(R2);
               FRAMESCORE := 10 + R2;
```

```
               WRITELN(B : 3, 'AFTER SPARE, FRAMESCORE =', FRAMESCORE : 2);
```

```
               ROLLSCORE := R2;
               if (FRAME < 10) then
                   READLN(R1)
            end
        else                                                       {open frame}
            begin
               FRAMESCORE := ROLLSCORE + R1;
```

```
               WRITELN(B : 3, 'OPEN FRAME, FRAMESCORE =', FRAMESCORE : 2);
```

```
               if (FRAME < 10) then
                   begin
                      READLN(ROLLSCORE);
                      READLN(R1)
                   end
            end
      end;
GAMESCORE := GAMESCORE + FRAMESCORE;
FRAME := FRAME + 1;
```

```
        WRITE(B : 3, 'LEAVING FRAMECALC WITH : ');
        WRITELN(B : 3, 'GAMESCORE FRAME ROLLSCORE R1');
        WRITELN(B : 32, GAMESCORE : 3, B : 4, FRAME : 4, B : 4,
                     ROLLSCORE : 5, B : 6, R1 : 2);
        WRITELN
```

```
    end; {procedure FRAMECALC}
    procedure GAMECALC(var GAMESCORE : integer);
        {Calculates GAMESCORE for the current game.
        Main variables:
                FRAME          —current frame
                GAMESCORE—score for the current game
                ROLLSCORE  —first roll score of current frame
                R1                —succeeding roll score after ROLLSCORE          }
    var
        FRAME, ROLLSCORE, R1 : integer;
    begin {procedure GAMECALC}
        GAMESCORE := 0;
        FRAME := 1;
        READLN(ROLLSCORE);
        READLN(R1);
        while (FRAME <= 10) do
            begin


                WRITE(B : 3, 'IN GAMECALC, GOING TO FRAMECALC WITH:');
                WRITELN(B : 3, 'GAMESCORE FRAME ROLLSCORE R1');
                WRITELN(B : 41, GAMESCORE : 6, B : 6, FRAME : 2, B : 3,
                            ROLLSCORE : 5, B : 5, R1 : 2);


                FRAMECALC(GAMESCORE, FRAME, ROLLSCORE, R1);


                WRITE(B : 3,
                        'IN GAMECALC, RETURNING FROM FRAMECALC WITH:');
                WRITELN(B : 3, 'GAMESCORE FRAME ROLLSCORE R1');
                WRITELN(B : 47, GAMESCORE : 6, B : 6, FRAME : 2, B : 3,
                            ROLLSCORE : 5, B : 5, R1 : 2);
                WRITELN


            end
    end; {procedure GAMECALC}
    procedure UPDATE(GAMESCORE : integer; var NUMBER, MIN, MAX, TOTAL : integer);
        {Prints GAMESCORE, and updates NUMBER, MIN, MAX, and TOTAL to reflect GAMESCORE.
        Main variables:
                GAMESCORE—score for the current game
                MAX           —current maximum game score
                MIN            —current minimum game score
                NUMBER    —current number of games played
                TOTAL         —accumulated total of all game scores                }
    begin {procedure UPDATE}
```

```
          WRITELN;
          WRITE(B : 3, 'BEGINNING TO UPDATE WITH:');
          WRITELN(B : 3, 'GAMESCORE NUMBER MIN MAX TOTAL');
          WRITELN(B : 32, GAMESCORE : 6, B : 4, NUMBER : 3, B : 4,
                      MIN : 3, B, MAX : 3, B, TOTAL : 4);
```

```
NUMBER := NUMBER + 1;
TOTAL := TOTAL + GAMESCORE;
if (GAMESCORE < MIN) then
     MIN := GAMESCORE;
if (GAMESCORE > MAX) then
     MAX := GAMESCORE;
```

```
          WRITE(B : 6, ' LEAVING UPDATE WITH:');
          WRITELN(B : 3, 'GAMESCORE NUMBER MIN MAX TOTAL');
          WRITELN(B : 29, GAMESCORE : 6, B : 4, NUMBER : 3, B : 4,
                      MIN : 3, B, MAX : 3, B, TOTAL : 4);
          WRITELN
```

```
end; {procedure UPDATE}

begin {BOWLINGSCORES}
     NUMBER := 0;
     MIN := 300;
     TOTAL := 0;
     MAX := 0;
     while (not EOF) do
          begin
```

```
          WRITELN;
          WRITELN('CALLING GAMECALC FOR GAME #', NUMBER + 1 : 2);
          WRITELN('----------------------------------------');
```

```
          GAMECALC(GAMESCORE);
```

```
          WRITELN('-= = = > RETURNING FROM GAMECALC WITH', B,
                      'GAMESCORE =', GAMESCORE : 3, B, 'FOR GAME #',
                      NUMBER + 1 : 2);
          WRITELN('CALLING UPDATE WITH;   MIN TOTAL MAX', 'NUMBER');
          WRITELN(B : 23, MIN : 3, TOTAL : 5, B, MAX : 3, B, NUMBER : 3);
```

```
          UPDATE(GAMESCORE, NUMBER, MIN, MAX, TOTAL);
```

```
        WRITELN('- = = = > RETURNING FROM UPDATE :     MIN TOTAL',
                'MAX NUMBER');
        WRITELN(B : 29, MIN : 3, B, TOTAL : 5, B, MAX : 3, B, NUMBER : 3)
```

```
      end;
    AVERAGE := TOTAL/NUMBER;
    WRITELN('FINAL RESULTS FOR ALL GAMES FOLLOW:');
    WRITELN('*********************************');
    WRITELN;
    WRITELN(B : 5, 'ACCUMULATED TOTAL =', TOTAL : 5);
    WRITELN;
    WRITELN(B : 10, 'MINIMUM GAME =', MIN : 5);
    WRITELN(B : 10, 'AVERAGE GAME =', AVERAGE : 10 : 4);
    WRITELN(B : 10, 'MAXIMUM GAME =', MAX : 5);
    WRITELN;
    WRITELN('NUMBER OF GAMES PLAYED =', NUMBER : 3);
end. {BOWLINGSCORES}
```

```
CALLING GAMECALC FOR GAME # 1
    IN GAMECALC, GOING TO FRAMECALC WITH:    GAMESCORE  FRAME  ROLLSCORE  R1
                                                 0          1        5        4
        STARTING FRAMECALC WITH:    GAMESCORE  FRAME  ROLLSCORE  R1
                                        0          1        5        4
OPEN FRAME, FRAMESCORE = 9
    LEAVING FRAMECALC WITH:    GAMESCORE  FRAME  ROLLSCORE  R1
                                   9          2        6        4
    IN GAMECALC, RETURNING FROM FRAMECALC WITH:    GAMESCORE  FRAME  ROLLSCORE  R1
                                                       9          2        6        4
    IN GAMECALC, GOING TO FRAMECALC WITH:    GAMESCORE  FRAME  ROLLSCORE  R1
                                                 9          2        6        4
        STARTING FRAMECALC WITH:    GAMESCORE  FRAME  ROLLSCORE  R1
                                        9          2        6        4
AFTER SPARE, FRAMESCORE = 12
    LEAVING FRAMECALC WITH:    GAMESCORE  FRAME  ROLLSCORE  R1
                                   21         3        2        4
    IN GAMECALC, RETURNING FROM FRAMECALC WITH:    GAMESCORE  FRAME  ROLLSCORE  R1
                                                       21         3        2        4
    IN GAMECALC, GOING TO FRAMECALC WITH:    GAMESCORE  FRAME  ROLLSCORE  R1
                                                 21         3        2        4
        STARTING FRAMECALC WITH:    GAMESCORE  FRAME  ROLLSCORE  R1
                                        21         3        2        4
OPEN FRAME, FRAMESCORE = 6
    LEAVING FRAMECALC WITH:    GAMESCORE  FRAME  ROLLSCORE  R1
                                   27         4        1        4
    IN GAMECALC, RETURNING FROM FRAMECALC WITH:    GAMESCORE  FRAME  ROLLSCORE  R1
                                                       27         4        1        4
    IN GAMECALC, GOING TO FRAMECALC WITH:    GAMESCORE  FRAME  ROLLSCORE  R1
                                                 27         4        1        4
```

```
        STARTING FRAMECALC WITH:       GAMESCORE  FRAME  ROLLSCORE  R1
                                          27        4        1        4
OPEN FRAME, FRAMESCORE = 5
        LEAVING FRAMECALC WITH:        GAMESCORE  FRAME  ROLLSCORE  R1
                                          32        5        3        4
        IN GAMECALC, RETURNING FROM FRAMECALC WITH:       GAMESCORE  FRAME  ROLLSCORE  R1
                                                             32        5        3        4
        IN GAMECALC, GOING TO FRAMECALC WITH:       GAMESCORE  FRAME  ROLLSCORE  R1
                                                       32        5        3        4
        STARTING FRAMECALC WITH:       GAMESCORE  FRAME  ROLLSCORE  R1
                                          32        5        3        4
OPEN FRAME, FRAMESCORE = 7
        LEAVING FRAMECALC WITH:        GAMESCORE  FRAME  ROLLSCORE  R1
                                          39        6        8        1
        IN GAMECALC, RETURNING FROM FRAMECALC WITH:       GAMESCORE  FRAME  ROLLSCORE  R1
                                                             39        6        8        1
        IN GAMECALC, GOING TO FRAMECALC WITH:       GAMESCORE  FRAME  ROLLSCORE  R1
                                                       39        6        8        1
        STARTING FRAMECALC WITH:       GAMESCORE  FRAME  ROLLSCORE  R1
                                          39        6        8        1
OPEN FRAME, FRAMESCORE = 9
        LEAVING FRAMECALC WITH:        GAMESCORE  FRAME  ROLLSCORE  R1
                                          48        7        9        0
        IN GAMECALC, RETURNING FROM FRAMECALC WITH:       GAMESCORE  FRAME  ROLLSCORE  R1
                                                             48        7        9        0
        IN GAMECALC, GOiNG TO FRAMECALC WITH:       GAMESCORE  FRAME  ROLLSCORE  R1
                                                       48        7        9        0
        STARTING FRAMECALC WITH:       GAMESCORE  FRAME  ROLLSCORE  R1
                                          48        7        9        0
OPEN FRAME, FRAMESCORE = 9
        LEAVING FRAMECALC WITH:        GAMESCORE  FRAME  ROLLSCORE  R1
                                          57        8       10       10
        IN GAMECALC, RETURNING FROM FRAMECALC WITH:       GAMESCORE  FRAME  ROLLSCORE  R1
                                                             57        8       10       10
        IN GAMECALC, GOING TO FRAMECALC WITH:       GAMESCORE  FRAME  ROLLSCORE  R1
                                                       57        8       10       10
        STARTING FRAMECALC WITH:       GAMESCORE  FRAME  ROLLSCORE  R1
                                          57        8       10       10
AFTER STRIKE, FRAMESCORE = 29
        LEAVING FRAMECALC WITH:        GAMESCORE  FRAME  ROLLSCORE  R1
                                          86        9       10        9
        IN GAMECALC, RETURNING FROM FRAMECALC WITH:       GAMESCORE  FRAME  ROLLSCORE  R1
                                                             86        9       10        9
        IN GAMECALC, GOING TO FRAMECALC WITH:       GAMESCORE  FRAME  ROLLSCORE  R1
                                                       86        9       10        9
        STARTING FRAMECALC WITH:       GAMESCORE  FRAME  ROLLSCORE  R1
                                          86        9       10        9
AFTER STRIKE, FRAMESCORE = 19
        LEAVING FRAMECALC WITH:        GAMESCORE  FRAME  ROLLSCORE  R1
                                         105       10        9        0
        IN GAMECALC, RETURNING FROM FRAMECALC WITH:       GAMESCORE  FRAME  ROLLSCORE  R1
                                                            105       10        9        0
```

```
IN GAMECALC, GOING TO FRAMECALC WITH:     GAMESCORE  FRAME  ROLLSCORE  R1
                                             105        10       9       0
   STARTING FRAMECALC WITH:     GAMESCORE  FRAME  ROLLSCORE  R1
                                  105        10       9       0
OPEN FRAME, FRAMESCORE = 9
   LEAVING FRAMECALC WITH:     GAMESCORE  FRAME  ROLLSCORE  R1
                                 114        11       9       0
   IN GAMECALC, RETURNING FROM FRAMECALC WITH:     GAMESCORE  FRAME  ROLLSCORE  R1
                                                     114        11       9       0
– = = = > RETURNING FROM GAMECALC WITH GAMESCORE = 114 FOR GAME # 1
CALLING UPDATE WITH;     MIN  TOTAL  MAX  NUMBER
                         300    0     0     0
   BEGINNING TO UPDATE WITH:     GAMESCORE  NUMBER  MIN  MAX  TOTAL
                                   114        0      300   0     0
   LEAVING UPDATE WITH:     GAMESCORE  NUMBER  MIN  MAX  TOTAL
                              114        1      114  114   114
– = = = > RETURNING FROM UPDATE:     MIN  TOTAL  MAX  NUMBER
                                     114   114   114    1



CALLING GAMECALC FOR GAME # 2
   IN GAMECALC, GOING TO FRAMECALC WITH:     GAMESCORE  FRAME  ROLLSCORE  R1
                                               0         1        9       1
   STARTING FRAMECALC WITH:     GAMESCORE  FRAME  ROLLSCORE  R1
                                  0          1        9       1
AFTER SPARE, FRAMESCORE = 20
   LEAVING FRAMECALC WITH:     GAMESCORE  FRAME  ROLLSCORE  R1
                                 20         2       10       7
   IN GAMECALC, RETURNING FROM FRAMECALC WITH:     GAMESCORE  FRAME  ROLLSCORE  R1
                                                     20         2       10       7
   IN GAMECALC, GOING TO FRAMECALC WITH:     GAMESCORE  FRAME  ROLLSCORE  R1
                                              20         2       10       7
   STARTING FRAMECALC WITH:     GAMESCORE  FRAME  ROLLSCORE  R1
                                  20         2       10       7
AFTER STRIKE, FRAMESCORE = 20
   LEAVING FRAMECALC WITH:     GAMESCORE  FRAME  ROLLSCORE  R1
                                 40         3        7       3
   IN GAMECALC, RETURNING FROM FRAMECALC WITH:     GAMESCORE  FRAME  ROLLSCORE  R1
                                                     40         3        7       3
   IN GAMECALC, GOING TO FRAMECALC WITH:     GAMESCORE  FRAME  ROLLSCORE  R1
                                              40         3        7       3
   STARTING FRAMECALC WITH:     GAMESCORE  FRAME  ROLLSCORE  R1
                                  40         3        7       3
AFTER SPARE, FRAMESCORE = 19
   LEAVING FRAMECALC WITH:     GAMESCORE  FRAME  ROLLSCORE  R1
                                 59         4        9       0
   IN GAMECALC, RETURNING FROM FRAMECALC WITH:     GAMESCORE  FRAME  ROLLSCORE  R1
                                                     59         4        9       0
   IN GAMECALC, GOING TO FRAMECALC WITH:     GAMESCORE  FRAME  ROLLSCORE  R1
                                              59         4        9       0
```

```
        STARTING FRAMECALC WITH:     GAMESCORE  FRAME  ROLLSCORE  R1
                                        59        4        9       0
OPEN FRAME, FRAMESCORE = 9
        LEAVING FRAMECALC WITH:      GAMESCORE  FRAME  ROLLSCORE  R1
                                        68        5       10      10
        IN GAMECALC, RETURNING FROM FRAMECALC WITH:    GAMESCORE  FRAME  ROLLSCORE  R1
                                                          68        5       10      10
        IN GAMECALC, GOING TO FRAMECALC WITH:     GAMESCORE  FRAME  ROLLSCORE  R1
                                                     68        5       10      10
        STARTING FRAMECALC WITH:     GAMESCORE  FRAME  ROLLSCORE  R1
                                        68        5       10      10
AFTER STRIKE, FRAMESCORE = 25
        LEAVING FRAMECALC WITH:      GAMESCORE  FRAME  ROLLSCORE  R1
                                        93        6       10       5
        IN GAMECALC, RETURNING FROM FRAMECALC WITH:    GAMESCORE  FRAME  ROLLSCORE  R1
                                                          93        6       10       5
        IN GAMECALC, GOING TO FRAMECALC WITH:     GAMESCORE  FRAME  ROLLSCORE  R1
                                                     93        6       10       5
        STARTING FRAMECALC WITH:     GAMESCORE  FRAME  ROLLSCORE  R1
                                        93        6       10       5
AFTER STRIKE, FRAMESCORE = 19
        LEAVING FRAMECALC WITH:      GAMESCORE  FRAME  ROLLSCORE  R1
                                       112        7        5       4
        IN GAMECALC, RETURNING FROM FRAMECALC WITH:    GAMESCORE  FRAME  ROLLSCORE  R1
                                                         112        7        5       4
        IN GAMECALC, GOING TO FRAMECALC WITH:     GAMESCORE  FRAME  ROLLSCORE  R1
                                                    112        7        5       4
        STARTING FRAMECALC WITH:     GAMESCORE  FRAME  ROLLSCORE  R1
                                       112        7        5       4
OPEN FRAME, FRAMESCORE = 9
        LEAVING FRAMECALC WITH:      GAMESCORE  FRAME  ROLLSCORE  R1
                                       121        8        6       4
        IN GAMECALC, RETURNING FROM FRAMECALC WITH:    GAMESCORE  FRAME  ROLLSCORE  R1
                                                         121        8        6       4
        IN GAMECALC, GOING TO FRAMECALC WITH:     GAMESCORE  FRAME  ROLLSCORE  R1
                                                    121        8        6       4
        STARTING FRAMECALC WITH:     GAMESCORE  FRAME  ROLLSCORE  R1
                                       121        8        6       4
AFTER SPARE, FRAMESCORE = 20
        LEAVING FRAMECALC WITH:      GAMESCORE  FRAME  ROLLSCORE  R1
                                       141        9       10      10
        IN GAMECALC, RETURNING FROM FRAMECALC WITH:    GAMESCORE  FRAME  ROLLSCORE  R1
                                                         141        9       10      10
        IN GAMECALC, GOING TO FRAMECALC WITH:     GAMESCORE  FRAME  ROLLSCORE  R1
                                                    141        9       10      10
        STARTING FRAMECALC WITH:     GAMESCORE  FRAME  ROLLSCORE  R1
                                       141        9       10      10
AFTER STRIKE, FRAMESCORE = 30
        LEAVING FRAMECALC WITH:      GAMESCORE  FRAME  ROLLSCORE  R1
                                       171       10       10      10
        IN GAMECALC, RETURNING FROM FRAMECALC WITH:    GAMESCORE  FRAME  ROLLSCORE  R1
                                                         171       10       10      10
```

```
IN GAMECALC, GOING TO FRAMECALC WITH:      GAMESCORE  FRAME  ROLLSCORE  R1
                                               171        10        10     10
      STARTING FRAMECALC WITH:     GAMESCORE  FRAME  ROLLSCORE  R1
                                      171        10      10       10
AFTER STRIKE, FRAMESCORE = 28
      LEAVING FRAMECALC WITH:     GAMESCORE  FRAME  ROLLSCORE  R1
                                      199       11      10       8
      IN GAMECALC, RETURNING FROM FRAMECALC WITH:      GAMESCORE  FRAME  ROLLSCORE  R1
                                                          199       11      10     8
 – = = = > RETURNING FROM GAMECALC WITH GAMESCORE = 199 FOR GAME # 2
CALLING UPDATE WITH:     MIN  TOTAL  MAX  NUMBER
                         114   114   114    1
      BEGINNING TO UPDATE WITH:     GAMESCORE  NUMBER  MIN  MAX  TOTAL
                                       199        1     114  114   114
      LEAVING UPDATE WITH:     GAMESCORE  NUMBER  MIN  MAX  TOTAL
                                  199        2     114  199   313
 – = = = > RETURNING FROM UPDATE:     MIN  TOTAL  MAX  NUMBER
                                      114   313   199    2

FINAL RESULTS FOR ALL GAMES FOLLOW:
*****************************************
      ACCUMULATED TOTAL =      313
          MINIMUM GAME =      114
          AVERAGE GAME =      156.5000
          MAXIMUM GAME =      199
NUMBER OF GAMES PLAYED =      2
```

1.10 Historical Notes

The study of data structures owes a great debt to Donald Ervin Knuth, who virtually created the field with the publication of the first volume of his series of influential books [Knuth, 1973a], the first edition of which appeared in 1968. His text assembled and organized most of the existing information on data structures plus a great deal of original material, and became an instant success because of its thoroughness and clarity. It is highly recommended for serious computer scientists.

Knuth chose to use assembly language to illustrate the implementation of data structures. In the late 1960s when his text appeared, assembly language played an important role in computer science because high-level languages performed less rapidly, required greater memory, and carried greater restrictions on control of a computer than did assembly language. Programming teams were often forced to use assembly language for implementation simply because their programs had to run in real time, had to occupy only 4K words, or had to satisfy a similar requirement that could not be met with high-level languages for the existing machines. Despite the advantages of programming in a high-level language, they simply could not use one in their applications.

Much has changed since 1968, when Knuth's book first appeared. Machines are faster and memories are larger, so neither performance nor memory utilization is as critical now as two decades ago. Moreover, compiler technology has changed as well.

Optimizing compilers can produce programs that are better than those produced by a programmer with average ability, and they come close to doing as well as an expert. So modern instruction in data structures depends strongly on high-level languages instead of assembly language. One of the themes of Knuth's work is that choosing the right algorithm and data structure for the job to be done is the most critical factor in determining running time and memory requirements. Given an algorithm and data structure for a particular problem, a programmer can write a program that builds the data structure and performs the algorithm in almost any reasonable computer language. Thus, many of Knuth's ideas and the fruits of over a decade of subsequent research in computer science now appear in popular texts that use high-level languages in place of assembly language.

High-level languages have evolved, too, in the past two decades. The late 1950s marked the development and emergence of the first two widely used computer languages, FORTRAN for scientific computations and COBOL for business computations. The computer science community, realizing the shortcomings of FORTRAN and COBOL, tended to favor ALGOL, a block-structured language. It was used widely in books and journals as a language for describing programs and was used in universities for instruction, but was never a strong contender in commercial computing. The ALGOL 60 report [Naur, 1963] defined the language standard that was the most influential form of ALGOL in the early 1960s. Niklaus Wirth created a dialect of ALGOL known as ALGOL-W and produced a compiler that was widely used in universities by the end of the decade but still failed to be a major influence in commercial computation. The beginning of the 1970s found computer science instruction going in diverse directions because no one computer language was strong enough to serve as the language of choice. Meanwhile, the commercial world tenaciously held to COBOL and FORTRAN.

The computer science community produced a number of candidates for a new universal computer language. ALGOL 68 [van Wijngaarden et al., 1975] was proposed as a successor to ALGOL 60, but was poorly received because of its complexity. Meanwhile, Wirth used his experience with ALGOL-W and other languages for which he had written compilers to produce Pascal, a language that was both simple and powerful [Wirth, 1971a, 1971b]. Meanwhile, the virtues of structured programming were reaching the world at large, and influencing the training of programmers in both universities and the commercial world. Since neither COBOL nor FORTRAN was designed for structured programming, their use interfered with the programmer's ability to do structured design. Pascal is well suited to structured programming and was slowly growing in popularity as the primary language of instruction in computer science curricula.

One more major force turned the tide toward Pascal. With the microcomputer revolution of the 1970s came an immediate need for high-level languages on small machines. The mid-1970s found the state of affairs in great turmoil since there were twenty to thirty new microprocessors on the market, each with a unique instruction set, and therefore with a unique need for systems software and compilers. Computer programmers were greatly handicapped by the lack of software tools for the new microcomputers. Kenneth Bowles of the University of California at San Diego became an enthusiast of Pascal and of microcomputers almost simultaneously. Through his leadership, a team at UCSD was able to construct a Pascal compiler and operating system that was both compact and portable [Bowles, 1980]. Bowles' team managed to "port" their Pascal system to a half dozen of the most popular microcomputers. The project had a tremendous influence on the success of Pascal as a language because it introduced the language to hundreds of thousands of microcomputer users who had not been exposed to the language through university instruction. The wide availability of Pascal compilers from UCSD supplied the additional impetus to make Pascal a leading language, both commercially and academically. Ada, a powerful new language greatly influenced by Pascal and supporting data abstraction, may eventually supplant Pascal.

Horowitz [1983] is a collection of reprints of the landmark papers in programming languages. For background in Pascal, see the language definition [Jensen and Wirth, 1978] and texts such as Keller [1982] and Koffman [1985]. For interesting reading in structured programming, the reader should study the text by Dahl, Dijkstra, and Hoare [1972] and Wirth [1973]. Many texts on Ada have appeared in recent years. Barnes [1982] provides an easily assimilated view of the language. For more information on particular algorithms in Pascal, see Sedgewick [1983] for general-purpose algorithms and Kernigan and Plaugher [1981] for software tools. Bentley's monograph on writing efficient programs is a very good text for the experienced programmer who wants to obtain the greatest possible performance from programs [Bentley, 1982].

1.11   Summary

Structure is important for algorithms, programs, and data. Structured programming is a philosophy as well as a defined methodology to guide the construction of algorithms and programs. It involves a top-down approach: starting with a given problem and then using stepwise refinement, breaking problems into smaller component problems that may then be solved independently and subsequently combined. The overall goal is to write programs that are more easily understood, debugged, and changed. Data abstraction and modularity are important elements of programming style to be incorporated into this approach. Algorithm and program structure have been stressed in this chapter and will continue to be emphasized throughout the book, as will the equally important choice of data structures. The next chapter discusses record and array information and pointers.

☐ Exercises

1. In Figure 1.1 suppose there are $N = 100$ houses and you must visit houses 3, 10, 50, 7, and 82 in this order. How much distance must you travel in each town?

2. Why do no more nonprimes remain in C when FACTOR $> \sqrt{N}$?

3. Explain the difference between a module and program segment implementation of a refinement.

4. Discuss any significant differences between INSERT, OMIT, and BELONGS for the set and array implementation of C.

5. Change PRIMES so that even numbers, except 2, are not considered as values for FACTOR or NEXTMULTIPLE.

6. Change your solution to Exercise 5 so that even numbers, except 2, do not appear in C (C must use only enough storage for 2 and the odd numbers between 2 and N).

7. This is the same as Exercise 6 except C must use only enough storage for 2 and the odd *primes* between 2 and N.

8. Change REMOVE so that, instead of increasing FACTOR by 1, FACTOR is increased to the value of the next prime in C. You may choose to do this by starting with REMOVE from your solution to Exercise 7.

9. Analyze the time and storage required for your solutions to Exercises 5 to 8.

10. Find a solution to the prime problem which stores no primes.

11. Explain why we must know the data type of the information stored in variables A and B in order to multiply their contents correctly.

12. Suppose that *integers* are represented as in the example of Section 1.6.2. Write an algorithm, in English, that will allow someone who knows addition tables up to 9 to compute the correct sum of the contents of A and B. The algorithm must yield the correct result no matter what integers are stored in A and B.

13. This is the same as Exercise 12 except that *reals* are represented and the algorithm should yield the correct sum represented as a real number.

14. Express the bowling program just as the prime number solution is expressed in Figure 1.3. What are its local, nonlocal, and global variables?

15. Modify the flowcharts and program for the bowling problem to obtain flowcharts and a program that solve the same problem but also print out the number of rolls for each game.

16. What modules might be inserted in bowling scores to check the validity of its input and output? Where would they go in the program?

17. What elements of style have been incorporated in the programs of Sections 1.9.2 and 1.9.3?

2 Records, Arrays, and Pointers

2.1 Bricks

The context in which problems will be solved and programs written having been presented, it is time to start studying seriously the effect of choice of data structure on the problem solution. Before we explore some simple examples, the two basic data structures — records and arrays — must be understood, along with the two basic operations on them — selection and traversal.

A *record* is a data structure made up of a fixed number of information items, not necessarily of the same type. An *array* is a data structure made up of a fixed number of information items *in sequence*, with all items required to be the same type. Records and arrays have boundless applications. Records are useful when the items are to be referred to by name, while arrays are useful when the items are to be referred to by their position in the sequence. The fundamental importance of the array was recognized quite early in the development of programming languages; the record has only more recently been incorporated in a diversity of languages. **Pointers** are variables that refer, or point, to data structures or link the components of a data structure together. Records and arrays are the bricks out of which more complex data structures are built, and pointers are the mortar holding them together.

Just as a builder asks for bricks, mortar, and other construction material, programmers in a high-level language ask for data structures to help build their solutions. Specifying a data structure is done by declaring a variable name to be of a specific **type.** Some languages restrict the choice of type to individual variables or to arrays of type integer, real, boolean, or char. Pascal includes these, plus other types such as records, pointers, and sets. Pascal even allows the user to define new types. Pascal requires the programmer to describe the format of the record, which may be almost limitlessly complex. Thus the memory of Pascal is a truly flexible and marvelous invention. As we proceed, you will glimpse how such a memory was achieved, but for now we simply use it.

Records and arrays allow related items of information to be treated as a group. In the case of records, the individual pieces of information are called *fields,* while for arrays they are called *entries.* The merit of records and arrays lies in the fact that they allow random access to any one of their fields or entries. *Random access* is accomplished by direct location of the desired piece of information without regard to sequence. Random access to an item means that access to the item may be accomplished in a fixed amount of time, no matter what item was previously accessed. This contrasts with *sequential access,* where the time to access an item depends on the number of items stored between that item and the last item accessed because each of these must be accessed first. With random access, no matter which field of a record or which entry of an array is wanted, access to it may be accomplished in a fixed amount of time, typically a few millionths or billionths of a second.

Both records and arrays provide the means to treat related items as a unit, and both generalize the idea of variables containing one item to variables containing many items. However, records do not contain the additional concept of a "sequence" of items, so we discuss records first.

2.1.1 Pascal Records

The Pascal memory can be thought of as consisting of storage elements of different lengths and complexity. Their complexity is determined by their type. The simplest storage elements have one of the four basic types, *integer, real, boolean,* and *char.* Up one level in complexity are storage elements that have type *record.* Among these, the simplest have exactly one field, that field having one of the basic types. A storage element of type record for a book would be more complex and might include fields for its title, author, cost, and number of pages. Fields are not restricted to have one of the basic types but may themselves have type record.

Consider the following Pascal declarations:

```
type                      type                        type
   balance = record          name = record               book = record
            amount : real          last : characters;          title : characters;
   end;                            middle : characters;        author : name;
                                   first : characters          cost : real;
                           end;                                pages : integer
                                                       end;
```

```
var
   AMOUNT : real;
   BANKBALANCE : balance;
   TEXT : book;
```

Storage elements for the three variables, AMOUNT, BANKBALANCE, and TEXT, may be pictured as in Figure 2.1. From the figure it is clear that storage elements must differ in complexity for different variables. The simplest element is obviously

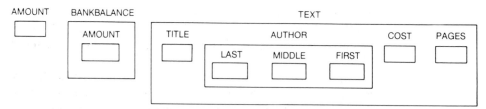

Figure 2.1   Records of Three Variables

the one that stores only one piece of information, as does the storage element for the variable AMOUNT. The element for BANKBALANCE is obviously more complex; it could also be made longer by adding more fields such as LASTDEPOSIT and LASTWITHDRAWAL. And of course more memory is needed to store the variable TEXT than to store BANKBALANCE. The type record generalizes the idea of an individual variable containing only one piece of information, to variables containing related pieces of information. The amount of storage required determines the *length* of a record, while the record's structure determines its *complexity*.

It is possible to write Pascal statements that refer to the entire record TEXT, its AUTHOR field, or its LAST field using the names TEXT, TEXT.AUTHOR, and TEXT.AUTHOR.LAST, respectively.

2.1.2 Arrays in Pascal

The array provides another way to group either individual items or records. An array stores a sequence of entries; any entry in an array is referred to and located by its position in the sequence. An array has a fixed size and is homogeneous (that is, its entries must all be of the same type, say of type integer or book). This contrasts with a record, whose fields may be of different types. An array entry is identified by qualifying the array name by the entry's position. In contrast, to identify a field in a record, the record name is qualified by the field name. (Note that arrays can have entries of record type and records can have fields of array type.)

Suppose the following type and variable declarations were added to those in Section 2.1.1.

```
type
     subject = (history, computer, philosophy, novel, biography)
var
     CLASS : array [21..80] of subject;
     AUTHORS : array [subject] of name;
     LIBRARY : array [21..80] of book;
```

The declaration specifies the name of each variable (e.g., CLASS) and its type (array) for each of three variables. It also specifies the range of values for an array index for each of the three arrays. An *array index* refers to a position of the array. CLASS, AUTHORS, and LIBRARY have array indexes that may take on values in the range

21 to 80, history to biography, and 21 to 80, respectively, Then CLASS (30), AUTHORS (philosophy), and LIBRARY (21) refer, respectively, to their tenth, third, and first entries. Notice that the type of an array index is specified by the array's declaration.

It has already been mentioned that arrays are very useful when entries must be randomly accessed. This occurs when the order in which requests for access to entries cannot be predicted. Suppose an array stores the initial mileage for each car of a fleet of rental cars. As a car is returned its initial mileage is needed to prepare a bill based on mileage used. The next car to be returned can be *any* rented car, and to access its initial mileage directly requires the random access capability of arrays. Processing time is saved since the information entry is located directly and no time is lost searching through other entries to find it. When information is thus accessed directly, in a constant time, it is said to be **selected**. Thus, any array entry whose position is known can be selected.

Instead of accessing a single array entry, a programmer may wish to process an entire array by accessing and processing each entry in turn. In this case, the program is said to **traverse** the array. Such a traversal would be required in order to print out, in order, the initial mileage of *each* car in the fleet. A complete traversal is accomplished when each entry has been processed exactly once. A simple loop, starting at the first entry and finishing at the last, will accomplish this. Another use of traversal is to find an array entry whose position is unknown. In this case, the loop is terminated when the entry is found; if the traversal is completed, it means the desired entry was not present.

Selection and traversal are two ways to access an array entry. If the entry's position is known, selection is the efficient way to access it. When successive array positions must be examined to find the entry, selection is not possible, but traversal may be used.

If the traversal terminates at the Ith entry (because it is the desired one), then a time proportional to I is required since the $(I - 1)$ preceding entries must be accessed before the Ith is obtained. Selection, on the other hand, takes constant time. This is an important distinction between these two basic operations on arrays. Selection means you can go directly to what is wanted; traversal means you must rummage around to find it. Use selection when one or more accesses must be made in arbitrary order and traversal when each entry is to be accessed in sequence.

Example 2.1 Suppose that data, such as integers in the range 1 to 100, are stored in an array A as shown in Figure 2.2. Given any valid index value in the variable I, print the number stored in the Ith entry of the array A. □

This may be done by executing the Pascal statement,

```
WRITELN (A[I])
```

This is a concise, easy-to-understand solution to Example 2.1. It takes a constant amount of time to execute since it selects the desired entry of A. Note that when the

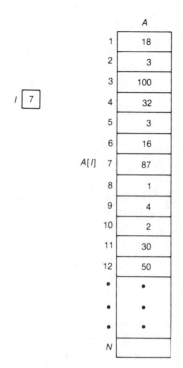

Figure 2.2   The Array for Example 2.1

value of the index I is 7, then the array entry with the value 87 is printed; when the value of I is 5, then the entry with the value 3 is printed. The index I is a variable that *points to* a particular entry of A. The current value of the index I determines the entry currently selected. Changing the value of I changes the entry to which it points. Thus the solution can be interpreted as the command "Print the entry of A to which the index I currently points."

Example 2.2   Let A be an array of length N, and let K be a variable containing an integer in the range 1 to 100. If there is some value of I for which $A[I]$ contains K, then print that value of I; if there is more than one such value, print any one of them. If the value of K is nowhere in A, then print a zero. □

Array A might represent the information kept by a car rental agency, with $A[I]$ containing the account number, K, of the individual or firm currently renting car I. Example 2.1 thus requires finding the account now leasing car I. Example 2.2 requires finding the car being used by account K.

Example 2.2 could certainly be solved by traversing the array A, searching for an entry whose value equals the value of K. If one is found, its position in A would be printed. If the traversal is completed without success, a zero would be printed. This solution is easy to code and could be written as follows:

```
FOUND := false;
LOC := 1;
while ((not FOUND) and (LOC <= N)) do
    if (A[LOC] <> K) then
        LOC := LOC + 1
    else
        FOUND := true;
if FOUND then
    WRITELN(LOC)
else
    WRITELN(ZERO);
```

Although this program segment for array traversal is simple, it is more complex than that for Example 2.1. Its execution time is proportional to the number of entries searched before the number in K is found, and if it is not found, the execution time is proportional to N.

Is it possible to find another way to solve this problem, one that will be as concise and clear as that for Example 2.1 and also execute in constant time? The answer is yes, if the information stored in A is represented so that the program can *select* the correct value to print.

Such a program would start with creation of an array POINTER of length 100 as follows. For each integer K between 1 and 100, if K does not appear in A, place a zero in POINTER[K]. If K *does* appear in A, place in POINTER[K] the position of an entry of A that contains K. Thus, in Figure 2.3, POINTER[3] contains 5, since $A[5]$ contains 3.

With array POINTER available, the solution to Example 2.2 may be written as

```
WRITELN(POINTER[K])
```

This is the concise, easy-to-understand solution desired, and it executes in constant time. Again, the way in which the relevant information was represented in the program — that is, the way in which the data was structured — allows this solution to be achieved. Even in such a simple example, the way data is represented has a substantial impact on the resulting program.

Note that the use of the POINTER array instead of A may cause some information available in A to be lost. This is because POINTER captures only one of A's positions that contains a specific number, even though that number may appear in A more than once. Finally, a price in execution time must be paid to create POINTER from A in the first place. However, if the solution to Example 2.2 needed to be executed repeatedly, for many values of K, then it might be worth the price. It is frequently the case that prior processing to extract or restructure data saves later processing time.

In terms of storage required, A takes up N storage entries, and POINTER takes up 100 storage entries. If N is much larger than 100, then POINTER even saves storage; if N is much smaller, it requires more storage. Thus it may be necessary to trade time for storage. It will become apparent that this is generally true, that saving execution time requires more storage and vice versa.

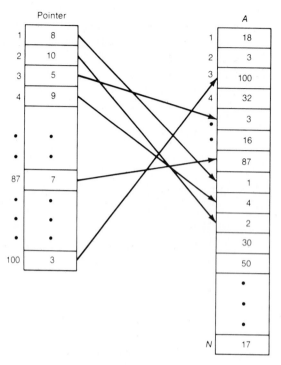

Figure 2.3 A Pointer Array for Example 2.2

When the choice of data structure was the array A, Example 2.1 was solved using selection, but traversal was required to find a solution to Example 2.2. When we chose the POINTER array to represent information, we were able to use selection to solve Example 2.2 more efficiently. However, if we had wanted to know *all* the cars leased by account K, POINTER would not have been sufficient. It would have been necessary to traverse A to find *all* the occurrences of account number K. Can you find a way to avoid this traversal?

Pascal and high-level languages in general also provide arrays of more than one dimension. Thus the Pascal declaration,

   A : **array** [1..5, 1..3] **of** integer;

defines a two-dimensional array of 5×3 or 15 entries, each of type integer. A can also be viewed as a collection of 5 one-dimensional arrays, each of length 3, or 3 one-dimensional arrays, each of length 5. Again, we can think of two variables I and J of the correct index type as pointing to an entry of the array. Thus $A[I, J]$ refers to the entry of the Ith row and Jth column, or to the entry of A currently pointed to by I and J. We assume that the (I, J)th entry can be accessed in constant time, no matter what the value of I or J. That is, the (I, J)th entry may be selected. Traversal of two-dimensional arrays may also be easily done.

Example
2.3

Suppose a collection of N^2 numbers, representing the distances between N (≤ 50) cities, is stored in a two-dimensional array A. Thus $A[I, J]$ contains the distance between city I and city J. A two-dimensional array is *symmetric* if $A[I, J]$ and $A[J, I]$ contain the same value for all I and J between 1 and N. For this example, which involves distances, the array must be symmetric. Array A shown in Figure 2.4 is not symmetric because $A[3, 4]$ does not equal $A[4, 3]$. The N entries $A[1, 1], A[2, 2], \ldots,$ $A[N, N]$ are called its **diagonal entries.** In the city–distance array, the diagonal entries must, of course, be zero. $\square$

Suppose a programmer wished, perhaps as part of an input validation module for the data of A, to check the array for symmetry. The programmer might choose to write a boolean function CHECK to return the value *true* if A is symmetric and *false* otherwise. A simple traversal, as follows, will carry out the task of checking.

```
type
    collection = array [1..50, 1..50] of real;
function CHECK(A : collection; N : integer) : boolean;
var
    I, J : integer;
begin
    CHECK := true;
    for I := 1 to N do
        for J := 1 to N do
            if A[I, J] <> A[J, I] then
                CHECK := false
end;
```

This program does a complete traversal of the appropriate N^2 entries of the array A. However, it is inefficient as a solution for a number of reasons. First, it does not exit immediately from the loops, even though it may have just found that A could not be symmetric. Second, it checks the diagonal elements, which will *always* satisfy $A[I, J] = A[J, I]$. Finally, it double checks each off-diagonal entry. For instance, when $I = 3$ and $J = 4$ it checks $A[3, 4]$ against $A[4, 3]$, and when $I = 4$ and $J = 3$ it checks $A[4, 3]$ against $A[3, 4]$ again. A better version would be a modified traversal such as

A

	1	2	3	4
1	1	5	-7	10
2	5	2	6	11
3	-7	6	0	8
4	10	11	9	3

Figure 2.4 An Asymmetric Two-Dimensional Array

```
function CHECK(A : collection, N : integer) : boolean;
var
    I, J : integer;
    CK : boolean;
begin
    CK := true;
    I := 1;
    while ((I <= N) and CK) do
        begin
            J := 1;
            while ((J < I) and CK) do
                begin
                    if A[I, J] <> A[J, I] then
                        CK := false;
                    J := J + 1
                end;
            I := I + 1
        end;
    CHECK := CK
end;
```

Be sure you understand why this eliminates the inefficiencies.

2.1.3 Representation of Records in Arrays

In Pascal and COBOL the record is a basic data structure. In other languages, such as FORTRAN, the record is not a built-in feature but must be constructed from the structures that are available. To see how this construction might be done, assume Pascal designers had provided the integer, real, boolean, and char data types, and only *one*-dimensional arrays. Not only would records have to be constructed, but so would arrays of more dimensions if they were needed. There are two reasons for looking at ways to build data structures.

1. It affords insight into how compilers implement records and higher dimensional arrays.
2. It demonstrates how programmers build new structures from those that are given in order to tailor data structure to specific needs.

Moreover, even though records and higher dimensional arrays *are* available in Pascal, there are times when programmers find it preferable to use these construction techniques.

Let us consider how to represent N records, each composed of M fields of some fixed type. Suppose M is 3. A natural solution is to take an array, of length $3*N$, of the same type as the fields, and store the records in the array. The first record takes up the first three entries, the second record the next three entries, and so on as in Figure 2.5. Each field of a record will be stored in the corresponding one of its three entries.

The Ith record begins in position $1 + 3*(I - 1)$ of the array. Thus we may *select* the Ith record.

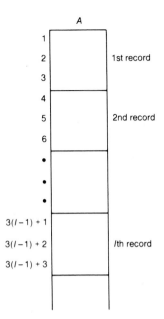

Figure 2.5 An Array of Records (of Length 3)

It is also easy to traverse the records using a *loop*, starting with I at 1 and ending with I at N. Of course, to access a specific field of the Ith record, say the third, position $1 + 3*(I-1) + 2$ of the array must be accessed. For example, the following procedure traverses the N records stored in the array A and prints the value in their Kth field, where K may be 1, 2, or 3.

```
procedure PRINTFIELD(A : recordarray; N,K : integer);
const
    LENGTH = 3;
var
    I : integer;
begin
    for I := 1 to N do
        WRITELN(A[1 + LENGTH * (I − 1) + (K − 1)])
end;
```

In Pascal, since arrays must be homogeneous (consisting of entries of the same type), this method is applicable only to homogeneous records, records whose fields are all of the same type. The method is useful in FORTRAN, since there are ways to represent a variety of data types in a single array. The following, more general example, demonstrates how the Pascal compiler might treat records:

Example 2.4 Consider Figure 2.6, which represents an array CARS containing a record for each car of an automobile rental agency. The record for each car has a field for the make

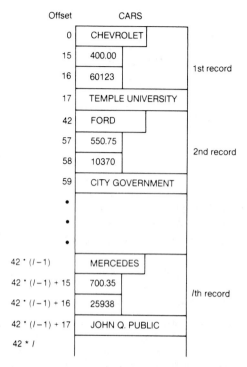

Figure 2.6   Records of a Car Rental Agency Stored in an Array CARS

(characters), monthly rate (a real number), current mileage (an integer), and the rentee (characters). This array, with entries of different types, could only be constructed in languages without strong typing constraints. All the records in the array are 42 elements long, using 15 elements for the make, 1 element each for the monthly rate and current mileage, and 25 elements for the rentee field. □

An offset gives the position of a data item with respect to a given reference point. When you say, "the third house from the corner," you are using an offset reference point. Each field has a *field offset* from the beginning of the record. In this case, the field offsets are 0, 15, 16, and 17, respectively, for make, monthly rate, current mileage, and rentee. The Ith record has a *record offset* of $42 * (I - 1)$ from the beginning of the array. The offset for its rentee field from the beginning of the array is $42 * (I - 1) + 17$, the sum of the record offset for the Ith record and the field offset for the rentee.

In order to reference, say, the current mileage field of the Ith record, the programmer may refer to CARS $[1 + 42 * (I - 1) + 16]$, assuming the first record starts in element one of the array. Only the fields may be referred to by the programmer; the record itself cannot be dealt with directly as a unit. This contrasts with the Pascal capability to define a carrecord as

```
type
    carrecord = record
        make : array [1 .. 15] of char;
        rate : real;
        mileage : integer;
        rentee : array [1 .. 25] of char
    end;
```

and CARS as an array of carrecords. Then the Pascal programmer may refer to the *I*th record as a unit, as CARS[*I*], and to its mileage field, by CARS[*I*].MILEAGE. The FORTRAN programmer cannot refer to a record in this way as a unit since FORTRAN does not provide the record data structure. Treating a record as a unit allows intentions to be stated more clearly in a program; it also allows for the contents of one record to be assigned to the storage for another record more efficiently. This is analogous to being able to refer to an automobile, to say "Move that automobile from here to there," rather than specifying the automobile or the move by referring to each of its parts individually.

Note that the record referred to during the execution of a program may be changed merely by changing the value of *I*, but the field referred to cannot be changed, since field names may not be changed during execution. This means that code referring to the *I*th entry of an array, such as CARS[*I*], may refer to different array entries as a program executes by computing a new value for *I*. Code using a field name will always refer to that particular field.

This example gives a technique for storing records in languages without strong typing constraints. It could not be used by the Pascal programmer. Still, a Pascal *compiler* might implement CARS in the actual computer memory as illustrated in Figure 2.6. In this case, if the initial array address in memory is 100 rather than 1, then the offset (or relative position) for the *I*th record is added to 100 instead of to 1. The compiler can produce commands that calculate the actual position in memory of any field of the *I*th record by adding the record offset and field offset to 100. Then a programmer's reference to CARS[2] is interpreted as a reference to the 42 consecutive locations 142 to 183. Similarly, CARS[2].RATE refers to the entry in location 157. This assumes the array starts at memory location 100. The offsets are independent of the starting location. When applied to homogeneous records, this method requires that CARS be defined to be the same type as the record's fields.

Observe that the CARS array preserves the homogeneity of type that is required of all arrays in Pascal. Its entries are now all of the same specific record type. The array entries just happen to be of type carrecord even though a record itself is not homogeneous. Both COBOL and Pascal allow operations to be performed directly on records, treating them as a unit. Of course, the compiler hides the details of the records' implementation from readers of the program, and provides facility in handling records.

The method just discussed is a single-array implementation. The second method of representing the *N* records is a straightforward multiarray implementation, shown in Figure 2.7. The method simply uses a different array for each field. Each array

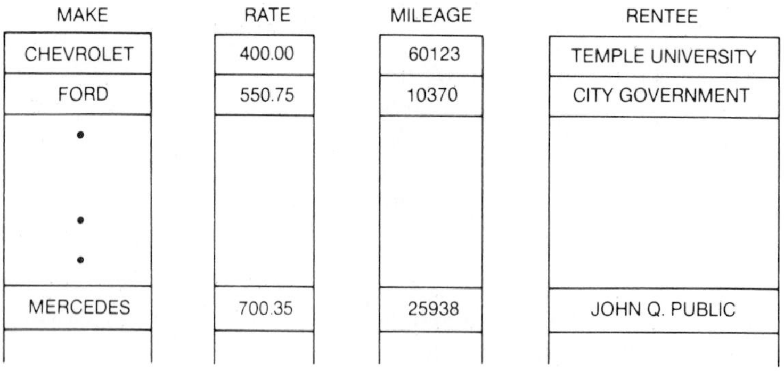

MAKE	RATE	MILEAGE	RENTEE
CHEVROLET	400.00	60123	TEMPLE UNIVERSITY
FORD	550.75	10370	CITY GOVERNMENT
•			
•			
•			
MERCEDES	700.35	25938	JOHN Q. PUBLIC

Figure 2.7   A Multiarray Storage of Records of a Car Rental Agency

then contains information of the appropriate type only. Again, there is no *direct* way to refer to the collective notion CARS[2]. Instead its data are given by MAKE[2], RATE[2], MILEAGE[2], and RENTEE[2]. Selection of the *I*th record and traversal through the records is possible for this method also.

The single-array technique causes problems when all entries are not of the same type. These may be overcome to some extent in FORTRAN but not in Pascal. However, Example 2.4 shows the offset calculations done by the Pascal compiler, which are invisible to the Pascal programmer. The multiple-array technique is useful in any language that provides arrays. Both techniques fail to give the programmer means to refer directly to, or to manipulate as a unit, an entire record composed of more than one field. The Pascal approach provides the record data structure, makes the underlying details transparent to the Pascal programmer, and thus provides an elegant solution to the problem of treating information of different types as a unit.

2.1.4 Variable-Length Records

When the records of a collection are not necessarily of the same length, they are called **variable-length records.** Looking back at the single-array and the multi-array representations for a collection of records, it is clear that selection of the *I*th record was possible only under the tacit assumption that the records were all the same length.

Suppose a field is added to carrecord for each previous rentee. Surely some newer cars will have few previous rentees and older cars will have a long history of rentees. The programmer could decide to represent each car's record by using a single-length record large enough to accommodate the largest possible number of past rentees. This would aid in processing, as uniformity always does, but could waste a great deal of storage if many records actually have short histories.

With variable-length records, shorter records use fewer locations than longer records, as shown in Figure 2.8. Details of the implementation of such a collection of records must somehow specify where one record ends and the next starts. Separators between records would do, or a field associated with each record could give its total length. Using separators, the last element of the storage for a record would

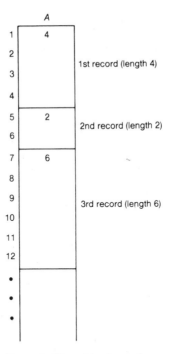

Figure 2.8 Variable-Length Records Stored in Array *A*

contain a special value denoting the end of the record's storage, while using an associated field with each record to store its length in its first storage element would allow a determination of the last element of its storage. In either case, the *I*th record may no longer be selected because its location cannot be calculated. However, given the position of the *I*th record, one can calculate the position of the $(I + 1)$th record.

Assuming the first element of each record contains its length, as in Figure 2.8, the following procedure accomplishes the traversal. A record of zero length is used as a sentinel to indicate there are no more records in the array.

```
procedure TRAVERSE(A : recordarray);
const
    ZERO = 0;
var
    I : integer;
begin
    I := 1;
    while (A[I] <> ZERO) do
        begin
            PROCESS(A, I);
            I := I + A[I]
        end
end;
```

The recordarray here is simply an array of individual elements; the programmer *imposes* the record structure. Each field of the record must thus have the same type in Pascal. PROCESS is a procedure that does whatever processing is called for. Thus, traversal through the records can be used to access the Ith record, but this takes time proportional to I.

2.1.5 Variant Records

This situation is avoided in Pascal, since records of variable length are stored in arrays as *variant records.* Pascal compilers implement variant records by assigning the maximum possible variant record length to each record. The records are then stored using the single-array method. Since each record is now of the same length, selection is still possible. Another way to implement records in Pascal is the *heap*, which tailors the length to the variant.

Variant records are used in this way only when the number of distinct record lengths is small. When many lengths are involved, lists (see Chapter 3) would be preferred to variant records. Lists, although created out of fixed-length records, may have varying lengths.

2.1.6 Address Calculation without Access

Calculating the address of an item of data is not the same thing as accessing the item of data. The *address* of an item is its storage position, not its value. To *access* the item means to read its current value from memory or to store a value in its memory location.

Many authors associate the process of selection with the idea of access to an item, rather than with the calculation of the storage address of the item. They say that the Ith item of a structure can be selected if, given the value of I, the program can access the item in a time that is independent of I. Such a structure is called a *random access* structure. This definition served well for early computers, in which arrays could reside in a single homogeneous memory. However, current practice includes radically different memory architectures.

Modern computers have memory hierarchies—that is, different kinds of memory—whose access times vary by one or two orders of magnitude from one level of the hierarchy to the next. It may well be the case that some portion of an array is stored in fast memory, such as high-speed cache memory, and some portion in slower central memory. Then the access time for an array element would depend on the index of the element (that is, its position in the sequence of the array). But the time required to *compute the storage address* would still be independent of the value of the index. Consequently, the process of address calculation should be thought of as separate from the process of access to the data. *Selection* thus denotes address calculation without access. Although it is important to grasp this distinction between address calculation and actual access, it is generally ignored in the explanations here, as in other texts, for convenience of exposition.

Our interest in the effect of data structures on program efficiency concerns the *timing* of various algorithms. Because access times may vary depending on features of the physical computer that are completely hidden from the language, we will

boolean
True or false
0 +1
≠
< >
:= assigns a value

measure time as if each program were executed on a computer that has a single homogeneous central memory.

The special techniques that are required to write efficient programs for computers with hierarchical memories are not in the scope of this text. Some computers even allow the exploitation of any parallelism inherent in an algorithm. This means that more than one operation may be carried out at a time. The text also largely ignores this possibility of parallel processing, although it is currently a topic of computer research.

If this array of material leaves you in disarray, keep going—pointers will point the way!

2.2 **Mortar**

2.2.1 **Pointers**

In Pascal, records can be stored in arrays. They can also be stored in a special area of memory called the **Pascal heap. Pointers** are variables that point to data items. Those that point to array entries have already been called array indexes. Those that point to heap records are called **pointer variables.** By following a pointer, you can access a record. Sometimes it is necessary to access a record by following a sequence of pointers.

Pointers and pointer variables afford flexibility in structuring data but must be used with great care, since they can introduce subtle errors that cause difficulty in the debugging of a program. The errors are problems that arise when collections of records can expand or contract in unpredictable ways. Storage for such records must be managed carefully.

To understand pointers and pointer variables, it is practical to examine them in a more static context. They are useful, even then, in solving problems involving variable-length records, and the representation of arrays. A good way to become familiar with the workings of pointers and pointer variables is to solve the following problem: *Is there a way to store* N *variable-length records in a one-dimensional array so that traversal through the records is possible, and, more important, so that the* Ith *one can be selected?*

The solution is not difficult in a programming language that lacks the strong typing constraint on arrays that is a feature of Pascal. Suppose a pointer array P is created, as in Figure 2.9. The information in $P[I]$ should state where the base, or origin, of the Ith record is in A. Thus $P[4]$ is 13 because the fourth record begins in $A[13]$. One describes this by saying that $P[I]$ contains a pointer to the Ith record in A. I can be thought of as pointing indirectly to a record in A; to get to it requires an access to P along the way.

Recall that records are represented by a sequence of consecutive entries, so $P[I]$ points to the first entry of the Ith record, its base. Once the base of a record and its field offsets are known, any field of the record can be selected. This technique of using pointer arrays is an old and very important technique in computer science. This kind of pointer is just an array index; it is also known as a *relative* pointer, because it indicates the position of the record in relation to the other records within the same

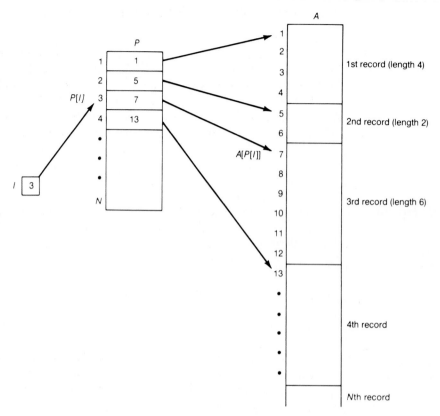

Figure 2.9   Pointer Array P, with Pointers to Records Stored in A

array. This is different from the other type of pointer in Pascal, the *pointer variable,* which refers to actual memory locations.

Selecting the *I*th record is now possible by accessing $P[I]$ and following the pointer found there to the entry of A in which the *I*th record begins. The base of this record has the name $A[P[I]]$. Note that selection is being applied first to array P, and then to array A. Each takes constant time, which is why we say the *I*th record may be selected. It is also easy to traverse through the records using P as shown by the following program.

```
procedure TRAVERSE(var A : recordarray; P : pointerarray; N : integer);
var
    I : integer;
begin
    for I := 1 to N do
        PROCESS(A, P, I)
end;
```

Using the pointerarray costs additional storage but solves the problem posed for variable-length records. Relative pointers to records stored in an array are easy to use when language typing constraints are not violated.

2.2.2 Pointer Variables and the Pascal Heap

As a programmer you may need to store a collection of records that are not all of the same type. In Pascal they cannot be kept in a single array, since that would violate the array typing constraint. But there is an easy way out: simply declare each different type to be one of the variants of a variant record. With this trick Pascal treats records of different types as records of the same type and the problem disappears! This solution sidesteps the issue of using less storage for shorter records and more storage for longer records, however. Another difficulty in Pascal is how to store a collection of records, even if they are all of the same type, when the maximum number of such records is not known in advance. Storing them in an array requires specifying the length of the array, but the programmer may not know what this should be. A practical solution to both of these difficulties is provided by the Pascal heap.

So far, by grouping records in arrays, it has been possible to refer to a record by its position in the array. This eliminates the need to attach a separate name to each record of the group. Imagine keeping track of all the names for a large collection, and imagine what a program segment for their traversal would look like. Its length would be proportional to the number of names!

The Pascal *heap* may be viewed as a collection of storage elements on call for the storage of record information. However, records stored in the heap do not have names or array positions to be used for their reference. Instead, *pointer variables* are used to point to an individual heap record. A heap record can be accessed only through its pointer variable. A pointer is like a string attached to a record: follow it and you get to the record. The pointers previously examined point to a record's position in an array, whereas pointer variables point to a record in the heap. Conceptually, both play the same role: they lead to a record.

Declaring a record type for records to be stored in the heap is the same as for individual records or records stored in arrays. However, an associated variable of type pointer must be declared and used to refer to the record. For example, to store a record of type carrecord to be referenced by the pointer variable CAR1 requires the following additional declarations,

```
type
    pointer = ↑ carrecord;
var
    CAR1 : pointer;
    CAR2 : carrecord;
```

The declaration of CAR2 is not needed, but an important distinction exists between the variable CAR1 of type pointer, CAR2 of type carrecord, and CARS of type array of carrecord. The variables CAR2 and CARS are not stored in the heap. Storage is allocated to them as soon as the component of the program in which they are declared is executed. The programmer need do nothing other than declare them to ensure this allocation of storage, and may immediately write statements to assign values to them.

This is *not* the case for the record pointed to by CAR1, which is to be stored in the heap. CAR1 itself is not stored in the heap, but the record it will point to is. This is because CAR1 was declared to be of pointer type. The prefix, ↑, denotes this. No storage is allocated for that record until a specific request made by the programmer is executed. This is done by an invocation of the Pascal standard procedure NEW. Thus,

    NEW(CAR1);

when executed, places a pointer value into CAR1 and also allocates storage in the heap to which that pointer value points. Until this is done, CAR1's value is undefined. After NEW(CAR1)'s execution, the situation may be pictured as in Figure 2.10.

The record itself may be referenced by CAR1↑, and its fields may be referenced as CAR1↑.MAKE, CAR1↑.RATE, CAR1↑.MILEAGE, CAR1↑.RENTEE. At this point, though, the contents of the fields are undefined. Storage has simply been allocated for them in the heap. The same, of course, is true for CAR1 and CARS. Just as they may be assigned values by using the assignment statement, so each field of the record pointed to by CAR1 can be given a value. Thus CAR1↑.RATE := 20 assigns a value of 20 to the rate field of the heap record pointed to by CAR1. Thus you must be sure that before values are assigned to a record stored in the heap, you have assigned a value to the pointer variable pointing to that record.

Remember that a pointer variable points to a record of a specific type and cannot be used to reference a variable of any other type. Pointer variables can be compared, and one can be copied into another, but both must point to records of the same type. This is necessary for your Pascal program to be syntactically correct. You don't want to spend your time correcting syntax errors. The advantages of using pointer variables, that is, of storing records in the heap, will appear as we proceed.

One disadvantage is that the value of a pointer variable cannot be printed out. This means that the programmer can never see the value of a pointer variable. Thus pointer variables cannot be looked at for debugging purposes; only the record they point to can be printed.

A significant savings of storage is possible when variant records are stored in the heap, because the particular variant is allocated only as much storage as it needs. This contrasts with the way variant records are treated when they are not stored in the heap. To achieve this savings, the NEW procedure must be invoked with a second parameter indicating the particular variant for which storage is being requested. This will be demonstrated in the next example.

Selection and traversal of a collection of records stored in the heap may be done by using an array of pointer variables. The array is then of type pointer, and its entries point to records in the heap.

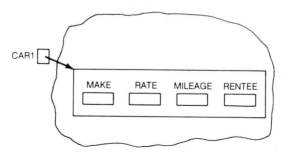

Figure 2.10   A Pascal Heap

Example
2.5 The record type "student" defines a record with four variant types. Each class, freshman through senior, has its own transcript type. The transcript is an array of enrollment records indicating courses the student has taken. Thus different variants have different lengths. The array STUDENTPOINTER is declared to be an array of pointers to student records. □

```
type
    classtype = (freshman, sophomore, junior, senior);
    courselist = array [1 .. 20] of enrollment record;
    pointer    = ↑student;
    student    = record
                    name : array [1 .. 30] of char;
                    address : array [1 .. 100] of char;
                    case transcript : classtype of
                        freshman : (freshmancourselist : courselist);
                        sophomore : (sophomorecourselist,
                                        freshmancourselist : courselist);
                        junior : (juniorcourselist,
                                    sophomorecourselist,
                                    freshmancourselist : courselist);
                        senior : (seniorcourselist,
                                    juniorcourselist,
                                    sophomorecourselist,
                                    freshmancourselist : courselist);
                end;
var
    STUDENTPOINTER : array [1 .. N] of pointer;
```

Executing,

```
NEW(STUDENTPOINTER[I], junior);
READIN(STUDENTPOINTER[I], junior);
```

creates storage for a junior variant and places in STUDENTPOINTER[I] a pointer to the newly created record, and the procedure READIN inputs information into that record. Repetition of these statements would fill the STUDENTPOINTER array, creating a directory of students.

Arrays of pointer variables to records in the heap are not as easy to use as relative pointers to records in an array but provide the flexibility to deal with different data types by using variant records. You shall see, though, that considerable care is needed to use them properly.

2.3 Representations of Two-Dimensional Arrays

It is time to return to the problem of how to represent higher dimensional arrays in terms of one-dimensional arrays. For simplicity, only two-dimensional arrays are discussed, but the techniques can be readily extended for higher dimensions. Two techniques will be studied: 1) rowwise and columnwise representation and 2) pointer array representation.

What exactly is meant by representing a two-dimensional array A in terms of a one-dimensional array, say DATA, and why is it done? The idea is that the problem to be solved may involve the use of A, but the language being used may not provide two-dimensional arrays, or for some other reason we may choose not to use them. Instead, we store the entries of A in DATA. This must be done so that whenever we want to refer to the (I, J)th entry of A in our program, we refer instead to the corresponding position of DATA in which it is stored. For example, the CHECK functions of Example 2.3 referred to a two-dimensional array A. If its information were stored in DATA, then the functions would have to be rewritten, replacing each reference to $A[I, J]$ by a reference to the correct entry in DATA which corresponds to it. Of course, the declarations involving A would also have to be replaced by declarations involving DATA.

2.3.1 Rowwise and Columnwise Representation

Suppose A has R rows and C columns, with row index range $1 . . R$ and column index range $1 . . C$. A *rowwise representation* for A uses a DATA array of length $R \times C$ and stores the first row of A in the first C consecutive entries of DATA, the second row in the next C entries, and so on.

Rowwise representation in arrays is similar to the first method discussed for storing records. In fact, it is logically the same as viewing each row as a record of length C. Thus the offset of the (I, J)th entry of A is $(I - 1) * C + (J - 1)$ in DATA. This is because $(I - 1)$ rows precede the Ith row in DATA, and take up $(I - 1) * C$ entries. The Jth entry of the Ith row is offset an additional $(J - 1)$ entries.

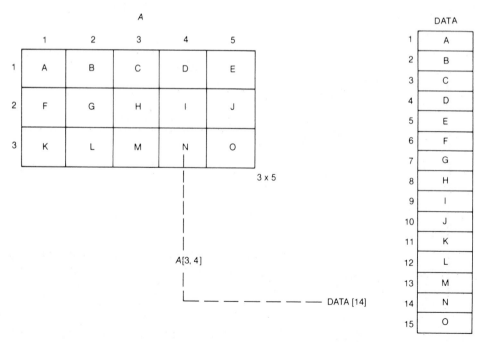

Figure 2.11   Representing a Two-Dimensional Array as a One-Dimensional Array

For the array A shown in Figure 2.11, with $C = 5$, the offset of $A[3, 4]$ is $(3 - 1) * 5 + (4 - 1)$ or 13, and the third row of A starts at DATA$[1 + 10]$, or DATA[11]. $A[3, 4]$ is represented by DATA$[1 + 13]$, or DATA[14].

If A were declared by $A :$ **array** $[3 . . 10, 6 . . 11]$ **of** carrecord; then $A[I, J]$ would be stored in DATA$[1 + ((I - 3) * (11 - 6 + 1) + (J - 6)) * 42]$. $A[4, 7]$ would be in DATA$[1 + ((4 - 3) * (6) + (7 - 6)) * 42]$, or DATA[295].

A simple formula, the ***address polynominal*** of A, can be derived for calculating the offset of the entry in DATA corresponding to the (I, J)th entry of A. This formula involves the column index range (CIR), the range starting values, $R1$ and $C1$, and the length, L, of the entry type of A. In the carrecord example, these are, respectively, $6(11 - 6 + 1)$, 3 and 6, and 42. The general formula is $((I - R1) * (CIR) + (J - C1)) * L$. Since the formula may be evaluated in constant time for any I and J values, the position to access in DATA for the (I, J)th entry of A may be calculated in constant time. In other words, the (I, J)th entry may be *selected*. This holds true for higher dimensions as well.

With this representation, function CHECK of Example 2.3 would be written as

```
type
    collection = record
                     data = array [1 . . 2500] of real
                 end;
function CHECK(A : collection; N : integer) : boolean;
var
    I, J : integer;
    CK : boolean;
begin
    CK := true;
    I := 1;
    while ((I <= N) and CK) do
        begin
            J := 1;
            while ((J < I) and CK) do
                begin
                    if (A.DATA[1 + (I − 1) * N + (J − 1)] <> A.DATA[1 + (J − 1) * N + (I − 1)]) then
                        CK := false;
                    J := J + 1
                end;
            I := I + 1
        end;
    CHECK := CK
end;
```

Notice that this way of defining collection allows the parameters of CHECK to be the same as in Example 2.3. Obviously, this representation in DATA allows A to be traversed, as well as allowing its (I, J)th entry to be selected.

The *columnwise representation* of a two-dimensional array is similar, except the columns rather than the rows of A are stored sequentially in DATA. The address polynomial for the columnwise representation is $((J - C1) * (RIR) + (I - R1)) * L$, where RIR is the row index range.

2.3.2 **Symmetric Array Representation**

Example 2.6
Suppose a program involves an $N \times N$ array A that is always symmetric. In other words, it is initially symmetric, and any processing performed on A does not disturb its symmetry. When N is small, both the rowwise and columnwise representations are feasible, even though roughly one-half of the information being stored is superfluous. For large values of N, say 400, the computer system may not provide the required 160,000 storage elements, so the program could not execute. One remedy may be to store only the diagonal entries of A and the entries below the diagonal (these are the entries whose row index I exceeds the column index J). This requires $(N^2 + N)/2$ entries, or 80,200 instead of 160,000.

Although high-level languages could have provided a data-type, symmetric array to be used in this way, no language does. Instead, the programmer can construct a DATA array of length $(N^2 + N)/2$ to store the entries. The idea is the same as for a rowwise representation, except that only those entries of a row in the lower half or on the diagonal of A are stored. Thus for row I, entries $A[I, 1], A[I, 2], \ldots, A[I, I]$ are stored in consecutive entries of DATA, each row's entries following those of the preceding row. □

To use this representation of A, the programmer needs to be able to refer, for given I and J, to the proper position of DATA that corresponds to $A[I, J]$, just as was done in the CHECK function. Finding the offset formula is a little more complex than for the rowwise representation but is done in the same way.

Preceding the entries for the Ith row are the $1, 2, 3, \ldots,$ and $(I - 1)$ entries for the first $(I - 1)$ rows. The Jth entry of the Ith row is then an additional $(J - 1)$ entries down in DATA. Thus the offset for $A[I, J]$ is $1 + 2 + 3 + \cdots + (I - 1) + (J - 1)$. Any reference we want to make to $A[I, J]$ is made, instead, by a reference to $DATA[1 + (1 + 2 + \cdots + (I - 1) + (J - 1)]$. This, of course, is true only for $I \geq J$ since $A[I, J]$, when $I < J$, is not stored in DATA directly. Its symmetric entry in A, $A[J, I]$ *is* stored in $DATA[1 + (1 + 2 + \cdots + (J - 1)) + (I - 1)]$. So if $I < J$, a reference to $A[I, J]$ must be achieved by referring to $A[J, I]$.

The polynomial $1 + (1 + 2 + \cdots + (I - 1)) + (J - 1)$ (or $(1 + 2 + \cdots + (I - 1) + J)$ appears at first glance to require a loop for its calculation, requiring time proportional to I. However,

$$1 + 2 + \cdots + (I - 1) \text{ is actually the same as } \frac{I * (I - 1)}{2} \text{ for } I \geq 1.$$

Hence the polynomial may be evaluated in constant time. This means that the (I, J)th entry of A can be *selected* using the index,

$$\frac{I * (I - 1)}{2} + J \qquad \text{when } I \geq J$$

and

$$\frac{J * (J - 1)}{2} + I \qquad \text{when } I < J.$$

Traversal may also be accomplished easily. Think of the entries stored in DATA for each row as records of variable length. Yet they can be selected and traversed conveniently with no pointer array. The reason is that their lengths, and the order in which they are stored, are regular enough so we can make the requisite calculations for positions. In the *general* case of variable-length records, there is no way to do this.

2.3.3 Pointer Array Representation

The second technique for representing a two-dimensional array in terms of one-dimensional arrays uses a pointer array *P*. **Pointer arrays** have pointers as their entries. The entries of the pointer array point to the rows of *A*, which may be stored in one of two ways: in DATA, a one-dimensional array, or in the Pascal heap. The number of rows, *R*, of *A* must be known. Then *P*, DATA, and *R* represent *A* when the array is used, and *P* and *R* represent *A* when the heap is used. In the array case, *P* is of integer type as in Section 2.2.1. In fact, this is just an application of that method.

Clearly, there is no need to store the rows one after another in DATA; they can be anywhere in the array as long as they do not overlap. This feature provides considerable flexibility in the use of storage.

A variation of the array technique would treat the rows stored in DATA as row records. In the heap case, *P* is of type pointer, and the row records are stored in the heap. Selection and traversal are thus both easily achieved. The corresponding versions (storing rows in DATA, storing row records in DATA, storing row records in the heap) of the function CHECK would appear as

```
type
    pointerarray = array [1..50] of integer;
    dataarray    = array [1..2500] of real;
function CHECK(P : pointerarray; DATA : dataarray; R : integer) : boolean;
var
    I, J : integer;
    CK : boolean;
begin
    CK := true;
    I := 1;
    while ((I <= R) and CHECK) do
        begin
            J := 1;
            while ((J < I) and CK) do
                begin
                    if (DATA[P[I] + J − 1] <> DATA[P[J] + I − 1]) then
                    CK := false;
                    J := J + 1
                end;
            I := I + 1
        end;
    CHECK := CK
end;
```

```
type
    rowrecord    = record
                        row : array [1..50] of real
                     end;
    pointerarray = array [1..50] of integer;
    dataarray    = array [1..50] of rowrecord;
function CHECK(P : pointerarray; DATA : dataarray; R : integer) : boolean;
var
    I, J : integer;
    CK : boolean;
begin
    CK := true;
    I := 1;
    while ((I <= R) and CK) do
        begin
            J := 1;
            while ((J < I) and CK) do
                begin
                    if (DATA[P[I]].ROW[J] <> DATA[P[J]].ROW[I]) then
                    CK := false;
                    J := J + 1
                end;
            I := I + 1
        end;
    CHECK := CK
end;

type
    rowrecord    = record
                        row : array [1..50] of real
                     end;
    rowpointer  = ↑rowrecord;
    pointerarray = array (1..50) of rowpointer;
function CHECK(P : pointerarray; R : integer) : boolean;
var
    I, J : integer;
    CK : boolean;
begin
    CK := true;
    I := 1;
    while ((I <= R) and CK) do
        begin
            J := 1;
            while ((J < I) and CK) do
                begin
                    if (P[I]↑.ROW[J] <>P[J]↑.ROW[I]) then
                        CK := false;
                    J := J + 1
                end;
            I := I + 1
        end;
    CHECK := CK
end;
```

The pointer array technique may be used storing columns instead of rows. Then P's entries point to the column records.

Example
2.7
It is often desirable to store information in an array in a specific order. Algorithms to rearrange the information to achieve the order require repeated interchange of rows. Suppose the programmer wants to interchange the Ith and Jth rows of the array A when it is represented using the pointer array P. This can be accomplished quickly, taking advantage of the pointers, by executing

```
begin
    TEMP := P[I];
    P[I] := P[J];
    P[J] := TEMP
end;
```

Note that the data in each row are not moved; only the pointers change. The time it takes the computer to switch rows is independent of their length. Contrast this with the processing involved for the rowwise method of representing A (Section 2.3.1). Even if A actually is available directly as a two-dimensional array, the pointer array representation is more efficient. Swapping columns, of course, is a much more involved task, unless the programmer has chosen to store columns rather than store rows. □

The pointer array method offers the advantage of convenience in storing rows of different lengths. Thus it can be used to construct arrays with rows of different lengths easily. Also, if many rows of A are the same, they need not be duplicated in DATA or in the heap. Their pointer entries in pointer array P need merely point to the same record, resulting in significant storage savings. The means should fit the ends as much as possible! In programming the ends, the desired operations, determine the means, the data structures to be used.

2.4 Advantages and Disadvantages of the Techniques

If you think of the rows (or columns) of a two-dimensional array as records, then what has been demonstrated amounts to five basic ways to store records so that selection and traversal are possible. The methods for storing a collection of records are as follows:

1. Fixed-length records of the same type are stored sequentially in a single array and accessed by calculating record and field offsets.
2. In the Pascal approach, each array entry is a record or a variant type.
3. Fixed-length records of the same type are stored in multiarrays, each of appropriate type to match a field type.
4. Relative pointer arrays to records stored in an array
5. Pointer variable arrays to records stored in the Pascal heap

The first approach is enlightening because it makes explicit the offset calculations that are usually provided invisibly by the compiler. A severe disadvantage of this approach is that the representation of different type records causes difficulties ranging from awkward (in FORTRAN) to impossible (in Pascal).

The second approach is the elegant form of this representation. It is possible in a language that provides the record data structure in which calculations are provided by the compiler. The disadvantage of the first approach then disappears.

The method of multiple arrays is applicable to all languages that provide arrays whether or not they have strong typing or the record data structure. This method, and the first, sacrifice the ability to refer to an entire record by a single term as provided by Pascal.

The two pointer-oriented methods work for collections of variable-length records but are convenient only when the number of distinct lengths is small. The more general case is treated in the next chapter. Relative pointers are easy to use but have the drawback that embedding records in a Pascal array raises the problems of clashes of data types.

Pascal pointers into the heap are more difficult and dangerous to use for reasons mentioned later, but provide extra flexibility. Since their values cannot be printed in Pascal, they cannot be looked at for debugging purposes. In any event, storing records in an array or in a heap eliminates the need to declare a variable name for them at the outset of a program, thus allowing records to be created dynamically during program execution.

The array is limited in the number of records it can store by its fixed length, which must be declared prior to program execution. The capacity of the heap can be much larger and need not be declared a priori but is determined by the computer system. As will become more apparent, the heap allows more efficient use of available storage.

In solving a problem we are free to use any data abstraction that is helpful. In deciding which data structure to use for its implementation, one must consider such factors as the possibility of carrying out the required operations, storage efficiency, execution time, and proneness to error. There is frequently a trade-off between storage efficiency and execution time. For example, pointers use extra storage and require some time to maintain, but typically give fast access. Developing the student's appreciation of such trade-offs in programming is one of the goals of this text.

2.5 Case Study: The Stable Marriage Problem

Consider Table 2.1. It represents for five men and five women, the preferences that each has expressed for the five members of the opposite sex. For example, the first man has ranked the women in the order 2, 4, 3, 1, 5.

Now suppose the group has paired off and married as in Table 2.2. M_i is said to be stable with respect to W_j if there is no other woman preferred by M_i to W_j who, in turn, prefers M_i to her mate. Similarly, W_j is stable with respect to M_i if there is

Table 2.1 Preferences

	Men's						Women's				
M_1	2	4	3	1	5	W_1	1	5	3	4	2
M_2	3	5	2	1	4	W_2	4	5	3	2	1
M_3	1	5	4	2	3	W_3	3	1	4	2	5
M_4	3	1	2	5	4	W_4	4	2	5	1	3
M_5	2	5	1	4	3	W_5	1	3	2	4	5

Table 2.2 Pairings

Men	Women
1	4
2	3
3	1
4	2
5	5

no other man W_j prefers to M_i who prefers W_j to his mate. *Any pair*, say M_i-W_j, *is stable* if each is stable with respect to the other. An *entire* pairing is stable if all its pairs are stable. Or, an entire pairing is *not* stable if there exists a man and a woman who are not mates, but who prefer each other to their mates.

Consider the pair M_3-W_1. Since M_3 prefers W_1 to all others, he is stable with respect to W_1. W_1 prefers M_1 and M_5 to M_3. M_1 is married to W_4 and does not prefer W_1 to W_4. M_5 is married to W_5 and does not prefer W_1 to W_5. Thus W_1 is also stable with respect to M_3. Hence the pair is stable. The entire pairing is *not* stable. For instance, M_2 and W_3 are paired, but W_3 prefers M_4 to her mate, and M_4 prefers W_3 to his mate. Hence M_2-W_3 is not a stable pair.

Suppose the problem is to write a program to check whether or not a given entire pairing is stable. The data consists of the N pairs and $2 * N^2$ preferences.

In these terms, the problem may appear frivolous, but it has other applications. The data might represent tasks and employees. Employees are ranked for each task by how well they perform it, and employees indicate their preferences for each task. Or students might provide their preferences for majors, and each major department gives its preferences for each student.

2.5.1 The Algorithm

The solution must traverse through the pairs and may be expressed as

1. Set man to 1.
2. Set check to "true."
3. While (check and man $\leq N$)
   a. set check to "false" if the man is not stable with respect to his wife or the wife is not stable with respect to her husband,
   b. increase man by 1.

An important module can be isolated and named STABLE. It must return true if a person is stable and false otherwise. A person is stable if every individual preferred by the person to the person's mate prefers his or her mate to the person. Refining STABLE we obtain,

1. Set STABLE to "true."
2. Set individual to whoever is most preferred by person.
3. While (STABLE and individual $<>$ person's mate)
       If the "individual prefers person to individual's mate, then
           set STABLE to false
       else
           set individual to whoever is next most preferred by person.

Note that STABLE requires

☐ Determining the mate of any person
☐ Choosing the individual most preferred by a person
☐ Determining if an individual prefers a person to the individual's mate
☐ Finding the individual next most preferred by a person

The solution follows the dictates of good programming style. The pairings and preference tables are treated as data abstractions, with their implementation put off until the basic operations on them have become clear. These operations correspond to the four tasks required of STABLE. These tasks will be implemented, respectively, as the modules MATE, MOSTPREFERRED, PREFERS, and NEXTPREFERRED. The implementation of the pairings and the preference data must now be selected before these modules may be written.

Task 1 is to determine a person's mate. If the pairings are kept in an array MPAIRS, then the mate of a man can be selected from the array, but the mate of a woman requires that the array be traversed. Instead, trading storage for time, we choose to create another array WPAIRS, so selection may be used in the latter case too. For this example, these arrays would be

MPAIRS		WPAIRS	
1	4	1	3
2	3	2	4
3	1	3	2
4	2	4	1
5	5	5	5

These may be created before the solution is invoked and so are assumed given.

Task 2 is to find out who is most preferred by a person. Suppose the preference tables are implemented as two-dimensional arrays MPREF and WPREF. Task 2 is then straightforward.

To perform task 3, determining if an individual prefers a person to the individual's mate, the row for that individual in the proper preference array may be traversed until either the person or the individual's mate is encountered. If the person is encountered first, PREFERS must be set to true, and otherwise to false.

Finally, task 4, finding the next preferred individual, can be done using an index to point to the current individual, and, after increasing the index by 1, selecting the (person, index) entry from the appropriate preference array.

STABLE can now be refined.

1. Set STABLE to "true."
2. Set individual to MOSTPREFERRED(person, PREF1).
3. Set person's mate to MATE(person, PAIRS1).
4. Set index to 1.
5. While (STABLE and individual <> person's mate)
   a. set individual's mate to MATE(individual, PAIRS2),
   b. if PREFERS(individual, person, individual's mate, PREF2), then
         set STABLE to "false"
      else
         i. Increase index by 1,
         ii. Set individual to NEXTPREFERRED(person, index, PREF1).

STABLE is assumed to include PAIRS1, PAIRS2, PREF1, and PREF2 among its parameters. These must be specified carefully when STABLE is invoked. For instance, if STABLE is called to work on a male person, then they must be MPAIRS, WPAIRS, MPREF, and WPREF, respectively. When STABLE is called to work on a female person, they must be WPAIRS, MPAIRS, WPREF, and MPREF, respectively.

The implementation for the modules used by STABLE can now be written.

```
function MATE(PERSON : integer; var PAIRS : mates) : integer;
begin
    MATE := PAIRS[PERSON]
end;

function MOSTPREFERRED(PERSON : integer;
                      var PREF : preferences) : integer;
begin
    MOSTPREFERRED := PREF[PERSON, 1]
end;

function PREFERS(INDIVIDUAL, PERSON, INDIVIDUALSMATE : integer;
                var PREF : preferences) : boolean;
var
    INDEX, NEXT : integer;
begin
    PREFERS := false;
    INDEX := 1;
    NEXT := PREF[INDIVIDUAL, 1];
    while ((NEXT <> PERSON) and (NEXT <> INDIVIDUALSMATE)) do
        begin
            INDEX := INDEX + 1;
            NEXT := PREF[INDIVIDUAL, INDEX]
        end;
    if NEXT = PERSON then
        PREFERS := true
end;

function NEXTPREFERRED(PERSON, INDEX : integer;
                      var PREF : preferences) : integer;
begin
    NEXTPREFERRED := PREF[PERSON, INDEX]
end;
```

To get an idea of the time required for this solution, note that STABLE's **while** loop can require a traversal through a row of PREF1. The **while** loop task may thus be executed $(N - 1)$ times since rows of PREF1 are of length N. During each of these executions, PREFERS is invoked and can traverse through a row of PREF2, which is also of length N. STABLE can thus take $O(N^2)$ time. Since STABLE may be invoked $2N$ times (twice for each pair), the total time of this solution could be $O(N^3)$. We can do better!

PREFERS' traversal through PREF2 can be eliminated. It is done simply to determine if the current individual prefers person to individual's mate. This information can be ferreted out beforehand from PREF2 and summarized in a priority array.

This needs to be done only *once*. Thus the priority array can be produced before the solution is invoked (so it is assumed to be given), or can be created initially in the main module before man is set to one.

One priority array must be created from MPREF and another from WPREF. MPRIORITY can be created from MPREF by traversing MPREF, and processing its (I, J)th entry by setting MPRIORITY[I, MPREF[I, J]] to J. Similarly, WPRIORITY can be obtained from WPREF. Then an individual prefers person to individual's mate if PRIORITY[individual, person] < PRIORITY[individual, individual's mate]. For our example, these arrays are as follows:

		MPRIORITY					WPRIORITY		
4	1	3	2	5	1	5	3	4	2
4	3	1	5	2	5	4	3	1	2
1	4	5	3	2	2	4	1	3	5
2	3	1	4	5	4	2	5	1	3
3	1	5	4	3	1	3	2	4	5

This version of PREFERS may be expressed as

```
function PREFERS(INDIVIDUAL, PERSON, INDIVIDUALSMATE : integer;
                PRIORITY : preferences) : boolean;
begin
    PREFERS := (PRIORITY[INDIVIDUAL, PERSON] < PRIORITY[INDIVIDUAL,
                INDIVIDUALSMATE])
end;
```

When person is male (female), the parameter PRIORITY must be WPRIORITY (MPRIORITY). The priority arrays result in $O(N)$ time for this STABLE, since one traversal is avoided. This reduces the total time of the solution to $O(N^2)$. Again we have traded storage for time. Extracting precisely the relevant information and implementing it properly, just as was done in Example 2.2, is what produced this time saving. Also, this version is more concise and clearer.

2.5.2 The Program

The solution expressed as a function STABILITYCHECK is

```
function STABILITYCHECK(N : integer; var DATA : information) : boolean;
var
    MAN; WIFE : integer;
    CHECK1, CHECK2, CHECK : boolean;
begin
    with DATA do
        begin
            MAN := 1;
            CHECK := true;
            while (CHECK and (MAN <= N)) do
                begin
```

```
                   WIFE := MPAIRS[MAN];
                   CHECK1 := STABLE(MAN, MPAIRS, WPAIRS, MPREF,
                                 WPRIORITY);
                   CHECK2 := STABLE(WIFE, WPAIRS, MPAIRS, WPREF,
                                 MPRIORITY);
                   CHECK := CHECK1 and CHECK2;
                   MAN := MAN + 1
               end
         end;
      STABILITYCHECK := CHECK
   end;
```

The function STABLE becomes

```
   function STABLE(PERSON : integer; var PAIRS1, PAIRS2 : mates;
                   var PREF1, PRIORITY : preferences) : boolean;
   var
      INDEX, PERSONSMATE, INDIVIDUAL, INDIVIDUALSMATE : integer;
      RESULT : boolean;
   begin
      RESULT := true;
      PERSONSMATE := MATE(PERSON, PAIRS1);
      INDIVIDUAL := MOSTPREFERRED(PERSON, PREF1);
      INDEX := 1;
      while (RESULT and (INDIVIDUAL <> PERSONSMATE)) do
         begin
            INDIVIDUALSMATE := MATE(INDIVIDUAL, PAIRS2);
            if PREFERS(INDIVIDUAL, PERSON, INDIVIDUALSMATE,
                       PRIORITY) then
               RESULT := false
            else
               begin
                  INDEX := INDEX + 1;
                  INDIVIDUAL := NEXTPREFERRED(PERSON, INDEX, PREF1)
               end
         end;
      STABLE := RESULT
   end;
```

Notice the symmetry apparent in STABILITYCHECK shown by the two calls to STABLE. The declarations for the data types may be taken as

```
   type
      mates       = array [1..MAXN] of integer;
      preferences = array [1..MAXN, 1..MAXN] of integer;
      information = record
                       mpairs, wpairs : mates;
                       mpref, wpref : preferences;
                       mpriority, wpriority : preferences
                    end;
```

It was not necessary to pass DATA and its fields as **var** parameters, since they are never changed. It was done to save storage that would otherwise be required for local copies.

The program checks an entire pairing for stability. The usual form of the stable marriage problem is to *find* a stable pairing for given preferences. Some simple cases allow stable pairings to be written by inspection:

1. *People have a unique way of looking at the world.* This case comes up when the first column of MPREF has N distinct entries: every man most prefers a different woman. Simply pair each man with his heart's desire. The case where WPREF has this property is similar.

2. *People are all the same.* This case occurs when the rows of MPREF are all exactly alike: every man has exactly the same preferences. Pair the most preferred woman with the man she most prefers. Pair the next most preferred woman with the man she most prefers among those not yet paired, and so on. For example:

MPREF				WPREF			
2	4	3	1	3	1	2	4
2	4	3	1	3	1	4	2
2	4	3	1	4	2	1	3
2	4	3	1	4	3	2	1

Pair W2 with M3, W4 with M4, W3 with M2, and W1 with M1. The case where WPREF has this property has a similar solution.

Not only is an algorithm for finding a stable pairing not apparent, it is not even evident that a stable pairing can always be found. It is true though, and the following algorithm constructs one. You might try your hand at convincing yourself that it always produces a stable pairing.

1. Set man to 1.
2. While (man is not paired)
    a. find the woman most preferred by man who is not yet paired, or, if paired, prefers man to her current mate,
    b. if the woman is not yet paired, then
        i. pair man to woman,
        ii. set man to an unpaired man if there is one
      else
        i. break the pair between the woman and her current mate,
        ii. pair woman to man,
        iii. set man to her ex mate.

For our example, the sequence of pairs is as shown in Table 2.3. Circles indicate conflicts that cause breaks when they occur. The final pairings are then 3–1, 4–3, 2–5, 5–2, 1–4.

This is a good example of a correct algorithm that surely requires both a proof of correctness (produces the proper result) and a proof that it will eventually stop. These are the essential ingredients of an algorithm. The proofs are left as exercises.

Table 2.3 Sequence of Pairs

Man	Man	Active Pairs	
1	1	1	2
	2	2	③
	3	3	1
	4	4	③
2		1	②
		3	1
		4	3
	2	2	5
	5	5	②
3		3	1
		4	3
		2	5
		5	2
	1	1	4

☐ Exercises

1. a. Do users of the subway system of a large city reach their destinations by a process analogous to selection or a process analogous to traversal and why?

b. Do users of the telephone system of a large city reach their parties by a process analogous to selection or one like traversal and why?

2. Suppose you are interested in processing English text in the following way:

a. Input is in the form of an English sentence.

b. The program is to check the sentence looking for violations of the spelling rule,

"'*I*' before '*E*' except after '*C*'"

(Do not worry about exceptions such as *neighbor, weigh,* etc.)

Would an array be a convenient data structure to use in your program and would traversal be a relevant process?

3. Write a Pascal program to print out how many elements of an integer array (of length N) contain *even* integers. Did you use the process of traversal?

4. In Example 2.2 suppose the POINTER array were stored in memory and there were no A itself. If you are told that $A[5]$ (row 5) and $A[9]$ have been interchanged, then what changes would you have to make to POINTER to reflect this interchange? What if $A[2]$ and $A[5]$ were interchanged?

5. Write a Pascal procedure to update the POINTER array of Example 2.2 to reflect the fact that the Ith and Jth columns of A have been interchanged.

6. a. Suppose the CARS array (Example 2.4) represents the fleet information for the cars of one rental agency. For a group of several such agencies, would the record data structure be convenient to represent all the information?

b. Assume the information is represented in an array that stores records, with each record containing all the information for a particular agency. In general, are these records fixed or variable length?

7. For Example 2.4 assume the alternate multiarray implementation. Write a Pascal procedure to interchange the Ith and Jth records.

8. Create a Pascal procedure that prints out the rentees of all cars that have been driven more than 50,000 miles for the multiarray implementation of Example 2.4.

9. Write a Pascal procedure to read in a sequence of at most twenty characters into an array. They are all digits (0, or 1, or 2, . . . , or 9) except for one character that will be a decimal point. After execution of the procedure the variable DP should point to the array element that contains the decimal point, and variable L should point to the last digit of the input sequence. The decimal point will always have at least one digit on each side.

10. Produce a Pascal procedure similar to that of Exercise 2.3 except that the array of integers is two-dimensional.

11. Suppose a checkerboard is represented as a two-dimensional array. Write a Pascal boolean function that is given the current configuration of the board and the move to be made by the player whose turn it is. The function is to return the value true if the move is legal and false otherwise. (Do not forget that a move can consist of many jumps.)

12. **a.** Is there an analogy between tabs in your home telephone directory and pointers?

b. If a song on a tape cassette is like a record data structure type, can a particular song be indexed or must a traverse be used to find it? How about a song on a phonograph record?

13. Explain the differences between a record stored in an array and in the Pascal heap.

14. Define a procedure to copy the student directory of Example 2.5 into an array STUDENTDIRECTORY, indexed by a pointer array of integers.

15. Write a procedure to interchange two records of the student directory of Example 2.5.

16. What procedure will create the student directory of Example 2.5?

17. Create a procedure to output from the student directory of Example 2.5 the names of all students who are seniors.

18. Assume the row representation for two-dimensional arrays has been extended to three-dimensional arrays. Determine the formula for the offset of $A[I, J, K]$.

19. The array A with R rows and C columns is stored using the rowwise representation with $A[1, 1]$ corresponding to the actual base location of A, ABASE. Given an integer number K (ABASE $\leq K \leq$ ABASE $+ R * C - 1$), write formulas that will yield the row and column of A to which actual location K corresponds. That is, if $A[I, J]$ is stored in K, then your formula for the row will yield I and for the column will yield J.

20. An *antisymmetric* array A is a square array that satisfies the condition that $A[I, J] = -A[J, I]$ for all $1 \leq I, J \leq N$. Hence the diagonal elements must be zero. Storing the antisymmetric array can be done just as storing the symmetric array was done except that now the diagonal entries can be omitted since they are known. Determine the formula for the offset of $A[I, J]$.

21. An array A is said to be *tridiagonal* if the nonzero entries of A fall along the three diagonals $A[I, I]$, $A[I, I + 1]$, and $A[I, I - 1]$ where I goes, respectively, from 1 to N, 1 to $N - 1$, and 2 to N.

a. Construct a rowwise representation of the nonzero entries of A, and find a formula for the offset of $A[I, J]$ in this array.

b. Construct a *diagonal* representation of the nonzero entries of a tridiagonal array, and find a formula for the offset of $A[I, J]$ in the array.

22. Write a Pascal procedure that takes a two-dimensional array represented in terms of P and DATA, as in Section 2.3.3, and changes P so that any duplicate rows of A are stored only once in DATA. Thus, if rows 2 and 7 are identical, the contents of $P[2]$ and $P[7]$ are made equal.

23. Define a Pascal procedure to output the N diagonal elements of the array A of Section 2.3.3 when the array is represented in terms of P and DATA.

24. Produce a Pascal procedure to print out the Jth column of array A when it is represented in terms of P and DATA as in Section 2.3.3.

25. Write a Pascal procedure to interchange $A[I, J]$ and $A[J, I]$, for all I, J, when A is represented in terms of P and DATA as in Section 2.3.3.

26. Create a Pascal procedure that takes any array A of integers with at most twenty entries and creates a pointer array P that has in $P[I]$ a pointer to the Ith largest entry of A. Thus $P[1]$ points to the largest entry of A.

27. Do the same as in Exercise 26 except the array A will be two-dimensional and the Ith record in P must contain two pointers, one for the row and one for the column of A's Ith largest entry.

28. Do Exercises 22 to 27 except use Pascal pointers and the Pascal heap. (Of course P cannot be printed.)

29. What pairs are not stable in the example pairings?

30. Give a procedure to create WPAIRS from MPAIRS.

31. Write a procedure to create a PRIORITY array given a PREF array.

32. What procedure will create a PREF array given a PRIORITY array?

33. a. Give a procedure to produce stable marriages.
   b. How much time does your answer to Exercise 33a require?

34. a. Why must the algorithm to produce stable marriages terminate eventually?
   b. Why does it produce stable marriages?

☐ Suggested Assignment

Suppose the amount of precipitation has been recorded over a region at N locations. In general each record consists of one to five numbers. You are to write and run six programs. Each is to produce the average precipitation. For example, if the input is

```
3.6
2.1
2.7
record sentinel
.67
1.2
record sentinel
1.9
record sentinel
final sentinel
```

the output should be the sum $[(3.6 + 2.1 + 2.7) + (.67 + 1.2 + 1.9)]$ divided by 6. Always *echo print* the input (that is, output the input as it is read in) and annotate all output so that you, or anyone, will know what the output means. Assume $N \leq 100$.

a. Two of the programs should assume all records are the same length, say 3. Program 1 will represent the records as fixed-length homogeneous records stored in a single array (method 1 of Section 2.4). Program 3 will represent them as fixed length records stored in multiarrays (method 3 of Section 2.4). For method 3, assume an additional record field giving the specific location where it was recorded.

b. Three of the programs should assume the general case of record lengths between 1 and 5. Program 2 will represent the records using Pascal variant records stored in an array (method 2 of Section 2.4). Program 4 will use a relative pointer array whose entries point to variant records stored in an array (method 4 of Section 2.4). The fifth program uses pointer variable arrays whose entries point to variant records stored in the Pascal heap. For method 4, output the content of the pointer array and the records to which each pointer points. For method 5, print only the record pointed to by each pointer. Your program for method 4 should work correctly no matter where the records are stored in the one-dimensional array.

c. Finally, one program should assume all records are of length 1 and represent entries in an $N \times N$ symmetric array. This program uses the symmetric array representation of Example 2.6. No two-dimensional array should be used in your solution.

The input and output for each program might appear as follows:

Input			Output
Programs A	1.	3.6	Echo print of the precipitation records:
		2.1	3.6, 2.1, 2.7
		2.7	.67, 1.2, 1.9
		RS	The average precipitation of the 6 values
		.67	is 2.028 inches. The number of records is 2.
		1.2	
		1.9	
		RS	
		FS	
	3.	White House	Echo print of the precipitation records:
		3.6	White House 3.6, 2.1, 2.7
		2.1	Lincoln Memorial .67, 1.2, 1.9
		2.7	The average precipitation of the 6 values
		RS	is 2.028 inches. The number of records is 2.
		Lincoln Memorial	
		.67	
		1.2	
		1.9	
		RS	
		FS	
Programs B	2.	3.6	Echo print of the precipitation records:
		2.1	3.6, 2.1, 2.7
		2.7	.67, 1.2
		RS	1.9
		FS	
		1.2	
		RS	The average precipitation of the 6 values
		1.9	is 2.028 inches. The number of records is 3.
		RS	
		FS	

4.   3.6
      2.1
      2.7
      RS
      .67
      1.2
      RS
      1.9
      RS
      FS

Echo print of the precipitation records:
   3.6, 2.1, 2.7
   .67, 1.2
   1.9

Pointer array		Data array	
1	10	10	3.6
2	1	11	2.1
3	16	12	2.7
		1	.67
		2	1.2
		16	1.9

The average precipitation of the 6 values is 2.018 inches. The number of records is 3.

5. This is all the same as for 4 except the pointer array will not appear and the data array will not be shown, only the heap records.

Heap records

3.6	.67	1.9
2.1	1.2	
2.7		

Programs C

3.6	2.1	2.7
.67	1.2	1.9
0.0	1.1	.15

Echo print of the precipitation records as a 3 × 3 array:

3.6	2.1	2.7
.67	1.2	1.9
0.0	1.1	.15

The average precipitation of the 9 values is 2.028 inches.

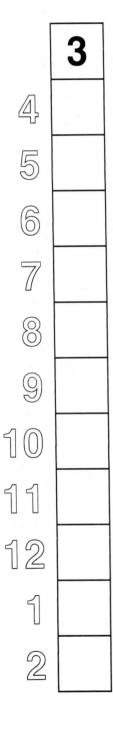

3 | Lists

3.1 Why Are Lists Needed?

Imagine you are a financial wizard and want to store information about your stock portfolio as records. Table 3.1 lists the information.

Table 3.1 A Stock Portfolio

Name	# Shares	Value	Date Bought
Apple	300	$ 7,512.46	3/15/84
CBS	100	8,000.55	6/16/83
Digital	200	18,400.00	9/20/83
IBM	100	11,213.25	1/20/83
IBM	200	21,400.00	4/17/84
Sears	100	3,100.00	2/10/82
Sears	100	3,200.00	4/6/84

How should these records be stored? The book so far has shown how to store them in

☐ Individual storage elements with individual names
☐ An array, so they can be referenced by position or from a pointer array
☐ The heap, where they can be referenced by individual pointer variables or from an array of pointer variables

Having more than a few records rules out using individual names, a method that would also be inadequate because it does not allow the records to be treated as a group. The same is true for individual pointer variables.

The other three methods, two kinds of array and the heap, allow not only grouping but also selection of records, as well as traversal through all the records. Figure 3.1 represents storage of the stock portfolio in each of these three ways. The three methods are called (a) sequential arrays, (b) sequential pointer arrays, and (c) sequential pointer variable arrays. Collectively they are known as *sequential array methods* for record storage.

The sequential array methods are not convenient for recording the daily transactions common in the buying and selling of stocks. These methods provide neither easy nor rapid insertion or deletion capability for the records involved in these transactions. Suppose Chrysler stock is bought, and its new record must be inserted into the portfolio. When the records are kept in arbitrary order, a new record can be inserted directly as the new last record. This means that in the method of sequential arrays (Figure 3.1(a)), a new record is inserted after Sears. In the method of sequential pointer arrays (Figure 3.1(b)), it can be placed in any unused slot, but the corresponding pointer goes in the eighth position of *P*. For the method of sequential pointer variable arrays (Figure 3.1(c)), the procedure NEW provides heap storage that is available to store the record; but again, its associated pointer variable value also goes in position 8 of *P*.

Usually order *does* matter. The stocks in fact are kept in alphabetic order. Thus Chrysler must be inserted in its proper place as the new third record. In sequential arrays this means all five records below its new position must be moved down; in the two pointer array methods, this means the five pointers below its new location (position 3) must be moved down. Although the pointer array methods afford flexibility of record storage position, they still require shifting, although it is pointers that are moved and not records. Shifting takes time proportional to the number of records moved. If *N* records are to be inserted, then the total time can be proportional, not to *N*, but to N^2. For example, suppose the *N* records each require insertion at the top. Even if there are no records stored initially, insertion of *N* records requires $0 + 1 + 2 + \ldots + (N - 1)$ moves. The time adds up to $N(N - 1)/2$, and so the time is $O(N^2)$. Even if each insertion requires only half the information to be shifted, the time is reduced merely by a factor of 2; it is still $O(N^2)$. When *N* is large this can take significant time. Of course, for one trader, *N* will be small, but for large brokerage houses *N* might be hundreds of thousands. If they were not designed to be efficient, these insertions might take hours or even days ($(300,000)^2$ operations $\times 10^{-6}$ seconds/operation = 25 hours).

Selling a stock, say Digital, requires that its record be deleted in sequential array (a) or that its pointer entries be set to 0 or NIL in the pointer arrays (b) and (c). Either course would leave gaps of unused storage, which is undesirable. Leaving gaps soon uses up all the slots in an array, and unless waste of storage is tolerable and affordable, this is impractical. Of course, the array could be declared to be so large that for sure it would not run out of space. Instead, the gap can be filled by moving up all the records below a deleted record. But again, this could take $O(N^2)$ time for the deletion of *N* records.

What is needed is a way to store records so their number can grow or shrink in response to an arbitrary number of insertions and deletions, in such a way that storage is not wasted and the time for insertion and deletion is reduced. The *list* data

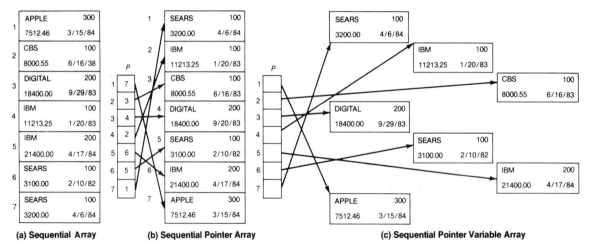

Figure 3.1   Sequential Methods of Storing Records in Arrays

structure introduced in this chapter provides one solution to this inefficiency. A *list* is a collection of records linked by pointers. Even with lists, it is still necessary, as with the sequential array methods, for the program to spend time deciding where to make an insertion or deletion in the first place. To make these operations efficient when large numbers of records are involved requires more advanced data structures (which are introduced later). For a moderate number of records, the time taken to locate the point of insertion or deletion is tolerable. Lists called *stacks* and *queues*, where insertion and deletion occur only at the ends of the lists, are especially useful even when there are many records. These will be considered in the next chapter.

Chapter 2 showed that the key advantage of the sequential array methods is selection in constant time. As just shown in this chapter, the disadvantage is that inserting or deleting entries from the interior of an array is costly. Another drawback is that arrays have fixed lengths that must be declared to the compiler. Thus, the maximum number of items to be stored in the array must be known in advance of execution. No such a priori limit need be declared for the number of items on a list. Lists provide the pliability to insert new items or to delete existing ones at a known point of the list, in constant time. However, selection of an arbitrary *I*th list item will take time proportional to *I*.

3.2 Keeping Track of List Pointers

The pointers in lists are what is manipulated by programs because lists are collections of records linked by pointers. A special element, called the **head** or **name** of the list, points to the beginning of the list, and each record in the list has a pointer to the next one. The final record, which has no successor, has an empty link, denoted by a special pointer value called the **null pointer.**

The stock portfolio example is represented in a list in Figure 3.2. The variable labeled HEAD contains a pointer to the first record in the list. Each record is composed of two fields: 1) an **information field,** which may itself be made up of subfields

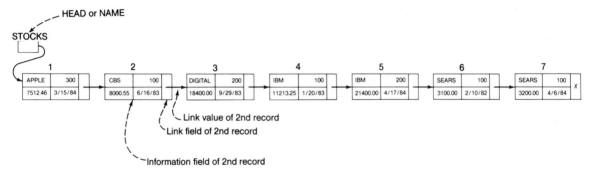

Figure 3.2 Graphic Representation of the List STOCKS

such as NAME, SHARES, VALUE, DATABOUGHT (or ACCOUNTNUMBER, BALANCE, ADDRESS); and 2) a **link field,** which contains the pointer to the next record. The X in the link field of the last record denotes the null pointer, and indicates that this is the last record on the list. The list with no records is called the **null list,** and is denoted by a head containing the null pointer.

It does no good to know that a phone number (say, 642-3715) contains the digits 1, 2, 3, 4, 5, 6, and 7, unless the order 6, 4, 2, 3, 7, 1, 5 is retained as well. Notice that the list data structure not only is a new way to store information, but also allows the information to be remembered in a specific order—the order in which the records appear on the list. Arrays provide this ability as well. The order in which records, or the pointers to them, are stored does this. But the operations that make lists interesting and powerful are insertion and deletion.

In effect, a list works as if the pointers from a pointer array were incorporated into the records to which they point. This is the crucial advantage of lists compared to arrays. The price of the added convenience is the loss of the capability to select an arbitrary record. Instead of access to the list records being through the pointer array, the list records must now be accessed via the pointer to the first list record (in head or name). That is, not just *any* record of a list can be directly accessed, only its first record. Knowing only the head of a list means that only the first record is immediately visible. To access another list record, the chain of pointers linking list records must be followed until the desired record is encountered.

Consider the simple list L in Figure 3.3(a). Two situations are depicted in Figure 3.3(b,c): (b) is the case when the list head L is known, and (c) the case when a pointer, PTR, to a list record is known. In each case only the record to which the known pointer points is visible.

If only one pointer points to a record, and that pointer value is changed, then the record cannot be accessed. It is as if the programmer had stored something somewhere but had no hope of remembering where. If that pointer happens to be in the head of a list, then access to the list is lost. Suppose the programmer must start with the situation depicted in Figure 3.3(a) and must create two lists. One, L, is to consist of all records of the original list, from the record pointed to by PTR to the last record. Another, NEWL, is to consist of the original list records, from the first to the record prior to that pointed to by PTR. Simply copying the value of PTR into L

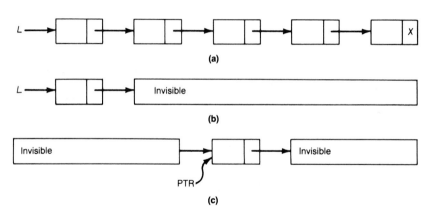

(a)

(b)

(c)

Figure 3.3   Simple Lists

creates the correct modified version of *L*. However, *NEWL* cannot be created since the pointer to the original first record that had been stored in *L* has been lost. Such a predicament must be avoided.

Keeping track of pointers in processing lists is extremely important. One reason is that more than one pointer can point to a record. The only way to see if two pointers point to the same record is to see if their pointer values are equal, since two records can be identical but use distinct storage elements.

3.2.1   Insertion and Deletion of Records in Lists

Consider the effects of inserting and deleting on a conceptual list. The effect of inserting a new record is shown in Figure 3.4. The new record is inserted between the records labeled PREDECESSOR and SUCCESSOR. This requires changing PREDECESSOR's link to point to the new record, and setting the new record's link to point to SUCCESSOR.

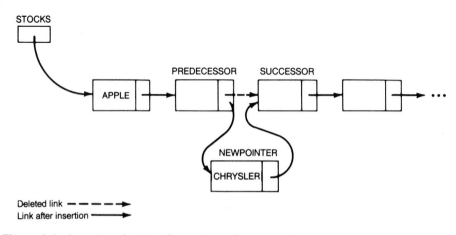

Figure 3.4   Insertion of a New Record in a Conceptual List

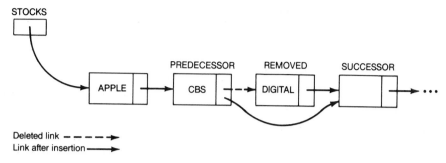

Figure 3.5 Deletion of a Record from a Conceptual List

The deletion of a record from a list is shown in Figure 3.5. The record labeled REMOVED is deleted from the list by arranging PREDECESSOR's link to point to SUCCESSOR. The rearrangement of links for insertion or deletion is independent of where in the list the operation occurs. Each operation can be performed in constant time. Lists, unlike arrays, readily accommodate change; they exhibit no growing pains (or contraction pains).

3.3 Expanding and Contracting Lists

3.3.1 Insertion

Suppose you wish to insert a new record for CHRYSLER. It is always a good idea to sketch an image like Figure 3.6(a) to show both the situation at the outset and the situation desired after the task is carried out. Since only the head of the list, STOCKS, is assumed known, normally each record of the list must be accessed in turn, starting from the first, in order to determine where to do the insertion. For now, assume that a pointer PREDECESSOR is given which points to the record after which the new record is to be inserted. In the example, this is the second record. The value of its link field must be copied into the link field of the new record, so the new record's link field points to the successor of the predecessor record. The link field of the PREDECESSOR record must end up pointing to the new record, so the value of NEWPOINTER must be copied into the predecessor's link field. The code to accomplish this may be written as

```
SETLINK(NEWPOINTER, NEXT(PREDECESSOR));
SETLINK(PREDECESSOR, NEWPOINTER);
```

where SETLINK is a procedure that copies the value of its second parameter into the link field of the record pointed to by its first parameter, and NEXT is a function whose value is a copy of the link field value of the record pointed to by its parameter. Why is it incorrect to interchange these two statements?

Notice that no assumptions have been made about the implementation of the list. The code is thus independent of how the list is implemented. Of course

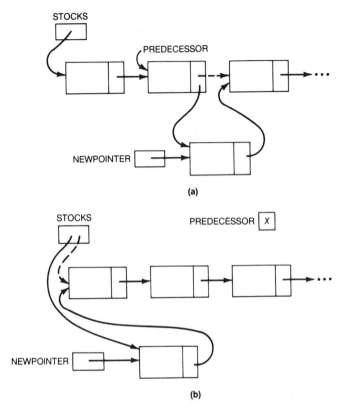

Figure 3.6   Insertion of a New Record (a) in the Interior of a List and (b) at the Front of a List

SETLINK can be written only when the implementation is known, and it *will* depend on the details. But this code *will not*. The list is thus a data abstraction with insertion as one of its operations. Deletion is another.

3.3.2 Special Cases

It is evident that this code is correct for insertion into the interior of the list or at its end. Special cases must always be sniffed out and dealt with. By definition, a special case means a situation requiring code different from the current solution. The existing solution must be modified to handle special cases. The special case here is shown in Figure 3.6(b), and represents insertion at the front of the list. Obviously there is no predecessor record, so the solution cannot properly handle this case. It is reasonable to assume that this special condition is represented by a null value for PREDECESSOR. Then it is the value of head that must be copied into the link field of the new record. Also, it is the head itself that must receive the copy of NEWPOINTER and end up pointing to the new record. The correct module to handle all situations is as follows:

```
procedure INSERT(var HEAD : listpointer;
                     PREDECESSOR, NEWPOINTER : listpointer);
var
    NULL : listpointer;
begin
    SETNULL(NULL);
    if PREDECESSOR = NULL then
        begin
            SETLINK(NEWPOINTER, HEAD);
            HEAD := NEWPOINTER
        end
    else
        begin
            SETLINK(NEWPOINTER, NEXT(PREDECESSOR));
            SETLINK(PREDECESSOR, NEWPOINTER)
        end
end;
```

where SETNULL returns with its parameter set to the null value. What is used for the null value is determined by the list implementation (Section 3.6).

3.3.3 Header Records

An alternative to this assigns a special record, called a **header record,** to every list. This record is a **dummy** record. The dummy is so called because it is not part of the conceptual list of records being created. Used to make processing easier, the dummy record is never deleted and no record is ever inserted in front of it. Then the special case never occurs, and the original code, requiring no check for the special case, can be used. Actually the header record can be a smart dummy, used to contain important information about the list, such as the number of records. When this alternative is used, the null list can no longer be recognized by a null value in the list head.

3.3.4 Deletion

To delete the record following PREDECESSOR (Figure 3.7(a)), only the link field value of its successor must be copied into the predecessor's link field:

```
SETLINK(PREDECESSOR, NEXT(NEXT(PREDECESSOR)));
```

Thus, NEXT(NEXT(PREDECESSOR)) is the value that must be copied into the predecessor's link field. It is clearer to write the code as

```
SUCCESSOR := NEXT(PREDECESSOR);
SETLINK(PREDECESSOR, NEXT(SUCCESSOR));
```

even if it is slower, requiring an additional memory access. Again, either code is independent of any implementation for the list. After checking for special cases (Figure 3.7(b)), the correct module is found to be

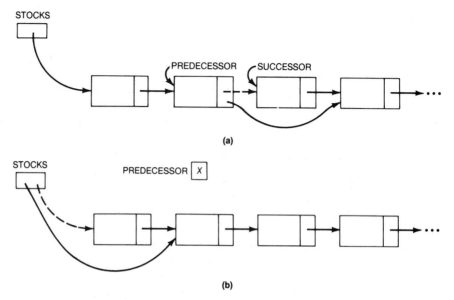

Figure 3.7   Deletion of a Record (a) from the Interior of a List and (b) from the Front of a List

```
procedure DELETE(var HEAD : listpointer; PREDECESSOR : listpointer);
var
    SUCCESSOR, NULL : listpointer;
begin
    SETNULL(NULL);
    if PREDECESSOR = NULL then
        HEAD : = NEXT(HEAD)
    else
        begin
            SUCCESSOR : = NEXT(PREDECESSOR);
            if SUCCESSOR <> NULL then
                SETLINK(PREDECESSOR, NEXT(SUCCESSOR))
        end
end;
```

Sometimes, instead of having a pointer to the predecessor of a record to be deleted, only a pointer to the record itself is available. Deletion can still be accomplished; all that is required is to copy the *entire* successor record (the successor to the record to be deleted, that is) into the record to be deleted. It is necessary to assume, however, that the last list record is never deleted. Why? Whether or not this is better than keeping track of the predecessor depends on how much time is required to effect this copying operation. The larger the record, the greater the time. However, if the information field of a record is kept elsewhere, and a pointer to it stored in the record itself, then the operation reduces to copying just this pointer and the value of the link field.

Are you listing from all this list information?

3.4 Traversal of Lists

Traversing a list's records is another operation performed on the data abstraction called the list. Traversal is useful when the records are to be processed one after another in the same order in which they appear in the list. A traversal may be accomplished by following the pointer in the list's head to the first record and processing it, then following the first record's link field pointer to the next record and processing it, and so on, until the last record has been processed.

3.4.1 List Reversal Using a Loop

Example 3.1

Consider the list L in Figure 3.8(a). The task is to write a procedure REVERSE, to reverse such a list. This means that when REVERSE is applied to L the result should be as shown in Figure 3.8(b). □

At first glance, this may seem to be a complicated task involving a great deal of record and pointer manipulation. But there is a simple solution: The information fields of each record need not be considered at all. Instead, as in Figure 3.8(c), the link field of F can be set to null, the link field of O can be set to point to F, the link field of R can be set to point to O, and so on. Finally, L itself can be set to point to D. The result would be as sketched in Figure 3.8(c), the correct reversed list. This procedure can be stated more generally:

1. Set the link field of the first record to null.
2. Set the link field of each record to point to its original predecessor.
3. And finally, set the list head to point to the original last record.

Even without the details of implementing the list and carrying out the procedure, it is easy to be certain that this procedure, when successfully carried out, does solve the problem. Clearly, this is so except for the case of a null list; the procedure does not specify what is to be done since there is no first record in a null list. Since the

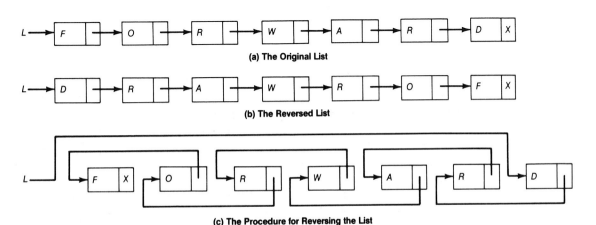

(a) The Original List

(b) The Reversed List

(c) The Procedure for Reversing the List

Figure 3.8 A List before, after, and during Reversal

first record of any list has no predecessor, the procedure can be specified somewhat differently.

1. Set the link field of each record to point to its original predecessor.
2. Then set the list head to point to the original last record.

Now we have a procedure that is correct for all cases.

The next step is to detail how this procedure is actually to be done. The basic
structure involved is a *loop*, since the same process is to be carried out repeatedly, but on a different record each time. In general, loops need a beginning
(*initialization*), and an end (*finalization*). The finalization here is specified explicitly
in the procedure: namely, set the list head to point to the original last record. The
initialization, as usual, cannot be specified until the loop is specified in more detail.

To implement the loop requires a pointer (call it RECORDPOINTER) to keep
track of the current record to be processed within the loop by its loop task. Imagine
that the first three records have already been processed correctly and the fourth is
about to be processed. It is pointed to by RECORDPOINTER, as depicted in
Figure 3.9(a).

Processing W requires setting its link field to point to W's predecessor R. To
do this requires knowing where its predecessor R is located. Thus another pointer,
PREDECESSOR, is needed. It is so named because it will contain a pointer to the
predecessor of the current record to be processed. (See Figure 3.9(b).)

Suppose someone attempts to process W now, copying PREDECESSOR into
W's nextpointer field to set it properly. The result is shown in Figure 3.9(c).

PREDECESSOR and RECORDPOINTER must now be updated so that they
point, respectively, to W and A, so that A can be processed next when the loop is
repeated. However, the link field of W no longer points to A, but instead points to
R. Thus the location of A has been lost. Care is required when changing pointer
values so that such important information is not lost. To remedy this, introduce
another pointer HOLD in which the pointer to A can be saved before changing W's
link field value. The processing of the record pointed to by RECORDPOINTER
may now be done by sequentially copying its link field value into HOLD, copying
PREDECESSOR into RECORDPOINTER's link field, and copying HOLD into
RECORDPOINTER. This produces the result depicted in Figure 3.9(d).

The test or condition for another repetition of the loop becomes
(RECORDPOINTER <> Null). The initialization involves setting RECORD-
POINTER to L so that it points to the first record and setting PREDECESSOR to
Null. Why is it unnecessary to initialize HOLD?

When the loop is exited, PREDECESSOR will point to the original last record
so the finalization can be accomplished by copying PREDECESSOR into L. This
solution may be expressed in two steps.

1. Set the link field of each record to point to its original predecessor.
2. Set the head of the list to point to the original last record.

Refining task 1 makes the algorithm read as follows:

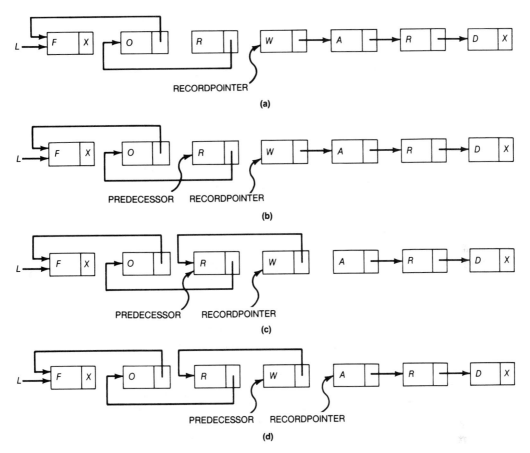

Figure 3.9   Achieving Proper Loop Implementation

1. Initialization
    While (there is a current record)
    a. set the link field of the current record to point to its original predecessor, and
    b. update the current record.
2. Set the head of the list to point to the original last record.

Refining again:

1. Set PREDECESSOR to NULL.
    Set RECORDPOINTER to *L*.
    While (RECORDPOINTER is not NULL),
    a. set HOLD to the link field value of the record pointed to by RECORDPOINTER,
        set RECORDPOINTER's link field to PREDECESSOR,
    b. set PREDECESSOR to RECORDPOINTER, and
        set RECORDPOINTER to HOLD.
2. Set *L* to PREDECESSOR.

This algorithm actually involves a complete traversal through the records of the list L. As it is carried out, RECORDPOINTER accesses each record of L in turn and processes it within the **while** loop. The processing is done by the loop task. In order for the loop to work correctly, some initialization had to be done, and some finalization was required after each record of the list had been processed.

3.4.2 A General List Traversal Using a Loop

Our intention is to write a general procedure TRAVERSE, to carry out a traversal of a list, given its head, LISTNAME. The code for TRAVERSE should be independent of the list implementation, as was the code for insertion and deletion. To make TRAVERSE independent of the particular application as well, the processing to be done on each record will be modularized in a procedure PROCESS. Its details are thus irrelevant; simply invoke PROCESS within TRAVERSE. However, to do its job, this procedure may need access to the list head, LISTNAME. It will surely need to know what record it is to currently process; RECORDPOINTER will be used to point to this record.

Often, the traversal must proceed through *all* the list records. To allow for the possibility of a partial traversal, however, a variable DONE can be introduced. DONE may be set by PROCESS so that the traversal does not continue beyond the current record. Finally, PROCESS cannot retain any information between calls unless that information is kept nonlocal to it, or passed as one of its parameters. So, PROCESS is given the parameters LISTNAME, RECORDPOINTER, DONE, and OTHER. OTHER denotes those parameters whose values must be preserved between calls to PROCESS.

The heart of a traversal is repeated access of the record pointed to by RECORDPOINTER, processing of the record, and updating of RECORDPOINTER to point to the next record. Clearly a loop is its main construct. The procedure for a general traversal of a list is as follows:

```
procedure TRAVERSE(var LISTNAME : listpointer);
var
    RECORDPOINTER : listpointer;
    OTHER : moreparameters;
    DONE : boolean;
begin
    INITIALIZE(LISTNAME, OTHER);
    RECORDPOINTER := LISTNAME;
    DONE := false;
    while (not DONE and ANOTHERRECORD(LISTNAME, RECORDPOINTER)) do
        begin
            PROCESS(LISTNAME, RECORDPOINTER, OTHER, DONE);
            RECORDPOINTER := NEXT(RECORDPOINTER)
        end;
    FINALIZE(LISTNAME, OTHER)
end;
```

INITIALIZE may be used to set the initial value of any of the "OTHER" parameters. ANOTHERRECORD is a function returning "true" if RECORD-

POINTER points to the next record to be processed, and returning "false" if the last record has already been processed. FINALIZE is used to carry out any tasks required after all list records have been processed, for instance, to print an appropriate message.

It is a good idea to check a program for correctness, in lieu of a formal proof, by seeing if it handles all special cases, and the typical case, correctly. You should check TRAVERSE in this way for the case of a null list, a one-record list, and a list with more than one record. For example, if the list is null, the **while** loop is never executed as long as ANOTHERRECORD is correct (which is assumed), and the program properly terminates as long as FINALIZE is correct (which is assumed). So TRAVERSE does work correctly for the special case of a null list.

3.4.3 The Merits of Modularization

TRAVERSE has been written in this general way so that it can be used as a tool readily adaptable to the solution of a large class of problems. How to adapt this procedure to the solution of seemingly disparate problems is the purpose of the next section. It is important to recognize the basic technique used to render the program independent of the list implementation: embedding those details in lower level modules. This is the reason for ANOTHERRECORD and NEXT. INITIALIZE, PROCESS, and FINALIZE are modules that allow TRAVERSE to be adapted to specific applications.

All the modules that must reflect implementation and application details in their definitions are lower level modules. Changes to them do not affect the correctness of TRAVERSE, but do affect what TRAVERSE does. The modules call attention to *what* is being done instead of how it is being done. Furthermore, if the programmer consistently uses a function such as NEXT, or a procedure such as PROCESS, to carry out specific tasks, then no matter how many places the task is required in a program, the definition of that task is localized in *one* place and it is clear where to look for the code that implements it—in NEXT or in PROCESS. The modules may then all be written independently to suit the immediate purpose. As long as they are correct, TRAVERSE must be correct too.

3.5 Using the TRAVERSE Procedure for Lists

Sometimes a solution to a new problem can be obtained by modifying a known program that solves another related problem. Maintenance or adaptation of programs also frequently involves small changes to current programs. Changes are easier, quicker, and more likely to be error free if exactly that function or task that requires change has been localized as a program module.

TRAVERSE adheres to two important elements of programming style.

1. High-level descriptions and programs should be as independent of the details of data abstraction implementation and of the application as possible.
2. High-level descriptions and programs should be modular so that special lower level functions or tasks carried out within the high-level description or program may be easily isolated.

To illustrate the use of TRAVERSE, and the effect of these principles, this section presents four examples. Although each could be solved in isolation, from scratch, a different approach is taken here. In each case it should be easy to see that TRAVERSE may be adapted to provide an almost immediate solution. This will be done by writing specific versions of TRAVERSE's modules for each application, so that these modules turn TRAVERSE into a solution. This means it will then do the required task when executed. Of course, the modules, when invoked by TRAVERSE, will do exactly what the programmer specifies in their definition.

Example 3.2

A sentence is stored in a list, with each record storing one character. Thus the sentence, THIS SENTENCE HAS EXACTLY 60 CHARACTERS COUNTING BLANKS AND., is stored in a list with 60 records. For simplicity, assume the period character, . , does not occur within a sentence (as it does in this one). The task is to write a procedure to print the length of the sentence. □

The solution can be achieved by traversing the list and counting the number of records. INITIALIZE can set a counter, LENGTH, to zero, and PROCESS can increment it by 1 each time it is invoked. FINALIZE can do the printing. The modules are readily defined.

```
procedure INITIALIZE(LISTNAME : listpointer; var LENGTH : moreparameters);
begin
    LENGTH := 0
end;
procedure PROCESS(LISTNAME, RECORDPOINTER : listpointer; var LENGTH :
moreparameters; DONE : boolean);
begin
    LENGTH := LENGTH + 1
end;
procedure FINALIZE(LISTNAME : listpointer; LENGTH : moreparameters);
begin
    if LENGTH = 0 then
        WRITELN('THERE IS NO SENTENCE')
    else
        WRITELN('THE SENTENCE HAS LENGTH', LENGTH)
end;
```

Either ANOTHERRECORD and NEXT must be supplied to the programmer, or the details of the list implementation must be specified so the programmer can write them. The task of the example is then carried out by the invocation TRAVERSE(SENTENCE).

There are two ways to view TRAVERSE. One is as a program that can be used but not modified in any way. This would require that the procedures be written as they appear and the type moreparameters be declared, nonlocal to TRAVERSE, as integer. The second is as a program that may be used or changed in any desirable way. In this case, for clarity, the module names can be changed: TRAVERSE to COUNT-CHARACTERS, change INITIALIZE to ZEROCOUNTER, PROCESS to INCREMENTCOUNTER, FINALIZE to PRINTCOUNTER, and ANOTHER-RECORD to ANOTHERCHARACTER, for example. It may be desirable to remove parameters that are not needed. Since LISTNAME is not needed by INITIALIZE, PROCESS, or FINALIZE, and RECORDPOINTER is not needed by PROCESS, they may be omitted from the definitions and invocations of these modules. OTHER may be changed to LENGTH, and moreparameters to integer. Finally, DONE may be eliminated, since it is not needed. Having made this distinction, the programmer is free to take either view. The one chosen should be clear from the context.

Suppose the sentence were stored in the list with three characters per record instead of just one per record. The solution would require a new version of PROCESS to reflect this change, but INITIALIZE and FINALIZE remain as is. NEXT might have to reflect the new record format. The new process procedure is

```
procedure PROCESS(LISTNAME, RECORDPOINTER : listpointer;
                      var LENGTH : moreparameters; var DONE : boolean);
var
    LASTRECORD : boolean;
begin
    LASTRECORD := not ANOTHERRECORD(LISTNAME,
                                    NEXT(RECORDPOINTER));
    if not LASTRECORD then
        LENGTH := LENGTH + 3
    else
        if CHAR1(RECORDPOINTER) = '.' then
            LENGTH := LENGTH + 1
        else
            if CHAR2(RECORDPOINTER) = '.' then
                LENGTH := LENGTH + 2
            else
                LENGTH := LENGTH + 3
end;
```

where CHAR1 returns a copy of the first character in the record pointed to by its parameters, and CHAR2 returns a copy of the second character in the record pointed to by its parameters. Like NEXT and ANOTHERRECORD, they must be supplied or the programmer must write them given list implementation details.

Finally, suppose the list is implemented as a circular list (Figure 3.10). In *circular lists,* the null pointer of the last record is replaced by a pointer that points to the first record. Illustrating the effect of such list implementation details are the two versions for ANOTHERRECORD, first for the standard list and second for the circular list:

```
Standard list
function ANOTHERRECORD(LISTNAME, RECORDPOINTER : listpointer) :
                              boolean;
var
    NULL : listpointer;
begin
    SETNULL(NULL);
    ANOTHERRECORD := (RECORDPOINTER <> NULL)
end;
```

Circular list

```
function ANOTHERRECORD(LISTNAME, RECORDPOINTER : listpointer) :
                        boolean;
begin
    ANOTHERRECORD := (LISTNAME <> RECORDPOINTER)
end;
```

Actually, the solution is not as general as possible. Suppose the list were implemented using a dummy header record. Then PROCESS must recognize when it is processing this record (the first), and not change LENGTH, since no characters are stored in the header record. You should modify PROCESS to account for this possibility. It is necessary to assume that the header may be distinguished from the other records in some way.

Example 3.3 TRAVERSE may be turned into a solution for the list reversal task of Example 3.1 by defining INITIALIZE, PROCESS, and FINALIZE as

```
procedure INITIALIZE(LISTNAME : listpointer; var SAVE, PREDECESSOR :
                        moreparameters);
begin
    SETNULL(SAVE);
    SETNULL(PREDECESSOR)
end;
procedure PROCESS(var LISTNAME, RECORDPOINTER : listpointer;
                  var SAVE, PREDECESSOR : moreparameters;
                  var DONE : boolean);
var
    NULL : listpointer;
begin
    SETNULL(NULL);
    if PREDECESSOR <> NULL then
        SETLINK(PREDECESSOR, SAVE);
    SAVE := PREDECESSOR;
    PREDECESSOR := RECORDPOINTER
end;
procedure FINALIZE(var LISTNAME : listpointer;
                   SAVE, PREDECESSOR : moreparameters);
var
    NULL : listpointer;
begin
    SETNULL(NULL);
    if PREDECESSOR <> NULL then
        begin
            SETLINK(PREDECESSOR, SAVE);
            LISTNAME := PREDECESSOR
        end
end;
```

□

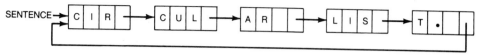

Figure 3.10 A Circular List

Example 3.4

Insert a new record into a list STOCKS, which is kept in alphabetic order by name. Assume the data for the new record may be accessed by a procedure GETNEXTRECORD. □

To turn TRAVERSE into a solution requires simply that PROCESS compare the new record's name field value with that of the current record. If it precedes the current record's name field value, it must be inserted before the current record and DONE set to true. To do the insertion conveniently, a pointer, PREDECESSOR, to the predecessor of the current record will be kept by PROCESS and updated each time PROCESS is invoked. INITIALIZE must allocate storage for the new record, set its data field values, and set PREDECESSOR to null. Assume that a procedure AVAIL is given which returns with its parameter pointing to a storage element that may be used to store the new record. FINALIZE must insert the new record in the event that the list is null. The solution for these modules follows:

```
procedure INITIALIZE(var NEWPOINTER, PREDECESSOR : listpointer);
var
    INFORMATION : infofield;
    NULL : listpointer;
begin
    AVAIL(NEWPOINTER);
    GETNEXTRECORD(INFORMATION);
    SETINFO(NEWPOINTER, INFORMATION);
    SETNULL(NULL);
    PREDECESSOR := NULL
end;
```

where SETINFO copies the value of its second parameter into the information field of the record pointed to by its first parameter, so it depends on the list implementation details.

```
procedure FINALIZE(var LISTNAME : listpointer;
                       PREDECESSOR, NEWPOINTER : listpointer);
var
    NULL : listpointer;
begin
    SETNULL(NULL);
    if LISTNAME = NULL then
        INSERT(LISTNAME, PREDECESSOR, NEWPOINTER)
end;
```

```
     procedure PROCESS(var LISTNAME : listpointer;
                     RECORDPOINTER, NEWPOINTER : listpointer;
                     var PREDECESSOR : listpointer; var DONE : boolean);
var
    NULL : listpointer;
begin
    SETNULL(NULL);
    if PRECEDES(NAME(NEWPOINTER), NAME(RECORDPOINTER)) then
        begin
            INSERT(LISTNAME, PREDECESSOR, NEWPOINTER);
            DONE : = true
        end
    else
        if NEXT(RECORDPOINTER) = NULL then
            begin
                INSERT(LISTNAME, RECORDPOINTER, NEWPOINTER);
                DONE : = true
            end
        else
            PREDECESSOR : = RECORDPOINTER
end;
```

where NAME returns a copy of the name field value of the record pointed to by its parameter, and PRECEDES returns true if its first parameter value precedes its second parameter value in alphabetical ordering. To insert a new record, invoke TRAVERSE(STOCKS). A better name for this procedure would be ORDEREDINSERT.

Suppose you wanted to insert the new record into a list of stocks kept in order by date bought, instead of by name. Rather than keep another list distinct from STOCKS, you could add another link field to its records. Call it the DATELINK field, and assume each record's DATELINK field points to the correct successor as in Figure 3.11. STOCKSDATE is a new head, pointing to the first record of that list when date bought is used as the criterion for ordering.

To solve this problem 1) replace each reference to the NAME function by a reference to a DATEBOUGHT function; 2) replace each reference, in INSERT, to the SETLINK module by a reference to the SETDATEBOUGHT module; and 3) redefine NEXT to return a copy of the DATELINK field of the record pointed to by its parameter. A call TRAVERSE(STOCKSDATE) to this modified TRAVERSE then carries out the task.

Example
3.5   Create a list STOCKS, to store a portfolio of stock records. □

To solve this problem, assume the data are already stored on some input medium and GETNEXTRECORD gives access to each record in turn, as it is invoked. The desired list may be created by traversing the records stored on the input medium. The job of PROCESS is to fill in the information field of the storage allocated for the new record, and fill in the link field of the new record with a pointer to storage allocated for the next new record. However, it is assumed that the last input data is a sentinel value indicating there are no more records. A function SENTINEL returns

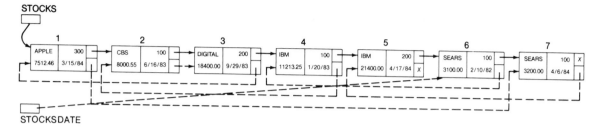

Figure 3.11 Two Orders for a List Using Two Heads and Two Link Fields

true in this case, and false otherwise. Consequently, PROCESS must first check for this sentinel value, and simply return after setting the link field of the last record to null. INITIALIZE must allocate storage for the first record and set LISTNAME to it. FINALIZE may simply return to the procedure invoking it. We have

```
procedure INITIALIZE(var LISTNAME : listpointer);
var
    NULL : listpointer;
begin
    SETNULL(NULL);
    AVAIL(LISTNAME)
end;

procedure PROCESS(var LISTNAME, RECORDPOINTER : listpointer);
var
    INFORMATION : infofield;
    NEXTPOINTER, NULL : listpointer;
begin
    GETNEXTRECORD(INFORMATION);
    if not SENTINEL(INFORMATION) then
        begin
            SETINFO(RECORDPOINTER, INFORMATION);
            AVAIL(NEXTPOINTER);
            SETLINK(RECORDPOINTER, NEXTPOINTER)
        end
    else
        begin
            SETNULL(NULL);
            SETLINK(RECORDPOINTER, NULL)
        end
end;
```

Invoking TRAVERSE(STOCKS) creates the list. Notice that this TRAVERSE will copy a list whenever GETRECORD obtains its information from the next record of the list to be copied. A better name for this procedure would be READLIST or COPYLIST.

Suppose the records are given in arbitrary order, but the STOCKS list must be created, with the records appearing in alphabetic order. To turn TRAVERSE into a solution to this problem, INITIALIZE, FINALIZE, and ANOTHERRECORD are not needed; neither are the variables RECORDPOINTER and OTHER. The PROCESS module is

```
procedure PROCESS(var LISTNAME : listpointer; var DONE : boolean);
var
    INFORMATION : infofield;
begin
    GETNEXTRECORD(INFORMATION);
    if not SENTINEL(INFORMATION) then
        INSERTINORDER(LISTNAME, INFORMATION)
    else
        DONE := true
end;
```

INSERTINORDER has the task of creating and inserting the new record into its proper place in LISTNAME; INFORMATION contains the value to be placed in the new record's information field. INSERTINORDER requires a traversal of LISTNAME. The version below is a modification of ORDEREDINSERT obtained by getting the new information field value in INITIALIZE and adding a second parameter, INFORMATION.

```
procedure INSERTINORDER(var LISTNAME : listpointer;
                            INFORMATION : infofield);
var
    RECORDPOINTER : listpointer;
    PREDECESSOR : listpointer;
    DONE : boolean;
procedure INITIALIZE(var NEWPOINTER, PREDECESSOR : listpointer;
                        INFORMATION : infofield);
begin
    NEW(NEWPOINTER);
    SETINFO(NEWPOINTER, INFORMATION);
    SETNULL(NULL);
    PREDECESSOR := NULL
end;
procedure PROCESS(var LISTNAME : listpointer;
                    RECORDPOINTER, NEWPOINTER : listpointer;
                    var PREDECESSOR : listpointer; var DONE : boolean);
var
    NULL : listpointer;
begin
    SETNULL(NULL);
    if PRECEDES(NAME(NEWPOINTER), NAME(RECORDPOINTER)) then
        begin
            INSERT(LISTNAME, PREDECESSOR, NEWPOINTER);
            DONE := true
        end
    else
        if NEXT(RECORDPOINTER) = NULL then
```

```
            begin
                INSERT(LISTNAME, RECORDPOINTER, NEWPOINTER);
                DONE : = true
            end
        else
            PREDECESSOR : = RECORDPOINTER
end;

procedure FINALIZE(var LISTNAME : listpointer;
                        PREDECESSOR, NEWPOINTER : listpointer);
var
    NULL : listpointer;
begin
    SETNULL(NULL);
    if LISTNAME = NULL then
        INSERT(LISTNAME, PREDECESSOR, NEWPOINTER);
end;
begin
    INITIALIZE(NEWPOINTER, PREDECESSOR, INFORMATION);
    RECORDPOINTER : = LISTNAME;
    DONE : = false;
    while (not DONE and ANOTHERRECORD(LISTNAME, RECORDPOINTER))
    do
        begin
            PROCESS(LISTNAME, RECORDPOINTER, NEWPOINTER,
                    PREDECESSOR, DONE);
            RECORDPOINTER : = NEXT(RECORDPOINTER)
        end;
    FINALIZE(LISTNAME, PREDECESSOR, NEWPOINTER)
end;
```

Our problem is solved by the procedure EXPAND.

```
procedure EXPAND(var LISTNAME : listpointer);
var
    DONE : boolean;

procedure PROCESS(var LISTNAME : listpointer; var DONE : boolean);
var
    INFORMATION : infofield;
begin
    GETNEXTRECORD(INFORMATION);
    if not SENTINEL(INFORMATION) then
        INSERTINORDER(LISTNAME, INFORMATION)
    else
        DONE : = true
end;

begin
    DONE : = false;
    while (not DONE) do
        PROCESS(LISTNAME, DONE);
end;
```

When EXPAND is called with LISTNAME set to null, it creates an ordered list. The name EXPAND was chosen for this procedure because, when called to work on an ordered nonnull list, it simply expands that list by adding the new inputs to it in order.

It is very important to recognize that TRAVERSE is a *tool* that could be used in solving the example problems. The tool was applicable because

☐ It was written using data abstractions that allowed writing or using required implementation modules without changing TRAVERSE.

☐ It was written modularly, which allowed isolation of modules for relevant tasks so they could be written to satisfy specific needs.

Recognizing and applying tools is a major aspect of programming methodology. In order for a tool to be convenient to use, it must be written according to the two elements of programming style just stated. Of course, in the simple examples, using the tool may not save much time, effort, and cost, but for complex tasks, the savings can be great.

Note that the use of GETNEXTRECORD makes the solutions to Examples 3.4 and 3.5 independent of the input medium or the format of the input. Thus any changes in the input are not reflected in TRAVERSE; only GETNEXTRECORD and SENTINEL can require modification. In fact, the same should be done for any output. It is better to use a module rather than specify READLN or WRITELN, in case the input or output medium is changed.

3.6 Implementing Lists

So far this chapter has covered lists in the abstract. Lists are implemented in two basic ways, differentiated by where the records of the lists are stored: 1) in an array of records or 2) in the Pascal heap. These are similar, but the Pascal heap allows for more efficient use of storage and is easier to use.

3.6.1 Lists Stored in the Pascal Heap

The simplest implementation is to store all list records in the Pascal heap. The declarations required are illustrated for the example of the stock portfolio.

```
type
    date         = record
                        month, day, year : integer
                   end;
    listpointer  = ↑stockrecord;
    infofield    = record
                        name : array [1..MAXSIZE] of char;
                        shares : integer;
                        value : real;
                        datebought : date
                   end;
    stockrecord = record
                        info : infofield;
                        link : listpointer
                   end;
var
    STOCKS : listpointer;
```

In other words, for storage in the heap, the records of a list are defined as usual, and an additional field is added to contain the link field pointer. Since it will point to a successor record stored in the heap, its type must be listpointer. In this case, the null value for a pointer is always given by the Pascal constant **nil**.

For illustration, some of the implementation modules that have been used are defined as follows:

```
function NEXT(POINTER : listpointer) : listpointer;
begin
    NEXT := POINTER ↑.LINK
end;

procedure SETNULL(var POINTER : listpointer);
begin
    POINTER := nil
end;

procedure SETLINK(POINTER1, POINTER2 : listpointer);
begin
    POINTER1 ↑.LINK := POINTER2
end;

procedure SETINFO(POINTER : listpointer; INFORMATION : infofield);
begin
    POINTER ↑.INFO := INFORMATION
end;

procedure AVAIL(var POINTER : listpointer);
begin
    NEW(POINTER)
end;
```

3.6.2 Lists Stored in an Array of Records

Instead of being stored in the heap, list records may be stored in an array of records. The declarations required are illustrated for the example of stocks.

```
type
        listpointer  = 0..MAX;
        date         = record
                            month, day, year : integer
                       end;
        infofield    = record
                            name : array [1..MAXSIZE] of char;
                            shares : integer;
                            value : real;
                            datebought : date
                       end;
        stockrecord = record
                            info : infofield;
                            link : listpointer
                       end;
        recordarray = array [1...MAX] of stockrecord;
    var
        STOCKS : listpointer;
        RECORDS : recordarray;
```

For this implementation the null pointer value is zero. The implementation for the modules corresponding to those of Section 3.6.1, except for AVAIL, are

```
function NEXT(POINTER : listpointer) : listpointer;
begin
    NEXT := RECORDS[POINTER].LINK
end;

procedure SETNULL(var POINTER : listpointer);
begin
    POINTER := 0
end;

procedure SETLINK(POINTER1, POINTER2 : listpointer);
begin
    RECORDS[POINTER1].LINK := POINTER2
end;

procedure SETINFO(POINTER : listpointer; INFORMATION : infofield);
begin
    RECORDS[POINTER].INFO := INFORMATION
end;
```

This implementation assumes that RECORDS is declared nonlocally to these modules, so that they may reference it. With this implementation, the RECORDS array plays the role of the heap. Since the procedure NEW, which allocates storage from the heap, is not usable here, it is necessary to write an AVAIL procedure that, in effect, is equivalent to NEW. AVAIL must keep track of those slots in RECORDS that are not in use, and hence can be allocated when record storage is requested.

3.6.3 Lists Stored in Languages without Records

In some languages, such as FORTRAN, there are no heaps, nor are there pointer variables or records. In such a language, the records themselves must be implemented by the programmer. They may be stored in single or multiple arrays as discussed in Chapter 2. Since the records now have an additional link field indicating their successor, they need not be stored sequentially and may be located anywhere in the array or multiarrays, as long as they do not overlap. An additional variable is needed for the head of the list. Once these arrays are set up, the programmer may write functions to access each field of a record and procedures to copy one record's value into another record, or to copy a record's field value into another record's field. These might be

NEXT(POINTER)
Returns a copy of the link field value of the record pointed to by POINTER.
INFO(POINTER)
Returns a copy of the information field value of the record pointed to by POINTER.
NAME(POINTER)
Returns a copy of the name field value of the record pointed to by POINTER.

SETLINK(POINTER1, POINTER2)

Sets the value of the link field of the record pointed to by POINTER1 to POINTER2.

SETINFO(POINTER1, POINTER2)

Sets the value of the information field of the record pointed to by POINTER1 to the value of the information field of the record pointed to by POINTER2.

SETNAME(POINTER1, POINTER2)

Sets the value of the name field of the record pointed to by POINTER1 to the value of the name field of the record pointed to by POINTER2.

In FORTRAN, the array or multiarray in which the records are kept would be declared to be stored in the FORTRAN common area or else must be passed as parameters to these modules. Once they are written, for all intents and purposes, the language has records. These records can be accessed, copied, or modified by using these modules. Although the programmer must do all this work initially, from this point on the situation is conceptually the same as in Section 3.6.2. That is, the actual implementation of the records may be forgotten; they are treated as if stored in an array of records just as in Pascal. The problem of writing an AVAIL procedure still remains, and it is addressed in the next section.

In FORTRAN, although storage for records kept in lists must be managed, the programmer does not need to manage storage for individual elements or for arrays of elements. To refer in a program to an element N, or an array DATA, simply declare N to be an element, and DATA to be an array. Then use the operations available in FORTRAN to enter specific values into N or DATA. This works because individual elements and arrays are data structures directly available in FORTRAN. Lists, on the other hand, must be built up explicitly by storing their records in arrays. Consequently, the programmer must determine where storage is available to create a record when the need arises.

In newer languages, such as Pascal, it is not necessary to explicitly implement records of lists in arrays, as done here. It is also not necessary to be concerned with the problems of storage allocation or reclamation. Instead, dynamic data structures may be used. A data structure is dynamic if it is built during execution of a program and storage is allocated for its components at that time. Dynamic data structures are built simply by asking for storage to be allocated for a record in the heap. A pointer will then be assigned to point to that storage. Using the pointer, appropriate values may be assigned to the fields of the new record. These fields may be referred to directly, using naming conventions in the language. Special functions to store or access information from the fields of the record need not be written.

Records still need to be inserted properly in a dynamic data structure. Commands directly available in the language may be used to create or reclaim records, or reclamation may be left to implicit storage reclamation provided by the language. Thus the definition, creation, reclamation, and manipulation of dynamic data structures becomes easier.

3.7 Keeping Track of Available Records

Keeping track of and allocating storage that is needed during the execution of a program is called *dynamic storage management.* In some languages, notably FORTRAN, storage for arrays is allocated storage before the program's execution, and no dynamic storage management is necessary. In block-structured languages like Pascal, storage is allocated to the local variables of a component (or block) at the start of its execution and remains assigned until the component (or block) completes its execution. The space can then be reassigned to the next executing component (or block). In effect, it disappears as far as the component (or block) is concerned. This is why values of local variables are not preserved between invocations of a module. Management of this storage during the execution of a program is not what is meant by dynamic storage management. Contrast this situation to heap storage, which is assigned or taken away from records in the heap during the execution of a component (or block) itself. This captures the true flavor of dynamic storage allocation.

If the array in which records are to be kept (as in Sections 3.6.2 and 3.6.3) is to function as a heap, then allocating storage in the array for a record requires dynamic storage management. In fact, this amounts to an implementation of a Pascal-like heap. But although storage can thus be managed explicitly for a specific program, the heap may manage storage for many programs and is hence more efficient use of storage. The difference is that one large array may function as a heap to be used by all the programs, instead of dedicating separate smaller arrays to each program.

3.7.1 **Why Heap? (Using Dynamic Storage Management)**

Why is storage efficiency important? Why not find storage for a new record in the array simply by placing it sequentially below the last new record's storage? After all, this would be very easy to do and would certainly use the storage as efficiently as possible. The answer is that this simple solution is a great idea — provided that all the storage needed to declare the array to be of sufficient length is available. The catch is that this proviso is rarely the case. Often, the amount required isn't known in advance, and even when it is known, not enough storage may be available.

Reconsider the prime number example of Chapter 1. It is probably evident by now that the list is a good data structure to use for the collection C. The program to generate all the primes between 2 and N uses very little storage besides that needed for the list. But how large should you make the array in which to store the list? It is possible to modify the program so it need not actually store all integers between 2 and N in the list, only those that are prime. Still, how many primes are there no greater than N? It is even possible to write such a program so it efficiently generates and prints all primes $\leq N$ yet stores only those $\leq \sqrt{N}$ in the list. But again, how many of these are there?

Suppose you are a programmer asked to store the contents of ten manuscripts in ten lists. If each can have a maximum length of 50,000 words, then storage for 500,000 words is needed. How long is the longest word? You see the problem. Even if the amount of storage could be estimated, sufficient storage may not be available. You might either conclude that the task cannot be done, or you might use secondary storage (magnetic tape, disks). But because secondary storage is not random access, it is slow, and it requires different techniques than those described so far. One possibility remains. Maybe the manuscripts to be stored, perhaps even more than 10, are compatible in the sense that they are not all of great length simultaneously. Perhaps the lengths will vary as the manuscripts are processed by a program, so that at any one time the manuscripts being stored can fit. This means they may be growing and shrinking in length at different points in the program. If the storage no longer needed for one manuscript is relinquished and reused for another, then the total array length may not ever be exceeded. In other words, if storage can be allocated, then reused for new allocations when no longer needed for its original purpose, problems may be solved that are otherwise out of range. This is the reason to manage storage.

This also explains why the heap makes better use of storage than individual program management using arrays of records. Each program may, to ensure its execution, ask for a large amount of storage to be used for its array. The total amount needed by all the programs may not be at hand. It is better to take all available storage and dole it out to each program as needed, the hope being that whenever some programs need a great deal of storage, the others need little. Instead of dedicating amounts to each user for each one's worst case, the programmer manages the heap and gives out only what is needed at any moment.

3.7.2 How to Heap

Having taken this relevant digression, let's return to the job of managing a miniheap. This will show how the heap itself might function, and give us the means to create our own when desirable. In fact, you will see when this might be advantageous.

Pointer variables are used in Pascal, and new high-level languages such as Ada and Modula-2, to eliminate the problem of dynamic storage management for the programmer. Pointer variables allow the declaration of a variable of a complex data type, and allocate storage for it by merely assigning to its pointer variable a value that points to that storage. The Pascal procedure NEW is given for this purpose. This section develops a procedure AVAIL that will have the same effect as NEW, but will manage storage in the RECORDS array for Section 3.6.2.

In the general case of list processing, records need to be inserted in *and* deleted from lists. It is deletion, you may recall, that makes the solution of larger problems feasible. When records are deleted, their storage in the RECORDS array may be reused. Reclaiming storage in this way allows larger problems to be solved than would otherwise be possible, by allowing the program to execute to completion.

Records of one or more lists may be stored in the RECORDS array at any moment during the execution of a program. Assume that all these records have the same length, and that no sharing of storage occurs. No sharing means that no list record has more than one pointer to it at any time. The more typical case of variable-length records and sharing of storage is also more complex, and will be dealt with in a later chapter. How to implement AVAIL is now the issue.

Suppose that, by looking at a record, you can tell whether or not it is in use. This would be the case if, whenever a record were deleted from a list, it were marked *unused*. An available record could be found by traversing the RECORDS array until a record marked unused were found. AVAIL could then return with its parameter NEW pointing to that record, after marking it as now in use. In Figure 3.12, this would require the first three records to be accessed before AVAIL could return with NEW set to 3. The time to carry out this procedure is proportional to the length of the RECORDS array in the worst case.

A very significant improvement would be to keep track of the available records so that the search may be avoided, and the time for AVAIL to do its task reduced to a constant. This is achieved by using the link fields of each unused record to create

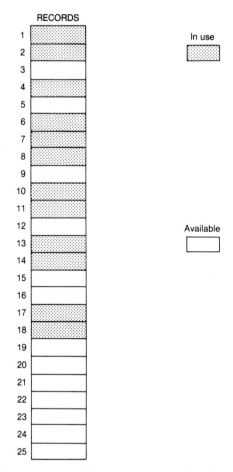

Figure 3.12 Typical Configuration of Used and Unused List Records in the RECORDS Array

a list of available records. Initially all entries of RECORDS are unused, so the list should contain every record of the array. Figure 3.13 shows how this list might appear for the configuration of Figure 3.12 with AVAILIST taken as its head. AVAIL now carries out its task by simply deleting the first record from AVAILIST and returning with its parameter pointing to the deleted record. This yields the desired constant time for AVAIL.

When records are deleted from a list in programs, it is convenient to keep track of their storage for future reuse. This requires inserting the deleted records' storage on AVAILIST. Again, this operation can be done in constant time if the newly available record is inserted at the front of AVAILIST—as its new first record. The module that carries out this task will be called RECLAIM. What time is required for insertion if the record is inserted in the list other than at the front?

The programmer invokes AVAIL(P) to request storage for a record to be stored in RECORDS, and P points to that storage when AVAIL returns. The programmer invokes RECLAIM(P) to request that the storage in RECORDS pointed to by P be

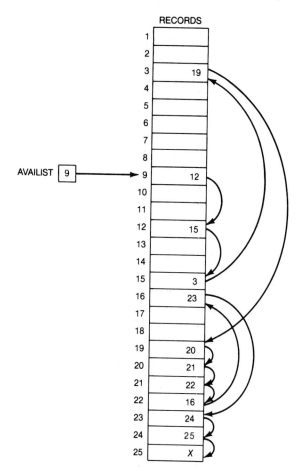

Figure 3.13 The List of Available Records Corresponding to Figure 3.12

inserted on AVAILIST. By employing AVAIL and RECLAIM appropriately, the programmer can dynamically allocate and reclaim storage for lists. This means that RECORDS can be viewed as the repository of all list records, thus acting as a miniature Pascal heap. Such routines are the heart of storage management algorithms. When the records of a list are not all the same length, then more complex management techniques must be used. When records can be shared, still more complexity is added to the storage management problem, as will be illustrated subsequently.

NEW is the general Pascal allocation procedure provided for the programmer's use, so that the heap appears as an abstract facility for storing records. When no memory is available to be allocated by NEW, what happens depends on the system. Some systems cause an abort of the program execution and print an error message; others return with the parameter of NEW set to **nil**. It is illegal in Pascal to refer to a heap record using a pointer variable whose value is **nil**. AVAIL may be written to abort or return **nil**, or to do whatever is best for your application.

The Pascal procedure DISPOSE is provided to carry out the general task of RECLAIM. However, what it does also depends on the computer system. At one extreme, there are systems for which DISPOSE does nothing but return, so no storage is actually reclaimed. In other systems, it may do just what RECLAIM does. Chapter 12 shows how DISPOSE might work in the most general case. But you can see that, even in Pascal where the heap, NEW, and DISPOSE are provided, you may choose to use the RECORDS array technique with AVAIL and RECLAIM, as your system may not actually implement DISPOSE to reclaim storage. Certainly in languages such as FORTRAN, you would implement lists in this way. Once AVAIL and RECLAIM are written, for all intents and purposes the language has a "heap" for record storage. You have tailored it to your needs.

3.8 Sequential Arrays versus Lists for Record Storage

Arrays allow records to be stored contiguously and to be accessed randomly. With pointer arrays, random access is possible even for variable-length records. Lists are also data structures containing records. Lists provide the flexibility, when needed, to separate records—enhancing the ability to insert or delete, but reducing the capability of accessing records at random. Stored records can be traversed using either the sequential array or list implementation. The time to carry out the traversal need not be significantly different for the two methods.

Suppose that instead of processing the records in sequential order, as in a traversal, your program must access the records in arbitrary order. (In an airplane reservation system, for example, seat reservations must be processed immediately, in random order.) Having to access the records in arbitrary order means that the program must access and process the records even though the programmer cannot predict the order in which this must be done. The sequential representation, because it allows selection for fixed-length records, allows this random accessing to be accomplished in constant time. The list representation requires that random accessing be done by traversing to the needed record, starting from the first and accessing each succeeding record until the desired one is reached. If the required record is the ith, traversal will take time proportional to i. Thus randomly accessing records takes constant time for each record access with the sequential implementation, but time proportional to the desired record number for the list representation. This can result in significantly greater processing time for the list implementation when you are randomly processing records.

To insert one record in the collection, say after the ith record, when using the sequential implementation, all succeeding records (the $(i + 1)$th, $(i + 2)$th, . . . , nth) must be moved down in the DATA array. This operation will take time proportional to the number of succeeding records $(n - i)$. Adding a record as the new first record gives the worst case time, which is proportional to n. Inserting a new record using the list implementation, again assuming you have determined where it is to be inserted, takes a constant time—the time to change two pointers.

To delete one record, say the ith, using the sequential representation, requires that the succeding $n - i$ records be moved up. Thus the time required is proportional to $n - i$. Using the list implementation requires a constant time for this deletion—the time to change one pointer. The time for deletion with a sequential implementation in the worst case is also proportional to n. It is obvious that insertion and deletion of one record can result in much greater execution time for the sequential implementation as compared to the list implementation.

The contrast is especially striking when record accesses, insertions, or deletions are performed on m records. The worst case time to randomly access an *entire* collection of m records becomes proportional to m and m^2, for the sequential and list implementations, respectively. For random insertions and deletions, these are reversed in favor of lists. This means that if m is doubled or tripled, the respective times increase fourfold or ninefold instead of merely doubling or tripling.

When selecting an implementation, the basic considerations are comparative execution times and relative frequencies for a random access, insertion, or deletion.

The list implementation will require at least as much memory as the sequential implementation. For instance, if each record requires one element for the information field, and the list implementation requires another element for the link field, then lists would require twice as much storage. It is possible that part of the storage used to implement a record would be left unused in any case, so that using it for the link field requires no extra storage.

3.9 Case Study: Merging and the Perfect Shuffle

Consider two sequences of numbers that are ordered, largest to smallest:

100	80	65	30
90	85	50	10

They may be merged to produce a new sequence containing all the numbers in order. For example, compare the two largest and place the larger one first in the final sequence. Continue comparing the two current largest and placing the larger in the next spot in the final sequence until all numbers have been placed. The result, of course, is

100	90	85	80	65	50	30	10

This merging algorithm takes $2n$ basic operations when there are n numbers in each original sequence. It is possible to merge the sequences using a different algorithm which, when parallel processing is possible, can reduce the time to $O(\lg 2n)$ rather than $O(2n)$ when n is a power of 2. It is not obvious how to do this. The solution involves a "perfect shuffle" operation plus a compare-and-exchange operation.

3.9.1 The Perfect Shuffle

Using gambling terminology, a **perfect shuffle** of $2n$ cards occurs when the deck of cards is split into two halves and the shuffle interleafs the two halves perfectly. An original configuration of eight cards, with the configurations after two consecutive perfect shuffles, is shown in Figure 3.14. A third perfect shuffle would produce the original configuration.

Suppose a sequence of perfect shuffles is made for $2n$ cards. Eventually the original configuration must reappear. How many shuffles will it take before this happens? One way to find out is to execute code that performs such a sequence of shuffles, keeping track of how many are made, and printing this total when the original configuration occurs again. A program segment to do this can be written as follows:

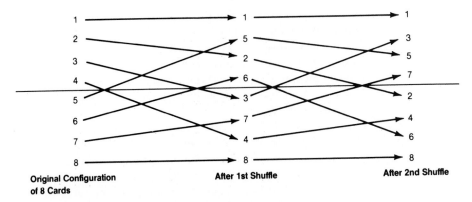

Figure 3.14   The Result of Two Perfect Shuffles

```
INITIAL(CONFIGURATION, N);
PERFECTSHUFFLE(CONFIGURATION, N);
NUMBERSHUFFLES := 1;
while (not ORIGINAL(CONFIGURATION, N))do
    begin
        PERFECTSHUFFLE(CONFIGURATION, N);
        NUMBERSHUFFLES := NUMBERSHUFFLES + 1
    end;
```

INITIAL initializes CONFIGURATION. ORIGINAL returns "true" if CONFIGU-
RATION is the original, and "false" otherwise. PERFECTSHUFFLE changes
CONFIGURATION so it reflects the new configuration resulting from a perfect
shuffle. As written, this code is independent of how the configuration is actually
implemented.

3.9.2 Array Implementation of the Perfect Shuffle

Suppose we decide to implement CONFIGURATION as an array and use N as a
pointer to the nth card. Then INITIAL and ORIGINAL may be defined, respectively, by

```
for I := 1 to (2 * N) do
    CONFIGURATION[I] := I;
```

and

```
TEMPORIGINAL := true;
I := 1;
while (I < N + 1) and TEMPORIGINAL do
    if CONFIGURATION[I] < > I then
        TEMPORIGINAL := false
    else
        I := I + 1;
ORIGINAL := TEMPORIGINAL;
```

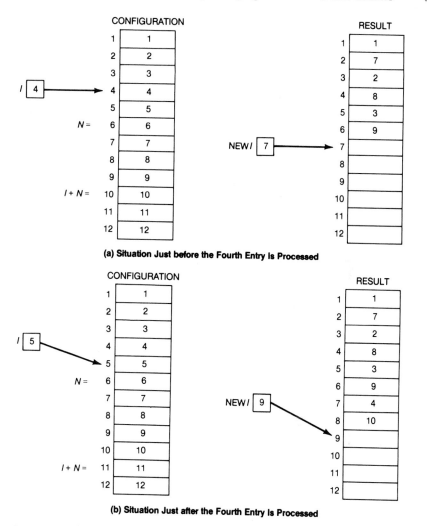

(a) Situation Just before the Fourth Entry Is Processed

(b) Situation Just after the Fourth Entry Is Processed

Figure 3.15 Two Arrays for a Perfect Shuffle of Twelve Elements

PERFECTSHUFFLE is somewhat more complex. The first and last cards, 1 and $2N$, never change position in CONFIGURATION. After the shuffle, cards 1 and $N + 1$, 2 and $N + 2$, 3 and $N + 3$, . . . , I and $I + N$, . . . , and N and $2N$ will appear in consecutive positions in the resultant configuration. An array, RESULT, is used to hold the new configuration. In traversing the first N positions of CONFIGURATION, its Ith entry is processed by copying CONFIGURATION[I] and CONFIGURATION[$I + N$] into their proper new consecutive positions in RESULT. I serves as a pointer to the current entry of CONFIGURATION being processed, and NEWI will point to the new position of that entry in RESULT. The situation, when N is 6, is depicted in Figure 3.15(a) just before the fourth entry is to be processed.

If the following statements are executed

```
RESULT[NEWI] := CONFIGURATION[I];
RESULT[NEWI + 1] := CONFIGURATION[I + N];
I := I + 1;
NEWI := NEWI + 2
```

then the program will have properly processed the Ith and $(I + N)$th cards. It will also have updated I and NEWI so that they are pointing to the proper new positions, respectively, in CONFIGURATION and RESULT. The situation after the fourth element has been processed is as shown in Figure 3.15(b).

To complete the shuffle, RESULT can be copied into CONFIGURATION. A program segment for PERFECTSHUFFLE might be

```
I := 1;
NEWI := 1;
while I < (N + 1) do
    begin
        RESULT[NEWI] := CONFIGURATION[I];
        RESULT[NEWI + 1] := CONFIGURATION[I + N];
        I := I + 1;
        NEWI := NEWI + 2
    end;
CONFIGURATION := RESULT;
```

Notice that the solution involves four array traversals, each traversal processing accessed elements in a different way.

3.9.3 List Implementation of the Perfect Shuffle

Suppose you decided to implement CONFIGURATION as a list of records stored in the heap, and to use N as a pointer to the nth record of the CONFIGURATION list. Figure 3.16 depicts these assumptions graphically for ten cards.

PERFECTSHUFFLE must, consecutively, move 6 before 2, 7 before 3, 8 before 4, and finally 9 before 5. Two pointers $L1$ and N are shown in Figure 3.16. Traversing CONFIGURATION and processing the records pointed to by $L1$ and N will accomplish the movements, if the processing deletes the successor of the record pointed to by N, inserts this deleted record after the record pointed to by $L1$, and updates $L1$ to point to it. MOVE carries out this processing task.

CONFIGURATION

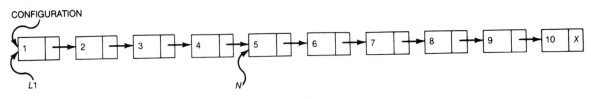

Figure 3.16 The List Implementation for CONFIGURATION

PERFECTSHUFFLE may now be implemented by

```
const
    NULL = nil;
var
    L1, NEWN : configurationpointer;
begin
  L1 := CONFIGURATION;
  NEWN := L1;
  while L1 <> N do
     begin
        MOVE(L1, N);
        L1 := L1↑.LINK;
        NEWN := NEWN↑.LINK
     end;
  N := NEWN
end;
```

PERFECTSHUFFLE in this form is a refinement of TRAVERSE. MOVE plays the role of PROCESS. It uses local variables HOLD1 and HOLD2 to keep track of the successors needed:

```
procedure MOVE(var L1 : configurationpointer; N : configurationpointer);
var
    HOLD1, HOLD2 : configurationpointer;
begin
   HOLD1 := L1↑.LINK;
   HOLD2 := N↑.LINK;
   L1↑.LINK := HOLD2;
   N↑.LINK := HOLD2↑.LINK;
   HOLD2↑.LINK := HOLD1;
   L1 := L1↑.LINK;
end;
```

Two complete programs that output the number of shuffles are presented at the end of this paragraph. The first is based on an array, and the second on a list implementation. In this case there is nothing to recommend the list implementation over the array implementation since the configuration does not grow or shrink, except for the artificial limit on the array size that would be required by the array implementation. The two versions of PERFECTSHUFFLE are both useful for the application to which we return in the section that follows the programs.

```
program PERFECTSHUFFLE(input, output);
type
    arraytype = array [1..52] of integer;
var
    CONFIGURATION : arraytype;
    N, NUMBERSHUFFLES : integer;
```

```
procedure INITIAL(var CONFIGURATION : arraytype; var N : integer);
var
    I : integer;
begin
    for I := 1 to (2 * N) do
        CONFIGURATION[I] := I
end;
procedure PERFECTSHUFFLE(var CONFIGURATION : arraytype; N : integer);
var
    RESULT : arraytype;
    NEWI, I : integer;
begin
    I := 1;
    NEWI := 1;
    while I < (N + 1) do
        begin
            RESULT[NEWI] := CONFIGURATION[I];
            RESULT[NEWI + 1] := CONFIGURATION[I + N];
            I := I + 1;
            NEWI := NEWI + 2
        end;
    CONFIGURATION := RESULT
end;
function ORIGINAL(CONFIGURATION : arraytype; N : integer) : boolean;
var
    TEMPORIGINAL : boolean;
    I : integer;
begin
    TEMPORIGINAL := true;
    I := 1;
    while (I < N + 1) and TEMPORIGINAL do
        if CONFIGURATION[I] <> I then
            TEMPORIGINAL := false
        else
            I := I + 1;
    ORIGINAL := TEMPORIGINAL
end;

begin
    WRITELN('N = ?');
    READLN(N);
    INITIAL(CONFIGURATION, N);
    NUMBERSHUFFLES := 1;
    PERFECTSHUFFLE(CONFIGURATION, N);
    while (not ORIGINAL(CONFIGURATION, N)) do
        begin
            PERFECTSHUFFLE(CONFIGURATION, N);
            NUMBERSHUFFLES := NUMBERSHUFFLES + 1
        end;
    WRITELN('NUMBERSHUFFLES = ');
    WRITELN(NUMBERSHUFFLES)
end.
```

```
program PERFECTSHUFFLE(input, output);
type
    configptr = ↑configrec;
    configrec = record
                      info : integer;
                      link : configptr
                end;
var
    CONFIGURATION, N : configptr;
    NUMBERSHUFFLES : integer;
    NUM : integer;


procedure INITIAL(var CONFIGURATION, N : configptr);
var
    P, Q : configptr;
    I : integer;
begin
    NEW(CONFIGURATION);
    P := CONFIGURATION;
    I := 1;
    while I <> 2 * NUM + 1 do
        begin
            P↑.INFO := I;
            if I = NUM then
                N := P;
            I := I + 1;
            NEW(P↑.LINK);
            Q := P;
            P := P↑.LINK
        end;
    Q↑.LINK := nil;
    WRITELN('first, n, last');
end;


procedure MOVE(var L1 : configptr; N : configptr);
var
    HOLD1, HOLD2 : configptr;
begin
    HOLD1 := L1↑.LINK;
    HOLD2 := N↑.LINK;
    L1↑.LINK := HOLD2;
    N↑.LINK := HOLD2↑.LINK;
    HOLD2↑.LINK := HOLD1;
    L1 := L1↑.LINK
end;

procedure PERFECTSHUFFLE(var CONFIGURATION, N : configptr);
const
    NULL = nil;
var
    L1, NEWN : configptr;
```

```
begin
    L1 := CONFIGURATION;
    NEWN := L1;
    while L1 <> N do
        begin
            MOVE(L1, N);
            L1 := L1 ↑.LINK;
            NEWN := NEWN ↑.LINK
        end;
    N := NEWN
end;

function ORIGINAL(CONFIGURATION, N : configptr) : boolean;
var
    TEMPORIGINAL : boolean;
    I : integer;
    P : configptr;
begin
    TEMPORIGINAL := true;
    I := 1;
    P := CONFIGURATION;
    while (P <> N ↑.LINK) and TEMPORIGINAL do
        if P ↑.INFO <> I then
            TEMPORIGINAL := false
        else
            begin
                I := I + 1;
                P := P ↑.LINK
            end;
    ORIGINAL := TEMPORIGINAL
end;

begin
    WRITELN('NUM = ?');
    READLN(NUM);
    INITIAL(CONFIGURATION, N);
    NUMBERSHUFFLES := 1;
    PERFECTSHUFFLE(CONFIGURATION, N);
    while (not ORIGINAL(CONFIGURATION, N)) do
        begin
            PERFECTSHUFFLE(CONFIGURATION, N);
            NUMBERSHUFFLES := NUMBERSHUFFLES + 1
        end;
    WRITELN('NUMBERSHUFFLES = ');
    WRITELN(NUMBERSHUFFLES)
end.
```

3.9.4 Merging Sequences of Entries

Set the first *n* entries of CONFIGURATION to one of the sequences to be merged, and the second *n* entries of CONFIGURATION to the other, but enter the second in reverse order.

Consider the following algorithm for merging two sequences of ordered (largest to smallest) entries each of length n:

Apply PERFECTSHUFFLE and COMPAREEXCHANGE to CONFIGURATION a total of $2n$ times.

COMPAREEXCHANGE is a procedure that compares each of the n pairs of adjacent configuration entries and exchanges their values whenever the second is larger than the first. Table 3.2 shows the results obtained as this algorithm is applied to our sample sequences of length 4. Since $\lg 2n = \lg 8 = 3$, the algorithm terminates after the third perfect shuffle and compare-and-exchange operation. Notice that this results in CONFIGURATION containing the correct merged sequence.

When $2n$ is a power of 2, say 2^k, then the k iterations always produce the correct merge. This is certainly not obvious, and it is not proven here. But one point is important. If this merge is implemented as a **for** loop, and carried out conventionally (that is, sequentially), it will take time $O(n \lg n)$. The straightforward sequential merge discussed earlier takes only $O(n)$ time. However, if the n moves of PERFECTSHUFFLE and the n pair comparisons and interchanges of COMPARE-EXCHANGE are all done in parallel (at the same time), then the total time will be just $O(\lg n)$.

Parallel processing is beyond the scope of this text, but this application illustrates its power and some of the difficulties involved. Doing parallel processing correctly is tricky since care must be taken to do the right thing at the right time. For instance, one could dress in parallel fashion, but certain constraints must be observed. Socks and shirt can be put on at the same time (a valet is needed of course,

Table 3.2 The Result of Merging Two Sequences of Ordered Entries of Length 4

Initial configuration	After first perfect shuffle	After first compare exchange	After second perfect shuffle
100	100	100	100
80	10	10	85
65	80	80	10
30	50	50	65
10	65	85	80
50	85	65	90
85	30	90	50
90	90	30	30

After second compare exchange	After third perfect shuffle	After third compare exchange
100	100	100
85	90	90
65	85	85
10	80	80
90	65	65
80	50	50
50	10	30
30	30	10

since a person has only two hands) followed by pants, with shoes and jacket next and in parallel. But shoes and pants cannot go on prior to socks and shirt.

The perfect shuffle, and the topic of parallel processing, is pursued further in Stone [1971, 1980] and Ben-Ari [1982]. An application of these ideas to the stable marriage problem appears in Hull [1984].

☐ Exercises

1. What record of a list has no pointer pointing to it from another list record? What record of a list has a null pointer in its link field?

2. If each record of a list has, in addition to its information and link fields, a "pred" field, then the list is called a *two-way list*. The pred field contains a pointer to the preceding record. The first record's pred field contains a null pointer. Write insertion and deletion procedures corresponding to those of Section 3.3 for a two-way list.

3. A *circular list* is a list whose last record's link field contains a pointer to the first list record rather than a null pointer. Write insertion and deletion routines corresponding to those of Section 3.3 for a circular list.

4. Modify the solution to Example 3.1 so it is correct for
   a. A two-way list
   b. A circular list

5. Write a procedure to interchange the records of a list that are pointed to by $P1$ and $P2$.

6. The solution developed for Example 3.1 essentially cycles pointers from one list record to the next. Instead, a solution could cycle information field values from one record to the next. Modify the solution so it does this, and compare the two execution times. What if the information field contains only a pointer to the actual information field value?

7. Consider the three arrays below — DATA, P, and S.

	DATA	P	S
1	1	0	6
2	12	5	7
3	18	7	9
4	4	6	10
5	7	10	2
6	3	1	4
7	12	2	3
8	100	9	0
9	20	3	8
10	5	4	5

An ordering of the integers in DATA is specified by P and by S. $P[I]$ and $S[I]$ point to the predecessor and successor of the integer stored in DATA[I]. A zero indicates no predecessor or successor. Assume the first I elements of DATA, P, and S are properly set, as above, to reflect the usual ordering of integers. Suppose a new integer is placed into DATA[$I + 1$].

   a. If I is 10 and the new integer is 15, what will the new P and S arrays be after they are properly updated to correctly reflect the ordering among the eleven integers? The DATA array, except for 15 being placed in element 11, is to be unchanged.

   b. Write a program segment to properly update P and S after the $(I + 1)$th integer is placed in DATA[$I + 1$]. You might want to assume that FIRST and LAST point, respectively, to the element of DATA containing the first and last integers in the ordering.

8. a. What does TRAVERSE (Section 3.4) do when PROCESS interchanges the record that RECORDPOINTER points to with its successor record?
    b. Same as Exercise 8(a) except, in addition, PROCESS then sets RECORD-POINTER to the link field value of the record to which it points.
    9. Write a procedure to delete all the records from list $L1$ that also appear on the list $L2$.

(In Exercises 10–13 you must turn TRAVERSE of Section 3.4 into a solution to the exercise by defining its modules properly. You may not change TRAVERSE itself other than by selecting proper parameters for "OTHER".)

    10. Write a procedure to delete all duplicate records from an alphabetic list such as that of Example 3.4.
    11. Write a procedure to insert a new record in *front* of the record pointed to by PTR. You should not keep track of a predecessor nor traverse the list to find a predecessor. A "trick" is involved here (see Section 3.3.4).
    12. This is the same as Example 3.4, but assume the list is implemented as a two-way list.
    13. Create a new list that is the same as L except that each record has been duplicated, with the duplicate inserted as the new successor of the record it duplicates.
    14. Create a list L that consists of all the records of the list $L1$ followed by all the records of the list $L2$.
    15. Write a procedure to print out the number of words for a list such as that of Example 3.2.
    16. Write the required modules for TRAVERSE of Section 3.4 when list records are stored in the Pascal heap and the list is implemented as
        a. A two-way list
        b. A circular list
    17. A hospital has 100 beds. The array RECORDS contains records that represent, by floor and bed number, those beds that are not occupied. The first, second, and third elements of a record contain, respectively, the floor number, bed number, and link value. How many beds are not occupied and what is the lowest floor with an available bed?

	RECORDS			RECORDS
1	5		13	5
2	10		14	2
3	4		15	0
4	7		16	2
5	10		17	5
6	13		18	22
7	3		19	5
8	6		20	10
9	4		21	2
10	7		22	7
11	3		23	1
12	16		24	1

BEDS 10

    18. Change the appropriate pointers for Exercise 17 so that the records are kept in order by floor and bed number.
    19. Show what the arrays FLOOR, BED, and NEXT might have in their entries if the BEDS list of Exercise 17 were implemented using three corresponding words of these arrays.

20. How would the RECORDS array of Exercise 17 change if bed 2 on the fifth floor became occupied?

21. Suppose bed 10 on the sixth floor became empty. Assuming that the RECORDS array is used only for the BEDS list, what changes might be made to it to reflect this new information?

22. This is the same as Exercise 16 except the list records are stored in an array RECORDS.

23. A *palindrome* is a sequence of characters that reads the same from front to back as from back to front. ABCDDCBA, ABCBA, and NOON are palindromes. Write a boolean function PALINDROME to return the value *true* if the list it is called to check represents a palindrome, and the value *false* otherwise. The list records are stored in the Pascal heap.

24. Suppose four records, 13, 7, 1, and 2, were deleted from lists whose records are stored in RECORDS of Figure 3.13. Then three records were inserted. If RECLAIM returns records at the front of AVAILIST, depict the AVAILIST and RECORDS after this processing.

25. Do the same as in Exercise 24, but assume that RECLAIM returns records at the rear of AVAILIST.

26. a. Why isn't it reasonable for AVAIL to delete a record from anywhere on AVAILIST except the front or rear?

b. Why isn't it reasonable for RECLAIM to insert a record anywhere on AVAILIST except the front or rear?

27. Suppose a record is deleted from a list stored in RECORDS, but RECLAIM is not invoked to return it to AVAILIST. Is it ever possible to reuse the storage relinquished by that record?

28. Suppose records with different lengths are stored in RECORDS using the techniques of Chapter 2. The AVAILIST contains the available records in arbitrary order. Describe how AVAIL and RECLAIM might be implemented.

29. This is the same as Exercise 28, except the AVAILIST contains the available records ordered by length.

30. Write a procedure to create a list whose records are defined by

```
type
    pointer = ↑listnode;
    listnode = record
                   info : whatevertype;
                   linkptr : pointer;
                   prevptr : pointer
               end;
```

The input should consist of a sequence of information field values given in the order they should appear in the list. LINKPTR points to the next record on the list and PREVPTR points to the preceding record on the list.

31. Explain why pointer variables and the procedure NEW remove the need for the programmer to manage storage for list records.

32. Both the sequential array and list representations for ordered records use arrays. Why are they different?

33. Suppose you are asked to store records that represent an inventory of books that are currently signed out from the library. Assume that frequent requests are made for output that includes the book title and the current borrower in alphabetic order by the borrower name. Of course, books are frequently taken out and returned. Should a sequential array be used for the records or a list representation, and why?

34. Suppose records are stored using the sequential array implementation. Initially 1,000 records are stored. You are asked to delete every other record, starting with the first. After this deletion you must insert records before every third record starting with the first record. Find an expression for the total number of shifts of records that must take place to accomplish these insertions and deletions.

35. Do Exercise 34, but instead of assuming a sequential implementation assume a list implementation.

36. Suppose you must access records in the order tenth, first, twelfth, thirtieth, and fiftieth. How much time will the five accesses take with a sequential representation, and how much time will they take with a list representation?

37. Describe a real-life situation in which the sequential array representation of ordered records is clearly more desirable, another in which the list representation is clearly favored, and a third situation that involves trade-offs between the two representations.

38. a. Write the INITIAL and ORIGINAL routines for the array implementation of the perfect shuffle and for the list implementation of the perfect shuffle in Section 3.9.

b. Can ORIGINAL be reduced to checking only the nth card to see if it has returned to the initial configuration?

39. a. Why must the "perfect shuffle" cause the original configuration to appear?

b. Show that the number of shuffles that will produce the original configuration is given by the smallest positive integer k for which $2^k - 1$ is a multiple of $(2n - 1)$. For instance, for eight cards $n = 4$ and $2^3 - 1 = 1 \times 7$; for fifty-two cards $n = 26$ and $2^8 - 1 = 5 \times 51$.

c. Show that k is never greater than $2n - 2$.

d. Can you write a procedure for PERFECTSHUFFLE that does not use the RESULT array (one that only uses CONFIGURATION)?

40. Justify the $O(n \lg n)$ and $O(\lg n)$ times claimed to be correct in Section 3.9.

☐ Suggested Assignment

Write and execute a program to input a series of lists such as those of Example 3.2. After inputting all the lists, the program should invoke a procedure SHORTEN to work on each list. SHORTEN is to print each sentence of the list it is to deal with whose length exceeds 25, and delete such sentences from the list. You *must* write SHORTEN by defining the modules of TRAVERSE so as to turn TRAVERSE into SHORTEN. Use the Pascal heap for record storage. Don't forget to echo print all input and annotate all output. Make up some fun sentences.

Modify your program (and run the new version) when three characters, instead of one, are stored per record.

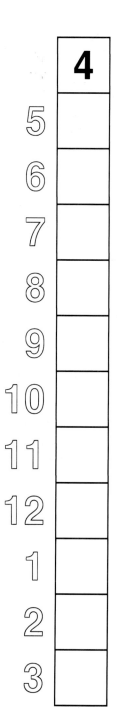

4 Introduction to Recursion, Stacks, and Queues

4.1 What Is Recursion?

People can't help but use themselves—their own life experiences—as a point of reference for understanding the world and the experiences of others. Definitions, algorithms, and programs may also refer to themselves, but for a different purpose—to express their meaning or intention more clearly and concisely. They are then said to be *recursive*. Languages, such as Pascal, that allow modules to call themselves are called *recursive languages*. When no self-reference is invoked they are said to be nonrecursive or *iterative*.

Self-reference is not without its pitfalls. You have most likely encountered the frustration of circular definitions in the dictionary, such as, "Fashion pertains to style" and "Style pertains to fashion." From this you conclude "Fashion pertains to fashion." This kind of self-reference conveys no information and is to be avoided. "This sentence is false" is another type of self-reference to be avoided, for it tells us nothing. If true it must be false, and if false it must be true. Nevertheless, self-reference is an important technique in finding and expressing solutions to problems.

Recall that the top-down approach to problem solving entails breaking down an initial problem into smaller component problems. These components need not be related except in the sense that putting their solutions together yields a solution to the original problem. If any of these component problems is identical in structure to the initial problem, the solution is said to be recursive and the problem is said to be solved by recursion. If the solution and its components are modularized, then the solution will refer to itself. Recursion is thus a special case of the top-down design methodology.

Suppose a traveler asks you, "How do I get there from here?" You might respond with a complete set of directions, but if the directions are too complex, or you are not sure, your response might be: "Go to the main street, turn left, continue for one mile, and then ask, 'How do I get there from here?'" This is an example of recursion. The traveler wanted directions to a destination. In solving the problem, you provided an initial small step leading toward the traveler's goal. After taking that step, the traveler will be confronted with a new version of the original problem. This new problem, while identical in form to the original, involves a new starting location closer to the destination.

Cursing is often used to belittle a problem; recursing has the same effect! Recursion, when appropriate, can give relatively easy-to-understand and concise descriptions for complex tasks. Still, care must be taken in its use, as with all powerful methods, or efficiency of storage and execution time will be sacrificed.

4.2 Using Recursion

Applying the recursive method is just like applying the top-down approach but can be tricky and presents conceptual difficulties for many students. The purpose of this section is to show how to develop and how to understand recursive solutions. Some illustrative examples are provided to help you "get the idea." Practice will help you become skilled and facile in use of recursion.

4.2.1 The Towers of Hanoi

A game called the Towers of Hanoi was purportedly played by priests in the Temple of Brahma, who believed that completion of the game's central task would coincide with the end of the world. The task involves three pegs. The version considered here has n disks initially mounted on peg 1; the priests dealt with 64 disks. The n disks increase in size from top to bottom, the top disk being the smallest. The problem is to relocate the n disks to peg 3 by moving one at a time. Only the top disk on a peg can be moved. Each time a disk is moved it may be placed only on an empty peg or on top of a pile of disks of larger size. The programmer's task is to develop an algorithm specifying a solution to this problem *no matter what the value of* n.

Consider the case when $n = 4$, shown in Figure 4.1(a). The following sequence of instructions provides a solution.

1. Move the top disk from peg 1 to peg 2.
2. Move the top disk from peg 1 to peg 3.
3. Move the top disk from peg 2 to peg 3.
4. Move the top disk from peg 1 to peg 2.
5. Move the top disk from peg 3 to peg 1.
6. Move the top disk from peg 3 to peg 2.
7. Move the top disk from peg 1 to peg 2.
8. Move the top disk from peg 1 to peg 3.
9. Move the top disk from peg 2 to peg 3.
10. Move the top disk from peg 2 to peg 1.
11. Move the top disk from peg 3 to peg 1.
12. Move the top disk from peg 2 to peg 3.
13. Move the top disk from peg 1 to peg 2.
14. Move the top disk from peg 1 to peg 3.
15. Move the top disk from peg 2 to peg 3.

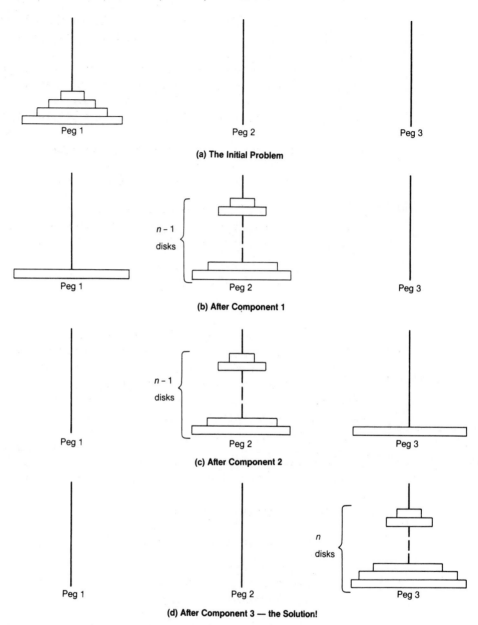

(a) The Initial Problem

(b) After Component 1

(c) After Component 2

(d) After Component 3 — the Solution!

Figure 4.1   The Towers of Hanoi Problem

It is not difficult to arrive at such a solution for a specific small value of n. Try to find a solution for $n = 5$. You will find that, even though you succeed (after some trial and error), creating a solution in a similar fashion for $n = 25$ is indeed a formidable task.

You may even be too old to care by the time you finish. If a particular value of n gives so much trouble, how does one specify a solution for *any* n, when one does not even know what value n will have?

The answer is to apply the technique of recursion. This means attempt to break down the problem into component problems that can be solved directly, or that are identical to the original problem but involve a smaller number of disks. The three component problems below fit the requirements of this framework.

1. Relocate the top $n - 1$ disks from peg 1 to peg 2.
2. Relocate the top disk from peg 1 to peg 3.
3. Relocate the top $n - 1$ disks from peg 2 to peg 3.

If these three problems can be solved, and their solutions are applied in sequence to the initial situation, then the result is a solution to the original problem. This can be seen from parts a–d of Figure 4.1, which show the consecutive situations after each is applied.

We now generalize the original problem:

Relocate the top n disks from peg I to peg F.

I denotes the initial peg on which the top n disks to be relocated reside, and F denotes the final peg to which they are to be relocated. Let A denote the third available peg. It is now apparent that the original problem, and the components 1, 2, and 3, have structure identical to the generalized problem, but the components involve fewer disks. They also involve different initial, available, and final pegs; this is why it was necessary to generalize the original problem.

Suppose you have found a solution to the generalization and denote it by TOWERS(n, I, A, F). Then, as just shown, the application of the solutions to components 1, 2, and 3, in sequence, will be a solution to the original problem. A recursive definition for TOWERS(n, I, A, F) can now be expressed as follows.

To obtain TOWERS(n, I, A, F):
If $n = 1$ then
   move the top disk from peg I to peg F
else
   apply TOWERS($n - 1, I, F, A$)
   apply TOWERS($1, I, A, F$)
   apply TOWERS($n - 1, A, I, F$).

This is the recursive algorithm for the Towers of Hanoi problem. Notice the definition gives an explicit solution when $n = 1$ and an implicit solution for any other case.

To use the method of recursion we must recognize when it is applicable and find a correct way to generalize and then to decompose the original problem. We have been successful and have found a recursive algorithm. The solution to component 2, TOWERS($1, I, A, F$) can be given directly: Move the top disk from peg I to peg F. Because no further refinement is needed, the corresponding recursive program can be written directly using modularization:

```
        procedure TOWERS(N, I, A, F : integer);
        begin
           if N = 1 then
                WRITELN(I, '→', F)
           else
                begin
                    TOWERS(N – 1, I, F, A);
[1]                 WRITELN(I, '→', F);
                    TOWERS(N – 1, A, I, F)
[2]             end
        end;
```

The labels [1] and [2] are not part of the program but are used later in references to this program. It is essential to see that this procedure has been written just like any other; whenever a component task is available as a module, we invoke it to carry out that task. The feature that distinguishes it and makes it a recursive procedure is that the required modules happen to be the procedure itself. The references within TOWERS to itself are allowed in recursive languages.

Any time a module calls itself during its execution we say a ***recursive call*** has been made. The two invocations of TOWERS within TOWERS represent such recursive calls. In general, when a recursive program executes on a computer, or when its execution is simulated by a programmer, many recursive calls will be made. Simulation of a program or module call means carrying out its instructions by hand and keeping track of the values of all its variables. These are referred to as the first, second, etc. recursive calls. The initial call to the module precedes the first recursive call.

4.2.2 Verifying and Simulating a Recursive Program

The verification of a recursive program is done just as for a nonrecursive program, by formal proof or by checking all cases. With recursion, the cases given explicitly are checked first. Also, it is assumed that each module individually works correctly. For TOWERS(N, I, A, F), the only explicit case is when $N = 1$ and the procedure clearly outputs the proper result and terminates.

For the case when N exceeds 1, Figure 4.1 has already confirmed that as long as the three component modules work properly then TOWERS(N, I, A, F) will also. Note that these components correspond to smaller values of N. Mathematically inclined readers may recognize that this really amounts to a proof of correctness for TOWERS using mathematical induction on N. One of the advantages of recursive programs is that they may be proven correct more easily in this way.

In order to understand how a recursive program actually executes, it is necessary to simulate its execution. We will go through the first few steps of the simulation for a call to TOWERS(4, 1, 2, 3). It will soon become apparent that considerable bookkeeping is involved and we will need an organized way to do it.

Since n is greater than 1, the procedure requires the sequential execution of

```
TOWERS(3, 1, 3, 2),
WRITELN(1, '→', 3),
```

and

| TOWERS(3, 2, 1, 3).

To do this requires suspending the execution of TOWERS(4, 1, 2, 3) at this point in order to simulate the first recursive call, TOWERS(3, 1, 3, 2). Note that after this recursive call is completed, 1→3 is to be output (1→3 means "Move the top disk from peg 1 to peg 3"), and then another recursive call must be simulated, TOWERS(3, 2, 1, 3).

Dealing with TOWERS(3, 1, 3, 2), since $n > 1$, the commands

| TOWERS(2, 1, 2, 3),
| WRITELN(1, '→', 2),

and

| TOWERS(2, 3, 1, 2)

must be carried out sequentially. Now the execution of TOWERS(3, 1, 3, 2) must be suspended in order to simulate the second recursive call, TOWERS(2, 1, 2, 3). Note that after this recursive call is completed, 1→2 is to be output, and then another recursive call must be simulated, TOWERS(2, 3, 1, 2).

Dealing with TOWERS(2, 1, 2, 3), since $n > 1$,

| TOWERS(1, 1, 3, 2),
| WRITELN(1, '→', 3),

and

| TOWERS(1, 2, 1, 3)

must be carried out sequentially. The two calls to TOWERS represent the third and fourth recursive calls. They both complete without generating any new recursive calls. The three statements result in the outputting of 1→2, 1→3, and 2→3 respectively. This completes the second recursive call (TOWERS(2, 1, 2, 3)) so we must pick up the simulation at the proper point which is to output 1→2 and then make the fifth recursive call to simulate TOWERS(2, 3, 1, 2).

Enough is enough! At this point you may feel like a juggler with too few hands and too many recursive calls. Figure 4.2 represents a convenient way to keep track of the complete simulation and may be generated as the simulation proceeds. Each recursive call is numbered to show whether it is the first, second, . . . , or fourteenth. The bracketed return values indicate the labeled statement of procedure TOWERS at which the preceding recursive call is to resume when the next call is completed. For example, when TOWERS(3, 1, 3, 2) is completed, TOWERS(4, 1, 2, 3) resumes at [1]. Our simulation stopped just as the fifth recursive call was to be carried out. The figure uses shorthand for the output. For example, 1→2 means, move the top disk from peg 1 to peg 2. The solution is the same as our earlier one.

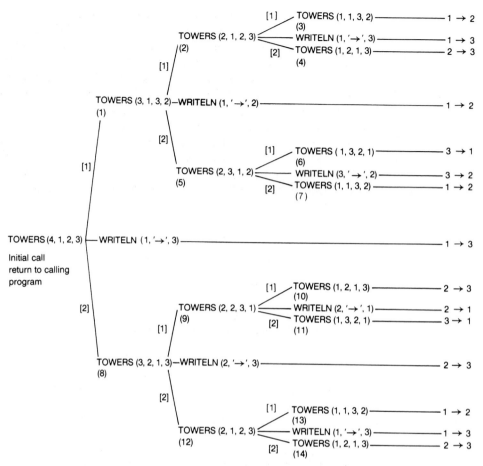

Figure 4.2 Bookkeeping for the Simulation of a Recursive Program

Figure 4.2 indicates very clearly what information must be available at each point in the simulation (or execution of the program) in order to carry it out. Specifically, it is necessary to know

☐ The four parameter values of the call currently being carried out
☐ Where to resume when the call currently being carried out is completed

For example, when the third recursive call is completed, resumption must be at the WRITELN statement of the second recursive call; when the fifth recursive call is completed, resumption must be at the **end** statement of the first recursive call; and finally, after the initial recursive call is completed, resumption must be at the proper point in the program that called TOWERS originally.

Notice that the last three parameters are never modified by TOWERS, but the first parameter, which corresponds to the number of disks for the current problem, is modified. For instance the first recursive call to TOWERS(3, 1, 3, 2) has modified the first parameter making it 3 rather than 4 as it was initially. It is important that this modification be kept local to TOWERS(3, 1, 3, 2) and not be reflected back to

TOWERS(4, 1, 2, 3), the initial call. In other words, the first parameter must be treated exactly as a non-**var** parameter in calls to TOWERS.

It is not always possible to find a recursive solution to a problem, nor is it always desirable to use one when available. Sometimes a recursive solution is the *only* one we can find. For the Towers of Hanoi problem it is difficult to find a nonrecursive solution, but a number are known. Recursive solutions normally make it easier to see why they are correct, probably because to achieve them requires that you make the structure inherent in the problem more explicit.

To make this point clearly, the recursive algorithm and a nonrecursive algorithm are repeated here. Convince yourself that the nonrecursive algorithm correctly solves the Towers of Hanoi problem (see Exercise 8). The nonrecursive program is taken from Walsh [1982]; another nonrecursive program appears in Buneman and Levy [1980].

A recursive solution for the Towers of Hanoi

To obtain TOWERS(n, I, A, F):
    If $n = 1$ then
        move the top disk from I to F
    else
        apply TOWERS($n - 1, I, F, A$)
        move the top disk from I to F
        apply TOWERS($n - 1, A, I, F$).

A nonrecursive algorithm for the Towers of Hanoi

1. Label the disks $1, 2, \ldots, N$ in increasing order of size.
2. Label the pegs I, A, and F, $N + 1$, $N + 2$, and $N + 3$, respectively.
3. Move the smallest disk onto another disk with an even label or onto an empty peg with an even label.
4. While all disks are not on the same peg
    a. move the second smallest top disk onto the peg not containing the smallest ring
    b. move the smallest disk onto another disk with an even label or onto an empty peg with an even label.

The Tower of Babel failed for lack of communication. The construction workers did not speak the same language. While recursion allows the solution to the Towers of Hanoi to be specified conveniently, it is execution time that causes trouble. The diagram of Figure 4.1 shows that the construction of the new tower of disks will take $2^4 - 1$ or fifteen moves. It is not difficult to generalize the diagram to n disks to conclude that $2^n - 1$ moves will be needed for n disks (see Exercise 7). Even with Olympic-caliber construction workers, it would take over one thousand years to complete the tower for 50 disks.

4.2.3 The Length of a List

Clearly a list may be thought of as being either a null list, a one-record list, or one-record followed by a nonnull list (the link field of the record plays the role of the head of this nonnull list). This is nothing but a way to define a list recursively. Consider the recursive function defined by

```
function LENGTH(LISTNAME : listpointer) : integer;
var
    NULL : listpointer;
begin
    SETNULL(NULL);
    if LISTNAME = NULL then
        LENGTH := 0
    else
        LENGTH := 1 + LENGTH(NEXT(LISTNAME))
end;
```

This function returns the length of the list, LISTNAME. To verify that this is correct we must check

1. The null list. It returns with LENGTH = 0.
2. A one-record list. It returns with LENGTH = 1 + 0 = 1.
3. A one-record list followed by a nonnull list. It returns LENGTH = 1 + the length of the nonnull list.

It is correct, since its value is correct for each case. Of course it is correct—after all, the length of a null list is zero, and the length of a list with at least one record is 1 for the record, plus the length of the rest of the list beyond the first record! This was how LENGTH was written in the first place.

4.2.4 Copying a List

Consider procedure COPY, which creates a list SECOND that is a copy of a list FIRST:

```
procedure COPY(FIRST : listpointer; var SECOND : listpointer);
var
    NULL, REST : listpointer;
begin
    SETNULL(NULL);
    if FIRST = NULL then
        SECOND := NULL
    else
        begin
            AVAIL(SECOND);
            SETINFO(SECOND, INFO(FIRST));
            COPY(NEXT(FIRST), REST);
            SETLINK(SECOND, REST)
        end
end;
```

When FIRST is the null list, COPY faithfully terminates with the copy also a null list. When FIRST is a one-record list, AVAIL sets SECOND to point to storage allocated for a record and sets the information field value of this record to the value of the information field in FIRST's first record. The recursive call to COPY (NEXT(FIRST),

REST) is then an invocation of COPY to copy the null list, since NEXT(FIRST) is null in this case. Assuming it performs its task correctly, REST will be null when it returns. The link field of the record pointed to by SECOND is then set to the value of REST (the null pointer) and the initial call to COPY terminates correctly.

Similarly, had there been more than one record in FIRST's list, the recursive call to COPY would have returned with REST pointing to a correct copy of the list pointed to by NEXT(FIRST). SETLINK would correctly place a pointer to that correct copy into the link field of the record pointed to by SECOND and the initial call would terminate correctly. This verifies that COPY is correct in all cases. Again, to copy the null list is easy, and to copy a list with at least one record, simply copy that record, copy the rest of the list beyond the first record, and append that copy to the copy of the first record. This is how copy was written!

If you are confronted with a recursive program and want to understand it, approach it in the same way as you would a nonrecursive program. Assume that any modules that are called perform their functions correctly, and then attempt to see what the program itself does. Sometimes this will be apparent as it was for TOWERS and COPY, and sometimes a simulation of the program helps to increase comprehension. Imagine, for example, that you were not told what COPY did. It wouldn't have been so easy to find out without simulation of some simple cases.

4.2.5 var versus Non-var Parameters

In order to understand what happens as a recursive program executes, it is necessary to know how local, nonlocal, and global variables are treated, and also how parameters are treated. In particular, the effect of declaring a parameter as **var** or non-**var** must be known. This must also be known to understand what happens when *any* program executes.

In nonrecursive programs, references to nonlocal or global variables always refer to the current actual storage assigned to them. Hence any changes to their values during the execution of the program will be reflected back in their values. Local variables are treated differently. Local copies are made, and these are referred to during the execution of the program. Just as for non-**var** parameters in Pascal, the storage for these local copies disappears when the procedure terminates or returns. The only difference for recursive programs is that each recursive call produces its own local copies.

Recall that in Pascal there are two kinds of formal parameters, **var** parameters and non-**var** parameters. A formal parameter is declared to be **var** in the definition of the procedure that uses the parameter, such as SECOND in the COPY procedure, by placing **var** before SECOND. Any formal parameter with no **var** before it is assumed to be a non-**var** parameter. FIRST is such a parameter.

As the invoked procedure executes, every reference to a **var** formal parameter is treated as if it were a reference to the *actual* parameter used at the point of the procedure call. This implies that any change to a **var** parameter during execution of the procedure is reflected back to the storage used for the corresponding actual parameter's value. The effect is as if the actual parameter were used in the procedure instead of the formal parameter.

Non-**var** parameters are treated differently. New storage is used for each non-**var** parameter. This storage is initially set to the value of the corresponding actual parameter when the procedure is invoked. In effect, this storage represents a *local copy* of the actual parameter. Any reference in the procedure is then interpreted as a reference to the local copy only. This implies that any change to a non-**var** parameter during the execution of the procedure will *not* be reflected back to the storage used for the actual parameter; it cannot have its value changed by the procedure.

Here is a simple example.

```
procedure SIMPLE(X : integer; var Y : integer);
begin
    X := 1;
    Y := 2;
    Y := X + Y
end;
```

Suppose that SIMPLE is invoked with actual parameters A and B containing 0 and 1 respectively. It is invoked by the statement, SIMPLE(A, B). Within the procedure, X initially has a copy of A as its value, 0 in this case. Y refers to the storage for B. The first statement of SIMPLE causes X to assume the value 1, the second statement causes the storage for B to contain 2, and the third statement sets the storage for B to 3. When the calling program continues, A will still be 0 but B will be 3.

In recursive programs, **var** and non-**var** parameters will be treated in just this way. Any time a recursive call is made within a recursive program, the recursive call acts just like a call to any procedure. The only difference is that, since a recursive procedure may generate many recursive calls during its execution, many local copies of its non-**var** parameters will be produced. References to a non-**var** parameter during the execution of each recursive call will then mean the current local copy of that parameter. Reference to a **var** parameter always means the same actual parameter.

In the recursive version of COPY note that

☐ NULL and REST are local variables of the initial call to COPY and remain local variables in all subsequent recursive calls. Local copies of NULL and REST are thus made on *any* call to COPY.

☐ FIRST is a non-**var** parameter and SECOND a **var** parameter of COPY.

☐ Whenever COPY is executing and generates a recursive call to copy (NEXT(FIRST), REST), the actual first parameter is the current copy of NEXT(FIRST), the copy associated with the currently executing call to COPY. Any references to the first parameter during the generated recursive call refer to the new local copy associated with that call.

When FIRST is given by Figure 4.3, the sequence of effects, as a call to COPY (FIRST, SECOND) is executed, appears in Figure 4.4. FIRST0, FIRST1, FIRST2,

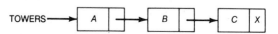

Figure 4.3 The List for COPY to Process

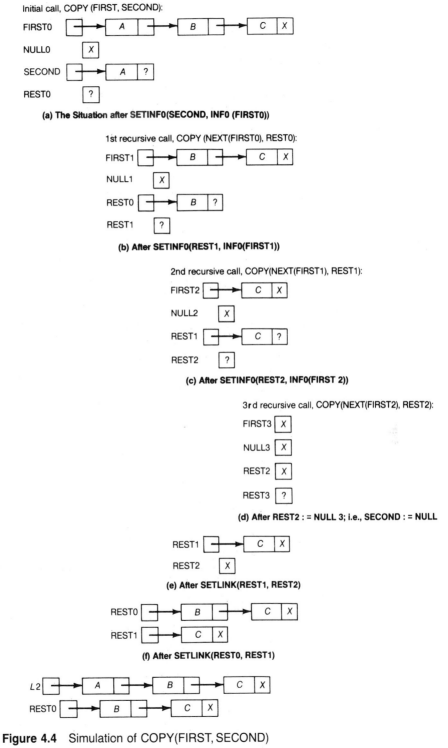

Initial call, COPY (FIRST, SECOND):

(a) The Situation after SETINFO(SECOND, INFO (FIRST0))

1st recursive call, COPY (NEXT(FIRST0), REST0):

(b) After SETINFO(REST1, INFO(FIRST1))

2nd recursive call, COPY(NEXT(FIRST1), REST1):

(c) After SETINFO(REST2, INFO(FIRST 2))

3rd recursive call, COPY(NEXT(FIRST2), REST2):

(d) After REST2 : = NULL 3; i.e., SECOND : = NULL

(e) After SETLINK(REST1, REST2)

(f) After SETLINK(REST0, REST1)

Figure 4.4 Simulation of COPY(FIRST, SECOND)

FIRST3 refer to the local copies of the actual first parameter associated with the initial, first, second, and third recursive calls to copy, respectively. Similarly for the other variables. A question mark indicates an as yet undefined value. Be sure you understand Figure 4.4 and how it represents the execution of COPY.

4.2.6 Counting Squares

Consider an $n \times n$ checkerboard and determine the number of ways a 4×4 checkerboard can be placed on it. For example, if $n = 5$, there are four ways to place a 4×4 checkerboard. This problem can be solved using recursion. Suppose you know the number of ways, $f(n - 1)$, in which the 4×4 board can be placed on an $(n - 1) \times (n - 1)$ board. An additional $(n - 3) + (n - 4)$ placements result from an $n \times n$ board, because of the n cells added at the top and left sides of the $(n - 1) \times (n - 1)$ board, as shown in Figure 4.5. There are a total of $f(n) = f(n - 1) + (n - 3) + (n - 4)$ placements for the $n \times n$ board, when $n \geq 5$. If $n = 4$, $f(4) = 1$. So the following is true.

$f(n)$ is
$$1 \quad \text{if} \quad n = 4$$
$$f(n - 1) + (n - 3) + (n - 4) \quad \text{if} \quad n \geq 5$$

It is easy to write a recursive function F, with parameter N, to return the correct result for any $N \geq 4$.

```
function F(N : integer) : integer;
begin
    if N = 4 then
        F := 1
    else
        F := F(N − 1) + (N − 3) + (N − 4)
end;
```

If $n = 7$, the program would execute as follows:

$$f(7) = f(6) + (7 - 3) + (7 - 4)$$
$$f(6) = f(5) + (6 - 3) + (6 - 4)$$
$$f(5) = f(4) + (5 - 3) + (5 - 4)$$
$$f(4) = 1$$
$$f(5) = 1 + 2 + 1 = 4$$
$$f(6) = 4 + 3 + 2 = 9$$
$$f(7) = 9 + 4 + 7 = 20$$

A simpler, more direct solution can be obtained by noticing that the top left corner of the 4×4 board can be placed in the first, second, . . . , $(n - 3)$rd position of the top row of the $n \times n$ board, resulting in $(n - 3)$ different placements. The second row also allows $(n - 3)$ placements. In fact, each of the first $(n - 3)$ rows allows $(n - 3)$ placements, for a total of $(n - 3) \times (n - 3)$ distinct placements. Thus, $f(n) = (n - 3)^2$ for $n \geq 4$. The program for this solution would be

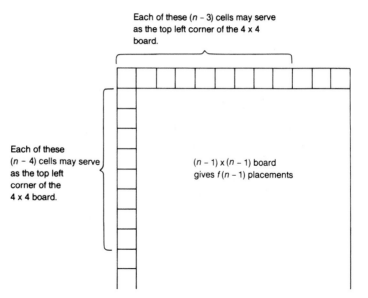

Each of these (n – 3) cells may serve as the top left corner of the 4 x 4 board.

Each of these (n – 4) cells may serve as the top left corner of the 4 x 4 board.

(n – 1) x (n – 1) board gives f (n – 1) placements

Figure 4.5   An $n \times n$ Checkerboard

```
function F(N : integer) : integer;
begin
    F := (N − 3) * (N − 3)
end;
```

The recursive solution will take time and storage $O(N)$, whereas the nonrecursive solution requires constant time and storage. You will see later why this is so. Obviously, this solution is better in every way than the recursive solution to this problem. Hence recursion does not always yield the best solution. Just as with any powerful tool, it must be used judiciously. You wouldn't use a bulldozer to dig a two-foot hole in your yard.

4.2.7 Permutations

Suppose you are a programmer asked to find a stable pairing for the n men and women of the stable marriage problem in Chapter 2 but you aren't aware of the algorithm discussed in Section 2.5. Probably the most straightforward approach is to search through all the possible pairings until a stable one is found. Each possible pairing may be thought of as a specific permutation of the n women. Thus the example pairing of that section corresponds to the permutation (or listing) 4, 3, 1, 2, 5. In general there are $n!$ such permutations (where $n!$ means n factorial).

This approach yields a program that traverses the collection of permutations, processing each one and halting when a stable permutation is encountered. STABLE may be conveniently invoked to check a permutation for stability. In contrast, the algorithm of Section 2.5 avoids such an exhaustive search by eliminating some permutations from consideration altogether. Still, many problems require just such an exhaustive search and contain a component to produce the permutations. The prob-

lem is to write a program to carry out the traversal. The procedure PERMUTATIONS
does this

```
procedure PERMUTATIONS(N : integer);
var
    DONE : boolean;
begin
    DONE := false;
    INITIALIZE(N);
    while not DONE do
        begin
            PROCESS(N);
            NEXT(N, DONE)
        end
end;
```

where NEXT(N, DONE) must return, having updated the current permutation to the
next permutation. If the current permutation is the last one, it simply sets DONE
to "true."

The problem is now to refine NEXT. Suppose $n = 4$ and the first permutation
is 3 2 1. Inserting 4 in all possible positions among 1, 2, and 3 gives the first four
permutations of 1, 2, 3, and 4.

$$\begin{array}{cccc} \underline{4} & 3 & 2 & 1 \\ 3 & \underline{4} & 2 & 1 \\ 3 & 2 & \underline{4} & 1 \\ 3 & 2 & 1 & \underline{4} \end{array}$$

Removing 4 leaves 3 2 1. The next four permutations for $n = 4$ can be obtained by first
obtaining the next permutation after 3 2 1 for $n = 3$. But this next permutation for
$n = 3$ can similarly be obtained by shifting 3 to the right one place, yielding 2 3 1.
Then the next four permutations for $n = 4$ are

$$\begin{array}{cccc} \underline{4} & 2 & 3 & 1 \\ 2 & \underline{4} & 3 & 1 \\ 2 & 3 & \underline{4} & 1 \\ 2 & 3 & 1 & \underline{4} \end{array}$$

Removing 4 leaves 2 3 1. Again, the next permutation after 2 3 1, 2 1 3, is obtained by
shifting 3 right. The next four permutations for $n = 4$ are

$$\begin{array}{cccc} \underline{4} & 2 & 1 & 3 \\ 2 & \underline{4} & 1 & 3 \\ 2 & 1 & \underline{4} & 3 \\ 2 & 1 & 3 & \underline{4} \end{array}$$

Continuing this process will produce, in turn,

$$\begin{array}{cccccccccccc} \underline{4} & 3 & 1 & 2 & & \underline{4} & 1 & 3 & 2 & & \underline{4} & 1 & 2 & 3 \\ 3 & \underline{4} & 1 & 2 & & 1 & \underline{4} & 3 & 2 & & 1 & \underline{4} & 2 & 3 \\ 3 & 1 & \underline{4} & 2 & & 1 & 3 & \underline{4} & 2 & & 1 & 2 & \underline{4} & 3 \\ 3 & 1 & 2 & \underline{4} & & 1 & 3 & 2 & \underline{4} & \text{and} & 1 & 2 & 3 & \underline{4} \end{array}$$

Generalizing, we see that, given a permutation of the n integers from 1 to n, the next permutation can be generated by shifting n to the right whenever possible. The only time this is not possible is if n is already at the right end. The next permutation must then be generated by removing n, and replacing the leftmost $n - 1$ integers, which must be a permutation of the integers from 1 to $n - 1$, by their next permutation. If n is 1, then the last permutation has been produced. This provides a recursive definition for NEXT.

```
NEXT(N, DONE) :
If N is not 1 then
    If N is not at the right end of the current permutation of 1,.., N then
        shift it right one position
    else
        remove "N" from the current permutation of 1,.., N
        NEXT(N − 1, DONE)
        Insert "N" at the left end of the current permutation of 1,.., N − 1
else
    set DONE to true.
```

In order to proceed, an implementation for the permutation must be chosen. To illustrate the effect of this selection, we first store the permutation in an array P. Searching for the location of N in P will be avoided by keeping an array L of pointers. $L[N]$ points to the location of N in P when NEXT(N, DONE) is invoked. INITIALIZE must set $P[I]$ to $N - I + 1$ and $L[I]$ to 1 for $1 \le I \le N$. NEXT may be defined as

```
procedure NEXT(N : integer; var DONE : boolean);
var
    I : integer;
begin
    if N > 1 then
        if L[N] < N then
            begin
                P[L[N]] := P[L[N] + 1];
                P[L[N] + 1] := N;
                L[N] := L[N] + 1
            end
        else
            begin
                NEXT(N − 1, DONE);
                for I := N − 1 downto 1 do
                    P[I + 1] := P[I];
                P[1] := N;
                L[N] := 1
            end
    else
        DONE := true
end;
```

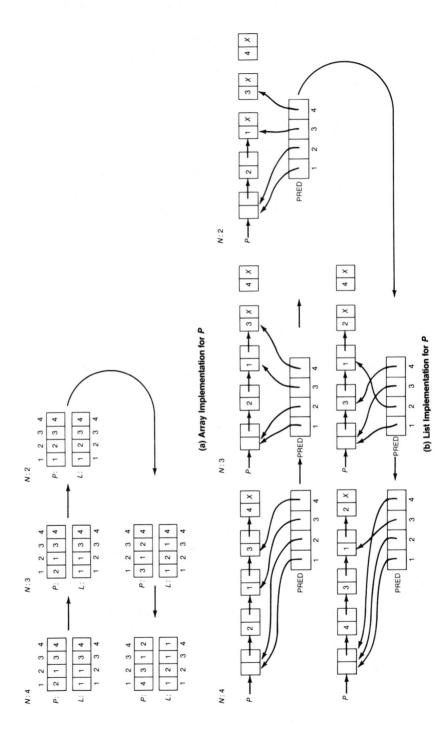

Figure 4.6   Simulation of NEXT(4, DONE) When *P* is 2134

Figure 4.6(a) simulates the execution of NEXT(4, DONE) when the current permutation is 2 1 3 4.

Now suppose P is implemented as a list whose records are stored in the heap. PTR[N] will contain a pointer to the record containing N in its information field and PRED[N] will contain a pointer to the predecessor of that record in P when NEXT(N, DONE) is invoked. To simplify list shifts and the insertion of a record at the front of P, a dummy record is used as the first record of P. PRED[K] will initially contain a pointer to the dummy record, and PTR[K] will initially contain a pointer to the record of P that contains K, for $1 \leq K \leq N$. Now NEXT may be defined as

```
procedure NEXT(N : integer; var DONE : boolean);
begin
    if N > 1 then
        if PTR[N] ↑.LINK <> nil then
            begin
                PRED[N] ↑.LINK := PTR[N] ↑.LINK;
                PRED[N] := PRED[N] ↑.LINK;
                PTR[N] ↑.LINK := PRED[N] ↑.LINK;
                PRED[N] ↑.LINK := PTR[N]
            end
        else
            begin
                PRED[N] ↑.LINK := nil;
                NEXT(N − 1, DONE);
                PTR[N] ↑.LINK := P ↑.LINK;
                P ↑.LINK := PTR[N];
                PRED[N] := P
            end
    else
        DONE := true
end;
```

Figure 4.6(b) simulates the execution of NEXT(4, DONE) when the current permutation is 2 1 3 4.

The advantage of the list implementation is that the **for** loop required by the array implementation is no longer needed. Inserting N at the left end of the current permutation thus takes only two pointer changes rather than time proportional to N. Other permutation algorithms are explored in Sedgewick [1977]. Two complete programs using procedure PERMUTATIONS, one for an array and one for a list implementation, are given below. The PROCESS module prints each permutation.

```
program PERMUTATIONS(input, output);
type
    arraytype = array [1 .. 20] of integer;
var
    N : integer;
    P, L : arraytype;
```

```
procedure INITIALIZE(N : integer);
var
    I : integer;
begin
    for I := 1 to N do
        begin
            P[I] := N - I + 1;
            L[I] := 1
        end
end;

procedure NEXT(N : integer; var DONE : boolean);
var
    I : integer;
begin
    if N > 1 then
        if L[N] < N then
            begin
                P[L[N]] := P[L[N] + 1];
                P[L[N] + 1] := N;
                L[N] := L[N] + 1
            end
        else
            begin
                NEXT(N - 1, DONE);
                for I := N - 1 downto 1 do
                    P[I + 1] := P[I];
                P[1] := N;
                L[N] := 1
            end
    else
        DONE := true
end;

procedure PROCESS(P : arraytype);
var
    I : integer;
begin
    for I := 1 to N do
        WRITELN(P[I]);
    WRITELN
end;

procedure PERMUTATIONS(N : integer);
var
    DONE : boolean;
begin
    DONE := false;
    INITIALIZE(N);
    while not DONE do
        begin
            PROCESS(P);
            NEXT(N, DONE)
        end
end;
```

```
    begin
        WRITELN('N = ?');
        READLN(N);
        PERMUTATIONS(N);
    end.



    program PERMUTATIONS(input, output);

    type
        listpointer = ↑listrecord;
        listrecord = record
                         info : integer;
                         link : listpointer
                     end;
        pointerarray = array [1 .. 20] of listpointer;
    var
        PTR, PRED : pointerarray;
        P : listpointer;
        N : integer;
    procedure INITIALIZE(N : integer);
    var
        I : integer;
        Q : listpointer;
    begin
        NEW(P);
        Q := P;
        for I := 1 to N do
            begin
                NEW(Q↑.LINK);
                Q := Q↑.LINK;
                Q↑.INFO := N − I + 1;
                PTR[N − I + 1] := Q;
                PRED[I] := P
            end;
        Q↑.Link := nil
    end;

    procedure NEXT(N : integer; var DONE : boolean);
    begin
        if N > 1 then
            if PTR[N]↑.LINK <> nil then
                begin
                    PRED[N]↑.LINK := PTR[N]↑.LINK;
                    PRED[N] := PRED[N]↑.LINK;
                    PTR[N]↑.LINK := PRED[N]↑.LINK;
                    PRED[N]↑.LINK := PTR[N]
                end
            else
                begin
                    PRED[N]↑.LINK := nil;
                    NEXT(N − 1, DONE);
                    PTR[N]↑.LINK := P↑.LINK;
```

```
                        P↑.LINK := PTR[N];
                        PRED[N] := P
            end
      else
            DONE := true
end;
procedure PROCESS(P : listpointer);
var
    Q : listpointer;
begin
    Q := P↑.LINK;
    while Q <> nil do
        begin
            WRITELN(Q↑.INFO);
            Q := Q↑.LINK
        end;
    WRITELN
end;

procedure PERMUTATIONS(N : integer);
var
    DONE : boolean;
begin
    DONE := false;
    INITIALIZE(N);
    while not DONE do
        begin
            PROCESS(P);
            NEXT(N, DONE)
        end
end;

begin
    WRITELN('N = ?');
    READLN(N);
    PERMUTATIONS(N);
end.
```

4.3 A Close Look at the Execution of Recursive Programs

When any program invokes one of its components it is because the task performed by that component must now be carried out. The component's **var** parameters and any nonlocal variables to which it refers specify storage that is not local to the component but which it may reference and change. This storage thus represents the *data* the component is to process. Any changes by the component to the data are reflected back in the data's storage.

The component's non-**var** parameters also specify storage that is not local to it, but these parameters are treated differently. When the component is invoked, their values are copied into storage that is local to the component. It is these local copies that are referenced, and perhaps changed, by the component as it executes, but such changes are not reflected back to the non-**var** parameters' nonlocal storage. In this way the information given by the non-**var** parameters is made accessible to the component, which may even change the local copies, but such changes are kept local; the original nonlocal values are untouched.

In effect, these copies are treated as if they were additional local variables of the component. The actual local variables of the component represent temporary information that the component uses to do its job. Both the local copies and local variables disappear when the task is completed. This storage for local copies and local variables serves as a "scratchpad" for use by the component. The scratchpad contains information used temporarily by the component to perform its task on the data. This view of the data and scratchpad of a component is depicted in Figure 4.7.

The component may, in turn, invoke another component, which may invoke still another, and so on. Each time this is done, the calling component suspends its operation, so all components of the sequence, except the last, are waiting.

When the last component completes its task, the component that invoked it then continues. In order for this to happen, each component must remember from whence it was called. Also, upon return to the correct place, the scratchpad of the calling component must be the same as before the call. For nonrecursive programs, the important point is that each component must retain only *one* returning point, and the scratchpad of a component is automatically retained when it invokes another component.

With recursive programs the situation is considerably different, as evidenced by Figures 4.2, 4.4, and 4.6. First, when a recursive module is invoked, this may be the initial, first, second, or *n*th recursive call to it. If it is the *n*th recursive call, there may be as many as $(n + 1)$ returning places to be retained, not just one. Second, there may

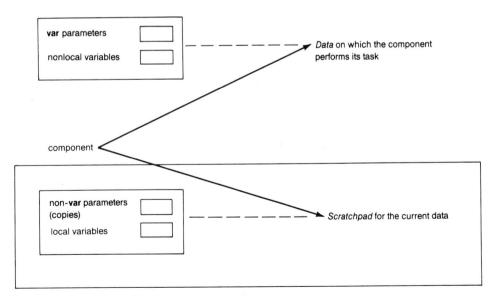

Figure 4.7 Data and Scratchpad for a Component

be $(n + 1)$ scratchpads to be retained. How many there are is determined by the number of calls that are currently suspended.

Suppose that this number is k, that the return for the initial call is handled separately, and also that the scratchpad for the currently executing call is associated with the module. The number of sets of additional returns and scratchpads that must be retained is then k. The *depth* of a recursive program is given by the maximum value of k. It is the depth that determines the amount of storage required by the module. The following examples illustrate these ideas.

Example 4.1 In Figure 4.2, when the tenth recursive call $(k = 3)$ is made to TOWERS, there are three returns and three sets of scratchpads to remember in addition to the initial call's return.

> [2] and $N = 4$, $I = 1$, $A = 2$, $F = 3$ for the initial call
> [1] and $N = 3$, $I = 2$, $A = 1$, $F = 3$ for the eighth recursive call
> [1] and $N = 2$, $I = 2$, $A = 3$, $F = 1$ for the ninth recursive call

$N = 1$, $I = 2$, $A = 1$, $F = 3$ for the tenth recursive call are stored, by our assumption, local to TOWERS. In general, the depth of recursion will be $N - 1$. Using our terminology, there are no data. □

Example 4.2 In Figure 4.4, when the third recursive call is made to COPY, there are three returns and three sets of scratchpads to be retained beside the initial call's return:

> FIRST0, NULL0, REST0 for the initial call
> FIRST1, NULL1, REST1 for the first recursive call
> FIRST2, NULL2, REST2 for the second recursive call

No returns are shown since they all return to the same place: the statement SETLINK(SECOND, REST). The depth of the recursion is one less than the length of the list to be copied. The data for the initial call is SECOND, while for the $(n + 1)$th recursive call it is RESTn. A change to REST in the $(n + 1)$th call is reflected in the scratchpad for the nth call. Storage could be saved by making NULL nonlocal to COPY. □

Example 4.3 In Figure 4.6 the situation corresponds to a point in the initial call when the second and then the third recursive calls to NEXT are made. The local variable I is not shown and the three scratchpad values are

> $N = 4$ for the initial call
> $N = 3$ for the second recursive call
> $N = 2$ for the third recursive call

Again, the returns are all the same, to the statement following the recursive call to NEXT, so they are not shown. The depth of the recursion is $N - 1$. The data consist of P, PTR, PRED, and DONE. □

It should by now be quite clear that the storage required by a recursive module is proportional to its depth. The execution time, on the other hand, has to do with the total number of recursive calls that are required to complete the initial call. Can you see why the recursive solution to Counting Squares (Section 4.2.6) is so inefficient both in time and in storage?

4.4 Implementing Recursive Programs

Recursion is a powerful tool for the development of algorithms and leads to concise, clear recursive programs that can be more easily checked for correctness. Complex algorithms may be expressed using relatively few program statements, which at the same time emphasize the structure of the algorithm. This will become even more apparent later in the text as more difficult problems are solved.

A module that invokes itself is *directly recursive*. If any sequence of calls to modules can lead to a call to the original module, then the original module is *indirectly recursive*. Some high-level languages such as FORTRAN and COBOL do not allow recursion. Pascal, LISP, ALGOL, and Ada are examples of languages that do. The compiler for such recursive languages must translate recursive as well as nonrecursive programs. It is not necessary to understand how a recursive program is translated, any more than it is necessary to know how a nonrecursive program is translated, in order to understand or to write the program itself. But it *is* necessary to know how the program will execute. This amounts to being able to simulate its execution.

The programmer constrained to a nonrecursive language can still use the power of recursion. This is done by writing a program as if the language allowed recursion, and then translating the program into an equivalent nonrecursive program. This is what compilers for recursive languages do and is one reason for spending time finding out how to translate, or implement, a recursive program.

As shown in the discussion of Counting Squares, some problems should not be solved using recursion under any circumstances. Sometimes, as in the Towers of Hanoi problem, the only solution we can think of may be a recursive one. Often we can find both a recursive and a nonrecursive solution which may be compared for trade-offs in clarity, conciseness, storage, and execution time.

Even though a recursive solution may not be best, it can suggest an approach that turns out to be better. In fact, its translated version can be helpful in finding desirable modifications. This is another reason for looking at the translation process.

Normally, if a recursive approach is right for a problem, and is applied intelligently, further refinements of the program do not improve its efficiency significantly. This is especially so when the program is to be run on new computers, and it will be even more the case in the future. The newer computers support the operations required for the execution of recursive programs with hardware tailored to their needs. In the history of computer design, hardware innovations have typically eliminated software inefficiencies in this way.

Breaking up a problem as required by the recursive approach (or the top-down approach in general) creates the possibility of doing certain tasks in parallel. For instance, the three components of the Towers of Hanoi solution may all be done at the same time, whenever the computer supports such parallel processing. Languages and computer systems that allow advantage to be taken of such concurrent processing will surely become more prevalent. While we have referred to these possibilities on occasion (Section 3.9), this text will not pursue these techniques, although perhaps your interest and curiosity have been piqued.

If each successive call to a recursive module were implemented by creating a new copy of the module with its own storage for the return and its scratchpad values, then, in effect, the module becomes exactly like any module in a nonrecursive program. With the advent of cheaper and larger storage and microprocessors, this may well occur in the future. But until then, another means of managing the generated returns and scratchpad values is needed.

The essential difference between nonrecursive (or iterative) programs and recursive programs is the storage needed for the returns and scratchpad values of the latter. Figures 4.2, 4.4, and 4.6 actually represent the bookkeeping needed to simulate the execution of a recursive program. The basic idea in translating such programs is to simply implement this bookkeeping procedure as follows:

1. Each time a recursive call is made to the module,
   a. save the proper return place and the current scratchpad values,
   b. set the scratchpad values to their new values.
2. Each time a recursive call is completed,
   a. restore the current return and scratchpad values to those that were last saved (and save them no longer),
   b. return to the proper place in the recursive module or to the original calling component if it is the initial call that has just finished.

Notice that the information to be retained (return and scratchpad values) must be recalled in the order opposite to the order in which it is generated. This is no different for nonrecursive programs, except then the information is saved locally with each component. It is helpful to think of return and scratchpad values as the entries of a record. Then the collection of records corresponding to each suspended recursive call must be stored in some data structure. The data structure must not only retain these records, but must retain the correct order.

In step 1 above, the record to be saved must become the new first record in the order. In step 2, the current first record (the last saved) must be removed from the data structure. A data structure for storing information so that new information can be inserted, so that a deletion always removes the last piece of information inserted, and which can be tested to see if it is empty (contains no information) is called a *stack*. We shall discuss it in more detail later; for now we simply use it.

4.4.1 A Sample Implementation of TOWERS

The stack is the most convenient data abstraction to use for all the bookkeeping entailed by recursion. To illustrate the translation, and the possibility of enhancing efficiency, we translate the recursive TOWERS and NEXT procedures.

In TOWERS there are two recursive calls. The idea in implementing it is to write a nonrecursive program that executes just as the recursive program would, while managing the additional records generated by the recursion. This amounts to implementing the procedure described for a simulation. Each recursive call will be replaced by code to insert the proper return indicator onto a stack, as well as the current scratchpad values. Whenever an **end** statement signifies completion of a recursive call, the proper return indicator and the scratchpad values last put on the stack will be removed and restored to the program's local storage. The recursive version and the implementation are as follows.

```
procedure TOWERS(N, I, A, F : integer);         procedure TOWERS(N, I, A, F : integer);
begin                                           label 2, 100;
    if N = 1 then                               var
        WRITELN(I, '→', F)                          RETRN : integer;
    else                                            S : stack;
        begin                                   begin
            TOWERS(N − 1, I, F, A);       100:      if N = 1 then
            WRITELN(I, '→', F);                         WRITELN(I, '→', F)
            TOWERS(N − 1, A, I, F)                   else
        end                                             begin
end;                                                        STACK(1, N, I, A, F);
                                                            SETVAR1(N, I, A, F);
                                                            goto 100
                                                        end;
                                                2:      if not EMPTY(S) then
                                                            begin
                                                                RESTORE(RETRN, N, I, A, F);
                                                                case RETRN of
                                                                    1 : begin
                                                                            WRITELN(I, '→', F);
                                                                            STACK(2, N, I, A, F);
                                                                            SETVAR2(N, I, A, F);
                                                                            goto 100
                                                                        end;
                                                                    2 : goto 2
                                                                end
                                                            end
                                                end;
```

STACK is a routine that inserts its arguments, as fields of a record, onto the stack. EMPTY(S) returns "true" if the stack contains no records and "false" otherwise. The SETVAR routines do the proper setting of the current scratchpad values for the ensuing recursive call. RESTORE(RETRN, N, I, A, F) restores the proper scratchpad values when a return is to be made after completion of some recursive call. (Note: The spelling RETRN is used here to prevent confusion with the FORTRAN reserved word RETURN.)

SETVAR1(N, I, A, F) sets N to N − 1 and interchanges the values of F and A.
SETVAR2(N, I, A, F) sets N to N − 1 and interchanges the values of A and I.

The "end;" statement of the recursive program has been replaced in the implementation by a more complex sequence of statements. This is because "end;" must, in effect, transfer control to the proper place in the calling program. If the stack itself is empty at this point, this means that it is the initial call to TOWERS that has been completed. Return should then be to the calling program. Otherwise, it is some recursive call to TOWERS that has been completed. At this point, the top stack record contains the four scratchpad values to be restored and the return location in the recursive calling program.

You should simulate the execution of this implementation to see that it really works correctly. The statement labeled 100 corresponds to the first executable statement of the recursive program, and is the statement that is invoked in the implementation to represent a recursive call. It is only invoked, however, after the scratchpad values of the current call and proper return location have been saved on the stack, and the scratchpad values for the upcoming recursive call have been correctly set.

Notice that the implementation requires a stack that can hold the stored information for up to $N-1$ recursive calls. The stack must be initialized to empty. Its contents must be preserved between calls. We will not dwell on its implementation details.

It should now be apparent that considerable overhead is involved in executing recursive programs. Time is consumed because variables must be stacked and unstacked for each recursive call and its return. It is often possible to discover a more efficient nonrecursive algorithm for a problem, even though the recursive algorithm is evident. Nonetheless, the recursive version is frequently clearer, easier to understand, and more concise as well as easier to verify. Thus programmers frequently prefer recursive solutions to problems even if they are less efficient than the non-recursive versions.

Another approach is to attempt to increase the efficiency of the iterative program (the implementation) translated from a recursive program. This attempt can be made whether or not there is a competing nonrecursive routine.

How can we create a more efficient version of a translated program such as TOWERS? The reason for the stack in the first place is to save return codes and to save scratchpad values that are needed when the suspended call is ready to resume (after the saved values have been unstacked and restored, and the proper program segment is to be executed). If the programmer can determine where the return should be, or what the scratchpad values that are to be restored should be, then this information does not have to be stacked. It may not be necessary to save the values of some other variables. It may also be possible to eliminate some return codes. If no variables need to be saved, and there is only one return code, then the stack itself is not needed. Let us attempt to reach this goal for the implementation of the recursive TOWERS routine.

Notice that in the case statement, when RETRN is 1, the call to STACK $(2, N, I, A, F)$ saves the values of the current variables in the suspended call, in order to make the recursive call to TOWERS$(N-1, A, I, F)$. When this new recursive call is completed, these current values will be restored, and the RETRN will be 2. The statement labeled 2 will then be executed.

If the stack is empty, the initial call is complete. Otherwise RESTORE will be called immediately and control transferred to the new value of RETRN. The current values saved by STACK$(2, N, I, A, F)$ will never be used, and so need not be saved at all. Thus the call to STACK$(2, N, I, A, F)$ may be eliminated from the program. This means that the only return code appearing will be 1 in the call to STACK $(1, N, I, A, F)$. However, the value of RETRN after RESTORE is called will always be 1. Therefore, no return code needs to be stored on the stack; the case structure may be removed. RETRN is not needed at all. This new program then looks like

```
        procedure TOWERS(N, I, A, F : integer);
        label 100;
        var
            S : stack;
        begin
100:        if N = 1 then
                WRITELN(I, '→', F)
            else
                begin
                    STACK(N, I, A, F);
                    SETVAR1(N, I, A, F);
                    goto 100
                end;
            if not EMPTY(S) then
                begin
                    RESTORE(N, I, A, F);
                    WRITELN(I, '→', F);
                    SETVAR2(N, I, A, F);
                    goto 100
                end
        end;
```

The **if–else** structure can be more clearly written as a **while** loop:

```
100:  if N = 1 then                      100:  while N > 1 do
          WRITELN(I, '→', F)                       begin
      else                                            STACK(N, I, A, F);
          begin                                       SETVAR1(N, I, A, F)
              STACK(N, I, A, F);                   end;
              SETVAR1(N, I, A, F);             WRITELN(I, '→', F);
              goto 100
          end;
```

```
        procedure TOWERS(N, I, A, F : integer);
        label 100;
        var
            S : stack;
        begin
100:        while N > 1 do
                begin
                    STACK(N, I, A, F);
                    SETVAR1(N, I, A, F)
                end;
            WRITELN(I, '→', F)
            if not EMPTY(S) then
                begin
                    RESTORE(N, I, A, F);
                    WRITELN(I, '→', F);
                    SETVAR2(N, I, A, F);
                    goto 100
                end
        end;
```

The procedure can be written in more structured form as follows:

```
procedure TOWERS(N, I, A, F : integer);
var
    DONE : boolean;
    S : stack;
begin
    DONE := false;
    while not DONE do
        begin
            while N > 1 do
                begin
                    STACK(N, I, A, F);
                    SETVAR1(N, I, A, F)
                end;
            WRITELN(I, '→', F);
            if not EMPTY(S) then
                begin
                    RESTORE(N, I, A, F);
                    WRITELN(I, '→', F);
                    SETVAR2(N, I, A, F)
                end
            else
                DONE := true
        end
end;
```

Because the number of stack operations has been reduced, this is a more efficient version than the compilerlike direct translation.

4.4.2 A Sample Implementation for PERMUTATIONS

Now for the NEXT procedure: a straightforward translation is

```
procedure NEXT(N : integer; var DONE : boolean);
label 2, 100;
var
    I, RETRN : integer;
    S : stack;
begin
100:    if N > 1 then
            if L[N] < N then
                begin
                    P[L[N]] := P[L[N] + 1];
                    P[L[N] + 1] := N;
                    L[N] := L[N] + 1
                end
            else
                begin
                    STACK(1, N, I);
                    SETVAR(N, I);
```

```
                        goto 100
                end
        else
            DONE := true;

2:      if not EMPTY(S) then
            begin
                RESTORE(RETRN, N, I);
                case RETRN of
                    1 : begin
                            for I := N − 1 downto 1 do
                                P[I + 1] := P[I];
                            P[1] := N;
                            L[N] := 1;
                            goto 2
                        end
                end
            end
    end;
```

where SETVAR(N, I) simply sets N to $N - 1$.

The same program can be written in a more structured way by noticing that the statement labeled 2 and the **goto** 2 statement create a **while** loop. The overall structure of the program becomes

```
100:    If C1  then
            if C2 then
                task for C1 and C2 both true
            else
                task for C1 true but C2 false
            goto 100
        else
            task for C1 false;
        while not EMPTY(S) do
            loop task
```

This can be written as

```
        While (C1 and not C2) do
            task for C1 true but C2 false
        If C1  then
            task for C1 and C2 both true
        else
            task for C1 false
        while not EMPTY(S) do
            loop task.
```

Surely the logic of this version is much easier to follow. You can now see at a glance that the segment is a loop, followed by a decision, followed by a loop. The iterative version of NEXT, translated from the recursive NEXT, thus becomes

```
procedure NEXT(N : integer; var DONE : boolean);
var
    I, RETRN : integer;
    S : stack;
begin
    while ((N > 1) and not (L[N] < N)) do
        begin
            STACK(1, N, I);
            SETVAR(N, I)
        end;
    if N > 1 then
        begin
            P[L[N]] := P[L[N] + 1];
            P[L[N] + 1] := N;
            L[N] := L[N] + 1
        end
    else
        DONE := true;
    while not EMPTY(S) do
        begin
            RESTORE(RETRN, N, I);
            case RETRN of
                1 : begin
                        for I := N − 1 downto 1 do
                            P[I + 1] := P[I];
                        P[1] := N;
                        L[N] := 1
                    end
            end
        end
end;
```

In general, when the value of a scratchpad variable does not change or does not
need to be maintained between recursive calls, it need not be stacked. This is the case
with the variable I of NEXT. Also, when there is only one return place from a
recursive call, there is no need to stack a return indicator. This is the situation with
NEXT. Finally, the value of N varies in a predictable fashion. Its restored value will
always be 1 greater than its current value. Thus there is no need to stack N. Each time
a recursive call returns, N may be correctly restored by adding 1 to its current value.

Therefore, the stack is unnecessary, since no information must be retained on
it. The STACK procedure can be removed, SETVAR can be replaced by the statement $N := N − 1$, and RESTORE can be replaced by the statement $N := N + 1$. Still,
the stack controls the second **while** loop in our translated version. Even though no
information needs to be stacked, it is still necessary to know when the stack would
have been empty so the loop may be properly exited.

Notice that the first **while** loop decreases N by 1 every time a stack entry would
have been made and the second **while** increases N by 1 every time an entry would
have been deleted from the stack. Hence, if an integer variable S is set to N initially,
prior to the first **while** loop, the test to see if the stack is empty in the second **while**
loop becomes $S = N$. The final version of NEXT is an iterative program that has no

stack. It is an example of the translated version giving us a better solution. This four-step solution is efficient and is also clear.

1. Set S to N.
2. Set N to the rightmost entry in the permutation that can still be shifted right.
3. If that entry is not 1 then
    Shift it right
else
    set DONE to "true"
4. Place the S − N entries that could not be moved to the right in the proper order at the left end of the permutation.

The final program is as follows:

```
procedure NEXT(N : integer; var DONE : boolean);
var
    I, S : integer;
begin
    S := N;
    while (N > 1 and not (L[N] < N)) do
        N := N − 1;
    if N > 1 then
        begin
            P[L[N]] := P[L[N] + 1];
            P[L[N] + 1] := N;
            L[N] := L[N] + 1
        end
    else
        DONE := true;
    while S > N do
        begin
            N := N + 1;
            for I := N − 1 downto 1 do
                P[I + 1] := P[I];
            P[1] := N;
            L[N] := 1
        end
end;
```

(steps 1., 2., 3., 4. marked in left margin)

A little insight can help a lot. For more on recursion, see Barron [1968] and Bird [1977a, 1977b]. It may now be time for you to make a recursive call on all preceding material!

4.5 Stacks

Frequently programmers encounter situations requiring the retention and recall of information in a specific order. One instance of such a situation is simulation and implementation of recursion. Another is the manipulation of dynamic data structures such as more complex lists and trees (see Chapters 5 and 6). In both cases the information is being removed in a last-in, first-out order (LIFO for short). Removing tennis balls from a can is also LIFO. The situation occurs when a programmer must postpone obligations, which must later be fulfilled in *reverse order* from that in which they were incurred. This is the precise situation in which the data abstraction called the *stack* is very convenient.

Information is kept in order in a **stack**. Additional information may be inserted on the stack, but only at the front or top end. Thus the information at the top of the stack always corresponds to the most recently incurred obligation. Information may be recalled from the stack, but only by removing the current top piece of information. The stack acts like a pile of playing cards to which we can only add a card at the top and from which we can only remove the top card. Of course, this is not what is meant by a "stacked deck."

The stack, with the operations of front-end insertion and deletion, initialization, and an empty check, is a data abstraction. It is used frequently in algorithms developed throughout the rest of this book. Stacks used to be called "pushdown stacks"; insertion of data onto the stack was referred to as "pushing" the stack and deleting data was known as "popping" the stack. Of the many implementations possible for the stack, the following subsections illustrate the three most straightforward.

4.5.1 Array Implementation of a Stack

A stack may be implemented using arrays by first declaring:

```
type
    stackrecords = whatever;
    stack        = record
                       stackarray : array [1..LIMIT] of stackrecords;
                       top : 0..LIMIT
                   end;
var
    S : stack;
```

Let us assume LIMIT is a global constant, fixing the maximum number of items the stack can hold. To store integers in the stack, declare "whatever" to be of integer type. Suppose 6, 45, 15, 32, and 18 were pushed onto the stack. Figure 4.8 illustrates the meaning attached to the declaration.

Addition or insertion of a new element to the stack will be accomplished by a module PUSH. Removal or deletion of the current top stack element will be accomplished by a module POP. Executing PUSH(NEWRECORD, S) results in the contents of NEWRECORD being placed on the stack as a new first element. A call to the procedure POP(S, VALUE) causes the removal of the current top stack element, with VALUE returning a copy of that value. A routine SETSTACK sets the stack to empty so that it initially contains no entries.

Example
4.4

Suppose NEWRECORD contains the number 5 and we execute

```
POP(S, Y);
POP(S, Z);
PUSH(NEWRECORD, S);
```

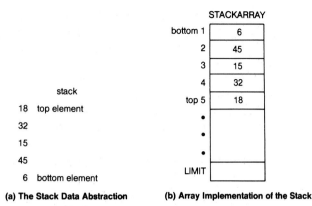

Figure 4.8   Stack before Insertion of a New Element

If Figure 4.8 indicates the current stack, then Figure 4.9 shows the new situation after this execution. □

Stack underflow occurs when a program attempts to remove an element from an empty stack. It normally indicates either an error or the termination of a task. *Stack overflow* occurs when a program attempts to add an element to a full stack. Although conceptually the stack as a data structure *has no limit*, an actual implemented stack *does* have a limit. In the present implementation it is termed LIMIT. PUSH and POP should test, respectively, for stack overflow and underflow and take appropriate action whenever these conditions occur. Such precautionary measures are an example of defensive programming.

It is also necessary to test the stack to determine whether or not it is empty. This may be accomplished by invoking a boolean function EMPTY(S), which will return the value "true" when the stack is empty and "false" otherwise.

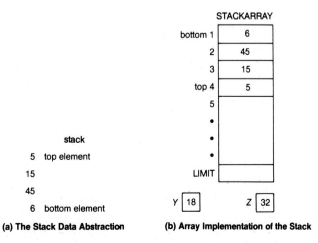

Figure 4.9   Stack after Insertion of a New Element

These routines may be implemented as

```
procedure SETSTACK(var S : stack);
begin
    S.TOP := 0
end;
function EMPTY(S : stack) : boolean;
begin
    EMPTY := (S.TOP = 0)
end;
procedure PUSH(NEWRECORD : whatever; var S : stack);
begin
    if S.TOP = LIMIT then
        OVERFLOW(S)
    else
        begin
            S.TOP := S.TOP + 1;
            S.STACKARRAY[S.TOP] := NEWRECORD
        end
end;
procedure POP(var S : stack; var VALUE : whatever);
begin
    if EMPTY(S) then
        UNDERFLOW(S)
    else
        begin
            VALUE := S.STACKARRAY[S.TOP];
            S.TOP := S.TOP − 1
        end
end;
```

The procedures OVERFLOW and UNDERFLOW are assumed to take appropriate action when they are invoked. Notice that the elements of the stack will be of "whatever" type.

The idea of program modularity is to isolate or localize the code of a program that is invoked in a particular task, such as an operation on a data structure. The implementation of the stack data abstraction that we have discussed has achieved modularity, with respect to the PUSH, POP, SETSTACK, and EMPTY operations on the stack, by embodying them in individual routines. Encapsulation may be achieved by placing the definitions of these operations together in one place in a program.

4.5.2 List Implementation of the Stack with an Array of Records

Notice that the AVAILIST (Section 3.7) actually acts as a stack. When AVAIL is invoked, it removes the top record from the AVAILIST, in addition to returning the pointer P. P points to the popped record. RECLAIM may return a record to the *front* of the AVAILIST if the record is deleted from a list whose records were stored in RECORDS. Doing so, RECLAIM is essentially pushing a new record onto the

AVAILIST. AVAILIST serves as the head of a list, which itself serves as a list implementation of a stack. Of course, appropriate overflow and underflow checking must be built into AVAIL and RECLAIM, respectively.

4.5.3 List Implementation of the Stack with Records in the Pascal Heap

The third stack implementation is also as a list, but a list that involves dynamic storage allocation of the records in the Pascal heap. That is, the records are stored in the storage area set aside by Pascal to store records referenced by pointer variables. First, the following declaration must be made.

```
type
    stackptr    = ↑ stackrecord;
    stackrecord = record
                        entry : whatever;
                        link : stackptr
                  end;
    stack = stackptr;
var
    S : stack;
```

Defining S as type *stack* allows code to be written that is independent of its implementation. SETSTACK must initialize the stack to empty. This means setting S, the head of the list implementing the stack, to **nil**. PUSH must now use NEW to allocate storage for the entry to be pushed onto the stack before setting its ENTRY field and inserting that record as the new first record on the stack. POP must copy the ENTRY field value of the top record into VALUE and then delete that record from the stack.

These stack operations are implemented as

```
procedure SETSTACK(var S : stack);
begin
    S := nil
end;

function EMPTY(S : stack) : boolean;
begin
    EMPTY := (S = nil)
end;

procedure PUSH(NEWRECORD : whatever; var S : stack);
var
    P : stack;
begin
    NEW(P);
    P↑.ENTRY := NEWRECORD;
    P↑.LINK := S;
    S := P
end;
```

```
procedure POP(var S : stack; var VALUE : whatever);
begin
   VALUE := S ↑.ENTRY;
   S := S ↑.LINK
end;
```

Notice that the third implementation removes the artificial restriction imposed by LIMIT in the first implementation using an array. This is one of the advantages of using dynamic allocation by means of pointer variables.

It is very important to see that no matter what the implementation, as long as the stack is treated as a data abstraction when writing programs, the programs need not be changed, even if the programmer decides to change the implementation of the stack.

The problem of implementing many stacks simultaneously is introduced in the suggested assignment at the end of this chapter. More sophisticated algorithms for the management of the stacks are explored in Garwick [1964], Knuth [1973], and Korsh [1983].

4.6 Case Study: Checking Sequences for Proper Nesting

Every computer programming student has gotten error messages saying "incomplete loop structure" or "a missing parenthesis." You now have enough background to write a program that checks for such errors. Let's see how it is done.

Arithmetic expressions, as well as a program text, consist of sequences of symbols. Complex arithmetic expressions may be composed by properly combining simpler arithmetic expressions delineated by matching left and right parentheses. The simpler expressions are said to be "nested" within the more complex expressions that contain them. The complex expression (A ∗ (B + [C/D]) + B) contains two pairs of nested expressions. Pascal programs contain compound statements delimited by matching **begin** and **end** pairs. Every program, procedure, and function header statement must have a matching "**end**." or "**end**;" statement as well. Ignoring all other symbols, these matching pairs must satisfy rules of nesting to be syntactically correct.

Nesting means that one matching pair is wholly contained within another. When pairs are nested they cannot overlap as do the two pairs in ([)]. The rules of nesting are the same for any sequence that is built by combining simpler sequences. They require that the start and end of each component be specified. Checking complex sequences to determine that these **begin–end** pairs do not overlap is an important operation. It provides an interesting application of the stack data abstraction as well as recursion. An intimate connection exists among such sequences, stacks, recursions, and trees; it will be explored more fully in later chapters.

We will consider two abstractions of this problem. The second is a generalization of the first. To begin, assume only one kind of left parenthesis and one kind of matching right parenthesis, and consider sequences composed of these. Thus, at first, expressions such as ([]) are not allowed since they involve more than one kind of parenthesis.

Given a sequence of left and right parentheses, determine if they may be paired so that they satisfy two conditions:

    i. Each pair consists of a left and right parenthesis with the left parenthesis preceding the right parenthesis.

    ii. Each parenthesis occurs in exactly one pair.

If a sequence has a pairing satisfying both of these conditions, we will say the sequence and pairing are **valid**. The problem is to determine whether a given sequence is valid or not. No sequence starting with a right parenthesis, ")", can be valid, since there is no preceding left parenthesis, "(", to pair with it. Any valid sequence must therefore begin with some series of n "(" parentheses preceding the first appearance of a ")" parenthesis, such as Figure 4.10(a), for which n is 3. Suppose we remove this adjacent pair, the nth "(" parenthesis, and the immediately following first ")" parenthesis. This would be pair 1 in Figure 4.10(a). If the new sequence thus obtained is valid, then adding the removed pair to it results in a valid pairing. Thus the original sequence is valid.

    Suppose you find that the resultant sequence is not valid. Can you conclude that the original sequence is not valid? In other words, has constraining one of the pairs to be the first adjacent "(" and ")" parentheses made a pairing of the original sequence satisfying i and ii impossible? The answer is no. To see this, assume that there *is* some valid pairing of the original sequence, in which the first ")" parenthesis is *not* paired with the immediately preceding "(" parenthesis, but there is *no* valid pairing in which it *is*. In general, the first ")" parenthesis must then be paired with an earlier "(" parenthesis, and the immediately preceding "(" parenthesis must have been paired with a later ")" parenthesis, as in Figure 4.10(b). These two pairs can then be rearranged by interchanging their "(" parentheses. The resultant pairing satisfies conditions i and ii, yet it has the first adjacent "(" parenthesis paired with the immediately following ")" parenthesis, but this is the nesting constraint that has been specified. This contradicts the assumption that no valid pairing satisfies the constraint.

    Consequently, the conclusion is that a solution to the problem is obtained as follows:

1. Pair the first adjacent left, "(", and right,")", parentheses and remove the pair.

2. If the resultant sequence is valid, then so is the original sequence; otherwise the original sequence is not valid.

Think of a left parenthesis as denoting an incurred obligation, and a right parenthesis as the fulfilling of the most recently incurred obligation. This is the

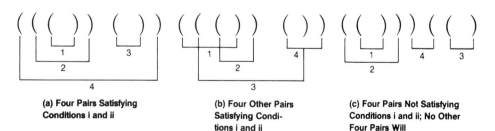

(a) Four Pairs Satisfying Conditions i and ii

(b) Four Other Pairs Satisfying Conditions i and ii

(c) Four Pairs Not Satisfying Conditions i and ii; No Other Four Pairs Will

Figure 4.10 Valid and Invalid Nesting of Parentheses

precise situation for which a stack is useful. As the program scans a sequence from left to right, it pushes each "(" parenthesis onto a stack, representing an incurred obligation. Task 1 of the solution may then be carried out by popping the stack when the first ")" parenthesis is encountered, to fulfill the most recently incurred obligation.

Carrying out task 2 requires first determining if the resultant sequence is valid. Notice, however, that had the resultant sequence been processed in this same way, the contents of the stack would be *exactly* what they are now. Consequently, the program can continue to scan the original sequence (which is exactly what would be seen if it were scanning the resultant sequence), pushing whenever it encounters a "(" parenthesis, and popping whenever it comes to a ")" parenthesis. If the stack is empty when the entire scan is completed, then we have determined that the original sequence is valid; otherwise it is not. During the scan, any attempt to pop an empty stack means that no "(" parenthesis is available to be paired with the ")" parenthesis that caused the attempt (that is, the sequence is invalid).

This solution may be implemented as in the procedure DETERMINE, which follows this paragraph. Note the stack is treated as a data abstraction. READCHAR is a procedure that reads in the next character of the input sequence. When DETERMINE returns, the entire input sequence has been read. VALID will be true if a pairing satisfying i and ii exists, false otherwise.

```
procedure DETERMINE(var VALID : boolean);
var
    CURRENTCHAR : whatever;
      TOPCHAR : whatever;
begin
    VALID : = true;
    SETSTACK(S);
    while not EOF do
        begin
            READCHAR(CURRENTCHAR);
            if LEFTPAREN(CURRENTCHAR) then
                PUSH(CURRENTCHAR, S)
            else
                if RIGHTPAREN(CURRENTCHAR) then
                    if not EMPTY(S) then
                        begin
                            POP(S, TOPCHAR);
                            if not MATCH(TOPCHAR, CURRENTCHAR) then
                                VALID : = false
                        end
                    else
                        VALID : = false
                else
                    PROCESS(CURRENTCHAR, S)
        end;
    if not EMPTY(S) then
        VALID : = false
end;
```

LEFTPAREN returns the value "true" if its parameter is a left parenthesis and false otherwise. RIGHTPAREN is defined similarly. MATCH returns the value *"true"* if its parameters TOPCHAR and CURRENTCHAR are left and right parentheses, respectively.

DETERMINE is actually more complex than need be. In fact, a stack is not even necessary. All that is really needed is to keep a tally of "(" parentheses, decreasing the tally by 1 every time a ")" parenthesis is read. If the tally *ever* becomes negative, then DETERMINE should, from that point, simply read in the rest of the input sequence and return "false" for the test named VALID. Otherwise, if the tally is zero after the entire input sequence has been read, it should return with VALID true. DETERMINE is implemented as shown in the procedure listed above, because it will serve as the solution to the next problem for which "paired parentheses" will be a special case.

Suppose, instead of containing only "(" and ")" parentheses, the input sequence could consist of any characters. Assume that each character could be either a left or a right character but not both, and also that each left character has a unique right character with which it matches. For instance, A, (, [, and L might be "left" characters and the unique "right" characters with which they match Z,),], and R, respectively.

Given a sequence of left and right characters, determine if they may be paired so that

i. Each pair consists of a left and a right matching character, with the left character preceding the right character.

ii. Each character occurs in exactly one pair.

iii. The sequence of characters between the left and right characters of each pair must also satisfy i and ii.

If a sequence of left and right characters satisfies conditions i, ii, and iii, the sequence and the pairing are *valid*. Condition iii then says that the sequence of characters between the left and right characters of each pair must be valid.

Let's see if this definition makes sense. Consider the above sample "matching" involving A, Z, (,), [,], L, and R and the sequences of Figure 4.11.

Both the pairings of Figure 4.11(a) and Figure 4.11(b) satisfy i and ii. However, only the pairing of (a) satisfies iii. The pairing of (b) fails because the left and right

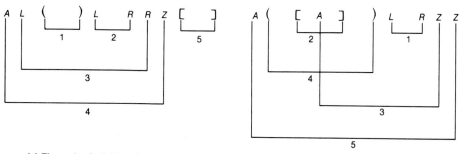

(a) Five pairs Satisfying Conditions i–iii

(b) Five Pairs Not Satisfying Conditions i–iii; No Other Five Pairs Will

Figure 4.11 Valid and Invalid Nesting of Matched Characters

characters of pair 3 are A and Z, and the sequence of characters between them is
$]$ $)$ L R. This sequence does not satisfy conditions i, ii, and iii because none of the six
possible ways to form two pairs will be valid. It is also apparent that the pairing of (b)
fails because the left and right characters of pair 2 are "[" and "]" and the sequence
of characters between them, A, is not valid. One would have to be sure no other
pairings for (b) are valid before concluding that (b) is not a valid sequence.

It is not immediately apparent that this problem generalizes the first problem,
even if the characters are restricted to be just left and right parentheses. This is
because condition iii does not appear in the first problem. However, the reasoning
used there shows that adding the condition does not change the problem. In fact, if
the left and right matching characters are thought of as different kinds of parentheses,
the same reasoning applied in the first problem can be applied to the present problem.

Again, any valid sequence must start with some series of $n > 0$ left parentheses
preceding the first appearance of a right parenthesis. Suppose its matching left
parenthesis does not immediately precede it. This is the situation, for example, in
Figure 4.11(b), where there are four left parentheses, A, [, [, A, appearing before "],"
the first right parenthesis. In order for this first right parenthesis to satisfy i and ii,
it must then be paired with a previous matching left parenthesis. But then the
immediately preceding left parenthesis is the last character in the sequence between
that pair of parentheses. In order to satisfy iii, this sequence must be valid. *This
sequence cannot be valid since this last left parenthesis has no matching right parenthesis in* this *sequence, as indicated in Figure 4.12.*

In conclusion, a solution may be obtained as follows:

1. Pair the first adjacent left and right parentheses that match, and remove
   the pair.
2. If the resultant sequence is valid, then so is the original sequence; otherwise
   the original sequence is not valid.

Procedure DETERMINE is also an implementation of this solution using a stack,
assuming LEFTPAREN, RIGHTPAREN, and MATCH reflect the different left
parentheses, right parentheses, and matched pairs, respectively. The stack is needed
in order to implement this solution. It is no longer simply a question of increasing or
decreasing a tally, depending on whether the program reads a "(" or ")" parenthesis,
and making sure it never goes below zero and ends at zero. It is not even enough to
keep a distinct tally for each of the different kinds of "left" and "right" parentheses.

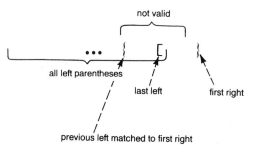

Figure 4.12   An Invalid Nesting Sequence

This would not result in Figure 4.11(b), for example, being recognized as invalid because each of the four numbers would satisfy the requirements just mentioned. It is condition iii, and more than one kind of left and right parentheses, that makes the stack mandatory. Consider a pair satisfying conditions i and ii. To satisfy condition iii, the sequence of characters between the "left" and "right" parentheses of the pair must also be valid. In effect, a new set of tallies must be kept for that sequence, and they must satisfy the three conditions. The stack is actually holding *all* of these tallies. Each time a "left" parenthesis appears, it becomes a character in many sequences, in general, and the tally for it, associated with each of those sequences, must be increased by one. Pushing it onto the stack, in effect, increases all these tallies by one simultaneously. Similarly, popping the stack decreases them all simultaneously.

The definition of a valid sequence may be restated to show its structure more clearly. A *valid sequence* is

- □ A null sequence
- □ A left and right matching pair of parentheses with a valid sequence between them
- □ A valid sequence followed by a valid sequence

The following recursive version of DETERMINE is based on this definition.

```
procedure DETERMINE(var VALID : boolean; LAST : char);
var
    CURRENTCHAR : char;
    DONE : boolean;
begin
    DONE := false;
    while (not EOF and not DONE) do
        begin
            READCHAR(CURRENTCHAR);
            if LEFTPAREN(CURRENTCHAR) then
                DETERMINE(VALID, CURRENTCHAR)
            else
                if RIGHTPAREN(CURRENTCHAR) then
                    if not MATCH(LAST, CURRENTCHAR) then
                        VALID := false
                    else
                        begin
                            DONE := true;
                            LAST := SPECIALCHAR
                        end
                else
                    PROCESS(LAST, CURRENTCHAR)
        end;
    if LAST <> SPECIALCHAR then
        VALID := false
end;
```

DETERMINE must be called initially with VALID true and LAST set to SPECIAL-CHAR, a character that does not match any right parentheses. (See Chapter 10 for another approach.)

Both this recursive solution and the iterative solution work from the inside out. They look for the first adjacent matching left and right parenthesis in the interior of the sequence. Another recursive solution could be written which would work from the outside in, looking for a rightmost mate to the first left parenthesis and then checking the sequence between them for validity. This would lead to a less efficient solution because parentheses could be considered more than once. When using recursion there is often this dual possibility, so both should be explored.

4.7 Queues

The queue, like the stack, is a useful data abstraction for retaining information in a specific order. A *queue* is a data structure with restricted insertion and deletion operations. Additional information may be inserted on the queue, but only at the *rear end*, or *bottom*. Information may be removed from the queue, but only at the *front end*, or *top*.

The queue acts like the pile of Community Chest cards in Monopoly. The top card is the only one that can be removed, and insertions to the pile can be made only at the bottom. If we think of the information stored as representing postponed obligations, then the queue gives access to the obligations in the *order* in which they were incurred. A popular mnemonic for helping to remember this characteristic is FIFO—first in, first out. Like LIFO, this is a common term in accounting and inventory control systems.

4.7.1 Array and Circular Array Implementation of the Queue

A queue may be implemented using arrays by first declaring

```
type
    queuerecords = whatever;
        queue      = record
                        queuearray : array [1..LIMIT] of queuerecords;
                        front, rear : 0..LIMIT
                    end;
var
    Q : queue;
```

Overflow and underflow should always be checked in a general implementation. A typical queue situation is depicted in Figure 4.13(a) for the array implementation. Figure 4.13(b) shows the situation after 18, 32, and 15 have been removed and 17 and 20 have been inserted.

Storage for insertion of more records is available at the top of the QUEUE-ARRAY, but not at the bottom. To ensure that all the relocated storage for QUEUE is used before overflow occurs, programs "wrap around." That is, the queue is implemented so that the QUEUEARRAY is viewed as a circle of records, with 1 following the LIMIT, 8.

The insertion operation may then be implemented as

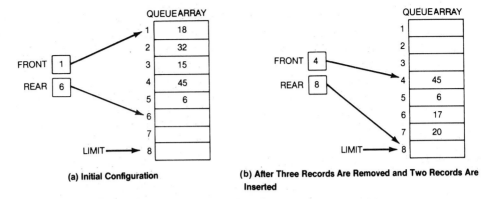

Figure 4.13 Typical Queue Configuration for an Array Implementation

```
procedure INSERT(NEWRECORD : whatever; var Q : queue);
begin
    if Q.FRONT = 0 then
        begin
            Q.FRONT := 1;
            Q.QUEUEARRAY[1] := NEWRECORD;
            Q.REAR := 2
        end
    else
        if Q.REAR = Q.FRONT then
            WRITELN('overflow')
        else
            begin
                if Q.REAR <= LIMIT then
                    begin
                        Q.QUEUEARRAY[Q.REAR] := NEWRECORD;
                        Q.REAR := Q.REAR + 1
                    end
                else
                    begin
                        if Q.FRONT = 1 then
                            WRITELN('overflow')
                        else
                            begin
                                Q.QUEUEARRAY[1] := NEWRECORD;
                                Q.REAR := 2
                            end
                    end
            end
end;
```

SETQUEUE must set FRONT and REAR to zero. EMPTY will return the value "true" when FRONT = 0, and "false" otherwise. The removal of a record can be implemented by a function REMOVE, which returns the value of the record that was deleted from the queue.

```
procedure REMOVE(var Q : queue; var VALUE : whatever);
begin
    if EMPTY(Q) then
        WRITELN('underflow')
    else
        begin
            VALUE := Q.QUEUEARRAY[Q.FRONT];
            if Q.FRONT < LIMIT then
                Q.FRONT := Q.FRONT + 1
            else
                Q.FRONT := 1;
            if Q.FRONT = Q.REAR then
                begin
                    Q.FRONT := 0;
                    Q.REAR = 0
                end
        end
end;
```

4.7.2 List Implementation of the Queue with an Array of Records

AVAILIST actually acts as a *queue* if RECLAIM returns a record to the *rear* of the AVAILIST. Thus queue can be implemented as a list of records stored in an array.

4.7.3 List Implementation of the Queue with Records in the Pascal Heap

The third queue implementation is also a list, but one involving dynamic storage allocation of the records in the Pascal heap. First, the following declaration must be made:

```
type
    queueptr    = ↑queuerecord;
    queuerecord = record
                      entry : whatever;
                      link : queueptr
                  end;
    queue       = queueptr;
var
    Q : queue;
```

SETQUEUE must set Q to **nil**. INSERT will first request storage for the new record to be inserted by invoking NEW. It will then set its ENTRY field, and insert it as the new last record in the queue. REMOVE must delete the first record of the queue and return its ENTRY field value.

Your deck has now been "stacked," you've been "queued" into queues, and you mustn't postpone your obligation to use them!

☐ Exercises

1. Let I and J be two integers and define $Q(I, J)$ by

$$Q(I, J) = \begin{cases} 0 & \text{if } I < J \\ Q(I - J, J) + 1 & \text{if } I \geq J \end{cases}$$

    a. What is the value of $Q(7, 2)$?
    b. Can we determine $Q(0, 0)$?
    c. Can we determine $Q(-3, -4)$?

2. Let A be an array of type real and I and N be positive integers. The function $M(A, I, N)$ is defined by

$$M(A, I, N) = \begin{cases} A(I) & \text{if } I = N \\ \max(M(A, I + 1, N), A[I]) & \text{if } I < N \end{cases}$$

    a. Find $M(A, I, N)$ if $I = 1$, $N = 6$, and A is

        1.   3.2
        2.   −5.0
        3.   14.6
        4.   7.8
        5.   9.6
        6.   3.2

    b. What does $M(A, I, N)$ do?

3. Let A be an array of type real, and I and N be positive integers. The function $M(A, I, N)$ is defined by

$$M(A, I, N) = \begin{cases} A[I] & \text{if } I = N \\ \max\left(M\left(A, I, \left\lfloor \dfrac{I + N}{2} \right\rfloor \right), M\left(A, \left\lfloor \dfrac{I + N}{2} \right\rfloor + 1, N \right) \right) & \text{if } I < N \end{cases}$$

$\lfloor (I + N)/2 \rfloor$ means, "Do an integer divide of $(I + N)/2$."

    a. Find $M(A, I, N)$ for $I = 1$, $N = 6$, and A the array of Exercise 2.
    b. What does $M(A, I, N)$ do?

4. Let I be a nonnegative integer. Find $b(4)$ where

$b(0) = 1$
$b(n) = b(0) \times b(n - 1) + b(1) \times b(n - 2) + b(2) \times b(n - 3) + \ldots + b(n - 1)$
    $\times b(0)$

5. Write a recursive function MAX corresponding to Exercise 2.
6. Write a recursive function MAX corresponding to Exercise 3.
7. **a.** Why does the recursive solution to the Towers of Hanoi problem use the minimum number of moves?
    b. What is the number of moves it uses?
8. Consider the following nonrecursive algorithm for the Towers of Hanoi problem.

    1. Label the disks $1, 2, \ldots, N$ in increasing order of size.
    2. Label the pegs I, A, and F, respectively, $N + 1$, $N + 2$, and $N + 3$.
    3. Move the smallest disk onto another disk with an even label or onto an empty peg with an even label.

   4. If all disks are on the same peg, then terminate. Move the second smallest
      top disk onto the peg not containing the smallest ring. Go to 1.

   a. Convince yourself that this correctly solves the Towers of Hanoi problem.
   b. Is the recursive solution or this nonrecursive version easier to understand?
9. Suppose a fourth peg is added to the Towers of Hanoi problem.
   a. Write a recursive solution for this problem.
   b. Can you find a recursive solution that uses the minimum number of moves for
this problem?
10. Mark any n distinct points on the circumference of a circle. How many triangles may
be drawn whose vertexes lie on three of the n points?
11. How many ways may k distinct points be selected from the n points of Exercise 10?
12. Given a permutation of $1, 2, \ldots, n$ let N_i be the number of integers to the right
of i which exceed i. For the permutation 2134, $N_1 = 2$, $N_2 = 3$, $N_3 = 1$, $N_4 = 0$. Write a
PROCESS procedure that will turn PERMUTATIONS into a program that prints $N_1, N_2, \ldots$,
N_n for each permutation.
13. Suppose L is implemented as a two-way list. Write a recursive procedure to reverse L.
14. Implement the function of Exercise 5.
15. Implement the function of Exercise 6.
16. Compare the requirements for the stack storage required during execution for the
implementations of Exercises 5 and 6.
17. Why are the more efficient versions of Section 4.4 more efficient?
18. The Fibonacci sequence is defined by

$$F_0 = 0, \qquad F_1 = 1$$
$$F_n = F_{n-1} + F_{n-2} \quad \text{for} \quad n = 2, 3, 4, \ldots$$

   a. Write a recursive program FIBONACCI(N) to compute and print F_N.
   b. Analyze its time and storage requirements.
19. **a.** Translate the program of Exercise 18 and obtain as efficient a version as you can.
   b. Analyze its time and storage requirements.
20. Write a nonrecursive program FIBONACCI(N) which takes $O(N)$ time and uses
only four local variables.
21. **a.** Write a function ELEMENT with parameter K which returns the value of the
Kth element on the stack of integers implemented as in Figure 4.8. For instance, if K is 1, it
returns the value of the current first stack element. It does not disturb the stack at all. Assume
you do not have access to the stack directly, but only through the PUSH, POP, and EMPTY
routines.
   b. Same as Exercise 21a except assume you do have direct access to the stack.
22. Two stacks are implemented in one array of length 1,000 as shown.

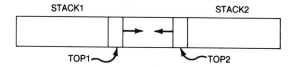

The tops of the stacks are pointed to by TOP1 and TOP2, and grow toward each other. Write
a procedure PUSH that pushes the contents of V onto the stack indicated by S. S will have a
value of 1 or 2. If the stack to which V is to be added is full, then PUSH should not add it, but
should return with S set to 0.

23. Write a boolean function MAXSTACK that returns in M the maximal element on a stack of integers implemented with pointer variables. MAXSTACK will return "true" when the stack is not empty and "false" otherwise.

24. What does

```
POP(S, VALUE);
PUSH(S, VALUE);
```

do?

25. What will the pairing generated by the procedure DETERMINE be for the input sequence $AA([[]()])ZZ$?

26. Modify the procedure DETERMINE so that it outputs the pairs as follows,

```
  12345678
if ( ( ( ) ) ( ) ) is the input sequence then the
output will be the pairs 3 4, 2 5, 6 7, 1 8.
```

27. Modify procedure DETERMINE so that it also outputs $((()))(())$, for example, if the input is $((()))(())$.
                                                                      42112334

28. How must DETERMINE be modified if some left characters may also be right characters, and they will always match each other? For example, let the left characters be A, (, [, B with the "right" characters being A,),], B. Here A is matched with A, B with B, (with), and [with]. Then $A[A]$ is not valid, but $A[CC](AA)A$ and $AB()AAB[]A$ are.

29. Write the REMOVE procedure for the array implementation of a queue.

30. Write the INSERT procedure for the pointer variable implementation of a queue.

31. Write the REMOVE procedure for the pointer variable implementation of a queue.

32. Suppose procedure BUFFER has three parameters, Q of type queueptr, E of type whatever, and OP of type character. If OP is R, then BUFFER returns after removing the top record of the queue and copying its value into E. If OP is n, then BUFFER returns after inserting the value in E at the bottom of the queue. Write an implementation of BUFFER assuming that access to the queue is only through the EMPTY, REMOVE, and INSERT routines.

33. What does the following procedure do?

```
procedure EXERCISE(var S : stack : var Q : queue);
var
    X : whatever;
begin
  SETQUEUE(Q);
  while not EMPTY(S) do
     begin
         X := POP(S, VALUE);
         INSERT(X, Q);
     end;
  while not EMPTY(Q) do
     begin
         REMOVE(Q, X);
         PUSH(X, S)
     end
end;
```

34. A *deque* (pronounced like "deck") is a data abstraction that retains ordered information, but allows insertion and deletion at both its front and rear.

    a. Develop an array-based implementation of a deque and write corresponding SETDEQUE, INSERTF, INSERTR, REMOVEF, REMOVER, and EMPTY routines.

    b. Do the same as in Exercise 34a, except use pointer variables with dynamic storage allocation for the deque implementation.

    35. Suppose there is a program to keep track of the current board configuration in a game of Monopoly by using a circular array of records, each record representing a board position (such as Boardwalk), and queues for Community Chest and Chance. Discuss how the records should be defined, what pointers to records will be convenient, and how these pointers and the circular array should be processed on each turn.

☐ Suggested Assignment

    a. Write and simulate a recursive program to reverse a list.

    b. In order to use storage efficiently when N stacks are needed during the execution of a program, it may be desirable to implement all the stacks in one array as shown here for $N = 4$.

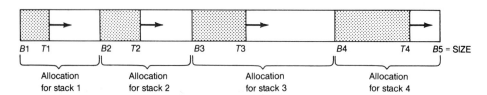

The B_i's and T_i's point to the bottoms and tops of the stacks, which grow to the right as indicated. Think of the total storage currently allocated to stack i as being from B_i to B_{i+1}. Stack i is actually using $T_i - B_{i+1} + 1$ positions of the array. If $B_1 = 1$, $B_2 = 10$, $B_3 = 15$, $B_4 = 25$, $B_5 = $ SIZE of the array $= 35$, $T1 = 3$, $T2 = 12$, $T3 = 20$, and $T4 = 33$, then the stacks are using, respectively, 3, 3, 6, and 9 entries, while they are allocated 9, 5, 10, and 10 entries.

When an entry is to be inserted into a stack that is currently using all its allocated storage, the stack is said to have overflowed. Stack i overflows if $T_i = B_{i+1} - 1$. Write a procedure to manage the storage provided by the array. Whenever a stack overflows, the procedure is to be invoked. If there is any unused space in the array, then the stack with an unused but allocated position which is "closest" to the overflow stack is to give up one of its unused positions. This position is then used by the overflow stack to accommodate its entry. This procedure must be written to shift stacks around. If no unused space exists in the array, then the procedure should print an "out of stack storage" message.

More Complex Lists

5.1 Imposing List Structure on Data

So far in this book, records in lists have had information fields and link fields. These are **simple records**. The lists themselves have looked like simple **chains** of records. Such lists may be used to store the records or to both store and impose an ordering on them. This chapter presents **complex records**, which contain fields that are themselves names of lists. The fields are called **sublist fields**. Lists composed of such records have more complex structure than chains and are known as **complex lists**. Several such lists are depicted schematically in Figure 5.1. The following examples illustrate the use of complex lists and show how they provide one means of organizing data to capture certain inherent relations among the list records.

Example 5.1

The ACCOUNTS list in Figure 5.1(a) consists of three records. The first two are complex, the third simple. The first record points to a sublist. This sublist consists of two records; the first of these is complex and the second is simple. ACCOUNTS might actually represent three companies' user accounts. The first user account is billed for two distinct computer services, $100 for last month's computing and $75 for this month's software consulting. The second user account owes $200 for the month's computing and $250 for the month's consulting. The third user account has a credit of $46. The X in the sublist field of the complex record "200" means its sublist is null. □

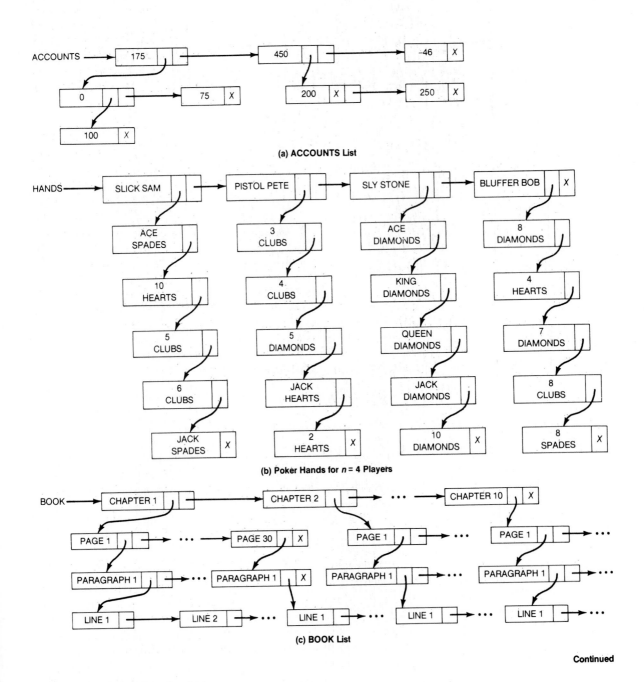

(a) ACCOUNTS List

(b) Poker Hands for *n* = 4 Players

(c) BOOK List

Continued

Figure 5.1 More Complex Lists

Example 5.2 A programmer asked to simulate a card game with n players might choose to represent the current configuration of the n individual hands by using a list composed of complex records. A typical configuration is shown in Figure 5.1(b) for four poker players. The sublist that makes up each complex record contains all the cards of a particular player's hand, each card represented as a record. Insertions and deletions into an individual hand require insertions and deletions from the appropriate sublist. ☐

Example 5.3 A book might be represented as the BOOK list shown in Figure 5.1(c). Records for the individual lines of text would be simple; the records for paragraph, chapter, and page would be complex.

    The data processing for word processing or text editing might involve inserting and deleting chapters, paragraphs, or lines. Creating an index for the book would require even more complex processing. This could be done by making a special "dictionary" listing the key words relevant to the book's topic, then searching the text for all instances of key words. If the book were a computer science text, then the dictionary would include all key technical computer science words. The index could be created by accessing and processing each page. This processing would involve checking the page for occurrences of the key words, and keeping track, for each such word in the dictionary, of the pages on which it occurred. (Unfortunately, such automatic indexing creates too large an index and one that may not be very useful, since not every mention of a key term is especially relevant.) ☐

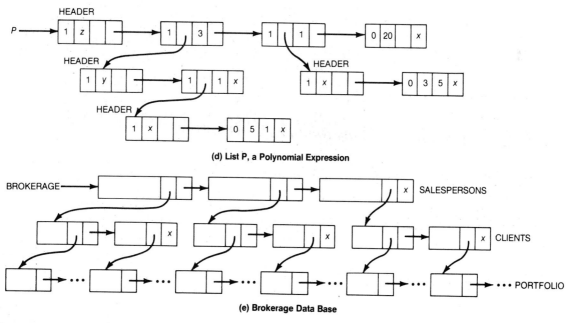

(d) List P, a Polynomial Expression

(e) Brokerage Data Base

Figure 5.1 *(continued)*

Example 5.4 — A polynomial in x, y, and z may be represented using a list-structure. Suppose the polynomial $P(x, y, z)$ is $3zx^5 + 5z^3yx + 20$. We can write this as

$$P(x, y, z) = z^3(y(x(5))) + z(x^5(3)) + 20$$

This, in turn, can be represented as P of Figure 5.1(d).

Each record of P has four fields, as shown in Figure 5.2(a). A TAG field value of 1 indicates that the record is complex, while a TAG field of 0 indicates that the record is simple.

Each sublist, including the main list, has a header record and represents a polynomial. The main list, for example, is a polynomial in z composed of three terms. The record (Figure 5.2(b)) on the main list indicates that this term contains z to the power 3, and a coefficient that is pointed to by the pointer in the COEFF field. Its successor record is similarly expressed. The last record on the main list (Figure 5.2(c)) is simple, meaning that the value in the COEFF field is to be interpreted as a constant. Sublists are interpreted in the same way. □

Example 5.5 — Each record on BROKERAGE's main list in Figure 5.1(e) represents a sales representative (a financial advisor) of a brokerage firm. The sublist of each salesperson contains information about each of his or her clients. Each client's sublist is the client's stock portfolio. □

Each of the example lists organizes information by collecting related data on sublists. They are a step up in complexity from the chains of Chapter 3 but do not illustrate the most complex lists, which allow sharing of records and sublists. **Sharing** means more than one record can point to another record or sublist. Records can also have additional pointer fields linking records to form intertwined lists. However, this chapter concentrates primarily on list-structures. They may be defined formally by either of two equivalent definitions:

☐ A **list-structure** is a collection of simple and complex records linked by pointers in the following way.
The link and sublist fields of each record contain pointers to records of the collection.
Each record of the collection has no more than one pointer to it from any record of the collection.

☐ A **list-structure** is a list of simple and complex records whose complex record's sublist fields point to distinct list-structures called sublists. The successor of each record must be unique.

The first definition treats list-structures as a collection of linked records but does not convey their inherent structure. The recursive definition emphasizes this structure, making clear how a list-structure is itself built from other list-structures.

(a) General Form of a Record   (b) Main-List Record   (c) Last Record on Main List

Figure 5.2   Records of the List-structure for a Polynomial

It is evident that each list of Figure 5.1 satisfies the first definition. To see that they also satisfy the second definition, consider the ACCOUNTS list. The main list consists of a list of simple and complex records, so it is necessary to check that the complex record's sublists are themselves list-structures. The first main-list record's sublist is a list-structure since the sublist's main list satisfies the definition and its complex record points to a list-structure, a single list record. The second main-list record's sublist is itself a list whose complex record's sublist is a list-structure, the null list-structure.

The lists SAM and SALLY in Figure 5.3 are *not* list-structures, since they fail to satisfy the definitions. SAM has shared sublists; SALLY has a loop.

5.2 Traversal of List-structures

Inserting or deleting a record from a list-structure, once it is decided where, is done using the same procedures as in Chapter 3. In order to determine where to insert or delete, the typical prior processing involves a traversal through the records. Unlike the chain, for which there is a natural order in which to traverse the records, list-structures have no simple natural order. Instead, the order in which records are to be accessed and processed is defined as follows:

> To *traverse a list-structure*,
>
> access each record on the main list in order and
> 1. Process the record
> 2. If the record is complex, then
>   *traverse the complex record's sublist.*

Notice that the definition is actually recursive, since a complex record's sublist is itself a list-structure. To see how to apply it, consider FORMULA in Figure 5.4. The records are numbered for ease of reference.

To determine the order in which records are accessed and processed in a traversal of the list-structure FORMULA, apply the definition. It specifies that records 1 and 2 on the main list be accessed and processed in sequence. Since record 2 is complex, sublist 1 must be traversed. At the finish of traversal of sublist 1, it will be necessary to continue where processing left off on the main list. To know where to resume, save P1. To traverse sublist 1, apply the definition to it, and access

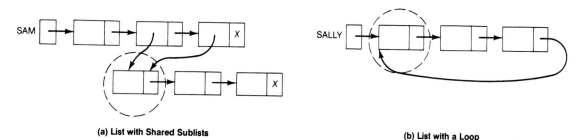

(a) List with Shared Sublists   (b) List with a Loop

Figure 5.3 Two Lists That Are *Not* List-structures

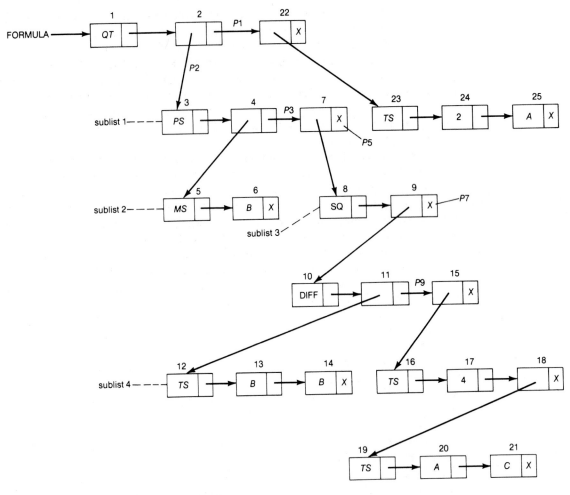

Figure 5.4   The List-structure FORMULA

and process records 3 and 4 in order. Since record 4 is complex, traverse sublist 2. Save P3 to know where to resume when its traversal is complete.

To traverse sublist 2, apply the definition of traversal to it, and so access and process records 5 and 6. Since the link field of record 6 is null, no records remain on this sublist, so its traversal is complete.

Which task should be done now? Step 2 of the traversal definition has just been applied to sublist 2. The next record of some sublist must now be accessed. *What record?* It is the successor record of the complex record whose sublist traversal was just completed—record 4. P3, which was saved for just this moment, points to record 7, so let the program follow it. Since P3 is no longer needed, discard it. Since record 7 is complex, traverse sublist 3. Continuing in this way, the program would access and process the records in the order in which they are numbered.

From this example it can be seen that whenever the link field of the record just accessed and processed is null, the traversal of some sublist has been completed and the program must determine where to go next. Each time the processing of a complex record was finished, the contents of its link field were saved before traversing its sublist. In FORMULA, this leads to saving P1, then P3. After record 6 comes a null link field signifying the completion of the traversal of sublist 2. P3 then tells the program where to go, so it is followed and can then be forgotten. P1 is still remembered, and P5, P7, and P9 need to be remembered in turn. After dealing with record 14, the program encounters its null link value, which signifies completion of sublist 4's traversal. Where does it go? It follows P9 and needs to remember only P7, P5, and P1, and so on.

Each pointer that is saved represents an obligation that must be postponed — the obligation to apply steps 1 and 2 of the definition of traversal of list-structures to successive records on the list pointed to by the pointer. The definition requires that the corresponding complex record's sublist be traversed immediately. In carrying out the traversal of that sublist, further obligations may be incurred and subsequently fulfilled. Each time step 2 is completed, the most recently saved pointer provides the information to determine *what* record to deal with next and is then discarded. This implies that any pointers saved during the complex records' traversal will have been discarded when its traversal is complete. Consequently, the most recently saved pointer must point to the record to be processed each time step 2 is completed. If there is no remaining saved pointer, it *must* mean that it is the main list of the original list-structure for which step 2 has been completed. The entire traversal is then complete.

Traversing a list-structure thus requires retention, recall, and deletion of information in a specific order. The pointer information retained represents postponed obligations. These obligations must be fulfilled in reverse order from that in which they were incurred. This is the precise situation in which the *stack* data abstraction is very convenient.

It is important to recognize that the definition of a list-structure traversal does not merely explain how to traverse a *specific* list-structure, such as FORMULA, but describes a procedure that may be applied to *any* list-structure. This is, of course, true for any algorithm or program. Programs and algorithms specify a procedure for *any* input and not just for a *specific* input. The definition of traversal of list-structures is really an algorithm, an initial description of a procedure for list-structure traversal.

5.2.1 An Iterative Procedure

We will now develop a program TRAVERSE to traverse a list-structure LS. In applying the definition it became clear that such a traversal may be described by the following algorithm.

1. Initialize the current record.
2. Initialize the stack of postponed obligations to "empty."
3. While there is a current record or a postponed obligation,
   if there is a current record, then
   a. process the current record, and
   b. update the current record to the next record to be processed.
   else
   c. remove the top obligation from the stack and update the current record to it.

To update the current record, task 3b needs to be specified in greater detail. If the record just processed was simple, then the next record to be processed is the successor of the current record. Otherwise—if the record just processed was complex—its successor record represents a postponed obligation that must be placed on the stack. In that case the next record to be processed is the first record on the current record's sublist. This gives a refinement for task 3b that is incorporated in the revised algorithm.

1. Initialize the current record.
2. Initialize the stack of postponed obligations to *empty.*
3. While there is a current record or a postponed obligation,
       if there is a current record, then
       a. process the current record, and
       b. if the current record is complex, then
            i. save an obligation to its successor record on the stack
            ii. update the current record to the first record on its sublist,
          else
               update the current record to its successor record
       else
       c. remove the top obligation from the stack and update the current record to it.

A new variable (call it PTR) is needed to contain a pointer to the current record. The stack can now be treated as a data abstraction with the usual operations SETSTACK, EMPTY, PUSH, and POP. The details for implementing the stack are built into the routines implementing these operations.

Assume that each record is processed by calling a routine PROCESS with parameters LS and PTR. To treat the list-structure as a data abstraction, assume the functions COMPLEX, NEXT, and SUBLIST, each with PTR as a parameter. COMPLEX returns a value "true" if the record to which PTR points is complex; the value "false" otherwise. NEXT and SUBLIST return, respectively, a copy of the link and sublist field value of the record pointed to by PTR.

A more detailed refinement of the algorithm can now be written.

1. Set PTR to LS
2. SETSTACK(S)
3. While PTR is not null or not EMPTY(S)
       if PTR is not null, then
       a. PROCESS(LS, PTR)
       b. If COMPLEX(PTR), then
            i. PUSH(NEXT(PTR), S)
            ii. Set PTR to SUBLIST(PTR)
          else
               Set PTR to NEXT(PTR)
       else
       c. POP(S, PTR)

Notice that if all records of LS are simple, then tasks i, ii, and c will never be invoked. This procedure is then essentially the same as the list traversal of Chapter 3, as it should be. As written, it does not provide for partial traversal (DONE is not involved in the loop control) but could be easily modified when necessary.

TRAVERSE may be implemented as in the following iterative, nonrecursive procedure. This implementation uses data abstraction and has been written modularly.

```
procedure TRAVERSE(var LS : liststructure);
var
    PTR, NULL : liststructure;
begin
    SETNULL(NULL);
    PTR := LS;
    SETSTACK(S);
    while ((PTR <> NULL) or not EMPTY(S)) do
        if PTR <> NULL then
            begin
                PROCESS(LS, PTR);
                if (COMPLEX(PTR)) then
                    begin
                        PUSH(NEXT(PTR), S);
                        PTR := SUBLIST(PTR)
                    end
                else
                    PTR := NEXT(PTR)
            end
        else
            POP(S, PTR)
end;
```

In this chapter and subsequently where stack operations are required, to avoid cluttering the programs, they have been omitted. However, to encapsulate, stack operations should be defined within TRAVERSE. It is important to see that the program is modular and independent of the implementation of the data abstractions to which it refers. To use TRAVERSE, the programmer must either be given the modules it uses or else write them.

5.2.2 A Recursive Procedure

To develop a recursive implementation for TRAVERSE, begin by considering a refinement of the defining algorithm for traversing a list-structure.

1. Initialize the current record.
2. While there is a current record,
   a. process the current record;
   b. if the current record is complex, then
      i. traverse the current record's sublist;
   c. update the current record to its successor record.

The variable PTR can now be introduced to point to the current record, and the variable NEXTSUBLIST can be introduced to point to a sublist. Again, the list-structure is treated as a data abstraction. Also, to modularize, assume the procedure TRAVERSE to implement task i. The algorithm can now be refined again:

1. Set PTR to LS.
2. While PTR is not null,
   a. PROCESS(LS, PTR);
   b. if COMPLEX(PTR), then
      i. set NEXTSUBLIST to SUBLIST(PTR),
         TRAVERSE(NEXTSUBLIST);
   c. set PTR to NEXT(PTR).

This refinement is implemented in the following recursive procedure.

```
procedure TRAVERSE(var LS : liststructure);
var
    PTR, NEXTSUBLIST, NULL : liststructure;
begin
    SETNULL(NULL);
    PTR := LS;
    while PTR <> NULL do
        begin
            PROCESS(LS, PTR);
            if COMPLEX(PTR) then
                begin
                    NEXTSUBLIST := SUBLIST(PTR);
                    TRAVERSE(NEXTSUBLIST)
                end;
            PTR := NEXT(PTR)
        end
end;
```

A number of comments are in order about the two implementations of TRAVERSE. First, imagine that the recursive procedure TRAVERSE is presented to you with the comment that it is a refined version of the definition of traversal of a list-structure. It is easy to see that this is so. Contrast this with the effort involved in seeing that the iterative, nonrecursive procedure TRAVERSE is also a refined version of the same defining algorithm. Second, the recursive version is more concise than the nonrecursive. Third, the recursive TRAVERSE is almost a direct translation of the defining algorithm. It required very little effort to achieve it in this case, because the definition is itself a recursive description.

These comments usually hold for algorithms that process data structures that can be recursively defined, such as list-structures. This is not an accident but can be expected when we deal with complex data structures. Recursive definitions allow concise descriptions of complex algorithms and data structures. Concise descriptions allow us to deal more easily with their complexity. As an example, now that you know what is meant by a list-structure traversal, try to give a definition for such a traversal that involves *no* vagueness, allows its application to *any* list-structure, and does *not* involve recursion. Recursive definitions are especially useful to the programmer dealing with complex data structures because they lead systematically and directly to recursive programs for their processing.

5.3 Using a TRAVERSE Procedure for List-structures

Use of the general list-structure traversal procedures just developed is illustrated in the following examples. The examples are intended to convey the flavor of list-structure applications and their processing.

Example 5.6 Print the information field of each stock record of the list-structure BROKERAGE shown in Figure 5.1(e) which was bought prior to DATE. A solution may be obtained by traversing BROKERAGE and printing the relevant stock records.

The module PROCESS can be written to turn the recursive traversal procedure into a solution to this problem. The task is straightforward except for the determination, within PROCESS, of whether the record it is to process currently is a stock record. Since only stock records are simple, a test for complexity of the current record will provide this information. PROCESS may be written as

```
procedure PROCESS(PTR : liststructure);
begin
    if(not COMPLEX(PTR)) and PRIOR(DATEBOUGHT(PTR), DATE) then
        PRINTINFO(PTR)
end;
```

where PRIOR returns "true" if DATEBOUGHT is prior to DATA and "false" otherwise, and PRINTINFO prints the information field value of the record pointed to by PTR. Note that PROCESS may also be used with the interative version of TRAVERSE. □

Example 5.7 Consider again the list-structure BROKERAGE in Figure 5.1(e). The task is to print, for each client, the total value of his or her portfolio. □

The idea of the solution to Example 5.7 is to traverse BROKERAGE, and each time a client's record is encountered, print the name, then accumulate the total value of the portfolio as it is being traversed and print this total when the portfolio has been completely traversed.

While this seems simple enough, some details require attention. Let us adapt a general traversal procedure, the iterative one, to this task. Thus PROCESS must be written to turn this traversal into a solution. Consequently, PROCESS must be able to recognize when the record it is to work on is a client's record. At this point, it must initialize the accumulated total to zero. For each ensuing record of the client's portfolio, it must then update the accumulated total by the value of that record's stock. Finally, PROCESS must recognize the end of the portfolio list and print the accumulated total.

If TOTAL is used to store the accumulated value, then it must be preserved between calls to PROCESS. This can be achieved by making TOTAL a variable of TRAVERSE and a parameter of PROCESS and initializing it properly in TRAVERSE, or making TOTAL nonlocal to TRAVERSE. If the latter is chosen, PROCESS may be written as

```
procedure PROCESS(PTR : liststructure);
begin
    if COMPLEX(PTR) then
        begin
            if SUBLIST(PTR) <> NULL then
                if not COMPLEX(SUBLIST(PTR)) then
                    begin
                        TOTAL := 0.0;
                        PRINTNAME(PTR)
                    end
        end
    else
        begin
            TOTAL := TOTAL + VALUE(PTR);
            if NEXT(PTR) = NULL then
                PRINTTOTAL(TOTAL)
        end
end;
```

The **if** conditions are used to determine if this is the first call to PROCESS for a portfolio and, if so, to initialize and print the client's name or, after updating a client's total, to see if the record is the last of a portfolio. Assume NULL is nonlocal to PROCESS. PROCESS will also work with the recursive version of TRAVERSE.

Example 5.8   Suppose BOOK, the list-structure shown in Figure 5.1(c), stores the current version of a text. A new paragraph, stored as a list NEWP, is to replace the current paragraph P of page PG of chapter C. To solve this problem we will write a new traverse procedure tailored to the situation since not all records of BOOK need to be accessed. Two versions are presented. In both versions the idea is to search for chapter C on the main list, then traverse its sublist until page PG is found, search its sublist to find paragraph P, and finally replace it by NEWP and terminate. The first version assumes records contain numbering information for chapter, page, or paragraph in a number field. The second assumes that these records are indistinguishable and contain no such information, so a count of list records must be maintained to determine when the appropriate record is encountered. ☐

```
procedure PARAGRAPHINSERT(BOOK, NEWP : liststructure; C, PG, P : integer);
var
    CURRENTNUMBER : integer;
    CURRENTLIST : (CH, PAGE, PAR);
    PTR, NULL : liststructure;
    FOUND : boolean;
begin
    SETNULL(NULL);
    PTR := BOOK;
    CURRENTNUMBER := C;
    CURRENTLIST := CH;
```

```
                    FOUND := false;
                    while (not FOUND and (PTR <> NULL)) do
                        begin
                            if CURRENTNUMBER <> NUMBER(PTR) then
                                PTR := NEXT(PTR)
                            else
                                case CURRENTLIST of
                                    CH : begin
                                            CURRENTLIST := PAGE;
                                            CURRENTNUMBER := PG;
                                            PTR := SUBLIST(PTR)
                                         end;
                                    PAGE : begin
                                            CURRENTLIST := PAR;
                                            CURRENTNUMBER := P;
                                            PTR := SUBLIST(PTR)
                                          end;
                                    PAR : FOUND := true
                                end
                        end;
                    if PTR <> NULL then
                        SETSUBLIST(PTR, NEWP)
                    else
                        WRITELN('PARAGRAPH NOT FOUND')
                end;
```

SETSUBLIST sets the sublist field of the record pointed to by its first parameter to the value of its second parameter. Just before SETSUBLIST is invoked, code (not shown here) could be inserted to reclaim the storage used by the replaced paragraph. This is also true for the second version.

```
            procedure PARAGRAPHINSERT(BOOK, NEWP : liststructure; C, PG, P : integer);
            var
                CURRENTNUMBER, COUNT : integer;
                CURRENTLIST : (CH, PAGE, PAR);
                PTR, NULL : liststructure;
                FOUND : boolean;
            begin
                SETNULL(NULL);
                PTR := BOOK;
                CURRENTNUMBER := C;
                CURRENTLIST := CH;
                FOUND := false;
                COUNT := 1;
                while (not FOUND and (PTR <> NULL)) do
                    begin
                        if CURRENTNUMBER <> COUNT then
                            begin
                                COUNT := COUNT + 1;
                                PTR := NEXT(PTR)
                            end
```

```
              else
                case CURRENTLIST of
                  CH : begin
                         CURRENTLIST := PAGE;
                         CURRENTNUMBER := PG;
                         COUNT =:0;
                         PTR := SUBLIST(PTR)
                       end;
                  PAGE : begin
                           CURRENTLIST := PAR;
                           CURRENTNUMBER := P;
                           COUNT :=1;
                           PTR := SUBLIST(PTR)
                         end;
                  PAR : FOUND := true
                end
            end;
        if PTR <> NULL then
            SETSUBLIST(PTR, NEWP)
        else
            WRITELN('PARAGRAPH NOT FOUND')
      end;
```

Example 5.9 Arithmetic expressions such as $(A + B)/C$ may be represented by a list-structure, as shown in Figure 5.5, where A, B, and C represent numeric values. $\square$

Consider again the list-structure FORMULA (Figure 5.4). It may be interpreted as representing the formula $(-B + \sqrt{B^2 - 4AC})/2A$. This happens to be the root of the quadratic equation $AX^2 + BX + C = 0$. In FORMULA the symbols QT, PS, TS, MS, DIFF, and SQ stand for, respectively, the operations of division, addition, multiplication, changing sign, taking the difference, and taking the square root. The square root and sign change operations apply to one operand. The others apply to two operands.

The main list, and each sublist, represent an arithmetic expression. Their first records contain an arithmetic operator; their remaining list records represent the operand values of that arithmetic operator. The expression represented by such a list is to be evaluated by applying the operation to its operands. Notice that each complex record's sublist is an arithmetic expression that must be evaluated. Thus the operand each represents must be obtained before the operator represented by the list on which it appears may be evaluated. For example, the sublists of complex records 2 and 22 must be evaluated before QT of record 1 can be applied to them.

The programming task is to write a function EVALUATE to return the value of an arithmetic expression represented by a list-structure. With FORMULA as a prototype, the evaluation can be accomplished by traversing its main list and, whenever a complex record is encountered, evaluating its sublist. When the last list record has been processed in this way, the operator and each of its operands are known. The final result is obtained by applying the operator to its known operands. Of course, in

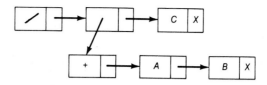

Figure 5.5 List-structure Representing the Arithmetic Expression $(A + B)/C$

evaluating an operand, more complex records may be encountered, such as record 4, and they must then be evaluated before continuing. A little thought should convince you that a PROCESS procedure can be written to turn either the recursive or the nonrecursive traversal program into EVALUATE.

One important detail remains: how to store the operands that are generated during the traversal so that they are available when needed. Suppose each operand encountered by PROCESS is stored in an operand stack and each operator encountered is stored in an operator stack. If the current record being processed is the last record of a list (its link value is null), then the operator currently at the top of the stack will have its operands at the top of the operand stack. PROCESS can then pop both these stacks, apply the operator to the operands, and place the result back onto the operand stack. If the record being processed represents the last record on the main list (the operator stack will then be empty), instead of placing the result on the operand stack it should copy it into EVALUATE.

A detailed description of PROCESS follows.

```
If NEXT(PTR) is not NULL and the record pointed to by PTR is simple, then
    if it contains an operator, then
        place the operator on the operator stack
    else
        place the operand on the operand stack
else
        pop the operator stack, remove the top K operands from the operand
        stack (K is the number of operands of the operator just popped), and
        apply the operator to the K operands.
        If the operator stack is not empty then
            push the result onto the operand stack
        else
            set EVALUATE to the result.
```

This solution may also be applied to the evaluation of logical or boolean expressions. In fact, it forms the basis of the interpretive language LISP.

Example 5.10 Suppose polynomials are represented as P was in Figure 5.1(d). It is then possible to write procedures to perform important algebraic operations on polynomials such as the addition and multiplication of two polynomials. Even symbolic differentiation can be performed. These operations are not discussed in detail here. Simply note that traversal of the list-structures representing the polynomials forms the heart of such procedures. □

5.4 Implementing List-structures

The graphic depictions of list-structures mirror the conceptual image of them. To implement list-structures in a high-level language such as Pascal, you may store their records, just as you may store any records, in an array (RECORDS) or in the Pascal heap. The list heads are stored outside of the array or heap. Normally a list-structure will be implemented using pointer variables, so two illustrative examples are given. The main difference in the declaration of the records, compared to those of a chain, is that an additional field becomes necessary for the sublist pointer.

The actual implementation of a list-structure record may invoke two distinct types of records with different field formats for simple and complex records. The use of the variant record in Pascal is appropriate for this case. Alternatively, both simple and complex records may have the same format with a field provided to indicate whether the record is simple or complex. The essential point is that these two kinds of records must be distinguishable. Programs that process list-structures, such as those written in the preceding sections, should be independent of the list-structure implementation; such details should be reflected only in low-level modules such as NEXT, SUBLIST, SETSUBLIST, and PRINTINFO.

The records for polynomials (Example 5.4) might be declared by

```
type
     kindtype          = (header, coeff, value);
     polynomialpointer = ↑polynomial;
     polynomial        = record
                              tag, exp : integer;
                              nextterm : polynomialpointer;
                              case kind : kindtype of
                                  header : (unknown : character);
                                  coeff : (sublist : polynomialpointer);
                                  value : integer
                              end
                         end;
var
     P : polynomial;
```

This uses the variant record implementation of Pascal, so there is a fixed part for fields common to all records' realizations and a variant part to describe the fields of each variant of the record. An alternative implementation would be

```
type
     polynomialpointer = ↑polynomial;
     polynomial        = record
                              tag, exp : integer;
                              nextterm, sublist; polynomialpointer;
                              kind : (header, coeff, value);
                              unknown : character;
                         end;
var
     P : polynomial;
```

The records for BOOK (Example 5.3) might be declared by

```
type
    kindtype     = (chapter, page, paragraph, line);
    bookpointer = ↑booklist;
    booklist      = record
                         number : integer;
                         link : bookpointer;
                         case kind : kindtype of
                             chapter, page, paragraph : (sublist : bookpointer);
                             line : ( )
                         end
                    end;
var
    BOOK : bookpointer;
```

The alternative would be

```
type
    bookpointer = ↑booklist;
    booklist      = record
                         kind : (chapter, page, paragraph, line);
                         link, sublist : bookpointer;
                         number : integer
                    end;
var
    BOOK : bookpointer;
```

It is also possible to implement the main list and sublists of a list-structure as two-way lists. This is convenient, just as for chains, when it is necessary to go back and forth during the processing of a list-structure or to make the predecessor of any record easily accessible. In this case an additional field would be needed for the backward pointer.

More complex lists occur frequently in applications and involve the sharing of list records as well as the sharing of sublists. List-structures may require large amounts of storage for their implementation. A natural idea is to avoid the duplication of identical sublists or records. At times, it is convenient to use additional fields linking records or sublists so that the resultant structure contains records with more than one pointer to them, and the structure may even contain loops. That is, by following pointers from a record we can arrive back at the record. You will see examples of this next, in the case study. Whenever these possibilities occur, the structures created are still lists but are no longer list-structures. These more general lists provide extensive flexibility but lead to more difficult storage management problems, considered later in the text.

5.5 Case Study: Information Retrieval

The simplest retrieval of information occurs when the name of the desired record, or a pointer to it, is known. It may then be directly accessed and processed to suit our needs. Slightly more difficult is the retrieval of a desired record that can be recognized when encountered but whose location is unknown. Traversing the records until the desired one is encountered then leads to its retrieval.

When large collections of records are involved, traversing all the records to find one is no longer feasible. The problem is not so much that retrieving one desired record takes too long but that many retrievals in rapid succession results in too much delay for the later retrievals. Imagine 1,000 computer terminals linked to a central computer and suppose 200 requests occur in rapid succession for the retrieval of records. The banking terminals known as "automatic tellers" are an example. If 1 million records need to be traversed, the retrieval of an individual record could easily take a second, so the last of the 200 requests to be processed would be honored only after more than 3 minutes of elapsed time. No one wants to wait at a terminal for 3 minutes before each request is answered. In the meantime, even more requests become backlogged.

The basic technique to avoid traversing all stored records is to focus the search on a smaller group of records known to contain the desired one. This is the essence of all faster retrieval algorithms. In the case study considered here lists will be used to organize the data so that this may be done. In Chapter 7 the search problem is presented in a more general context for information stored in random access internal memory and in Chapter 8 for information stored in external memory. External memories are cheaper and slower than internal memory but can hold vast amounts of data.

5.5.1 Family Relationships

The central problem in this case study concerns information about a collection of individuals. The collection might represent everyone who graduated from a specific university, all registered voters in a given region, or all individuals known to have contracted a particular disease that is being researched.

The information about each individual is given as a record with name, sex, birthdate, father's name, and mother's name fields. Other relevant fields may be present but are ignored for our purposes here.

To simplify, assume the following: no duplicate records appear, no two individuals have exactly the same name, all siblings have the same parents, all parents are married, there are no divorces, and no one remarries — truly a noteworthy collection of people living in an idyllic world! The violation of these assumptions would create serious problems that could not be ignored. However, their consideration would detract from our immediate aims.

The task is to input a sequence of these records and represent the collection in memory so that questions involving certain relationships among individuals may be answered. Examples of possible questions are

☐ How many children does John Smith have?
☐ Who are the uncles of John Smith?
☐ Who are the siblings of John Smith?

5.5.2 A First Solution

Perhaps the most straightforward approach to a solution for this information retrieval problem is to represent the collection of information by its image in memory as an array of records. To answer the question, "How many children does John Smith have?" requires a simple traversal of the records. Have a program look at the fathersname field in each record and, whenever it comes to JOHN SMITH, increment a counter that represents the number of John Smith's children. When the traversal is complete, the program would print the counter value. To answer the question, "Who are the uncles of John Smith?", first the program must traverse, looking at the name field of each record, to find JOHN SMITH. It would note the father's name, which is in the fathersname field of that record. Similarly, it finds JOHN SMITH's grandfather's name. Then it would traverse again, looking at the fathersname fields. Each time John Smith's grandfather's name appears, and "male" is listed as the corresponding sex field value, the program must print the name that appears in the corresponding name field. The same sequence would be repeated for John Smith's mother.

The execution time for these traversals can be proportional to the total number of records. This makes the solution time proportional to the amount of information represented in the system. For large systems, this would be impractical, as noted earlier.

What is the least amount of time that could be taken by *any* solution for these kinds of questions? Clearly, identifying the brothers of John Smith requires printing the names of the brothers. To display who the uncles of John Smith are, the program must print the names of each of his uncles. The least amount of time required for *any* solution would thus be proportional to the length of the answer to any given question. In the next section, you will see whether a different way of representing the information allows a solution that is closer in execution time to this length. This is much better than being proportional to the entire amount of information stored.

5.5.3 A Better Solution

To find answers to relationship questions quickly, you must be able to localize the search and get to the relevant records without considering *all* of them. You can, if you somehow link records together in a meaningful way. The problem deals with family relationships. Suppose you set up a record in memory to correspond to each individual name in the system, each record having seven fields, five of the fields containing pointer information. You will also have a table of names, called nametable. Figure 5.6 summarizes the form of the two kinds of records. Each record of the nametable will have a NAME and RECORDPTR field.

The seven fields of each individual's record will be NAMEPTR, FNAMEPTR, MNAMEPTR, SIBLINGPTR, CHILDRENLIST, SEX, and BIRTHDATE. No assumptions are made about the implementation of the nametable, but the individual records will be kept in storage separate from the nametable records.

The memory would appear as shown in Figure 5.7, after all information has been input. The CHILDRENLIST field of a record F contains a pointer to the first record on the list of children of the individual represented by F. The SIBLINGPTR

(a) Nametable Record

(b) Individual's Record

Figure 5.6 Format of the Nametable and Individual Records

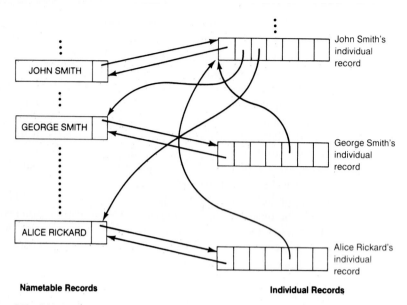

John Smith's individual record

George Smith's individual record

Alice Rickard's individual record

Nametable Records   **Individual Records**

Figure 5.7   Memory in the Family Relationships Problem

field plays the role of a link field for records on the list of siblings of *F*. The different lists are intertwined as shown in Figure 5.8.

Records *F* and *M* are assumed to be husband and wife, so their CHILDREN-LIST pointers are identical. It might be convenient to keep the lists of children in order by birthdate or to make them *circular*, so that the null pointer signifying the last record would instead point to the first record of the list.

If the assumptions about an "ideal" world were violated, it would be possible to have shared records, and even loops could appear; *with* those assumptions we see list-structures. The main list of any sublist consists of siblings. All records are complex, with sublist fields (CHILDRENLIST fields) pointing to sublists representing children of the individual represented by the complex record. Sublist sharing, however, does occur because the fathers and mothers share the lists of children.

5.5.4 Updating the System

How are the records and nametable created originally? Suppose you have already dealt with the first hundred records and that the situation in memory accurately reflects all the information they contain. You now attempt to input the next record, the one hundred first. If there is none, the information base in memory is complete. If it is not, the program should check the record for validity (input validation) and, if valid, the data representation in memory must be updated to reflect the new information. Then the program should read the next record and so on. Clearly an important component of the solution is an update module, which must function as follows.

It is possible that one or more of the three names in the name fields of the newly input record are already in the nametable, with individual records having been

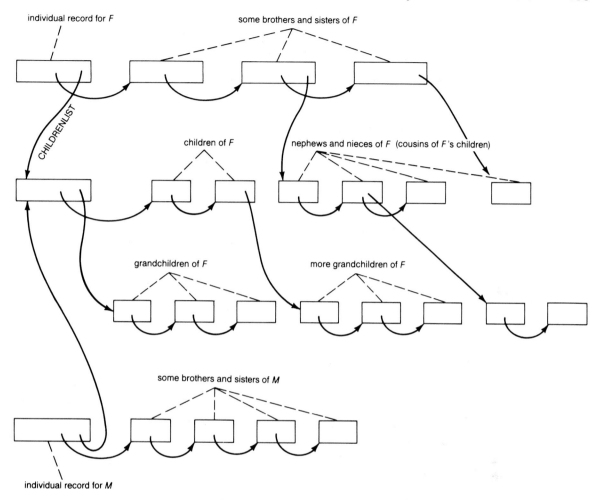

individual record for *F*

some brothers and sisters of *F*

CHILDRENLIST

children of *F*

nephews and nieces of *F* (cousins of *F*'s children)

grandchildren of *F*

more grandchildren of *F*

some brothers and sisters of *M*

individual record for *M*

Figure 5.8 Typical Configuration of Individual Records

created for them. For instance, the father's name might have been dealt with earlier when it appeared in the name field of another record. Assume first that each *distinct* name appearing in any field of the previously processed records has been entered into the nametable and has had an individual record created for it. Thus the nametable entry for each of these distinct names has the correct name in its name field, and a correct pointer in its RECORDPTR field to the corresponding individual record. This individual record also has a pointer in its name field back to the record in the nametable which it represents. Some fields of the individual record may not yet have been filled with appropriate information.

In general, we cannot assume that *any* name in the new input record has been seen before. Suppose JOHN SMITH is in the name field of the new record. Search the nametable to see if there is an entry for John Smith. If there is, remember where it is by placing a pointer to it in NTPTR and then copy the pointer in the RECORD-PTR field into a variable NPTR. Then NPTR reveals where the individual record is that corresponds to JOHN SMITH. If there is no entry, you know that there is not yet an individual record created for JOHN SMITH. Create such a record, and also create an entry in the nametable corresponding to it. Store John Smith's name and a pointer to his corresponding record in the RECORDPTR field of the nametable entry. Also place a copy of the pointer to this entry in the NAMEPTR field of the individual record. Then copy the pointer to the individual record into NPTR.

At this point, whether or not information on John Smith was already in the system, both an entry in the nametable and an individual record for him exists. The nametable record is completely filled in, and the individual record has its NAMEPTR field filled in. Also NPTR points to the individual record.

Suppose that four pointers are available and contain the following values:

FPTR
A pointer to the individual record representing John Smith's father
MPTR
A pointer to the individual record representing John Smith's mother
FTPTR
A pointer to the nametable entry for John Smith's father
MTPTR
A pointer to the nametable entry for John Smith's mother

How do we now complete the update properly? That is, which individual records and nametable entries must be modified and how are the modifications done?

Consider the individual record for John Smith. The sex and birthdate fields can easily be filled in, as well as the FNAMEPTR field, copying FTPTR into it. The same can be done for MNAMEPTR.

Now the individual record for the father of John Smith must be updated. Fill in the sex field (you know he is male). There is no additional information on his birthdate. (It may already be known. Why?) John Smith's record must be added to the list of children of his father. Assuming that the children are not kept in any special order, add his record at the front of the list. This requires copying the CHILDRENLIST pointer of his father's record into the SIBLINGPTR of John Smith's record, and then copying the pointer in NPTR into the CHILDRENLIST field of his father. This implies that whenever individual records are created, they must have their CHILDRENLIST and SIBLINGPTR fields set to null.

The mother's record can be treated similarly, except we may simply copy the father's CHILDRENLIST pointer (or NPTR) into her CHILDRENLIST field. This completes the update, which consisted of a search of the nametable, and the updating of pointers in nine fields after the nametable entries and individual records were created. These nine fields were

☐ FNAMEPTR, MNAMEPTR, SEX, BIRTHDATE, SIBLINGPTR—for the individual record of John Smith
☐ SEX, CHILDRENLIST—for the individual record of George Smith and Alice Rickard, the father and mother

**Example
5.11**   Suppose the input data so far consisted of the information shown in Table 5.1.

Table 5.1 Input Data for Example 5.11

NAME	SEX	BIRTHDATE	FATHERSNAME	MOTHERSNAME
ALBERT EINSTEIN	M	3/14/1879	HERMANN EINSTEIN	PAULINA KOCH
LEO TOLSTOY	M	9/9/1828	NIKOLAI TOLSTOY	MARIE VOLKRONSKII
GEORGE ELIOT	F	11/22/1819	ROBERT EVANS	CHRISTINA PEARSON
MARGARET TRUMAN	F	2/17/1924	HARRY TRUMAN	BESS TRUMAN
WILHELM BACH	M	11/22/1710	JOHANN S. BACH	MARIA BACH
JIMMY CARTER	M	10/1/1924	JAMES EARL CARTER	LILLIAN CARTER
SIR ISAAC NEWTON	M	12/25/1642	ISAAC NEWTON	HANNAH NEWTON
HARRY TRUMAN	M	5/8/1884	JOHN TRUMAN	MARTHA YOUNG
BILLY CARTER	M	3/29/1937	JAMES EARL CARTER	LILLIAN CARTER
JOHANN S. BACH	M	3/21/1685	JOHANN AMBROSIUS BACH	ELIZABETH LÄMMERHIRT
JOHANN GOTTFRIED BACH	M	5/11/1715	JOHANN S. BACH	MARIA BACH

For this example we use an array to hold the individual records, and an array for the nametable entries. □

The actual implementation of the nametable would be appropriately selected from the methods of Chapter 7. The individual records would be stored in the Pascal heap. The situation in memory will then be as shown in Table 5.2.

The next input is

| JOHN SMITH M 1/2/1579 GEORGE SMITH ALICE RICKARD

Since none of these names appears in the nametable, an entry in the nametable and an individual record must be created for each of the names.

After this has been done, the new nametable entries, individual records, and saved pointers will appear as shown in Figure 5.9(a). Updating the nine fields of the individual records yields the result shown in Figure 5.9(b).

The next input is

| CARL BACH M 3/8/1714 JOHANN S. BACH MARIA BACH

JOHANN S. BACH and MARIA BACH already appear in the nametable and have individual records. An entry in the nametable and an individual record must, however, be created for CARL BACH.

When this has been completed, the nametable entries, individual records, and saved pointers related to this input appear as in Figure 5.9(c).

Updating the nine fields of the individual records yields the result shown in Figure 5.9(d). The time required to complete an update is the constant time for the pointer manipulations plus the time to search the nametable.

The following is an algorithm for updating the information base given another input record.

Table 5.2 The NAMETABLE and Individual Records (for Example 5.11) after Initial Input Data Are Processed

NAMETABLE Records		Individual Records						
NAME	RECORDPTR	NAMEPTR	FNAMEPTR	MNAMEPTR	SIBLINGPTR	CHILDRENLIST	SEX	BIRTHDATE
1 ALBERT EINSTEIN	1	1	2	3	0	0	M	03141879
2 HERMANN EINSTEIN	2	2			0	1	M	
3 PAULINA KOCH	3	3			0	1	F	
4 LEO TOLSTOY	4	4	5	6	0	0	M	09091828
5 NIKOLAI TOLSTOY	5	5			0	4	M	
6 MARIE VOLKRONSKII	6	6			0	4	F	
7 GEORGE ELIOT	7	7	8	9	0	0	F	11221819
8 ROBERT EVANS	8	8			0	7	M	
9 CHRISTINA PEARSON	9	9			0	7	F	
10 MARGARET TRUMAN	10	10	11	12	0	0	F	02171924
11 HARRY TRUMAN	11	11			0	10	M	
12 BESS TRUMAN	12	12			0	10	F	
13 WILHELM BACH	13	13	14	15	0	0	M	11221710
14 JOHANN S. BACH	14	14	25	26	0	27	M	03211685
15 MARIA BACH	15	15			0	27	F	
16 JIMMY CARTER	16	16	17	18	0	0	M	10011924
17 JAMES EARL CARTER	17	17			0	16	M	
18 LILLIAN CARTER	18	18			0	16	F	
19 SIR ISAAC NEWTON	19	19	20	21	0	0	M	12251642
20 ISAAC NEWTON	20	20			0	19	M	
21 HANNAH NEWTON	21	21			0	19	F	
22 JOHN TRUMAN	22	22				11	M	
23 MARTHA YOUNG	23	23				11	F	
24 BILLY CARTER	24	24	17	18		0	M	03291937
25 JOHANN AMBROSIUS BACH	25	25			16	14	M	
26 ELIZABETH LÄMMERHIRT	26	26			0	14	F	
27 JOHANN GOTTFRIED BACH	27	27	14	15	13	0	M	05111715

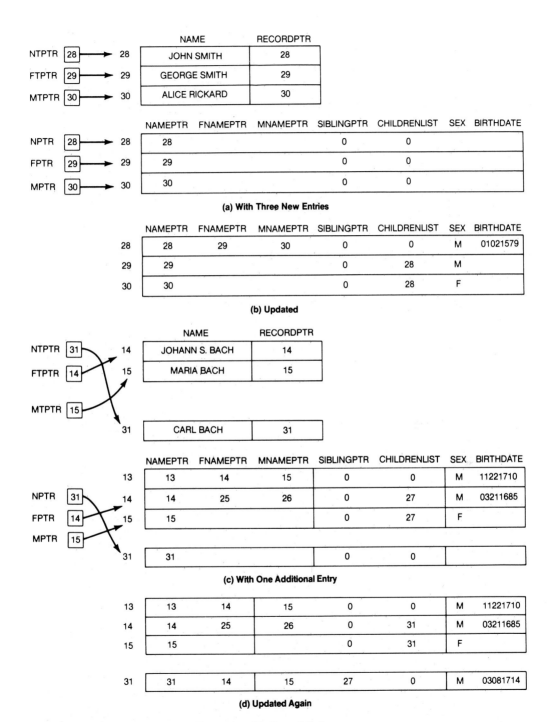

Figure 5.9 Nametable and Individual Records with Saved Pointers

1. Search the NAMETABLE.
   a. Create entries in the NAMETABLE and create individual records for any of the three input names not present in NAMETABLE.
   b. Set their RECORDPTR and NAMEPTR fields.
   c. Set their CHILDRENLIST and SIBLINGPTR fields to null.
   d. Set NTPTR, FTPTR, MTPTR, NPTR, FPTR, and MPTR.
2. Update the following fields of the individual record pointed to by NPTR:
   SEX to input sex
   BIRTHDATE to input birthdate
   FNAMEPTR to FTPTR
   MNAMEPTR to MTPTR
3. Update:
   SEX.FPTR (the sex field of the record pointed to by FPTR) to *M*
   SIBLINGPTR.NPTR to CHILDRENLIST.FPTR
   CHILDRENLIST.FPTR to NPTR
   SEX.MPTR to *F*
   CHILDRENLIST.MPTR to NPTR

5.5.5 Retrieving Information from the System

Now that we have built the system, how do we answer questions about family relationships?

Example 5.12   How do we determine who are the children of John Smith? Search the nametable for JOHN SMITH. If the name is not there, print an appropriate message. If it is there, follow the pointer to John Smith's individual record. Traverse his list of children and count the number of records on it, or output the individual names. In any case, ignoring the search of nametable, the time required is proportional to the length of the answer — that is, it is proportional to the number of children of John Smith. □

Example 5.13   How do we find all the uncles of John Smith? Search the nametable, and follow its pointer to the record for John Smith. Then, follow the FNAMEPTR pointer to the entry in the nametable for his father and follow its RECORDPTR back to the father's record. Do this again for the father to get to the grandfather's record. Repeat the procedure for the mother. □

Simply following the sibling pointer of the father's record doesn't work, because the traversal may have begun in the middle of this sibling list. To ensure starting at the beginning of the sibling list, it is best to use the children's list of the grandfather's record. If the sibling lists were circular, this would not be necessary; it would suffice to traverse the grandfather's list of children (John Smith's father's siblings), and output the name of each male. The same processing must be done for John Smith's mother, to output all his uncles on his mother's side.

The total time, again ignoring the nametable search, is proportional to the answer, the number of uncles. Excluding the nametable search, this is certainly close to the minimal time that would be desirable. You will see in the chapter on searching and sorting how long it would take to search the nametable!

5.5.6 Other System Components

To complete design of the system, in addition to the nametable implementation and search module, components are needed for deletion of records. We will not pursue this topic here, but clearly the issues of storage reclamation and allocation would have to be considered.

There are some more basic unresolved problems. Exactly how are questions asked of the system?

One way is for anyone wanting answers to questions to bring them to the system's designers. The designers then write programs to output the solutions. This is feasible in certain situations, and in fact, many organizations do information retrieval in this way. A related solution would be to give the data representation to questioners and have them write their own programs.

Instead, a simple "menu," or list, of questions that might be asked could be designed. Users could then "check off" their questions, and previously written programs could be run to answer them. This solution proves satisfactory as long as the questions people want answered are on the menu.

A more sophisticated scheme would be to design a general query language. Questioners could then ask their questions in this language. A built-in language translator would interpret the question and automatically produce a program to print the answer. Achieving this solution might challenge the state of the art at the present time.

The issue of security has been ignored. It would be of major concern in any retrieval system. User access to, and ability to modify, specific information would have to be limited.

This simplified case study illustrates the use of the basic concepts this book has stressed so far. These include the top-down approach, data abstraction, modularization, traversal of list-structures, the use of pointers, and the selection of appropriate data structures to achieve clear, concise, and efficient programs.

☐ Exercises

1. a. Draw a picture, like that of Figure 5.1(b), corresponding to Example 5.2 for an actual configuration of hands for the game of poker with four players.

2. Draw pictures, similar to P of Figure 5.1(d), for the polynomials

$$z^2(y^2(x(8))) + z(y(3x)) + y(x) + 18 \quad \text{and} \quad x^3yz + 2xz + y^2xz^3$$

3. Give a recursive definition for a chain.

4. Why do the two definitions of list-structures not allow more than one pointer to a record, or loops, to occur in a list-structure?

5. Why does a null PTR and an empty stack indicate the end of the traversal of a list-structure?

6. What will be in the stack when record 20 of FORMULA (Figure 5.4) is accessed?

7. Simulate the execution of the iterative implementation of TRAVERSE on P of Figure 5.1(d).

8. Simulate the execution of the recursive implementation of TRAVERSE on P of Figure 5.1(d).

9. Give an example of a list containing loops for which the traversal procedures fail because they do not terminate.

10. a. Write a PROCESS module to turn the iterative traversal into a program that prints the number of sublists of a list-structure.

   b. Will your solution also work for the recursive traversal?

11. a. Write a procedure to return a pointer to the record of a list-structure which has the maximum information field value.

   b. Modify your solution to return a pointer to a list. The list should contain pointers to *all* records whose information field value coincides with the maximum value.

12. Give an algorithm to determine whether two list-structures whose records have the same format are identical.

13. Modify your solution to Exercise 12 so that the algorithm determines whether the two list-structures have the same "structure," independent of the information values stored.

14. Each complex record of a list-structure has a field pointing to the record's sublist. The sublist is composed of a main list (composed of the chain of records linked by their link fields). Suppose each complex record of a list-structure also has a field called NUMBER that contains the number of records on the complex records sublist. Write a PROCESS module to turn the traverse procedures into programs to insert a record after the record whose information field value is VALUE. The program must, of course, also correctly update the number field for the appropriate sublist.

15. Write a procedure to implement EVALUATE (Example 5.9).

16. Modify your solution to Exercise 15 so it outputs the evaluation of each operation as it occurs.

17. Modify your solution to Exercise 16 so that it prints out an appropriate message, such as "too many operands for operator PS of the sublist of record 7" or "missing operands for the operator PS of the sublist of record 7," whenever the list-structure does not represent a valid arithmetic expression.

18. Assume that P points to a record of Example 5.9 containing an operator or operand. Suppose PTR points to a record of a sublist after which the record pointed to by P is to be inserted. It is to be inserted as the first record of a sublist if it is an operator, and as the next record on the sublist if it is an operand. Write an INSERTION procedure to accomplish this. For example, suppose the list-structure, LS, is currently:

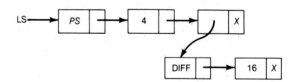

If PTR points to DIFF, and the record pointed to by P contains PS, then after insertion LS will be

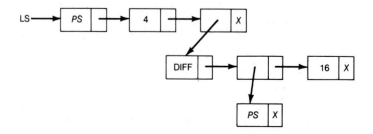

If the record pointed to by P contained 432.713, then after insertion LS would have been

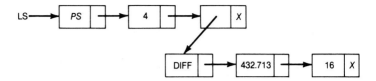

19. Insertion and deletion of records in list-structures is similar to their insertion and deletion in chains. However, the deletion of a *sublist* has ramifications for the RECLAIM procedure of Chapter 3. Discuss these, and explain how they might be resolved by modifying the definition of RECLAIM or by increasing the responsibility of the programmer. In either case, the idea is to be sure all unused records are returned to AVAILIST.

20. Modify PARAGRAPHINSERT (Example 5.8) so that *all* deleted records are returned to the AVAILIST.

21. Let PTR and PV point, respectively, to a record of a list-structure and to its preceding record. Write a procedure to delete the record pointed to by PTR if it is simple, and to replace it with the list-structure to which it points if it is complex. For example, consider the following list-structure.

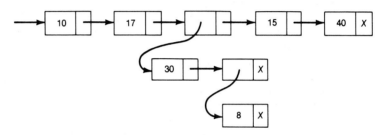

If PTR points to "17," then the procedure produces

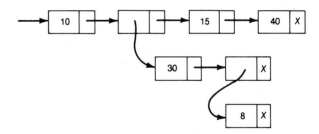

If PTR points to the complex record following "17," then the procedure produces

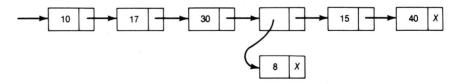

22. Give an implementation of NEXT and SUBLIST of the procedure TRAVERSE (Section 5.2.1) for each declaration of the polynomial *P*.

23. Give a declaration for the records of Example 5.8 using the Pascal heap, and write implementations for all the modules of TRAVERSE and PROCESS that depend on this implementation.

24. Draw a picture, corresponding to Table 5.2, for the complete input data (31 names) of Example 5.11.

25. Modify the answer to Exercise 24 to reflect the lists of children being kept as circular lists.

26. Show the complete situation in the arrays of your solution to Exercise 24 after the input below is processed.

JOHANN AMBROSIUS BACH M 2/22/1695   CHRISTOPH BACH   MARIA MAGDALENA GRABLER

27. Show the complete situation after the input of Exercise 26 is processed, when circular lists are used for the lists of children.

28. Suppose the records of Example 5.11 were to be kept in alphabetical order by the name in the name field. What would the arrays look like after all the input data were processed?

29. How does the algorithm for updating the information base given another input record (p. 204) have to be modified if inputs are allowed for which one or more field values are unknown?

30. Write two procedures for Example 5.11, CHILDREN(PERSON) and BROTHERS (PERSON). They should print out, respectively, the names of all children and all brothers of PERSON. Simulate the behavior of the procedures on the data of the example.

31. Modify your solutions to Exercise 30 so the procedures will work on circular lists of children.

32. Suppose the nametable is implemented as a list. How will your solutions to Exercises 30 and 31 be modified?

33. Write an algorithm to print out the names of the individuals who were born before 1900. How much time will your algorithm take?

34. Can you find a way to implement the information system so that a faster solution can be obtained for Exercise 33? If you find a faster solution, then determine how its update time will compare to that for Exercise 33.

35. Write a detailed description for a routine that will delete an individual record and its nametable entry from the system. This implies that all relevant pointers will be properly modified and storage will be reclaimed.

□ Suggested Assignment

Consider the following list-structure for a book. BOOK might represent the current structure of a textbook. Suppose we want to print this information as a table of contents. It would appear as follows:

```
CHAPTER 1
        1.1 ARRAYS
        1.2 RECORDS
            1.2.1 POINTERS
            1.2.2 EXAMPLE
        1.3 SUMMARY
CHAPTER 2
        2.1 LISTS
        2.2 USES
```

CHAPTER 3
   3.1 APPLICATIONS
      3.1.1 BACKGROUND
      3.1.2 RANKINGS
         3.1.2.1 FLOWCHART

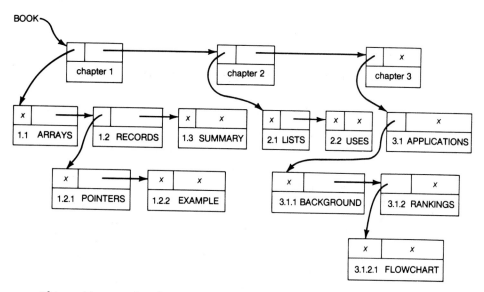

This problem can be abstracted to the printing out of a "picture" of a list-structure. Assume all records are declared as

```
type
    kind        = (smpl, cmplx)
    listpointer = ↑listrecord;
    listrecord  = record
                      info : whatever;
                      recordtype : kind;
                      link, sublist : listpointer
                  end;
```

Write a procedure PRINTLIST that will print out a "picture" of the list-structure pointed to by LS. Consider, for example, the list-structure ACCOUNTS of Section 5.1. The list-structure is

```
INFO          = 175
RECORDTYPE = COMPLEX
            INFO          = 0
            RECORDTYPE = COMPLEX
                        INFO          =  100
                        RECORDTYPE = SIMPLE
            INFO          = 75
            RECORDTYPE = SIMPLE
INFO          = 450
```

```
RECORDTYPE = COMPLEX
          INFO        = 200
          RECORDTYPE = COMPLEX
          INFO        = 250
          RECORDTYPE = SIMPLE
INFO           = −46
RECORDTYPE = SIMPLE
```

Your program should read in and echo print three list-structures. One should be null. It should then call on PRINTLIST to print out the "picture" for each of the three list-structures. The input data for ACCOUNTS might be

1		indicates a nonnull list-structure, 0 would indicate a null list structure.
175	CMPLX	
1	1	indicates the link and sublist fields of "175" are not null.
0	CMPLX	
1	1	
100	SMPL	
0		indicates the link field of "100" is null, it is thus the last record of a sublist.
75	SMPL	
0		
450	CMPLX	
1	1	
200	CMPLX	
1	0	indicates the link field of "200" is not null but its sublist field is null.
250	SMPL	
0		
−46	SMPL	
0		

Notice that the input is given in traversal order.

The PRINTLIST module is to have almost *exactly* the same detailed refinement as either the iterative TRAVERSE (Section 5.2.1) or the recursive TRAVERSE (Section 5.2.2). You must write the proper PROCESS routine, say PROCESS2, to turn TRAVERSE into PRINTLIST. You may add parameters to PROCESS2 if necessary.

For extra credit, do the reading in and echo printing of the three list-structures in the program by calling a procedure READECHOPRINT. It must also be obtained by writing the proper PROCESS routine, say PROCESS1, to turn TRAVERSE into a procedure for READECHOPRINT.

Of course it will be necessary for you also to write the stack operation routines SETSTACK, PUSH, POP, and EMPTY, as well as NEXT, SUBLIST, and COMPLEX.

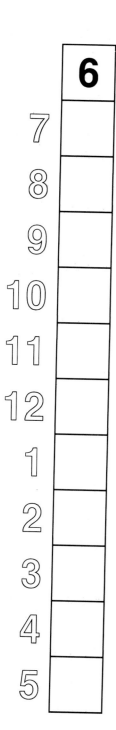

6 Trees

6.1 Branching Out

All data structures provide a way to organize data. Different structures serve different purposes. More complex lists, as shown by the information retrieval case study in the preceding chapter (Section 5.5), can result in considerable intertwining and sharing of lists and data. Everyone is familiar with the concept of a family tree. In fact, a nice exercise would be to print the family tree for an individual whose family history is stored in the data base of that case study. The family tree is actually embedded within the lists containing the family history. Trees may be viewed as a special case of lists in which no intertwining or sharing takes place. They deserve study in their own right because they are the basis for structures and operations used in all aspects of programming, from the structure of programs for compilers, to work in information retrieval and artificial intelligence. Trees are ubiquitous; they seem to sprout everywhere — even in the field of computer science!

Formally *trees* are collections of nodes. Trees derive both their appearance and their name from the lines, known as *branches*, that connect the nodes. Understanding how to represent trees, and how to perform certain operations on them, opens the door to an appreciation of many elegant algorithms and useful techniques in computer science.

Trees play a significant role in the organization of data for efficient information retrieval and are ideal candidates for fast searches, insertions, deletions, and sequential access. Efficiency and speed are possible because trees "spread out" the data they store so that different paths in the tree lead quickly to the relevant data. They are also convenient for conceptualizing algorithms.

Many problems can be solved by imagining all the possible answers represented as a tree. The algorithm or program is then viewed as a traversal through the tree, and a general procedure for such a traversal is adapted and taken as the basis for the program. This often results in easily created and efficient programs. In such cases the tree itself serves as a conceptual aid and need not actually be "grown" or stored in memory. Nevertheless, it provides the framework for obtaining the algorithm.

The mathematics of trees has always been of interest and is discussed quite thoroughly by Knuth [1973a]. In this chapter we consider fundamentals and introduce special trees as they are needed in subsequent chapters.

As indicated in Figure 6.1, there are many ways to depict inclusion or hierarchical relationships. Each figure part conveys the same information about the relations between objects A to J. Figure 6.1(a) uses indentation reminiscent of program structure, or Pascal and COBOL record structure, to convey inclusion. Figure 6.1(b) uses nested blocks or sets, while Figure 6.1(c) has nested parentheses. The last, Figure 6.1(d), uses lines that branch out like a tree turned upside down. This is how the data structure that is the topic of this chapter, the tree, is depicted.

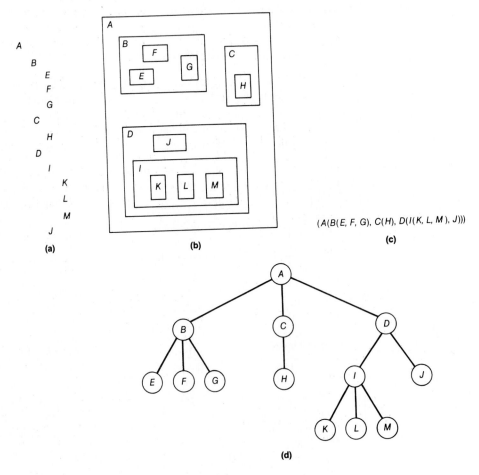

Figure 6.1   Capturing Inclusion Relationships

If Figure 6.1(a) represents the structure of a Pascal record, then only inclusion information is important; the data structure shows that record A includes three fields, B, C, and D, or that D includes two subfields I and J. If, instead, Figure 6.1(a) represents the structure of a whole Pascal program, then more information is needed. It is important that B come before C and that C precede D. When such ordering information is needed, we use **ordered trees**.

Much of the terminology for the tree data structure is taken from common botanical description and so is familiar and colorful. For instance, A of the tree in Figure 6.1(d) is at the **root** of the tree. The tree consists of three **subtrees**, whose roots contain B, C, and D. The entries in the tree, A to J, are each stored at a **node** of the tree, connected by lines called **branches**. The tree is **ordered** if each node has a specified first, second, or nth subtree. The order itself may be specified in many ways. In this example, the order is specified by taking the subtrees in alphabetic order determined by their root entries. Rearranging the order of the subtrees in Figure 6.1(d) results in the same tree but not the same ordered tree if we assume the ordering is specified for each node from left to right by the way the tree is pictured. A distinction will be made between *ordered trees* and *trees* throughout this text. Keep in mind that these terms refer to two distinct kinds of structures.

Besides these two kinds of trees, there are binary trees. A **binary tree** is either

- ☐ The null binary tree, or
- ☐ A root node and its left and right subtrees, which are themselves binary trees with no common nodes

This recursive definition emphasizes the fact that binary trees with at least one node are composed of a root and two other binary trees, called, respectively, the left and right subtrees. These subtrees, in turn, have the same structure. All binary trees consist of nodes, except for the null binary tree, which has no nodes. The null binary tree, just like the null list, cannot be "drawn." Both are used to make definitions more uniform and easier, and both represent the smallest data structure of their kind. There is exactly one binary tree with one node (its root); this tree has null left and right subtrees. Figure 6.2 pictures a binary tree. The two binary trees with exactly two nodes are pictured as in Figure 6.3.

The lines used to indicate a left and right subtree are called *branches*. In Figure 6.2 the branches are used in the same way to show the relationship between nodes and their subtrees. The nodes are numbered 1 to 20 for easy reference. Node 5 has a **predecessor** (node 2), a **left successor** (node 10), and a **right successor** (node 11). Every node has at most two successors, and every node, except the node labeled *root*, has exactly one predecessor. Predecessors are also known as "parents," successors can be called "children," and nodes with the same parent are (what else?): siblings. As far as is known, trees do not exhibit sibling rivalry.

Notice that starting from any node in the tree there is exactly one path from the node back to the root. This path is traveled by following the sequence of predecessors of the original node until the root is reached. For node 18, the sequence of predecessors is 9, 4, 2, and 1. There is, of course, exactly one path from the root to any node.

Follow the branch from node 1 to node 2 or 3 and you come to the left or right subtree of node 1 (Figure 6.4). Similarly, each node has a left and a right subtree. All nodes with at least one successor are called **internal** nodes. Those with no successors

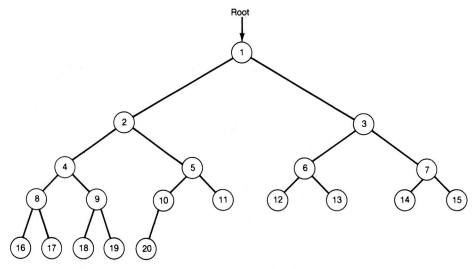

Figure 6.2   A Binary Tree

are called *terminal* nodes (also known as "external" nodes or "leaf" nodes). The left and right subtrees of a terminal node are always null binary trees.

By definition, the root of a binary tree is at *depth* 1. A node whose path to the root contains exactly $d - 1$ predecessor nodes has depth d. For example, node 10 is at depth 4. This is the *path length* of the node. The longest path length is called the *depth of the binary tree*; it is 5 for the tree of Figure 6.2. For many applications it is the depth of a binary tree, like the depth of a list-structure, that determines the required storage and execution time.

Suppose your program must count the number of occurrences of each character appearing in an input sequence of characters. This is easy. Store the count for each character of the allowed character set in an array indexed by the character set and increment the appropriate entry by 1 for each input character. Note that the efficiency of this solution derives from the selection operation for an entry, which is supported by the array data structure.

What if words, rather than characters, are to be counted? Sufficient storage is not available for an array to store counts for all possible words, even if these words could be agreed upon. What is required is a data structure that can be dynamically extended to accommodate each new word and its count as the word is encountered

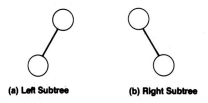

(a) Left Subtree   (b) Right Subtree

Figure 6.3   Two Two-Node Binary Trees

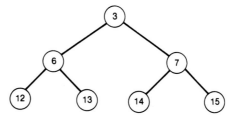

Figure 6.4   The Right Subtree of the Root of Figure 6.2

in the input. This data structure must be searched to see if the next word already appears; if it does, the count is increased by 1. Should the word not appear, it must be inserted with its count set to 1. A special tree, a binary search tree introduced in Chapter 7, is convenient to use for this data structure. This tree allows the search for a word to consider only nodes along a particular path. At worst, this path must be followed from the root to a terminal node. Thus the longest search time will be determined by the depth of the tree. The same data structure and the depth measure are important for the related problem, "Produce an index for a book." Now, instead of storing word counts, the position of each occurrence of a word must be retained. Do you see the possibility of storing dictionaries of modest size in binary search trees?

Binary trees need not have such a compact look as that of Figure 6.2 but can appear sparse, as in Figure 6.5. A compact binary tree like Figure 6.2 is called a *complete* binary tree. To be more precise, a binary tree of depth d is a ***complete*** binary tree when it has terminal nodes only at the two greatest depths, any nodes at the greatest depth occur to the left, and any nodes at depth less than $d - 1$ have two successors. In Figure 6.2, nodes 16 to 20 are the nodes at greatest depth; they occur to the left. The sparse tree has the same number of nodes but twice its depth.

6.1.1 Depth versus Capacity

Let us take a moment here to derive two important relations between the depth, d, and the number of nodes, N, in a binary tree.* First note that in any binary tree there is at most one node at depth 1, at most two nodes at depth 2, and, in general, at most 2^{k-1} nodes at depth k, since a node can give rise to at most two nodes at the next depth. The total number of nodes, N, is then at most $1 + 2^1 + 2^2 + \cdots + 2^{d-1}$. This sum is $2^d - 1$. So

$$N \le 2^d - 1$$

The minimum possible depth, d_{min}, for a binary tree with N nodes will be given by

$$d_{min} = \lceil \lg (N + 1) \rceil$$

where $\lceil x \rceil$ indicates the smallest integer that equals or exceeds x. If $N = 20$ then $d_{min} = \lceil \lg 21 \rceil = \lceil 4.39 \rceil = 5$, and if $N = 31$ then $d_{min} = \lceil \lg 32 \rceil = 5$. The binary tree corresponding to d_{min} may always be taken as a *complete* binary tree. Consequently,

---

*This section can be omitted on a first reading.

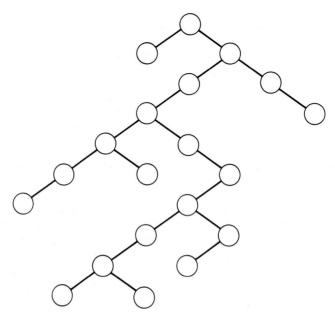

Figure 6.5   A Sparse Binary Tree

the depth of a complete binary tree will never exceed $(\lg N) + 1$. This contrasts sharply with the depth of the sparsest binary tree with N nodes, which is N. For instance, if N is 1,000, the complete binary tree has a depth of only 10 while the sparsest has depth 1,000. This has important implications for information retrieval, as shown in the next chapter.

6.2 Trees of Records

Nodes of binary trees may be used to store information. For example, the nametable of Section 5.5 could be implemented by storing each of its records at a node of a binary tree. Just as lists are referred to by name, the tree can be named, say NAMETABLE. Obviously, NAMETABLE must have records inserted into it, deleted from it, and records searched for in it. Insertion, deletion, search, and traversal are the basic tree operations.

Balanced trees, binary search trees, and heaps (the latter are discussed in the next chapter) are all binary trees with special properties that make them useful for storage of information. The properties that make them useful enable efficient searching, inserting, and deleting. Each of these types of binary tree requires its own algorithms for these operations in order to take advantage of or to preserve their characteristics. For now, to get the flavor of these operations, consider some simple examples.

6.2.1 Insertion and Deletion of Records in Binary Trees

Assume that each node of a binary tree is represented by a record containing an information field, a left pointer field, and a right pointer field. The notation NODE.P stands for the node or record pointed to by the variable P.

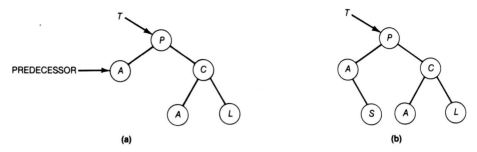

(a)   (b)

Figure 6.6 A Binary Tree *T* before and after the Insertion of *S*

To accomplish an insertion, storage must first be allocated for a new record, then its fields must be set correctly, and finally the proper pointer adjustments must be made in the tree to the predecessor of the new entry. Consider Figure 6.6, which shows a binary tree *T* before and after the insertion of a new entry *S*, which replaces PREDECESSOR *A*'s null right subtree. The information field entry of the new record is assumed to reside in VALUE; that is, *S* is stored in VALUE. Thus the new record must have its information field set to VALUE and its left and right pointer fields set to null. The predecessor's right pointer field must be set to point to the new record. This is accomplished by

```
AVAIL(P);
SETINFO(P, VALUE);
SETLEFT(P, NULL);
SETRIGHT(P, NULL);
SETRIGHT(PREDECESSOR, P);
```

SETINFO, SETLEFT, and SETRIGHT copy the contents of their second parameter into the proper field of the record pointed to by their first parameter. These modules reflect the binary tree's implementation details. The code itself is independent of the implementation.

If a new record is to replace a nonnull subtree (say, if *S* were to replace *C* in *T*), then the new record's left and right pointer fields would have to be adjusted accordingly. Furthermore, the storage for the replaced record might be reclaimable and, if so, care is required to do this before the pointer to it in its predecessor's left or right field is lost. The code below does this correctly assuming PREDECESSOR points to a record whose nonnull right subtree is to be replaced.

```
Q := RIGHT(PREDECESSOR);
AVAIL(P);
SETINFO(P, VALUE);
SETLEFT(P, LEFT(Q));
SETRIGHT(P, RIGHT(Q));
SETRIGHT(PREDECESSOR, P);
RECLAIM(Q);
```

RIGHT returns a copy of the right pointer field value of the record pointed to by its parameter. This code is for illustrative purposes. If the record is really reclaimable, it would be more efficient simply to replace its INFO field by the new INFO value. The statement SETINFO(Q, VALUE) would suffice. However, if the released and new records are two variants with different lengths, then code similar to this would be needed.

The deletion of a terminal node pointed to by P, whose predecessor is pointed to by PREDECESSOR, may be accomplished by

```
if LEFT(PREDECESSOR) = P then
    SETLEFT(PREDECESSOR, NULL)
else
    SETRIGHT(PREDECESSOR, NULL);
```

LEFT is analogous to RIGHT. The decision is required in order to know whether it is PREDECESSOR'S left or right successor that is to be deleted. Again, if the deleted node's storage may be reclaimed, RECLAIM must be invoked before the pointer to it is lost. Deletion of an internal node must take into account what is to be done with the node's subtrees.

The wary reader may have qualms about the code developed for insertion and deletion. *Remember:* special cases must always be checked. When insertion or deletion occurs at the root node, indicated by a null value in PREDECESSOR, it is the name of the tree whose pointer must be adjusted. The illustrative code fails in this case. You should modify the program segments so they also account for this special case.

6.2.2 Climbing Binary Trees

A traversal through the records stored in a binary tree is frequently the basis for a required algorithm just as it is in arrays and lists. Consider three distinct ways to traverse a binary tree: (1) preorder, (2) inorder, and (3) postorder.

Pre-, in-, and postorder traversals are often referred to mnemonically as root-left-right, left-root-right, and left-right-root traversals. The *pre, in,* and *post* prefixes refer to whether the root is accessed prior to, in between, or after the corresponding traversals of the left and right subtrees. In each case, the left subtree is traversed before the right subtree. When nodes are listed in the order in which they are processed, all nodes in the left subtree appear before all nodes in the right subtree no matter which traversal is used, but the type of traversal determines where the root appears. Because binary trees were defined recursively, it is convenient to give recursive definitions for these traversals.

To *preorder traverse a binary tree:*

if the binary tree is not the null binary tree, then
  1. access and process its root,
  2. traverse its left subtree in preorder,
  3. traverse its right subtree in preorder.

To *inorder traverse a binary tree:*

if the binary tree is not the null binary tree, then
  1. traverse its left subtree in inorder,

2. access and process its root, and
3. traverse its right subtree in inorder.

To ***postorder traverse a binary tree:***

if the binary tree is not the null binary tree, then
1. traverse its left subtree in postorder,
2. traverse its right subtree in postorder, and
3. access and process its root.

Let's apply these definitions to Figure 6.6(b).

To do a preorder traversal of T, since it is not null, requires that its root, P, be accessed and processed first. Next, the left subtree of T must be preorder traversed. Applying the definition to it, its root, A, is accessed and processed. Since A's left subtree is null, its right subtree is traversed next in preorder. This results in S being accessed and processed, terminating the preorder traversal of A's right subtree and also of T's left subtree. Completing T's traversal requires a preorder traversal of its right subtree, resulting in C, A, and L being accessed and processed in turn.

An inorder traversal of T requires its left subtree to be inorder traversed first. Applying the definition to this left subtree requires its null left subtree to be inorder traversed (note how easy that is), its root A to be accessed and processed next, and then its right subtree to be inorder traversed, which results in S being accessed and processed. This terminates the inorder traversal of T's left subtree. T's root, P, must then be accessed and processed, followed by an inorder traversal of T's right subtree. This causes A, C, and L to be accessed and processed in turn, completing the inorder traversal of T.

Try applying the postorder traversal definition to T yourself. The sequences below represent the order in which the records stored at the nodes of T are accessed and processed for each of the traversals.

PASCAL   preorder
ASPACL   inorder
SAALCP   postorder

Notice that the terminal nodes S, A, and L are dealt with in the same order for all three traversals. This is not just a coincidence but will always happen.

The trees of Figure 6.7 have natural interpretations as a table of contents, an arithmetic expression, and a program that invokes procedures that, in turn, invoke other procedures. Traversing these trees, respectively, in pre-, in-, and postorder results in the order of access to nodes shown in Figure 6.7(d–f). Each represents a natural application for one of the three traversals: a listing of the table of contents, an arithmetic expression in the usual notation, and a listing of the order in which the procedures may be written so that those procedures needed to test the one currently being written are already available.

Not all data structures need to be traversed. For example, stacks, queues, heaps, and the hash tables to be introduced in Chapter 7 are not normally traversed. Just as applications of arrays and, even more so, lists often reduce to traversals, applications of binary trees often do as well. Therefore procedures for their traversal merit study.

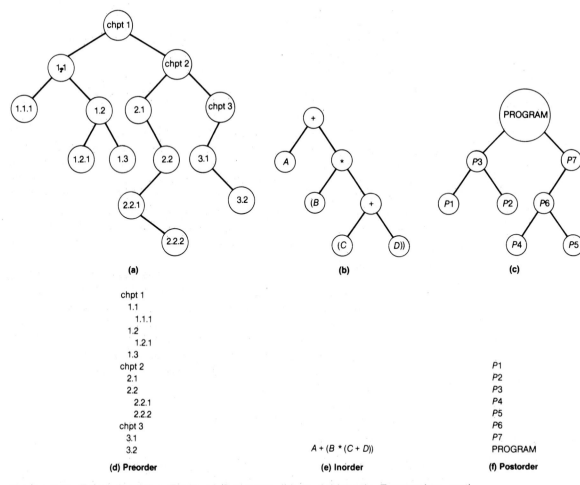

(a)

(b)

(c)

(d) Preorder

$A + (B * (C + D))$

(e) Inorder

P1
P2
P3
P4
P5
P6
P7
PROGRAM

(f) Postorder

Figure 6.7 Trees for (a) a Table of Contents, (b) an Arithmetic Expression, and (c) Components of a Program. Order of Access to Nodes is (d) for Preorder Traversal of (a), (e) for Inorder Traversal of (b), and (f) for Postorder Traversal of (c).

6.2.3 Three Preorder Traversals of a Binary Tree

It is easy to write a recursive procedure based on the recursive definition for preorder traversal (the same is true for the other inorder and postorder traversal).

```
procedure PREORDER(var TREE : binarytree);
var
    L, R, NULL : binarytree;
begin
    SETNULL(NULL);
    if TREE <> NULL then
    begin
```

```
        PROCESS(TREE);
        L := LEFT(TREE);
        PREORDER(L);
        R := RIGHT(TREE);
        PREORDER(R)
    end
end;
```

To develop an iterative procedure (for contrast with the recursive one or if the programming language you are using is not recursive), recall that the application of the definition of preorder traversal to Figure 6.6(b) required keeping track of the left subtree about to be traversed and remembering at which node to resume when that left subtree traversal terminated. Put another way, it was necessary to suspend the current traversal, incurring its completion as a postponed obligation, and begin a traversal of the proper left subtree. These postponed obligations must be recalled in order opposite to the order in which they were incurred. Obviously the stack is called for here. It seems to pop up everywhere.

Let P point to the root of the subtree about to be traversed. After the processing of NODE.P, a pointer to its right subtree can be pushed onto the stack before traversal of its left subtree. At the time that NODE.P's right subtree is to be processed (when its left subtree traversal terminates), the stack will contain pointers to all right subtrees whose traversals have been postponed (right subtrees of nodes already accessed), but the top stack entry will point to NODE.P's right subtree. Thus popping the stack and setting P to the popped value correctly updates P to point to the correct next record to be accessed.

```
procedure PREORDER(var TREE : binarytree);
var
    P; NULL : binarytree;
    S : stack;
begin
    SETNULL(NULL);
    SETSTACK(S);
    P := TREE;
    while ((P <> NULL) or not EMPTY(S)) do
        if P <> NULL then
            begin
                PROCESS(TREE, P);
                PUSH(RIGHT(P), S);
                P := LEFT(P)
            end
        else
            POP(S, P)
end;
```

The **while** loop condition is true whenever the traversal is not yet completed. A nonnull P means that a record is pointed to by P and is the next one to be accessed and processed. A null P value means no record is pointed to by P and some left subtree traversal must have just been completed. If the stack is not empty, then more needs to be done; but if it is empty, then no right subtrees remain to be traversed and the traversal is done.

The recursive procedure reflects the structure of binary trees and emphasizes that they are made up of a root with binary trees as subtrees. In order to develop the nonrecursive version, it is necessary to think of the binary tree as a collection of records. Writing the procedure then involves arranging for the correct next record to be accessed and processed within the while loop. This is a general strategy for attempting to find nonrecursive solutions. The recursive version deals with the special cases and the substructures of a recursive definition, while the nonrecursive version requires that the structure be viewed as a collection of its parts with each part treated appropriately and in the correct order. It's no wonder recursive versions are clearer.

An alternative nonrecursive procedure is based on saving on the stack the path from the root to the predecessor of the node currently being processed. This is useful, for instance, if the processing of a node requires accessing its predecessor node. This alternative will, at the time the node is processed, guarantee that its predecessor is at the top of the stack. However, the algorithm now requires some searching to find the proper right subtree to traverse next when a subtree traversal has terminated (indicated by P being null). Figure 6.8 shows a typical situation when such a termination has occurred. P is null, having been set to the null right pointer value of node 10 after node 10's left subtree has been traversed. Looking back along the path from node 10 to the root, it is not difficult to see that node 5's right subtree is where the traversal must resume. More generally, this path back must be followed until the present path node (node 6 in this example) is the left successor of its predecessor. P must then be set to the right subtree of that node and the traversal resumed. If no such node is found, the entire tree has been traversed. This is accomplished by the following procedure for nonrecursive preorder traversal saving the path to root on the stack. ITEM is assumed to return a copy of the top stack pointer without disturbing the stack.

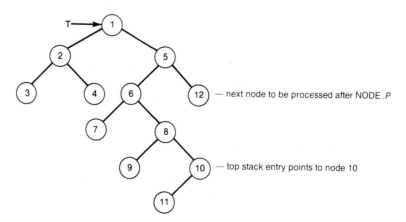

Figure 6.8 Node 5's Left Subtree Has Just Been Traversed.

```
procedure PREORDER(var TREE : binarytree);
var
    NULL, P, Q, RIGHTPOINTER : binarytree;
    S : stack;
begin
    SETNULL(NULL);
    SETSTACK(S);
    P := TREE;
    while ((P <> NULL) or not EMPTY(S)) do
        if P <> NULL then
            begin
                PROCESS(TREE; P);
                if LEFT(P) <> NULL then
                    begin
                        PROCESS(TREE : P);
                        if LEFT(P) <> NULL then
                    end
                else
                    begin
                        PUSH(P, S);
                        P := RIGHT(P)
                    end
            end
        else
            begin
                repeat
                    POP(S, Q);
                    if not EMPTY(S) then
                        RIGHTPOINTER := RIGHT(ITEM(S))
                    else
                        RIGHTPOINTER := NULL
                until (EMPTY(S) or (Q <> RIGHTPOINTER));
                if Q <> RIGHTPOINTER then
                    P := RIGHTPOINTER
            end
end;
```

Each of the three traversal procedures can be easily modified when a partial traversal is required, by including a variable DONE to signal termination just as for the list traversals. You should write similar procedures for the inorder and postorder traversals.

6.3 Using the Traverse Procedures for Binary Trees

In this section a number of examples are presented to show how to apply the traverse procedures developed thus far.

Example 6.1   Print the number of terminal nodes in a binary tree *T*. □

The preorder traversal procedure that saves right subtree pointers on the stack can be used to perform this task (the other procedures could be adapted as readily). One approach is to leave the procedure as it is and write PROCESS to turn PREORDER into a solution to the problem.

Evidently PROCESS must test each node it is to deal with to see if it is a terminal node. If so a counter, TNCOUNT, should be increased by 1. Making TNCOUNT a parameter of PROCESS allows its values to be preserved between calls to PROCESS. In addition to updating TNCOUNT, PROCESS must initialize it to zero and print its final value. PROCESS initializes TNCOUNT when it is processing the root node.

If P points to the current record to be processed, then when $P = T$, TNCOUNT must be set to zero. How does PROCESS recognize when P points to the last node so that TNCOUNT can be printed? To do this, PROCESS must have access to the stack S. When S contains no nonnull pointers and NODE.P is a terminal node, then NODE.P is the last node. Assume that a function LAST(S) returns true if S contains no nonnull pointers and false otherwise. Consequently S must be a parameter of PROCESS or nonlocal to it. Finally, we must assume that only nonnull binary trees T are to be considered since PROCESS is invoked by PREORDER only when T is not null. PROCESS may now be defined as

```
procedure PROCESS(T, P : binarytree; S : stack; var TNCOUNT : integer);
var
    NULL : binarytree;
begin
    SETNULL(NULL);
    if (P = T) then
        TNCOUNT := 0
    else
        if ((LEFT(P) = NULL) and (RIGHT(P) = NULL)) then
            begin
                TNCOUNT := TNCOUNT + 1
                if LAST(S) then
                    WRITELN('THE NUMBER OF TERMINAL NODES IS',
                            TNCOUNT)
            end
end;
```

It would certainly be more efficient to include NULL as a parameter so SETNULL would not be invoked for each node. Similarly, setting TNCOUNT to zero in PREORDER could remove the need for the $(P = T)$ test for each node. In fact, it would be easier to take a second approach to finding a solution. Namely, modify PREORDER so it sets TNCOUNT to zero initially, and after its **while** loop is exited, simply print TNCOUNT. This second solution is considerably more efficient, because the test performed by LAST is not needed. The second approach is better in every way here.

Example 6.2   Insert a new node in the binary tree T by replacing the first terminal node encountered in a preorder traversal of T by the new node. The information field value of the new node is in VALUE. □

PROCESS can be written to make a solution out of the PREORDER procedure that stores the path from the root to the node being processed. This is convenient since the predecessor of that node is required by PROCESS when the insertion is to be made, and it will be the top stack entry at that time.

```
procedure PROCESS(var TREE : binarytree; P, NULL : binarytree; var S : stack);
var
    Q, PTR : binarytree;
begin
    if ((LEFT(P) = NULL) and (RIGHT(P) = NULL)) then
        begin
            AVAIL(PTR);
            SETINFO(PTR, VALUE);
            SETLEFT(PTR, NULL);
            SETRIGHT(PTR, NULL);
            if P <> TREE then
                begin
                    POP(S, Q);
                    if LEFT(Q) = P then
                        SETLEFT(Q, PTR)
                    else
                        SETRIGHT(Q, PTR)
                end
            else
                TREE := PTR;
            SETSTACK(S)
        end
end;
```

VALUE is assumed to be nonlocal to PREORDER and to PROCESS. ITEM simply returns a copy of the top stack entry. SETSTACK allows TRAVERSE to exit once the insertion has been made.

Example 6.3   Write a function DEPTH to return the depth of a binary tree as its value. ☐

It is not difficult to turn the PREORDER procedure into such a function. Of course the header statement must be changed to make the procedure a function. When a node is being processed, its depth is one more than the number of stack entries at that moment. To determine DEPTH, initialize it to 1 and SIZE to zero before the *while* loop, increase SIZE by 1 after PUSH, and decrease it by 1 after POP. Give PROCESS access to DEPTH and SIZE. PROCESS must simply compare SIZE + 1 to DEPTH, and when greater, set DEPTH to SIZE + 1.

Another solution for DEPTH can be obtained by recursion. This requires a way to express the depth recursively. The *depth of a binary tree T* is

☐ Zero if T is null, else
☐ One more than the maximum of the depths of T's left and right subtrees

Now the function can be written directly as

```
function DEPTH(T : binarytree) : integer;
var
    NULL : binarytree;
begin
    SETNULL(NULL);
    if T = NULL then
        DEPTH := 0
    else
        DEPTH := 1 + MAX(DEPTH(LEFT(T)), DEPTH(RIGHT(T)))
end;
```

where MAX returns the maximum of its parameters as its value.

6.4 Implementing Binary Trees

This section introduces and illustrates a number of important binary tree implementations.

6.4.1 Sequential Representation

The sequential representation uses an array to store information corresponding to each node of a tree. Consider the binary tree shown in Figure 6.9. Its depth is 5 and it has fourteen nodes. The nodes are numbered in a special way. This numbering may be obtained by preorder traversing the tree and, as each node is accessed, assigning it a node number. The root is assigned 1, each left successor of a node is assigned twice the number of its predecessor, and each right successor is assigned one more than twice the number of its predecessor. With nodes numbered in this way, the predecessor of node I is numbered $I/2$ (integer divide), its left successor is numbered $2*I$, and its right successor $2*I + 1$.

The *sequential representation* of a binary tree is obtained by storing the record corresponding to node I of the tree as the Ith record in an array of records, as shown in Figure 6.9. A node not in the tree can be recognized by a special value in its corresponding array position (such as node 8) or by a node number (like 24) that exceeds the highest node number in the tree (20 in this example). Given a pointer P to a node in the array it is easy to determine the position of its predecessor $(P/2)$, its left successor $(2*P)$, and its right successor $(2*P + 1)$.

A binary tree with n nodes will require an array length between n and $2^n - 1$. The smallest length (n) is sufficient when the binary tree is complete and the greatest length $(2^n - 1)$ corresponds to the case of an extremely skewed binary tree whose nodes have only right successors. No space in the array is unused for a complete binary tree and the array length is proportional to the number of nodes in the tree. However, a sparse tree can waste a great deal of array space. The worst case requires $2^n - 1$ positions but uses only n. Thus the sequential representation is convenient for dealing with complete static binary trees. Such trees arise, for example, when you must put student records in alphabetic order by student name (Section 7.4). For cases when the tree may change size or shape drastically, the sequential representation is not appropriate. Word counting as in Section 6.1 is not an appropriate problem.

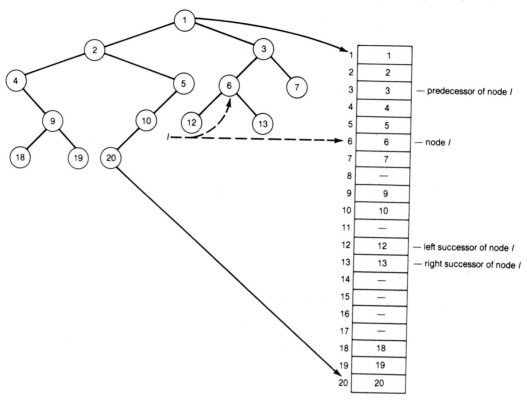

Figure 6.9 Sequential Representation of a Binary Tree

6.4.2 **Linked Representation**

A binary tree data structure can be implemented by representing each node of the tree as a record with three fields: (1) a left pointer field, (2) an information field, and (3) a right pointer field (called here the LEFTPTR, INFO, and RIGHTPTR fields). The left and right pointer fields link records of the tree just as the link and sublist fields of lists link their records. Another point of view is that the pointer fields specify a node's left and right subtrees just as the sublist field of a list specifies its sublist. The LEFTPTR and RIGHTPTR fields of a node point to the record that represents, respectively, the root of the node's left and right subtree. The INFO field contains the information stored at the node. A variable referred to as the name of the tree points to the record representing the root of the tree. A null pointer in the name denotes the null tree.

We can store each record of a binary tree using an array just as was done for the records of lists (Figure 6.10). The declarations may be

```
type
    binarytree      = integer;
    binarytreenode = record
```

```
                                info : whatever;
                                leftptr, rightptr : binarytree
                           end;
            recordsarray = array [1 .. max] of binarytreenode;
     var
            FRED, T : binarytree;
            RECORDS : recordsarray;
```

Instead of using an array, pointer variables may be used, and the records of the tree
stored in the Pascal heap. The record declarations are

```
     type
            binarytree      = ↑binarytreenode;
            binarytreenode = record
                                info : whatever;
                                leftptr, rightptr : binarytree
                           end;
     var
            FRED, T : binarytree;
```

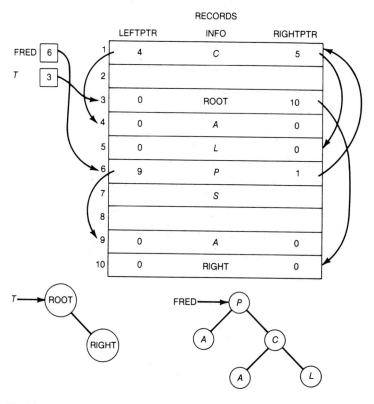

Figure 6.10   Linked Representation for Binary Trees with Records Stored in an Array

Such linked representations require storage proportional to the number of nodes of the binary tree represented, no matter what the shape of the binary tree. Contrast this with the sequential representation of binary trees. If a linked representation uses three elements per record, whereas a sequential representation uses one element per record, then for *complete* binary trees three times as much storage is used in a linked representation than in a sequential one. If the binary tree is not complete, then the sequential representation may require storage proportional to $2^d - 1$, where d is the depth of the binary tree. This could result in significant amounts of wasted space. There may not even be enough storage. Consequently, the sequential representation is more practical only when dealing with complete or nonsparse binary trees.

Using the linked representation, it is obviously possible to insert or delete records, once we know where to do so, by making changes in only a few pointer fields.

6.4.3 List-structure Representation

Another way to represent a binary tree is indicated in Figure 6.11. Each node's record is made complex. A complex record's sublist points to the representation of the node's left subtree. The result is that BTREE is implemented as the list-structure LSTREE. Abstractly, binary trees are a special case of list-structures. However, in computer science the term *tree* usually implies zero or restricted sharing of storage, whereas the term *list-structure* or *list* implies the possibility of more general sharing of storage.

6.5 Trees

So far we have considered only binary trees. Trees may have more than two successors, as does the tree in Figure 6.1. It is natural to assume that binary trees are a special case of trees, but the tree literature does not treat them this way. The formal definition of a *tree*, as opposed to a binary tree, is as follows: A *tree* is a root node with subtrees $T_1, T_2, \ldots, T_n$ which are themselves trees and have no nodes in common.

Formally there are no null trees (although there are null binary trees), so each tree has at least one node, its root. It is convenient nonetheless to refer to null trees, so the terminology applied to binary trees also applies to trees. The important distinction is that no order is imposed on the subtrees of a tree, whereas for binary trees there is a distinct left and right subtree. Consequently, when trees are pictured, it makes no difference in what order subtrees are drawn; any order represents the same tree. When order among the subtrees is to be imposed, then they are called *ordered trees*. For example the structures in Figure 6.12, when viewed as binary trees, represent two distinct binary trees, since their left and right subtrees differ, but they represent the same tree when viewed as trees.

6.5.1 Implementing Trees as Binary Trees

When a constraint is imposed limiting the number of successors of any node to at most k, the tree is called a **k-ary** tree. Such trees may be implemented by generalizing the sequential representation for binary trees. The nodes are numbered as before, except the jth successor of the node numbered I is now assigned node number

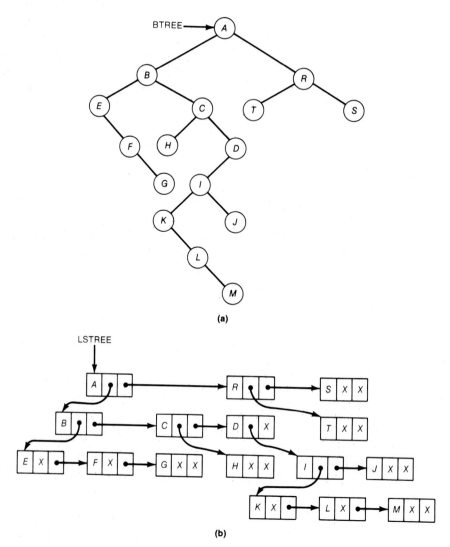

Figure 6.11   List-structure Representation (b) of a Binary Tree (a)

$k * (I - 1) + (j + 1)$. This implementation will not be pursued further, but is similar in character to the sequential implementation for binary trees. This means that formulas can be derived to compute the array position of a node's predecessor and successors which are important requirements for tree processing, and also, this representation is convenient for essentially static, healthy looking (nonsparse) trees.

Another representation is based on a natural generalization of the linked representation for binary trees. Simply expand each record so that it has as many pointer fields as it has subtrees. However, this leads to variable-length records, which are not desirable. The variable-length records occur because nodes need not all have the same number of successors. It may not even be possible to predict in advance what the greatest number of successors will be. When it is known that the tree will be a

Figure 6.12 Two Distinct Binary Trees or One General Tree

k-ary tree, then all records could be made the same length, large enough to accommodate k subtree pointers. But this can result in considerable wasted storage for unused pointer fields within records when the tree is sparse.

Perhaps surprisingly, there is a way to represent a tree as a binary tree, which then allows all records to be of fixed length. This is an important result because, since any tree has a binary tree representation, studying only binary trees is really no restriction at all.

Example 6.4 Consider the tree of Figure 6.13(a). The task in this example is to represent a tree as a binary tree. □

The binary tree is obtained as follows: First, create a root A of the binary tree to correspond to the root A of the tree. Next, pick any successor of A in the tree — say B — and create a node B in the binary tree as A's left successor. Then take the remaining siblings of B, which are C and D in this case, and let C be B's right successor, and D be C's right successor, in the binary tree. So far this yields the binary tree shown in Figure 6.13(b). If we view this procedure as the processing of node A of the tree, then the binary tree is completed by repeating this procedure for every other node of the tree. For example, after B is processed the result is Figure 6.13(c). The final binary tree created in this way appears in Figure 6.13(d).

Each tree will have a corresponding binary tree by the construction in the example, although the binary tree obtained will depend on the order in which successors are taken in the tree. For instance, had C been selected initially as the first successor of A, then the resultant binary tree would be different. If the ordering of each node's successors is specified and they are taken in the specified order, then the construction creates a *unique* binary tree for each tree. In any case, a tree with n nodes will correspond to a binary tree with n nodes. It is not difficult to find an algorithm that, given a binary tree with no right subtree, can reverse the construction and generate the tree it represents. This means that when the tree is ordered, there is a unique binary tree that can be constructed to represent it, and conversely, that given a binary tree with no right subtree, there is a unique tree that it represents which can also be constructed. Hence there are exactly as many trees with n nodes as there are binary trees with n nodes and no right subtrees.

If we define an *ordered forest* as an ordered collection of ordered trees, then each tree has its unique binary tree representation. Can you see how to append these binary trees to the binary tree representing the first ordered tree of the ordered forest to obtain a binary tree representing the forest? (*Hint*: Use the fact that the binary trees have no right subtrees.) For those of you who wish to count trees, pursuing this

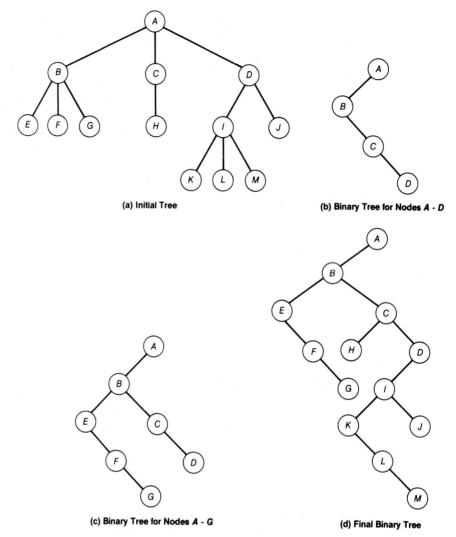

(a) Initial Tree

(b) Binary Tree for Nodes *A* - *D*

(c) Binary Tree for Nodes *A* - *G*

(d) Final Binary Tree

Figure 6.13   Representation of a General Tree as a Binary Tree

should lead to the conclusion that there are exactly as many ordered forests as there are binary trees.

6.6 Traversals of Trees

In this section algorithms are developed for traversing trees and are applied to two examples. The second example should be studied carefully because it illustrates an important modified traversal of trees that has many applications. Assuming the trees are ordered, it makes sense to refer to a tree's *first* subtree, *second* subtree, and so on. If an order is not given, the programmer can impose one.

When trees are used to store data at their nodes, then tree traversals give a means to access all the data. However, a tree might be used to represent a maze or all routes from Philadelphia to San Francisco. Traversal of the tree then provides the means to find exits from the maze or the shortest route across country. Of course the maze and the routes must not intersect. When they do, a more general data structure, a *graph*, is needed for their representation. Unlike trees, a **graph** allows more than one path between its nodes. It is not difficult to generalize tree traversal algorithms, once they are understood, to obtain graph traversal algorithms. Should a tree contain family relationships by storing an individual's record at a node, a traversal allows the parent (predecessor) or the children (successors) of an individual to be found.

The preorder and postorder traversals of binary trees generalize quite naturally to ordered trees.

To *preorder traverse an ordered tree*:
1. access and process its root, then
2. preorder traverse its subtrees in order.

To *postorder traverse an ordered tree*:
1. postorder traverse its subtrees in order, then
2. access and process its root.

There is no natural inorder traversal of trees. It is not difficult to see that a preorder and postorder traversal of a tree correspond, respectively, to a preorder and inorder traversal of its corresponding binary tree. The preorder and postorder access sequences for the tree of Figure 6.13(a) are ABEFGCHDIKLMJ and EFGBHCKLMIJDA. You should confirm that a preorder and inorder traversal of the binary tree of Figure 6.13 result in these respective access sequences. A preorder traversal is also called a *depth-first* traversal.

6.6.1 Obtaining the Binary Tree for a Tree

It should now be clear that confining attention to binary trees, their representation, and operations on them is not actually a restriction. That is, since trees can be represented as binary trees, any operations can be performed on them by performing equivalent operations on their binary tree representations. In this sense no generality is lost in dealing with binary trees. The binary tree corresponding to a tree can be represented using any of the methods discussed in Section 6.4.

Example 6.5   Develop an algorithm to generate the binary tree corresponding to a general tree. ☐

Let *T* point to the general tree, and let *BT* point to the binary tree generated by the algorithm. Recall the list-structure representation of a binary tree. Think of the leftpointer field of each node of *BT* as pointing to a sublist. This sublist contains all the successors of the corresponding node in *T*. Thus, in Figure 6.13(d) node *A* of the binary tree representation has a leftpointer field pointing to the sublist consisting of nodes *B*, *C*, and *D*. These are the successors of *A* in the general tree, Figure 6.13(a). Similarly, *D* has a leftpointer field pointing to the sublist consisting of *I* and *J*, the successors of *D* in the general tree.

Consequently, to produce *BT*, traverse *T*, create a sublist for each node in *T* consisting of all its successors, and set the leftpointer field of the corresponding node in *BT* to point to this sublist. The rightpointer fields of these nodes in *BT* serve as the link fields of this sublist. Also, the INFO field of the node in *T* must be copied into the INFO field of the corresponding node in *BT*.

Recall that, as we preorder traverse a general tree *T*, we are preorder traversing the binary tree, *BT*. That is, the order in which the nodes of *T* are accessed is exactly the same as the order in which the corresponding nodes of *BT* are accessed. Thus we can achieve a solution by preorder traversing *T*, preorder traversing *BT* at the same time, and processing the corresponding nodes as described above. For example, if this were carried out on the general and final binary tree of Figure 6.13, and nodes *A, B, E, F, G,* and *C* had been processed, we would have generated the binary tree shown as Figure 6.14(b).

Suppose *P* points to the node currently being processed in *T*. Let *PB* point to the corresponding node in *BT*. In the example, *P* would now point to *D* of *T* and *PB* to *D* of *BT*. To achieve a preorder traversal of *T*, use a stack, *TS*, to keep track of the postponed obligations. This was done in the second procedure PREORDER (Section 6.2.3), the preorder traversal saving right subtree pointers for a binary tree preorder traversal. The obligations, pointers to those right subtrees remaining to be traversed, were kept on the stack. For any node already processed, at most one subtree remained to be traversed—its right subtree.

In a general tree, since each node may have more than two successors, more than one subtree may remain to be traversed. After processing the node to which *P* points, we can update *P* to point to one of its successors, NEXT(*P*), and stack on *TS* all pointers to the remaining successors. These pointers represent the latest postponed obligations for the preorder traversal of *T*. We assume NEXT(*P*) is a function returning a pointer to the successor of *P* that is not stacked. At the same time, to keep track of the postponed obligations for *BT*'s preorder traversal, keep a parallel stack, *BTS*. At all times, pointers in corresponding positions of the two stacks will point to corresponding nodes—one in *T*, the other in *BT*. Storage can be created for the nodes of *BT* as the traversal proceeds by using the routine NEW to return a

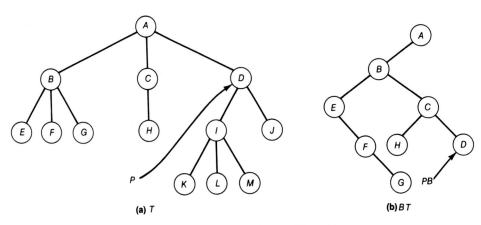

(a) *T*   (b) *BT*

Figure 6.14   Binary Tree *BT* Generated from General Tree *T*

pointer to the available storage for a node, since a pointer variable implementation is used for the binary tree.

One last detail remains. In order to do the processing required on NODE.P and NODE.PB a routine, PROCESS, will be invoked. PROCESS must copy INFO.P into INFO.PB, create a sublist consisting of new nodes corresponding to the successors of NODE.P in T, and set LEFTPTR.PB to point to that sublist. We assume that a procedure CREATE, given P, creates the required sublist, and returns with FIRST pointing to the first node of that sublist. The preorder traversal algorithm to create the binary tree corresponding to a general tree is as follows:

1. Set P to T
2. NEW(PB)
3. SETSTACKT(TS)
4. SETSTACKBT(BTS)
5. SET BT to PB
6. While P is not null or not EMPTY(TS),
    if P is not null, then
        a. PROCESS(T, BT, P, PB)
        b. For each successor pointer PS of NODE.P, except NEXT(P),
            NEW(PBS)
            PUSHT(PS, TS)
            PUSHBT(PBS, BTS)
        c. NEW(NEXT(PB))
        d. update P to NEXT(P) and PB to NEXT(PB)
    else
        e. POPT(TS, P)
        f. POPBT(BTS, PB).

The PROCESS algorithm to be used in the preorder traversal is simple:

1. Set $PB\uparrow$.INFO to INFO.P
2. CREATE(P, FIRST)
3. Set $PB\uparrow$.LEFTPTR to FIRST

Note that if the preorder traversal algorithm is modified so that all references to PB, BT, PBS, and NEXT(PB) are deleted, it becomes a description for a *general tree* preorder traversal.

The correspondence between an ordered tree and its binary tree can now be defined more formally. An ordered tree T may be represented by a binary tree BT as follows:

☐ Each node of T corresponds to a node of BT,
☐ If node N of T corresponds to node NB of BT, then
the leftmost successor of N in T corresponds to the leftsuccessor of NB in BT;
☐ All other siblings of N in T form a right chain from the node in BT corresponding to the leftmost successor of N in T.

We may now give a recursive definition specifying an algorithm for generating the binary tree BT representing the general ordered tree T.

To ***generate a binary tree corresponding to an ordered tree***:

1. Create the root node of *BT* corresponding to the root of *T*.
2. If *T* has a subtree, then *generate the binary tree BT.LEFT corresponding to the leftmost subtree of T, T.LEFTMOST,* and make the generated binary tree the left subtree of *BT*. For every other subtree of *T*, in order, *generate the binary tree corresponding to the subtree,* and insert it at the end of the right chain of *BT*.LEFT.

For illustration this algorithm is applied to the ordered tree *T*, in Figure 6.15(a).

First create the root of *BT* corresponding to the root of *T* shown in Figure 6.15(b). To carry out statement 2, note that *T* has three subtrees with *B* at the root of its leftmost subtree. We must thus generate *BT*.LEFT to correspond to Figure 6.15(c). To do this, apply the definition to this tree and obtain Figure 6.15(d) as its corresponding binary tree. Completing the first part of statement 2 for *T* yields the binary tree shown in Figure 6.15(e).

To complete the second part of statement 2, generate the binary tree for the next subtree of *T*, with *C* at its root, and then insert it at the end of the right chain of *B* to obtain Figure 6.15(f). Finally, do the same for the last subtree of *A*, with *D* at its root, and complete the application to *T*, to obtain the result shown in Figure 6.15(g).

This is another example for which we found a recursive solution. Compare the clarity and conciseness of the recursive solution with the nonrecursive solution.

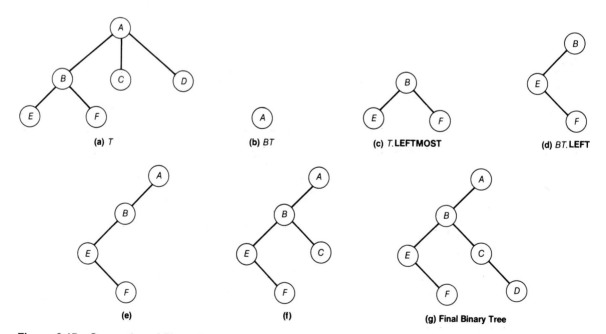

Figure 6.15   Generation of Binary Tree *BT* from an Ordered Tree *T*

6.6.2 **Backtracking: The *N*-queens Problem**

Chess is played on a square board with eight rows and eight columns, just like a checkerboard. We can think of the board as a two-dimensional array, BOARD (Figure 6.16).

A queen located in the Jth row and Kth column may move to a new position in one of the following ways:

- ☐ To the right, or left, along its row
- ☐ Up, or down, in its column
- ☐ Up, or down, along its $D1$ diagonal
- ☐ Up, or down, along its $D2$ diagonal

Example 6.6 The eight-queens problem is to find *all* ways to place eight queens on the chessboard so that no queen may take any other, that is, move into a position on its next move that is occupied by any other queen. ☐

The *N*-queens problem is a generalization of this problem, involving the placement of *N* queens on an $N \times N$ board, and is the one we want to solve. At first glance this problem has little relation to trees. Let us see.

Since a queen can be moved along one of its rows, columns, or diagonals, a solution clearly is achieved by specifying how to place the *N* queens so that *exactly* one queen appears in each row and column, and no more than one queen appears on any diagonal of the board. One could attempt to find a solution by searching through all possible placements of the *N* queens satisfying these restrictions. There are,

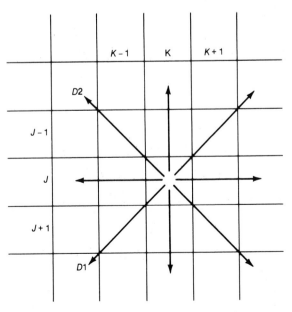

Figure 6.16 A Chessboard Represented as a Two-Dimensional Array, BOARD

however, $N!$ such placements. Even for moderate N, this is obviously not a practical solution. Instead, the programmer can construct a solution. In doing the construction the idea is to determine if the placements obtained for the first I queens cannot lead to a solution. If they cannot, abandon that construction and try another. This *may* avoid the need to consider all possible constructions. It is not even clear that a solution exists for all N.

To construct a solution involves testing a partial construction to determine whether or not it can lead to a solution or must be abandoned as a dead end. This testing is the next question.

Consider a general tree with each of its nodes representing a sequence of decisions on the placement of queens. Take the root to represent the initial situation, in which no decisions have yet been made. The root will have N successors. Each successor corresponds to a choice of row for the placement of the first queen. Each of these successor nodes, in turn, has N successors corresponding to a choice of row for the placement of the second queen and so on. The tree for the four-queens problem is shown in Figure 6.17.

Since exactly one queen must appear in each column in *any* solution, assume the Ith queen is placed in column I. Hence, each path, from the root to a node at depth I in the tree, specifies a partial construction in which the first I queens have been placed on the board. The path indicated in the four-queens tree specifies a partial construction in which the first, second, and third queens have been placed, respectively, in rows 2, 4, and 1 (and columns 1, 2, and 3).

Suppose a path has been found to a node at depth K. *The path is feasible* if none of the K queens whose positions are specified by the path can take any other. If the node at depth K is a terminal node, and the path is feasible, then a solution has been found and may be printed. If the node at depth K is not terminal, and the path is feasible, we want to extend the path to a node at depth $K + 1$. Let P point to such a node. Then NODE.P must be a successor of the node on the path at depth K.

P is feasible if the position that NODE.P specifies for the $(K + 1)$th queen does not allow it to take any of the other K queens. If P is feasible, the path can be extended downward in the tree to include NODE.P so there is now a feasible path of depth $K + 1$. If P is *not* feasible, then another successor of the node at depth K must be tried until a feasible one is found to extend the path, or until all have been tried and none are feasible. In the latter case, the choice of node at depth K cannot be extended to a solution and the computer backs up in the tree to a node representing a shorter path that has not yet been explored. This procedure to extend the new path is repeated until a solution is found or until all possibilities have been tried.

The procedure described amounts to a modified general tree traversal called *backtracking*. A different approach would be to create an algorithm for the problem by applying a general tree preorder traversal that uses a process routine. The process routine would check each node to be processed to see whether the node is terminal and represents a feasible path. If so, it prints the solution. This approach amounts to an exhaustive search of all $N!$ possibilities, since the preorder traversal backs up only when the preorder traversal of a subtree has been completed, that is, after a *terminal* node has been processed. The backtracking traversal need not access and process all nodes. It backs up when the traversal of a subtree has been completed *or* when it becomes known that no path involving the root of a subtree can be extended to a

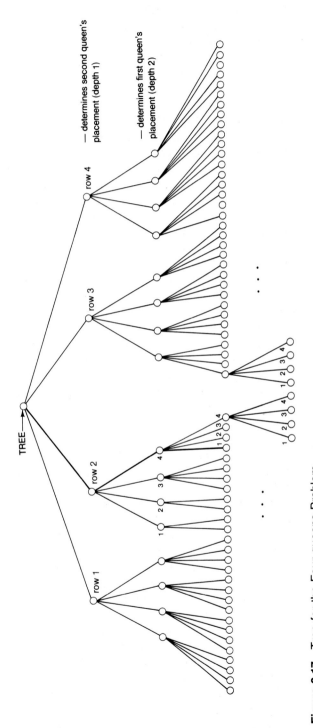

Figure 6.17   Tree for the Four-queens Problem

solution. The backtracking procedure generates only *feasible* paths — not *all* paths. In effect it prunes the tree by ignoring all nodes that cannot lead to a solution.

6.6.3 Depth-First

A backtracking algorithm can be derived by some modifications of a general tree preorder traversal algorithm. The "*P* not null" test in the loop body of the preorder traversal algorithm must be replaced by an appropriate test that *P* points to an existing node and a "*P* feasible" test to prune the tree. How this feasibility test is implemented is what determines the amount of pruning that occurs and hence the efficiency of the solution. The PROCESS routine called in the loop body must determine if NODE.*P* is terminal, and, if so, print the solution. If these were the only changes made, then nothing at all would be printed when no solution exists.

You, as the programmer, do not know whether a solution exists for every *N*. Therefore, initialize a flag, FOUND, to "false," and have PROCESS set FOUND to "true" if it finds a solution. Upon exiting from the loop body, test FOUND, and if it is false print "No solution." The resultant algorithm for a backtracking preorder traversal is as follows:

1. Set *P* to the root of *T*.
2. Set FOUND to false.
3. Set the stack to empty.
4. While *P* is not null or the stack is not empty,
    if *P* is not null, then
        if *P* is feasible, then
           a. PROCESS(*P*),
           b. push all successors of NODE.*P* onto the stack except NEXT(*P*),
           c. move down in *T* by setting *P* to NEXT(*P*),
        else
           backtrack in *T* by popping the stack and setting *P* to the popped value,
    else
        backtrack in *T* by popping the stack and setting *P* to the popped value;
  if not FOUND then
    print NO SOLUTIONS.

The function NEXT(*P*) is assumed to return a null value if NODE.*P* has no successors. If only one solution is to be found and printed, only the test of the **while** loop must be changed. It should become "(*P* not null or stack not empty) and (not FOUND)." The PROCESS algorithm to be used with the backtracking preorder traversal is as follows:

If   NODE.*P* is a terminal node, then

    1. Print the solution, and
    2. Set FOUND to true.

The algorithms developed in this section are quite general. They are applicable to any problem that can be reduced to a backtracking traversal (like the *N*-queens problem). They should be viewed as general tools for problem solving. We must now specialize them to the N-queens problem so they are detailed enough to implement as a procedure. Data structure decisions, specifically the implementation of the current board configuration, must be made along the way.

The tree is not actually stored in memory. It was used as a conceptual aid in formulating the problem abstractly. As a result the problem has been recognized as one that may be solved by a general tree backtracking procedure. It is not necessary to refer to the tree at all but we have done so here to place the problem in this more general context and continue with this approach.

Suppose P points to a node at depth K. The depth of the node specifies the placement for the Kth queen, column K. P itself determines the choice of row. In this way P corresponds to a particular ROW and COL pair and vice versa. A nonnull value for P corresponds to a column and row value $< N + 1$. Initializing P to the first successor of the root corresponds to setting ROW to 1 and COL to 1.

NEXT must have ROW and COL as parameters, and simply increases COL by 1 and sets ROW to 1. As the traversal proceeds, ROW and COL vary in a regular way. This can be used to advantage. Instead of pushing all successors of NODE.P onto the stack, which would involve $N - 1$ entries, simply push the current value of ROW. Then the backtracking task can be carried out by adding 1 to the current value of ROW when this value is less than N. If it equals N, the stack must be popped, ROW set to the popped value plus 1, and COL set to COL $- 1$.

To implement the crucial test, "P feasible," we use a boolean function FEASIBLE to return the value "true" when P is feasible and "false" otherwise. FEASIBLE must have ROW and COL as parameters, and access to information about the current board configuration. It must determine if placing a queen in the position specified by ROW and COL will allow it to "take" one of the currently placed queens. If a queen may be taken, it must return "false," otherwise "true."

We could use an $N \times N$ two-dimensional array BOARD to keep track of the current board configuration. If we did this, FEASIBLE would have to traverse through the row, column, and diagonals specified by ROW and COL in order to determine what value to return. This checking must involve all entries in many rows and columns. Since FEASIBLE is invoked in the loop body of the backtracking preorder traversal algorithm, it is executed once for every node of the tree that is accessed. Operations that appear in loop bodies should be done efficiently since they have a significant effect on the overall efficiency of the implementation.

To do its job, FEASIBLE must know whether or not the ROW, COL, and diagonals specified by ROW and COL are occupied. If this information can be efficiently extracted and made available, FEASIBLE will be more efficient. We now see exactly what information is required and proceed to the details involved in efficiently extracting it.

Consider Figure 6.16. Notice that entries $[J, K]$, $[J + 1, K - 1]$, and $[J - 1, K + 1]$ all lie along the $D1$ diagonal. Notice also that $J + K = (J + 1) + (K - 1) = (J - 1) + (K + 1)$. This means that all entries on the diagonal $D1$, determined by J and K, have the same ROW + COL sum: $J + K$. The same is true of differences along $D2$. That is, all entries on the diagonal $D2$, determined by J and K, have the same ROW minus COL difference: $J - K$. Suppose we keep information about the current board configuration as follows:

$R[J]$

Is true if the current board configuration has no queen in the Jth row, and is false otherwise.

$D1[J + K]$

Is true if the current board configuration has no queen along the diagonal $D1$ with ROW + COL sum $J + K$, and false otherwise.

$D2[J - K]$

Is true if the current board configuration has no queen along the diagonal $D2$ with ROW − COL sum $J - K$, and false otherwise.

FEASIBLE can now simply return the value of $(R[J]$ and $D1[J + K]$ and $D2[J - K])$. The arrays R, $D1$, and $D2$ require storage for N, $2N - 1$, and $2N - 1$ entries, respectively, and must be properly initialized, but FEASIBLE now takes constant time to execute. Also, when ROW and COL are changed, these changes must be reflected in R, $D1$, and $D2$. What we have done amounts to finding a way to store the current board configuration so that the operations performed on it by the algorithm are done efficiently.

Finally, we must implement the printing of a solution in PROCESS. This can be done by printing the sequence of values stored on the stack. They specify the rows in which queens 1 to N were placed.

The backtracking traversal algorithm that was developed and applied to this problem is a general tool for problem solving. It may be adapted, for example, to solving a maze, finding good game-playing strategies, and translating high-level language programs.

See Exercise 39 for another approach to the N-queens problem. The nonrecursive solution may be written as

```
program QUEENS(input, output);
var
    N : integer;
procedure QUEENS(N : integer);
const
    NLIMIT = 50;
type
    rowcheck       = array [1..NLIMIT] of boolean;
    diagonalcheck1 = array [2..2*NLIMIT] of boolean;
    diagonalcheck2 = array [−(NLIMIT − 1)..(NLIMIT − 1)] of boolean;
    whatever       = integer;
    stackrecords   = whatever;
    stack          = record
                         stackarray : array [1..NLIMIT] of stackrecords;
                         top : 0..NLIMIT
                     end;
var
    I, ROW, COL : integer;
    R : rowcheck;
    D1 : diagonalcheck1;
    D2 : diagonalcheck2;
    FOUND : boolean;
    S : stack;
```

```
procedure SETSTACK(var S : stack);
begin
    S.TOP := 0
end;

procedure PUSH(NEWRECORD : stackrecords; var S : stack);
begin
    if S.TOP = NLIMIT then
        WRITELN('stack overflow')
    else
        begin
            S.TOP := S.TOP + 1;
            S.STACKARRAY[S.TOP] := NEWRECORD
        end
end;

function EMPTY(S : stack) : boolean;
begin
    EMPTY := (S.TOP = 0)
end;

procedure POP(var S : stack; var VALUE : whatever);
begin
    if EMPTY(S) then
        WRITELN('stack overflow')
    else
        begin
            VALUE := S.STACKARRAY[S.TOP];
            S.TOP := S.TOP - 1
        end
end;

function ITEM(I : integer) : whatever;
begin
    ITEM := S.STACKARRAY[S.TOP - (I - 1)]
end;

function FEASIBLE(ROW, COL : integer) : boolean;
begin
    FEASIBLE := (R[ROW] and D1[ROW + COL] and D2[ROW - COL])
end;

procedure PROCESS(ROW, COL : integer; var FOUND : boolean; S : stack);
var
    I : integer;
begin
    if COL = N then
        begin
            for I := (N - 1) downto 1 do
                WRITELN('COL', N - I, '- - - -', 'ROW is', ITEM(I));
            WRITELN('COL', N, '- - - -', 'ROW is', ROW);
            FOUND := true
        end
end;
```

```
begin
    ROW := 1;
    COL := 1;
    for I := 1 to N do
        R[I] := true;
    for I := 2 to 2 * N do
        D1[I] := true;
    for I := -(N - 1) to (N - 1) do
        D2[I] := true;
    FOUND := false;
    SETSTACK(S);
    while (((COL < N + 1) and (ROW < N + 1)) or not EMPTY(S)) do
        if ((COL < N + 1) and (ROW < N + 1)) then
            if FEASIBLE(ROW, COL) then
                begin
                    PROCESS(ROW, COL, FOUND, S);
                    PUSH(ROW, S);
                    R[ROW] := false;
                    D1[ROW + COL] := false;
                    D2[ROW - COL] := false;
                    COL := COL + 1;
                    ROW := 1
                end
            else
                ROW := ROW + 1
        else
            begin
                POP(S, ROW);
                COL := COL - 1;
                R[ROW] := true;
                D1[ROW + COL] := true;
                D2[ROW - COL] := true;
                ROW := ROW + 1
            end;
    if not FOUND then
        WRITELN('NO SOLUTIONS')
end;

begin
    WRITELN('N = ?');
    READLN(N);
    QUEENS(N)
end.
```

ITEM(I) returns a copy of the Ith stack entry, which represents the row in which the Ith placed queen (the queen in column I) appears.

You may be tempted to try a more analytic approach to this problem to eliminate the need for all this searching. Be forewarned that famous mathematicians also attempted to analyze this problem but had difficulty solving it other than by backtracking! Actually, there are no solutions for $N = 1$, 2, and 3, and at least one solution for all $N \geq 4$. For the curious, the number of solutions for N up to 15 are

N	4	5	6	7	8	9	10
Solutions	2	10	4	40	93	352	724

N	11	12	13	14	15
Solutions	2,680	14,200	73,712	365,596	2,279,184

One final point about the backtracking traversal algorithm. Suppose the **while** loop task is replaced by the task:

    if P is not null, then
      if P is feasible, then
        a. PROCESS(P)
        b. push *all* successors of NODE.P onto the stack, except NEXT(P)
        c. update P to NEXT(P)
      else
        POP(S, P)
    else
      POP(S, P).

6.6.4 Breadth-First

The version also represents a preorder tree traversal. The stack is used to store and recall postponed obligations. Instead, modify it by changing the stack to a queue, replacing PUSH and POP by the corresponding queue operations. The result is another modified general tree traversal, a *backtracking breadth-first* traversal. It accesses the nodes in level order. In contrast, the backtracking preorder traversal might be called a *backtracking depth-first traversal*. Removing the "P is feasible" test of the backtracking breadth-first traversal turns it into a *breadth-first* traversal. You should convince yourself that this version leads to the nodes of Figure 6.13(a) being accessed and processed in the order A, B, C, D, E, F, G, H, I, J, K, L, M. Keep in mind that in this application the root node was never considered. The difference between a backtracking breadth-first traversal and a breadth-first traversal is that backtracking tests for feasibility. This allows tree paths to be ignored when it can be determined that they cannot lead to a solution.

6.6.5 Branch and Bound

A more general modified tree traversal, called a *branch and bound traversal*, is as follows:

    1. Set P to T.
    2. Set BAG to empty.
    3. While P is not null or the BAG is not empty,
        if P is not null, then
          a. if P is feasible, then
            i. PROCESS(T, P), and
            ii. add each successor pointer of P to the BAG;
      Select a pointer from the BAG and set P to it.

This algorithm uses a data abstraction consisting of a BAG data structure and operations on the BAG that set it to empty, test it for emptiness, select (and remove) a pointer from it, and add a pointer to it. The idea is to define the select operation so that it removes the pointer from the BAG that points to the node most likely to lead to a solution. The execution time required by the branch and bound traversal will be decreased when the select function does a better job of picking the next node to process, or when the feasible function does a better job of pruning the tree.

If the select function always selects the node most recently added to the BAG, then the data abstraction becomes a stack, and the algorithm is turned into a backtracking depth-first traversal. If the select function always selects the node that was added earliest to the BAG, then the data abstraction becomes a queue, and the algorithm is turned into a backtracking breadth-first traversal. Thus backtracking may be viewed as a special case of branch and bound.

Horowitz and Sakni [1978] contains extensive discussions of backtracking and branch and bound traversals, with many applications worked out in detail. Also see Golomb and Baumert [1965]. Wirth [1976] deals with these techniques for problem solving, in particular, the stable marriage problem and the eight-queens problems are solved recursively.

6.7   More on Recursion, Trees, and Stacks

Looking back at Figures 4.2 and 4.4 of Chapter 4 it now becomes clear that they are pictures of trees. In fact, any recursive program can be viewed as generating such a tree as it executes. The recursive program can be thought of as executing by traversing its corresponding execution tree. The processing done at each node in the course of this traversal is the carrying out of the program's task on a specific problem specified by its data and current scratchpad. Now that you know a good deal about tree traversals, is it any wonder that the stack appears in the translation of a recursive program? It is clearly the number of nodes in the tree that determines the execution time of the algorithm and it is the depth of the tree that determines the storage requirements. This point can become somewhat muddled when recursion is applied to trees themselves, but you must realize that this is the case even when no trees are apparent in the nature of the problem as in the Towers of Hanoi problem in Chapter 4.

Looking back from our enhanced perspective it is also evident that recursion clarifies because it hides the bookkeeping required by the tree traversal and because it elucidates the structure that must be inherent in the problem in order for a recursive solution to be found in the first place. Although an extremely powerful tool for these reasons, it must be applied with care. The purpose of this section is to provide some insight into the nature of those problems where a more skeptical approach is wise.

6.7.1   Balanced Binary Trees

In a *balanced* binary tree, no matter what node of the tree is considered, the left and right subtrees of that node have depths that differ by at most 1.

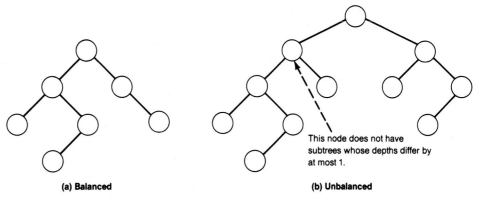

(a) Balanced   (b) Unbalanced

This node does not have
subtrees whose depths differ by
at most 1.

Figure 6.18 Balanced and Unbalanced Binary Trees

The binary tree (a) of Figure 6.18 is balanced; binary tree (b) is not. Balanced trees are important in information retrieval applications and will be discussed fully in the next chapter. In information retrieval the data are stored at the tree's nodes. The depth of the tree determines the search times for retrieval and, with balanced trees, the tree's depth is controllable and can be limited, as will be shown in Chapter 7. Here we consider the "worst case" of such trees.

A binary tree is a ***Fibonacci tree*** if it is balanced and has the minimum number of nodes among all balanced binary trees with its depth. Fibonacci trees represent the worst case for balanced trees since they contain the fewest nodes, and hence the least storage capacity, among all balanced trees with a specified depth. The binary tree in Figure 6.19 is a Fibonacci tree of depth 4. This is a Fibonacci tree because it is balanced, and no balanced binary tree with its depth (4) has fewer nodes (7). Any complete binary tree of depth 4, for example, will not be a Fibonacci tree because, while balanced, it will have more than the minimum number of nodes (7) for this depth.

The Fibonacci numbers are a well-known sequence of integers defined by the following recursive definition:

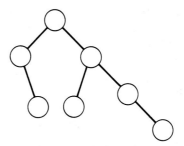

Figure 6.19 A Fibonacci Tree of Depth 4

$$F_0 = 0, \qquad F_1 = 1,$$

$$F_n = F_{n-1} + F_{n-2} \quad \text{for} \quad n > 1$$

The first few are $0, 1, 1, 2, 3, 5, 8, 13, 21, 34, \ldots$. These numbers seem to appear in the most unexpected places. In computer science they often arise in the analysis of algorithms. The number of nodes in a Fibonacci tree of depth d, $F(d)$, can be shown to be $F_{d+2} - 1$ (see Exercise 34b), hence their name.

Example 6.7   Develop an algorithm to generate a Fibonacci tree of depth d. Apply the method of recursion to find a recursive definition of the solution, if possible. □

Clearly if $d = 0$, there is only one Fibonacci tree of depth d, the null binary tree. If $d = 1$ there is only one Fibonacci tree of depth d, the tree with one node — its root.

Any subtree of a balanced binary tree must also be balanced (or else the tree itself would not be balanced). *Any* subtree of a Fibonacci tree must therefore be balanced and must also be a Fibonacci tree (or else it could be replaced by a Fibonacci tree of that depth with fewer nodes). This is the key to the recursive solution here. We can now construct a Fibonacci tree of depth $d > 1$ as follows: Since $d > 1$, the Fibonacci tree must have a root, and its two subtrees must be Fibonacci trees. One, say the right, must have depth $d - 1$ (so the tree itself has depth d). The other, the left subtree, must be a Fibonacci tree and must differ in depth from $d - 1$ by at most 1. Hence it must have depth $d - 2$ or $d - 1$. It has just been demonstrated that a Fibonacci tree of depth $d - 1$ has at least one subtree of depth $d - 2$. Hence the Fibonacci tree of depth $d - 1$ has more nodes than the Fibonacci tree of depth $d - 2$. Thus the left subtree of the Fibonacci tree being constructed must have depth $d - 2$. (Why?) This gives the complete recursive solution.

To **construct a Fibonacci tree** of depth d:
1. If $d = 0$, then
         construct the null tree and terminate,
2. else if $d = 1$, then
         construct the tree with one node, its root,
3. else if $d > 1$, then
      a. construct a root,
      b. *construct a Fibonacci tree* of depth $d - 2$ and
         make it the left subtree of the root, and
      c. *construct a Fibonacci tree* of depth $d - 1$ and
         make it the right subtree of the root.

The explicit constructions are given by the algorithm's statements 1 and 2 for $d = 0$ and $d = 1$. Statement 3 gives the implicit construction for $d > 1$. You should apply this definition to the case $d = 4$, and confirm that it constructs the example given earlier of a Fibonacci tree of depth 4. It should also be clear that other Fibonacci trees of depth 4 exist.

The recursive program can be written directly from the definition.

```
procedure FIBONACCITREE(D : integer; var T : binarytree);
const
    NULL = 0;
begin
    AVAIL(T);
    if D = 0 then
        T := NULL
    else if D = 1 then
        begin
            RECORDS[T].LEFTPTR := NULL;
            RECORDS[T].RIGHTPTR := NULL
        end
    else
        begin
            FIBONACCITREE(D − 2, RECORDS[T].LEFTPTR);
            FIBONACCITREE(D − 1, RECORDS[T].RIGHTPTR)
        end
end;
```

For concreteness, we have chosen to implement the constructed tree using a linked representation. The tree itself will be stored in the RECORDS array (Section 6.4.2) with the fields of a record being INFO, LEFTPTR, and RIGHTPTR. RECORDS is assumed to be a global variable. When the routine returns, T will point to its root record in the array representation.

If we choose to make RECORDS a parameter of the procedure, it becomes

```
procedure FIBONACCITREE(D : integer; var T : binarytree;
                                    var RECORDS : recordsarray);
const
    NULL = 0;
var
    TL, TR : binarytree;
begin
    AVAIL(T);
    if D = 0 then
            T := NULL
        else if D = 1 then
            begin
                RECORDS[T].LEFTPTR := NULL
                RECORDS[T].RIGHTPTR := NULL
            end
        else
            begin
                TL := RECORDS[T].LEFTPTR;
                FIBONACCITREE(D − 2, TL, RECORDS);
                RECORDS[T].LEFTPTR := TL;
                TR := RECORDS[T].RIGHTPTR;
                FIBONACCITREE(D − 1, TR, RECORDS);
                RECORDS[T].RIGHTPTR := TR
            end
end;
```

Here, the variables TL and TR are required by the Pascal syntax, because, without them, RECORDS[T].LEFTPTR and RECORDS[T].RIGHTPTR would be passed as non var parameters, while passing RECORDS as a **var** parameter in the recursive calls to FIBONACCITREE. This clutters the program.

Using an implementation with pointer variables for the binary tree, the procedure becomes

```
procedure FIBONACCITREE(D : integer; var T : binarytree);
begin
    NEW(T);
    if D = 0 then
        T := nil
    else if D = 1 then
        begin
            T↑.LEFTPTR := nil;
            T↑.RIGHTPTR := nil
        end
    else
        begin
            FIBONACCITREE(D − 2, T↑.LEFTPTR);
            FIBONACCITREE(D − 1, T↑.RIGHTPTR)
        end
end;
```

6.7.2 Trading Storage for Time

Consider the execution tree (Figure 6.20) for these procedures when $d = 6$.

It is a rather healthy looking (nonsparse) tree with depth $d = 6$. This holds true for any value of d and means that while the storage is not excessive, the number of

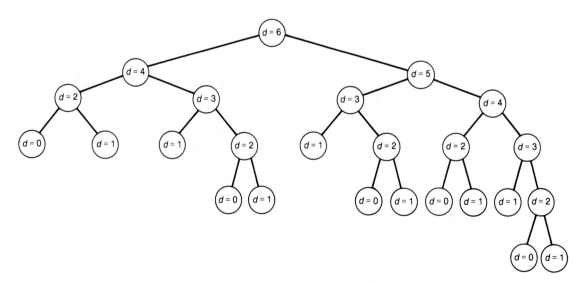

Figure 6.20   Execution Tree for Depth $d = 6$

nodes in the tree will be $O(2^d)$. Hence the execution time will increase exponentially with d. A close inspection reveals that many problems are solved repeatedly during its execution. For example, $d = 0, 1, 2, 3,$ and 4 are solved $5, 8, 5, 3,$ and 2 times, respectively. This is what causes the excessive execution time and illustrates the situation to be wary of. When the same problems occur repeatedly, the efficiency can be increased if the algorithm can be modified to save the results for these problems so they may be used directly when needed instead of being regenerated. Of course, if this requires excessive storage, then such an approach won't do. Still it represents a viable strategy when applicable, as is the case here.

Notice that a Fibonacci tree of depth d (≥ 2) can be constructed even if only Fibonacci trees of depth $d - 2$ and $d - 1$ are known. All that is necessary is to create a root node and append the tree of depth $d - 2$ as its left subtree and the tree of depth $d - 1$ as its right subtree. Consequently, the Fibonacci tree of depth d can be obtained by constructing the trees for depth $0, 1, 2, \ldots, d$ in turn, while retaining only the latest two. This gives the nonrecursive solution:

```
If d = 0, then
    set T to null
else if d = 1, then
    a. create a root node
    b. set T to point to the root node
else
    c. set TL to null,
    d. create a root node,
    e. set TR to point to the root node, and
    f. for k from 2 to d,
        i. create a root node with TL its left subtree and
           TR its right subtree
        ii. set T to point to the root node
        iii. set TL to TR and TR to T.
```

This solution is efficient in both execution time and storage (see Exercises 16 and 17 of Chapter 4 for a related example). Try analyzing the recursive solution of Section 6.6.1 to determine its efficiency for a contrast to the recursive version here.

Although it was possible to cut down drastically on the number of Fibonacci trees retained in this solution, such a saving is not always possible. Sometimes solutions to all the problems generated will need to be retained. Even so, when this number is not excessive and an appropriate data structure can be found in which to store and efficiently access a solution when needed, then execution time can be improved. This is another instance of what we have frequently seen: time may be traded for storage.

It is hoped that you do not feel we have been barking up the wrong trees! Perhaps you even agree with the humorist Ogden Nash:

> I think that I shall never see
> A billboard lovely as a tree.
> Indeed, unless the billboards fall
> I'll never see a tree at all.

☐ **Exercises**

1. a. What is the minimum number of nodes that a binary tree of depth d can have?
b. What is the maximum number of nodes that a binary tree of depth d can have?
2. Suppose T is a binary tree with n internal nodes and m terminal nodes. T is a *full binary tree* if each of its nodes has zero or two successors. What is the relation between m and n when T is a full binary tree?
3. There are 0, 1, 2, and 5 distinct binary trees with, respectively, 0, 1, 2, and 3 nodes.
a. How many distinct binary trees are there with four nodes?
b. Can you find a formula for the number of distinct binary trees with n nodes? This formula $BT(n)$ may be expressed in terms of $BT(k)$ for $k < n$.
4. Modify the program segments of Section 6.2.1 so they work correctly in all cases.
5. a. Suppose the binary tree below is preorder, inorder, and postorder traversed. List the order in which the nodes will be accessed for each.

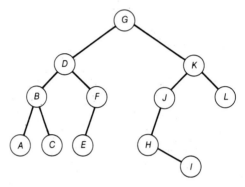

b. Do you notice anything striking about the inorder listing? Can you generalize your observation?
6. Prove that all terminal nodes will always be accessed in the same relative order for all three traversals.
7. a. Suppose the stack used in a pre-, in-, or postorder traversal is implemented as an array. What is the requirement for LIMIT in terms of the depth of the binary tree, to guarantee that the stack is large enough for the traversal to work?
b. What is the necessary value for LIMIT in order to guarantee that the traversal will work with the stack, for any binary tree with n nodes?
8. Suppose the following two binary trees are preorder and postorder traversed. The preorder and postorder listings are given for each tree.

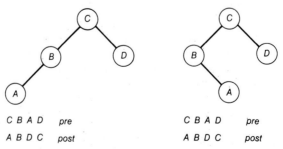

Both binary trees have *identical* listings. This cannot happen with preorder and inorder listings. That is, we *cannot* find two distinct binary trees that have *identical* preorder and inorder listings. The same is true for postorder and inorder listings. Find an algorithm that will create the unique binary tree that is thus determined by its preorder and inorder listings.

9. a. Can you find a way to use the left and right pointer fields of terminal and internal nodes that contain null pointers in a binary tree to create "threaded binary trees" so that they can be traversed without using a stack? (*Hint:* Consider pointers that point to the predecessor and successor of a terminal node in an inorder traversal.)

b. What about for inorder and postorder traversals?

10. Write inorder and postorder traversal routines (nonrecursive and recursive).

11. a. Suppose you wish to use a linked representation for binary trees with an array implementation as in Figure 6.10. Suppose that input is given as a name value followed by a sequence of records, each record representing a node of a binary tree. For the binary tree FRED of Figure 6.10 the input would be

```
6
9   P   1
0   A   0
4   C   5
0   A   0
0   L   0
```

Three records appear in the input in the order in which they would be accessed by a preorder traversal. Assume the head value is read into FRED, and PREORDER TRAVERSE is called. Write a PROCESS routine that will turn PREORDER TRAVERSE into a routine that reads the records of the binary tree into the LEFTPTR, INFO, and RIGHTPTR fields properly.

b. Same as Exercise 11a, but assume the records are given in the order in which they would be accessed in a postorder traversal.

12. The binary tree SAMPLE is stored using a linked representation. List the order in which its nodes will be accessed in a preorder traversal.

		LEFTPTR	INFO	RIGHTPTR
	1	0	R	0
	2	3	W	4
	3	5	R	0
SAMPLE 7	4	0	C	0
	5	4	E	6
	6	0	T	0
	7	10	C	3
	8	6	A	3
	9	1	B	4
	10	1	O	0

13. What will be in the stack during a preorder traversal of SAMPLE, in Exercise 12, when its rightmost node is accessed? What about when it is inorder and postorder traversed?

14. a. Suppose *every* subtree of SAMPLE of Exercise 12 is interchanged with its right subtree. What will LEFTPTR, INFO, and RIGHTPTR look like?

b. What would LEFTPTR, INFO, and RIGHTPTR look like if all the terminal nodes of SAMPLE were deleted in Exercise 12?

15. Suppose a binary tree is stored using the RECORDS array implementation as in Figure 6.10. If TREE points to its root node, write a procedure to print out the sequence of pointers that specify the path in the tree to the right most node in TREE. For example, in Figure 6.10 the rightmost node of FRED is L and the sequence of pointers to be printed out for FRED would be 6, 1, 5.

16. a. If the binary tree of Figure 6.5 were represented sequentially, what numbers would be assigned to its nodes?

b. What binary tree with n nodes will require the largest array for its sequential representation?

17. When dealing with *arbitrary* binary trees, would you use linked or sequential representation? Why?

18. a. Write a procedure that will return, given a binary tree T, with a pointer to a terminal node of T containing the largest value in its information field.

b. Write a function that, given a binary tree T and two pointers P and Q to nodes of T, returns a value "true" if NODE.Q is a successor of NODE.P and a value "false" otherwise.

c. Write a procedure that does the same thing as Exercise 18b, except the function returns a value "true" if NODE.Q is in the subtree of NODE.P and a value "false" otherwise.

19. Consider the binary tree that was produced by the transformation from a general tree to a binary tree as a general tree and find the binary tree produced by its transformation.

20. Consider again the solution to the information retrieval problem of Chapter 5. Suppose you create a record, R, in memory. R will have a pointer field pointing to the record for a father. You can then think of R as a record representing the node of a binary tree.

a. Describe this binary tree.

b. What general tree would have R as its binary tree under the transformation of Section 6.5.1?

21. a. Write a procedure to append a binary tree $T1$ to a binary tree $T2$ by replacing some terminal node in $T2$ at least depth by the whole tree $T1$. For example, see the figure.

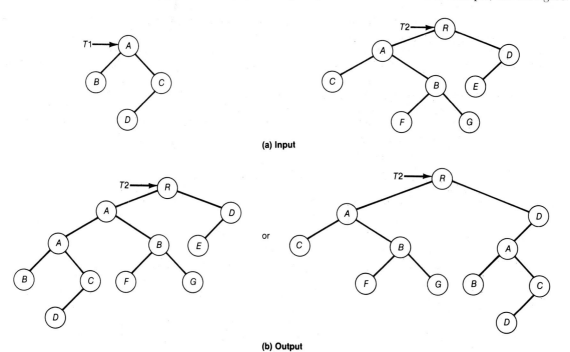

(a) Input

(b) Output

Use a linked representation with pointer variables.

b. What does your procedure do if $T1$ and $T2$ are the same tree?

    c. How will your solution change if a sequential representation is used?

  22. **a.** Write a procedure that deletes all the terminal nodes of a binary tree.

    b. Write a procedure that deletes NODE.Q if it is a successor of NODE.P in a binary tree.

  23. **a.** Write a procedure to interchange *all* left and right subtrees of a binary tree.

    b. Create a procedure to interchange all left and right subtrees except the interchanged version of the original tree will be created as a new tree, leaving the original tree unchanged. Assume pointer variables are used for its implementation.

  24. **a.** Modify the procedure PREORDER so it returns, in a variable IDENTICAL, a value "true" if $T1$ and $T2$ point to identical trees, and a value "false" otherwise. That is, the value is "true" if the two trees have the same structure and the same information field values.

    b. Do the same task, except that the binary trees need have only the same structure.

  25. **a.** Suppose you are given a maze with the structure of a binary tree. The maze has a starting point and an exit. A node is associated with the starting point, with the exit, and with every point in the maze where one of two paths must be taken. The maze is given as a two-dimensional array A. $A[I, J]$ is 1 if there is a path from node I to node J in the maze, and is 0 otherwise. There are N points in the maze. Adapt the procedure PREORDER to achieve an algorithm for solving the maze — that is, for printing out the path from the starting node to the exit node. Your solution should be detailed enough to write a procedure corresponding to it directly.

    b. If the maze has loops, what modifications must be made in your solution so that the algorithm works correctly?

  26. **a.** Modify the preorder traversal algorithm for creating a binary tree from a general tree (p. 235) and the PROCESS algorithm so the preorder traversal returns, in the variable TRANSFORM, a value "true" only if a binary tree BT is the transformed version of a general tree T.

    b. Modify the preorder traversal algorithm so that it produces the transformed tree by processing the nodes of T in breadth-first order. (*Hint:* Consider the queue.)

  27. Write the procedure CREATE used in the PROCESS algorithm.

  28. Modify the backtracking preorder traversal algorithm so that it does a backtracking *breadth-first* traversal.

  29. Suppose you are given a "map" of N cities and the distances between them. Can you find a way to modify the preorder traversal algorithm to determine the shortest distance between two cities? What is a feasible test to use to allow FEASIBLE to limit the execution time of the solution?

  30. **a.** Suppose a general tree is given as follows:

$$(A(B(E, F, G), C(H), D(I(K, L, M), J)))$$

This corresponds to the general tree:

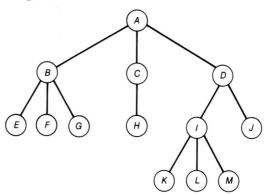

Suppose that input is given by such a parenthesized expression. Can you find an algorithm that will create the general tree from it? Assume the general tree will be represented in memory as a collection of lists of successors, with one successor list for each node.

b. What is the connection between parenthesized expressions and a listing of nodes in the order in which they are accessed by a preorder traversal?

31. T is a binary tree. RESULT(T) is defined by

$$\text{RESULT}(T)=\begin{cases} 0 & \text{if } T \text{ is null} \\ 1+\text{RESULT}(\text{LEFT}(T))+\text{RESULT}(\text{RIGHT}(T)) \end{cases}$$

LEFT(T) and RIGHT(T) are, respectively, the left and right subtrees of T.

a. If T is the binary tree below, then what is RESULT(T)?

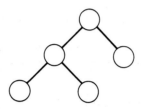

b. What does RESULT do?

32. $T1$ and $T2$ point to binary trees represented using pointer variables.

```
function CHECK(T1, T2 : pointer) : boolean;
begin
    if ((T1 = nil) and (T2 = nil)) or ((T1 <> nil) and (T2 <> nil))) then
        CHECK := CHECK(T1 ↑.LEFTPTR, T2 ↑.LEFTPTR) and CHECK(T1 ↑.RIGHTPTR, T1 ↑.RIGHTPTR)
    else
        CHECK := false
end;
```

a. Find the function value if it is invoked for trees $T1$ and $T2$.

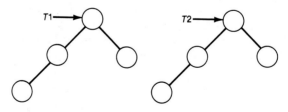

b. What does CHECK do?

33. a. Let I be a nonnegative integer. Find $b(4)$ where

$$b(0)=1$$

$$b(n)=b(0)\times b(n-1)+b(1)\times b(n-2)+b(2)\times b(n-3)+\cdots+b(n-1) \times b(0).$$

b. Find a connection between the number of distinct binary trees with n nodes and $b(n)$.

34. a. Give a recursive definition of balanced binary trees.

b. Find a recursive definition for $F(d)$, the number of nodes of a Fibonacci tree of depth d.

35. Write a recursive function RESULT corresponding to Exercise 31.

36. a. Write a recursive function COUNT to return the number of terminal nodes of a binary tree.

b. Write a recursive procedure TERMINAL to delete all terminal nodes of a binary tree using pointer variables.

37. Write a recursive procedure PARTIALEXCHANGE to interchange *all* subtrees of a binary tree whose left subtree INFO field value exceeds the right subtree field value. Assume the binary tree is represented using pointer variables.

38. Write a recursive procedure, using pointer variables, to transform a general tree into its binary tree representation.

39. Write a recursive procedure that produces a solution, if one exists, to the N-queens problem.

40. Write a recursive procedure to produce a copy of a binary tree. Both trees should be implemented using pointer variables.

☐ Suggested Assignment

a. Write a procedure to print the family tree for an individual whose family history is stored in the data base of the case study of Chapter 5. The individual is at the root of the family tree, and its subtrees are the family trees of all the individual's children. Print the tree using indentation as in Figure 6.1(a). Assume individual records are stored in the Pascal heap and that appropriate modules are available for searching and accessing the nametable. If this procedure is to also be executed, then this would be a good assignment for a group project.

Also discuss the connection between the lists used in the case study and the binary tree representation of a general tree.

b. Consider the problem of finding a stable pairing, given preferences, as discussed in Chapter 2. Describe a tree that represents all possible pairings, and write a backtracking traversal module to produce all stable pairings. Base your solution on the backtracking preorder traversal algorithm given in the text. Compare this solution with the solution given in Chapter 2.

c. Formulate a solution to the stable pairing problem as a traversal through all permutations of the men. Use the permutation traversal program of Chapter 4 as the basis for your algorithm. Compare this solution to your solution to part b of this assignment and also to the solution given in Chapter 2.

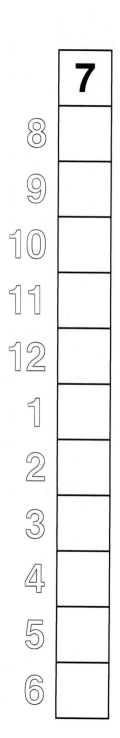

7 Searching and Sorting

7.1 Overview

So far in this book, arrays, lists, binary trees, and trees—the basic data structures—have been introduced and applied to a variety of problems. Selecting the appropriate data structure can only be done when the operations to be performed on it are known. The frequency with which these operations are required, the characteristics of the data to be stored, and the average or worst-case time and storage requirements all combine to determine this choice. Other considerations such as clarity and adaptability may also serve as criteria for deciding which data structures to use in programming. It is rarely possible to pick data structures that are best for all criteria. Instead, trade-offs must be made.

In the case study of family relationships in Section 5.5 one of the important operations was a search of the nametable data base. At that time no assumptions were made about its implementation. This chapter will show that many implementations are possible and that the appropriate choice is determined by the kinds of operations to be performed on a data base. Nametable might be organized as an array, list, binary search tree, balanced binary search tree, or hash table using the techniques to be introduced.

Searching and sorting masses of data to retrieve specific information and organize it for manipulation and presentation are nothing new. These basic operations were performed and studied even before the advent of computers. Volumes have been written on these topics, and yet they are still being researched. Even the general public and the press are evidently interested in searching, as you can see from the following letter and response:

> Dear Ann Landers:
>
>   Why is it that whenever I lose anything, it is always in the last place I look? —*Dizzy Lizzy*
>
> Dear Liz:
>
>   Because when you find it you stop looking—and that's the last place you looked.

Although searching and sorting may appear mundane, the speed with which they can be carried out largely determines whether a particular application of the computer is practical (and "cost-effective") or not. Estimates indicate that about one-fourth of the processing time in computer centers is spent just sorting. The relation between sorting and searching will become apparent in this chapter. If one can be done faster, so can the other. The choice of data structures is always important in algorithm design and is key to the evolution of good (that is, efficient) searching and sorting procedures. This chapter serves as an application of the basic data structures studied in the preceding chapters—arrays, lists, and binary trees, using them in the design of efficient procedures.

Normally, the objects stored, searched for, and sorted are records. In sorting, one field of the records, called the *sort key*, is chosen as the basis for the sort. Thus, in a payroll application an employee name field might be the key for an alphabetic ordering, while a salary field might serve as the basis for a sort to determine an ordering by amount of earnings. For simplicity it will always be assumed in this chapter that the objects being sorted are integer numbers. However, any objects could have been assumed. The only requirement, for sorting purposes, is that, given any two objects, it is possible to tell which precedes the other.

Searching normally involves comparing records to a given *search key* value, the goal being to determine whether there exists among the records of the data base a record with key equal to that of the search key. If the key value can be matched, then a pointer to the record with the matching value must be returned. The basic principle for shortening search times is to organize the data base so the search can be focused quickly on the part of the data base containing the desired record, if it is present.

We start with the simple linear, binary, and interpolation searches as well as a number of elementary sorting algorithms such as the *bubble sort* and the *insertion sort*. These lead to more advanced methods based on special binary trees: the *binary search tree* and the *heap*. An application of recursion yields *quicksort*. The final data structure used for search organization to be described is the *hash table*.

Many of the algorithms developed in the text are fairly complex and difficult, if not impossible, to analyze mathematically. The last topic is the use of simulation as a tool in discovering the behavior and efficiency of such complex algorithms. Simulation is a useful tool for investigating any algorithm, not just searches or sorts. not just searches or sorts.

The chapter concludes with a summary of the strengths and weaknesses of each data structure introduced. Knuth [1973b] and Wirth [1976] discuss many searching and sorting algorithms that are not dealt with in this text. Knuth contains mathematical analyses of many of these algorithms.

7.2 Elementary Searches

Three simple searches are applicable when records are stored in arrays: (1) linear search, (2) binary search, and (3) interpolation search. You probably have all used these methods in everyday activities. Understanding their limitations and how they work will help you see the need for the more complex structures and algorithms of later sections.

7.2.1 Linear Search

A *linear search* is so named because it proceeds in sequence, linearly through an array. Suppose DATA in Figure 7.1 is an array of integers. The task is to determine whether the number stored in the variable KEY is in the array, and if so, what its index is.

One obvious method would be to traverse the DATA array, checking each element of DATA to see if it contains the same value as KEY. If an element currently being processed did contain the same value as KEY, its index would simply be returned and the search would be complete. Arriving at the end of DATA without having found the KEY value would mean no element with that value is stored in the array. This procedure is easily implemented in a high-level language using a loop structure (as in the following procedure). The worst-case time required for its execution will be of the order N, written $O(N)$, where N is the length of the DATA array. In particular, if the value being sought is in element I of the array, it will take $O(I)$ time to find it. The linear search is implemented as follows:

```
procedure LINEARSEARCH(DATA : recordarray; N, KEY : integer;
                           var FOUND : boolean; var LOC : integer);
begin
   LOC := 1;
   while ((LOC <= N) and (DATA[LOC].KEY <> KEY)) do
      LOC := LOC + 1;
   FOUND := (LOC <> N + 1)
end;
```

As a special case, suppose the search is always for a key known to be stored in the array, and that each key stored is distinct and equally likely to be the search key. This is like standing in front of a locked door with a bunch of keys; you need to find the key that opens the door from among N keys in arbitrary order on your keyring. The average time for such a search would be $O(N/2)$. That is, on the average, you would look at half the keys, or half the elements of the array, before finding the right one.

Thus the procedure called *linear search* is so named, not only because it proceeds linearly through an array, but because its processing time increases linearly with N; when N is doubled, the time required to complete the search is doubled.

7.2.2 Saving Time: A Neat Trick

Occasionally programming tricks are used to enhance efficiency. In this case paying attention to some details produces a trick that can pay off in processing time saved. The straightforward implementation of the linear search requires a test $(LOC \leq N)$ for the end of the array before checking the next element. This is true whether the implementation is a **do** loop, a **for** loop, or a **while** loop. However, it is possible to avoid performing this test.

Place the search key in element $n + 1$ of DATA. Then, in implementing the linear search, there is no need to test for the end of the array before checking the next element. Since the array is now considered to be $(n + 1)$ elements in length, we are certain to find the search key before we "fall off the end." After the loop is exited, note

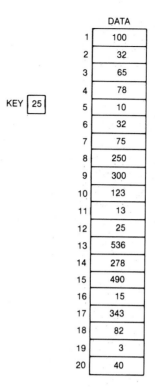

Figure 7.1 An Array of Integers to Be Searched for the Key Value 25

the element in which KEY was found, and test to see if it was the $(n + 1)$th element, which means that the search was unsuccessful. Thus, only one test (DATA [LOC].KEY $<>$ KEY) must be performed. This saves N tests in unsuccessful searches, and I tests in successful searches, when the search key appears in element I of DATA. This simple modification of the basic linear search can easily produce significant time savings (20 to 50 percent). In general, whenever loops are modified to reduce the tests or processing they perform, execution time is saved *each* time through the loop. The more efficient linear search implementation appears as follows:

```
procedure LINEARSEARCH(DATA : recordarray, N, KEY : integer;
                    var FOUND : boolean; var LOC : integer);
begin
    LOC := 1;
    DATA[N + 1].KEY := KEY;
    while DATA[LOC].KEY <> KEY do
        LOC := LOC + 1;
    FOUND := (LOC <> N + 1)
end;
```

When doing a linear search, it is reasonable to store the keys in decreasing order of frequency, when it is known how frequently each will be searched. Even such simple modifications sometimes significantly improve the efficiency of algorithms. In fact, if these frequencies decrease rapidly enough, the average search time for the linear search could be constant.

7.2.3 Binary Search

Certainly no one does a linear search to look for a phone number in the telephone directory. Imagine trying to do so in the directory for New York City or any other large city! But there are ways to carry out the search so that the name is found in a few seconds, even from among a few million names. The structure of the telephone directory is the clue to the solution, which takes advantage of the order of entries in the phone book for looking up a person's phone number.

Assume that the numbers stored in DATA are arranged in decreasing order as in Figure 7.2. They are said to be *sorted* in decreasing order. One of the things most people do by habit when using the telephone directory is to flip the directory open toward the front, middle, or back depending on the location in the alphabet of the name being sought. If the page opened to has names farther down in the alphabet, the search name cannot be on that page or anywhere in the directory to its right. This process of elimination is behind the binary search. It is not difficult to see why this search technique is called *binary*. Every time a test is made in the search, there are two choices: in this telephone book example, search either half of the remaining pages for the name.

Binary search is also a good strategy for the game of twenty questions, which is

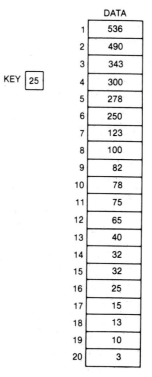

Figure 7.2   Array of Integers Sorted in Decreasing Order

to guess the identity of an object after finding out if it is in the animal, the mineral, or the vegetable category. Twenty questions with "yes" or "no" answers are allowed. Selecting each question so that about half the remaining possibilities are eliminated, no matter what the answer, is best (for example, "Is the object male or female?"). In this way 2^{20}, or over a million, objects can be distinguished.

When searching arbitrary keys, there is no reason to expect the search key to be in any particular region of an array of data; but when the data have already been sorted, the situation is different. It is possible to check the middle element to see if the search key is there. If it is, the program would note its location and terminate the search. If the key is not there, then if the search key is greater than the key in the middle element, eliminate the middle element and all elements below it from consideration. If the desired record is in DATA at all, it must be above the middle element. Similarly, if the search key is less than the key in the middle element, eliminate the middle element and all elements above it. In any event, at most half the elements remain to be considered and the same procedure can then be applied to the appropriate half, either elements 1 to [MID − 1] or elements [MID + 1] to N. MID is a variable that points to the middle element.

For example, if MID is 10, then the search key value, 25, is not greater than DATA[MID], 78. Hence, if it is in DATA at all, it must be between positions MID + 1 and N, 11 and 20. Taking 15 as the middle element of these, the new MID value is 15. KEY is less than DATA[MID], 32. Hence we need to search between MID + 1 and 20, 16 and 20. With a new MID value of 18, KEY is greater than DATA[MID], 13. Now search only between 16 and 17. The next MID value is 16 and the KEY is found.

The basic structure of the binary search algorithm is a *loop*, as shown in the following procedure.

```
procedure BINARYSEARCH(DATA : recordarray; N; KEY : integer;
                            var FOUND : boolean; var LOC : integer);
var
    TOP, MID, BOTTOM : integer;
begin
    TOP := 1;
    BOTTOM := N;
    FOUND := false;
    LOC := 0;
    while ((TOP <= BOTTOM) and not FOUND) do
        begin
            MID := (TOP + BOTTOM) DIV 2;
            if (DATA[MID].KEY = KEY) then
                begin
                    FOUND := true;
                    LOC := MID
                end
            else
                if DATA[MID].KEY < KEY then
                    BOTTOM := MID − 1
                else
                    TOP := MID + 1
        end
end;
```

MID is initialized to the middle element of DATA, TOP to 1, and BOTTOM to N. TOP and BOTTOM are variables that point to the top and bottom elements of the consecutive elements left to be searched, all others having been eliminated from consideration. In the loop body, test for KEY equal to DATA[MID]. If the equality is true, the program exits the loop and the search is done, since KEY has been found at element MID. If not, TOP and BOTTOM must be updated to reflect the new sequence of elements that are to be searched. This updating must set BOTTOM to MID − 1 whenever KEY is greater than DATA[MID], and TOP to MID + 1 other-wise. The test for continuing the loop involves checking whether KEY was found, and whether any elements are left to be searched between TOP and BOTTOM. The search is terminated as soon as the desired entry is found or as soon as it is concluded that the entry is not present. LOC will be zero if the key value was not found, and will index its location in DATA if found.

7.2.4 Timing the Binary Search

How much time is required by the binary search algorithm in the worst case? Each pass through the loop requires at most a constant amount of work. The time to execute the algorithm will then be determined by the number of passes through the loop, plus, of course, a constant time for initialization and finalization. What is the greatest number of loop iterations executed?

Each pass through the loop the search involves at most half the elements that were under consideration during the preceding pass through the loop. Starting with N elements, after one pass through the loop at most $\frac{1}{2}N$ elements are left, after two passes through the loop at most $\frac{1}{2}(\frac{1}{2}N)$ elements, after three passes at most $\frac{1}{2}(\frac{1}{2^2}N)$ elements, and after k passes at most $\frac{1}{2}([1/(2^{k-1})]N)$ or $\frac{1}{2^k}N$ elements. This number, $\frac{1}{2^k}N$, is less than 1 when $-k + \lg N < 0$ or when $k > \lg N$. This means the loop cannot be executed more than $\lceil \lg N \rceil$ times. If N is 20, for example, then $\lg 20 = 4.32$, and $\lceil 4.32 \rceil$ is 5. Thus in the worst case, the binary search is $O(\lg N)$. If each record stored is searched with equal frequency, then the average time to find a stored record is actually about $(\lg N) - 1$ (the proof is not given here).

7.2.5 Interpolation Search

Sometimes, telephone directories, like dictionaries and encyclopedias, have tabs so users can flip open the book to the beginning of the section containing entries with a specific first letter and gauge whether to search toward the front, middle, or back pages of the section. The tabs have been inserted or interpolated within the data to guide the search. This represents a generalization of the binary search called the *interpolation search*. The topic will not be pursued in detail, but note that this technique allows the elimination of greater fractions of the remaining names than does a binary search. Not surprisingly, this tends to reduce the execution time.

When N is large, the binary search takes much less time, in the worst case, than the linear search. This is because it makes $\lg N$ rather than N comparisons, going through its loop body $\lg N$ rather than n times. However, the steps performed in the loop body of the binary search are more complex and more time-consuming than the steps performed in the loop body for the linear search. Hence, it is possible, for smaller values of N, that the linear search will be faster. Similarly, the interpolation search will need to perform more complex steps in its loop body even though it may need to loop fewer times than the binary search.

7.3 Elementary Sorts

We now turn our attention to three simple sorting methods applicable to records stored in arrays: (1) maximum entry sort, (2) bubble sort, and (3) insertion sort. They are also applicable to records stored in lists. Understanding their limitations and how they work serves as motivation for the more complex structures and algorithms of the next section.

7.3.1 Maximum Entry Sort

Perhaps the most straightforward way to sort numbers in an array into decreasing order is to begin by placing the largest number in element 1. The next largest number is then placed into element 2, and so on. The *maximum entry sort* repeatedly finds the next largest array entry and places it into its proper position in the array. Suppose the point has been reached in this procedure where the k largest numbers have been properly placed into the first k elements of the array DATA. Assume a variable NEXT points to the element of DATA into which the next largest element is to be placed. NEXT must now be updated to NEXT + 1 so it contains the value $k + 1$ indicated in Figure 7.3.

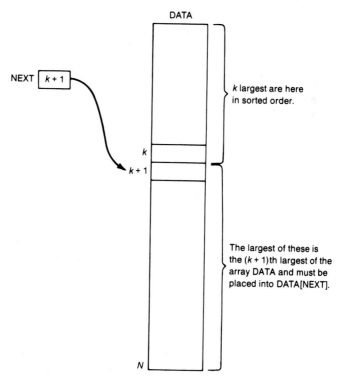

Figure 7.3 Ready to Determine the Next Largest

Assume that a function MAXLOC exists, with parameters DATA, NEXT, and N, the array length. MAXLOC returns with its value indexing the largest element between the NEXTth and the Nth elements of DATA. The sort may then be obtained by a loop in which MAXLOC is invoked $(N - 1)$ times, with NEXT taking on values $1, 2, \ldots, N - 1$, respectively, on each call. Within the loop, when each call to MAXLOC is made, an exchange between DATA[NEXT] and DATA[MAXLOC] occurs.

MAXLOC might be implemented by traversing the elements NEXT to N of DATA. Each time a new element is accessed, it is compared to a variable, LARGEST, containing the largest entry seen so far in this traversal. If the new element is greater than LARGEST, LARGEST is set to the new element value, and MAXLOC is set to point to the location of the new element in DATA.

This algorithm is probably similar to what most programmers do instinctively when confronted with a small sorting problem, and may be implemented as in the procedure MAXENTRYSORT.

```
function MAXLOC(DATA : recordarray; NEXT, N : integer) : integer;
var
     LARGEST, I : integer;
begin
     MAXLOC := NEXT;
     LARGEST := DATA[NEXT].KEY;
     for I := NEXT + 1 to N do
         if DATA[I].KEY > LARGEST then
             begin
                 MAXLOC := I;                        Comparison
                 LARGEST := DATA[I].KEY
             end
end;

procedure MAXENTRYSORT(var DATA : recordarray; N : integer);
var
     NEXT, LOC : integer;
     TEMPDATA : individualrecords;
begin
     for NEXT := 1 to N - 1 do
         begin
             LOC := MAXLOC(DATA, NEXT, N);
             TEMPDATA := DATA[NEXT];
             DATA[NEXT] := DATA[LOC];                Interchange
             DATA[LOC] := TEMPDATA
         end
end;
```

How much time does this implementation of the maximum entry sort take? One interchange is made on each call to MAXLOC for a total of $N - 1$ interchanges. The number of comparisons is $(N - k)$ on the call to MAXLOC, when NEXT has the value k. The total number of comparisons is $(N - 1) + (N - 2) + \cdots + 2 + 1$; which sums to $[N(N - 1)]/2$. Thus, the time is determined by the time of the $(N - 1)$ interchanges plus the time of the $[N(N - 1)]/2$ comparisons. Each interchange takes a constant amount of time, and each comparison takes, at most, a constant amount of time. The result is $O(N^2)$ time. This means that if N is doubled or tripled, the time will increase by a factor of about 2^2, or 4, and 3^2, or 9, respectively, when N is large. For $N = 10^5$, the time is roughly proportional to $\frac{1}{2} 10^{10}$, which is within a factor of 100 of 10^{13}, the guide for feasibility presented in Chapter 1. Quicker algorithms are needed for large N and even perhaps for small N. The next elementary sort technique is an improvement.

7.3.2 Bubble Sort

The **bubble sort** gets its name from the way smaller entries "sink" to the bottom of the array during the sort while larger entries "bubble up" to the top. To carry out the bubble sort on the array shown in Figure 7.4(a), traverse the array, comparing two adjacent elements, starting with the first two, and ending with the last two. If the $[I + 1]$th element value exceeds the Ith, interchange the two element values. When a traversal is completed, it is called a **pass** through the array. Continue making passes until a pass occurs in which no interchanges are required.

In the example, after pass 1, the array looks like Figure 7.4(b). Since at least one interchange was made, another pass is made, yielding Figure 7.4(c). Again, at least one interchange was made, so the program must make another pass.

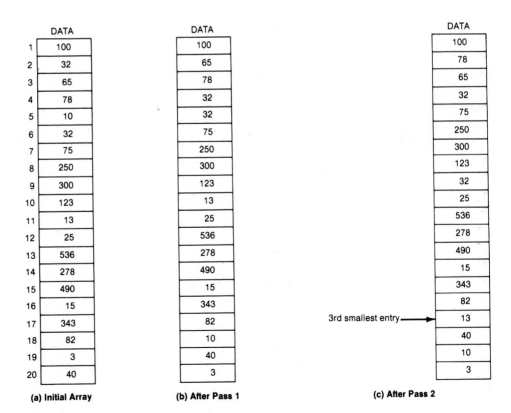

(a) Initial Array   (b) After Pass 1   (c) After Pass 2

Figure 7.4 Bubble Sort

Will this process continue forever making passes, or eventually stop? Clearly, once it stops since no interchanges were made on the last pass, the array is sorted. If any number were out of order, at least one interchange would have been made during that pass.

Notice that after the first pass, the smallest entry, 3, was at the bottom of the array. After the second pass, the two smallest entries, 10 and 3, were in order at the bottom of the array. This was not accidental. Notice that the two smallest entries will never be moved, and the third smallest element (13 in this case) will be encountered on the next pass. Once it is encountered, it will always be interchanged with the adjacent lower record to which it is compared. It will eventually come to rest just above the second smallest entry.

In general, after the kth pass, the k smallest entries will be in order in the bottom k elements of the array. Of course, more than the k smallest may be in order at this point, but only k can be guaranteed. Hence, the array will be in sorted order after at most $N - 1$ passes. The procedure can therefore be modified to compare down to only the $[N - k]$th element on the kth pass. The bubble sort is implemented with the following procedure.

```
procedure BUBBLESORT(var DATA : recordarray; N : integer);
var
    I : integer;
    TEMPDATA : individualrecords;
    DONE : boolean;
begin
    DONE := false;
    while not DONE do
        begin
            DONE := true;
            for I := 1 to N - 1 do
                if DATA[I + 1].KEY > DATA[I].KEY then
                    begin
                        TEMPDATA := DATA[I];
                        DATA[I] := DATA[I + 1];
                        DATA[I + 1] := TEMPDATA;
                        DONE := false
                    end
        end
end;
```

7.3.3 Timing the Bubble Sort

If the array were initially given in sorted order, only one pass would be required, and the time would be proportional to N. If the array were initially given in *reverse* sorted order, then $N - 1$ passes would be required, with $(N - 1 - k)$ interchanges and comparisons. This is the worst case, and takes time determined by the $\sum_{k=1}^{N-1}(N - k)$ interchanges and comparisons. This sum is $(N - 1) + (N - 2) + \cdots + 1$ or $[N(N - 1)]/2$ interchanges and comparisons.

The worst-case time for the bubble sort is $O(N^2)$, just as for the maximum entry sort. However, the maximum entry sort will always take time $O(N^2)$ since the number of comparisons it makes is not dependent on the data, while, for certain initial orderings, the bubble sort will take $O(N)$ time.

7.3.4 Insertion Sort

The *insertion sort* works by assuming all entries in the array are in sorted order already and inserting the next entry in its proper place in the order. Illustrating the insertion sort is Figure 7.5.

In this example the same array, DATA, is used as for the bubble sort, and each record is processed in turn, starting from the second. Figure 7.5(a) represents the situation after processing of the first six records; the seventh is yet to be processed. It is processed, as are all the other records, by assuming the preceding records are already in sorted order. Notice that records 1–6 are in order. To insert the seventh record, 75, into its proper place among the first seven records, compare record 7 with its predecessor, record 6. Since 75 exceeds 10, it should go somewhere higher up in the array, so compare it to the predecessor of record 6, record 5. Since 75 exceeds 32, compare it to the predecessor of record 5, record 4. Again, 75 exceeds that element's value of 32, so compare it to its predecessor's value, 65. The last comparison is with 78. Since 75 does not exceed 78, record 7 must be inserted between record 2,

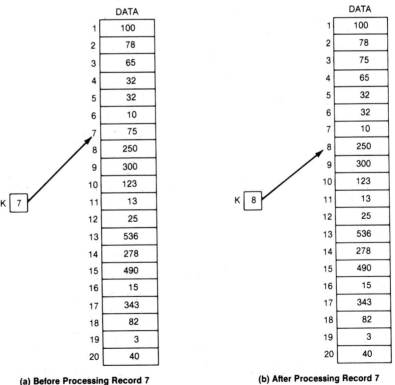

(a) Before Processing Record 7   (b) After Processing Record 7

Figure 7.5 Insertion Sort

where 78 is now, and record 3. To do this, move records 3 to 6 down one element, respectively, and place 75 in record 3. The result is Figure 7.5(b).

K has been updated by 1, so it points to the next record to be inserted. This algorithm for an insertion sort can be described by a loop structure in which K varies from 2 to N, as in the following procedure.

```
procedure INSERTIONSORT(var DATA : recordarray; N : integer);
var
    K, I : integer;
    TEMPDATA : integer;
    INSERTED : boolean;
begin
    for K := 2 to N do
        begin
            I := K;
            INSERTED := false;
            while (I > 1) and not INSERTED do
                if DATA[I − 1].KEY < DATA[I].KEY then
                    begin
                        TEMPDATA := DATA[I];
                        DATA[I] := DATA[I − 1];
                        DATA[I − 1] := TEMPDATA;
                        I := I − 1
                    end
                else
                    INSERTED := true
        end
end;
```

Within the loop process the Kth record by inserting it properly among the top K elements. This may be accomplished by another loop, in which record K is compared to each consecutive predecessor until it does not exceed the current predecessor record. It is inserted at that point in the array. As an exercise, you should modify the INSERTIONSORT program to incorporate the programming trick of Section 7.2. In Table 7.4 (see Section 7.9), this is referred to as the *modified* insertion sort.

7.3.5 Timing the Insertion Sort

If the initial array were given in sorted order, the insertion of the kth record would require one comparison and no insertions. The total time would be $O(N − 1)$. If the initial array were given in *reverse* sorted order, the insertion of the kth record would require $(k − 1)$ comparisons, and the insertion of the kth record at the top of the array. To accomplish this, each of the $(k − 1)$ records must be moved down one element. The total time will be the time for the $1 + 2 + \cdots + (N − 1)$ comparisons, plus the time for the $1 + 2 + \cdots + (N − 1)$ shifts down. Consequently, the total time is $O(N^2)$. This represents the worst case. Again we see that the time can vary with N^2 for large N. The insertion sort, like the bubble sort, performs better the closer the initial data is to being sorted. If each of the $N!$ possible initial orderings of the array with N

distinct entries is equally likely to occur, then the average time for all three of the sorts considered so far is also $O(N^2)$.

In the three implementations for the sorting algorithms, it was assumed that the interchanges taking place were actually interchanges of records. When records are large, significant amounts of time can be saved by keeping an array, P, of indexes or pointers to the records. The entries of this array can then be kept in order, so that $P[I]$ indexes or points to the Ith record in sorted order. In the procedures shown for maximum entry sort, bubble sort, and insertion sort, the interchange operations would then apply to the array P, and the comparison operations would apply to the actual records indexed or pointed to by I.

7.3.6 **Attempted Improvements**

We could try to improve the insertion sort. In effect, it traversed through records $[k-1]$ to 1 *linearly* to insert the kth record properly. Instead, we could do a binary search of the consecutive elements 1 to $[k-1]$. We will then know where to insert the kth record. This will reduce the $1 + 2 + \cdots + (N-1)$ comparisons to $\lg 2 + \lg 3 + \cdots + \lg(N-1)$, which is about $N \lg N$. It does not, however, alleviate the need for the $1 + 2 + \cdots + (N-1)$ shifts due to the insertions, so the time is still $O(N^2)$.

What else can be tried to improve the insertion sort? Aha, lists! Recall that lists are convenient for insertions, so simply represent the records in a list rather than an array. Then, once you know where to insert a record, merely change two pointers. Thus the $1 + 2 + \cdots + (N-1)$ or $[N(N-1)]/2$ insertion time is reduced to time $O(N)$. The list, coupled with the binary search reduction in comparison time to $N \lg N$, seems to give a new implementation of the insertion sort with worst-case time $N \lg N$. The fly in this ointment is that the ability to do a binary search has disappeared. It is no longer possible to locate the middle record by selection, which is what makes the binary search with sorted arrays so fast. Just the first record's location is known; the middle record can be found only by traversing the list and counting records until the middle one is reached.

Wait! We are not yet defeated in our quest for a faster insertion sort. Use a pointer array, assuming enough storage is available, to tell where all the records are on the list. This allows selection of the list records as in Chapter 2. The situation is then as shown in Figure 7.6.

NUMBERLIST is the head of the list of records in the illustration. Suppose the first six records have been properly processed as in the insertion sort, and the seventh is to be processed next. A binary search can now be done, since the middle record, among 1 to 6, will be indexed by the middle entry of elements 1 to 6 of the pointer array. Thus it is possible, in $\lg 6$ time, to determine where the seventh record is to be inserted. The insertion will require the changing of two pointers. But here's the rub: to maintain the pointer array, it must have its seventh element inserted in the corresponding position of the pointer array. We have merely succeeded in transferring the insertion problem to the pointer array — we have not eliminated it!

Although these attempts to find a faster sorting algorithm have so far not been successful, they provide greater insight into the binary search and sorting problems.

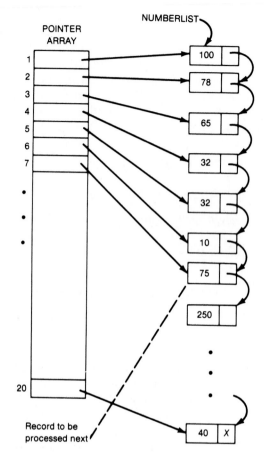

Figure 7.6   Selection of Records by Means of a Pointer Array

One observation is that to search in binary search time (lg N), a linked type structure is needed to do fast insertions and deletions, as well as some way to eliminate from consideration a significant fraction of records. A second observation is that the original insertion sort would be faster if the length of the array in which each insert is made were shorter. We must somehow break up the array of records to be sorted, so that the individual insertions do not involve *all* previous records. These observations lead naturally to the idea of heapsort and quicksort, two faster sorting algorithms, and to the idea of a binary search tree. Except for the binary search, all the searching and sorting algorithms so far considered may be applied to records stored in lists as well as in arrays.

7.4 Heapsort: A Faster Sort

In this section and the next (Section 7.5, Quicksort), two less obvious but faster sorts are considered. The heapsort and quicksort are fundamental sorts having distinct

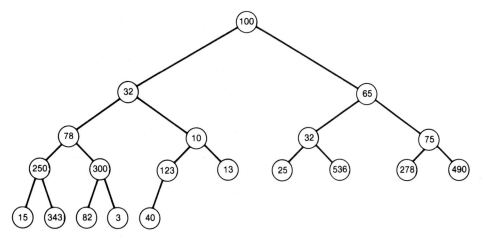

Figure 7.7 Not a Heap

advantages. They are developed from different points of view. An important application for sorting of heaps is given for priority queues.

7.4.1 Heapsorts

A *heap* is a binary tree with the property that all records stored in nodes are in sorted order along the path from each node back to the root. This heap is a completely different structure from the Pascal heap discussed in earlier chapters and has no relation to it. The tree of Figure 7.7 is not a heap, for example, since the path from node 10 (where 123 is stored) is not in sorted order. That path has records 100, 32, 10, and 123. (The nodes in this chapter are numbered like the nodes on trees in Chapter 6 and are referred to by their number.)

Notice that the tree has the same information as the DATA array, but the information has been spread out along different paths. Figure 7.8(a) is a heap storing the same information.

A heap is the basis for one of the faster sorts. Also, suppose you must store a collection of records, say bills due, to which new records are frequently being added or deleted. When you must support these operations and also gain access directly to the highest priority record, say the one with the shortest due date, then a heap is a convenient data structure for the collection.

Since the path from every node to the root is in sorted order, the record at the root of a heap must be at least as great as any other record in the tree. The same holds for all subtrees. The record at the root of any subtree must be at least as great as any other record in the subtree. The root record may then be taken as the first record in a sorted output of the information stored in the tree.

To sort, output 536 first, and then remove it from the tree. Now suppose that somehow the records can be rearranged in the tree to create a new heap — a process called *reheaping*. The result might look like Figure 7.8(b). This tree has one fewer node than the original. Clearly, this process of removing the root can be repeated, outputting it next in the sorted output, and reheaping. When all the records have

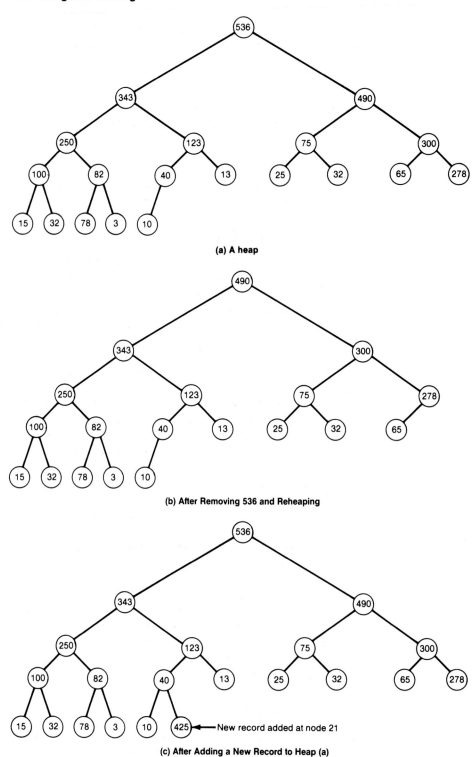

(a) A heap

(b) After Removing 536 and Reheaping

New record added at node 21

(c) After Adding a New Record to Heap (a)

Figure 7.8   Heaps

been output in sorted order, the remaining tree will be the null binary tree (the heap will be empty), and a sort will have been obtained. The algorithm is stated simply:

To **perform a heapsort**:
1. Create a heap.
2. While the heap is not empty
    a. output the record at the root of the heap,
    b. remove it from the heap, and
    c. reheap.

As currently stated, the algorithm is not detailed enough. It does not specify how to create a heap for step 1 and how to reheap for step 2.

7.4.2 Creating a Heap

Consider the heap of Figure 7.8(a) with one new record as in Figure 7.8(c). Notice that all paths are in order, except for the path from the new record at node 21 to the root. This prevents this tree from being a heap. To make it a heap, the insertion sort idea may be useful. Insert the new record at its proper place along the already sorted path from its predecessor node to the root, and allow 425 to work its way up along the path as far as it can go to reach its proper place. This can be done by comparing 425 to its predecessor, and interchanging if it exceeds its predecessor's value. In this case, it does exceed that value, so interchange to obtain the tree shown in Figure 7.9(a).

All other paths remain sorted, as before. Now compare 425 at node 10 with its predecessor. Since it exceeds 123, interchange again to obtain Figure 7.9(b). Finally, compare 425 with its predecessor's value, and interchange to obtain Figure 7.9(c).

At this point, when 425 is compared to its predecessor's value, the 425 has reached its proper place. *All* paths must now be in order, since the path from node 10 to the root is in order, and the interchanges have not disturbed the order along any other path.

This gives us the means *to create a heap*:

Start with records stored in the complete binary tree and process each node in turn, starting with node 2 and ending with node *N*.

The processing of the *I*th node is exactly the same processing as was done on the new record 425. Since nodes 1 to $I - 1$ will already have been processed prior to processing node *I*, the binary tree consisting of nodes 1 to $I - 1$ will already be a heap. Processing node *I* then, in effect, treats the record at node *I* as a new record, and creates a new heap. For the example of twenty records, this procedure leads to the heap of Figure 7.8(a).

7.4.3 Timing the Heap Creation

In order to analyze the time required, recall that the number of nodes *N*, and the depth of a complete binary tree, are related by

$$d = \lceil \lg_2(N + 1) \rceil$$

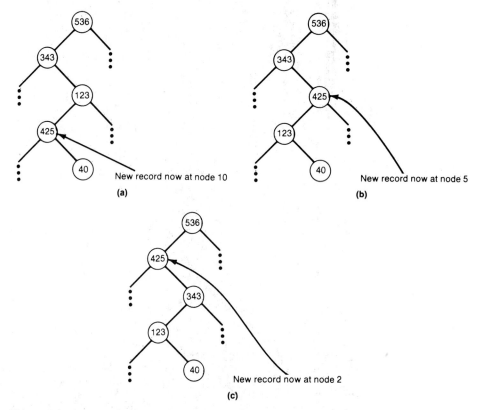

Figure 7.9   Heap Creation

This is important since the heaps dealt with initially in our heapsort algorithm are complete, their depth is $O(\lg(N))$.

We now analyze the time required to create a heap by this algorithm. Starting from a complete binary tree is important. For instance, if we started with the binary tree shown in Figure 7.10, this algorithm would be equivalent to the original insertion sort of Section 7.3.4.

The heap creation algorithm does a total amount of work determined by the sum of the number of comparisons and interchanges needed in processing each node. A node at depth k cannot require more than k comparisons and k interchanges in its processing. The worst-case time will be achieved for any initial tree in which the numbers stored at nodes 1, 2, 3, . . . , N form an increasing sequence. For instance, if the integer I is stored at node I, for $I = 1, 2, . . . , N$, we obtain such an increasing sequence. If N is 15, the tree will be as shown in Figure 7.11.

It should not be difficult to see that the total time for such a tree to be turned into a heap by the algorithm is proportional to $\sum_{k=0}^{d} k\, N_k$, where N_k is the number of nodes at depth k, d is the depth, and k is the number of comparisons and interchanges required for each node at depth k. This is because every record will work its way to the root of the tree when it is processed. Since $N_k = 2^{k-1}$, this sum will be proportional to $N \lg N$. The efficiency of this method can be increased somewhat by

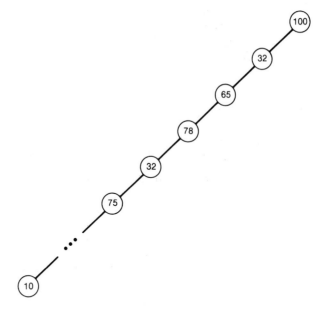

Figure 7.10 An Incomplete Binary Tree

first determining where a record to be processed will end up along its path to the root, and then shifting everything down before inserting it. This efficiency could also have been achieved with the insertion sort.

7.4.4 **Better Heap Creation**

For a tree of depth d, a better procedure for creating a heap is to start at node number 2^{d-1}, the rightmost node at depth $d - 1$. Even better, start at $\lfloor N/2 \rfloor$, the integer part of $N/2$, the first nonterminal node at depth $d - 1$. Process each node in turn, from node $\lfloor N/2 \rfloor$ to node 1. The processing at each node I is to turn the tree with node I

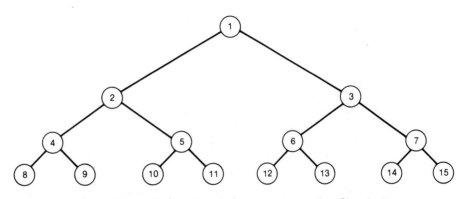

Figure 7.11 Binary Tree with Numbers Forming an Increasing Sequence

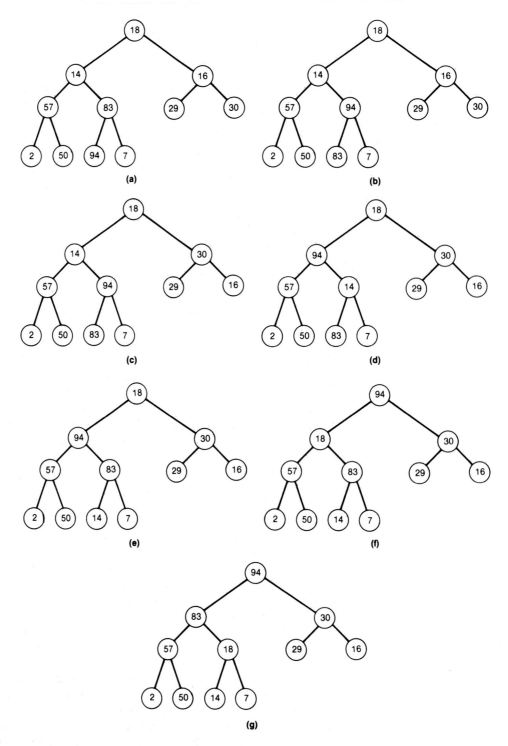

Figure 7.12 A Fast Heap Creation

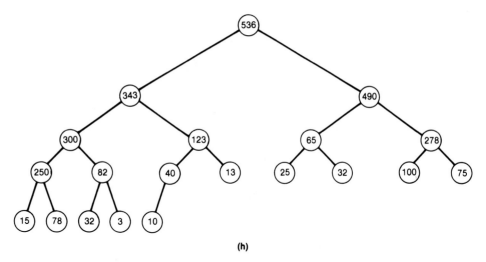

(h)

Figure 7.12 (*continued*)

as its root into a heap. This can be done assuming that its left and right subtrees are already heaps, as in the following example.

Consider the initial complete binary tree in Figure 7.12(a). Start at node 5 ($=\lfloor 11/2 \rfloor$) (83 is stored there) and compare its successors 94 and 7, determining that 94 is the larger. Compare 94 with 83 and since 94 exceeds 83 interchange 94 and 83 to obtain Figure 7.12(b).

The subtree with node 5 (94) as root is now a heap. Move to node 4 and the similar comparisons reveal that it is already a heap. Move to node 3, compare its successors 29 and 30, and then compare the larger to 16. Since 30 exceeds 16, interchange 30 and 16 to obtain Figure 7.12(c).

The subtree of node 3 is a heap, so move to node 2. Compare its successors 57 and 94, and then compare the larger to 14. Interchange 94 and 14 to obtain Figure 7.12(d).

At this point, notice that all nodes processed so far must be the roots of subtrees that remain heaps, except perhaps for the root of the subtree, where 14 now appears after the interchange. This subtree need not be a heap and, in fact, is not in this case. You can make it a heap by applying the same process to the node where 14 is currently stored, node 5. Compare its two successors and then compare the larger of those with 14. Then interchange 14 and 83 to obtain Figure 7.12(e).

The subtree with root node 2 is now a heap and the processing of node 2 is complete. Notice that all nodes processed so far are roots of subtrees that are heaps. The last node to be processed is now node 1. Compare its successors, 94 and 30. Since the larger, 94, exceeds 18, interchange to obtain Figure 7.12(f).

The 18 from the node being processed, node 1, has now moved down to node 2. Hence its subtree may no longer be a heap. Apply the process to node 2. The 18 can move down again and will continue to move down until it either becomes situated at a terminal node or becomes the root of a subtree that remains a heap. In this case, it should be compared with 83, the larger of its two successors, and interchanged to get Figure 7.12(g).

At this point, you can see that 18 is the root of a heap by comparing it to the larger of its two successors. Processing of node 1 has been completed, and the heap has been created. The heap obtained from the original example with this algorithm is Figure 7.12(h).

Without analyzing this heap creation algorithm in detail, its result can be stated. This procedure is actually only $O(N)$. This heap creation algorithm is faster than that of the last section because few nodes must move down long paths, while in the other algorithm, many nodes may move up long paths. A use for this linear time heap creation algorithm will be demonstrated in another context (in Section 7.6, Priority Queues).

7.4.5 Some Details of Heap Implementation

One way to implement the heap creation algorithm is to make use of a module, or routine, that works on a binary tree whose left and right subtrees are already heaps. The module does the "shifting" down of the root record until it becomes the root of a subtree that remains a heap, or until it reaches a terminal node. This "shift" routine need not do the interchanging along the way. Instead it can determine the final position of the root being shifted down, moving each record along that path to its predecessor, finally placing the root where it belongs.

Notice that the first heap creation algorithm requires testing the record being inserted along a path to the root against its current predecessor. Before this can be done, the program must test for whether or not there is a predecessor — that is, whether the record has already reached the root. This test must precede every comparison. Similarly, in the second heap creation algorithm the record being shifted down must be tested against its successors. Before doing this, it is necessary to test whether there are successors.

These tests can be avoided by always putting "plus infinity" at the root of the initial complete binary tree for the first algorithm, and "negative infinity" at the subtrees of all terminal nodes for the second algorithm. This is similar in effect to adding the search key to the end of the array in the linear search algorithm. **Plus infinity** and **negative infinity** stand for, respectively, any number larger or smaller than the numbers appearing in the binary tree. In this way, a record being inserted along a path in the first algorithm will never reach the root (so it will always have a predecessor with which it may be compared), and a record being shifted down in the second algorithm will always have successor nodes (since it will never become a terminal node).

7.4.6 Reheaping

Think of step 1 of the heap sorting algorithm as phase I, in which a heap is created. The execution of step 2 until the records are sorted is phase II. In phase II, the root element of the heap is removed and output. The program must then reheap. This may be done in two ways.

One is to allow the "gap" created at the root by removal of its record to shift down by comparing its two successors and interchanging the larger of the two successors with the gap, then repeating this process until the gap is at a terminal node. A convenient way to do this is to replace the record removed from the root by a "negative infinity," and invoke the shift down module referred to earlier for the second algorithm.

A second way to reheap is to replace the gap with the rightmost record at greatest depth (actually any record with no successors will do). The same shift module may be invoked to reheap.

Since the length of the longest path in a complete binary tree is $O(\lg N)$, the reheaping after each record is removed can take time at most $O(\lg N)$. Because N records will ultimately be removed, the total time required for phase II will be at most $O(N \lg N)$. For either implementation of phase I, the total heapsort time is $O(N \lg N)$. This was achieved by "spreading out" the records along paths of a complete binary tree, and, in effect, doing inserting only along the path from a record to the root.

We have been dealing with a **_max heap_**, in which the largest record is at the top. A **_min heap_**, with the smallest record at the top, is dealt with similarly. The only difference is that interchanging occurs when a successor's key is _smaller_, rather than larger.

7.4.7 An Implementation for Heapsort

You have now seen a number of ways to create a heap and to reheap. Picking a heap creation algorithm for phase I and a reheaping algorithm for phase II results in a more detailed version of the heapsort algorithm. To implement this algorithm in a high-level language, the programmer needs to decide on an implementation of the binary tree data structure.

The binary tree used in heapsort is initially complete. The required processing involves predecessors and successors of nodes. The sequential representation for the binary tree is thus ideal, and so we use it here. The binary tree is stored in the DATA array and consists of N records. We will use the second heap creation algorithm and the second reheaping method. They both use the SHIFT procedure.

Storage is needed for the sorted version of DATA. Although another array may seem necessary for this purpose, we will use only the DATA array. The algorithm, after creating a heap (in DATA), continually takes the root record as the next record in the sorted output, and then reheaps. Before reheaping, the rightmost record at the lowest level of the heap is placed at the root. The storage vacated by that rightmost record will no longer be needed. We choose to store the output record there. You should convince yourself that this will result in the records appearing in DATA in _reverse_ sorted order upon termination. To remedy this, we write SHIFT so that it produces MIN heaps. The records will then appear in correct sorted order upon termination.

SHIFT has parameters DATA, ROOT, and LAST. ROOT points to the root of a subtree, and LAST points to the node of the original heap that is currently the rightmost node at greatest depth. The nodes LAST + 1 to N are currently storing the already sorted N − LAST output records. Whenever SHIFT is invoked, the left and right subtrees of ROOT (excluding nodes LAST + 1 to N) are assumed to be heaps. SHIFT returns after reheaping, by allowing the ROOT record to move down to its final position. This is done by first storing the key value and record of the initial ROOT record in KEYVALUE and RECORDVALUE, respectively. PTR points to the node currently being considered as the final position for the initial ROOT record. This will be the final position if either of the following two conditions is met.

1. The successor record of PTR with minimum key value has a key value greater than or equal to KEYVALUE, or
2. PTR points to a terminal node or to a node whose successors are nodes among LAST + 1 to N.

Condition 2 can be recognized by the test (SUCC ≤ LAST), where SUCC points to the left successor node of PTR. Condition 1 requires finding the minimum key value for the successors of PTR. PTR may not have a right successor, or that successor may represent an output record. This can be tested for by the test (SUCC < LAST).

The heapsort is implemented with the following procedure.

```
procedure HEAPSORT(var DATA : recordarray; N : integer);
var
    TEMPRECORD : recordtype;
    ROOT, LAST : integer;
begin
    ROOT := N DIV 2;
    LAST := N;                              ⎫
    while ROOT > 0 do                       ⎬  Create the heap
        begin                               ⎭
            SHIFT(DATA, ROOT, LAST);
            ROOT := ROOT − 1
        end;
    ROOT := 1;                              ⎫
    while LAST > 1 do                       ⎪
        begin                               ⎪
            TEMPRECORD := DATA[1];          ⎪
            DATA[1] := DATA[LAST];          ⎬  Output and reheap
            DATA[LAST] := TEMPRECORD;       ⎪
            LAST := LAST − 1;               ⎪
            SHIFT(DATA, ROOT, LAST)         ⎭
        end
end;
```

The SHIFT procedure used in HEAPSORT is shown separately for clarity.

```
procedure SHIFT(var DATA : recordarray; ROOT, LAST : integer);
var
    PTR, SUCC : integer;
    KEYVALUE : whatevertype;
    RECORDVALUE : recordtype;
begin
    PTR := ROOT;
    SUCC := 2 * ROOT;
    if SUCC < LAST then
        if DATA[SUCC + 1].KEY < DATA[SUCC].KEY then
            SUCC := SUCC + 1;
    KEYVALUE := DATA[ROOT].KEY;
```

```
        RECORDVALUE := DATA[ROOT];
        while (SUCC <= LAST) and DATA[SUCC].KEY < KEYVALUE do
            begin
                DATA[PTR] := DATA[SUCC];
                PTR := SUCC;
                SUCC := 2 * PTR;
                if SUCC < LAST then
                    if DATA[SUCC + 1].KEY < DATA[SUCC].KEY then
                        SUCC := SUCC + 1
            end;
        DATA[PTR] := RECORDVALUE
    end;
```

When SHIFT determines that PTR is not the final position, it moves the record at PTR to its predecessor node. This is why the original record at root is saved. When the final position is found, the saved record is placed there. The initial heap and the situation after the first three entries have been output are shown in Figure 7.13 for the tree of Figure 7.7.

7.5 Quicksort: Another Fast Sort

As a final example of a sorting method, we consider an algorithm called *quicksort*. This algorithm is appropriately named, since its average execution is very quick. Its worst-case execution time is slow, but the worst case should occur rarely.

One way to develop quicksort is to attempt a recursive solution to the problem of sorting an array DATA of N records. The general recursive method immediately prescribes guidelines. Here, they dictate that the original array be broken down into component arrays which can then be sorted independently.

Thus DATA is to be separated into two components, an upper array and a lower array. We have two options for proceeding. One is to *combine* the resultant two sorted component arrays to achieve a final sorted solution. This method is the *merge sort*, which is not pursued here, but is applied to the sorting of files in Chapter 8. The second approach is to ensure that the resultant two sorted component arrays require *no further processing*, but directly yield the final sorted solution. This is the approach taken here.

Merely splitting DATA into two components and then sorting each component independently is not sufficient to guarantee that the resultant array is sorted, with no further processing required. This is because some entries in the upper component may be smaller than some entries in the lower component. For example, suppose the initial array is DATA, shown in Figure 7.14(a), and the upper and lower components consist, respectively, of entries 1 to 4, and 5 to 8. Sorting these components independently yields Figure 7.14(b), which is clearly not sorted.

Notice, however, that if *all* entries in the upper component were no less than *all* entries in the lower component, then sorting each component independently would always lead to a result which *is* sorted. For example, suppose the initial array is Figure 7.14(c). Taking the upper and lower components as entries 1 to 4, and 5 to 8, respectively, and independently sorting them produces Figure 7.14(d). This array is now sorted.

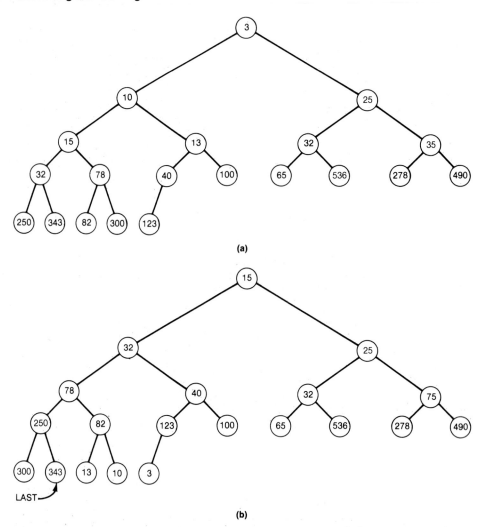

Figure 7.13   (a) Initial Heap and (b) Heap after First Three Entries Have Been Output

Note that the fifth entry, 13, occupies the same position in the sorted array as in the initial array. This is because all entries in the upper component are no less, and all entries in the lower component are no greater, than 13. The key value 13 actually occupied its proper position in the sorted version of DATA before the two components were sorted. Hence it need not be included in either component and may serve as a separator or ***partitioning entry*** between the two components to be sorted.

To carry out this procedure for an arbitrary array requires finding a partitioning entry. Normally a partitioning entry, such as 13 in position 5, will not occur in the initial array to be sorted. For example, no such partitioning entry (separating larger entries above from smaller entries below) occurs in Figure 7.14(a). This means that the initial array must be rearranged, so that a partitioning entry may be found and subsequently used to separate the components.

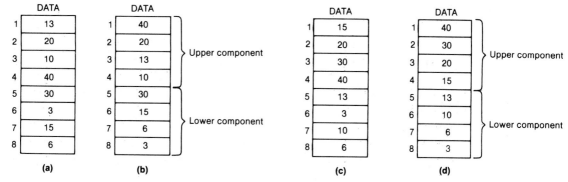

Figure 7.14   Sorting an Array by Component

Continuing the top-down approach, assume this task of rearranging the initial array and determining a partitioning entry is carried out by the integer function PARTITION(I, J). The arguments I and J contain pointers to entries of the array, as shown in Figure 7.15. PARTITION(I, J) returns a pointer to a partitioning entry of the array consisting of all entries between I and J. Thus, if PARTITION(I, J) returns a value P, then all entries between I and $P - 1$ are at least as great as DATA$[P]$.KEY, and all entries between $P + 1$ and J are no greater than DATA$[P]$.KEY. P separates the upper and lower components of I, J.

7.5.1   Two Quicksort Procedures

The procedure QUICKSORT may now be written, recursively, as

```
procedure QUICKSORT(I, J : integer);
var
    P : integer;
begin
    if I < J then
        begin
            P := PARTITION(I, J);
            QUICKSORT(I, P − 1);
            QUICKSORT(P + 1, J)
        end
end;
```

To sort a global array of N records, QUICKSORT$(1, N)$ is invoked. The crux of the algorithm is the PARTITION function, which will be discussed shortly. First, a nonrecursive version of QUICKSORT is developed.

Every time a call is made to QUICKSORT, two new obligations are incurred, and a current obligation is postponed. For instance, the initial call to QUICKSORT generates the initial obligation: sort the N entries of DATA. During the execution of this call, PARTITION determines a partitioning entry, and two new obligations are incurred. These are represented by the two recursive calls to QUICKSORT, one for each component. The current obligation must then be postponed to carry out these

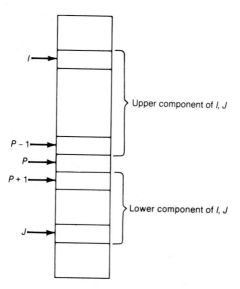

Upper component of *I, J*

Lower component of *I, J*

Figure 7.15   Array with a Partitioning Entry *P* Separating Upper and Lower Components

new obligations. Each recursive call also generates two new obligations, requiring the execution of the current recursive call to be postponed.

The **stack** is a convenient data abstraction for storing one of the new obligations, and the other can be processed immediately. It turns out that the choice of which of the two obligations to stack, and which to deal with immediately, is critical to the algorithm's storage requirements. Selecting the larger of the two components to stack results in a worst-case stack depth of $O(\lg N)$. An arbitrary choice instead leads to a worst-case stack depth of $O(N)$.

From this nonrecursive point of view, the algorithm structure amounts to a loop in which the smaller of the two new component arrays is processed, and the larger is stacked. The procedure may be written as

```
procedure QUICKSORT(I, J : integer);
var
    P, TOP, BOTTOM : integer;
    S : stack;
begin
    SETSTACK(S);
    PUSH(J, S);
    PUSH(I, S);
    while not EMPTY(S) do
        begin
            POP(S, TOP);
            POP(S, BOTTOM);
            while (TOP < BOTTOM) do
                begin
                    P := PARTITION(TOP, BOTTOM);
```

```
                    if (P − TOP) > (BOTTOM − P) then
                        begin
                            PUSH(P − 1, S);
                            PUSH(TOP, S);
                            TOP := P + 1
                        end
                    else
                        begin
                            PUSH(BOTTOM, S);
                            PUSH(P + 1, S);
                            BOTTOM := P − 1
                        end
                end
        end
end;
```

7.5.2   The Partition Module

We now return to the partitioning task. To determine a partitioning entry, and a corresponding rearrangement, the first array entry is selected as a basis. This is a somewhat arbitrary selection and will be discussed more fully later. In general, this first array entry will not be in its proper sorted position. It will need to be shifted, and the array rearranged, so that all larger entries appear in the upper component, and all smaller entries appear in the lower component.

A clever way to do this requires two pointers, UPPER and LOWER. Initially, UPPER is set to I, and LOWER to J, when the upper and lower components of I, J are to be determined. The initial situation is shown in Figure 7.16(a).

LOWER is now moved upward until an entry larger than DATA[UPPER].KEY is encountered. In this case, 15 will be that entry. It is then interchanged with DATA[UPPER]; see Figure 7.16(b). At this point, attention is shifted to UPPER, which is moved downward until an entry smaller than DATA[LOWER].KEY is encountered. This entry will be 10, and it is interchanged with DATA[LOWER], yielding Figure 7.16(c).

Attention now shifts back to LOWER, which is again moved upward until an entry greater than DATA[UPPER].KEY is encountered. This will be 30, and it is interchanged with DATA[UPPER], resulting in Figure 7.16(d).

UPPER is then moved downward until an entry smaller than DATA[LOWER].KEY is encountered. In this case no such entry appears, and when upper reaches LOWER, no such entry *can* appear. This is so because, at all times, any entries above UPPER are greater than the original first entry (13 in the example), and any entries below LOWER are less than the original first entry. Hence, whichever pointer is being moved, only entries between UPPER and LOWER can result in an interchange. When UPPER and LOWER coincide, no entries are left to interchange. Furthermore, when UPPER and LOWER coincide, they must be pointing to the original first entry or basis since at all times at least one of them points to it. The final situation, then, is as shown in Figure 7.16(e).

This procedure clearly carries out the task of PARTITION(I, J), which is to return the value of UPPER (or LOWER). Notice that, whether UPPER or LOWER

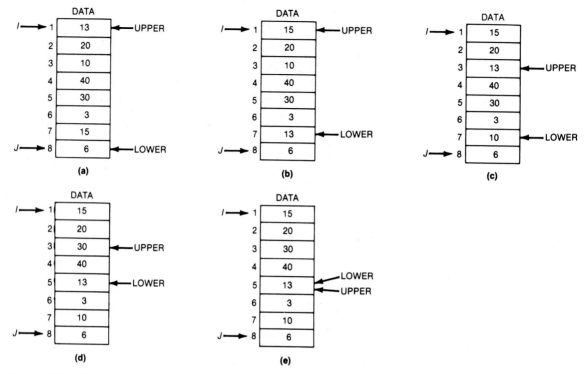

Figure 7.16   Sorting an Array by Means of a Partitioning Module

is the focus of attention, it is always the original first entry (13 here) that is the basis
for comparison. Instead of *interchanging* the basis with the larger or smaller entry
that has been found, the program simply *moves* the larger or smaller entry to the
position pointed to by the current stationary pointer. This is the position occupied by
the basis in the example. The basis will no longer appear in the array but must be
saved in a temporary variable, SAVERECORD. For the example, this would generate the sequence shown in Figure 7.17. When UPPER and LOWER meet, the
record stored in SAVERECORD must be copied into DATA[UPPER]. This version
of PARTITION may be implemented as follows:

```
function PARTITION(I, J : integer) : integer;
var
    UPPER, LOWER : integer;
    SAVERECORD : individualrecords;
begin
    UPPER := I;
    LOWER := J;
    SAVERECORD := DATA[I];
    while UPPER <> LOWER do
        begin
            while (UPPER < LOWER) and
                (SAVERECORD.KEY >= DATA[LOWER].KEY) do
```

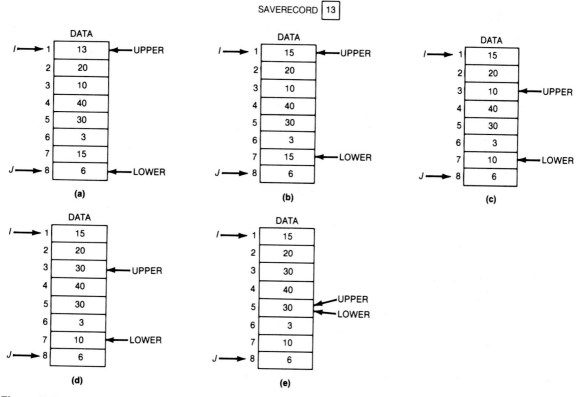

Figure 7.17   Partitioning an Array by Means of a Temporary Variable, SAVERECORD

```
            LOWER := LOWER − 1;
        if UPPER <> LOWER then
            DATA[UPPER] := DATA[LOWER];
        while (UPPER < LOWER) and
            (SAVERECORD.KEY <= DATA[UPPER].KEY) do
            UPPER := UPPER + 1;
        if UPPER <> LOWER then
            DATA[LOWER] := DATA[UPPER]
    end;
    DATA[UPPER] := SAVERECORD;
    PARTITION := UPPER
end;
```

It is important to recognize that, whenever PARTITION(I, J) is invoked, it processes only entries between I and J of the DATA array, and deals with each of these entries exactly once. Each entry is compared with SAVERECORD, and perhaps copied into DATA[UPPER] or DATA[LOWER]. Consequently, a call to PARTITION(I, J) takes time $O(J − I + 1)$, since there are $J − I + 1$ entries between I and J.

7.5.3 **Analyzing Iterative Quicksort**

We now want to analyze the nonrecursive version of quicksort to determine its time and storage requirements. To provide some insight into its behavior, we will simulate its application to our initial array, focusing on the changes that occur in this array and in the stack during execution.

Initially, the stack is empty, and the array is as shown in Figure 7.18(a). When QUICKSORT(1, 8) is invoked, it calls PARTITION(1, 8), which returns with P pointing to the partitioning entry. At this point, the rearranged array is Figure 7.18(b).

The upper component array is the larger, so $(1, 4)$ is placed on the stack, and the lower component array is processed. This leads to a call to PARTITION(6, 8). When PARTITION returns, the situation is Figure 7.18(c).

The *current* upper component array is larger, so $(6, 7)$ is placed on the stack, and the lower component array is processed. Note that the length of the component $(6, 7)$ is no greater than half the length of the preceding stack component $(1, 4)$. Since the lower component contains no entries, $(6, 7)$ is removed from the stack and PARTITION(6, 7) is invoked, returning the situation depicted in Figure 7.18(d).

Now $(6, 6)$ is placed on the stack, and the lower component is processed. Again, this component has no entries, so $(6, 6)$ is removed from the stack. Since TOP $(=6)$ is not less than BOTTOM $(=6)$, the outer **while** loop body is now executed, causing $(1, 4)$ to be removed from the stack. At this time the stack is empty, and the array is as shown in Figure 7.18(e). PARTITION(1, 4) is now invoked, and returns, yielding Figure 7.18(f).

Now $(1, 3)$ is placed on the stack. The lower component again contains no entries, so $(1, 3)$ is removed from the stack, and PARTITION(1, 3) is invoked. The result is Figure 7.18(g).

At this point $(2, 3)$ is placed on the stack, and since the upper component contains no entries, $(2, 3)$ is removed from the stack, and PARTITION(2, 3) is invoked. It returns with Figure 7.18(h).

Now $(2, 2)$ is placed on the stack. The lower component has no entries, so $(2, 2)$ is removed from the stack. Since TOP $(=2)$ and BOTTOM $(=2)$, the outer **while** loop test for an empty stack is made. As the stack is empty, QUICKSORT terminates.

It should now be clear that each time the inner loop body of QUICKSORT is executed, and TOP $<$ BOTTOM, P is set to point to an entry of the array that has been correctly placed in its final sorted position. If TOP $=$ BOTTOM then the one entry is already in its proper sorted position. The inner loop body is thus executed at most N times. Ignoring the time taken by PARTITION, the inner loop body takes a constant time to execute. Each time the inner loop body executes, it generates one new problem that is placed on the stack and another new problem that is processed immediately. As soon as this latter problem has fewer than two entries (TOP $\geq$ BOTTOM), the inner loop is exited. Unless the stack is empty, the outer loop removes the next problem from the stack, and the inner loop then functions again. Consequently, each entry that is placed in its proper position requires, at most, an execution of the inner loop body or an execution of the inner loop body plus the additional constant time required by the outer loop test plus removal of a problem from the stack. This means that the total time is, at most, $C_1 + C_2 \times N$ plus the total time taken by PARTITION, for some constants C_1 and C_2.

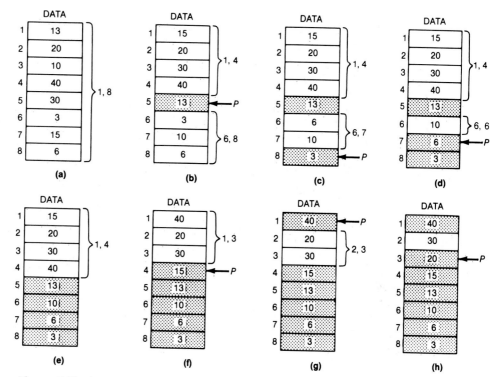

Figure 7.18   Iterative Quicksort

7.5.4   The Worst and Best Cases

To analyze the total time of PARTITION, recall that each execution takes time O (length of the component array it is called to work on). Since the length of a component is at most N, with PARTITION being invoked at most N times, total time is at most $O(N^2)$. Hence, QUICKSORT has a worst-case time $O(N^2)$. You should convince yourself that the worst case occurs whenever the initial array is in sorted or reverse sorted order.

The best case (fastest execution) actually occurs when the partitioning entry returned by PARTITION splits the array in half. In this case, PARTITION is called to work on one component array of length N, two component arrays of length $N/2$, four component arrays of length $N/4$, . . . , 2^k component arrays of length $N/2^k$, etc. By an argument similar to the worst-case analysis of the binary search, about $\lg_2 N$ such calls will be made to PARTITION. Its total time will then be $O(N \lg N)$.

While the worst-case time for QUICKSORT is poor, its best-case time is fast — in fact, better than HEAPSORT. The average time for QUICKSORT is also $O(N \lg N)$. This assumes that each ordering of the N entries is equally likely to appear in the initial array. Evidently, cases differing significantly from the best occur rarely, and this is why QUICKSORT is aptly named.

The storage requirements for QUICKSORT, beyond the initial array, are a few variables plus the stack depth. Since the larger of each generated component array problem is stacked, the next problem to be stacked must have length at most one-half the current top stack entry length. Again, by an argument similar to the worst-case binary search analysis, at most $O(\lg N)$ such problems can appear on the stack at any time, so the storage requirements for QUICKSORT are $O(\lg N)$. Thus, QUICKSORT, while faster on the average than HEAPSORT (by a factor of 2 or 3), does not have the guaranteed worst-case $O(N \lg N)$ time of HEAPSORT. Moreover, QUICKSORT requires additional storage $O(\lg N)$ to achieve its faster average time.

For smaller values of N, the simpler sorts, like the insertion sort, will be even faster than quicksort. Of course, if the initial array is known to be nearly sorted, the insertion sort will be faster anyway. Clearly, one way to speed up quicksort is to modify it by using a faster sort, such as insertion sort, when small component arrays are encountered. It is also possible to enhance the performance of quicksort by taking more care in the selection of the entry to be used as a basis by PARTITION. Instead of taking the first entry of a component as the basis, the median of three entries may be selected, or an entry may be selected at random.

7.5.5 Distributive Partitioning

Although sorting has been extensively researched, a new generalization of the quick-sort, *distributive partitioning,* has recently been discovered [Dobosiewicz, 1976]. It appears to be even faster than QUICKSORT. Recall that the quicksort was based on the idea of rearranging the initial array so that it could be split into *two* component arrays to be sorted independently. Each of these arrays was then recursively sorted in the same way. **Distributive partitioning** carries this idea to its logical limit, by splitting the initial array into N component arrays, to be sorted independently and recursively. The price paid by this new algorithm is that additional storage of size $O(N \lg N)$ is required. Note that all the sorting algorithms considered sort in place, except the quicksort and distributive partitioning. Quicksort and distributive partitioning require additional storage, limiting their use for large N. Since quicksort's additional storage increases $1/N$th as fast as that of distributive partitioning, it will not be as severely limited.

7.6 Priority Queues

Situations are frequently encountered in which n tasks are given, each with an associated priority. The n tasks are to be carried out in order of priority. When studying for examinations, most students review and prepare in order of priority determined by the date of the exam. Most people read the chapters of a book in order, with priority determined by chapter numbering. Computer centers process submitted programs by attaching a priority to each, and processing them in order of priority. It is usually necessary to add new tasks to the current collection.

A **priority queue** is a data structure with objects, their priorities, and two operations, insertion and deletion. **Insertion in a priority queue** means an object with its priority is added to the collection of objects, and **deletion from a priority queue** means an object with highest priority is deleted from the collection. A **stack** may be thought of as a priority queue with the highest priority object the one most recently added. (The stack would be used for the LIFO system of accounting: last in, first out.) A **queue** may be thought of as a priority queue with the highest priority object the

Table 7.1 Worst-Case Insertion
and Deletion Times for the Priority Queue

Implementation	Insertion	Deletion
Unordered		
Array	Constant	$O(N)$
List	Constant	$O(N)$
Ordered		
Array	$O(N)$	Constant
List	$O(N)$	Constant

earliest added. (The queue would be needed for the FIFO system of accounting: first in, first out.)

High-level programming languages do not have priority queues directly available in their memories. It is important to be able to implement such queues because they are of use in their own right, and, as will be shown later, they often appear as components of algorithms.

7.6.1 Simple Implementations

To implement a priority queue, first represent its objects and priorities as records with priority fields. Two ways to store the records come immediately to mind—an array and a list. In either case, the programmer may choose to store the records in arbitrary order, or in order of priority. Table 7.1 gives the worst-case insertion and deletion times for each of the four implementations, when N records are present in the priority queue. You should be able to justify the entries of the table. For example, when using the ordered array implementation, the top array record will have highest priority; thus deletion can be performed in constant time by using a pointer TOP to the current top record. Insertion of a record requires a search of the array to find its proper position. A binary search will allow this position to be found quickly, but to insert it requires $O(N)$ time because all records below it must be shifted down.

If insertions are more frequent than deletions, it is better to use unordered records. Another factor will be the amount of available memory. Less memory favors the array.

7.6.2 Using a Heap

You have seen how to implement a heap data structure efficiently so that storage is minimal, heap creation takes at most $O(N)$ time, and reheaping takes at most $O(\lg N)$ time. Another implementation for the priority queue is to store the records at the nodes of a heap that is ordered by priority field values. To insert a new record, place it as a new rightmost entry at the greatest depth of the heap. Then let it work its way up in the heap as in the first heap creation algorithm. Adding the new record in this way will take time at most $O(\lg N)$. To delete a record, simply delete the record at the root of the heap, and then reheap by invoking SHIFT. This takes time at most $O(\lg N)$. The time to create the heap initially will be at most $O(N)$ if the second heap creation algorithm is used, but this will also be the time required to create the initial unordered array or list of records. To create sorted arrays or lists will take time at most

$O(N \lg N)$. Referring to Table 7.1, you can see that the heap implementation affords a compromise solution. Either one operation can be done quickly (in constant time) and the other in $O(N)$ time, or both operations can be done in at most $O(\lg N)$ time.

7.6.3 Using Leftist Trees

Given two priority queues, suppose you wish to merge them, to produce a priority queue consisting of all entries from both queues. The implementations discussed so far do *not* allow this merge operation to be done in $O(\lg N)$ time, where N is the total number of entries in the two priority queues. Crane [1972] introduced *leftist trees* as a data structure that can be used to implement priority queues (see Knuth [1973a] for more details). Leftist trees do allow merging to be done in $O(\lg N)$ time. They also allow the other priority queue operations to be done in $O(\lg N)$ time. Moreover, they require only constant time for additions and deletions when the priority queue is acting as a stack.

A *leftist tree* is a null binary tree or is a binary tree with the following properties:

- ☐ It is a heap.
- ☐ Its left and right subtrees are leftist trees.
- ☐ The path, obtained by starting from the root and branching to the right until a node with no right successor is reached, is the shortest path from the root to any node with at most one successor.

For example, the tree (a) of Figure 7.19 violates condition 3 while the trees (b) and (c) are leftist trees.

As an exercise, you should prove, by induction on the number of nodes, N, in a leftist tree, that the shortest path in the tree, from the root to a node with at most one successor, contains at most $\lfloor \lg(N + 1) \rfloor$ nodes. Such a shortest path can always be obtained by traversing the right chain from the root.

Leftist trees are implemented using a linked representation. (See Figure 7.20.) Each node's record has an additional field, the distance field, containing the number of nodes along the right chain. The algorithm for merging two priority queues represented as leftist trees in $O(\lg N)$ time is as follows:

1. Make NODE.*P* the root of the merged tree, and merge *Q* with *P*'s right subtree.

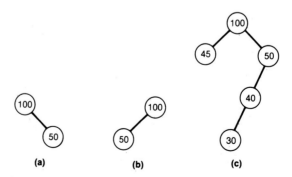

(a) (b) (c)

Figure 7.19 One Nonleftist and Two Leftist Trees

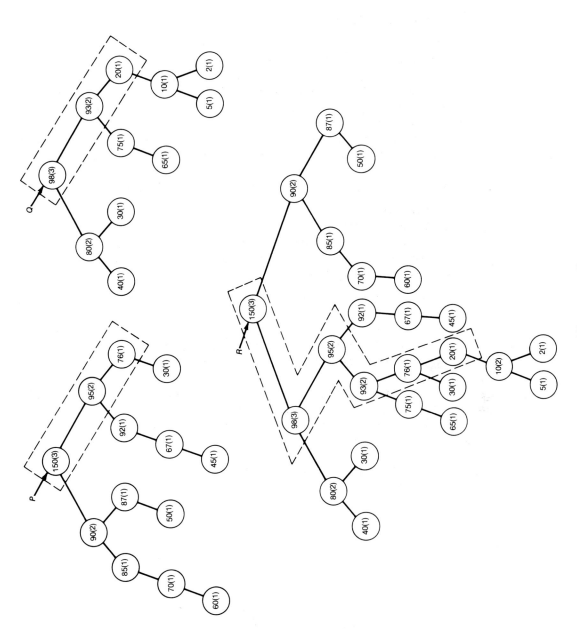

Figure 7.20 The Merging of Leftist Trees Implemented in Linked Representation

2. Update the distance field of NODE.*P.*
3. If the distance of the root of the left subtree is not at least as great as the distance of the root of its right subtree, then interchange the two subtrees.

P is assumed to point to the root of the two leftist trees to be merged containing the maximum of the two root key values, and *Q* points to the other root. The result of merging the two trees *P* and *Q* is shown as the tree *R.* The distance field values appear in parentheses. Notice that, in effect, the two right chains of *P* and *Q* are merged, with the other subtrees coming along for the ride. It is because only these two shortest paths participate in the algorithm, that the time is *O*(lg *N*).

7.7 Binary Search Trees

We return now to the problem of attaining binary search time *O*(lg *N*) while still being able to do efficient inserting and deleting. A **binary search tree** is a binary tree with the property that its left subtree contains records no larger than the root record, its right subtree contains records no smaller than the root record, and its left and right subtrees are also binary search trees. This is a recursive definition.

A binary tree fails to be a binary search tree if even *one* node contains a record in its left subtree or its right subtree that is, respectively, larger or smaller than the

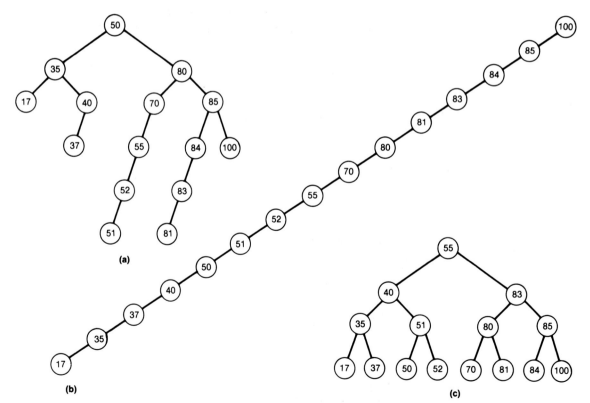

Figure 7.21   Three Binary Search Trees Containing the Same Data

record stored at the node. Figure 7.21 has three examples of binary search trees containing the same fifteen records.

Note that a binary search tree need not be a heap, and that a heap need not be a binary search tree. In general, they are different kinds of binary trees. There are many binary trees that can store the same records. Any binary tree with N nodes can store N records in such a way that the tree is a binary search tree (just do an inorder traversal of the binary tree and insert the records in sorted order).

7.7.1 Searching the Search Trees

In Chapter 6, three important traversals through the nodes of any binary tree were defined: 1) preorder, 2) inorder, and 3) postorder. In order to search a binary tree to determine if a particular key value is stored, any one of those traversals could be used to gain access to each node in turn, and the node tested to see if the search key value is there. This would be equivalent to a linear search.

The special nature of binary *search* trees allows for much more efficient search. Compare the search key with the root key. If it is there, the search is complete. If it is not there, determine whether it is smaller than the key at the root. If so, then if it is in the tree at all, it must be in the left subtree. If it is larger than the root key, it must be in the right subtree if it is in the tree at all. Thus, either the left or right subtree is eliminated from consideration. This procedure is repeated for the subtree not eliminated. Eventually, the procedure finds the key in the tree or comes to a null subtree and concludes that the key is not stored in the tree.

Assume that nodes of the binary search tree are represented as

```
type
    binarytree = ↑ node;
    node       = record
                     key : whatevertype;
                     leftptr, rightptr : binarytree
                 end;
```

This special search may be implemented as follows:

```
FOUND := false;
P := T;
PRED := nil;
while P <> nil and not FOUND do
    if KEYVALUE = P↑.KEY then
        FOUND := TRUE
    else if KEYVALUE < P↑.KEY then
        begin
            PRED := P;
            P := P↑.LEFTPTR
        end
    else
        begin
            PRED := P;
            P := P↑.RIGHTPTR
        end;
```

FOUND indicates whether the search key value was present in the tree. If so, *P* points to the node in which the search key was found, and PRED points to its predecessor. If the search key was not found, then PRED points to the node that would have been its predecessor had it been in the tree.

Notice that when (b) of Figure 7.21 is searched in this way, the search is equivalent to a linear search of an array in which the records are stored in sorted order. This search algorithm, applied to (c), would be equivalent to a binary search of an array in which the records are stored in sorted order. A search of (a) would fall somewhere between these two extremes.

What allows the search of Figure 7.21(c) to be equivalent to a binary search? It is the fact that the tree is "scrunched up" or near minimum possible depth, and not as straggly (unnecessarily deep) as the others. It has an intuitive kind of "balance," so that we eliminate from consideration about half the records each time we make a comparison. This should remind you of the game "twenty questions."

7.7.2 Growing the Search Tree "Simply"

This section develops an algorithm for creating or growing a binary search tree that stores records at its nodes. Imagine that you have already processed some records and created a binary search tree for them. Given the next input record, search the current tree for its key value. Assume no duplicates will occur in the tree, although this need not create any real problem since a node can contain a pointer to a list, stored separately, of records with identical key values. Eventually, since the new record is not in the tree, a null subtree will be reached. However, if this null subtree is replaced by a node that stores this record, the resultant tree will still be a binary search tree. For instance, inserting 45 by this procedure, in (c) of Figure 7.21, produces Figure 7.22. This gives an algorithm for growing a binary search tree. Start with the first input record at the root. For each additional input, search the tree. The search will reach a node whose left or right successor must be followed, but the successor is null. The record replaces that null subtree.

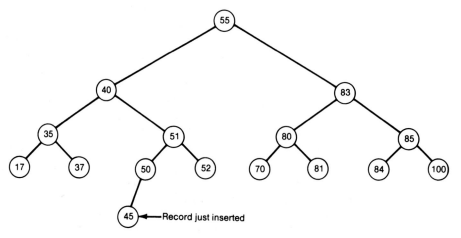

Figure 7.22   Binary Search Tree Created from Figure 7.21(c)

This can be accomplished by using PRED from the search implementation, and then invoking

```
NEW(P);
P↑.KEY := KEYVALUE;
P↑.LEFTPTR := nil;
P↑.RIGHTPTR := nil;
if KEYVALUE < PRED↑.KEY then
    PRED↑.LEFTPTR := P
else
    PRED↑.RIGHTPTR := P;
```

We now have algorithms for growing, searching, and inserting records into a binary search tree.

7.7.3 **The Shape of Simple Binary Search Trees**

The binary search tree grown by the algorithm of the preceding section will have its shape determined by the input order of the records to be stored. If they are input in sorted order, or reverse sorted order, the result is Figure 7.21(b) or its mirror image. If they are input in the order 55, 40, 83, 35, 51, 80, 85, 17, 37, 50, 52, 70, 81, 84, 100, the result is Figure 7.21(c). There are $N!$ possible input orderings of N distinct keys. Some of these may give rise to the same binary search tree. We know that the tree grown cannot have depth greater than N nor less than $\lceil \lg(N + 1) \rceil$. Suppose the input is selected so that each of the $N!$ possible orderings is equally likely to occur. This would be the case if the first input record is selected at random from among the N records, the second is selected at random from among the remaining $N - 1$ records, and so on. What will be the *average* depth of trees grown by the algorithm in this case? To calculate the average depth directly would mean to generate, for each of the $N!$ orderings of input records, the binary search tree grown and note its depth. Then add up the $N!$ depths and divide by $N!$ to obtain the average depth.

It is difficult to analyze this problem using probability theory. However, the average depth has been shown to be $O(C \lg N)$, where C is about 4. The **average search time** can be calculated for a randomly grown binary tree. It is the average time required to search for a record stored in the binary tree, assuming each record is equally likely to be searched. This average search time is $O(1.39 \lg N)$. In the case of random input, the average search of the binary search tree grown by the algorithm will be only 39 percent more than the smallest possible average search time! Moreover, the algorithm for growing the tree will take an average time at most $O(\lg N)$. If the records are given in sorted order instead of in random order, it will take the algorithm $O(N^2)$ time to grow the tree.

It is possible to grow "balanced" binary search trees, also called AVL trees, after the discoverers of these trees, Adelson-Velskii and Landis [1962]. The algorithm for growing AVL trees is slower and more complex, as is the insertion and deletion of records. However, they are guaranteed to have depth no greater than about $1.44 \lg N$. This is the *worst-case* depth. Consequently, AVL trees may be searched in time at most $O(1.44 \lg N)$. Such trees appear quite healthy and are never sparse. It always takes greater care to grow healthy trees, as will be seen later.

7.7.4 Deleting a Record "Simply"

All the important operations on binary search trees have been considered here except deletion. The purpose of this section is to derive an algorithm for deleting a record from a binary search tree so that the remaining tree is still a binary search tree. To delete a terminal record, simply replace it by a null tree. To delete a record with only one successor, simply insert the successor's subtree at the position occupied by the deleted node. For instance, in the tree shown in Figure 7.23(a), deleting 51 and 71 yields the tree shown in Figure 7.23(b).

Consider Figure 7.23 again. A difficulty occurs if you wish to delete 80, a record with two successors. The node 80 must be replaced by a record that will allow the tree to retain its binary search tree property. This means that the record replacing 80 must be at least as large as any record in the left subtree of 80, and no larger than any record in the right subtree of 80. There are two choices: replace 80 with the largest record in its left subtree or the smallest record in its right subtree.

Notice that the largest record in any binary search tree is always found by going to its root and following right successors until a null tree is reached. The smallest record is found by going to its root and following left successors until a null tree is reached. Thus, in the example, we may take either 77 or 81's record to replace 80's record. The record selected, say 77, must then be inserted in place of 80's record, which is then effectively deleted. Taking 77 requires that 74's record replace it. The result is Figure 7.23(c). It should be clear that searching, inserting, or deleting, using the procedures in a search tree of depth d, will take worst-case time proportional to d.

Binary search trees are treated in this chapter as abstract objects. A sequential representation for deep but sparse trees requires array lengths proportional to $2^d - 1$. Deletions for this representation require a great deal of shifting of records. For instance, to delete 85 requires shifting 84, 83, and 81. To save storage, and to achieve faster insertions and deletions, requires using a linked representation.

7.7.5 A Balancing Act

The "simple" algorithms for growing binary search trees and inserting and deleting records within them are relatively simple and have excellent time and storage requirements on the *average* when randomly done. While these randomly grown trees can be fine for compiler symbol tables, or for small data base applications such as dictionaries, or for creating indexes, there are situations where good average behavior is not enough. Suppose your rocket ship's computer must search a binary search tree for retro-rocket firing instructions, and must complete the search within a specific interval. This is not the time to find that the tree is out of shape and that a much longer than average time will ensue.

This section discusses AVL or balanced binary search trees in more detail. An **AVL tree** is a balanced binary tree that is also a binary search tree. (*Balanced binary trees* were defined in Chapter 6 in the discussion of Fibonacci trees.)

AVL trees have excellent *worst-case* time and storage requirements and allow access to the *I*th record to be performed quickly. The algorithms for the growth of such trees and insertion and deletion within them are considerably more complex than for "simple" binary search trees. Balanced trees are very useful whenever all

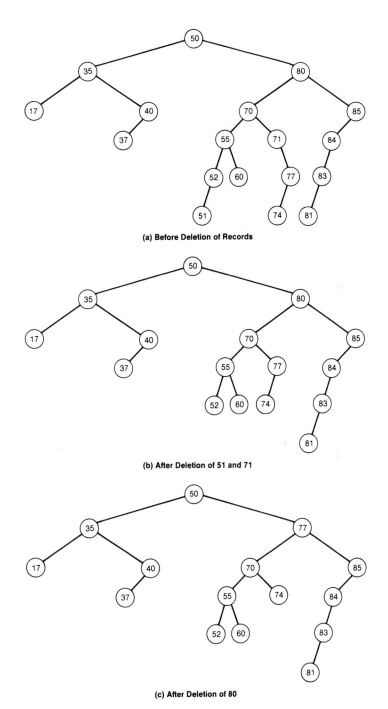

(a) Before Deletion of Records

(b) After Deletion of 51 and 71

(c) After Deletion of 80

Figure 7.23 A Binary Search Tree before and after Deletion of Records

four operations — searching, inserting, deleting, and accessing the *I*th record — are needed and worst-case rather than average time is important.

The next task is to construct a balanced binary search tree (AVL tree) of depth d, which has the least number of nodes among all AVL trees, of depth d. Such a tree will be a Fibonacci tree that is also a binary search tree. These trees represent the worst-case AVL trees, because we want to use AVL trees to store records. Thus it is desirable for the AVL tree to have as small a depth as possible and yet to store as many records as possible for that depth. The "best" AVL tree of depth d is complete and has $2^d - 1$ nodes. A Fibonacci AVL tree of depth d will, instead, store the minimum possible number of records. Suppose $N(d)$ represents the number of nodes of such a tree. Then, any AVL tree with depth d must have a number of nodes N that is at least $N(d)$. It is possible to prove that $N(d)$ is related to the $(d + 2)$th Fibonacci number, $F(d + 2)$. In fact, $N(d) = F(d + 2) - 1$. A great deal is known about the Fibonacci numbers. In particular, $F(d + 2) > (\phi^{d+2}/\sqrt{5}) - 1$, where $\phi = (1 + \sqrt{5})/2$. It follows from this that $N \geq N(d) > (\phi^{d+2}/\sqrt{5}) - 2$. Also, from Chapter 6, $N \leq 2^d - 1$. After some manipulation we may conclude that

$$d < 1.44 \lg (N + 2) - 0.328$$

This means that the depth of any AVL tree with N nodes is never greater than $1.44 \lg(N + 2)$. In other words, an AVL tree storing N records has a worst-case depth $O(\lg N)$. Since the best possible depth of a binary tree storing N records is $\lceil \lg(N + 1) \rceil$, the *worst depth* of an AVL tree storing N records is at most 44 percent more than the best achievable. Contrast this with the "simple" binary search tree for which the *average depth* is at least 39 percent more than the best achievable. Consequently, it is very desirable to be able to create and use AVL trees.

7.7.6 Maintaining Balance

Consider the AVL tree of Figure 7.24(a). To insert a new record into this tree, let us search for it and then replace a null tree by the new node. The dashed branches indicate the sixteen possible insertion positions for a new node. You should confirm that, of these, only an insertion of a new node as a successor of 45, 53, 81, or 100 will cause the new tree to fail to remain an AVL tree. An insertion at node 45 causes the subtrees with roots 55, 40, and 70 to become unbalanced. For example, the subtree with root 40 would have a left subtree of depth 2, while its right subtree would have depth 4. These differ by more than 1. Notice that 55, 40, and 70 lie along the search path from the root to the new node inserted as a successor of 45. If 43 were inserted, then the result would be the tree of Figure 7.24(b). Thus the "simple" insertion discussed earlier will not retain the balance of a search tree.

This imbalance is remedied by rearranging the subtree with root 55 as shown in Figure 7.24(c). Notice that the subtrees with roots 40 and 70 are no longer out of balance. In fact, the tree of Figure 7.24(c) is now an AVL tree. Notice also that the subtree in Figure 7.24(c) replacing the subtree of 55 in Figure 7.24(b) has *exactly* the same depth as the original subtree of 55 in Figure 7.24(a). If any of the other insertions that would have produced an imbalance in Figure 7.24(a) had occurred, they could have been remedied by similar rearrangements. You should confirm this by trying them all and finding the suitable rearrangements. Remember, the

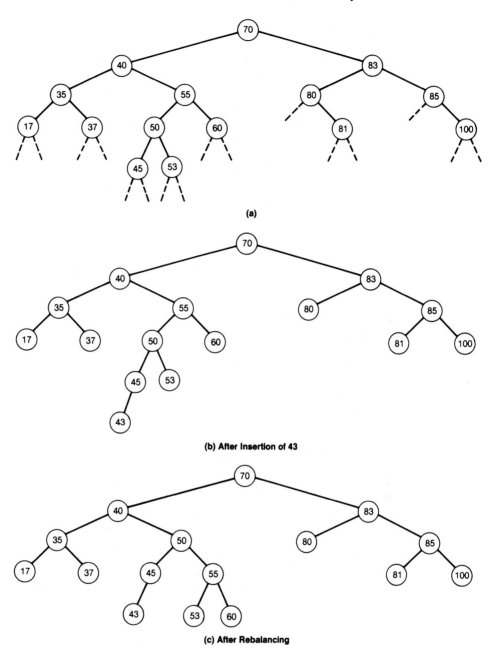

(a)

(b) After Insertion of 43

(c) After Rebalancing

Figure 7.24 An AVL Tree before and after Insertion

rearrangements not only must rebalance, but also must preserve the binary search tree property.

It is possible to analyze the general situation to determine exactly when an insertion will cause an imbalance, and what its remedy will be. An insertion into an AVL tree with zero or one node cannot cause an imbalance. When the tree has more

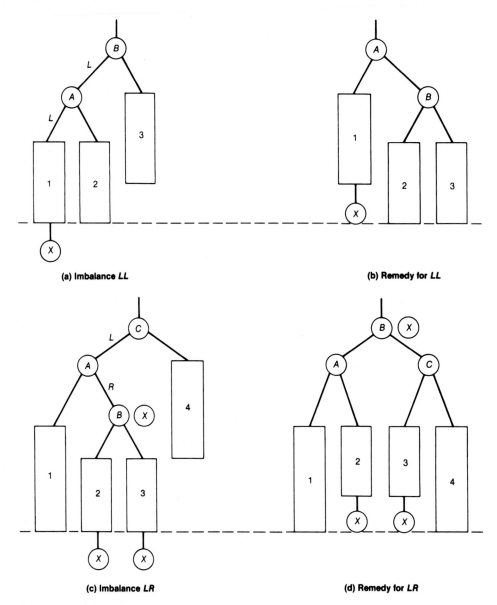

(a) Imbalance *LL*   **(b) Remedy for *LL***

(c) Imbalance *LR*   **(d) Remedy for *LR***

Figure 7.25   Two Imbalances and Their Remedies

than one node, the types of imbalance, and their corresponding remedies, reduce to the four indicated in Figures 7.25 and 7.26.

Each rectangle in Figures 7.25 and 7.26 represents an AVL tree; any of these may be null. An *X* represents the position of the inserted new record that has caused imbalance. Three *X*'s appear in imbalances *LR* and *RL*, actually representing three possibilities, although only one will have taken place. The *LR* and *RL* imbalances are meant to include the special case where *B* is actually the inserted node. This is why

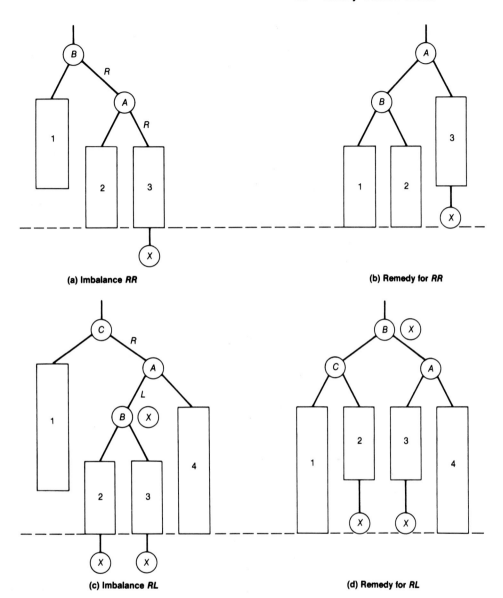

(a) Imbalance *RR*

(b) Remedy for *RR*

(c) Imbalance *RL*

(d) Remedy for *RL*

Figure 7.26 Two More Imbalances and Their Remedies

the X appears next to node B. Subtrees 1, 2, 3, and 4 must then be null. This fact is noted here, since it is not clear from the figures. In cases *LL* and *RR*, the subtree with root B represents the node closest to the inserted node, along the path from the inserted node to the root, where an imbalance occurs. In cases *LR* and *RL* the subtree with root C represents this node. In all remedies, the subtrees represented by the rectangles retain their relative positions. Note that all remedies preserve the binary *search* tree property. It is very important to see that, in each case, the depth

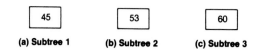

(a) Subtree 1   (b) Subtree 2   (c) Subtree 3

Figure 7.27   Rectangles 1–3 of Figures 7.26(a) and 7.26(b)

of the remedy is exactly the same as the depth of the original subtree before the new insertion was made. Consequently, *no* nodes on the path from the subtree root, *B* in cases *LL* and *RR*, and *C* in cases *LR* and *RL*, imbalanced by the new insertion, will be imbalanced after the remedy is applied. It is also important to see that these remedies are applied *locally;* they do not involve the creation of a new AVL tree in its entirety.

In Figure 7.24, when 43 was inserted, case *LL* occurred. The roles of *B* and *A* were taken by 55 and 50, respectively. The three rectangles, 1, 2, 3 of Figure 7.25 (a and b), represented, respectively, the subtrees shown in Figure 7.27. The *X* represented 43.

Consider imbalance *LL*. The remedy looks as though *A* has moved up to the root and *B* has moved to the right. This is called a *rotation to the right of the subtree with* B *at its root*. The remedy for imbalance *RR* would be described as a *rotation to the left of the subtree with* B *at its root*. To rectify imbalance *LR*, perform a rotation to the left of the subtree with root *A* to obtain Figure 7.28(a). A further rotation to the right of the subtree rooted at *C* produces (b) of Figure 7.28. Assume rotations are accomplished by procedures ROTATELEFT and ROTATERIGHT, each with a parameter that points to the root of the subtree to be rotated. Then the remedies for each imbalance may be obtained by

LL: ROTATERIGHT(LAST)	where LAST points to *B*
RR: ROTATELEFT(LAST)	where LAST points to *B*
LR: ROTATELEFT(LAST ↑.LEFTPTR)	where LAST points to *C*
ROTATERIGHT(LAST)	
RL: ROTATERIGHT(LAST ↑.RIGHTPTR)	where LAST points to *C*
ROTATELEFT(LAST)	

The procedure for ROTATERIGHT, for example, might be

```
procedure ROTATERIGHT(var LOCALROOT : binarytree);
var
    Q : binarytree;
begin
    Q := LOCALROOT ↑.LEFTPTR;
    LOCALROOT ↑.LEFTPTR := Q ↑.RIGHTPTR;
    Q ↑.RIGHTPTR := LOCALROOT;
    LOCALROOT := Q
end;
```

Note that the procedure also changes the pointer in LOCALROOT, so it points to the root of the new subtree. It is assumed that nodes of the AVL tree are represented as

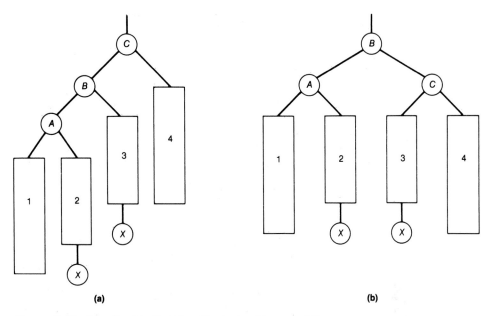

Figure 7.28 The Double Rotation Producing Remedy *LR*

```
type
    balancevalue = −1 .. + 1;
    binarytree   = ↑ node;
    node         = record
                       key : whatevertype;
                       leftptr, rightptr : binarytree;
                       balance : balancevalue
                   end;
```

The BALANCE field stores the node's right subtree depth minus the node's left subtree depth. In an AVL tree it will have values $-1, 0,$ or $+1$.

Consider the binary tree shown in Figure 7.29(a), which was balanced until the new node, marked by X, was inserted. The initial BALANCE values are also shown. Because of the insertion, the ROOT node and node C have become unbalanced. Since node C is closest to the inserted node, we remedy this imbalance by applying the remedy for *RL* to obtain Figure 7.29(b). The tree itself is now balanced, but the balances of nodes A, B, and C are now incorrect, as are the balances of the three nodes between X and A. The last node, however, does have the correct balance value.

In general, after rebalancing, one of the nodes involved in the remedy will be the new root of the subtree that was rebalanced (B in the example). If the remedy was *LL* or *RR*, all nodes along the path from this node to the inserted node, starting with its successor, need their balances reset. If the remedy was *LR* or *RL*, then all nodes along this path, starting with its successor's successor (the successor of A in the example), need their balances reset. The node not on this path involved in the remedy (C in the example) must have its balance reset, and, finally, the new root of the rebalanced subtree must have its balance set to 0. The special case when the

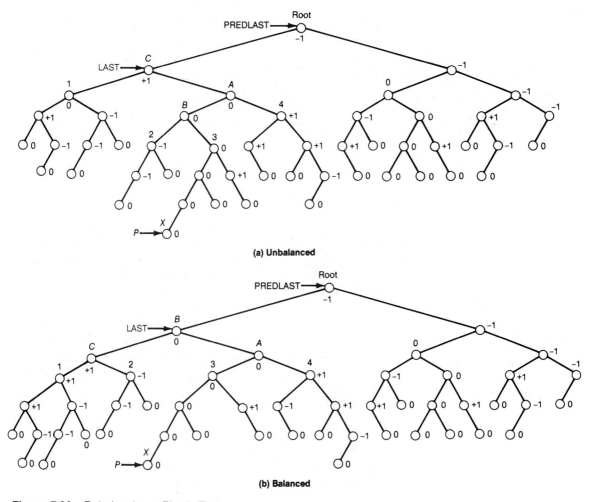

Figure 7.29   Rebalancing a Binary Tree

inserted node is at B requires only that C's balance be set to 0. All nodes *above* this new root need not be reset; they retain their original values. Any time the root node is involved, special processing is required, since the head of the tree must be modified rather than a left or right subtree pointer of a node.

The algorithm for ***inserting a node into an AVL tree*** can now be written.

1. Search for the keyvalue.
2. If it is not found, then
   a. Create a new node for it and set its field values.
   b. Insert the new node into the tree.
   c. If the tree has more than one node, then
      i. If it is not necessary to rebalance, then
         reset appropriate balances on the search path.
      ii. If it is necessary to rebalance, then
         apply the appropriate remedy and rebalance,

reset the balance of the node involved in the remedy but not on the
new search path,
reset the proper new search path balances,
set the balance of the root of the subtree at which rebalancing
occurred to 0.
If this root was the root of the tree itself, then
set the head of the tree to this root,
otherwise set its predecessor to this root;
else
reset the balance of the predecessor of the inserted node.

It has already been noted that, when a rebalance is necessary, once the subtree
whose root is nearest the newly inserted node has been rebalanced with the correct
remedy, all other subtrees along the path to the root of the entire tree will also be back
in balance. Again, this is because the smallest subtree causing the imbalance has been
modified by the remedy to have its original depth. All the subtrees were originally
balanced when it had that depth, so they must be balanced now. During the search
in step 1 for the insertion key, suppose you keep a pointer LAST. LAST is updated
to point to the node that may become imbalanced on the search path nearest the
insertion node. Only nodes with balance values of ±1 may become imbalanced due
to the insertion. It is necessary to rebalance only if LAST $\uparrow$.BALANCE was -1 and
the search path went left at LAST, or LAST $\uparrow$.BALANCE was $+1$ and the search path
went right at LAST, P is not T, and PRED $\uparrow$.BALANCE $= 0$. Only nodes on the
search path, between the inserted node and LAST, will need to have their balance
fields updated.

During the search, an updated pointer to the predecessor node of LAST should
be kept in PREDLAST. P will point to the node whose key field is currently being
compared with the search key, and PREDP points to its predecessor. An implementation of the AVL tree insertion is given in the INSERTAVL procedure. For
clarity, the procedures CREATENODE and SEARCH are then given separately,
followed by procedures INSERTNODE and RESETPATHBALANCES.

```
procedure INSERTAVL(KEYVALUE : whatevertype; var T : binarytree);
var
    P, PREDP, LAST, PREDLAST, Q : binarytree;
    FOUND : boolean;
begin
    SEARCH(KEYVALUE, T, P, PREDP, LAST, PREDLAST, FOUND);
    if not FOUND then
        begin
            CREATENODE(KEYVALUE, P);
            INSERTNODE(KEYVALUE, P, PREDP, T);
            if P <> T then
                if PREDP↑.BALANCE = 0 then
                    if KEYVALUE < LAST↑.KEY then
                        case LAST↑.BALANCE of
                            0 : begin
                                LAST↑.BALANCE := -1;
                                RESETPATHBALANCES(KEYVALUE, LAST↑.LEFTPTR, P)
                            end;
```

```
+1 : begin
         LAST↑.BALANCE := 0;
         RESETPATHBALANCES(KEYVALUE, LAST↑.LEFTPTR, P)
    end;
-1 : begin
         Q := LAST↑.LEFTPTR;
         if KEYVALUE < Q↑.KEY then
             begin
                 ROTATERIGHT(LAST);
                 LAST↑.RIGHTPTR↑.BALANCE := 0;
                 RESETPATHBALANCES(KEYVALUE, LAST↑.LEFTPTR, P)
             end
         else
             begin
                 ROTATELEFT(LAST↑.LEFTPTR);
                 ROTATERIGHT(LAST);
                 if KEYVALUE < LAST↑.KEY then
                     begin
                         Q↑.BALANCE := 0;
                         LAST↑.RIGHTPTR↑.BALANCE := +1;
                         RESETPATHBALANCES(KEYVALUE,
                                           LAST↑.LEFTPTR↑.
                                           RIGHTPTR, P)
                     end
                 else
                     if KEYVALUE > LAST↑.KEY then
                         begin
                             Q↑.BALANCE := -1;
                             LAST↑.RIGHTPTR↑.BALANCE := 0;
                             RESETPATHBALANCES(KEYVALUE,
                                               LAST↑.RIGHTPTR↑.
                                               LEFTPTR, P)
                         end
                     else
                         LAST↑.RIGHTPTR↑.BALANCE := 0
             end;
         LAST↑.BALANCE := 0;
         if PREDLAST = nil then
             T := LAST
         else
             if KEYVALUE < PREDLAST↑.KEY then
                 PREDLAST↑.LEFTPTR := LAST
             else
                 PREDLAST↑.RIGHTPTR := LAST
    end
end
else
    case LAST↑.BALANCE of
        0 : begin
                LAST↑.BALANCE := +1;
                RESETPATHBALANCES(KEYVALUE, LAST↑.RIGHTPTR, P)
            end;
```

```
                              -1 : begin
                                      LAST↑.BALANCE := 0;
                                      RESETPATHBALANCES(KEYVALUE, LAST↑.RIGHTPTR, P)
                                   end;
                              +1 : begin
                                      Q := LAST↑.RIGHTPTR;
                                      if KEYVALUE > Q↑.KEY then
                                         begin
                                            ROTATELEFT(LAST);
                                            LAST↑.LEFTPTR↑.BALANCE := 0;
                                            RESETPATHBALANCES(KEYVALUE, LAST↑.RIGHTPTR, P)
                                         end
                                      else
                                         begin
                                            ROTATERIGHT(LAST↑.RIGHTPTR);
                                            ROTATELEFT(LAST);
                                            if KEYVALUE > LAST↑.KEY then
                                                begin
                                                    Q↑.BALANCE := 0;
                                                    LAST↑.LEFTPTR↑.BALANCE := -1;
                                                    RESETPATHBALANCES(KEYVALUE,
                                                    LAST↑.RIGHTPTR↑.LEFTPTR, P)
                                                end
                                            else
                                                if KEYVALUE < LAST↑.KEY then
                                                    begin
                                                        Q↑.BALANCE := +1;
                                                        LAST↑.LEFTPTR↑.BALANCE := 0;
                                                        RESETPATHBALANCES(KEYVALUE,
                                                        LAST↑.LEFTPTR↑.RIGHTPTR, P)
                                                    end
                                                else
                                                    LAST↑.LEFTPTR↑.BALANCE := 0
                                         end;
                                      LAST↑.BALANCE := 0;
                                      if PREDLAST = nil then
                                         T := LAST
                                      else
                                         if KEYVALUE < PREDLAST↑.KEY then
                                             PREDLAST↑.LEFTPTR := LAST
                                         else
                                             PREDLAST↑.RIGHTPTR := LAST
                                   end
                    end
                else
                    PREDP↑.BALANCE := 0
        end
end;

procedure CREATENODE(KEYVALUE : whatevertype; var P : binarytree);
begin
    NEW(P);
```

```
        P↑.KEY := KEYVALUE;
        P↑.LEFTPTR := nil;
        P↑.RIGHTPTR := nil;
        P↑.BALANCE := 0
end;
procedure SEARCH(KEYVALUE : whatevertype; T : binarytree; var P, PREDP, LAST,
                    PREDLAST : binarytree; var FOUND : boolean);
begin
    FOUND := false;
    P := T;
    LAST := T;
    PREDP := nil;
    PREDLAST := nil;
    while ((P <> nil) and not FOUND) do
        if KEYVALUE < P↑.KEY then
            begin
                if P↑.BALANCE <> 0 then
                    begin
                        PREDLAST := PREDP;
                        LAST := P
                    end;
                PREDP := P;
                P := P↑.LEFTPTR
            end
        else
            if KEYVALUE > P↑.KEY then
                begin
                    if P↑.BALANCE <> 0 then
                        begin
                            PREDLAST := PREDP;
                            LAST := P
                        end;
                    PREDP := P;
                    P := P↑.RIGHTPTR
                end
            else
                FOUND := true
end;

procedure INSERTNODE(KEYVALUE : whatevertype; P, PREDP : binarytree; var T : binarytree);
begin
    if PREDP = nil then
        T := P
    else
        if PREDP = T then
            if KEYVALUE < T↑.KEY then
                T↑.LEFTPTR := P
            else
                T↑.RIGHTPTR := P
```

```
        else
            if KEYVALUE < PREDP↑.KEY then
                PREDP↑.LEFTPTR := P
            else
                PREDP↑.RIGHTPTR := P
end;

procedure RESETPATHBALANCES(KEYVALUE : whatevertype; START, P : binarytree);
var
    Q : binarytree;
begin
    Q := START;
    while Q <> P do
        if KEYVALUE < Q↑.KEY then
            begin
                Q↑.BALANCE := −1;
                Q := Q↑.LEFTPTR
            end
        else
            begin
                Q↑.BALANCE := +1;
                Q := Q↑.RIGHTPTR
            end
end;
```

For contrast with the nonrecursive implementation just given, a recursive version is presented next. A recursive solution may be based on the following formulation.

To **insert a node in T:**

If *T* is null then
    create the new node, set its field values and set *T* to it
else
    if KEYVALUE < *T* ↑.KEY, then
        insert the node in T↑.*LEFTPTR*
        if *T* is balanced then
            reset its balance
        else
            rebalance *T* and reset the balances of the nodes involved in the remedy
    else if KEYVALUE > *T* ↑.KEY then
        insert the node in T↑.*RIGHTPTR*
        if *T* is balanced then
            reset its balance
        else
            rebalance *T* and reset the balances of the nodes involved in the remedy.

The recursive INSERTAVL procedure is as follows:

```
procedure INSERTAVL(KEYVALUE : whatevertype; var T : binarytree;
                    var INCREASE : integer);
var
    Q : binarytree;
begin
    if T = nil then
        begin
            CREATENODE(KEYVALUE, T);
            INCREASE := 1
        end
    else
        if KEYVALUE < T↑.KEY then
            begin
                INSERTAVL(KEYVALUE, T↑.LEFTPTR, INCREASE);
                if INCREASE = 1 then
                    case T↑.BALANCE of
                        0 : T↑.BALANCE := −1;
                        +1 : begin
                                T↑.BALANCE := 0;
                                INCREASE := 0
                             end;
                        −1 : begin
                                Q := T↑.LEFTPTR;
                                if KEYVALUE < Q↑.KEY then
                                    begin
                                        ROTATERIGHT(T);
                                        RESET1BALANCE(T↑.RIGHTPTR)
                                    end
                                else
                                    begin
                                        ROTATELEFT(T↑.LEFTPTR);
                                        ROTATERIGHT(T);
                                        RESET2BALANCES(Q, T, T↑.RIGHTPTR)
                                    end;
                                T↑.BALANCE := 0;
                                INCREASE := 0
                             end
                end
            end
        else
            if KEYVALUE > T↑.KEY then
                begin
                    INSERTAVL(KEYVALUE, T↑.RIGHTPTR, INCREASE);
                    if INCREASE = 1 then
                        case T↑.BALANCE of
                            0 : T↑.BALANCE := +1;
                            −1 : begin
                                    T↑.BALANCE := 0;
                                    INCREASE := 0
                                 end;
```

```
            +1 : begin
                    Q := T↑.RIGHTPTR;
                    if KEYVALUE > Q↑.KEY then
                        begin
                            ROTATELEFT(T);
                            RESET1BALANCE(T↑.LEFTPTR)
                        end
                    else
                        begin
                            ROTATERIGHT(T↑.RIGHTPTR);
                            ROTATELEFT(T);
                            RESET2BALANCES(T↑.LEFTPTR, T, Q)
                        end;
                    T↑.BALANCE := 0;
                    INCREASE := 0
                end
        end
    end
end;
```

In order to determine the balance of T upon return from the recursive calls (these are italicized in the algorithm), we will need to know if the subtree in which the node was inserted has increased in depth. A flag, INCREASE, with values 1 or 0 indicates an increase. INCREASE may be nonlocal to, or a parameter of, the procedure; but it must be initialized to 0 before the procedure is invoked. We make it a parameter.

The procedures for resetting balances are

```
procedure RESET1BALANCE(Q : binarytree);
begin
    Q↑.BALANCE := 0
end;

procedure RESET2BALANCES(Q, T, P : binarytree);
begin
    if T↑.BALANCE = −1 then
        P↑.BALANCE := +1
    else
        P↑.BALANCE := 0;
    if T↑.BALANCE = +1 then
        Q↑.BALANCE := −1
    else
        Q↑.BALANCE := 0
end;
```

Suppose you wanted to create an AVL tree by reading and echo printing a sequence of key values. The code below creates the AVL tree using the recursive version of INSERTAVL; it prints the key and balance field values of the resultant tree nodes in preorder access order, as the tree is created. The PREORDER traversal routine is assumed to call a PROCESS routine, as in Chapter 6, that prints out the KEY and BALANCE field values of a node it is called to work on.

```
NEW(T);
T := nil;
READLN(KEYVALUE);
while KEYVALUE <> SENTINEL do
   begin
      INCREASE := 0;
      INSERTAVL(KEYVALUE, T, INCREASE);
      PREORDER(T);
      READLN(KEYVALUE)
   end;
```

Deletion procedures for AVL trees are not developed in detail here, but the basic ideas will be illustrated. Consider the AVL tree of Figure 7.30(a). The tree is a Fibonacci tree of depth 5. Suppose the rightmost node of its right subtree, 12, is deleted, as in a simple binary search tree. The result is Figure 7.30(b).

Node 11, the predecessor of 12, is now unbalanced. Rebalancing can be achieved by applying remedy *LR* at node 11 to obtain Figure 7.30(c). Node 8, the predecessor of 11 before rebalancing, is now unbalanced. Rebalancing can be done by applying remedy *LL* at node 8 to obtain Figure 7.30(d).

This tree is finally an AVL tree. Deleting the rightmost node from any such Fibonacci tree will always lead to a rebalance at every node along the search path.

The basic algorithm for deletion of a node from an AVL tree is first to delete as in a simple binary tree. Then, the search path must be retraced, from the deleted node back to the root. If an imbalance occurs, it must be remedied. Deletion can require $O(\lg N)$ rebalances, while insertion can require at most one rebalance.

A recursive deletion algorithm is sketched below.

To delete a node from T:

If *T* is not null then
    if KEYVALUE < T↑.KEY, then
        delete the node from T↑.*LEFTPTR*
        if T is balanced, then
          reset its balance
        else
          rebalance T and reset balances
    else
        if KEYVALUE > T↑.KEY, then
          delete the node from T↑.*RIGHTPTR*
          If *T* is balanced then
            reset its balance
          else
            rebalance *T* and reset balances
        else
          delete the node with the largest key value in T↑.*LEFTPTR*
          replace the root of *T* by that deleted node
          if *T* is balanced then
            reset its balance
          else
            rebalance *T* and reset balances.

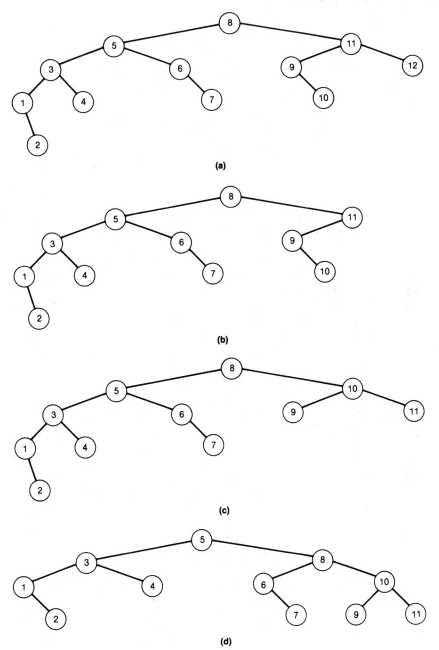

Figure 7.30 A Fibonacci Tree of Depth 5 and Deletion

7.7.7 Random Access in AVL Trees

Given a key value to find, it is easy to search the AVL tree for it. However, consider the records stored at the nodes as ordered by their processing positions in an inorder traversal of the AVL tree. For instance, in the AVL tree of Figure 7.24, the ordering is

1.	17	9.	60
2.	35	10.	70
3.	37	11.	80
4.	40	12.	81
5.	45	13.	83
6.	50	14.	85
7.	53	15.	100
8.	55		

By *access to a node* is meant that, given an index, say 10, produce the tenth record (key value 70 above). The difficulty is that it is not immediately apparent where node 10 is nor what its key value is. One way to access this node is simply to inorder traverse the tree, counting nodes. Arriving at the tenth node, produce it. This will take time $O(I)$ if the index is I. In the worst case this is $O(N)$, if N nodes are stored in the tree. Since AVL trees with N nodes have maximum depth $1.44 \lg N$, any key search, insertion, or deletion can be done in at most $O(\lg N)$ time. There is also a simple way to index in at most $O(\lg N)$ time. To accomplish this, add an INDEX field to each node. It will contain an integer that is 1 plus the number of nodes in its left subtree. The INDEX field thus contains the nodes' index. For example, the INDEX field value of 70 would be 10. It is then possible to search the tree for an index value much as it is searched for a key value. The index search thus takes time at most $O(\lg N)$. Of course, the insertion and deletion algorithms must be modified to keep the INDEX fields updated correctly.

Creating an AVL tree is done by growing it as was done for the simple binary search tree: start with a null tree and insert each input record, one at a time. The difference is that a "simple" insertion is used to grow the simple binary search tree, whereas the INSERTAVL procedure is used to grow an AVL tree. The AVL tree may be grown in $O(N \lg N)$ time. Also, since it may then be inorder traversed in $O(N)$ time, we have another way to sort in $O(N \lg N)$ time.

7.8 Hash Tables

A hash table is a data structure for the storage of records. It is intended to provide rapid search for a record with a given key value as well as the insertion and deletion of records. Compilers, for example, use hash tables in the implementation of symbol tables. They are also used in information retrieval systems. Thus NAMETABLE of Chapter 5 or a dictionary of words might be implemented in a hash table.

Example
7.1

How may records be stored, when key values are assigned by the system, so that access to a record may be accomplished by selection? □

Suppose we want to store 1,000 records representing 1,000 customer accounts. Assume that each record has an account number as its key, and, since we control account numbers, they range from 1 to 1,000. Store the record with key value I in element I of an array DATA. Then, given a key value to search for, say 836, go directly to element 836 of DATA to find it. What could be a quicker search? We are given a record and know immediately where to go to find it. The search time here is a constant, independent of the number of records stored. This kind of search requires the ability to assign key values so that all keys are within a range of array indices (1 to 1,000 in this case). It also requires that we have enough storage to accommodate all records.

Suppose we were dealing with records representing information about our employees, and that the keys were social security numbers. Even with only 1,000 employees, there are 10^9 possible social security numbers. It is not possible to know in advance which of the 10^9 social security numbers our 1,000 employees will actually have. If we were to allocate storage using social security numbers as addresses, we would run into two problems. First, there would not be enough storage. Second, if we did have sufficient storage, 999,999,000 ($10^9 - 10^3$) storage elements would be wasted! Nonetheless, it is extremely attractive to be able to look at the search key value and to know where to find it.

This is the goal of hash tables and hash searching—to find a record directly, given its key value. No attempt at an exhaustive or deep discussion of hash tables is made here, but some examples are given so that the basic concepts should become clear.

7.8.1 Building a Hash Table

This section deals with a scaled down version of the social security example, using eighteen key values, each a three-digit number. The eighteen key values will be given in some order, normally unpredictable. We are to build a table, implemented in an array, in which the eighteen key values will be stored. This table will then be searched for given key values. The table is called a *hash table*. To build it requires a hashing function and a collision resolution policy. A *hashing function* is a method of calculating an array or table address for any key. To be useful, the address must be quickly calculable.

The hash function should have other properties that will become evident. The hash function used here assigns to any key the remainder after division of the key by the table size. If the table size is M and the key value is K then $K\ MOD\ M$ denotes this remainder. The starting table or array size is 23. The eighteen key values and their order are given in Table 7.2, along with the hashing function values assigned to each.

Table 7.2 Hash Addresses

Key Value		Hashing Address	Key Value		Hashing Address
019	→	19	468	→	08
392	→	01	814	→	09
179	→	18	720	→	07
359	→	14	260	→	07
663	→	19	802	→	20
262	→	09	364	→	19
639	→	18	976	→	10
321	→	22	774	→	15
097	→	05	566	→	14

The hashing address for 019 is found, for example, by dividing 019 by the table size 23, to obtain $019 = 0 \times 23 + 19$. The remainder, 19, is the assigned hashing address. As each key value is input, its hashing address is calculated, and the key value is placed into that element of the table. After the first four key values are entered, the table is as shown in Figure 7.31(a).

When the fifth key value, 663, is input, its hashing address is 19; however, element 19 of the table is already occupied by another key value. This event is called a *collision*. The *collision resolution policy* is the method used to determine where to store a value that underwent collision. The most straightforward policy for resolving the conflict is called *linear probing*. It entails proceeding through the table from the collision element, and placing 663, the colliding entry, into the first unoccupied element found. The hash table is assumed to have been initialized, so that each element was "unoccupied" or "empty." If the search for an empty element reaches the end of the table, it proceeds from the top of the table. In this case, 663 is entered at element 20. The final table is shown in Figure 7.31(b). A total of eight initial collisions occurred in building it.

Each time a location of the table is accessed in an attempt to insert a key value, *one probe* has been made. To enter the first key value required one probe; to enter the fifth key value required two probes. To enter keys 1 through 15 required, respectively, 1, 1, 1, 1, 2, 1, 4, 1, 1, 1, 2, 1, 5, 4, 7, 3, 1, 3 probes. You should build the table and confirm these probe numbers.

7.8.2 Searching a Hash Table

How would you search a hash table when asked to find a given key, such as 627? If the key were stored in the table, it would either be found at its hashing address or at the end of a linear probe. If its hashing address were empty, or if the search came to an empty element in the linear probe before finding the key, you might conclude that it was not stored in the table. In this case, the hash address of 627 is 21. Element 21 is not empty but does not have 627 as its value. If you do a linear probe, you will eventually come to element 3, which is empty, without finding 627 and conclude that 627 is not in the table.

If the key searched for were 802, you could go to its hash address (20), find that element occupied with a different key, and start the linear probe finding 802 at element 0.

Notice that if the search key value is present in the table, the search will require *exactly* as many probes to find it as were required to enter it into the table. The search traces out the same path. Instead, if the search is for a key value that is not present, the search will take *exactly* as many probes as would be required to enter it into the current table.

A search that finds a key value is called *successful*, and one that fails to find a key value is *unsuccessful*. Theoretically, one can calculate the number of probes required for every possible key value. Knowing the frequency with which each possible key value (there are 1,000 in our example) will be searched for, one can determine the average number of probes required to search the table. The maximum number of probes can always be determined given the table. In the example, a successful search would require at most seven probes, while an unsuccessful search,

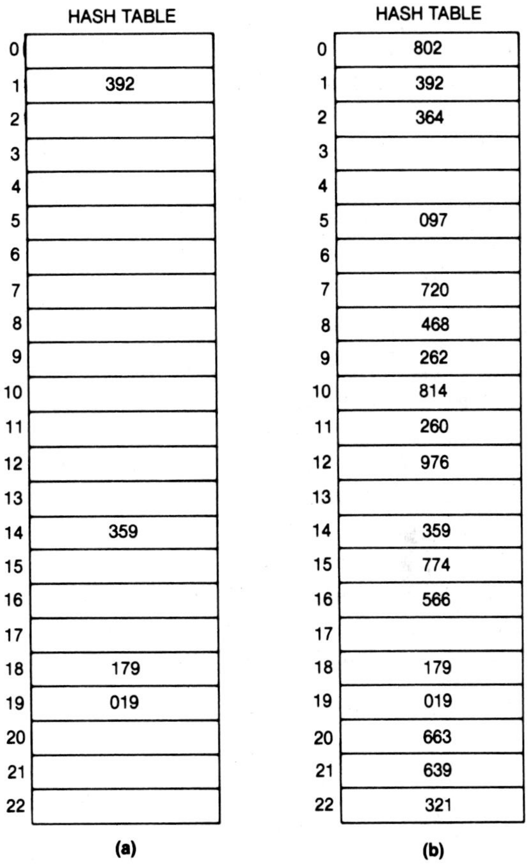

	HASH TABLE		HASH TABLE
0		0	802
1	392	1	392
2		2	364
3		3	
4		4	
5		5	097
6		6	
7		7	720
8		8	468
9		9	262
10		10	814
11		11	260
12		12	976
13		13	
14	359	14	359
15		15	774
16		16	566
17		17	
18	179	18	179
19	019	19	019
20		20	663
21		21	639
22		22	321

(a)   (b)

Figure 7.31   Hash Table after Four Entries (a) and Finally (b)

for example, for key value 248, could require nine probes. If one never had to search for a key not stored, and all stored keys were searched for with equal frequency, the average number of probes would be

$$\frac{1}{18} \times 1 + \frac{1}{18} \times 1 + \frac{1}{18} \times 1 + \frac{1}{18} \times 1 + \frac{1}{18} \times 2 + \frac{1}{18} \times 1$$
$$+ \frac{1}{18} \times 4 + \frac{1}{18} \times 1 + \frac{1}{18} \times 1 + \frac{1}{18} \times 1 + \frac{1}{18} \times 2 + \frac{1}{18} \times 1$$
$$+ \frac{1}{18} \times 5 + \frac{1}{18} \times 4 + \frac{1}{18} \times 7 + \frac{1}{18} \times 3 + \frac{1}{18} \times 1 + \frac{1}{18} \times 3$$

or $\frac{40}{18} = 2.22$ probes. This calculation involves multiplying the frequency of search for each record by the number of probes required to enter it, and then adding all these products. In this case, each frequency was $\frac{1}{18}$, and the required probes were noted when the hash table was built.

If no collisions occurred in building the table, *every* successful search would take *exactly* one probe. If the hash function actually assigned every key value not stored in the table to an empty address, *exactly* one probe would be required for *any* search. This would be the ideal situation. It is apparent now that a desirable hashing function will "scatter" or distribute the key values throughout the table, so relatively few collisions ensue.

The hash table was of length 23 and stored eighteen key values. Its usage ratio is $18/23$; the table is 78 percent full. Intuitively, the lower this ratio, the greater the storage wasted, but the lower the likelihood of a collision. The selection of appropriate hashing functions must be done with care in real applications, but it is possible to achieve very quick searches using hash tables.

7.8.3 Random Hashing

A great deal of literature in computer science is devoted to the selection of hashing functions and collision resolution policies. To give some idea of what can be achieved, this section states results for an idealized scheme that assumes the hashing function is perfectly random. Given any key value, the scheme assigns an address to that key value by picking randomly from among all the addresses of the table. This random selection is made so that each of the M addresses in a table of size M is equally likely to be selected. The table is built by inserting, in turn, each given key value. A key value is stored by determining its hash address. If that address is empty, the key value is stored there. If that address is occupied, the collision resolution policy works as follows. Another random hash function again selects an address at random. If that address is empty, the key value is stored there. If it is occupied, this procedure is repeated until the key value is finally entered. Thus, an insertion of a key value may require the generation of a sequence of hash addresses ending with the actual final storage address.

After the table is built, searches are performed as follows. Trace the sequence of hash addresses that were generated to store the search key (if it is in the table) or that would have been generated (had the key been stored). The basic assumption made here is that the hash functions generate precisely the same sequence of hash addresses for the search as for building the table. This may seem like a strange way for *random* hash functions to work, but it is our assumption nevertheless. Table 7.3 shows the theoretical results for such a scheme, when N keys are stored in the table of size M.

Table 7.3 Average Number of Probes for Searches

Usage Ratio N/M	A Successful Search	Unsuccessful Search
.25	1.15	1.33
.50	1.39	2.00
.75	1.85	4.00
.80	2.01	5.00
.90	2.56	10.00
.95	3.15	20.00

The successful search and unsuccessful search columns are given approximately by the functions $(1/\alpha) \ln \alpha$ and $1/(1 - \alpha)$ where $\alpha = N/M$. The remarkable fact is that the *average* search time does not depend on N, the number of records stored in the table, but only on the usage ratio, N/M. Thus storage can be traded for speed in hash table search. For example, if N is 10,000 and M is 11,112, α is about 0.90, and an average of only 2.56 probes will be required for a successful search. Contrast this with the 5,000 comparisons or probes for the linear search in the random case, or the 12.29 comparisons or probes for a binary search. Actual hashing functions and collision resolution policies can achieve this kind of average behavior. The worst-case times for hash table searching can, however, be quite large.

Hash tables are not a searching panacea. One disadvantage is that there is no convenient way to determine the sorted order of records stored in a hash table, except by sorting them.

7.8.4 Other Collision Resolution Policies

The linear probing collision resolution policy is a special case of *open addressing*. The idea of open addressing is to resolve collisions by following a specific *probe sequence*, whenever a collision occurs, in order to determine the insertion location for a new key. Let K_i denote the key stored in the ith location of a hash table of size M. Assume at least one table location is unoccupied, and set all unoccupied locations to the "null" key value. This prevents "falling off" the table when searching for a key, and reduces the search time, because an end of table search test need not be made.

Let $h(K)$ denote the hash function value for search key K. The sequence of indexes determined by

$$[h(K) + i \times p(K)] \bmod M, \quad \text{for} \quad i = 0, 1, 2, \ldots, M - 1$$

is a probe sequence if the indexes are all distinct. This implies that, as i goes from 0 to $M - 1$, the generated indexes form a permutation of the indexes $0, 1, 2, \ldots,$ $M - 1$. Consequently, in attempting a new key insertion, all locations of the hash table will be accessed in some order, before deciding the key cannot be inserted. It also ensures that, in attempting to search for a key, all locations of the table will be accessed in some order, before concluding the search key is not in the table, or until a null key is encountered.

Linear probing is the special case obtained by taking $p(K) = 1$ for all keys K. In general, a key is inserted by accessing the table locations given by its probe sequence, determined by $[h(K) + i \times p(K)] \bmod M$ as i goes from 0 to $M - 1$, until a null key is encountered. The key is then inserted in place of that null key. A search is done the same way. The algorithm for a *hash table search using a probe sequence* is as follows:

1. Set i to $h(K)$
2. While K_i is not the search key K and K_i is not the null key
       set i to $[i + p(K)] \bmod M$.
3. If $K_i = K$, then
       set FOUND to "true"
   else
       set FOUND to "false."

Notice that $p(K)$ represents a displacement from the current probe address.

With linear probing, large clusters of keys stored in adjacent locations of the hash table tend to get larger as insertions are made. This is because large clusters have a greater probability of the new keys' hash address falling within the cluster, assuming a "random" hash function and "random" keys. A cluster gets larger when a new key is inserted at either end of the cluster, or when two separated clusters become connected because of the new key insertion. Both of these events occurred in the scaled down social security number example. This phenomenon is called ***primary clustering***. As the table usage ratio increases, this leads to greater search and insertion times. This is clearly undesirable. It happens because the large clusters must be traversed, with the average time being proportional to half the cluster length when keys are searched with equal frequency. Thus, the insertion, or search for a key, begins to look like a linear search through a cluster.

To avoid primary clustering, try taking the next probe to be in a position removed from the current one, instead of being adjacent to it as in linear probing. Taking $p(K) = \alpha$, for some integer α that is not a factor of M, will give such a probe sequence. To see this, take $M = 13$ and $\alpha = 5$. The probe sequence is then generated by $[h(K) + i \times 5]$ mod 13 for $i = 0, 1, 2, \ldots, 12$. If $h(K) = 7$, this gives the probe sequence

$$7, 12, 4, 9, 1, 6, \underline{11}, 3, 8, 0, 5, 10, 2$$

Note that any key K, whose hash address is 7, will have *exactly* the same probe sequence. *Even worse*, suppose a key's hash address is 11, and 11 is occupied upon its insertion. The next probe for this key will be in location $[11 + 1 \times 5]$ mod 13, which is location 3. A collision at 3 will result in a further probe at $[3 + 1 \times 5]$ mod 13 or 8, then 0, 5, etc. Thus the key that originally hashed to address 11 picks up at the intersection of 11 with the probe sequence for any key hashing to 7, and follows that same probe sequence from 11 onward. Similarly, any key that collides, upon insertion, with a key already occupying its hash address, will continue along this exact probe sequence from its point of entry.

In effect, there is exactly one probe sequence for all keys; they just enter, or merge into it, at different positions specified by their hash addresses. This means that, as a "cluster" builds up along this probe sequence, say at 11, 3, 8, 0, and 5, as they become occupied, it has the same tendency to grow as a cluster of physically adjacent occupied addresses did with linear probing. This is just primary clustering, although the clusters do not appear in adjacent locations.

We need effective techniques for dealing with this problem. Figure 7.32 gives the hash tables that result from their application to our example. The hash tables produced by linear probing, and the displaced linear probing just discussed, appear in tables (a) and (b) of the figure, corresponding to $\alpha = 1$ and $\alpha = 4$, respectively. In addition, the number of probes required for the insertion of each key is indicated for each table. You should create these tables yourself to confirm their correctness, and to aid in understanding the discussion.

The average number of probes for a successful search of this table is $\frac{1}{18} \times (11 \times 1 + 5 \times 2 + 1 \times 3 + 1 \times 12) = \frac{36}{18}$ or 2.00, which is an improvement over linear probing for this example. However, for the reasons stated previously, the theoretical average number of probes in a successful search will be the same as for linear probing.

Example 7.2   Find a way to eliminate or break up large clusters. ☐

How can these results be improved? Consider the following analogy. Suppose there are M stores, each selling a certain specialty item, and each with exactly one such item in stock. Assume N people decide to buy that item the same day, and they,

Keys	Hash Address
019	19
392	01
179	18
359	14
663	19
262	09
639	18
321	22
097	05
468	08
814	09
720	07
260	07
802	20
364	19
976	10
774	15
566	14

	Hash Table (a)		Hash Table (b)		Hash Table (c)		Hash Table (d)		Hash Table (e)	
0	802	(4)	663	(2)	364	(5)	364	(4)		
1	392	(1)	392	(1)	392	(1)	392	(1)	392	(1)
2	364	(7)								
3			321	(2)						
4			364	(3)	566	(3)				
5	097	(1)	097	(1)	097	(1)	097	(1)	097	(1)
6					260	(3)	260	(3)	663	(3)
7	720	(1)	720	(1)	720	(1)	720	(1)	720	(1)
8	468	(1)	468	(1)	468	(1)	468	(1)	468	(1)
9	262	(1)	262	(1)	262	(1)	262	(1)	262	(1)
10	814	(2)	976	(1)	976	(1)	814	(2)	976	(1)
11	260	(5)	260	(2)			976	(2)	364	(2)
12	976	(3)	566	(12)	814	(3)			321	(2)
13			814	(2)			566	(3)		
14	359	(1)	359	(1)	359	(1)	359	(1)	359	(1)
15	774	(1)	774	(1)	774	(1)	774	(1)	774	(1)
16	566	(3)							566	(3)
17					639	(2)	639	(3)	260	(4)
18	179	(1)	179	(1)	179	(1)	179	(1)	179	(1)
19	019	(1)	019	(1)	019	(1)	019	(1)	019	(1)
20	663	(2)	802	(1)	663	(2)	663	(2)	802	(1)
21	639	(4)			802	(2)	802	(2)	814	(2)
22	321	(1)	639	(2)	321	(1)	321	(1)	639	(2)
	linear probing		displaced linear probing		secondary clustering		quadratic residue		double hashing	
Average number of probes for a successful search	2.22		2.00		1.72		1.72		1.61	

Figure 7.32 Typical Hash Tables for the Five Open-Addressing Techniques Considered (Usage Ratio 78 Percent)

in turn, each select one of the M stores at random. If a customer finds the item in stock at the shop of his or her choice, he or she buys it. However, if someone has already bought the item, it will be out of stock, and the person may ask the store manager for directions to another store. Let the stores be numbered from 0 to $M - 1$, and, whenever this occurs, suppose the manager of the ith shop sends the customer to the $(i + 1)$th shop. Of course, the manager of the $(M - 1)$th store refers people to the zeroth store. The result of all this feverish activity is that *all* customers arriving at an out-of-stock store are sent to the same next store. Again, at that store, they are *all* sent to the same next store whenever its item has been sold. It seems clear that this results in *primary clusters* of customers being formed. The physical locations of the stores is irrelevant to this process.

Suppose each store manager, instead of giving identical directions to each dissatisfied purchaser, sends customers to another store depending on which store they tried originally, and depending on the number of stores they have already been to. The effect, apparently, will be to disperse the unhappy customers. Rather than *all* these people being sent on to the same sequence of shops, only those with the same initial shop and the same number of previous attempts at buying are given identical directions. Clusters should still appear, but they should tend to be smaller than the primary clusters. This is, in fact, what happens, and the clusters that appear after such dispersion are called *secondary clusters*.

Translating this remedy to the problem involves choosing $p(K)$ so that it becomes a function of $h(K)$, the initial hash address of key K. This implies that only keys hashing to the same address will follow identical probe sequences. Unlike linear or displaced linear probing, keys whose probe sequences intersect do not merge into the same probe sequence at intersection; they go their separate ways. Again, to ensure that $p[h(K)]$ generates a probe sequence, it is necessary to choose it carefully. As long as $p[h(K)]$ is not a factor of M, for each key K, a probe sequence will result. If M is a prime number, this will always be the case when $p[h(K)]$ is between 0 and $M - 1$.

As an example, take

$$p(K) = \begin{cases} [h(K) + 4] \bmod M & \text{if it is not zero} \\ 1 & \text{otherwise} \end{cases}$$

Using our $h(K) = K \bmod M$ and $M = 13$, any key with hash address 7, say key 137, has the probe sequence,

7, 5, 3, 1, 12, 10, 8, 6, 4, 2, 0, 11, 9

Any key hashing to 11 now, say key 258, has the probe sequence,

11, 0, 2, 4, 6, 8, 10, 12, 1, 3, 5, 7, 9

Notice that a collision at 11, for such a key, does *not* result in the probe sequence for keys with hash addresses 7 being followed from its intersection with 11. It follows the sequence 11, 0, 2, ... instead of 11, 9, 7, 5, ...

The hash table for this secondary clustering remedy is hash table (c) of Figure 7.32. The average number of probes for a successful search in this table is $\frac{1}{18} \times [(11 \times 1) + (3 \times 2) + (3 \times 3) + (1 \times 5)] = \frac{31}{18}$ or 1.72. This gives an improvement over hash tables (a) and (b), as expected, and occurs because the secondary clusters tend to be shorter than the primary clusters. Notice that the "physically adjacent" clusters in the table are deceiving; they are not relevant. It is the clustering along the probe sequences that is important. In linear and displaced linear probing there is, in effect, only *one* probe sequence. With the secondary clustering techniques, there is a distinct probe sequence for each distinct hash address.

The *quadratic residue* technique attempts to break up primary clusters in a similar way, although it generates a probe sequence somewhat differently. The probe sequence for key K starts with $h(K)$ and follows with

$$[h(K) + i^2] \bmod M, \quad [h(K) - i^2] \quad \text{for } i = 1, 2, \ldots, (M - 1)/2$$

Again, to ensure that M distinct indexes are generated, care must be taken in the choice of M. If M is prime and of the form $(4 \times j) + 3$, then M distinct indexes are guaranteed. Since $M = 23$ in our example, $j = 5$ and $(M - 1)/2 = 11$. The probe sequence for key K is then

$$h(K), [h(K) + 1^2] \bmod 23, [h(K) - 1^2] \bmod 23,$$
$$[h(K) + 2^2] \bmod 23, [h(K) - 2^2] \bmod 23, \ldots,$$
$$[h(K) + 11^2] \bmod 23, [h(K) - 11^2] \bmod 23.$$

If K is 364, $h(K) = 19$ and the probe sequence is

$$19, 20, 18, 0, 15, 5, 10, 12, 3, 21, 17, 9, 6, 22, 16, 12, 1, 8, 7, 4, 11, 2, 13$$

This is really a secondary clustering technique, since keys that hash to the same address will still have identical probe sequences. The hash table for this technique appears as hash table (d) of Figure 7.32, which gives an average number of probes of $\frac{1}{18} \times [(10 \times 1) + (4 \times 2) + (3 \times 3) + (1 \times 4)] = {}^{31}\!/_{18}$ or 1.72 for a successful search. When a key is inserted with these secondary clustering techniques, the result may be the lengthening or connecting of two clusters. These events may occur simultaneously along more than one probe sequence when the key is inserted.

Returning to the example of the out-of-stock specialty item, we might look for a remedy that avoids even these secondary clusters, as they also tend to increase search and insertion times. It now seems reasonable to try to disperse these secondary clusters by giving each dissatisfied customer a separate set of directions. Perhaps this may be done by having store managers randomly select the next store for a customer to try. This idea is known as **double hashing**. The technique uses a second hash function for $p(K)$. To be most effective, this should be as "random" as the initial hash function and should assign a value to key K by selecting this value independently of the value assigned to key K by the initial hash function.

The theoretical analysis for this technique has not been carried out as fully as for other methods, but the results indicate that double hashing gives the best results among the open addressing techniques. Empirically, it gives results that are the same as those for "random" hashing (see Table 7.3). This is somewhat surprising, since random hashing corresponds to our store remedy. Double hashing, instead of picking a store randomly, over and over again, until a customer is satisfied, merely picks an individual displacement at random for each key. This displacement then determines the probe sequence for a given hash address.

Again, care must be exercised in the selection of the second hash function so that a desirable probe sequence is generated. If M is a prime, then one possibility that ensures the generation of such a probe sequence is

$$p(K) = \begin{cases} Q \bmod M & \text{where } Q \times M + r = K, \quad r \text{ is } K \bmod M, \quad \text{and} \quad Q > 0 \\ 1 & \text{if } \quad Q = 0 \end{cases}$$

For instance, $p(657) = 11$ since $657 = 50 \times 13 + 7$ when $M = 13$. Hence the probe sequence for 657 is

$$7, 5, 3, 1, 12, 10, 8, 6, 4, 2, 0, 11, 9$$

Key 137 also has hash address 7, but $p(137) = 10$ since $137 = 10 \times 13 + 7$. Its probe sequence, however, is distinct from 657's, and is

$$7, 4, 1, 11, 8, 5, 2, 12, 9, 6, 3, 0, 10$$

Now, *even keys with the same hash address* are unlikely to have the same probe sequence. The idea is that, statistically, probe sequences should appear to be approximately independently and randomly generated for two distinct keys. The hash table produced by this technique is given as hash table (e) of Figure 7.32 and the average number of successful probes is $\frac{1}{18} \times [(11 \times 1) + (4 \times 2) + (2 \times 3) + (1 \times 4)] = \frac{29}{18}$ or 1.61.

As a further illustration, suppose key 582 is to be inserted in the hash tables of Figure 7.32. Its hash address, 582 mod 23, is 7, since $582 = 25 \times 23 + 7$. The sequence of probed locations, and the number of probes required for each table, is given below.

Linear probing	7, 8, 9, 10, 11, 12, 13	(7)
Displaced linear probing	7, 11, 15, 19, 0, 4, 8, 12, 16	(9)
Secondary clustering	7, 18, 6, 17, 5, 16	(6)
Quadratic residue	7, 8, 6, 11, 3	(5)
Double hashing	7, 9, 11, 13	(4)

It is interesting that the average number of probes required to make an insertion is the same as the average number of probes required to carry out an unsuccessful search and is useful in the analysis of hashing. The results of the example are typical of the behavior of open addressing techniques. As the usage ratio of the table increases, the secondary clustering and quadratic residue methods provide considerable improvement over the primary clustering methods. The double hashing techniques improve the results even more. For lower usage ratios, the improvements are much less noticeable. These improvements in average numbers of *probes* do not translate directly into similar improvements in average *times*, which depend on implementation details.

Chaining is another method of collision resolution. The idea is to link together all records that collide at a hash address. These may be kept separately or within the hash table itself. *Separate chaining* treats each location of the hash table as the head of a list, the list of all keys that collide at that location. Separate storage is used to store records of the list which consist of key values and link pointer values. When a collision occurs, an insertion is made at the front of the corresponding list. Using this technique for our example yields the hash table shown in Figure 7.33 with corresponding numbers of probes (key comparisons). The table's average number of probes for a successful search is $\frac{1}{18} \times [(12 \times 1) + (5 \times 2) + (1 \times 3)] = \frac{25}{18}$ or 1.39.

In contrast to open addressing, separate chaining allows clusters to form only when keys hash to the same address. Hence, the lengths of the lists should be similar to the lengths of clusters formed with secondary clustering techniques. A comparison of the 1.39 probes to the 1.72 probes with secondary clustering is somewhat unfair, since the hash table with separate chaining really uses additional storage. The actual amount of additional storage depends on the record lengths. When they are small, and storage that would otherwise be unused is available for the link pointer values, then the usage ratio should more properly be measured as $N/(N + M)$. This is $\frac{18}{41}$, or 44 percent, in the example. When the link field takes up the same amount of storage as a record, then the usage ratio should more properly be measured as $N/(2N + M)$. This is $\frac{18}{59}$ or 31 percent in the example.

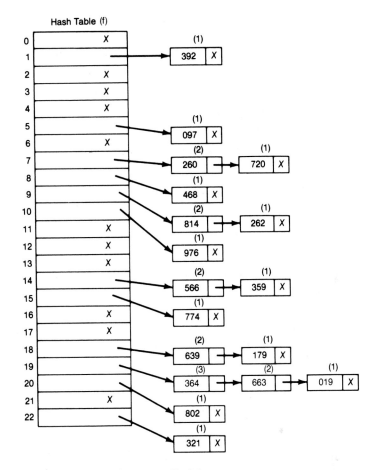

Figure 7.33 Hash Table for Separate Chaining

Coalesced chaining maintains lists of records whose keys hash to the same address. These lists are stored *within* the hash table itself. Whenever two such lists "intersect," they coalesce. This is analogous to two separated clusters becoming connected when a new key is inserted in the location that separated them. Each hash table entry is now a record containing a key value and a link value to the next record on its associated list.

A key is inserted into the table by going to its hash address and traversing its list until a null key is found, the key itself is found, or no records remain on the list. If the null key is found, the new key is inserted in the record stored at that location, and its link field is set to null. If the key itself is found, no insertion is necessary. If no records remain on the list, then an unoccupied location must be found, the new key inserted there, and its link field set to null. This new record must then be appended at the end of the traversed list.

In order to create this new record to be appended, a pointer P is kept updated. Initially, P points to location M (which is just off the table). Whenever a new record must be found, P is decremented by 1 until the location it points to is unoccupied.

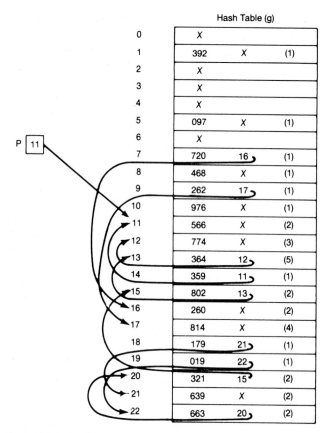

Figure 7.34   Hash Table for Coalesced Chaining

If P "falls off" the table (becomes less than 0), then the table is full and no insertion is possible.

Figure 7.34 illustrates coalesced chaining for the example. P is initially 23 and the first four keys are inserted directly into their hash addresses. Key 663 collides at its hash address, 19. P is then decremented by 1 and, since location 22 is empty, 663 and a null next pointer are inserted there. This new record is then appended at the end of the list beginning in 19, by setting the link field of location 19 to 22. Key 262 is inserted directly into its hash address, 09. The next entry is 639, but its hash address, 18, contains an entry. P is then decremented by 1, and since location 21 is empty, 639 and a null link value is inserted there. This record is then appended at the end of the list beginning in 18 by setting the link field of location 18 to 21.

Figure 7.34 shows the resultant hash table, the number of probes for each key insertion, and the value of P after all eighteen keys are entered. The average number of probes for a successful search of this table is $\frac{1}{18} \times [(9 \times 1) + (6 \times 2) + (1 \times 3) + (1 \times 4) + (1 \times 5)] = \frac{33}{18}$ or 1.81. If extra storage is available for the link fields, then N/M is a reasonable measure of the table usage here. These 1.81 probes are not as good as the 1.61 or 1.72, for double hashing and quadratic residues in the example. Theoretical results, however, show that coalesced chaining does yield better average results than "random" hashing, when link pointer fields' storage is available. You may expect coalesced chaining to give results that are not as good as separate chaining, better than linear or displaced linear probing, not as good as "random" or double hashing, but perhaps comparable to the secondary clustering techniques. If the link fields take additional storage, it should be taken into account in the usage factors for comparison. Note that coalesced chaining generally yields more but shorter lists (or clusters) than linear or displaced probing, because connecting or coalescing of cluster occurs to a lesser extent with coalesced chaining.

A third method of collision resolution will be discussed in Chapter 8 in connection with external memory, or secondary storage, where it is especially appropriate and useful.

7.8.5 Searching in Ordered Hash Tables

If keys are entered into a hash table in sorted order, then the open-addressing and chaining techniques will always result in searches along a probe sequence, or along a list, in which the keys appear in the same or reverse order, respectively. In both cases, the search algorithm may be easily modified so that, whenever a key is encountered that precedes the search key in the relevant ordering, the search is immediately terminated unsuccessfully. This can significantly decrease search times for unsuccessful searches, but will not affect successful search times. You should generate the new hash tables (a) through (g) of Figures 7.32 to 7.34 to see the effect of the keys appearing in sorted order on the tables.

Of course, one cannot normally control the order in which keys to be inserted appear. It is not difficult, however, to modify the insertion algorithms, so that the resultant hash table is exactly the same as the hash table resulting when keys *are* given in sorted order. The idea of the algorithm is clever and simple. For open addressing, simply insert a key, as usual, unless, in following a probe sequence, a key is encountered that precedes the new key in the ordering. Then, the search key is inserted in *that* position, and the insertion proceeds as though the replaced key were being inserted using the displaced key instead of the new key. For separate chaining, it is necessary to traverse the list at which a collision occurs, and insert the new key in its proper position of the list.

This technique does not work directly for coalesced chaining, because the insertion of a new key in a list may start from the interior of the list when a collision occurs. In order to keep coalesced lists in order, it is necessary to find the first list record or be able to traverse the list in either direction. To achieve this, the lists might be implemented as circular lists or two-way lists. Circular lists take more traversal time but less storage than two-way lists.

Keeping ordered hash tables yields significant improvements in the average number of probes required for unsuccessful searches with open addressing. These improvements are especially striking for high usage ratios.

7.8.6 Deletion from Hash Tables

Deletion in hash tables using separate chaining is straightforward, since it amounts to the deletion of a record from a list. With open-addressing and coalesced chaining, the deletion of a key is *not* so straightforward, since a key of the table will be needed to reach another key when it is on that key's probe sequence or list. Deleting it would break this path. One solution to this problem is to mark a deleted key location as "deleted," so that the path is not broken. When a significant fraction of keys has been deleted, the actual usage ratio of the resultant table is low, but search times will still reflect the original higher usage ratio. New insertions, when encountering a "deleted" location, may recapture this wasted storage by occupying such "deleted" locations. However, if "deleted" locations build up, without being recaptured by insertions, search times deteriorate to a linear search for unsuccessful searches and are larger than necessary for successful searches. The only remedy is to rebuild the hash table. Although the algorithm is not given here, this may be done in place, by using only storage allocated to the table in order to carry out the creation of a new table. Hash tables can also be expanded or decreased in size, and recreated. Again, this can be done in place.

7.9   Simulation of an Algorithm

It is often difficult, if not impossible, to mathematically analyze an algorithm and determine its time and storage requirements. Simulation is a useful basic tool for determining the behavior of an algorithm for this purpose. To illustrate, an algorithm for a simulation of the heapsort is constructed in this section.

The storage required by the heapsort algorithm in the implementation is $O(N)$. A reasonable measure for the time required is given by the number of interchanges and comparisons necessary to produce a sort. Assume that a procedure TREESORT has been written that is one of the detailed implementations discussed previously for heapsort. It has parameters N, A, SA, INT1, INT2, COMP1, and COMP2. These represent, respectively, the number of records, the input array of records to be sorted, the output array of sorted records, the number of interchanges required in phases I and II, and the number of comparisons required in phases I and II.

The simulation program to be written must explore the time requirements, as measured by INT1, INT2, COMP1, and COMP2, for various values of N, such as 20, 40, 60, 80, and 100. This will suggest how the execution time depends on N. Alternatively, the actual execution times could be measured. Intuitively, the algorithm will have fastest execution time when the input is nearly sorted, and slowest time when the input is nearly reverse sorted. For random initial orderings, the time can be expected to be between these two extremes. This may not be the case but seems likely a priori. Consequently, we want to generate a number of samples from each of these three distinct classes of input, execute the TREESORT routine for each sample, and collect statistics on the numbers of interchanges and comparisons based on the samples taken.

We will choose twenty-five samples of each type of input, for a total number of executions of TREESORT of (twenty-five samples for each input class and value of N) $\times$ 3 input classes $\times$ 5 values of N, or 375 runs. One way to see if twenty-five samples is enough to achieve good statistics is to run an additional twenty-five. If the results do not vary significantly, then the twenty-five samples, or perhaps even fewer, are sufficient. If necessary, we can use a larger number of samples. Remember, the twenty-five samples are taken from a possible number of $N!$ samples. It may seem the height of foolishness to base estimates on such a ridiculously small fraction of the possibilities. Thank goodness for statistics (when properly applied).

For each of the twenty-five samples for a given input class, the task is to find the following statistics for INT1, INT2, COMP1, and COMP2: their minimum, average, and maximum overall twenty-five sample values. Other statistics, such as the range and standard deviation, could be calculated if needed. We will have the simulation program print this information for each value of N as indicated below for $N = 40$.

INPUT CLASS	N = 40			
		MIN	AVE	MAX
	INT1	x	x	x
	INT2	x	x	x
"NEARLY SORTED"	COMP1	x	x	x
	COMP2	x	x	x
	INT1	x	x	x
	INT2	x	x	x
"RANDOM"	COMP1	x	x	x
	COMP2	x	x	x
	INT1	x	x	x
	INT2	x	x	x
"NEARLY REVERSE SORTED"	COMP1	x	x	x
	COMP2	x	x	x

The x's represent actual numeric values that will be output. A total of thirty-six values will be printed for each N; $5 \times 36 = 180$ statistics.

The program will keep statistics tables, one table for each input class for the current value of N. An algorithm for the simulation program is as follows:

1. Set N to 20.
2. While $N \leq 100$
   a. Set NS to 1.
   b. Initialize statistics tables.
   c. While $NS \leq 25$,
      i. Generate a sample from each input class, call TREESORT to work on each input, and then update the appropriate statistics tables. Set NS to $NS + 1$.
   d. Output the statistics tables for the current value of N and for each input class.
   e. Set N to $N + 20$.

Task i may be carried out as follows:

a. Generate a "random" sample for A of size N and call TREESORT(N, A, SA, INT1, INT2, COMP1, COMP2).
b. Update the statistics table for "random" input.
c. Generate a "nearly sorted" input for A of size N by making 20 percent of N random interchanges on SA. Copy SA into A.
d. Generate a "nearly reverse sorted" input for A of size N by copying SA, in reverse order in RA. Call TREESORT(N, A, SA, INT1, INT2, COMP1, COMP2).
e. Update the statistics tables for "nearly sorted" input.
f. Call TREESORT(N, RA, INT1, INT2, COMP1, COMP2).
g. Update the statistics table for "nearly reverse sorted" input.
h. Set NS to $NS + 1$.

It may be necessary to explain in more detail what is meant by the three classes of input. Assume that all input arrays, A, will contain integers between 1 and 1,000. Random inputs for A of size N are generated by placing the N integers into A in such a way that all orderings of the N numbers are equally likely. Consider the two arrays shown in Figure 7.35.

Array (b) has been obtained from array (a), which is sorted, by making two interchanges. These were interchanging A1[2] with A1[6], and interchanging A1[4] with A1[9]. These two interchanges represent 20 percent of N interchanges, since N is 10. A *nearly sorted* input for A of size N is obtained by making 20 percent of N such interchanges in an initially sorted array. The interchanges are to be selected at random. This means that each interchange is obtained by picking a value for I at random, so that each of the locations 1 to N of SA is equally likely to be selected. An integer J may be similarly obtained. Then SA[I] and SA[J] are interchanged. The only details still left to implement in the simulation algorithm are how to generate the required random integers to be placed in A and used for interchange locations, how to update the statistics tables, and how to finalize the tables before printing them.

Assume that a function RNG is available that returns a real number as its value. This real number will be greater than 0.0 and less than 1.0 and whenever a sequence of these numbers is generated by consecutive calls to RNG, the numbers appear, from a statistical point of view, to have been selected independently. Also assume that the returned value will lie in a segment of length L between 0 and 1, with probability L. For example, if L is of length 0.25, then the returned value will lie in that interval, say, between 0.33 and 0.58, 25 percent of the time. The random number generator RANF of FORTRAN is an example of such a function.

To generate an integer between 1 and 1,000, take the value RNG returns, multiply it by 1,000, take the integer part of the result, and add 1 to it. For example, if the value returned is 0.2134 then multiplying by 1,000 gives 213.4. Its integer part is 213; adding 1 yields 214. In fact, if any number strictly between 0.213 and 0.214 had been returned, 214 would have been generated. Hence 214 would be generated

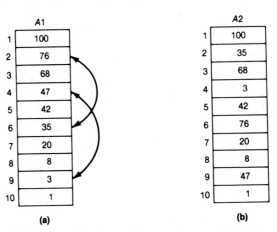

Figure 7.35   Array (b) Obtained from Sorted Array (a) by Two Interchanges

Table 7.4 Simulation Results in Actual Execution Time

N	Bubble					Insertion					Modified Insertion				
10	1	4	6	7	9	1	2	5	6	7	1	2	4	6	7
20	1	9	23	34	40	2	6	11	25	28	1	5	10	23	27
40	2	45	101	138	153	4	15	51	103	113	3	13	47	95	105
100	6	282	700	901	965	10	96	343	629	712	8	86	268	578	656
200	11	1,093	2,824	3,476	3,879	21	374	1,317	2,508	2,856	16	340	1,204	2,302	2,627
400	23	5,085	11,822	14,267	15,554	41	1,403	5,658	10,089	11,440	32	1,280	5,182	9,255	10,503

N	Heap					Iterative Quicksort					Recursive Quicksort				
10	6	5	5	5	5	7	6	5	6	8	5	3	4	4	4
20	14	14	13	12	12	19	14	13	14	20	13	9	9	9	14
40	34	33	32	29	28	55	33	27	30	56	44	24	19	22	45
100	104	102	98	90	89	266	126	80	89	268	238	102	61	69	239
200	238	235	225	206	204	958	364	179	190	961	901	317	141	151	904
400	541	531	510	481	478	4,190	1,187	396	422	3,625	4,026	1,094	319	338	3,511

with probability 1/1,000, the length of the interval from 0.213 to 0.214. The same is true for each integer between 1 and 1,000. Carrying out this procedure N times will fill the array A to generate a "random" input.

To generate a *nearly sorted* or *nearly reverse sorted* input, select each of the 20 percent of N interchanges as follows. Call RNG twice. Multiply the two returned values by N, take the integer part and add 1. This gives two integers, I and J, between 1 and N. Interchange $SA[I]$ with $SA[J]$.

The statistics tables can keep current running minimums, maximums, and the accumulated sum of the appropriate statistic. When each call to TREESORT returns, the minimum, maximum, and accumulated sum may be updated for each statistic, INT1, INT2, COMP1, and COMP2. When the inner loop of the flowchart is exited, and task d is to be carried out, the statistics tables are ready to be printed, except for the twelve averages. They must be finalized in task d by dividing the accumulated sums by 25.

Table 7.4 gives simulation results (in actual execution time measured in 1/60 second intervals). It should be carefully studied. Note that the $O(N)$ and $O(N \lg N)$ sorts may be easily identified. The best and worst input cases are also evident, as well as the relatively uniform behavior of heapsort. Each entry in Table 7.4 is the average of 20 runs on a DEC Rainbow under UCSD Pascal. For each N the five values correspond to input in sorted order, half sorted–half random, random, half reverse sorted–half random, and reverse sorted.

7.10 Synopsis of Search and Sort Efficiencies

We have consistently viewed the record as the basic unit of data. Collections of records usually appear in problems, and their processing typically reduces to traversing through the records of the collection, inserting or deleting records, randomly accessing records, accessing records in sorted order, or searching the collection for a given record. The basic data structures are available for storage of the collection and each supports some operations well at the expense of others. Arrays are excellent for random access and traversal but poor for general insertions and deletions. Lists support traversal, insertions, and deletions well but are poor for random access.

Linear searches of arrays and binary searches of sorted arrays can be performed, respectively, in $O(N)$ and $O(\lg N)$ time. Under special conditions, linear searches can be fast. Easily constructed binary search trees allow efficient insertion and deletion and can also be searched in *average time* $O(\lg N)$. More complex construction, insertion, and deletion algorithms for balanced binary search trees guarantee search, insertion, and deletion in *worst-case time* $O(\lg N)$. Binary search trees allow easy access to records in sorted order, and balanced binary search trees also allow $O(\lg N)$ random access to the Ith record in sorted order. Hash tables can be searched very quickly, on the average, when properly constructed but do not allow records to be easily enumerated in sorted order.

Simple sorting algorithms such as the bubble and insertion sort have worst-case time $O(N^2)$ but are $O(N)$ when dealing with almost sorted data. Quicksort gives very fast average times and heapsort does sorting in worst-case time $O(N \lg N)$.

It is important to recognize that in this chapter we have been considering *comparative* searches and sorts. This means that we have assumed no special knowledge of the key values involved, and have used only comparisons between key values in each search or sort algorithm. It is possible to prove that such searches and sorts have worst-case times $O(\lg N)$ and $O(N \lg N)$, respectively. Other kinds of search and sort algorithms are possible and may take significantly less time. For example, suppose you must sort N distinct keys whose values are known to be integers between 1 and 1,000. Simply store the record with key value I as the Ith record in an array of records. This places the records in the array in (decreasing) sorted order and takes $O(N)$ time. Sorts that place records in groups, depending on their *actual* key values, and then attempt to sort further within the groups, are called *distributive sorts*. These are not considered in this text. We did, however, consider a very important noncomparative search in Section 7.8.

Simulation is a basic tool for the analysis of the storage and timing requirements of algorithms although we have used it only for analyzing heapsorts.

Trees find numerous applications ranging from storing data to aiding in the conceptualization of algorithms. Binary trees are not only useful themselves but can serve as the representation for general trees. You have seen that stacks and queues underlie the important tree traversal operations.

This chapter has provided examples of the effective use of appropriate data structures with their appropriate implementations. These include the use of a heap for priority queues, the use of a binary tree for a heap, the use of a heap for sorting, and the use of binary search trees for searching.

The top-down approach to problem solving, with recursion as a special case, has been consistently adhered to. A number of basic strategies have also been illustrated repeatedly. These included searching through the collection of all possible solutions, constructing a solution, and adapting a previously written algorithm to a new but related problem. The rest of this book deals with the same concepts but applies them to more advanced problems.

As searching as this chapter may have been, it is hoped that it didn't leave you out of sorts!

☐ **Exercises**

1. a. If all comparisons and assignment statements take the same amount of time to execute, then compare the execution times of the first linear search procedure and the procedure revised for greater efficiency.

    b. For what values of N will the binary search be faster than the linear search of the improved procedure in the worst case?

2. When you look up a book by author in the library, what kind of a search are you doing?

3. In a *ternary search* of a sorted array, the array is divided into three "nearly" equal parts and searched. Key values are examined "near" 1/3 and "near" 2/3, and compared with the search key to determine in which third to search further. Determine the worst-case time for this search and compare it to the worst-case time of a binary search.

4. Suppose a sorted array stores 1,000 integers between 0 and 1,000,000. A pointer array indicates where the least integer greater than $1,000 \times (I - 1)$ but not greater than $1,000 \times I$ appears in the array. $P[I]$ contains that pointer for $I = 1, 2, , \ldots, 1,000$. If no such integer is in the array, then $P[I] = 0$. Write a procedure to do an interpolation search, coupled with a binary search.

5. Assuming all comparisons and assignments take the same time to execute, do the following.

    a. Determine the worst-case times for the sorts of the procedures given in the text for the maximum entry sort, the bubble sort, and the insertion sort.

    b. For each value of N, determine which of the three sorts has least worst-case time.

6. What input order produces the worst case time for

    a. The bubble sort and

    b. The insertion sort?

7. Write a procedure to carry out the bubble sort when the integers are stored in a chain.

8. Write a procedure to carry out the insertion sort when the integers are stored in a chain.

9. Modify the INSERTIONSORT procedure so it does a binary search for the proper insertion position, and then does the insertion.

10. Modify the procedure so it does not deal with the last I elements after the Ith pass.

11. Suppose input is given in the order

    16, 18, 22, 15, 4, 50, 17, 31, 4, 90, 6, 25

Create the heap produced by

    a. The first heap creation algorithm of Section 7.4 and

    b. The second heap creation algorithm of Section 7.4.

    c. How many comparisons and interchanges were required in Exercise 11a and Exercise 11b?

12. For each heap of Exercise 11a and 11b, produce

    a. The reheaped heap after the root element is removed using the first reheaping algorithm of Section 7.4, and

    b. The reheaped heap after the root element is removed using the second reheaping algorithm of Section 7.4

    c. How many comparisons and interchanges were required in Exercises 12a and 12b?

13. Why does the pointer array of Section 7.3.6 fail to help?

14. Show the entries of the DATA array, for the input of Exercise 11, when the HEAP-SORT procedure is applied, after the first three elements have been output.

15. Modify the HEAPSORT procedure so that it counts the number of interchanges and comparisons in each phase and returns their values as parameters.

16. Modify the HEAPSORT procedure so it sorts a DATA array of pointers to records, instead of the records themselves.

17. What input sequence will cause the second heap creation algorithm to take worst-case time? Calculate the number of comparisons and interchanges it requires.

18. Determine the number of comparisons and copies required by QUICKSORT for an initial array of N records which is

    a. In sorted order

    b. In reverse sorted order

    c. In order so that PARTITION always produces two component arrays whose lengths differ by at most 1

19. Modify PARTITION so it selects an entry at random to be used as the basis entry.

20. Modify PARTITION so it selects the median of the first, middle, and last entries as the basis entry.

21. Explain why the implementation given for QUICKSORT requires a stack depth $O(\lg N)$.

22. Modify QUICKSORT so it sorts all component arrays of length at most 20 by using INSERTIONSORT.

23. Justify all the entries of Table 7.1 for the priority queue implementations.

24. Write two procedures to, respectively, insert and delete records from a priority queue implemented as a heap.

25. Take the NAMETABLE names of Chapter 5 and grow a simple binary search tree as in Section 7.7 when the names are input in the order in which they appear in that figure. The order is determined alphabetically by last name, first name, and then middle initial. Thus ROBERT EVANS precedes HARRY TRUMAN. If a duplicate name occurs, do not enter it again in the tree.

26. Delete PAULINA KOCH from the binary search tree of Exercise 25, using the simple deletion algorithm of Section 7.7.

27. Write a procedure, SEARCH, with parameters KEYVALUE, P, and T, a pointer to the root node of a binary search tree. SEARCH is to return with P pointing to the node of T in which KEYVALUE equals P↑.KEY. If no such node exists, P should return with its value **nil**.

28. Write a procedure, INSERTBST with parameters KEYVALUE and T. It is to insert a node with KEYVALUE into the simple binary search tree T if no node exists with that KEY.

29. Write a procedure, DELETEBST, with parameters KEYVALUE and T. It is to delete a node whose KEY equals KEYVALUE in the simple binary search tree T, if such a node exists.

30. Should a linked or a sequential implementation be used for binary search trees grown "simply" when they will contain fifty integers picked at random from the first 1,000 integers? Why?

31. What is the minimum depth of a binary search tree storing 137 entries, and how may it be constructed in time $O(N)$ for N entries?

32. Should a linked or a sequential implementation be used for a binary search tree grown as an AVL tree when it will contain fifty integers picked at random from the first 1,000 integers? Why? (Cf. Exercise 30.)

33. Follow the same directions as in Exercise 25, but grow a binary search tree that is an AVL tree. It should be the same AVL tree that would result if it were grown by invoking INSERTAVL of Section 7.7.6 for each input name.

34. Create a binary search tree, with the names of Exercise 33 in it, which has minimum possible depth.

35. Delete the rightmost node of the AVL tree grown in Exercise 33, using the recursive deletion algorithm of Section 7.7.6.

36. Modify the nonrecursive procedure INSERTAVL so indexing can be done as described in Section 7.7.6.

37. Modify the recursive procedure INSERTAVL so indexing can be done as described in Section 7.7.6.

38. Why does growing and then inorder traversing an AVL tree correspond to an $O(N \lg N)$ sort?

39. Write a procedure, SEARCH, with parameters INDEXVALUE, P, and T. It is to return with P pointing to the node, if it exists, in the AVL tree T, whose INDEX field is equal to INDEXVALUE. P should be **nil** if there is no such node.

40. a. Build a hash table for the twenty-seven names of the NAMETABLE of Chapter 5. Do not store duplicates. The table will be of size 31. Assign to each letter of this alphabet the integer corresponding to its position in the alphabet. For example A is assigned 1, E is assigned 5. Add the integers corresponding to every letter of a name and divide the sum by 31. The remainder is then the hash address of the name. For example, JIMMY CARTER has the sum $(10 + 9 + 13 + 13 + 25 + 3 + 1 + 18 + 20 + 5 + 18) = 135$. Its hash address is 11. Use linear probing when a collision occurs.

b. How may probes were needed to insert each name?

41. Criticize the choice of hash function in Exercise 40.

42. Search the hash table of Exercise 40 for JOHN SMITH, and write down the probe addresses needed.

43. Discuss the advantages and disadvantages of storing the NAMETABLE entries of Chapter 5 in a sorted array, sorted chain, binary search tree, AVL tree, and hash table.

44. Show the state of hash tables (a) through (g) of Section 7.8 when key 019 is deleted.

45. Suppose that the eighteen keys are entered into the hash table of Section 7.8 in order from largest to smallest. As you search for a key, you conclude it is not in the table whenever you encounter a key value smaller than the search key as you trace out the linear probe path. Convince yourself that this is true, and that it will result in fewer probes for an unsuccessful search.

46. Write a procedure to build a hash table for each of the open-addressing and chaining techniques of Section 7.8.

47. Run each procedure of Exercise 46 with the input data and hash function of Exercise 40.

48. What is the maximum number of probes for an unsuccessful search of each of the hash tables (a)–(g)?

49. Can you find a way to build a hash table as in Exercise 45, so that the sorted search can be done, even if the input was not actually in sorted order?

50. How might we estimate the relation between the average depth of a simple binary search tree grown randomly and, N, the number of inputs?

51. Suppose AVL trees are grown randomly. That is, each of the $N!$ arrangements of N distinct inputs is equally likely to occur. Starting with the null tree, INSERTAVL is invoked for each input. How might the average depth of such AVL trees be estimated as a function of N?

52. How might the average number of probes be studied for a given hash function as in Exercise 40?

53. Generation of N integers to fill the array A in Section 7.9 randomly was really only an approximation of a random input. This is because duplicate values might occur. While the effect of this duplication may be negligible for the simulation results, a "true" random input *can* be generated. You can fill array A as follows: pick an integer at random between I and N, and store it in $A[I]$, for I from 1 to N.

    a. Convince yourself this will generate a "true" random input.

    b. Write a procedure to generate this "true" random input.

    54. Consider the "perfect shuffle" example of Chapter 3. When $2n - 1$ is a prime number p, then the number of shuffles required is $p - 1$. The initial configuration is in sorted order, and so is the final configuration after $p - 1$ shuffles. The configurations produced along the way represent different permutations of the initial input. With successive reshufflings, the configurations seem more and more like a "random" arrangement, and then less and less like a "random" arrangement. Take $p = 101$ and use the one hundred configurations produced by the hundred shuffles required to reproduce the original, as inputs to the heapsort algorithm. Output the statistics table based on one hundred samples of an input of size 101.

    55. For $M = 107$, generate N random key values between 000 and 999 and build (by executing a program) hash tables (a) to (g) for these keys. Do this twenty-five times for each N and output the average number of probes to insert the N keys over the twenty-five samples. Do this repeatedly for a series of N values corresponding to usage ratios of approximately 0.50, 0.55, 0.60, . . . , 0.90, 0.95. Compare results of this simulation to your expectations.

☐ Suggested Assignment

    a. Design the nametable for the case study of Chapter 5. Discuss the relative merits of arrays, lists, binary search trees, AVL trees, and hash tables for its implementation.

    b. Write and run the HEAPSORT procedure of Section 7.4.7. A main program should read in examples for the input array A. For each example, N and the array A should be printed, and HEAPSORT should be called to sort A. When HEAPSORT returns, the output array, SA, should be printed along with the values for INT1, INT2, COMP1, and COMP2. At least two examples for small N should be worked through by hand to test the correctness of HEAPSORT.

8 Files

8.1 The File Data Structure

A *file* is a collection of records. This is a loose definition of a file. Almost all of the data structures discussed in the preceding chapters satisfy it. The term *file*, however, is usually reserved for large collections of information stored on devices outside the computer's internal memory. It usually implies that the records are stored in the computer's external memory, on the tapes or disks also known as secondary storage. As a result, the ways in which the file must be organized so that operations on it can be carried out efficiently are determined by the characteristics of the secondary storage devices used to implement the file. The basic operations on a file are to insert and delete records, process or update records, and search for, or retrieve, records. The operations are the same as the basic operations used for arrays, lists, trees, list-structures, and more complex lists, which are stored in the computer's internal memory. And similarly, in designing algorithms that use files, programmers must weigh the trade-offs between the time and storage required to support these operations on files stored in external memory just as they weigh trade-offs between time and storage for operations on data structures stored in internal memory. More time spent in organizing information results in faster operations, but this efficiency must be weighed against the increased care required to nurture and maintain the better organized data structure. For example, balanced trees are faster to use in the worst case but harder to grow. Similar effects pertain with file manipulations.

8.2   Internal and External Memory

Computer memories are normally thought of as falling into two basic categories, internal and external. Which memory is used to store data depends on the trade-off of efficiency of access to data versus the cost of that efficiency.

The data structures and algorithms considered thus far are all appropriate to the *internal memory* of a computer. This memory is also referred to as *main* memory or *random access* memory. A program can process only information stored in its internal memory. If the program is to process information stored in external memory, that information must first be read into its internal memory. Except for the instructions involved in this transfer of information, all program instructions refer to variables that name internal memory locations.

By means of random access, it is possible to access *any* individual internal memory element in exactly the same length of time — typically one-millionth of a second or less. This access time is extremely fast and is independent of the past history of accessed elements. However, random access memory is expensive and, although available in increasingly larger sizes, is still relatively small in size compared to the storage needs of many applications.

External memory, also referred to as *secondary storage*, is so called because it is physically outside the computer itself. It is relatively inexpensive and is available in very large amounts, but access to an arbitrary record is slow. *Magnetic tapes*, *floppy disks*, and *magnetic disks* (the latter are also known as *hard disks*) are the usual devices for external storage of data. The characteristics of these devices that are essential for efficient use of data structures are discussed in this chapter. The access capability of secondary storage devices is distinctly different from that of random access, or internal, memory. Similarly, the data structures and the algorithms required to process them are distinct from those for internal memory. However, many of the same concepts and techniques of good design and implementation of algorithms are still applicable and form the basis for representing and operating on information stored in external memory, normally in files.

8.2.1   Operating Systems

High-level programming languages such as Pascal or COBOL do not ordinarily allow direct manipulation of external storage elements. Instead, as with internal storage, they provide commands that allow programmers to deal with external memory conceptually. Pascal provides very limited kinds of operations to be performed on its conceptual external memory, whereas COBOL provides very extensive operations; FORTRAN falls between these extremes. Whatever high-level language is used, the operating system of a computer installation provides commands to make files available for processing by a program. Operating systems allow permanent storage of files generated by a program during its execution; the stored files can then be easily retrieved for later use.

You may have used the DOS, MVS, VM, or NOS operating system on a mainframe computer; RT-11, RSTS, RSX, TSX, VAX/VMS, or UNIX on a mini-computer; or MS-DOS, PC-DOS, or CP/M on a micro- or personal computer. In effect, operating systems provide repositories of files that may be added to, or referenced by, programs. Such files are used to store data or information to be processed, sometimes very large data bases. They are also used to store algorithms, such as programs to be executed, compilers to be invoked, or even other operating systems to be used when needed. Thus operating systems support the development of libraries of data and algorithms that programmers use, add to, or delete from. They should support the general programming strategy recommended and demonstrated in this book, whereby in solving a problem, the programmer should always begin by attempting to apply an already known algorithm, either directly or after appropriate modification.

8.2.2 Filters

Frequently, a solution to a problem is readily found by starting with one or more files of data and repeatedly applying available programs to these files. These programs, in turn, produce output data in the form of files, which then become the input files for other programs. The basic idea behind this kind of solution is a filter. A *filter* is a program whose input is one file and whose output is another file. Frequently, a solution to a problem may be found by starting with an input file and applying a sequence of filters. Each filter takes its input to be the output file of the preceding filter. System commands allow this *composition* of filters, so that complex programs can be generated with few commands.

Example 8.1   The bowling scores problem is revisited in this example. Suppose an input file contained the roll scores for the bowling problem of Chapter 1. Structure the solution so that processing this file produces an output file of statistics. ☐

Suppose GAMESCORES is a filter that takes the input file and produces an output file of game scores. A statistical package, available in the library of the computer's operating system, might be used to process an input file as data, producing appropriate statistics. Applying this program, or filter, to the game scores file would result in an output file containing the required information. This file could be stored for future use, or processed by a printing routine, directly producing printed output.

The two filters, GAMESCORES and STATISTICS, applied sequentially, produce the desired output file. Note that this solution is written so that the calculation of the game scores is done first, independently of the calculations producing the statistics. In the solution of Chapter 1 these tasks were intertwined.

The idea behind filters is to allow the construction of complex programs by sequencing simpler but powerful programs. The next example illustrates this more forcefully.

Example 8.2   Use filters to produce a simplified index for a book. The index should consist of the important words of the book in alphabetic order and the pages on which they appear. ☐

One way to achieve a solution is to apply the following filters in sequence.

1. WORD-COUNT REFERENCES
2. TRUNCATE
3. SORT

The first takes a file consisting of the book text (organized as a sequence of pages) and produces an output file of records. Each record contains a word, the number of pages on which it appears, and the pages on which it appears. TRUNCATE takes a file of records as its input and outputs a file that is identical to its input file, except that all records with a designated key field value greater than N are deleted. Here, the key field is the number-of-pages field, and a reasonable value for N might be 10. This should eliminate frequently occurring but not relevant words such as "the," "a," "and," and so on. SORT takes an input file of records and creates an output file in which the records appear in sorted order by designated key field value, in this case, the word field. The sequencing of these three relatively simple filters provides a quick and effective solution.

Using these system capabilities to store and access files of data or programs provides a new framework in which to approach the entire task of problem solving. In effect, a computer installation provides a *programming environment* that determines the tools available for program construction. Such tools include text editors, file management utilities, ways to create a new program from existing programs already stored as files, and debugging aids. The enhancement of such programming environments is currently one of the major research and development areas of computer science. The *command languages*, also known as *job control languages*, provided by operating systems, are used to operate on general files.

8.3 Organization of Files

During the execution of high-level language programs, operations typically deal only with files treated as data. Operations include traversing and processing all the records of a file, randomly accessing and processing individual records selected in random order, or some combination of these two modes. The basic function of a file system, in addition to providing storage facilities, is to allow files to be searched efficiently and conveniently, so that records of an entire file may be sequentially retrieved, or a portion of the file's records, perhaps only one record, may be retrieved. In Example 8.1, after the bowling game scores file has been obtained, one may want to retrieve the scores of a particular game or individual. Of course, the file being processed as data might actually represent the text of a program.

This chapter briefly discusses the file processing facilities provided by Pascal. It shows a number of ways in which more flexible and powerful file processing may be implemented. The literature on files would itself require a large file for its storage, and file storage and manipulation is currently an active area of research. This book considers a *very* small portion of that file. The entire discussion deals only with the case of fixed-length records that are to be retrieved on the basis of a single field value, the *primary key field,* which is intended to uniquely identify a record. It is the field normally used as the search key and the key by which records are sorted.

Just as with data structures that are stored in internal memory, the programmer must take great care to keep related records of files stored in external memory physically contiguous or linked by pointers. In internal memory, the time requirement of an algorithm is measured by the number of operations performed. These might be arithmetic operations or assignments, comparisons between two records (keys), or comparisons between two variables. When dealing with external memory, the time requirements are measured by the number of accesses to secondary storage.

8.3.1 Sequential Files

The simplest organization for a file is sequential. A *sequential file* is a sequence of records. The records may or may not be kept in sorted order in the sequence. In Pascal all files are sequential files and consist of records of the same type. A record of a file is not necessarily declared to be of type *record* of Pascal. Although typically file records are of type record, a file record may also be declared to be of type *integer, real, boolean, character,* or any other Pascal type, excluding type file. Files of characters are called *text files*.

The name of any file to be saved in secondary storage after the execution of the program must be included in the parameter list of the *program* statement. The name of any file already in secondary storage which is referenced by the program must also appear in this parameter list. The standard names, INPUT and OUTPUT, are names of text files, and normally appear in the parameter list, but should not be declared in the program.

Example 8.3 Suppose you are asked to keep a master file, BOOKINVENTORY, consisting of records representing all books currently in stock in a book store. Each record is to contain a title, author, publisher, price, and currentstock field. The declarations that may be used are

```
type
    bookrecords = record
                      title : array [1 .. MAXTITLE] of char;
                      author : array [1 .. MAXAUTHOR] of char;
                      publisher : array [1 .. MAXPUBLISHER] of char;
                      price : real;
                      currentstock : integer
                  end;
var
    BOOKINVENTORY : file of bookrecords;
    □
```

The name of a file is a variable within a Pascal program. Unlike other variables, it represents stored information that may have been available before the execution of the program or that may be available after the execution of the program. A file named *F* is depicted in Figure 8.1.

Associated with each file is a *file pointer*, which always points to a record or is positioned prior to the first record or after the last record. A record may be read from a file or written to a file. A READ or WRITE statement always refers to the record indicated by the current position of the file pointer. Each file also has a variable stored in main memory, called the *buffer variable*, associated with it. When the file pointer

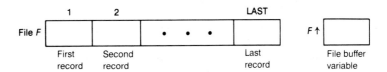

Figure 8.1   File *F* and *F*↑

is pointing to a file record, the file buffer contains a copy of that record's contents. A file named F will have the buffer variable named $F\uparrow$ associated with it.

Before reading from a file, it is necessary to prepare the file by executing *one* RESET statement. Similarly, before writing to a file, it is necessary to prepare the file by executing *one* REWRITE statement. Executing the RESET statement causes the file pointer to be positioned to the first record, and the file buffer variable to be initialized so it contains the value of the first record. If the file is initially empty (contains no records), then the file buffer variable may be undefined. Attempting to read from an empty file, or from a file whose file pointer is positioned after the last record, elicits an error message. (The message might say, "Attempting to read beyond the file." or "GET attempted after end-of-file.") For this reason, it is a wise policy always to invoke the Pascal end-of-file function, EOF(F), and test it before reading a file F. EOF(F) returns the value "true" when the file pointer is positioned after the last record (the case when the file is empty), and "false" otherwise. Executing the REWRITE statement causes the file to be initialized to empty and positions the file pointer to the file storage area where the next record to be written will appear.

Execution of the statement READ(F, V) will cause the value of the record pointed to by the file pointer for F to be copied into variable V, the file pointer to be moved to point to the next record of the file (or after the last record if that was the record just read), and the file buffer variable to be set to the value of the record in the new file pointer position. V must be of the same type as the records of the file F.

Execution of the statement WRITE(F, V) will cause the value of V to be copied into the storage pointed to by the file pointer of F, and the file pointer moved to point to the storage to be used for the next record. The file buffer variable is then undefined. V must be of the same type as the records of the file F.

Reading from a file thus causes information in secondary storage (the file) to be transferred to variables whose values are stored in internal memory. Writing to a file causes the information stored in internal memory to be transferred to secondary storage.

The values of file buffer variables are stored in internal memory. The file buffer variable can be treated just like any other variable in Pascal programs; two special operations are provided by Pascal to manipulate it. GET(F) causes the file pointer of F to be advanced to the next record (or after the last record), and the value of that next record to be copied into $F\uparrow$. PUT(F) causes the file F to be extended by appending a new record to it. The value of the new record is a copy of $F\uparrow$. The file pointer is also advanced to the next record of the file. After execution of a PUT statement, the file buffer variable is undefined.

The READ and WRITE statements can be defined in terms of GET and PUT as follows:

READ(F, V) is equivalent to

```
begin
    V := F↑;
    GET(F)
end
```

and WRITE(F, V) is equivalent to

```
begin
    F↑ := V;
    PUT(F)
end
```

Example
8.4

To illustrate the effect of the file operations, suppose there is a file PRIME consisting of the first ten prime numbers, and the following program segment is executed. ☐

```
RESET(PRIME);
I := 1;
while not EOF(PRIME) do
    begin
        READ(PRIME, A[I]);
        I := I + 1
    end;
REWRITE(REVERSEDPRIME);
I := I − 1;
while I > 0 do
    begin
        WRITE(REVERSEDPRIME, A[I]);
        I := I − 1
    end;
```

PRIME and REVERSEDPRIME are files of integer type records, and A is an array of integer type records. The records have one field, the INFO field.

After RESET is executed, the file called PRIME, its file pointer, and its buffer variable can be depicted as in Figure 8.2(a). After nine executions of the first **while** loop body, the situation will be as shown in Figure 8.2(b).

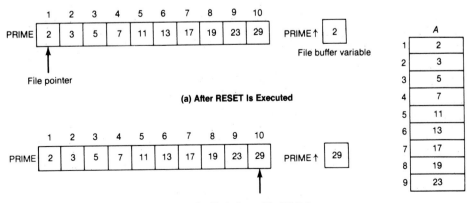

(a) After RESET Is Executed

(b) After Nine Executions of the While Loop

Figure 8.2 File PRIME

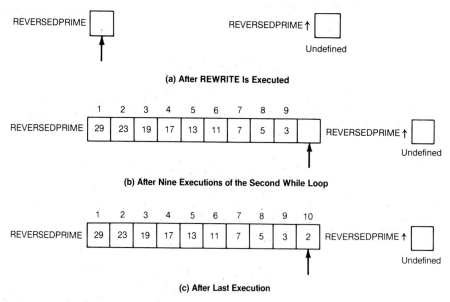

REVERSEDPRIME

REVERSEDPRIME ↑
Undefined

(a) After REWRITE Is Executed

	1	2	3	4	5	6	7	8	9	
REVERSEDPRIME	29	23	19	17	13	11	7	5	3	

REVERSEDPRIME ↑
Undefined

(b) After Nine Executions of the Second While Loop

	1	2	3	4	5	6	7	8	9	10
REVERSEDPRIME	29	23	19	17	13	11	7	5	3	2

REVERSEDPRIME ↑
Undefined

(c) After Last Execution

Figure 8.3   File REVERSEDPRIME

The tenth execution sets $A[10]$ to 29, and moves the file pointer beyond the last file record. The buffer variable is then undefined, and the EOF test yields the value "true," so the loop is exited with I set at 11.

After REWRITE is executed, the file REVERSEDPRIME appears as in Figure 8.3(a). After the second **while** loop body has been executed nine times, REVERSEDPRIME looks like Figure 8.3(b). The last execution yields the file shown in Figure 8.3(c).

Suppose you wished to append the eleventh prime, 31, to PRIME, after 29. This cannot be done directly. Instead, a new file, TEMP, with the desired records would have to be created. This could be done as follows:

```
REWRITE(TEMP);
RESET(PRIME);
while not EOF(PRIME) do
    begin
        TEMP ↑ := PRIME ↑ ;
        PUT(TEMP);
        GET(PRIME)
    end;
TEMP↑.INFO := 31;
PUT(TEMP);
```

Executing REWRITE and RESET would yield the file shown in Figure 8.4(a). Execution of TEMP ↑ := PRIME ↑, PUT(TEMP), and GET(PRIME) yields, respectively, Figure 8.4(b), (c), and (d). The last execution of the loop body yields the two files shown in Figure 8.4(e) and (f). Finally, the execution of the last two statements produces, in turn, Figure 8.4(g) and 8.4(h).

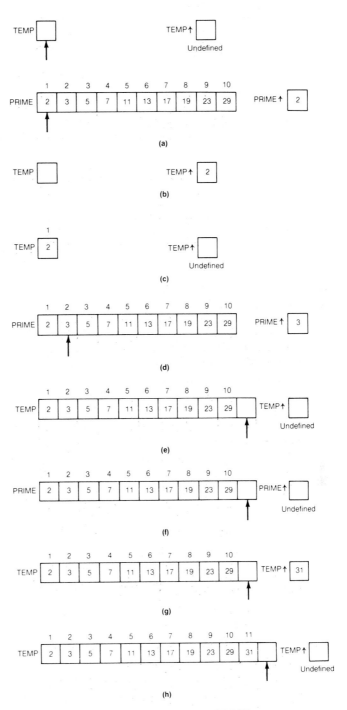

Figure 8.4 Appending the Eleventh Prime to File PRIME

To copy TEMP into PRIME, a simple procedure called COPY could be invoked.

```
procedure COPY(var TEMP, PRIME : recordsfile);
begin
     REWRITE(PRIME);
     RESET(TEMP);
     while not EOF(TEMP) do
          begin
               READ(TEMP, PRIME ↑ );
               PUT(PRIME)
          end
end;
```

Notice that it was possible to use an array to produce the REVERSEDPRIME file, presumably because the maximum length of the PRIME file was known. Because A could be declared of sufficient length to hold its records, storage in internal memory was available for A. Typically, this is not possible, however, and it would be necessary to use a more complicated algorithm, since A would be able to hold only a tiny portion of the records of the file.

Example 8.5   Suppose there are two files with records of the same type in sorted order based on key value. Merge the two files. □

Producing a new file consisting of all the records of the two files, and itself in sorted order, is called **merging** the two files. The merging of two files is a basic component of efficient methods of external sorting. The task in Example 8.5 is to write a procedure to produce a merged file assuming records are ordered with the smallest key value appearing in the first record.

The basic idea is straightforward: Read a record from each sorted file, and append the record with the smaller key value to the merged file. Read the next record of the file that had the record with the smaller key value. Compare it with the record that has not yet been appended; append the record with the smaller key value to the merged file. Repeat this process of reading and comparing records from the two files, until one of the files becomes empty. Then append the records on the remaining file to the merged file.

Assume that the files to be merged are not empty, and are of type *recordsfile* = file of filerecords, with *key* the field of filerecords on which sorting is to be based. The merge procedure may be written as follows:

```
procedure MERGE(var FILE1, FILE2, MERGEDFILE : recordsfile);
var
     RECORD1, RECORD2 : filerecords;
     FLAG : integer;
begin
     FLAG := 0;
     RESET(FILE1);
     RESET(FILE2);
     REWRITE(MERGEDFILE);
```

```
        READ(FILE1, RECORD1);
        READ(FILE2, RECORD2);
        while FLAG = 0 do
            if RECORD1.KEY < RECORD2.KEY then
                begin
                    WRITE(MERGEDFILE, RECORD1);
                    if not EOF(FILE1) then
                        READ(FILE1, RECORD1)
                    else
                        begin
                            FLAG := 1;
                            WRITE(MERGEDFILE, RECORD2)
                        end
                end
            else
                begin
                    WRITE(MERGEDFILE, RECORD2);
                    if not EOF(FILE2) then
                        READ(FILE2, RECORD2)
                    else
                        begin
                            FLAG := 2;
                            WRITE(MERGEDFILE, RECORD1)
                        end
                end;
        if FLAG = 1 then
            while not EOF(FILE2) do
                begin
                    READ(FILE2, RECORD2);
                    WRITE(MERGEDFILE, RECORD2)
                end
        else
            while not EOF(FILE1) do
                begin
                    READ(FILE1, RECORD1);
                    WRITE(MERGEDFILE, RECORD1)
                end
    end;
```

8.3.2 Text Files

Text files are sequential files composed of a sequence of characters. The standard names INPUT and OUTPUT denote text files in Pascal. They should not be declared in a Pascal program since this can cause conflicts with their standard meanings. Further, when reading from the INPUT file, RESET(INPUT) should not be invoked; when writing to the output file, REWRITE(OUTPUT) should not be invoked. In fact, any READ statement with its file name parameter omitted is assumed by the computer to refer to the INPUT file. Similarly, any WRITE statement appearing without its file name parameter is assumed by the computer to refer to the OUTPUT file. Thus READ(V) and WRITE(V) mean READ(INPUT, V) and WRITE(OUTPUT, V),

	1	2	3	4	5	6	7	8	9	10	11	12
	L	I	N	E	1	eoln	L	I	N	E	2	eoln

Figure 8.5   Example of a Text File

respectively. When a program is reading from INPUT, V must be of character type, integer type, or real type. When a program is writing to OUTPUT, V may be of integer, real, or boolean type, or it may be a string of characters. Other files may be declared to be of type file of char, and are then text files.

Every sequential file that is a text file has associated with it a symbol called an end-of-line (eoln) marker. This symbol is not accessible to the user but is used in the file to denote the end of a line. Executing WRITELN(F) causes an eoln marker to be inserted in file F and the file pointer to be advanced. A text file may thus be thought of as being segmented into lines. A file F with five characters per line, and two lines, would appear as in Figure 8.5. If the file pointer is positioned at an eoln position, then executing READ(F, V) results in the blank character being placed in V (since the eoln character is stored as a blank), and the file pointer being advanced to the next character position.

Two special statements are available for use with text files, READLN and WRITELN. Executing READLN(F, V) results in V being set to the next character on the current input line, the file pointer being advanced to the first character of the next line, and F↑ being set to that character. Executing WRITELN(F, V) has the same effect as WRITE(F, V), plus the insertion of an end-of-line marker after the character appended to the file.

In order to appreciate the limitations of external memory, as well as its possibilities, it is necessary to understand something of the nature of the devices used for such storage, the topic of the next section. The section also provides a glimpse into the nature and implementation of other kinds of files typically provided by computer installations.

8.4   Sequential Access in External Memory

A range of devices is now available for use as secondary storage. The most common devices are magnetic tapes and disks. Tape cassettes like the ones you use to listen to your favorite rock groups are prototypical of the magnetic tape used for secondary storage. If a song is being played on such a tape, the time required to access another song on the tape depends on how far away from the current position that song is. This accessibility is the same for magnetic tapes used as secondary storage. Such a tape can be pictured as containing a sequence of fixed-length *blocks* (Figure 8.6). Each block

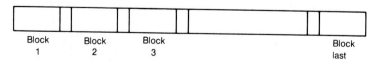

| Block
1 | Block
2 | Block
3 | | Block
last |

Figure 8.6   Sequential Access on Magnetic Tape

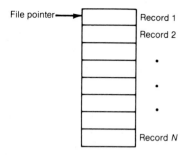

Figure 8.7 Input Buffer for the File

contains a fixed number of records of a file, say N per block. One or more *input buffer areas* (reserved storage areas) are set aside in internal memory, each large enough to hold one block of records. These buffers are required in order to allow for efficient reading and writing of files.

Suppose one buffer is set aside. To read a block of records into the buffer, the tape must be moved at sufficient speed past a read head. This speed determines the rate at which data are transferred to the buffer. If a Pascal sequential file is stored on magnetic tape, then executing RESET(F) causes the buffer storage to be allocated, the tape to be rewound so the first block may be read, and the first block to be read into the buffer. After these operations have occurred, the buffer and the file pointer can be visualized as in Figure 8.7.

At this moment the storage used for the first record actually represents the file buffer variable. If READ(F, V) is executed, the first record is copied into V, the file pointer is advanced to the next buffer position, and this buffer position now contains the value of the file buffer variable. Consecutive executions of READ for this file cause similar actions. Finally, when N such reads have occurred, the next block of records from the tape is placed into the buffer, the file pointer is automatically repositioned at the first record of the buffer, and the process is repeated. A similar procedure takes place for the WRITE command, with respect to an output buffer for the file. In this way the buffer is being filled, when reading from a file (or emptied, when writing to a file), at the same time that the computer is carrying out other commands of a program. Blocking of records is done because N records can be read or written as a block much faster than individually since there is no starting and stopping tape. Today's computers, whether mainframe or personal, can execute on the order of 100,000 commands in the time it takes for a block to be read into or written from the buffers. A program may actually process N records of the file while the next block is being transferred to the buffer. For example, the records may be sorted or individually processed during this transfer time. In this case, the time required to process the entire file is determined by the time required to scan the file in this fashion. Thus, the number of accesses to secondary storage determines the execution time of the program. This may take minutes, a very long time in computer terms.

The sequential file data structure of Pascal is meant to model this kind of magnetic tape storage for file records. It should now be clear why sequential files should not be used when records must be accessed in an order other than the order in which they appear on the file. Attempting to access the records in arbitrary order may mean spending great amounts of computer time, since minutes may be required for each access. Instead, the typical use for such sequential files is when records may be processed in turn, starting from the first record. In other words, when the processing to be done can be accomplished by a traversal through the records of the file, then sequential files are appropriate. This is typical of external sorting, copying, and updating of each record.

As a practical example, suppose you are given the master file, BOOK-INVENTORY, of Example 8.3, and another transaction file, BOOKTRANS-ACTIONS. BOOKTRANSACTIONS consists of records representing the arrival of new book inventory, and sales of books in the last week. If both files are sorted on the same key, say title, then it is possible to traverse the files and update each master file record to reflect new arrivals and sales. Of course, a new file must be created for this updated master file. This step would actually be advantageous for security purposes, since the old master file and BOOKTRANSACTIONS file could be saved. If anything were to happen to the new master file, the procedure could be repeated and the file could be reconstructed.

8.5 Sorting Tape Files

Once again, one picture — in this case, a good example — is worth a thousand words. The different merging techniques demonstrated for the following example illustrate some of the complexities of sorting files stored on magnetic tape, when all records of the file cannot fit into internal memory at the same time. Detailed analysis of the sorting algorithms discussed here, and others, may be found in Knuth [1973b]. We begin with an extreme case.

Example 8.6   Sort an original file of twenty-one records that are stored sequentially on a tape file. The records have integer key values. Assume that only two records can be kept in internal memory at any one time. Storage for the two records is in addition to input and output buffers. □

Suppose the sequence of records in the original file is as follows:

2 12 17 16 14 30 17 2 50 65 20 32 48 58 16 20 15 10 30 45 16

It is not possible simply to read all the records into internal memory, and then apply one of the internal sort algorithms of Chapter 7, since no available internal storage is assumed. Instead, the general strategy, given that two sorted files can always be merged as shown in Section 8.3, is to create sorted subfiles repeatedly and merge them repeatedly until a final merged file containing all the original records is produced. The literature contains many ingenious algorithms for external sorting. This chapter gives only the flavor of the solutions. One major constraint on a solution is the number of tapes available for use in the sort. Assume three available tapes.

8.5.1 Straight Merge

Perhaps the most straightforward sorting technique is the straight merge. The *straight merge* distributes the initial records onto two tapes, *a* and *b*, so that they contain the same number of records, or so that one tape contains only one more record than the other. If this is done for the original file in Example 8.5, then the configuration of tapes *a* and *b* will appear as the *initial distribution:*

$$a \quad 2\,|17\,|14\,|17\,|50\,|20\,|48\,|16\,|15\,|30\,|16$$
$$b \quad 12\,|16\,|30\,|\ 2\,|65\,|32\,|58\,|20\,|10\,|45\,|$$

Now *a* and *b* can be thought of as being composed of subfiles, each of which is sorted and of length 1. A subfile is a **run of length r** if it consists of *r* records in sorted order. Here, *a* contains eleven subfiles, or *runs* of length 1, and *b* contains ten runs of length 1.

Apply a merge procedure to each pair of runs, each pair containing a run from *a* and the corresponding run from tape *b*, thus

$$\frac{2}{12}\,,\ \frac{17}{16}\,,\ \frac{14}{30}\,,\ \text{etc.}$$

are "paired." The merge procedure consecutively merges each pair (consisting of a sorted subfile of length 1 from *a*, and a corresponding sorted subfile of length 1 from *b*). The resultant merged files are written consecutively to tape *c*. The result of the *first merge of a and b to c is*

$$c \quad 2\ 12\,|\,16\ 17\,|\,14\ 30\,|\,2\ 17\,|\,50\ 65\,|\,20\ 32\,|\,48\ 58\,|\,16\ 20\,|\,10\ 15\,|\,30\ 45\,|\,16$$

Think of *c* as containing ten subfiles or runs of length 2 and one run of length 1 and distribute these to *a* and *b* equally to obtain the *second distribution.*

$$a \quad 2\ 12\,|\,14\ 30\,|\,50\ 65\,|\,48\ 58\,|\,10\ 15\,|\,16$$
$$b \quad 16\ 17\,|\,2\ 17\,|\,20\ 32\,|\,16\ 20\,|\,30\ 45\,|$$

By now there are five paired runs of length 2, and one run of length 1. These may again be consecutively merged, and written to *c* to obtain the *second merge of a and b to c.*

$$c \quad 2\ 12\ 16\ 17\,|\,2\ 14\ 17\ 30\,|\,20\ 32\ 50\ 65\,|\,16\ 20\ 48\ 58\,|\,10\ 15\ 30\ 45\,|\,16$$

Another distribution to *a* and *b* yields the *third distribution.*

$$a \quad 2\ 12\ 16\ 17\,|\,20\ 32\ 50\ 65\,|\,10\ 15\ 30\ 45$$
$$b \quad 2\ 14\ 17\ 30\,|\,16\ 20\ 48\ 58\,|\,16$$

These pairs of length 4 can now be merged to obtain the *third merge of a and b to c.*

$$c \quad 2\ 2\ 12\ 14\ 16\ 17\ 17\ 30\,|\,16\ 20\ 20\ 32\ 48\ 50\ 58\ 65\,|\,10\ 15\ 16\ 30\ 45$$

It takes two more distributions and merges to complete the sort. The *fourth distribution*

$$a \quad 2\ \ 2\ 12\ 14\ 16\ 17\ 17\ 30\,|\,10\ 15\ 16\ 30\ 45$$
$$b \quad 16\ 20\ 20\ 32\ 48\ 50\ 58\ 65\,|$$

is followed by the *fourth merge.*

$$c \quad 2\ 2\ 12\ 14\ 16\ 16\ 17\ 17\ 20\ 20\ 30\ 32\ 48\ 50\ 58\ 65\,|\,10\ 15\ 16\ 30\ 45$$

The *fifth distribution* is next. It is followed by the *fifth merge*.

```
a    2   2 12 14 16 16 17 17 20 20 30 32 48 50 58 65
b   10 15 16 30 45
c    2   2 10 12 14 15 16 16 16 17 17 20 20 30 32 45 48 50 58 65
```

This completes the sort, which has taken five distributions and five merges. The sort is described as a *five-pass* sort, with five distribution phases and five merge phases, using three tapes. Programming this process is not a trivial task. Ignoring details, the basic time requirements can be seen to be determined by the number of times files must be reset or rewritten, and the number of records that must be accessed from secondary storage (tapes). This assumes the internal memory processing will be done so quickly that it does not add to the total time for the sort. Before the original file, c, can be distributed to tapes a and b, those tapes must be rewritten (that is, rewound), and the original file must be reset (that is, rewound). Before a and b can be merged to c, they must be reset, and c must be rewritten. Also, in each phase, whether distribution or merge, each record must be accessed from secondary storage. Thus the total time is proportional to the number of passes (five here). If the access time of a record is T_A, and the rewind time is T_R, then the total time is $5 \times (2 \times 21 \times T_A + 3 \times T_R)$. Note the factor of 2 associated with the twenty-one records and the access time. The factor is 2 because there are two phases, distribution and merge.

8.5.2 Natural Merge

The straight merge sort does not take advantage of any natural ordering that may exist in the original file. Even if that file were given in sorted order, the straight merge would proceed as before. A *natural merge sort* distributes the records of the original file to a and b, so that sorted subfiles or runs are preserved and treated as a unit. Such a distribution would assign 2 12 17 to a, since they form a run. The 16 terminates this run, and goes to b. The 14 terminates this run and goes to a as the beginning of its second run, followed by 30. So far the result is

```
a    2 12 17 | 14 30
b   16
```

The 17 now terminates the 14 30 run and goes to b. Note that this extends the first run of b to 16 17. At this point, 2 terminates this run, with the following result.

```
a    2 12 17 | 14 30
b   16 17
```

If *balance* is to be maintained, each file must end up with a number of runs differing by no more than 1 from the other files, then the next run (starting with 2) must go to b. Subtleties of this kind must be carefully watched for in the actual implementation of merge sorting algorithms. The resultant distribution will be the *initial distribution*.

```
a    2 12 17 | 14 30   | 20 32 48 58 | 15 16
b   16 17    |  2 50 65 | 16 20       | 10 30 45
```

Merging these pairs of runs, and writing the merged result to c yields the *first merge*.

c 2 12 16 17 17|2 14 30 50 65|16 20 20 32 48 58|10 15 16 30 45

Another distribution and merge gives the *second distribution*,

a 2 12 16 17 17|16 20 20 32 48 58
b 2 14 30 50 65|10 15 16 30 45

which is followed by the *second merge*.

c 2 2 12 14 16 17 17 30 50 65|10 15 16 16 20 20 30 32 45 48 58

A third and final distribution and merge complete the sort. The *third distribution* yields

a 2 2 12 14 16 17 17 30 50 65
b 10 15 16 16 20 20 30 32 45 48 58

The result of the *third merge* is as follows:

c 2 2 10 12 14 15 16 16 16 17 17 20 20 30 30 32 45 48 50 58 65

This is a three-pass, two-phase sort, using three tapes. The total time is $3 \times (2 \times 21 \times T_A + 3 \times T_R)$. Any inherent ordering of the initial data allows the number of passes to be reduced, compared to the straight merge sort.

Note that to merge runs embedded in a file, the procedure of Section 8.3.1 requires modification.

8.5.3 Replacement-Selection

Since typically there is room for a reasonable number of records in internal memory, both the straight and natural merge sorts can be speeded up. For instance, if m records can be sorted in internal memory, then the straight merge sort can start with the distribution of runs of length m on each of the tapes a and b.

There is a clever way to produce runs for distribution (perhaps with the natural merge sort) without actually sorting the m records. This is the **replacement-selection sort**, which uses a heap of size m and works as follows. Start with the first m keys of the original file of Example 8.6 in internal memory, and create a heap to obtain Figure 8.8(a) ($m = 7$).

Remove the root key from the heap and output it to an output file. The next input file key, 2, is inserted at the root of the heap, and the heap is reheaped giving Figure 8.8(b).

Again, the root key is removed and written to the output file. The next record key of the input file, 50, is inserted at the root, and reheaping occurs. Figure 8.8(c) results.

Continuing in this way generates a run on the output file of length 8, which would be terminated when 16 from the input file is inserted at the root of the heap. The situation at that point is shown in Figure 8.8(d). Instead of terminating the run at length 8, treat 16 as associated with the next run, since 16 is less than the last output value, 20. This means that 16 must be distinguished from the heap entries for the

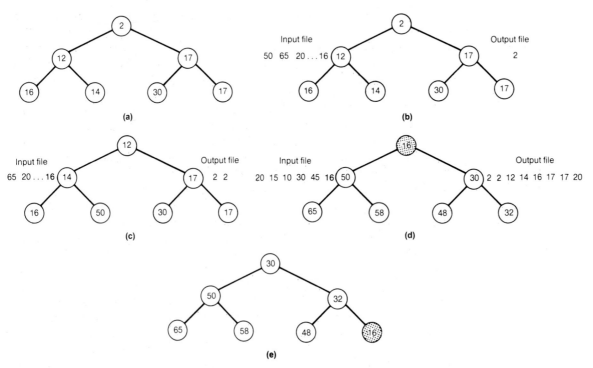

Figure 8.8   Replacement-Selection Sort

current run. Thus, 16 is shaded in Figure 8.8(d). In reheaping, current run entries are considered smaller than next run entries. Figure 8.8(e) shows the heap after reheaping. Each input smaller than the last output is handled in this way. Eventually the heap becomes filled with entries of the next run and the process repeats.

Notice that the length of the output run will always be at least m (with the possible exception of the last run generated). Continuing this process, called *replacement-selection*, we obtain the output file,

2 2 12 14 16 17 17 20 30 32 48 50 58 65 | 10 15 16 16 20 30 45

The original file consisted of ten runs; the output file after replacement-selection consists of 2 runs. With randomly ordered input files, this replacement-selection generates runs whose average length is $2m$. The example exhibits this behavior in an exemplary fashion.

Notice that both the straight and natural merges spend half their time accessing records for the distribution phase. Spending this time can be avoided by using another tape. By this technique, each time two runs are merged, they can be written, alternately, to tapes a and b. This eliminates the need for extra, basically unproductive, time spent in distribution from c.

8.5.4 Polyphase Sort

Rather than use more tapes, it is possible to incorporate the distribution phase (except for the initial distribution) along with the merge phase. Such a sort is called a *polyphase sort*. In this type of sort, the tapes being merged, and the tape to which the merged subfiles are written, vary continuously throughout the sort. In this technique, the concept of a pass through the records is not as clear-cut as in the straight or the natural merge. A distribution, merge, and pass all blend together. This might have more properly been called an *amorphous* sort, except it has considerable character and is one of the better sorts.

The polyphase sort starts with an initial distribution of runs on tapes a and b. The initial distribution is critical to its proper execution. For the case of the original file of twenty-one records in Example 8.6, the initial distribution should be thirteen runs to tape a, and eight runs to tape b, each run of length 1. It is the *number*, not the length, of the runs on each tape that is critical. The number of records for the example is twenty-one because the first few Fibonacci numbers are 0, 1, 1, 2, 3, 5, 8, 13, 21. The Fibonacci numbers are crucial to the polyphase sort because the number of records must be a Fibonacci number to make the polyphase sort work.

When a three-tape polyphase sort is used, the original number of runs should be a Fibonacci number, with the distribution of runs between tapes a and b the two preceding Fibonacci numbers, which add to the original number of runs. In the present case, $8 + 13 = 21$. When more tapes are used, *generalized* Fibonacci numbers, which specify the required number of records, become the basis for the initial run distribution among the tapes. No programs will be shown for implementation of the details of the external sorting algorithms discussed in this section. Therefore it is unnecessary to resolve in detail the question of how to proceed when the actual number of runs is not a Fibonacci number. The remedy, though, involves adding an appropriate number of "dummy" runs [Knuth, 1973b].

Getting back to the workings of the polyphase sort, the initial situation after distribution will be an *initial distribution*.

```
a    2 | 12 | 17 | 16 | 14 | 30 | 17 | 2 | 50 | 65 | 20 | 32 | 48    13 runs of length 1
b   58 | 16 | 20 | 15 | 10 | 30 | 45 | 16 |                          8 runs of length 1
c
```

This distribution required twenty-one record accesses.

We now proceed by merging the first eight runs of a and the eight runs of b to c to obtain the *merge of the first eight runs of a and b to c*.

```
a   50 | 65 | 20 | 32 | 48                                          5 runs
b
c    2 58 | 12  16 | 17  20 | 15  16 | 10  14 | 30  30 | 17  45 | 2  16   8 runs
```

Notice that b is now empty, a total of $8 + 8$, or sixteen, records have been accessed, and a and c contain $5 + 8 = 13$ runs. All three tapes had to be rewound before the initial distribution, but only b need be rewound now. It is possible to continue by merging the first five runs of c, and the five runs of a to b. This results in a *merge of the first five runs of a and c to b*.

```
a
b    2 50 58 | 12 16 65 | 17 20 20 | 15 16 32 | 10 14 48    5 runs
c   30 30    | 17 45    | 2 16     |                         3 runs
```

Notice that a is empty, a total of $5 + 5 \times 2 = 15$ records have been accessed, and b and c contain $5 + 3 = 8$ runs. Tape a is now rewound, and the first three runs of b are merged with the three runs of c. The result is the *merge of the first three runs of b and c to a*.

```
a    2 30 30 50 58|12 16 17 45 65|2 16 17 20 20    3 runs
b   15 16 32|10 14 48                              2 runs
c
```

Tape c is now empty and must be rewound. A total of $(3 \times 3) + (3 \times 2) = 15$ records were accessed, and a total of $2 + 3 = 5$ runs remain. Merging the first two runs of a and b to c yields

```
a   2 16 17 20 20                                              1 run
b
c   2 15 16 30 30 32 50 58|10 12 14 16 17 45 48 65   2 runs
```

This leaves b empty, so we rewind it. A total of $(2 \times 3) + (2 \times 5) = 16$ records were accessed, and $1 + 2 = 3$ runs remain. Merging the run of a and the first run of c to b yields

```
a
b   2  2 15 16 16 17 20 20 30 30 32 50 58   1 run
c  10 12 14 16 17 45 48 65                   1 run
```

A total of $(1 \times 5) + (1 \times 8) = 13$ record accesses occurred, and $1 + 1 = 2$ runs are left. Tape a is rewound. Then a final merge produces

```
a   2 2 10 12 14 15 16 16 16 17 17 20 20 30 30 32 45 48 50 58 65
b
c
```

This final merge of b and c to a took $13 + 8 = 21$ record accesses. A total of $117\ (= 21 + 16 + 15 + 15 + 16 + 13 + 21)$ record accesses is required. These 117 record accesses represent an effective $^{117}/_{21}$, or $5\,^4/_7$, passes. The total time for this algorithm is $117 \times T_A + 8 \times T_R$. The straight merge sort and natural merge sort required $210 \times T_A + 15 \times T_R$ and $126 \times T_A + 9 \times T_R$ time, respectively.

The polyphase sort, until completion, results in exactly one empty tape, so that the remaining tapes may be partially merged to it. After each merge, the distribution of runs is made up of two consecutive Fibonacci numbers ($13 + 8$, $8 + 5$, $5 + 3$, $3 + 2$, $2 + 1$, $1 + 1$, $1 + 0$). With more tapes, this is also true, but generalized Fibonacci numbers appear.

8.6 Direct Access in External Memory

Accessing a song on a phonograph record is different from accessing a song on a tape cassette. Think of the songs as stored along the grooves of a record rather than along the tape of a cassette. Instead of going through each song between the current arm position and the location of the desired song (and scratching the record!), the arm is moved directly to the proper groove. Once the arm is placed, it is necessary to wait until the record revolves, so the beginning of the song appears under the arm. The movable arm eliminates the need to pass through all songs that intervene between its current and desired position. The magnetic disk works the same way: it is the reading head that moves to the desired storage location, thus saving access time compared to the magnetic tape.

Magnetic disks and disk packs (also known as *hard* disks) are examples of *direct access* devices used for secondary storage. In this context, **direct access** means a program can go straight to desired information stored on a given surface and cylinder. Although this access time is not constant, it is slower than random access in internal memory, but generally much faster than the sequential access time for tapes. A floppy disk has similar access capability, but is slower and has much less storage capacity. Thus, in terms of access time, direct access storage devices fall between sequential access devices, such as magnetic tapes, and random access memory. Hard disks are used by mainframes and minicomputers, while microcomputers or personal computers vary from no disks through floppy disks to hard disks.

A random access memory allows very fast access to any element of the memory. The access time is the same for all stored elements, no matter which element was last accessed. Sequential devices allow fast access "locally," but all elements between the currently accessed element and the next desired element must be passed through before the next element may be accessed. Consequently, the time to access the next desired element is proportional to its distance from the currently accessed element. Direct access devices are intermediate between these two extremes. They act like sequential devices with tabs. Just as using the alphabetic tabs in a dictionary allows a person seeking a word to find it quickly, so do "tabs" allow one to close in, relatively quickly, on the desired area of the sequential storage. In direct access devices, the "tabs" are movable read/write heads and surfaces.

Sequential devices are convenient for tasks that may be accomplished by traversing records. However, when the order in which records must be processed cannot be predicted, sequential devices are not useful. Tasks requiring random access to records cannot be accomplished efficiently using sequential memory devices. The introduction of economical direct access devices made random access feasible. As a result, airline reservation systems, interactive computing, and instant updating of bank accounts have become commonplace. This was made possible by the development of appropriate technology for direct access memory.

A **magnetic disk** is a flat, circular platter on whose two surfaces information can be stored and accessed. It can be pictured as a phonograph tone arm and record, with its concentric *tracks*, corresponding to the grooves of the phonograph record, and its **movable read/write head**, corresponding to the tone arm. A **disk pack** consists of a pile of such magnetic disks, and a read/write head for each record surface — that is, one head for each side of a record (see Figure 8.9). The read/write heads are typically coupled so that they all move at the same time, and are positioned over the same track of their respective surfaces, although only one head is actually reading or writing at any moment. There may be twenty magnetic disks and a hundred tracks on each disk.

Each track of a surface in a disk pack stores records in blocks, similar to the blocking of records on a magnetic tape. Each track behaves as a sequential access device, like a magnetic tape. That is, each block must be passed through, as the disks rotate, before another block farther along the track can be accessed by the surface read/write head.

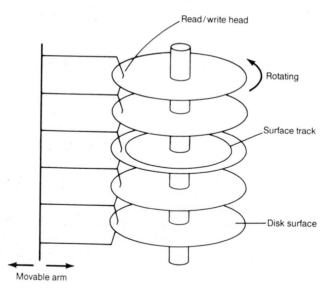

Figure 8.9   A Disk Pack

If we focus on the same track on each surface, then the pile of tracks form a conceptual cylinder in space as shown in Figure 8.10. Assuming tracks are numbered from, say, 1 to 100, a cylinder consists of all tracks with the same number. Thus the disk pack can be viewed as composed of one hundred concentric cylinders.

A cylinder is important because it allows any block of records stored on a surface of the cylinder to be accessed without moving the read/write heads. Accessing a block stored on a different cylinder (or track) requires moving the read/write heads. The time required to move the heads from one cylinder to another is called **seek time**; it is proportional to the distance between the cylinders. This time typically may take a significant fraction of a second (1/10th to 1/20th). It is the dominant factor in dealing with time requirements for accessing blocks on magnetic disks.

Once the read/write heads are positioned over the desired cylinder, the time required for the desired block to rotate under the heads is called **latency time**, and can be on the order of one hundredth of a second.

8.7 Sequential and Random Access of Disk Files

Often large amounts of information, too much to fit into internal memory, must be organized so that random requests for specific pieces of information can be readily satisfied. The methods of organization that are useful in internal memory are not adequate for external memory implemented using magnetic disks.

8.7.1 Sequential Access

There is a natural way to store records sequentially on a magnetic disk pack to minimize total seek time for a traversal through the records. This storage technique is based on the cylinder concept. It starts by filling blocks of the top surface track of

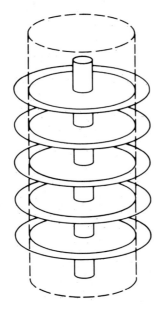

Figure 8.10 Conceptual Cylinder

the outermost cylinder with records, allocating records to blocks sequentially. When the track is full, the same process is repeated with the track of the next surface, and the next, and the next, until the lowest surface track is filled. Continuing, in the same way, records are stored on each of the inner cylinders, starting with the next adjacent cylinder. This is similar to storing records sequentially on a magnetic tape. In fact, we can picture the surfaces and cylinders laid out linearly as in Figure 8.11. This arrangement has all the inherent drawbacks of magnetic tape, whenever random accessing of records is required.

Storage could be made more efficient by taking advantage of the tab feature of the disk, which allows the read head to go, directly, to any cylinder and surface. The problem is how to determine exactly where to go. If one knew that the record to be retrieved were the *I*th record, then it would be easy to calculate on which cylinder and surface it would be located. This is not often the case, since the search is conducted by means of key value, not by order in the sequence.

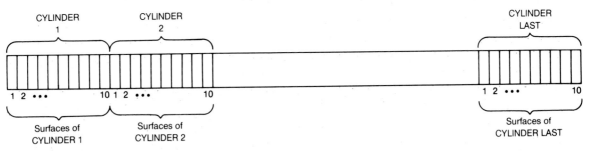

Figure 8.11 Sequential Access on a Magnetic Disk Pack

A linear search of the file could be done, but might take $O(N)$ time, when N records are stored in the file. This could take minutes. If the records are stored in sorted order by key value, a binary search of the file might be done. The difficulty here is that lg N accesses are required. A million-record file would require twenty accesses, and each access might require a seek. While the binary search is better, it still might take seconds. This is reasonable for isolated requests, but during this time there may be many requests for desired retrievals. Waiting requests may build up interminably, with unlimited waiting time before all are processed. The need to insert or delete records further compounds the problem.

Just as in internal memory, keeping records in blocks, with pointers to succeeding blocks, is a possibility based on the concept of lists. While this may avoid insertion and deletion difficulties, it does not alleviate the problem of searching. We encountered this same problem with lists in internal memory. What about binary search trees? Even if kept balanced, a million records may need as much as $20 \times c$ seeks, where c is a small constant.

8.7.2 Random Access

We still have hash tables in our arsenal. Using hash tables in secondary storage requires some accommodation to its access capabilities. **Buckets**, an extension of the chaining policy for collision resolution with internal memory, are appropriate. The idea is to create a hash table based on key values. The hash table will contain pointers to lists. Each list, referred to as a bucket, contains all records that hash to the same hash table address. The lists are stored in blocks on the disk, each block holding a fixed number of records and a pointer to the next block containing other records on the list. When a key is to be inserted into the hash table, the program determines its hash address and then inserts the key into the bucket pointed to by that address. The key may be inserted into the bucket by traversing the list of linked blocks until a block is encountered with room for the record. If no such block is found, a new block is appended to the list, and the record is inserted in that block. Care should be taken to avoid wasting seek time (and latency time) when these lists are being traversed. This means blocks of a bucket should be on the same cylinder. Searching for a key is similar to making an insertion. Deletion involves the usual deletion from a list, with care taken to release unneeded blocks when possible. When small enough, the hash table itself is kept in internal memory to avoid one disk access.

In practice, such hash tables can be devised so that one or two disk accesses are required for either successful or unsuccessful searches. This is accomplished by selecting a good hash function, an appropriate fixed number of records per block, and an appropriate number of buckets. The usage factor of such a hash table is given by N/Bk, where N is the number of records stored, B is the number of buckets, and k the fixed number of records per bucket. If the performance of the table degrades as insertions are made, the table may be reorganized.

Other interesting and important external hashing methods are presented in Larson [1978], Litwin [1980], and Fagin, Nievergelt, Pippenger, and Strong [1979].

8.7.3 Indexed Sequential Access

While the hash table solution may yield fast average access times, there is no guarantee for the worst case, and no convenient way to access records in sorted order by key value. To achieve the ability to access records in unpredictable order or in sorted order, as necessary, we must incorporate an old idea familiar to all. Suppose a visitor from outer space wanted to find the location of a particular street, say Bond Street in London. The visitor might go to a world atlas and determine first where London's country, England, is situated. The intergalactic traveler might then find a map of the country, and locate London. Finally, a city map of London gives the creature the exact location of the street. On a more mundane level, suppose a student wants to locate a particular book in a university library. The student would go to the file cabinet of authors and find the drawer that contains authors' last names with the appropriate beginning initial. She would then search for the card with the correct author and title, which gives a library call number. Next she would consult a library directory to learn the floor and location of those call numbers. Finally, she would go to that location and search for the book with that particular call number. The critical concept in such searches is the availability of one or more *directories* to be used to determine quickly the location of the particular item desired.

The magnetic disk supports the use of such a directory to focus the search. It can be used to find a particular cylinder and surface relatively quickly, eliminating the need for traversing sequentially through intervening records. Until recently, when B-trees (see the next section) were introduced, the most popular method of creating and maintaining such a directory used the natural sequential storage of records, so they appear in sorted order by key value. This is known as the *indexed sequential access method* (ISAM), and may be implemented in various ways, typically using three or four levels of directories. A first directory, known as the *master index*, may be searched to determine the cylinder on which a particular search key appears. If a disk pack has two hundred cylinders (tracks), then the master index has two hundred entries, one for each cylinder. The entry for the *i*th track gives the highest key value appearing on that track. A search of the master index then readily determines the cylinder on which a search key may reside. That cylinder is accessed, and contains a *cylinder index* directory. If a disk pack has ten surfaces, the cylinder index has ten entries, one for each surface. The entry for the *i*th surface gives the highest key value appearing on that surface. A search of the cylinder index determines the surface on which a search key may reside. Finally, the track of the cylinder on that surface may be searched sequentially for the desired key, resulting in a successful or unsuccessful search. With such an implementation, unused storage initially is left in blocks so that the insertion of new records may be more easily accommodated. If a block is full, records can be shifted to the right to other blocks, so that the new record is inserted in proper sorted order.

Overflow areas must also be available and maintained on the disk, in case this track storage is exhausted due to insertions. Tracks and cylinders are set aside for this purpose. Insertions may require the master or cylinder index to be updated. Similarly, deletions of records, leaving vacated storage to be reclaimed, may require updating of directories and shifting of records. Deletions may also be treated simply by marking a record as deleted, but this may eventually lead to the need for reclamation of this storage, degrading the efficiency of the implementation. Because of overflow from insertions, performance may degrade, necessitating reorganization, allocation of more disk storage, and reconstitution of the file.

The overflow areas may be maintained as lists of records in sorted order, linked by pointers. When the proper cylinder index is searched, the pointer to be followed

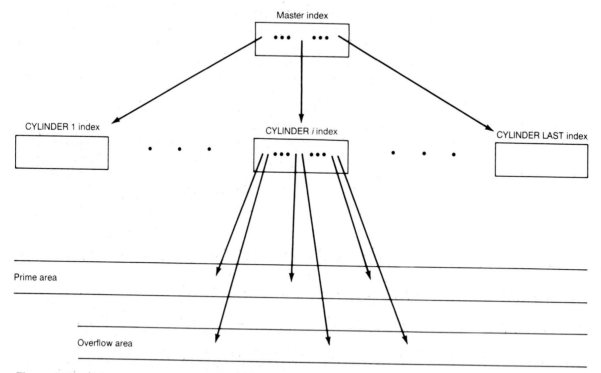

Figure 8.12   Organization of Indexed Sequential Files

may point to an overflow area, in which case the search amounts to a traversal of a list of records. Otherwise, the record is said to reside in the *prime area,* and the search amounts to a sequential traversal of records on a track. The **prime area** consists of reserved tracks on cylinders designated as prime cylinders.

For a given number of records to be stored, there is no guarantee that overflow will not degrade the system, unless a high price is paid by dedicating large amounts of track storage to reduce this possibility.

Each cylinder index actually has additional entries giving the highest key value in its overflow area for each surface, and a pointer to the first record of the overflow list for that surface. Conceptually, we may visualize the organization of such implementations as shown in Figure 8.12.

8.7.4   **B-trees for Sequential and Random Access**

A more recent method allows for achieving both the random access of records and a traversal through the records in sorted order. This method allows a more flexible use of the disk and guarantees excellent worst-case performance for a given number of records, with an acceptable amount of dedicated disk storage. It is known as the *virtual sequential access method* (VSAM). To see how it might be implemented we study its basis, *B-trees.* VSAM and many data base management systems use trees that are modified B-trees in their implementation. The basic reference for B-trees is the classic paper by Bayer and McCreight [1972]. Hash trees are an alternative to

B-trees for the organization of large files of data. They are discussed and compared to B-trees by Bell and Deen [1984]. Tremblay and Sorenson [1984] discuss many file structure organizations. See Ullman [1982] for more on data base systems. Wirth [1976] gives Pascal programs for the basic B-tree operations.

Figure 8.12 shows that the directories (the master index and the cylinder indexes) form a tree structure that guides the search for a record. Programmers try to find specialized trees leading to efficient searches, efficient use of storage, and relatively easy maintenance. Since the depth of the tree determines the worst-case search times, the goal is to find trees with short paths to terminal nodes. This implies that the nodes of the tree generally will have many successors. B-trees satisfy these requirements.

A **B-tree of order** m has the following four properties:

1. Every node of the tree, except the root and terminal nodes, has at least $\lceil \frac{1}{2} m \rceil$ subtrees.
2. Every terminal node has the same depth.
3. The root node has at least two subtrees, unless it is a terminal node.
4. No node has more than m subtrees.

Each node of a B-tree will have the form shown in Figure 8.13. This represents storage for m keys and $m + 1$ pointers, although the storage may not all be used at any given time. If n is less than m, not all m keys are present in the node. Each pointer P_i points to a subtree of the node. The keys $K_1, K_2, \ldots, K_n$ are kept in sorted order, so $K_1 < K_2 < \ldots < K_n$ within the node. The subtree pointed to by P_{i+1} contains all records of the file whose key values are less than K_{i+1} and greater than or equal to K_i. P_1 and P_{n+1} point, respectively, to subtrees containing records with key values less than K_1, and greater than or equal to K_n. For example, if the keys are

$$1, 3, 5, 6, 7, 8, 13, 20, 21, 23, 24, 30, 37, 40, 56, 60, 62, 63, 70, 80, 83$$

then the tree of Figure 8.14(a) is a B-tree of order 4 storing these keys and their records.

The terminal nodes of the B-tree in Figure 8.14 are not shown. Instead, the pointers to them have been replaced by null pointers. This reflects the way the tree might be represented in external storage. Notice that, in general, null pointers will appear at the same depth in the tree, depth one less than the terminal nodes. A generalized inorder traversal (see Chapter 6) of the B-tree accesses the keys in sorted order. Associate with each null pointer, the key value accessed immediately after the pointer is considered in such a traversal. A unique key is then associated with every null pointer except the last, and each key has a unique null pointer associated with it. For example, the first three null pointers have keys 1, 3, and 5 associated with them. The fourth null pointer (to the right of 5) has key 6 associated with it. Con-

| P_1 | K_1 | P_2 | K_2 | $\cdots$ | P_i | K_i | P_{i+1} | K_{i+1} | $\cdots$ | P_n | K_n | P_{n+1} | $\cdots$ | | |

Figure 8.13 Form of Each Node on a B-Tree

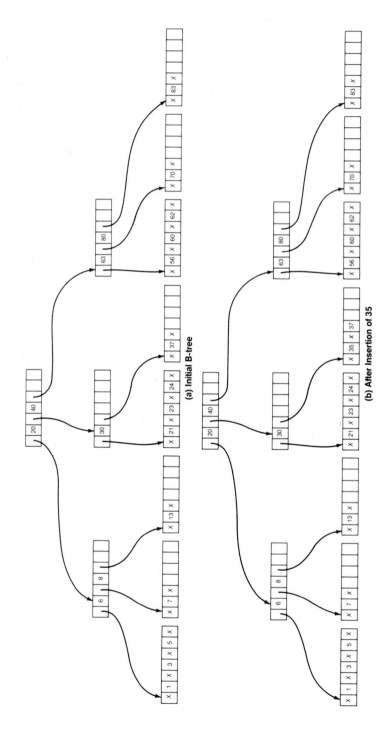

(a) Initial B-tree

(b) After Insertion of 35

Figure 8.14 A B-Tree of Order 4 with Twenty-one Records and after Insertion and Deletion

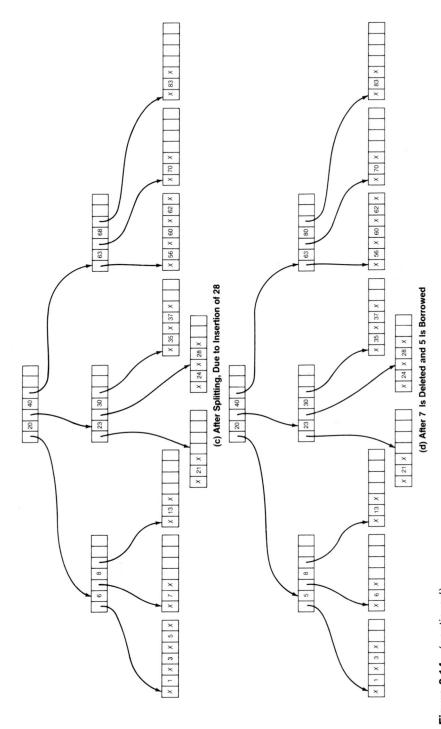

(c) After Splitting, Due to Insertion of 28

(d) After 7 Is Deleted and 5 Is Borrowed

Figure 8.14 *(continued)*

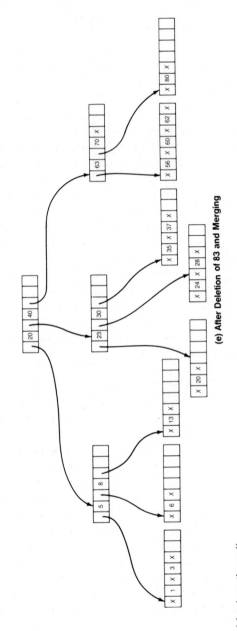

(e) After Deletion of 83 and Merging

Figure 8.14   *(continued)*

sequently, the number of null pointers, and the number of terminal nodes, are exactly one greater than the number of keys stored in the tree.

Any B-tree has a root node with at least two successors. Each successor has at least $\lceil \frac{1}{2} m \rceil$ successors. Thus, there are at least $2\lceil \frac{1}{2} m \rceil^{d-2}$ nodes at depth $d \geq 3$ of any B-tree. A B-tree of depth $d \geq 3$ has at least $2\lceil \frac{1}{2} m \rceil^{d-2}$ terminal nodes, so

$$N + 1 \geq 2\lceil \tfrac{1}{2} m \rceil^{d-2}$$

This implies that $d \leq 2 + \lg_x[(N + 1)/2]$, where $\lg_x$ denotes logarithm with base x and $x = \lceil \frac{1}{2} m \rceil$. If $N = 2^{24} - 1 = 16,777,215$ and $m = 2 \times 2^8 = 512$, then $(N + 1)/2 = 2^{23}$ and $\lg_x[(N + 1)/2] = \lg_{256}(2^{23}) < 3$.

A B-tree storing $16,777,215$ records will therefore have depth ≤ 4. We shall see that $d - 1$ is the maximum number of nodes that must be accessed when searching a B-tree for a search key. Thus, we are guaranteed that no more than three node accesses are required to search for a key in the B-tree with $16,777,215$ records!

A B-tree may be viewed as a generalization of a binary search tree, with a special imposed balance requirement to ensure against too great a depth. To search a B-tree for a search key value, say 22, entails accessing its root node, and traversing the node's keys until 22 is encountered, a key that exceeds 22 is reached, or the last key stored in the node is passed. If 22 is found, the search is complete. In Figure 8.14(a) the key value 40 is reached. The pointer to its left points to a subtree that must contain the search key, if it is in the tree at all. That subtree is then searched in the same way. Its root node is accessed, and 30 is reached. Following its left pointer, the final subtree root is accessed. Its key value, 23, is reached. Its left pointer is null, which means that the search terminates unsuccessfully.

Property 1 ensures that, except for the root and terminal nodes (which don't appear anyway), every node of a B-tree will be at least half full. Property 2 ensures that the B-tree will not be scraggly; all paths to terminal nodes must have the same length. The idea is to store information of a node on blocks of a cylinder on the disk, so that accessing a node requires one seek time and all keys of the node may be read into internal memory. The search through the keys of a node, to determine the next node to access, then takes place rapidly in internal memory, using an appropriate search technique.

Of course, after an insertion or deletion, the tree must be maintained as a B-tree. This may be done making *local* modifications that are simpler than those required for AVL trees. For insertion, the key to be inserted is searched until a null pointer is to be followed. This assumes that only one record with a given key value appears in the tree, and is similar to the initial insertion in AVL trees. If the node containing the null pointer has unused storage, then the key is simply inserted at the proper place in this node. This may require the shifting of keys in the node, but is accomplished quickly in internal memory. For example, if key 35 is inserted in the tree of Figure 8.14(a), the result is the tree of Figure 8.14(b).

All insertions will be made in this way, in nodes at the lowest level, until the node becomes full. For example, if 28 is to be inserted next in the tree of Figure 8.14(b), no room exists in the node x 21 x 23 x 24 x. The $m + 1$ key values (the m old keys and the 1 new key) can be split by leaving $\lceil m/2 \rceil - 1$ in the old node, and moving the remaining records, except the middle one, the $\lceil \frac{1}{2} m \rceil$th, to a newly created node. The middle record is inserted in the predecessor (parent) of the old node. The result is the B-tree of Figure 8.14(c).

Had the predecessor been full, it would have been split in the same way in turn. Splitting may be necessary at every node of the search path, back to, and including, the root. If this occurs, the depth of the resultant B-tree is one greater than the original B-tree.

Deletion is done similarly. A key is simply deleted from a lowest level node, and the keys shifted over, if the resultant number of keys satisfies the constraint that the node contain at least $\lceil m/2 \rceil - 1$ keys. If the constraint is violated, a key can be borrowed from a "neighbor" node, provided this may be done without violating the constraint for that node. In this case, the predecessor or successor key of the borrowed key moves into the deletion node, and the borrowed key takes its place in the predecessor node. For example, if key 7 is deleted from the tree of Figure 8.14(b), key 5 is borrowed from its neighbor (13 cannot be borrowed). The result is Figure 8.14(d).

If no neighbor can spare a key, the total number of keys between a neighbor and the deletion node will be less than m. These nodes may then be merged, along with a key from their predecessor. In the tree of Figure 8.14(d), if 83 is to be deleted, this situation will occur. The result is Figure 8.14(e).

It is possible for the predecessor to become too sparse, although this did not happen in our example. It is then treated as though its key were deleted, and so on, until the entire process is complete. This may go all the way to the root, in which case the root disappears, and the depth of the tree decreases by 1.

If the key to be deleted were not in a lowest level node, it would be replaced by its successor, and the successor node treated as if the successor were being deleted.

These insertion and deletion procedures preserve the B-tree properties. The B-tree is an external memory data structure that plays the same role as AVL trees in internal memory. In practice, a modification of the basic B-tree is used to ensure better storage utilization, and to increase the efficiency of traversal through the records in sorted order for VSAM. With B-trees, the generalized inorder traversal must be used for sequential access. This is time consuming and requires stack storage. Instead of sorting some key records in higher level nodes, the idea is to store all records only in lowest level nodes, and chain the lowest level nodes by pointers. For example, in Figure 8.14(a) all nodes at depth 3 could be linked in a chain, with the leftmost node first, and the rightmost node last, on the list. A traversal then amounts to a traversal of this chain.

It is clear that storage management is needed for external memory, just as for internal memory. This problem is not discussed here, but the internal memory techniques are applicable, when properly modified to take into account the structure of disks.

8.8   Summary

Files are stored in secondary storage and provide powerful facilities for the temporary and permanent storage of large amounts of information. Magnetic tapes and magnetic disks are two important devices on which to store files. These are typical of sequential and direct access devices, respectively.

Because of the structure and resultant access capabilities of these devices, internal memory techniques must be modified in order to deal efficiently and conveniently with files stored on them. It is possible to sort efficiently, even with sequential files, by using external sorting techniques. Primarily, these are merge sorts, such as straight, natural, and polyphase sorts. Other merge sorts may also decrease sorting time. In general, sequential files are suitable for tasks that can be accomplished by traversing the records of the file. These tasks include sorting and updating master files.

It is possible to achieve efficient random accessing of records with direct access devices when access is by a specific key. Hash tables are useful for this purpose. To achieve a combined capability of random plus sequential access in sorted order by a specific key requires considerable file organization. This organization involves the creation of a file directory, which may consist of a number of levels. The directory guides the search efficiently to the desired record with specific search key value. A number of directory implementations are possible, with directories based on B-trees becoming increasingly popular. Such directories may be searched relatively quickly, allowing efficient insertion and deletions, while utilizing storage well.

At this point, you should have filed away the substance of this book. It is hoped that you have done so to allow quick retrieval, while maintaining room for insertions. Deletions may be necessary but should be minimal.

☐ Exercises

1. Suppose a procedure reads in each record of Example 8.4 and creates a file consisting of every other prime number on the file. Show the state of the input and output files, their file pointers, and buffer variables after the fourth record of the output file has been written.

2. Write a procedure to create the output file of Exercise 1.

3. Write a procedure to create REVERSEDPRIME of Example 8.4, assuming the array A may only be of length 10.

4. How many writes and reads will be executed by PROCEDURE MERGE if FILE1 and FILE2 are, respectively,

 1 2   8 10 13 15 40
 3 7 10 12 17 20 45 50 60 ?

5. Write a procedure to create a sequential file that is the same as FILE1, except all records on FILE1 that are also on FILE2 do not appear.

 a. Assume FILE1 and FILE2 records appear in sorted order based on the KEY field.

 b. Assume FILE1 and FILE2 are not sorted, and you do not know how to sort a file.

6. Write a procedure to produce a new file that is the same as an input file except all blanks have been deleted from it.

7. Write a procedure that takes two sequential files and appends the second file to the first.

8. Write a procedure to read a text file consisting of the twenty-six letters of the alphabet, plus the blank character, and produce an output file consisting of the corresponding Huffman code (see Chapter 11).

9. Why are the sort procedures of Chapter 7 inappropriate for files?

10. Why does the number of passes required by a straight sort not depend on any initial ordering among the records?

11. Write a procedure for the straight merge.

12. Modify the merge procedure of Section 8.3 so it merges two runs embedded in files.

13. Write a procedure to distribute records as required by the natural merge.

14. Write a procedure for the natural merge.

15. Simulate the behavior of replacement-selection to verify that the average length run produced is $2\ m$.

16. Why must Fibonacci numbers govern the number of initial runs for three tapes in the polyphase sort?

17. **a.** If four tapes are used in a polyphase sort, what is the relation determining the initial distribution of runs?

   b. Can you generalize to n tapes?

18. Write a procedure for a polyphase sort using three tapes.

19. Why do the movable read/write heads and surfaces act as tabs for a disk?

20. Suppose the master index of Section 8.7.3 does not fit on one cylinder. How may another directory level be created to serve as an index to the master index?

21. Why do B-trees allow more flexible use of a disk than directories implemented using prime and overflow areas?

22. Create a B-tree of order 4 to store the nametable records of Chapter 5. The records are to be ordered alphabetically so the B-tree can be searched with the NAME field as key.

23. Write a procedure to insert a record into a B-tree of order m that is stored in internal memory.

24. Can you write the procedure of Exercise 23 so it is independent of whether the B-tree is stored in internal or external memory? If so, write it, if not, explain why not.

25. Write a procedure to delete a record from a B-tree of order m that is stored in internal memory.

26. Why does the chaining of lowest level nodes discussed in Section 8.7.4 allow more efficient traversal through the file?

27. Write a procedure to create a B-tree stored in internal memory.

28. Suppose we want to store variable length records in B-trees. How may this be done?

29. Why is it not feasible to store all records in the root node of a B-tree so that only one seek is required?

30. A B-tree of order 3 is called a 2-3 tree since each node has two or three successors. Although not useful for external storage, such a tree may rival AVL trees for an internal memory structure in which to store records. Compare its search, insertion, and deletion algorithms, and time requirements with those for AVL trees.

31. Write a search procedure for a B-tree of order m.

32. Write a procedure to traverse through the records of a B-tree in order by key value.

33. Suppose the individual records of Figure 5.6 are to be stored on a disk with the RECORDPTR field of the NAMETABLE pointing to the address of an individual record on the disk. The address is a cylinder and surface specification. What is a reasonable way to allocate disk storage to the individual records?

34. Suppose records of a file were stored in a hash table, with buckets for random access by key, and linked in sequential order by pointers, for sequential access. Compare the insertion and retrieval times of such an implementation with the use of B-trees.

☐ Suggested Assignment

This assignment is appropriate for a group of students to do together. It involves a task of reasonable size, which must be partitioned so that each member of the group knows just what to do, and so that, when all the parts are put together, the final solution works correctly. The idea is to produce an "index" for a book. This involves

1. The creation of files, using the sequential files available in Pascal
2. The creation of appropriate procedures and functions that will allow the records of a file to be accessed randomly, or in sequential order, by key value

One file, the BOOK file, is to consist of records that represent the pages of a book. Each page contains one hundred lines, and each line consists of one hundred characters. The key consists of a page number and a line number. A second file, the DICTIONARY file, is to consist of records representing words to appear in an index for the book represented on the BOOK file. When the solution is run, it should use a scaled down version of the BOOK file which will consist of a few pages of ten lines and twenty characters each with the dictionary containing relatively few words, say twenty-five.

The DICTIONARY file is to be a sequential file with the file implemented using B-trees. Instead of a disk, assume enough internal memory exists to store the BOOK file. The index for the book should be output so the words of the index appear in alphabetic order, followed by the page and line numbers on which the word appears in the book. Also, an input file consisting of page and line numbers appearing in random order should result in an output consisting of the text for each record of this input file.

9

Topological Sorting:
An Archetypal Solution

9.1 Background

Topological sorting requires ranking a set of objects subject to constraints on the resultant topology, that is, on the placement of the objects. It occurs in many practical situations. For example, textbooks are often written so that each chapter builds on material covered earlier and cannot be understood without this base of information. Determining the order in which to present topics to ensure that all prerequisite material has been covered requires finding a topological sort of the topics. Several other examples involving topological sorting are presented below.

In this chapter the topological sorting problem is solved by application of arrays and lists. The solution is intended to serve as a prototype, demonstrating its characteristics and methodology. The problem is substantial and the algorithm developed important, but it is the process by which it is achieved that is most important. In this complex example of the application of structured programming concepts, data structure selection plays a significant role.

The topological sorting program to be developed is a model solution, representing nearly the best programmers can hope to achieve. Few solutions to problems have all its characteristics. It is concise and clear. Correctness is easy to determine, and the storage and execution time requirements can be analyzed. Invalid input data are not difficult to deal with. What more can we ask?

The following are some examples of problems whose solutions require topological sorting.

Example 9.1

A large skyscraper is to be constructed. Imagine that you must write a program to prescribe the order in which all the tasks are to be performed. Tasks such as T_3 — install windows; T_{50} — install floors; T_8 — install window sashes; T_{1000} — clear the ground; T_7 — build the foundation; T_9 — install doors. For any two tasks, it is possible to specify whether one should be done before the other. Clearly, T_8 must be done before T_3, and T_{1000} must be done before T_7, while it makes no difference whether or not T_3 is done before T_9. The constraint that T_i be done before T_j is represented as the pair (i, j). $\square$

Example 9.2

Imagine that you want to write a book on data structures. All technical words used must be defined. First write down all the relevant words. If word w_j uses w_i in its definition, represent this constraint by the pair (i, j). $\square$

Example 9.3

As a student you must take a number of courses to graduate. Represent the fact that course c_j has course c_i as a prerequisite by the pair (i, j). $\square$

Example 9.4

A number of books must be read for a course you are taking. Represent the fact that you prefer to read book i before book j by the pair (i, j). $\square$

If you proceed to carry out the construction tasks, use the technical words, take the courses, or read the course books in arbitrary order, then you may not be able to, respectively, do the next task (since those tasks that had to precede it may not yet be finished), define the next word (because words used in its definition have not yet been used and defined), take the next course (not all prerequisites may have been taken), or read the next book (because you want to honor your preferences). A topological sort gives an order in which to proceed so that such difficulties will never be encountered.

9.1.1 Binary Relations and Partial Orders

Some mathematical concepts and terminology must be defined before the topological sorting problem can be stated and solved in abstract terms. As with the solution to any problem, stating this solution abstractly is desirable so that it will not be tied to a particular application.

Most English-speakers would readily understand what is meant by the statements: "Fred *is related to* Sam"; "John *is taller than* Sue"; "3 *is the square root of* 9." The italicized phrases each specify a connection or relation between two objects. In the first two cases the relations refer to two people; in the third case the relation refers to numbers. Each is a binary relation on a set of objects.

Mathematics abstracts from such examples to define a **binary relation R on a set S**. S is taken as the set or collection of objects referred to by the relation. R contains information, for any two of these objects, on whether or not they are related. R is a set of pairs of objects (a, b), where a and b belong to S. If the pair (a, b) belongs to R, then this is interpreted to mean that a is related to b. This is written as $a R b$. If (a, b) does not belong to R, then a is not related to b. This is written as $a \not R b$.

For instance, specify S to be the set of integers between 2 and 10, so $S = \{2, 3, \ldots, 10\}$; and take $R = \{(4, 2), (6, 2), (8, 2), (8, 4), (9, 3), (10, 2), (6, 3), (10, 5)\}$.

Then R captures the "is divided evenly by but is not equal to" relation on S, since a pair (a, b) will belong to R only if a "is divided evenly by but is not equal to" b. By looking at R, we can determine if $a R b$ or $a \not R b$ for any a and b in S.

Of particular interest are the kinds of binary relations called *partial orders*.

A binary relation R on S is called a ***partial order on* S** if it has the following properties:

- ☐ **Irreflexivity.** For any a in S, $a \not R a$
- ☐ **Asymmetry.** For any two distinct a and b in S, $a R b$ implies $b \not R a$
- ☐ **Transitivity.** For any three distinct a, b, and c in S, $a R b$ and $b R c$ implies $a R c$.

These properties specify that whenever certain pairs are in R, then other pairs must necessarily be included in R or excluded from R. The "is divided evenly by but is not equal to" relation on S in the preceding paragraph fulfills all three properties of a partial order.

- ☐ It is irreflexive, since a is divided evenly by but *is* equal to a for all a in S.
- ☐ It is asymmetric, since if a "is divided evenly by" b, then b cannot be divided evenly by a when a is not equal to b.
- ☐ It is transitive, since whenever a is divided evenly by b and b is divided evenly by c, then a must also be divided evenly by c.

To show that a relation does not have a property requires only one counterexample.

Two extreme binary relations on a set S are the null relation, which contains no pairs at all, and the universal relation, which contains all possible pairs. The null relation is a partial order. This is because no counterexamples can be found. The universal relation will never be irreflexive (unless S has no objects in it), or asymmetric (unless S has only one object), but will always be transitive.

9.1.2 Graphic Representation of Partial Orders

One can graphically represent any binary relation R on a set of n objects as in Figure 9.1. Let S consist of ten objects, the integers $1, 2, 3, \ldots, 10$. Take R to contain

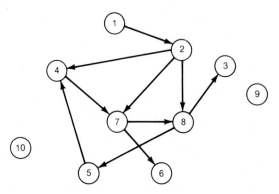

Figure 9.1   Binary Relation R on a Set of $n = 10$ Objects

the pairs (1, 2), (8, 3), (7, 6), (2, 7), (5, 4), (7, 8), (2, 4), (4, 7), (2, 8), (8, 5). Create a node for each object in S and draw arrows between two nodes for each pair in R. For example, an arrow will appear from 7 to 8 for the pair (7, 8).

Any such diagram can be interpreted as representing a binary relation on a set S. For such a diagram to represent a partial order requires

- ☐ That no arrows appear from any node to itself (irreflexivity)
- ☐ That no arrows appear from any node i to another node j and back from j to i (asymmetry)
- ☐ And if arrows appear from i to j and from j to k, then an arrow must appear from i to k (transitivity)

In depicting partial orders, it is unnecessary to draw all the arrows needed to represent transitivity. They need not be shown because they are always assumed. With this understanding, it is not difficult to see that a diagram represents a partial order if and only if it contains no loops. This means that no node can be found such that one can follow a series of arrows starting from that node and ending at that node. In Figure 9.1, there is a loop involving nodes 5, 4, 7, and 8. Hence, the diagram does not represent a partial order. Note that if one starts with a diagram representing a partial order (no loops), erasing a node and all arrows emanating from it results in a diagram that represents a new partial order on the set of remaining nodes.

9.1.3 Topological Sorts: Consistent Rankings

Partial orders are important. They are meant to capture abstractly any concrete example in which the pairs of R (or arrows of the diagram) mean "is greater than," "precedes," "is ranked higher than," or "comes before." A special case of a partial order is one whose diagram looks like

$$3 \rightarrow 5 \rightarrow 1 \rightarrow 2 \rightarrow 4 \rightarrow 6 \rightarrow 8 \rightarrow 7$$

For such a diagram, it seems clear what would be meant by a listing or ranking of the eight objects that is consistent with the given partial order. Such a ranking would be 3, 5, 1, 2, 4, 6, 8, 7. No other ranking would be consistent with the given partial order. This can be generalized to any partial order by interpreting the arrows as constraints on the ordering of objects in a ranking. For example, an arrow from 3 to 5 would mean that 3 must be ranked higher than 5. Then, a *ranking consistent with a partial order* would mean a ranking of the n objects which violates no constraints (that is, a ranking that violates no arrows or pairs).

Example 9.5 Consider the partial order on the set of nine integers represented by Figure 9.2. ☐

The ranking 2, 3, 4, 5, 6, 7, 8, 9, 10 would not be consistent with this partial order, because it violates at least one of the constraints, namely that 6 be ranked higher than 3, or that 10 be ranked higher than 2. This diagram actually represents the "is divided evenly by but is not equal to" relation introduced earlier.

The definition of topological sorting can now be stated more formally than at the outset of the chapter: A *topological sort* is a ranking of the n objects of S that is consistent with the given partial order. Let us try to solve the following *topological sorting problem*.

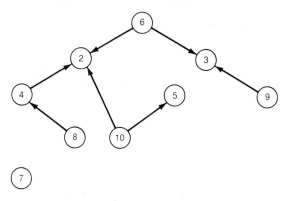

Figure 9.2   A Partial Order on the Integers 2, . . . , 9

Example   Given a partial order on a set S of n objects, produce a topological sort of the n
9.6   objects, if one exists. If no such ranking exists, then print out a message saying that
none exists.* ☐

Do you think a topological sort always exists? We shall see.
For simplicity assume that S is always the set of the first n integers $1, 2, 3,$
. . . , n, and the partial order is given as m pairs of integers representing arrows in
the corresponding diagram. Assume no pairs are replicated. For concreteness, take
the input to have the following form:

$$
\left. 10 \;\; \right\} \quad value\ of\ \text{n}
$$

$$
\left.
\begin{array}{cc}
7 & 3 \\
5 & 3 \\
2 & 10 \\
6 & 8 \\
5 & 6 \\
4 & 8 \\
7 & 1 \\
4 & 2 \\
7 & 6
\end{array}
\right\} \quad m = 9\ pairs
$$

This particular instance of the topological sorting problem will be referred to repeatedly throughout the chapter. Is there an obvious algorithm for this problem? Try to
think of one before continuing.

---

*If a relation is asymmetric and transitive but not irreflexive, then one can eliminate all pairs of the form
   (x, x) from the relation or, equivalently, erase all self-loops from its diagram. The resulting relation
   is a partial order and it still makes sense to find a topological sort with respect to it. The topological
   sort then satisfies constraints of the original relation involving distinct objects.

9.2 A Searching Solution

Consider the specific ranking 4, 8, 1, 2, 7, 10, 9, 5, 3, 6 of the 10 objects of the example. It is easy to determine whether or not this ranking violates any constraints of the partial order by checking each one. Since this ranking violates two of the nine constraints, $6 \rightarrow 8$ and $7 \rightarrow 1$, it is not a topological sort. Any ranking may be checked in this way. This leads to an obvious algorithm based on the generation of all rankings of the n objects.

> **A search-based algorithm:**
> If a ranking is found which violates no constraints, then the ranking is a topological sort, print it and stop. If all possible rankings have been tried and no topological sort found, then print out the message that none exists, and stop.

To implement this algorithm in a programming language requires finding a way to generate the rankings so that all the distinct rankings are eventually generated. The procedure PERMUTATIONS of Chapter 4 does this. Any implementation of the algorithm could take time proportional to the number of distinct rankings of n objects. A particular ranking can be constructed by selecting any one of the n objects to be first in the ranking, then selecting any one of the remaining $n - 1$ objects to be second in the ranking, and so on. Thus there are $n \times (n - 1) \times (n - 2) \times \cdots \times 2 \times 1$ distinct rankings of n objects. This product is n factorial. Consequently this solution can deal with values of n no greater than 16 (Section 1.8.2). For larger n, an algorithm must be found that need not consider all rankings.

9.3 A Constructed Solution

The first solution to Example 9.6 involved a search through all possible rankings. Another approach is to attempt the construction of the required ranking. To this end consider a ranking, OBJ_1, OBJ_2, ..., OBJ_n, of the n objects that is a topological sort with respect to a given diagram. What can be said about OBJ_1, the highest ranked object? Clearly there must be no objects that are constrained by the diagram to appear higher in the ranking than OBJ_1. Otherwise, those constraints would be violated, and the ranking would not be a topological sort. In terms of the diagram, this means that no arrows must point to OBJ_1. We describe this by saying that OBJ_1 must have no predecessors.

Now suppose the node corresponding to OBJ_1 is erased, as well as all the arrows emanating from OBJ_1. As noted earlier, this results in a new diagram that represents a new partial order on the remaining $n - 1$ objects. Consider the ranking of these $n - 1$ objects obtained by taking the original topological sort of the n objects and removing OBJ_1. That is, consider OBJ_2, OBJ_3, ..., OBJ_n. It must be a topological sort of the remaining $n - 1$ objects in the new diagram with respect to the new partial order. This is because any constraint in the new diagram that is violated by this ranking would have been violated in the original ranking of the n objects. Note that if *any* topological sort of the remaining $n - 1$ objects were taken with respect to the new partial order, and OBJ_1 were placed in front of it, the ranking of n objects thus obtained would be a topological sort with respect to the original partial order. Placing

OBJ_1 first in this ranking cannot violate any of the original constraints because they did not require that any object precede OBJ_1.

We have just discovered how to construct a topological sort:

A *construction-based algorithm:*
While S is not empty
1. Select any object with no predecessors.
2. Place it in the next position of the output ranking.
3. Remove that object from S, and
4. Remove its arrows from the partial order.

The output ranking produced will always be a topological sort.

9.3.1　Correctness

One difficulty remains. How can the programmer be certain the algorithm can actually be carried out? It may be impossible to carry out because at some point there may be no objects with zero predecessors. That this is indeed an algorithm requires showing that there will always be at least one object with no predecessors.

A method of proof for any proposition is to assume it is not true and then show that this assumption leads to a contradiction. This method of proof is applied here. The goal is to prove that every time the loop task is to be carried out, at least one object with no predecessors can be found among those remaining. To assume that this is not true means that at some point the task cannot be carried out because *every* object left has at least one predecessor. Recall that the original diagram, representing a partial order, had no loops. It will be shown that the assumption implies a loop in the diagram. This will be the contradiction.

Suppose i_1 is one of the remaining objects. Under the assumption, every object has at least one predecessor, so i_1 has a predecessor, say i_2. Note that i_2 cannot be the same object as i_1, or the irreflexivity property would not hold. Again, i_2 must have a predecessor, say i_3. The object i_3 cannot be i_1 or i_2. If it were i_1 or i_2, then a loop involving i_2 and i_1 or a loop with just i_2 would exist. Continuing with this argument, $i_1, i_2, i_3, i_4, \ldots$ must all be distinct objects. But, since there are only n objects in total, eventually an object must repeat. This implies that the repeated object is the starting and ending object of a loop. The conclusion is that the assumption was false. Therefore what we wanted to prove must be true, and we never get bogged down — there will always be an object with no predecessors.

This algorithm yields additional insight into the topological sorting problem. Since it is clear that the loop can always be carried out to completion, it will *always* produce a topological sort of the n objects. This was certainly not obvious before.

To be sure the algorithm is understood, it is applied next to Example 9.6, depicted again in Figure 9.3. Initially (see Figure 9.3(a)) 4, 7, 5, and 9 have zero predecessors.

The first step is to select and remove 5 (either 4, 7, or 9 could also have been removed) and its successor arrows, to obtain Figure 9.3(b). S is not empty so the loop must be repeated. Now, 4, 7, and 9 have no predecessors. Select and remove 7 and its successor arrows, and obtain Figure 9.3(c). S is still not empty and now 4, 9, 1, 3, and 6 have no predecessors. Select 4. Updating produces Figure 9.3(d).

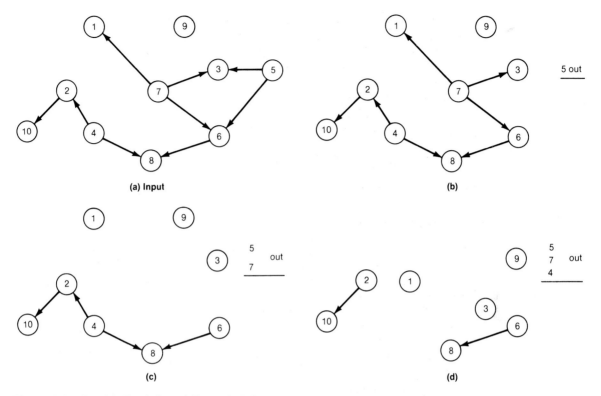

Figure 9.3 Graphic Depiction of Example 9.6

S is still not empty but 9, 1, 3, 6, and 2 now have zero predecessors. Continuing in this way, removing 1, 3, 6, 8, 9, 2, and, finally, 10 in succeeding iterations yields the final ranking: 5, 7, 4, 1, 3, 6, 8, 9, 2, 10.

Notice that every time an object is selected and removed, the diagram is updated to reflect the new S and the new partial order. As a result, some additional objects may end up with zero predecessors. Once an object has zero predecessors, it will remain in each succeeding diagram, always with zero predecessors, until it is removed.

The *first refinement* describes an implementation of the algorithm.

First refinement:
1. Read N.
2. Initialize for phase I.
3. While there is another input pair,
   a. record the information in the pair I, J   Phase I

___

4. Initialize for phase II   Phase II
5. While the set S is not empty,
   a. select an object with no predecessors, and output it as the next object in the output ranking;
   b. update the records to reflect the removal of the output objects.

Phase I reads into memory the information about the number of objects and the partial order. Every time an *I, J* pair is read in, the new information that this represents must be incorporated into a representation in memory. The "record the information" of task 3a refers to the modification of this representation to reflect the new arrow, $I \to J$.

Phase II describes the processing required by our algorithm. Task 5a involves the selection, removal, and outputting of an object. Task 5b involves modifying the partial order representation and S, to reflect the removal of an object and its arrows, and outputting it in the ranking. After task 5b is carried out, that representation should reflect the new set S and the new partial order resulting from the object's removal.

9.3.2 An Initial Implementation

A straightforward representation of the partial order would be to keep an image in memory of all input arrows. We might use two arrays, FIRST and SECOND, for this purpose. FIRST would contain the first integer, and SECOND would contain the second integer of an input pair. The "record the information" task would then involve putting *I* and *J* into the next available locations of FIRST and SECOND, respectively. For Example 9.6, after phase I was executed, the result would be the arrays shown in Figure 9.4.

Suppose the *while* loop of phase II is being executed and task 5a is to be carried out. An object with no predecessors must be selected. How is such an object found? Any object that has no predecessors will not appear in the SECOND array. Somehow the SECOND array must be searched to select an object with no predecessors. This can be accomplished by using an array S, traversing SECOND, and marking location *I* of S when object *I* appears in SECOND. Any location in S left unmarked corresponds to an object with no predecessors.

Suppose this is done, and object 5 is selected. Object 5 can then be output to the next place in the ranking. To accomplish task 5b, the "updating of the records," then requires that the array FIRST be traversed. As it is traversed, each time a 5 is encountered, the program must mark the location of FIRST in which it appears, and

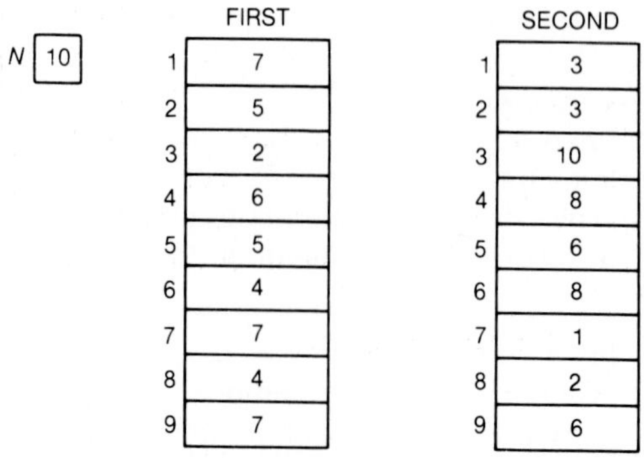

Figure 9.4   Result of Phase I of the First Refinement

the corresponding location of SECOND. The mark signifies that the corresponding arrow emanating from 5 has been removed from the representation. This completes one execution of the loop. This same processing must be repeated for each repetition of that loop. The loop will be repeated n times, once for each of the n objects. The FIRST and SECOND array must be traversed each time. This will take time proportional to their length, which, in general, will be m. Hence this implementation of the algorithm will take time proportional to $n \times m$. The storage required is roughly $2m$ locations for FIRST and SECOND, and n locations for S.

9.3.3 A Better Implementation

It is apparent that a lot of time is spent finding the information needed to carry out the processing in phase II. Efficiency can be improved by focusing on the following important question: *Precisely* what information is needed to carry out the processing?

Notice that each time through the loop, the program must *select an object with no predecessors*. To do this requires knowing which of the objects left in S have zero predecessors. Suppose that, before and after each execution of the loop body, exactly how many predecessors each remaining object has is known. With this knowledge an object with zero predecessor count can be selected. Once an object becomes eligible to be selected (has zero predecessors), it remains eligible until it is actually selected. Why not collect all those initially eligible in the initialization for phase II? The program could then select among them arbitrarily. Think of this collection as kept in a bag from which the object selected for output is pulled.

As the rest of the loop body is executed, *the records must be updated to reflect the removal of this object and its arrows*. Removing its arrows amounts to reducing the predecessor count of each successor of the object removed. Whenever the predecessor count of one of these successors becomes zero, that successor becomes eligible for selection on the next repetition of the loop. That successor is immediately added to the bag. Consequently, at the start of each loop repetition, the bag will contain exactly those objects eligible for selection, thus eliminating the need to search for them. In fact, the "S not empty" test is now equivalent to asking if the "bag is not empty." Keeping track of the successors of each object eliminates the need to search for them when that object is output. The precise information needed for processing has now been isolated. What must be known are the predecessor counts and successors for each object, and what's in the bag.

The loop body of phase I must update predecessor counts and successors. The input pair I, J contains the information that J has one more predecessor than currently reflected in J's predecessor count, and that I has one more successor, J, than currently reflected by I's successors. The loop body of phase II must update the predecessor counts of all successors of the removed object. It must also update the bag. We have developed the following *better refinement* of the algorithm.

The better refinement:
1. Read N.
2. Initialize
   a. Initialize the predecessor counts for each of the N objects to zero.
   b. Initialize current successors for each of the N objects to zero.

3. While there is another input pair,
   a. increase the predecessor count of *J* by 1;
   b. add *J* to the current successors of *I*.
4. Place all objects with zero predecessor count into the bag.
5. While the bag is not empty,
   a. remove an object from the bag and output it in the output ranking;
   b. for each successor of the output object, decrease its predecessor count by 1; if the predecessor count becomes zero, add the successor to the bag.

In order to refine the solution further, we must decide how to store *the prede-cessor counts, the successors of each object, the bag,* and *the output ranking.* These are data structure decisions. They should be based on the kinds of operations to be performed in tasks 1 through 5.

The implementation treats the predecessor counts, the collections of successor counts, the bag, and the output ranking as data abstractions.

```
1.    READLN(N);
2. a. PREDINITIALIZATION(N, COUNT);
   b. SUCCINITIALIZATION(N, SUCCESSOR);
3.    while NEXTPAIR(I, J) do
         begin
            a. INCREASE( J, COUNT);
            b. INSERT(I, J, SUCCESSOR)
         end;
4.    BAGINITIALIZATION(BAG, N, COUNT);
5.    while not EMPTYBAG(BAG) do
         begin
            a. REMOVE(BAG, OBJ, RANKING);
            b. UPDATE(SUCCESSOR, OBJ, BAG, COUNT)
         end;
```

Every operation performed in tasks 1 through 5 that involves the bag, any of the *N* predecessor counts or collections of successors, or the output ranking, has been implemented by a corresponding procedure or function. Note the use of a prefix to designate the structure involved in some of these operations. When written in this form, the program is independent of the specific details of implementation of each of these structures. This means that even if subsequent changes in the data structure implementations are ultimately adopted, this version of the solution will never need to be modified.

The next step is to decide on specific data structures for implementation of the data abstractions. This choice must be based on the procedures and functions which operate on the data structures. These procedures and functions are PREDINITIALIZATION, SUCCINITIALIZATION, INCREASE, INSERT, BAGINITIALIZATION, EMPTYBAG, REMOVE, and UPDATE.

At some future time a decision may be made to change the implementation of any data abstraction. This requires finding *all* definitions of the data structures and procedures or functions involved and replacing them by the new definitions. This modification may be made more easily and more reliably when the original definitions have been localized in the original program. Such localization is called *encapsulation*.

Not all high-level languages provide appropriate tools for achieving complete encapsulation. In the ideal final program the data abstractions are defined in precisely one place and, even more important, no operations are allowed on the corresponding data structures except those specified by the procedures and functions of the data abstraction. In the implementation above this means, for example, that only the BAGINITIALIZATION, EMPTYBAG, REMOVE, and UPDATE operations may be applied to the bag. This makes it easier to determine which operations may be affected by a new implementation of the bag. Neither Pascal nor FORTRAN ensures complete encapsulation. The greater the encapsulation and modularization, the more expeditious the process of achieving correct modifications and adaptations.

The programmer does not know, in advance, the order in which objects will be output. In task 5b of the better refinement, after an object is output, its successors must be accessed and their predecessor counts updated. This means that the *predecessor counts and the collections of successors must be accessed in arbitrary order*. Thus in the implementation, the predecessor counts are stored in an array COUNT, and pointers to each collection of successors in an array SUCC. COUNT[I] and SUCC[I] will then contain, respectively, the predecessor count and a pointer to the successors of object I. This allows the predecessor count and collection of successors of any object to be selected, taking constant time.

There are N collections of successors, one for each object. These may be stored separately or may share storage. This choice has important ramifications (discussed later). For now, it is best to share storage and to implement each collection of successors as a list of records. The records consist of two integer fields, SUCCOBJ, containing a successor object, and LINK, containing a pointer to the next list record. Either the Pascal heap or an array may be used to store the records. Selecting the array for storage means the programmer must manage its allocation himself or herself. The Pascal heap is probably a more natural choice, but an array of records is used to illustrate its simple management in this case and to make the later discussion comparing shared or separate storage for the list records more concrete. LISTS will be the array for record storage, and a variable T will keep track of the next available record in LISTS for task 3b. Since only insertions will be made into the lists, the entries of LISTS will be allocated one after another as needed, starting with the first. Thus T must be initialized to 1.

The apparent choice for the output ranking is an integer array RANK, with a variable NEXT specifying where the next output object is to be placed in the RANK array. For convenience, we use the record RANKING with the two fields RANK and NEXT.

The bag could be implemented similarly, in an array with BAG pointing to the next available element for a new bag entry. When an object is to be removed from the bag, we can store its value in OBJ and then decrease BAG by 1. Thus an object can be added or removed from the bag in constant time. This implementation is permissible because objects may be selected from the bag in any order. However, implementing the bag as in Figure 9.5 affords an advantage. By allowing the bag and the output ranking to share storage, it saves time. However, this selection is made primarily to emphasize a point, to be made later, about the independence of modules.

The X's represent nine objects placed in the rank array. NEXT, pointing to position 6, indicates that the next object to be selected from the bag will be the one

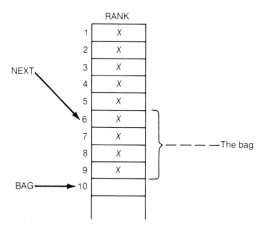

Figure 9.5   Data Structure Implementation of Bag and Output-Ranking Data Abstractions

in RANK[NEXT], RANK[6] in this case. BAG, pointing to 10, indicates that when a successor is to be added to the bag, it should be placed in RANK[BAG], RANK[10] in this case. In other words, the bag contains all objects in RANK between NEXT and BAG − 1.

The bag is initialized by traversing the COUNT array and placing any object with zero count into the location of the RANK array to which BAG points. BAG, of course, must then be updated by 1 to move its pointer down. BAG must initially be 1, and NEXT must initially be 1. Objects are then output in the order in which they are placed into the bag, easing processing and keeping the time constant for addition or removal of an object. Each time an object is selected, NEXT must be increased by 1 to move it down. The bag is empty when NEXT equals BAG.

Before proceeding, phase I is illustrated by applying it to Example 9.6. For this example, COUNT, SUCC, *T*, and LIST would appear as in Figure 9.6, after the first eight pairs have been input. Figure 9.7 graphically depicts the successor lists.

At the start of phase I, no information was processed yet on predecessors or successors for any object. The first pair, 7 3, contains the information that 3 has one more predecessor than was known, and that 7 has one more successor than was known, namely 3. One must be added to the COUNT for 3, and 3 to the list of successors of 7, and so on for the other seven pairs.

If the ninth pair input is 7 6, it is processed similarly. To update the COUNT for 6, add 1 to COUNT[6]. To create a record to contain the successor 6, place 6 into LISTS[9].SUCCOBJ, and add this new record to the current successor list for 7 by changing two pointers. First, copy the pointer from SUCC[7], the head of the list to which the new record is to be added, into the link field of the new record LISTS[9].LINK. Then place a pointer into SUCC[7] so it points to the new record. In this case, 9 is placed into SUCC[7]. Since successors need not be kept in any special order, always adding records at the front of successor lists saves processing time. Adding the record anywhere else on the list would require traversal time from

SUCCOBJ LINK
FIELD FIELD

	COUNT		SUCC		LISTS	
1	1	1	X	1	3	X
2	1	2	3	2	3	X
3	2	3	X	3	10	X
4	0	4	8	4	8	X
5	0	5	5	5	6	2
6	1	6	4	6	8	X
7	0	7	7	7	1	1
8	2	8	X	8	2	6
9	0	9	X	9		
10	1	10	X			
		11				
		12				

First 8 pairs

7	3
5	3
2	10
6	8
5	6
4	8
7	1
4	2

T 9

Figure 9.6 Data Structures Involved in Phase I after Input of First Eight Pairs

the head of the list to the insertion place. T is incremented by 1 so it points to the next available record in LISTS. The final situation after all nine input pairs have been read and processed is shown in Figures 9.8 and 9.9. An X indicates a null pointer.

We are now ready to consider the detailed implementations for the modules of the data abstractions. Following is the actual code that might be used for those modules whose implementation may not be apparent.

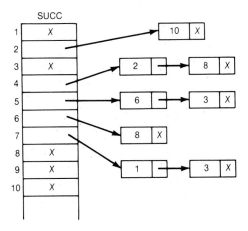

Figure 9.7 Graphic Depiction of Successor Lists

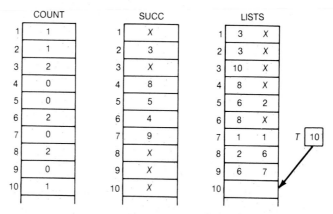

Figure 9.8 Data Structures of Figure 9.7 after Processing Last Input Pair of Phase I

INCREASE
  COUNT[J] := COUNT[J] + 1
INSERT
  LISTS[T].SUCCOBJ := J;
  LISTS[T].LINK := SUCC[I];
  SUCC[I] := T;
  T := T + 1
EMPTYBAG
  EMPTYBAG := (BAG = RANKING.NEXT)
REMOVE
  OBJ := RANK[NEXT];
  NEXT := NEXT + 1

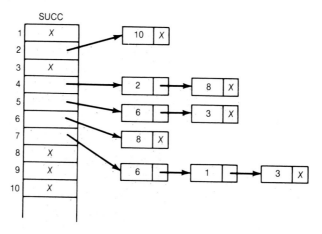

Figure 9.9 Graphic Depiction of Successor Lists of Figure 9.8

Note that SUCCINITIALIZATION must also set T to 1.

Task 5b of the better (or "bag") refinement of the algorithm could be done by writing the procedure UPDATE from scratch. Instead, it is done here using a tool that is available, the TRAVERSE procedure of Chapter 3. First TRAVERSE is modified by adding BAG and COUNT as additional parameters of both TRAVERSE and PROCESS. The code for UPDATE is then

```
UPDATE
    LISTNAME := SUCC[OBJ];
    TRAVERSE(HEAD, LISTS, BAG, COUNT)
```

PROCESS must now be implemented so that UPDATE does its job.

```
procedure PROCESS(HEAD : listpointer; var PTR : listpointer;
                    var LISTS : recordsarray; var BAG : integer;
                    var COUNT : integerarray);
const
    NULL = 0;
    ZERO = 0;
var
    CURRENTSUCC : integer;
begin
    if HEAD <> NULL then
        if PTR <> NULL then
            begin
                CURRENTSUCC := LISTS[PTR].SUCCOBJ;
                COUNT[CURRENTSUCC] := COUNT[CURRENTSUCC] − 1;
                if COUNT[CURRENTSUCC] = ZERO then
                    begin
                        RANK[BAG] := CURRENTSUCC;
                        BAG := BAG + 1
                    end
            end
end
```

A complete program using TOPSORT follows. Notice that TOPSORT has two parameters. It is the same as our version, except it copies the RANK field of RANKING into the output array as a last step.

Because of the implementation, some modules must have access to specific variables. Pascal requires these variables to be either nonlocal or global. For example, PROCESS must have access to RANK, and EMPTYBAG to NEXT. We will refer to this implementation of the *better refinement* algorithm as the **TOPSORT** procedure and define it to have two parameters, N and TOPOLOGICALSORT. Incidentally, as written, TOPSORT does not depend on the medium assumed for the input pairs. Normally, we want programs to be independent of the form of the input. This has been accomplished here for the pairs by using the function NEXTPAIR(I, J), which inputs the next pair and returns "true" if it is a nonsentinel pair. The program uses 0 0 as the sentinel pair.

```
program SAMPLETOPSORT(INPUT, OUTPUT);
const
    LIMIT = 20;
    RECORDLIMIT = (LIMIT * (LIMIT − 1)) DIV 2;
type
    outputarray = array [1 .. LIMIT] of integer;
var
    N, I, J : integer;
    TOPOLOGICALSORT : outputarray;

procedure TOPSORT(var N : integer; var TOPOLOGICALSORT : outputarray);
type
    integerarray     = array [1 .. LIMIT] of integer;
    listpointer      = integer;
    listrecords      = record
                            succobj : integer;
                            link : listpointer
                        end;
    recordsarray     = array [1 .. RECORDLIMIT] of listrecords;
    listpointerarray = array [1 .. LIMIT] of listpointer;
    successorrecord  = record
                            succ : listpointerarray;
                            lists : recordsarray;
                            t : listpointer
                        end;
    rankingrecord    = record
                            rank : outputarray;
                            next : integer
                        end;
var
    COUNT : integerarray;
    SUCCESSOR : successorrecord;
    BAG : integer;
    OBJ : integer;
    RANKING : rankingrecord;

procedure PREDINITIALIZATION(N : integer; var COUNT : integerarray);
var
    I : integer;
begin
    for I := 1 to N do
        COUNT[I] := 0
end;

procedure SUCCINITIALIZATION(N : integer;
                                        var SUCCESSOR : successorrecord);
var
    I : integer;
begin
    for I := 1 to N do
        SUCCESSOR.SUCC[I] := 0;
    SUCCESSOR.T := 1
end;
```

```
function NEXTPAIR(var I, J : integer) : boolean;
begin
    READLN(I, J);
    NEXTPAIR := not ((I = 0) and (J = 0))
end;

procedure INCREASE(J : integer; var COUNT : integerarray);
begin
    COUNT[J] := COUNT[J] + 1
end;

procedure INSERT(I, J : integer; var SUCCESSOR : successorrecord);
begin
    with SUCCESSOR do
        begin
            LISTS[T].SUCCOBJ := J;
            LISTS[T].LINK := SUCC[I];
            SUCC[I] := T;
            T := T + 1
        end
end;

procedure BAGINITIALIZATION(var BAG : integer; N : integer;
                            COUNT : integerarray);
var
    I : integer;
begin
    with RANKING do
        begin
            NEXT := 1;
            BAG := 1;
            for I := 1 to N do
                if COUNT[I] = 0 then
                    begin
                        RANK[BAG] := I;
                        BAG := BAG + 1
                    end
        end
end;


function EMPTYBAG(BAG : integer) : boolean;
begin
    EMPTYBAG := (BAG = RANKING.NEXT)
end;

procedure REMOVE(var BAG, OBJ : integer; var RANKING : rankingrecord);
begin
    with RANKING do
        begin
            OBJ := RANK[NEXT];
            NEXT := NEXT + 1
        end
end;
```

```
            procedure UPDATE(SUCCESSOR : successorrecord; OBJ : integer;
                            var BAG : integer; var COUNT : integerarray);
            var
                LISTNAME : listpointer;
            function ANOTHERRECORD(LISTNAME, RECORDPOINTER : listpointer) :
                                        boolean;
            const
                NULL = 0;
            begin
                ANOTHERRECORD := (RECORDPOINTER <> NULL)
            end;

            function NEXT(RECORDPOINTER : listpointer) : listpointer;
            begin
                NEXT := SUCCESSOR.LISTS[RECORDPOINTER].LINK
            end;

            procedure PROCESS(LISTNAME : listpointer; RECORDPOINTER : listpointer;
                            var L : recordsarray; var BAG : integer;
                            var COUNT : integerarray);
            const
                NULL = 0;
            var
                CURRENTSUCC : integer;
            begin
                if LISTNAME <> NULL then
                    if RECORDPOINTER <> NULL then
                        begin
                            CURRENTSUCC := L[RECORDPOINTER].SUCCOBJ;
                            COUNT[CURRENTSUCC] := COUNT[CURRENTSUCC] − 1;
                            if COUNT[CURRENTSUCC] = 0 then
                                begin
                                    RANKING.RANK[BAG] := CURRENTSUCC;
                                    BAG := BAG + 1
                                end
                        end
            end;

            procedure TRAVERSE(LISTNAME : listpointer; L : recordsarray;
                            var BAG : integer; var COUNT : integerarray);
            var
                RECORDPOINTER : listpointer;
            begin
                RECORDPOINTER := LISTNAME;
                while ANOTHERRECORD(LISTNAME, RECORDPOINTER) do
                    begin
                        PROCESS(LISTNAME, RECORDPOINTER, L, BAG, COUNT);
                        RECORDPOINTER := NEXT(RECORDPOINTER)
                    end
            end;
```

```
        begin
           with SUCCESSOR do
              begin
                 LISTNAME := SUCC[OBJ];
                 TRAVERSE(LISTNAME, LISTS, BAG, COUNT)
              end
        end;
        begin
           READLN(N);
           PREDINITIALIZATION(N, COUNT);
           SUCCINITIALIZATION(N, SUCCESSOR);
           while NEXTPAIR(I, J) do
              begin
                 INCREASE(J, COUNT);
                 INSERT(I, J, SUCCESSOR)
              end;
           BAGINITIALIZATION(BAG, N, COUNT);
           while not EMPTYBAG(BAG) do
              begin
                 REMOVE(BAG, OBJ, RANKING);
                 UPDATE(SUCCESSOR, OBJ, BAG, COUNT)
              end;
           TOPOLOGICALSORT := RANKING.RANK
        end;
        begin
           TOPSORT(N, TOPOLOGICALSORT);
           WRITELN('A TOPOLOGICAL SORT IS:');
           for I := 1 to N do
              WRITELN(TOPOLOGICALSORT[I])
        end.
```

9.4 Analysis of TOPSORT

We will now analyze the time requirements of this implementation. Refer to the refinement shown in the implementation that used data abstractions (see p. 386). Reading N takes constant time. The COUNT and SUCC array initialization take time proportional to n. The **while** loop read and test takes constant time. Reading the next input pair and tasks 3a and 3b, which involve executing five instructions, take constant time. Each repetition of the loop thus takes constant time. Since the loop is executed once for each of the m input pairs, the total loop time will be proportional to m. Phase I thus takes some constant time, plus time proportional to n, plus time proportional to m.

Initializing the bag at the start of phase II takes time proportional to n, since it involves traversing the COUNT array and placing each object whose count is zero into the bag. The **while** loop body of phase II, unlike that of phase I, does not take the same amount of time on every repetition. Task 5a takes constant time, but task 5b depends on the number of successors of the object that was removed by task 5a. The loop itself is executed n times, once for each object output.

How can we determine the total loop time required? Notice that each of the n objects will eventually be output in *some* loop execution. We do not know in what order the objects will be output. However, the time taken in its particular loop execution for each object output is the same. This time is at most a constant plus time proportional to the number of successors of the object. Thus, the total time for the *while* loop in phase II is the sum of the time required to output each object. The total time is then a constant times n plus time proportional to the sum,

[(number of successors of object 1) plus (the number of successors of object 2)...plus the (number of successors of object n)].

This sum is just the total number of successors, m. Hence the total time for phase II is made up of the same kinds of components as the total time for phase I. We conclude that the total time for this implementation has the same form.

Note that the search-based algorithm could take time $O(n!)$. The straightforward implementation of the construction-based algorithm could take time $O(n \times m)$. TOPSORT takes time of the form $c_1 + c_2 n + c_3 m$, and represents a very substantial improvement. It was made possible because we were able to determine precisely, and to obtain efficiently, the information required to do the processing steps of the algorithm. The topological sort problem is more complex than earlier ones in this book, but it illustrates the same theme. The processing to be done determines the data structures that are most appropriate. Clearly, any implementation of an algorithm that does topological sorting must take time of the form $a n + b m$, since it is necessary to read in all m input pairs and output all n objects.

How much storage does the implementation require? Suppose the program is to run correctly for values of n between 1 and 20. The only difficulty in determining the actual amount of storage required is in deciding what length to declare for LISTS. This depends on how large m may be. In general, if there are n objects, each object can have no more than $n - 1$ successors—that is, an arrow to every other object. There are then at most $n \times (n - 1)$ possible successors. Each successor requires one record of the LISTS array. Actually, because of the asymmetry property, at most one-half of the $n(n - 1)$ possibilities can appear. Hence, we need a total of at most $\frac{1}{2} \times n(n - 1)$ records for LISTS. If n is 20, then $(20 \times 19)/2$ records will do. The storage required is proportional to n^2.

Knuth [1973a] and Wirth [1976] give different implementations of the algorithm for the topological sorting problem. See Aho, Hopcroft, and Ullman [1983] for a somewhat different point of view on its solution.

9.5 Behavior for Replicated Pairs or Loops

In the solution to the topological sorting problem, it is assumed that each distinct input pair appears only once and also that the input contains no loops. Either assumption might be violated. Of course, more obvious errors could occur, for example, n or one of the input pair members could be negative or out of range. It is not difficult to add a validation routine to check for these kinds of input errors. Subtler errors, such as replication of pairs, or the occurrence of loops, are not as obviously remedied.

What does happen if pairs are replicated or loops occur in the input? How would you recognize loops? Replication of an input pair I, J causes the COUNT of J to be

1 larger than it should be. It also causes the successor J to appear on the list of successors of I one more time. When object I eventually is removed, its list of successors is traversed. This results in the COUNT of J being reduced one additional time so that the extra increase due to the I, J replication is cancelled. The implementation will thus work correctly as long as there is room for the extra successor records to appear in LISTS. If there is no room to accommodate these extra records, it is not possible to predict what will occur when the implementation is executed.

Loops, on the other hand, result in some objects never being output. Objects involved in a loop, or which are the successors of an object in a loop, will never have their counts go to zero, and will never appear in the bag of objects. In fact, had the test for completion been "S not empty" or "N objects output," loops in the input would cause an infinite loop in the program. It should now be clear that NEXT $-\,1$, when the loop in phase II is exited, will be the actual number of objects that were output by the loop. If this is less than n, then loops occurred in the input. This can provide a simple test for loops.

9.6 Final Comments on TOPSORT

Notice that the implementation of the output ranking and the bag are coupled because they share storage. As a result, they are not independent. This means that a change in the choice of implementation for one will affect the other. In general, such a situation is to be avoided, and as pointed out earlier, could have been avoided. Certainly the small saving in time and storage did not warrant the added complexity.

There are, however, some important storage considerations that were alluded to earlier. TOPSORT will run out of storage before it runs out of time, since storage requirements grow as n^2. The bulk of the storage needed is taken by the LISTS array. Suppose a maximum size, based on the available storage of the computer system, is declared for the LISTS array. Say its length is 50,000. Assuming each of its records takes two entries, this provides enough storage to guarantee the solution of any problem with no more than 25,000 successors ($m \leq 25,000$). It makes no difference how the successors are distributed among the objects. Only the total number is relevant.

Suppose, instead, that the decision had been to represent each collection of successors by dedicating an array to the collection. Since the programmer does not know in advance how the successors will be distributed, each of the required N arrays should have the same length. Lists are no longer necessary, since the successors can be placed sequentially in the proper array. Of course, a variable will be needed to keep track of the last successor in each array. An additional array may be used for these pointers. If N is to be no greater than, say 500, then each of the arrays containing the successors can be declared of length 50,000/500, or 100. The upshot is that the solution may now be guaranteed for a different class of problems. These problems must have $N \leq 500$, and each object may have no more than 100 successors. Even though the total number of successors may now be 50,000 (twice as many as before), their distribution is critical. When storage is at a premium, these kinds of considerations are important.

Had the Pascal heap been used, instead of the LISTS array, for storage of the successor records, then the program would contain no explicit storage limitation (other than the declarations for the length of COUNT, SUCC, and RANK). Still, the maximum heap size would have imposed a limit on the value of m for which the program would execute.

9.6.1 An Input Validation Module

One final point involving time and storage trade-offs. Suppose an input validation module must be added to TOPSORT just prior to the processing of the current I, J pair read in phase I. The module is to check whether I, J is a duplicate of an earlier input pair. If so, it is to be ignored, and processed otherwise. One way to accomplish this, which requires no additional storage, is to traverse the current list of successors of object I. If J appears on the list as a successor, then I, J is a duplicate, otherwise it is not. This takes time proportional to the current number of successors of I and thus adds a *total* time to phase I which is proportional to m^2. Instead, the module can work in constant time if $n \times (n - 1)$ additional storage is available. Use the storage for an $n \times (n - 1)$ array that is initialized to all zeros. When I, J is read, simply test the (I, J)th array entry. If it is zero, the pair is not a duplicate. Then set the entry to 1 to indicate that this I, J pair has been processed. In this way, an entry of 1 will mean that the pair is a duplicate from now on. This adds *total* time to phase I on $O(m)$, but requires $n \times (n - 1)$ additional storage.

9.7 Reviewing Methodology

A topological sort produces a ranking of objects which satisfies constraints on their allowable positions within the ranking. The obvious algorithm for finding a topological sort, *searching* through all rankings until one satisfying the constraints is found, is not feasible. Another algorithm was developed by *constructing* a ranking that satisfied the constraints. An initial implementation, which merely produced an image of the input data in memory, resulted in a feasible solution. However, the selection of an array to contain predecessor counts, the creation of lists of successors, and the bag proved to be significantly better. This solution was achieved by a process of stepwise refinement, stressing data abstraction, encapsulation, modularity, and the proper choice of data structures. The modularity of the final solution allowed immediate application of a routine developed earlier — the list traversal routine. Again, because of modularity, it was not difficult to determine where and how to build in appropriate checks of the input data.

More generally, the analysis of the storage and time requirements of a fairly complex program was demonstrated. Even though this cannot always be accomplished, or may be difficult for complex programs, it serves as an example of what we hope to be able to do.

□ Exercises

1. Within a textbook, chapters cover specific topics. The information required to understand each topic is expected to have appeared before the topic appears in the book. Suppose you are given a list of topics and the other topics on which each depends. How might you select an ordering of the topics for their appearance in the book?

2. Which of these binary relations is a partial order on S?
  a. "Square root of" on the set S of all real numbers
  b. "Square root of" on the set S of all real numbers greater than 1
  c. "Is older than" on the set S of all your relatives
  d. "Sits in front of" on the set S of all students in a class
  e. "Lives diagonally across from" on the set S of all people

3. Write down the graphic representation for the binary relation R on the first 10 integers. $R = (3, 2), (4, 6), (7, 6), (8, 1), (9, 7), (9, 8)$.

4. Write a detailed modification of the algorithm of Section 9.2 that will check if a given ranking is consistent with the given partial order.

5. Write a program to implement the refinement of Exercise 4 and determine its worst-case time and storage requirements.

6. Apply the construction-based algorithm of Section 9.3 to the following data to obtain a consistent ranking. Always select the smallest integer for output.

$$S = 1, 2, 3, \ldots, 12$$
$$R = (3, 2), (4, 6), (7, 9), (12, 10), (5, 6), (2, 4),$$
$$(8, 9), (2, 6), (3, 6), (7, 12), (3, 4), (7, 10)$$

7. If the second implementation of the construction-based algorithm is applied to the input of Exercise 6, then what integers are in the bag after 3 is removed?

8. State clearly and concisely what purpose the bag serves in the better "bag" refinement and why it was introduced.

9. Write an expanded version of the better refinement that will output integers from the bag by selecting the smallest possible integer first.

10. What will the SUCC, LISTS, and COUNT arrays have in them after phase I, when the input pairs of the running example appear in the order 7 6, 5 3, 2 10, 6 8, 5 6, 7 3, 4 8, 7 1, 4 2?

11. What will the COUNT, SUCC, and LISTS arrays look like after phase II as compared to after phase I?

12. Suppose the better implementation were modified, so that no COUNT array were stored in memory, and only the SUCC and LISTS arrays were available after phase I. Write a new phase II refinement under this constraint.

13. Suppose a solution to the topological sort problem had been constructed by determining what object should be at the bottom of the ranking. How would the better refinement be changed to reflect this new solution?

14. a. Suppose the bag is implemented in a separate record BAG instead of using the RANKING record. How must the data abstraction implementations change?
  b. Suppose the output ranking is not kept in the RANKING record, but, instead, each record is simply printed. How must the data abstraction implementations change?

15. The procedure PROCESS is itself dependent on the predecessor count and bag implementations. Modify it so that PROCESS becomes independent of these implementations.

16. Suppose task 5b of the better refinement is further expanded to:

  5b. i. For each successor of the output object, decrease its predecessor count by 1.
  5b.ii. For each successor of the output object, if its predecessor count is zero, add the successor to the bag.

  a. How should the implementation of the data abstraction algorithm (on p. 386) be modified to reflect this refinement?
  b. Write implementations for tasks 5b.i and 5b.ii which use TRAVERSE as a tool. This should include writing the corresponding two PROCESS procedures.

c. How will this expansion of task 5b affect the time required for the algorithm?

17. Suppose the input for Exercise 10 had the pairs below appended after 4 2. What would the graphic depictions of the successor lists be after phase I of TOPSORT?

7 3, 5 6, 4 2, 7 3, 6 8

18. For the input of Exercise 17 what would be in the COUNT array after phase I?

19. For the input of Exercise 17, show what will be in the COUNT array, the successor lists, and the bag after 7 is output.

20. Take as input the Example 9.6 with pairs 10 4 and 10 1 appended after 4 2. What will the second implementation of TOPSORT output in the rank array? What will be the value of NEXT after phase II?

☐ Suggested Assignment

a. Write and run a program whose input will be a series of topological sorting problems. For each problem the program should execute a slight modification of the TOPSORT procedure, called NEWTOPSORT. NEWTOPSORT has parameters N and TOPOLOGICALSORT. NEWTOPSORT is to read in and echo print N and all input pairs for the example it has been called to work on. It should print out the relevant portions of the COUNT, SUCC, and LISTS arrays as they appear after phase I. When NEWTOPSORT returns, the program prints the topological sort contained in the TOPOLOGICALSORT array. Except for the modifications needed to do the printing, NEWTOPSORT corresponds exactly to the sample implementation of TOPSORT with one exception, implement the bag as an array separate from RANK. Consequently, you must use TRAVERSE and the PROCESS routine, which it calls. NEWTOPSORT should work correctly for valid input and for any number of objects between 1 and 20. You should make up four input sample problems to use. Two should be valid. One should include replications and one should contain loops.

b. Suppose instead of using the sample implementation you do the following to keep successor information: Declare LISTS to be an $n \times (n - 1)$ two-dimensional array and keep the successors of object I in the Ith row of LISTS. For the example, after phase I, LISTS would be

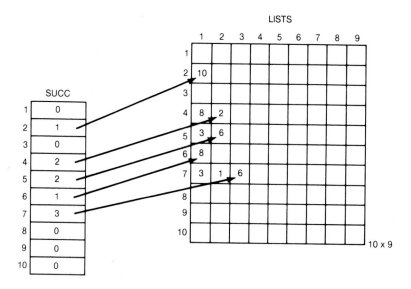

This two-dimensional LISTS array takes up the same total amount of storage as the one-dimensional LISTS array of the better implementation. For both implementations the limiting factor on whether or not the program will run might then be the value of n beyond which available storage is exhausted. Suppose you are willing to give up the guarantee that TOPSORT always run correctly. This means you may attempt to run problems whose n is large enough that you are not sure whether LISTS implementation can hold all successors. Discuss the relative advantage of the implementations.

      c. This is the same as part a except, instead of the LISTS array, use the Pascal heap to store the successor lists.

10 Compilers

10.1 How Compilers Work

Have you ever wondered how you can recognize an English sentence? Or how you can tell which sentences are grammatically correct? Or, given one that is correct, how you determine what it means, if it has a meaning at all? Compilers face such problems even though they deal with programming languages rather than English. In order to translate programs into efficient machine code, a compiler must "understand" a programming language.

Both English and high-level programming languages consist of sequences of allowable symbols. Grammatical rules (also called *rules of syntax*) specify which sequences are legitimate in both cases. When learning English or a high-level computer language, we do not consciously start from the grammar (or syntax). Typically, we pick up knowledge by mimicking and generalizing from examples. The better the examples provided, the luckier we are, because the more quickly we learn. The same process takes place in learning to write lucidly and concisely and with "style." No complete set of rules is presented; instead, over time, the elements of style become clearer.

The main difference between programming languages and English is that programming languages require a greater degree of precision, because they will be processed automatically by a computer. In fact, one of the foremost achievements of computer science was the development of ways to specify the grammars for high-level languages so that they are easily learned, expressive enough, and yet amenable to translation by a compiler. The study of this fascinating development is a practical and intellectually rewarding experience. In the 1950s, formal grammars were first defined by linguists and computer scientists. With these theoretical underpinnings the design of high-level languages and their compilers has been closer to a science than an art.

The purpose of this chapter is simply to give an inkling of the issues and difficulties involved in the creation of a compiler. Since compilers consist of tens of thousands of statements, they are complex, requiring considerable structure to make them comprehensible. Compilers apply many of the basic data structures in their implementation. This chapter presents a concise version of their tasks and discusses much smaller but related problems dealing with arithmetic expressions and sequences of assignment statements.

10.2 Language Specification

The very simple hypothetical language defined in this section illustrates the ideas involved in language specification and translation. The language consists of all arithmetic expressions obtained by correctly sequencing left and right parentheses, addition and multiplication signs, and letters.

The sequences (A), $A + B * C$, and $(A + B) * C$ are immediately recognizable as valid, while $(A + , (A + B))$, $( )$, and $A + * B$ are seen to be invalid. The first problem to be faced is specifying exactly those sequences that are valid arithmetic expressions. How this can be done for a high-level language was one of the major hurdles initially confronting computer scientists. It is also a hurdle even for a very simple language such as the hypothetical one. Since there are an infinite number of arithmetic expressions, they cannot simply be listed. Recursion using syntactic categories gives the solution as follows:

1. An *expression* is a term followed by a plus sign (+), followed by an expression, or it is just a term.
2. A *term* is a factor followed by a multiplication sign (*), followed by a term, or it is just a factor.
3. A *factor* is a left parenthesis, (, followed by an expression, followed by a right parenthesis,), or it is just a letter.
4. A *letter* is one of $A, B, C, \ldots, Z$.

The word *expression* is used as shorthand for arithmetic expression, the symbol + for addition, * for multiplication, and (and) for left and right parentheses. The definition thus makes use of four syntactic categories: expressions, terms, factors, and letters. This may seem excessive, but the reason for such expansiveness in categories will become clear.

A less wordy but equivalent way to convey the same information is used in formal grammars:

1. $E \rightarrow T + E \,|\, T$
2. $T \rightarrow F * T \,|\, F$
3. $F \rightarrow (E) \,|\, L$
4. $L \rightarrow A \,|\, B \,|\, C \,|\, \ldots \,|\, Z$

Statements 1 to 4 are called *productions* because they are used to produce sequences, starting from the initial one-character sequence E. For instance, the first statement means E can be replaced by either $T + E$ or by T. The other productions can be used

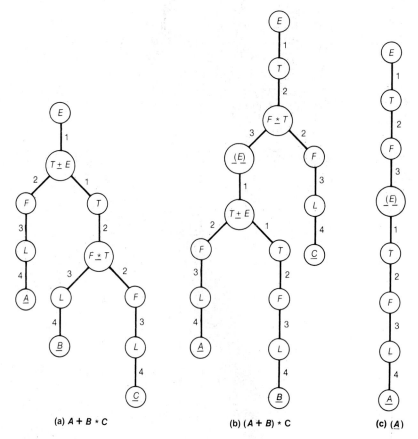

(a) *A + B * C*   (b) *(A + B) * C*   (c) *(A)*

Figure 10.1   Derivation Trees

similarly to replace syntactic categories *T*, *F*, and *L*. Together the four productions are a ***grammar***.

10.2.1 Derivations and Derivation Trees

The trees of Figure 10.1 show the derivation of $A + B * C$, $(A + B) * C$, and (A). It is natural to call them ***derivation trees***. They describe sequences of applications of the productions which produce their corresponding expressions. Each branch is labeled with the number of the production applied to produce its successor.

For instance, to derive $A + B * C$, start with *E*. Apply the first production to obtain $T + E$. Apply the second and first production again, substituting *F* for *T* and *T* for *E*, to obtain $F + T$. The third production allows *F* to be replaced by *L*, and the fourth allows *L* to be replaced by *A*, yielding $A + T$. $F * T$ replaces *T*, by the second production, so $A + F * T$ results. Finally, *F* is replaced by *L*, then *L* by *B* using productions 3 and 4, and *T* is replaced by *F*, *F* by *L*, and *L* by *C* using productions 2, 3, and 4. This produces $A + B * C$.

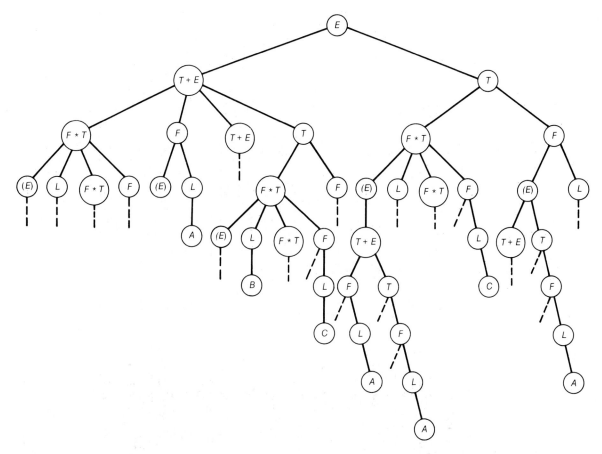

Figure 10.2 "Infinite" Tree

The *language* specified by the four productions, or grammar, consists of all sequences of (,), +, *, A, B, . . . , Z that have derivation trees. Be sure to understand how each tree of Figure 10.1 corresponds to a proper application of the productions, starting with E, and ending with the respective expressions.

Specifying a language formally, as done here, is important when dealing with high-level programming languages, since the designer, compiler writer, and user must all know precisely what statements are in the language — that is, which statements are grammatically correct. But this is not enough. The second major problem faced by compiler writers originally was how to recognize a valid statement.

The productions actually specify an "infinite" tree, which is partially drawn in Figure 10.2. *All* derivations are embedded in this tree, which explicitly shows the derivation trees of Figure 10.1. Finding a derivation for a given expression is tantamount to searching the tree for a derivation. On the other hand, to show that a sequence is *not* an expression requires a demonstration that no derivation exists in the tree.

10.2.2 Syntax and Semantics

We shall return to the recognition of valid statements soon, but first we deal with a related issue: the *meaning* of a valid statement. Languages are used to convey information. Speakers attach meaning to statements they utter and hear, although not all grammatically correct statements make sense. How to attach meaning to valid statements, or to interpret them, is determined by the **semantics** of a language. This area is still being researched and is not as fully understood as the syntactic analysis of language. Syntactic analysis has to do with the structure of a valid statement. And so does semantic analysis, in that the meaning of a statement is related to its syntax, and its syntax is related to its derivation. Consequently, when more than one derivation exists for a statement, its semantics is clouded. Ambiguity arises when more than one derivation exists.

Standing alone, the expression $A + B * C$ is ambiguous. Its two possible meanings correspond to "adding first" or "multiplying first." Two ways to avoid this ambiguity, typically learned in grade school or high school, are to use parentheses or to adopt the convention that multiplication is always done first unless this priority is overriden by parentheses. The first technique causes us to write $(A + B) * C$ when "adding first" is meant and $A + (B * C)$ when "multiplying first" is intended. The second requires $(A + B) * C$ when "adding first" is meant, but finds $A + B * C$ sufficient when "multiplying first" is intended. It is therefore reasonable to expect a language specification for expressions to honor these conventions. The use of syntactic categories gives productions the power to do this.

Look at the derivation tree for $A + B * C$ of Figure 10.1. It is easy to interpret $+$ as the main operator for the expression, with A and $B * C$ being its two operands. Thus the meaning to be attached to it agrees with convention and multiplication will be done first. Although it may not be apparent, the simple expression grammar is unambiguous and allows meaning to be attached in this way to *all* derivation trees. The meaning will always satisfy the conventions.

Other grammars can also be written for the simple language of expressions. Two such grammars are

$$E \rightarrow E + E \,|\, E * E \,|\, (E) \,|\, L$$
$$L \rightarrow A \,|\, B \,|\, C \,|\, \ldots \,|\, Z \tag{1}$$

and

$$E \rightarrow E + T \,|\, E * T \,|\, T$$
$$T \rightarrow (E) \,|\, L \tag{2}$$
$$L \rightarrow A \,|\, B \,|\, C \,|\, \ldots \,|\, Z$$

The first grammar is ambiguous. For example, $A + B * C$ has the two derivation trees shown in Figure 10.3.

The second grammar does not satisfy the priority rule for $*$ over $+$. For example, $A + B * C$ and $A * B + C$ have the derivation trees shown in Figure 10.4, respectively. The main operator of the first tree is $*$, so it gives priority to $+$, while the main operator of the second tree is $+$, so it gives priority to $*$.

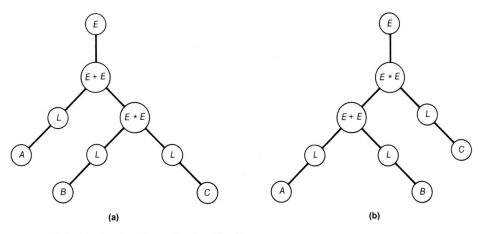

Figure 10.3 Derivation Trees for $A + B * C$

Another example of ambiguous grammar is the following, for **if-then-else** statements:

$S \rightarrow$ if C then S else $S \,|\,$ if C then $S \,|\, T$

where we do not further specify the syntactic categories C (for condition) and T (for task). Although this can be done, simply assume that C can be replaced by any logical expression, and T by any task. The sentence

If $C1$ then if $C2$ then $T1$ else $T2$

is ambiguous, having the two derivation trees shown in Figure 10.5.

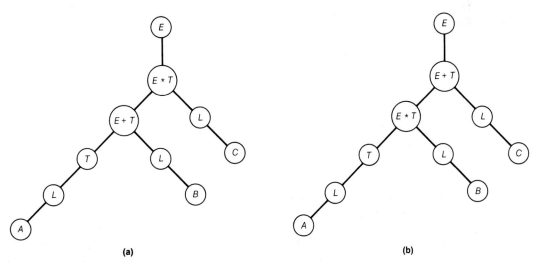

Figure 10.4 Derivation Trees for $A + B * C$ and $A * B + C$

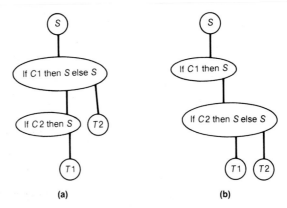

(a)   (b)

Figure 10.5   Two Derivation Trees

The same language can be specified by the following unambiguous grammar.

$S \rightarrow$ if C then $S \,|$ if C then S' else $S \,|\, T$

$S' \rightarrow$ if C then S' else $S' \,|\, T$

The ambiguity occurred because the **else** could be associated with either of the two **then**'s. Introducing another syntactic category S' allows the grammar to be written so that only S' precedes an **else**. This ensures that an **else** can be associated only with the last preceding **then**. The sentence now has only the derivation tree of Figure 10.6.

These examples demonstrate that it is the grammar, and not necessarily the language, that determines ambiguity and causes semantic difficulties. This leads to the realization that one of the important considerations for language specification, and compiler feasibility, is the development of grammars whose syntax allows the desired semantic interpretation to be selected. Since certain languages are inherently ambiguous (because *any* grammar for the language is ambiguous), it is fortunate that programming languages can be specified with unambiguous grammars.

10.2.3 Parsing

Finding either a derivation tree or its equivalent for a statement is known as *parsing* the statement. You may have learned to parse English sentences using syntactic categories such as *sentence, verb, adjective* in grade school or high school. Parsing lies at the heart of recognition algorithms for languages and is also needed so that meaning can be assigned to valid statements. Compilers use the parse of a statement to determine its proper translation. They also need additional information, and create a *symbol table* for this purpose. This section will demonstrate how a recognition program is developed. Consider again the unambiguous grammar of the simple expression language with this goal in mind:

1. $E \rightarrow T + E \,|\, T$

2. $T \rightarrow F * T \,|\, F$

3. $F \rightarrow (E) \,|\, L$

4. $L \rightarrow A \,|\, B \,|\, C \,|\, \ldots \,|\, Z$

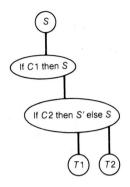

Figure 10.6 Derivation Tree for: If C1 Then If C2 Then T1 Else T2

The basic idea, given a sequence of symbols, is to search the infinite tree of the grammar to find a derivation tree for the sequence. As you will recall from Chapter 6, general tree traversals are the basis for tree searches and can entail considerable backtracking. Efficiency demands that backtracking be avoided. Because of specific properties of the simple expression language grammar, the search can be done very efficiently.

The general situation is made difficult because it is not possible to determine which branch of the tree to follow when a node has more than one successor, each leading to distinct possible decompositions of the sequence. For instance, beginning right at the root (Figure 10.2), does the sequence consist of a term, followed by a +, followed by an expression, or is the sequence just a term? Notice that, no matter which of these two possibilities is the case, an initial term must be found. It then becomes possible to decide which branch represents the correct decomposition by checking the next symbol. If it is a +, the left branch $(T + E)$ must be explored. Otherwise the sequence is a term, unless it contains more symbols and so cannot be a valid expression. Thus, searching for a term first costs nothing, since it must be done in any event.

A similar conclusion follows for branches from a term node. A factor must be found first, with the next symbol then indicating how to proceed with the search. An asterisk (*) means a term is to be searched for next; otherwise the term node is correctly decomposed into a factor.

Finally, once a factor node is reached, the correct branch is determined by whether or not the next symbol is a left parenthesis, (, or a letter. A left parenthesis means an expression is to be found, and then a right parenthesis,). A letter means a factor has been found.

With such analysis it is easy to determine at each node just the right path to take. Then, either the desired category is found or the sequence is judged invalid.

Given the recursive definition for the grammar, it should not be surprising that the *top-down* search of the tree can be implemented recursively. The following program gives such a recognizer for the simple expression language defined earlier. The input is assumed to be a sequence of symbols.

```
program EXPRESSIONRECOGNIZER(input, output);
const
    MAX = 100;
type
    chararray = array [1 .. MAX] of char;
    index = 0 .. MAX;
var
    STRING : chararray;
    LENGTH, J : index;

function NEXTCHAR(var C : char) : boolean;
begin
    READ(C);
    NEXTCHAR := not (C = ' # ')
end;

procedure READSTRING(var STRING : chararray; var LENGTH : index);
begin
    LENGTH := 0;
    while NEXTCHAR(STRING[LENGTH + 1]) do
        LENGTH := LENGTH + 1
end;

function LETTER(C : char) : boolean;
begin
    LETTER := (C in ['A' .. 'Z'])
end;

function FACTOR : boolean; forward;
function TERM : boolean; forward;
function EXPRESSION : boolean;
begin
    if TERM then
        if STRING[J + 1] = '+' then
            begin
                J := J + 1;
                EXPRESSION := EXPRESSION
            end
        else
            EXPRESSION := true
    else
        EXPRESSION := false
end;

function TERM;
begin
    if FACTOR then
        if STRING[J + 1] = '*' then
            begin
                J := J + 1;
                TERM := TERM
            end
        else
            TERM := true
```

```
          else
              TERM := false
     end;

     function FACTOR;
     begin
         if STRING[J + 1] = '(' then
             begin
                 J := J + 1;
                 if EXPRESSION then
                     if STRING[J + 1] = ')' then
                         begin
                             J := J + 1;
                             FACTOR := true
                         end
                     else
                         FACTOR := false
                 else
                     FACTOR := false
             end
         else
             if LETTER(STRING[J + 1]) then
                 begin
                     J := J + 1;
                     FACTOR := true
                 end
             else
                 FACTOR := false
     end;

     begin
         READSTRING(STRING, LENGTH);
         J := 0;
         if (EXPRESSION and (J = LENGTH)) then
             WRITE('VALID EXPRESSION')
         else
             WRITE('INVALID EXPRESSION')
     end.
```

You should simulate execution of this program for the input $(A + B) * C$ and convince yourself that it generates the derivation tree for this expression. At each point in the derivation tree requiring that a specific syntactic category be found, the program invokes the appropriate function — EXPRESSION, TERM, FACTOR, or LETTER. This type of search is known as *recursive descent*. Not all grammars allow such a search. Other grammars for the expression language may cause a recursive descent program to work incorrectly or go into infinite loops.

The theory of formal grammars, spurred on by the notation used by Backus, extended by Naur, and brought to fruition by Noam Chomsky, provides considerable insight into the design of high-level languages and their compilers. It has led to the recognition that efficient compilers require certain kinds of grammars. As a result, there is a delicate interplay between the design of a language, its grammar, and its compiler. Considerable care is required to ensure that an efficient compiler can be specified for a given grammar. This is one reason some seemingly arbitrary restrictions occur in high-level languages.

A special class of grammars, ***context-free grammars***, has been sufficient to specify most of the syntax rules for high-level languages. The productions in this chapter are all context-free. A grammar is said to be ***context free*** if each production allows the replacement of a syntactic category to be done independent of its context. Allowing context dependency to influence replacements yields a more general class of grammars, *phrase-structure* grammars.

For purposes of efficient compiler development, context-free grammars are too general. The way in which declarations are specified and used in programming languages actually introduces a form of context dependency in their grammars. Fortunately, efficient compilers can still be developed based on the incorporation of a symbol table. Perhaps this discussion has whetted your appetite sufficiently so you will pursue the theory further.

10.2.4 **Lexical Analysis and Symbol Tables**

The simple expression language allows operators to be named using only single letters. Pascal, of course, allows much greater freedom. Thus $(SUM + ONE) *$ $(COUNT + A2)$ is a proper Pascal expression. Extending the simple language to allow a more flexible choice for operator names requires a new syntactic category, identifier (I). Its grammar is

1. $E \rightarrow T + E \,|\, T$

2. $T \rightarrow F * T \,|\, F$

3. $F \rightarrow (E) \,|\, I$

where we have replaced the category L of the third production by I, for identifier. I itself can be specified by productions, but this would needlessly complicate the discussion. Sequences in I, the identifier, consist of a letter followed by any combination of zero or more letters or digits $(0, 1, 2, \ldots, 9)$.

Now $(SUM + ONE) * (COUNT + A2)$ is a legal expression in the extended language. Its derivation tree will contain the category I, and the expression recognizer program must be modified to work for this extended language. One approach is to use a function, *identifier*, employed similarly to *expression, term, factor,* and *letter*. The function **identifier** must recognize a sequence of symbols falling in its syntactic category.

It no longer suffices for the program to look merely at a next symbol. Instead it must look at the next sequence of symbols which, treated as a single entity, falls into the identifier category or else consists of a single (,), +, or *. Programming languages contain other sequences of symbols to be recognized and treated as a single entity, for example, the assignment symbol := and the reserved words **begin, end, case, while, if, then, procedure. Begin** and **end** play roles similar to left and right parentheses, serving to bracket meaningful segments. Identifiers and reserved words are examples of tokens. ***Tokens*** are sequences of symbols that are to be treated as single entities. Low-level syntactic categories such as identifiers, numeric and character string constants, some operators, reserved words, and parentheses are separated out from the others and their members are considered tokens.

From the point of view of a Pascal compiler, the entire statement

| AMOUNT := (SUM + ONE) * (COUNT + A2)

simply looks like a sequence of the thirteen tokens AMOUNT, :=, (, SUM, +, ONE,), *, (, COUNT, +, A2,). That is, the important information for the compiler is that AMOUNT, SUM, ONE, COUNT, A2, etc. are tokens. Similarly, the Pascal statement

| **while** (A <> B) **do**

must be viewed by the compiler as the sequence of the seven tokens **while**, (, A, <>, B,), **do**. In addition to parsing, one of the tasks for the compiler is to analyze the program into tokens. This task is called *lexical analysis*.

Incorporating a lexical analyzer into the parser gives another way to modify the expression recognizer program to obtain an extended expression recognizer. Instead of looking at the next character, it must look at the next token to make its decisions. In the simple recognizer, the only decision affected occurs in FACTOR. Instead of asking if STRING[J + 1] is a letter, it is necessary to know if the next token is an identifier. Thus it appears that the simplest approach is to replace the if statement involving LETTER by

| **if** IDENTIFIER **then**
| FACTOR := true;

and define IDENTIFIER by

```
function IDENTIFIER : boolean;
begin
    if LETTER(STRING[J + 1]) then
        begin
            J := J + 1;
            while (LETTER(STRING[J + 1]) or DIGIT(STRING[J + 1])) do
                J := J + 1;
            IDENTIFIER := true
        end
    else
        IDENTIFIER := false
end;
```

DIGIT must return "true" if its parameter is a digit, "false" otherwise. This represents the first approach to modifying the EXPRESSIONRECOGNIZER program. The simplicity of this approach is misleading. For the more complicated situation, where high-level language programs are to be recognized, the second approach, emphasizing a lexical analyzer, is better.

Pascal programs appear to the compiler as a sequence of characters. Their tokens must be ferreted out by the lexical analyzer, and the syntactic categories must be found by the parser. There are about fifty syntactic categories. Compilers are written so that there is interplay between the lexical analyzer and the parser.

Even for the simple extended expression language there is a need to retain information about the tokens that appear. This is necessary if a proper translation is to be made. For example, in the expression $(A + B) * (SUM + COUNT) * (ONE + A)$, the two occurrences of A must be recognized and treated as references to the same identifier. Thus distinct occurrences of the same identifier must be determinable.

In general, a good deal of information must be retained for each identifier in a high-level language. For instance, the type or syntactic category of each identifier must be kept, dimensions of arrays must be known, and parameters of functions must be accessible. Such information is stored in the symbol table.

Suppose the lexical analyzer is implemented by a procedure GETTOKEN, which finds the next token, moves the pointer corresponding to J of the simple parser to the last symbol of the token, and makes appropriate entries to the symbol table. The parser can invoke GETTOKEN when it is necessary, and can search the symbol table to find the token's syntactic category, as well as other required information, as needed. This additional information, such as array dimensions, is essential for proper translation. It is even needed in order to decide if a meaningful translation is possible. For instance, variables whose types are undeclared or conflict, or whose values are not set, should cause at least an error message. The lexical analyzer simplifies the structure of the parser, allowing the parser to work with tokens, while the task of finding the tokens and building the symbol table is given to the lexical analyzer.

In some programming languages, the lexical analyzer might need to look considerably beyond the last symbol of the next token in order to find the token. The task is made easier when tokens of more than one character are separated by single character tokens. Thus ; , (,), +, *, and = can serve this purpose, as well as blanks. When reserved words cannot be used as variables, the task is simpler. Again, some of the apparent arbitrariness of syntax rules is due to the desire to make lexical analysis easier.

Finally, the symbol table must support the insertion of new tokens and their data as they are encountered, as well as table searches, so that repetitions of tokens and access to their data can be quickly achieved. Symbol tables are generally implemented as hash tables or as binary search trees.

10.2.5 Translation

Once the symbol table has been built and the program parsed, its translation may take place. The translation is normally done as the parser proceeds, although it could be done as a separate phase. Translation, at the simplest level, involves the generation of assembly language code equivalent to the input program. In reality, compilers generally are designed to attempt to optimize this code for storage and time requirements. It was the ability of the FORTRAN compilers to generate code close to the efficiency of that produced by good programmers that led to the initial acceptance of compilers as a viable tool. Of course, at that time hardware was scarce and expensive, while programmers were relatively inexpensive.

Perhaps the most important but least understood aspect of compiler writing is the generation of error messages. Errors may be discovered and treated during lexical analysis, parsing, or translation. Although this discussion of compilers has been broad and brief, you should recognize and appreciate their complexity. The study of their theory and practice involves elegant theoretical developments, clever application of the principles of good algorithm design, and proper choice of data abstraction implementation. An extended treatment of the topics introduced here appears in Aho and Ullman [1972].

10.3 Evaluation and Translation of Expressions

FORTRAN was originally designed for use in scientific calculations. The name itself is an acronym standing for *formula* translation. People were accustomed to writing algebraic expressions in **infix notation**, where an operator appears between its operands. The new programming language was to allow such expressions, perhaps the historically earliest "user friendly" design decision. Thus the FORTRAN programmer could write

$$(((A + (B/C * D)) + (A/W)) * B)/(((A * C) + D) + A)$$

Even humans must scan such an expression carefully, more than once, before discovering that its basic syntactic structure is operand 1/operand 2. At the time, a serious problem for the compiler writers was how to translate such expressions without making many scans back and forth through them. The problem was compounded further since programmers were not required to write fully parenthesized expressions, so an additional dilemma was how to resolve ambiguity. We shall see that ambiguity may be resolved by using a notation other than infix.

Consider the two binary trees of Figure 10.7. Their access orders are shown in Table 10.1. These are all arithmetic expressions written in prefix, infix, or postfix notation. **Prefix** means the operator appears to the left, before its operands, and **postfix** means the operator appears to the right, after its operands. Although infix notation is what programmers normally use, there are contexts where prefix notation is more natural. For instance we write SQRT(X), $f(x, y)$, and minimum(x, y).

Table 10.1 Access Orders for Two Binary Trees

	Tree (a)	Tree (b)
Preorder	+ A * B C	* + A B C
Inorder	A + B * C	A + B * C
Postorder	A B C * +	A B + C *

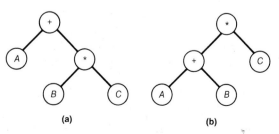

(a)   (b)

Figure 10.7 Two Binary Trees Representing Arithmetic Expressions

Note that the prefix and postfix expressions of tree (**a**) are equivalent ways to express the infix expression $A + (B * C)$, while the prefix and postfix expressions of tree (**b**) are equivalent to $(A + B) * C$. Unfortunately, the infix expressions of (**a**) and (**b**) are identical. This means that, unless parentheses are used, *there is no way to distinguish between* $A + (B * C)$ and $(A + B) * C$ using infix notation. Yet we *can* choose the proper prefix or postfix notation to make clear which of the two is intended. This is possible even though no parentheses (or special conventions) are used, and holds true in general for arithmetic expressions. For this reason, prefix and postfix notations are called **parentheses-free** notations. Compilers can easily process prefix and postfix expressions and, since postfix expressions are generally used, we concentrate on them.

10.3.1 Postfix Expressions

Given an infix expression that is *completely parenthesized,* such as

$$((A + B) * (C/D))$$

you know how to evaluate it. This is because you have grown accustomed to the rules for its evaluation, although you might be hard pressed to state those rules completely and precisely. In any case, parentheses signal how the operators are to be applied to the operands, indicating that $(A + B)$ and (C/D) must be evaluated first before applying the $*$ operator. Removing all parentheses yields

$$A + B * C/D$$

Unless conventions or rules are given, this expression is ambiguous. Its five distinct interpretations correspond to the ways in which parentheses may be placed,

$$((A + B) * (C/D))$$

$$(((A + B) * C)/D)$$

$$((A + (B * C))/D)$$

$$(A + ((B * C)/D))$$

$$(A + (B * (C/D)))$$

A postfix expression such as

$$AB + CD/*$$

makes little sense to us for we are not used to it, having little experience in interpreting or evaluating it. The rule to be used is as follows:

1. Scan the postfix expression from left to right.
2. Whenever an operator is encountered,
   replace it, and the immediately preceding number of operands required by that operator, with the result of applying that operator to those operands.

3. Treat this replacement as an operand, and continue scanning from this point.

Thus the postfix expression is equivalent to the infix expression

$$((A + B) * (C/D))$$

The rule, in generating this expression, produces the two intermediate expressions: $(A + B)CD/*$, $(A + B)(C/D)*$.

The following list shows the five fully parenthesized infix expressions representing the interpretations of $A + B * C/D$ and their corresponding postfix expressions.

$$((A + B) * (C/D)) \cdots AB + CD/*$$
$$(((A + B) * C)/D) \cdots AB + C * D/$$
$$((A + (B * C))/D) \cdots ABC *+ D/$$
$$(A + ((B * C)/D)) \cdots ABC * D/+$$
$$(A + (B * (C/D))) \cdots ABCD/*+$$

These examples emphasize two points:

1. The rule for evaluating postfix expressions allows no ambiguity. It precisely determines the meaning or interpretation of the postfix expression.
2. An infix expression, unless fully parenthesized, may be ambiguous in its meaning or interpretation.

It is because of statement 1 that postfix notation, or postfix expressions, are called parentheses-free. A similar rule allows prefix notation, or prefix expression, to be parentheses-free.

Furthermore, evaluating a postfix expression is easily accomplished by scanning the expression from left to right and using a stack to retain operands and results of intermediate evaluations. Any operand that is encountered is placed on an operand stack. When an operator is encountered, its operands are taken from the top of the stack, the operator is applied, and the result is put on the top of the stack. The process is illustrated in the following example.

Example 10.1 Table 10.2 shows the contents of the operand stack after each input is processed, simulating the procedure for evaluation of a postfix expression. The expression is $ABC * D/+$. □

Since the procedure for the evaluation of an arithmetic expression using a stack is relatively straightforward and requires no parentheses, why don't programmers write arithmetic expressions in postfix notation only? The reason is we are so used to infix notation, we don't want to change. As a result, high-level languages accept infix expressions rather than postfix. This leads back to the question of how infix expressions may be evaluated.

Table 10.2   Evaluation of a Postfix Expression

Input	Operand Stack
A	A
B	B
	A
C	C
	B
	A
*	$(B*C)$
	A
D	D
	$(B*C)$
	A
/	$((B*C)/D)$
	A
+	$(A+((B*C)/D)$

10.3.2 Infix Expressions

The rule to be used for a completely parenthesized infix expression is

1. Scan the infix expression from left to right.
2. When a "matched" pair of "left" and "right" parentheses is encountered, apply the operator to the operands enclosed within the pair of parentheses, and replace the paired parentheses and the contained operator and operands by the result. Continue scanning from this point.

The matched pairs referred to in this rule are exactly the same as in the case study of Chapter 4. Studying the rule, you can see that a right parenthesis signals that an operator and its operands are enclosed between the right parenthesis and its matching left parenthesis.

Procedure DETERMINE in Chapter 4 may be modified to obtain a function EVALUATE, with the same parameters as DETERMINE, by defining the PROCESS routine as follows:

1. When an operand is encountered, place the operand on top of an operand stack.
2. When an operator is encountered, place the operator on top of the operator stack.

It is also necessary, when a "right" parenthesis is encountered, and the operator stack is not empty, to pop the operator stack, remove the required number of operands from the top of the operand stack, apply the operator to those operands, and place the result on the top of the operand stack. This must be done just before the POP(S, TOPCHAR) statement. DETERMINE's stack, S, plays the role of the operator stack. An operand stack must be introduced and must be available to both the EVALUATE and PROCESS procedures.

One problem remains: How do we evaluate infix expressions that are *not* completely parenthesized? Recall that there are standard rules for interpreting infix expressions in this case. These rules are also incorporated in high-level languages. They are necessary because parentheses are not always available to signal what is to be done next. For example, if we apply EVALUATE to

$$A + B * C/D$$

then when the * is encountered, the stacks appear as

Operand Stack	Operator Stack
B	+
A	

The operator * signals that, had the expressions been completely parenthesized, a *left* parenthesis would have occurred just *before* the B or else a *right* parenthesis would have occurred just *after* the B. In other words, the appearance of the operator requires a decision as to whether B should be considered an operand of * or an operand of +. The standard rules resolve such ambiguities by assigning *priorities* or *precedence values* to operators, assuming a left-to-right scan of the expression. For the binary operators +, −, *, /, and ** (for exponentiation), the priorities are as follows:

1. Exponentiation (**) has the highest priority.
2. Multiplication and division (*, /) have the same priority, which is higher than that of addition or subtraction (+, −).
3. Addition and subtraction (+, −) have the same priority.

A left parenthesis also needs a priority, the lowest.

Whether B is an operand of * or + can then be resolved by taking B as an operand of the highest priority operator; * in this case. Again, parentheses may be used to override priorities. For example, in

$$(A + B) * C/D$$

B is to be associated with the + operator.

Example 10.2 In order to see how *any* infix expression is evaluated using priorities, and to develop an algorithm for this evaluation, consider the expression,

$$A + (B * C/D ** E) * F$$

☐

If EVALUATE is applied to it, when the first * is encountered the situation will be

Operand Stack	Operator Stack
B	(
A	+

In this case, since the left parenthesis is on top of the operator stack, the * should be placed on top of the operator stack, and scanning continued. After C, division (/) is encountered and the stacks become

Operand Stack	Operator Stack
C	*
B	(
A	+

At this point a decision must be made with respect to C: either it is to be associated with * (at the top of the stack) or with / (the current operator being processed). The standard rules associate C with the operator of highest priority. In this case, since * and / have equal priorities, associate C with the leftmost of the two operators in the input — that is, the top stack operator. Thus, the * must be popped, C and B must be popped, the * must be applied to B and C, and the result, $(B * C)$, placed on top of the operand stack. Then the / must be placed on the operator stack. Had the current operator been of higher priority, say **, then the current operator should simply be placed on the operator stack.

In the example, after / and D are processed, the stacks are as follows:

Operand Stack	Operator Stack
D	/
$(B * C)$	(
A	+

The ** becomes the current operator and D must be associated with it or with /. Since ** has higher priority, place it on the operator stack; the result after processing E is

Operand Stack	Operator Stack
E	**
D	/
$(B * C)$	(
A	+

The current input character being scanned is now a right parenthesis. This "matches" the topmost left parenthesis on the stack. The next steps are to pop the operator stack; pop the operand stack to obtain the top two operands; apply ** to them and place the result back on the top of the operand stack. Then pop the operator stack; pop the operand stack to obtain the top two operands; apply / to them and place the result back on top of the operand stack; pop the stack again; and notice that a left parenthesis has appeared signaling completion of the process for the current input character. The result is

Operand Stack	Operator Stack
$((B * C)/(D ** E))$	+
A	

Finally, the last * is processed; it has higher priority than +, so it is placed on the operator stack. *F* is then processed and placed on the operand stack, yielding

Operand Stack	Operator Stack
F	*
$((B*C)/(D**E))$	+
A	

Since the input is exhausted, the final steps are, for each remaining operator on the operator stack, to pop the operator stack, remove the required number of top operands from the operand stack, apply the operator and place the result back on top of the operand stack. The final result appears at the top of the operand stack.

The algorithm for the evaluation of *any* infix expression can now be written. The algorithm, which follows, assumes that a character, when read, will be an entire operand or operator. This means, for example, that ** should be interpreted as a "character."

1. Initialize the operand stack to empty.
2. Initialize the operator stack to empty.
3. While there is another input character,
    read the current character
    if the current character is (, then
        push it on the operator stack;
    else if the current character is an operand, then
        push it on the operand stack;
    else if the current character is an operator, then
        if the operator stack is not empty, then
            if the current character does not have greater priority than the top
            operator stack character, then
                pop the operator stack, remove the required number of oper-
                ands from the operand stack, apply the operator to them, and
                push the result on the operand stack
        push the current character onto the operator stack
    else if the current character is), then
        pop the operator stack and set topchar to the popped value
        while topchar is not (
            remove the number of operands required by topchar from the
            operand stack, apply topchar to them, and push the result onto the
            operand stack
            pop the operator stack and set topchar to the popped value
4. While the operator stack is not empty,
    pop the operator stack, remove the required number of operands from
    the operand stack, apply the operator to them, and push the result on the
    operand stack
5. Pop the operand stack and set EVALUATE to the popped value

Notice that the evaluation of an infix expression requires two stacks rather than the one stack required for the evaluation of a postfix expression. Other operators may be introduced and given appropriate priorities. For example, the assignment operator, :=, would be given a higher priority than **. Rather than modify the function EVALUATE, which is valid for completely parenthesized infix expressions, it seems easier to implement this directly.

10.3.3 Translating Infix to Postfix

Suppose, rather than evaluating an infix expression, a programmer wished to translate it and produce the corresponding postfix expression as output. The reason is that postfix expressions can be executed directly, whereas infix expressions are tricky to evaluate. Moreover, if the translation can be done, then the postfix expression may be easily embellished to produce a machine language program for the evaluation of the original infix expression.

You should convince yourself that the following modification of the evaluation algorithm will result in such a translation.

1. Eliminate the operand stack. Instead, any pushing onto the operand stack should be changed to outputting the same value.
2. Instead of applying operators to operands, simply output the operators.

10.4 Top-down and Bottom-up Compilers

It is not difficult to translate a postfix expression into equivalent assembly language code. Efficient code, however, is easier to generate for some computers than for others, depending on their architecture. Stack machines make this task more straightforward.

The algorithm just described in the last section can serve as the basis for a compiler that translates a language consisting of infix expressions to a language consisting of postfix expressions. The algorithm ensures that the input and its translation are equivalent, both evaluating to the same result. Adding a lexical analyzer to the algorithm allows more general operand names. The result is a parser, coupled with a translator.

This is an example of the *bottom-up* approach to parsing. Instead of searching the "infinite" tree of the grammar from the top down, it searches the tree starting from the leaf nodes. The idea is to find sequences of input tokens as the input is scanned from left to right, reducing them to their syntactic categories. The effect is to generate the derivation tree from its leaf nodes, working toward the root. This contrasts with the top-down approach, which determines the syntactic categories for which to search and then finds the appropriate sequence of input tokens for that category, working from the root to the leaf nodes.

The top-down approach decomposes the input into its highest level syntactic parts, each part being similarly broken down into its highest level syntactic components, and so on, until the lowest level categories are found. The bottom-up approach works from the lowest level categories, and the way they are put together in the input sequence, to generate the derivation tree.

Once the derivation tree has been obtained, the postfix expression may be generated by simply traversing it in postorder fashion, outputting leaf nodes (operands) and nodes representing operators as they are encountered. The algorithms in the chapter thus far do not actually construct the derivation tree and then

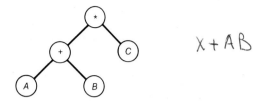

Figure 10.8 Derivation Tree for (A + B) * C Omitting Syntactic Categories

traverse it in this way. Instead they traverse the derivation tree and construct the translation as the traversal proceeds. This is evident in the bottom-up approach of Section 10.3. You will soon see how it can also be incorporated in the top-down approach of Section 10.2.

First, consider the derivation tree of $(A + B) * C$ of Figure 10.8. This is the derivation tree with syntactic categories and parentheses ignored. Looking closely at how the translation algorithm of the last section proceeds should convince you that the effect is an inorder traversal of the tree. The expression recognizer program given earlier also carries out an inorder traversal of this tree. It may be turned into a translator by outputting operands and operators. Operands must be output as they are encountered, but the outputting of an operator must be delayed until its operands have all been output. The following program segments show the changes that must be made to functions EXPRESSION, TERM, and FACTOR to accomplish output of the postfix translation.

```
function EXPRESSION : boolean;
begin
    if TERM then
        if STRING[J + 1] = '+' then
            begin
                J := J + 1;
                EXPRESSION := EXPRESSION;
                WRITE('+')
            end
        else
            EXPRESSION := true
    else
        EXPRESSION := false
end;

function TERM;
begin
    if FACTOR then
        if STRING[J + 1] = '*' then
            begin
                J := J + 1;
                TERM := TERM;
                WRITE('*')
            end
```

```
            else
                TERM := true
        else
            TERM := false
    end;

    function FACTOR;
    begin
        if STRING[J + 1] = '(' then
            begin
                J := J + 1;
                if EXPRESSION then
                    if STRING[J + 1] = ')' then
                        begin
                            J := J + 1;
                            FACTOR := true
                        end
                    else
                        FACTOR := false
                else
                    FACTOR := false
            end
        else
            if LETTER(STRING[J + 1]) then
                begin
                    J = J + 1;
                    FACTOR := true;
                    WRITE(STRING[J])
                end
            else
                FACTOR := false
    end;
```

10.5 A Simple Compiler

The more complex the input language, the more complex the compiler. In order to show how this complexity increases as the input language expands, we now develop a compiler for a still simple but expanded version of the expression language. The idea is to modify previous solutions to handle the new language.

To start, we present grammar for a simple programming language consisting of sequences of assignment statements separated by semicolons and ending with a period. The right side of assignment statements may consist of only a single digit, or it may be an expression of the extended expression language.

1. $P \rightarrow B$

2. $B \rightarrow I := E;\ B \mid I := E$

3. $E \rightarrow T + E \mid T$

4. $T \rightarrow F * T \mid F$

5. $F \rightarrow (E) \mid I \mid D$

where P, B, I, and D stand for program, block, identifier, and digit, respectively. An example of a valid program is

| ONE := 1; SUM := 7; B := 3; A := ((SUM * B) + ONE) * B; B := A + ONE.

Note that the language allows no blanks to appear in a program.

The compiler must assign memory storage addresses to each identifier and digit, and produce a sequence of postfix expressions separated by semicolons and ending in a period, which corresponds to the program. Assume the compiler assigns storage sequentially, starting at address 100. Thus the translated version of the input program should be

| 100 101 := ; 102 103 := ; 104 105 := ; 106 102 104 * 100 + 104 * := ;
| 104 106 100 + := .

The correspondence between identifiers and digits, and their addresses, is given by

ONE	100
1	101
SUM	102
7	103
B	104
3	105
A	106

In order for the program to "make sense" and to be executable, all identifiers appearing in an expression must have already been set to some numeric value by a previous assignment statement. The simple compiler will not make such checks, nor will it include any error messages. Of course, as already mentioned, this must be an integral part of real compilers. Notice that more than one occurrence of the same identifier must be recognized, with each being assigned the same address. Such requirements are not built into the grammar and represent context-dependent rules. Building and referring to a symbol table can handle such additional problems.

The lexical analyzer is assigned the task of producing the next token in a global variable TOKEN, creating the symbol table, and assigning addresses. For the hypothetical simple compiler the symbol table is a data abstraction with the operations INSERT and SEARCH. It contains records consisting of identifiers or digits, their syntactic category, and their assigned address. Only the first five characters of an identifier will be taken as relevant. Thus any identifiers with the same first five characters will be treated as being identical.

The compiler, PROGRAMTRANSLATOR, is shown below. Notice that its structure reflects the grammar and that it results from modifying the EXPRESSION-RECOGNIZER program, incorporating the modifications of functions shown before. For convenience it has been assumed that no assignment statement of the output requires more than one line. Also, the input must have a # character to serve as a sentinel. INSERT creates an entry in the symbol table for its parameter, while

SEARCH returns with FOUND true when its first parameter is already in the table and false if not. The third parameter will contain the address field value of the first parameter when FOUND is true. The implementation of the symbol table is only for illustration (see Exercises 19 and 20). The program does not output, as part of the translation, the instructions that cause the addresses corresponding to digits to be initialized to the numeric values of those digits. This would be necessary to produce a complete translation, but would detract from our main concerns.

```
program PROGRAMTRANSLATOR(input, output);
const
    MAX = 100;
    FIVE = 5;
    SIX = 6;
    HND = 100;
    FIVEHND = 500;
type
    chararray      = array [1..MAX] of char;
    index          = 0..MAX;
    alpha          = array [1..FIVE] of char;
    addressrange = HND..FIVEHND;
    entry          = record
                        name : alpha;
                        kind : char;
                        address : addressrange
                     end;
    symboltable  = array [1..HND] of entry;
var
    STRING : chararray;
    LENGTH, J : index;
    LOCATION, ADDRESS : addressrange;
    TOKEN : entry;
    TABLE : symboltable;
    T : integer;

function NEXTCHAR(var C : char) : boolean;
begin
    READ(C);
    NEXTCHAR := not (C = ' # ')
end;

procedure READSTRING(var STRING : chararray; var LENGTH : index);
begin
    LENGTH := 0;
    while NEXTCHAR(STRING[LENGTH + 1]) do
        LENGTH := LENGTH + 1
end;

procedure INSERT(TOKEN : entry);
begin
    TABLE[T] := TOKEN;
    T := T + 1
end;
```

```
function EQUAL(A, B : alpha) : boolean;
var
    I : integer;
begin
    EQUAL := true;
    for I := 1 to FIVE do
        if A[I] <> B[I] then
            EQUAL := false
end;
procedure SEARCH(TOKEN : entry; var FOUND : boolean; var ADDRESS : addressrange);
var
    I : integer;
begin
    FOUND := false;
    I := 1;
    while ((I < T) and not FOUND) do
        begin
            if EQUAL(TABLE[I].NAME, TOKEN.NAME) then
                begin
                    FOUND := true;
                    ADDRESS := TABLE[I].ADDRESS
                end;
            I := I + 1
        end
end;

procedure GETTOKEN;
var
    L, K : 1 .. SIX;
    FOUND : boolean;
begin
    if STRING[J + 1] in ['+', '*', '(', ')', ';', '.'] then
        begin
            TOKEN.KIND := STRING[J + 1];
            J := J + 1
        end
    else
        if ((STRING[J + 1] = ':') and (STRING[J + 2] = '=')) then
            begin
                TOKEN.KIND := 'A';
                J := J + 2
            end
        else
            if STRING[J + 1] in ['0' .. '9'] then
                begin
                    TOKEN.NAME[1] := STRING[J + 1];
                    TOKEN.KIND := 'D';
                    TOKEN.ADDRESS := LOCATION;
                    LOCATION := LOCATION + 1;
                    INSERT(TOKEN);
                    J := J + 1
                end
```

```
        else
            if STRING[J + 1] in ['A' .. 'Z'] then
                begin
                    TOKEN.KIND := 'I';
                    K := 1;
                    repeat
                        TOKEN.NAME[K] := STRING[J + 1];
                        J := J + 1;
                        K := K + 1
                    until (not ((STRING[J + 1] in ['A' .. 'Z', '0' .. '9']) and (K <= FIVE)));
                    for L := K to FIVE do
                        TOKEN.NAME[L] := ' ';
                    while (STRING[J + 1] in ['A' .. 'Z', '0' .. '9']) do
                        J := J + 1;
                    SEARCH(TOKEN, FOUND, ADDRESS);
                    if FOUND then
                        TOKEN.ADDRESS := ADDRESS
                    else
                        begin
                            TOKEN.ADDRESS := LOCATION;
                            LOCATION := LOCATION + 1;
                            INSERT(TOKEN)
                        end
                end
end;

function FACTOR : boolean; forward;
function TERM : boolean; forward;
function BLOCK : boolean; forward;
function EXPRESSION : boolean; forward;

function PROGRM : boolean;
begin
    if BLOCK then
        begin
            GETTOKEN;
            if TOKEN.KIND = '.' then
                begin
                    PROGRM := true;
                    WRITELN('.')
                end
            else
                PROGRM := false
        end
end;

function BLOCK;
begin
    GETTOKEN;
    if TOKEN.KIND = 'I' then
        begin
            WRITE(TOKEN.ADDRESS);
```

```
                    GETTOKEN;
                if TOKEN.KIND = 'A' then
                    begin
                        if EXPRESSION then
                            begin
                                WRITE(':=');
                                if STRING[J + 1] = ';' then
                                    begin
                                        WRITELN(';');
                                        GETTOKEN;
                                        BLOCK := BLOCK
                                    end
                                else
                                    BLOCK := true
                            end
                        else
                            BLOCK := false
                    end
                else
                    BLOCK := false
end;

function EXPRESSION;
begin
    if TERM then
        begin
            if STRING[J + 1] = '+' then
                begin
                    GETTOKEN;
                    EXPRESSION := EXPRESSION;
                    WRITE('+')
                end
            else
                EXPRESSION := true
        end
    else
        EXPRESSION := false
end;

function TERM;
begin
    if FACTOR then
        begin
            if STRING[J + 1] = '*' then
                begin
                    GETTOKEN;
                    TERM := TERM;
                    WRITE('*')
                end
```

```
            else
                TERM := true
        end
    else
        TERM := false
end;

function FACTOR;
begin
    if STRING[J + 1] = '(' then
        begin
            GETTOKEN;
            if EXPRESSION then
                begin
                    if STRING[J + 1] = ')' then
                        begin
                            GETTOKEN;
                            FACTOR := true
                        end
                    else
                        FACTOR := false
                end
            else
                FACTOR := false
        end
    else
        begin
            GETTOKEN;
            if TOKEN.KIND in ['I', 'D'] then
                begin
                    FACTOR := true;
                    WRITE(TOKEN.ADDRESS)
                end
            else
                FACTOR := false
        end
end;

begin
    READSTRING(STRING, LENGTH);
    J := 0;
    T := 1;
    LOCATION := HND;
    if (PROGRM and (J = LENGTH)) then
        WRITE('VALID EXPRESSION')
    else
        WRITE('INVALID EXPRESSION')
end.
```

Although the input language allows rudimentary programs to be written, it is a far cry from a real programming language. For example there are no arrays, no procedures or functions, and no conditional or looping constructs available. These could each be added to the language, resulting in a more complex grammar and in additional modifications of this compiler. Error checking and diagnosis would further complicate the solution, as well as the actual translation of the postfix program produced into actual assembly language code of a particular computer. Still, the simple compiler constructed here should demonstrate the flexibility of the top-down approach.

Although top-down recursive compilers may be easier to implement, bottom-up compilers may be more efficient. Aho and Ullman [1977] should be consulted for a thorough treatment of compiler design. Wirth [1976] gives a compiler for a more complex example than the one we have presented here.

10.6 Compiler Conclusions

Compilers are complex programs. Writing them requires all the basic tools of computer science, from the application of top-down design with modularity to the proper selection of data structures. Careful interplay between the design of a high-level language, the creation of its grammar, and the development of its compiler is needed.

The theory of formal grammars has contributed heavily to the understanding and implementation of languages and their processors. Context-free grammars play an especially important role, and special classes of these grammars form the basis for compilers, whether the top-down or bottom-up approach is used.

These grammars are needed to specify most of the syntax of high-level languages. The syntactic analysis of a language underlies its proper semantic translation.

This chapter again demonstrates the importance of trees to the creation and understanding of solutions to a wide range of problems, and serves as a concrete example of the intimate connection between recursion, trees, and stacks.

☐ Exercises

1. Draw the derivation trees for $((A * B) + (C * D))$ and $A * B + C * D$, based on the first grammar of Section 10.2.

2. Write an unambiguous grammar for the language of sequences of paired expressions of Chapter 4, and another when four different matching pairs are allowed.

3. Extend the grammar for the simple expression language to include division as an operation. The language should reflect its normal priority, which is the same as multiplication. Make sure your grammar is unambiguous and allows recursive descent to be used for its parser.

4. Write an unambiguous grammar for logical expressions containing only letters and the logical operators "and" and "or." Assume "and" has higher priority than "or."

5. Write a context-free grammar for the language consisting of all sequences of n 0's followed by n 1's for $n \geq 1$.

6. Simulate the execution of the EXPRESSIONRECOGNIZER program on the expressions of Exercise 1.

7. Explain why recursive descent parsers take execution time proportional to the length of the input.

8. Explain why, had EXPRESSION been written to call EXPRESSION first, or TERM to call TERM first, infinite loops would occur in the parser of the EXPRESSION-RECOGNIZER program.

9. Why are parentheses not needed when prefix or postfix notation is used?

10. How do conventions eliminate ambiguity in infix notation?

11. Evaluate the postfix expression 3 6 + 6 2/ ∗ 8 + .

12. Simulate the execution of the algorithm of Section 10.3.2 for evaluation of an infix expression on $(A * B/(C + D)) + E ** F$.

13. Simulate the execution of the translation algorithm of Section 10.3.3 on $(A * B/(C + D)) + E ** F$.

14. What priority must be given to the assignment operator, $:=$, if the evaluation and translation algorithms for infix to postfix are to work on assignment statements as well as arithmetic expressions?

15. Write the function EVALUATE.

16. Describe how EVALUATE must be modified if arithmetic expressions are allowed to include function calls.

17. Explain why the structure of the EXPRESSIONRECOGNIZER program parallels that of the grammar.

18. Simulate the execution of the simple compiler for $(A + B) * C + D$.

19. Implement the symbol table of the simple compiler as a hash table.

20. Implement the symbol table of the simple compiler as a binary search tree.

21. Syntax diagrams given in Pascal texts are another means of specifying the grammar of a language. Consult such a text and write a function to recognize Pascal expressions. Assume functions are available to recognize other needed syntactic categories.

☐ Suggested Assignment

a. Modify the grammar of Section 10.5 and the compiler program so that instead of allowing only single digits, sequences of digits up to length 5 can be used.

b. Modify the grammar of Section 10.5 and the compiler program so that any number of blanks can appear between tokens.

c. Modify the grammar of Section 10.5 and the compiler program to obtain a recursive descent compiler that also allows the operations of subtraction, division, and exponentiation. The grammar must reflect the usual priority among the operators and must be unambiguous.

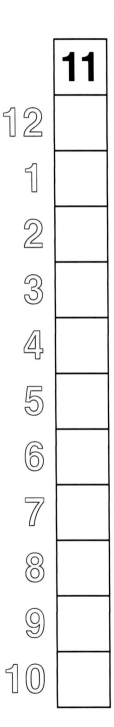

11 Huffman Coding and Optimal and Nearly Optimal Binary Search Trees

11.1 Techniques for Compressing Text or Storing Records

Many important techniques are available for the compression of text. Such compression is important when dealing with large collections of information, since internal memory is scarce and access to external memory is slow. Huffman coding is one elegant method that can be used profitably when text characters do not all appear with equal frequency (as is the case with the letters of the alphabet in English text).

Binary trees can be used as the basis for encoding text and for the creation of Huffman codes. Binary search trees can also be used. They generate codes of comparable efficiency but codes that can be found more quickly.

The application of binary search trees for key storage was demonstrated in Chapter 7. It was shown there that excellent average search times are achievable under random input when keys are accessed equally often and that AVL trees guarantee excellent worst-case search time. Optimal binary search trees are useful when the keys have known, even unequal frequencies, and when the trees, once grown, remain unchanged. An optimal binary search tree could be applied, for example, as a dictionary storing the 500 most frequently used English words, along with their definitions and their common misspellings. A search of the tree would then yield the definitions and misspellings.

This chapter shows that the problem of finding Huffman codes and the problem of finding optimal or nearly optimal binary search trees are related. The solutions illustrate the use of trees, heaps, and list-structures in the construction of good algorithms. The chapter also introduces the "greedy" heuristic. This is a method that leads to an optimal solution for finding Huffman codes and to a nearly optimal solution for finding binary search trees. In both cases, the proper selection of data structures plays a significant role.

11.2 Weighted Path Length

An important measure associated with binary trees is the weighted path length. This measure underlies the entire development in this chapter. Suppose a numeric weight is assigned to each node of a binary tree T.

These weights are related to the relative number of occurrences of characters in a text-compression application of binary trees or to the relative number of search requests for key values in a record-storage application. These weights must be estimated or else determined empirically for a specific application. The ***weighted path length of a node in T*** is the product of its depth and its assigned weight. The ***weighted path length of T***, $W(T)$, is the sum of the weighted path lengths of all nodes of T. As an example, consider the binary tree in Figure 11.1(a) with assigned weights indicated for each node. Its weighted path length is

$$(1 \times 3) + (2 \times 17) + (2 \times 10) + (3 \times 15) + (3 \times 0) + (3 \times 20) + (4 \times 31) + (4 \times 4)$$

or 302. This was calculated directly from the definition of the weighted path length.

Another way to determine the weighted path length is to determine first the value of each node of the tree. The ***value*** of a node is the sum of the assigned weights of all nodes in the subtree with that node as root. Thus the root of a tree is assigned a value that is the sum of all the weights of the tree. The example would have values assigned to each node as indicated in Figure 11.1(b). The weighted path length of the tree is then calculated by adding up the values of the nodes. Thus, from Figure 11.1(b), the weighted path length is

$$100 + 67 + 30 + 15 + 35 + 20 + 31 + 4 = 302$$

It is easy to see that adding the node values must always yield the weighted path length, since the weight of any node is counted once for every subtree in which it appears. For example, the weight 31 is counted in the value attached to each node from the node to which it is assigned to the root. This is a total of four nodes, exactly the number of times that the node's weight should count in the weighted path length.

The weighted path length can be viewed in still another way. It is given by the value of the root plus the weighted path length of the two subtrees of the root node. For the example shown in Figure 11.1(b) this is given by $100 + 152 + 50$, where 100 is the root's value and 152 and 50 are the left and right subtree's respective weighted path lengths.

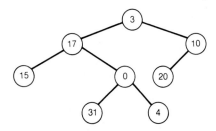

(a) Nodes Labeled with Assigned Weights

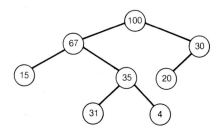

(b) Nodes Labeled with Values Derived by Adding Assigned Weights

Figure 11.1   Binary Tree T

11.3 Huffman Coding

Consider any binary tree with n terminal nodes. Assign a zero to every left successor branch, and a one to every right successor branch of the tree. *Encode* each terminal node with the sequence of 0's and 1's encountered when following the path from the root to the terminal node. Since this path is unique, the sequence or code assigned to each node must be unique. The code for the leftmost terminal node (N) in Figure 11.2, for example, is the sequence 00000. Any character, word, or information associated with a terminal node thus is encoded with the unique code for that node.

For example, in binary tree $T1$ shown in Figure 11.2 the twenty-six letters of the alphabet and the space character Δ were assigned to the terminal nodes.

The code assigned to the letter S in $T1$ is the sequence 00011 of length 5, one less than the depth of the encoded node to which S is assigned. In this way, a code is automatically generated for the twenty-seven characters associated with the terminal nodes of $T1$. Any string of these characters can then be encoded into a string

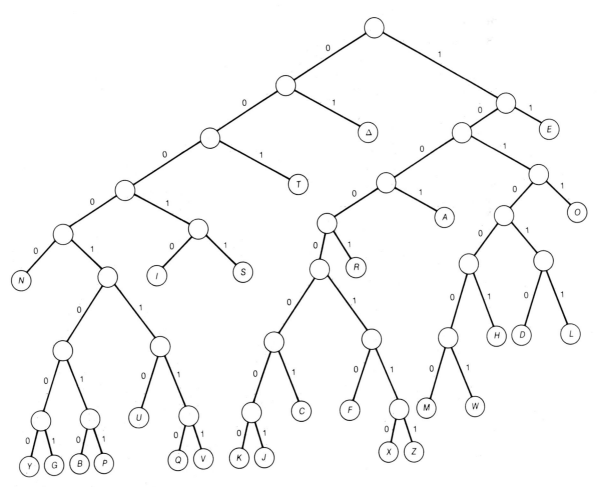

Figure 11.2 Binary Tree $T1$

of 0's and 1's. This string is simply the sequence of the combined sequences of 0's and 1's that constitute the codes for each of the characters in the string. For instance, the string of six characters "AΔTREE" will be encoded

100101001100011111

of length 18. Again, because each path is unique, given any two code words, one can never be an extension of another. Consequently no other sequence of code words will yield exactly this sequence of eighteen 0's and 1's and any sequence starting with these eighteen 0's and 1's must start with AΔTREE.

The tree $T1$ generates a *variable-length code*, since it does not assign the same length sequences of 0's and 1's to each character. A *fixed-length code* assigns equal-length strings of 0's and 1's to each character. A fixed-length code would be generated by a tree if each terminal node of the tree had the same depth.

One reason for encoding information might be to send it across a communication channel that transmits only sequences of 0's and 1's. Another reason might be to store character information in the memory of a computer. Since elements of computer memory actually store only sequences of 0's and 1's (by design), character information *must* be encoded. One way to encode the character set of a computer is by means of a standard fixed-length code, which uses six 0's and 1's per character.

The character set of a computer is the alphabet of characters that it can accept. For example, not all computers accept braces, that is, {}. Two important standard character sets are ASCII (American Standard Code for Information Exchange) and EBCDIC (Extended Binary Coded Decimal Interchange Codes). External BCD is used for storing information on magnetic tape and uses a six-bit code (six 0's and 1's) while ASCII and EBCDIC use seven and eight bits, respectively. An n-bit code can distinguish 2^n characters, and a sequence of L characters would then be represented by a sequence of $L \times n$ 0's and 1's. Variable-length codes are not constrained to using the same number of 0's and 1's for each character.

Storing a text in which the characters occur with different frequencies can be accomplished by compressing the text by using a variable-length code. Shorter length sequences would be assigned to characters used more frequently, and longer length sequences to characters used less frequently. This is the idea behind the Morse code. Morse, in fact, estimated the relative frequencies of characters by looking at the frequency with which printer's boxes containing the different characters of the alphabet needed to be refilled.

The use of fixed-length codes makes it easy to decode a sequence of 0's and 1's to recover the original sequence of characters or text. A variable-length code must be chosen with care, if it is to allow proper decoding and avoid ambiguity. One way to achieve such a code is to use the scheme outlined for Figure 11.2, which associates a code to each binary tree. Decoding the code generated by a given binary tree would then proceed as follows:

1. Start at the root of a binary tree that is identical to the one used for encoding the original text.
2. Follow the branches according to the dictates of the sequence of 0's and 1's to be decoded — go left for a 0 and right for a 1.

3. When a terminal node is reached, the sequence of 0's and 1's that led to it is decoded as the character associated with that terminal node.
4. Start again at the root to decode the remainder of the sequence in the same way.

The relative frequency with which each of twenty-six characters of the alphabet and the blank space between words occur in English text is as follows:

Δ	A	B	C	D	E	F	G	H	I	J	K	L	
186	64	13	22	32	103	21	15	47	57	1	5	32	
M	N	O	P	Q	R	S	T	U	V	W	X	Y	Z
20	57	63	15	1	48	51	80	23	8	18	1	16	1

These relative frequencies are used to assign weights to the nodes of a tree such as $T1$. Each internal node is assigned weight 0 and each terminal node is assigned the relative frequency of the character associated with it. Thus, node S of $T1$ is assigned weight 51. The *average amount of compression* is measured by the weighted path length of the tree. In this way, the amount of compression achieved with different codes can be compared, since each tree has associated with it a unique code. The *average length* of the assigned codes is obtained by subtracting 1 from the weighted path length when the weights are normalized to sum to 1. Weights are normalized by dividing each weight by the sum of all the weights. The designer of a compression scheme can make this calculation directly or write a program for this purpose.

The weighted path length of $T1$ can be improved. Take the subtree with root at depth 5, and I and S as its successors, and interchange it with T to obtain binary tree $T2$ (shown in Figure 11.3). The weights of I and S, 57 and 51, will now each contribute one less time to the weighted path length of $T2$ than to $T1$, while T, with weight 80, will contribute one more time to the weighted path length of $T2$ than to $T1$. The result is that the weighted path length of $T2$ will be $(57 \times 51) - 80$ less than that of $T1$.

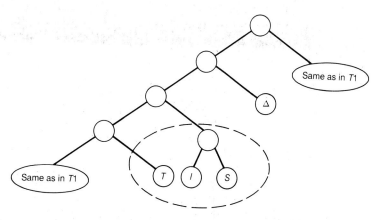

Figure 11.3   Binary Tree $T2$, Obtained by Interchanging Two Subtrees

The programmer's goal should be to find that binary tree, called the *optimal binary tree*, which has minimal weighted path length when the characters of the alphabet are stored at its n terminal nodes. Incidentally, the references here are to characters associated with the terminal nodes, but more generally, they can be words or messages. A straightforward algorithm for finding this optimal binary tree is to generate each binary tree with n terminal nodes, associate the alphabetic characters with these n nodes, and calculate the weighted path length of the tree. A tree that yields the minimal weighted path length is optimal. Unfortunately, this algorithm is feasible only for small n. If $n = 13$, there are more than 10^{12} such trees, and the number of trees increases by a factor of almost 4 each time n increases by 1.

11.3.1 The Huffman Algorithm

An optimal binary tree generates what is called a *Huffman code*. The searching just described is not needed to find it. It can be constructed as follows.

1. Start with a collection of n trees, each with just a root. Assign an alphabetic character to each of these nodes; the weight of the node is thus the weight associated with a certain character of the alphabet. The value of each of these root nodes is equivalent to its weight. (*Value* in this case equals the weight of the root itself since these trees have no other nodes.)
2. Find the two trees with smallest values. Combine them as the successors of a tree whose root has a value that is the sum of their values. Remove the two combined trees, and add the new tree obtained to the current collection of trees. Repeat the second step $n - 2$ times to obtain exactly one tree. This will be the optimal tree and will give the assignments of characters to terminal nodes.

When this algorithm is applied to the twenty-seven characters with their weights, the first combination made is J with Q, since each has weight 1. The resultant tree has value 2. Next X and Z, also each of weight 1, are combined, yielding another tree with value 2. These two trees are combined, yielding a tree with value 4. The current collection now consists of twenty-four trees. The next combination involves weights 4 and 5 and yields value 9. A final optimal tree that might result from the construction is shown in Figure 11.4. Other optimal trees could have been constructed, but they will all have the same weighted path length of 5,124. This means the average number of 0's and 1's needed per character will be 4.124, saving almost 20 percent over a fixed-length code of length 5 (the shortest fixed-length code that can distinguish twenty-seven characters).

This construction procedure is the *Huffman algorithm*. A proof is given later which shows that it does, in fact, produce an optimal binary tree. Notice that a cumulative total weight can be kept as the algorithm is carried out. To do this, start with the variable WEIGHT set at the sum of all the weights of the alphabetic characters. Every time two trees are combined, add the value of the resultant tree to WEIGHT. When the algorithm terminates, after making $(n - 1)$ combinations, WEIGHT will contain the weighted path length of the optimal binary tree constructed.

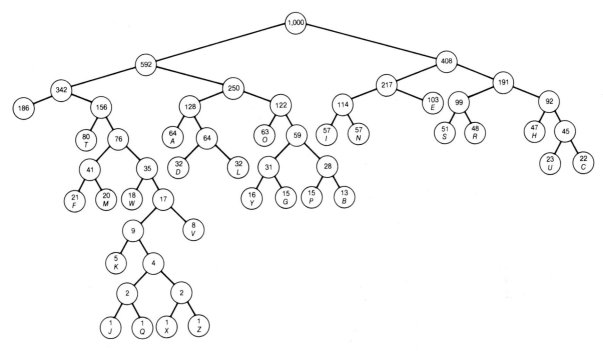

Figure 11.4 A Final Optimal Tree

The algorithm chooses that combination of current trees which yields a minimal value for the combined trees. It is in this sense that it is a "greedy" algorithm: it doesn't consider future ramifications of the current choice of subtrees to combine but takes the current two "best" subtrees. In this instance, *best* means "of smallest value." The algorithm makes a "local" best or greedy decision. It is an example of the *greedy* method of algorithm design which involves making choices on the basis of the immediate best alternative. This may lead to later choices being constrained to such poor alternatives as to lead to an overall suboptimal result. Being less greedy now may lead to better choices later, which in turn may yield better overall results. Hence it is not obvious that taking the best possible next combination, as done here, must lead to an optimal tree.

The greedy method does *not* yield optimal solutions in all situations. A traveler who applied the greedy method to selecting a route might always choose the next road because it is the shortest of all the current possibilities. This method will clearly not always yield the shortest *overall* route. When making change in U.S. currency using our system of 1-, 5-, 10-, 25-, 50-cent pieces and dollar bills, we normally use a greedy algorithm. For instance, to give $3.70 change most people would give three $1 bills, one 50-cent piece, and two dimes (not seven 50-cent pieces, one dime, and two nickels). The algorithm is greedy because it always takes as many pieces of currency of the next largest value as possible. This always minimizes the total number of pieces of currency used to make change in our system. If a system had 1-, 5-, 11-cent pieces and dollar bills, then making change "greedily" to give $3.70 would require three

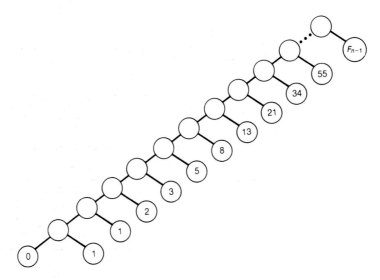

Figure 11.5 Tree Constructed by the Huffman Algorithm for Fibonacci Weights

$1 bills, six 11-cent pieces, and four pennies. Fewer pieces of currency result from using three dollar bills, five 11-cent pieces, and three nickels. Fortunately, the greedy method does yield optimal binary trees.

11.3.2 Representation of Huffman Trees

The Fibonacci sequence is the sequence of integers $F_0, F_1, F_2, \ldots$ that starts with $F_0 = 0$ and $F_1 = 1$, with each succeeding integer found by adding its two predecessors. Thus the sequence is $0, 1, 1, 2, 3, 5, 8, 13, 21, 34, 55, \ldots, F_{n-1}, \ldots$, where $F_0 = 0$, $F_1 = 1$, $F_{n+2} = F_{n+1} + F_n$, $n \geq 0$.

Example
11.1

Suppose that the first n Fibonacci numbers are assigned as weights to characters of an alphabet represented as terminal nodes in a tree. The task is to generate a Huffman code. □

The Huffman algorithm would construct the tree shown in Figure 11.5. This tree has depth n. Hence the Huffman algorithm may generate trees whose depth is $O(n)$. If a sequential representation were used for such trees, considerable storage would be wasted; for large n, the storage would not even be available. A good alternative is a linked representation of the tree.

11.3.3 Implementation

In this section the Huffman algorithm is implemented so that the Huffman tree and its weighted path length are generated. For a list of n records, a linked representation of the tree is illustrated in Figure 11.6(a) for $n = 5$ and weights 4, 3, 10, 2, 6.

The X's in the figure represent null pointers. The information field of each list record contains a pointer to a record representing the root of a binary tree. The

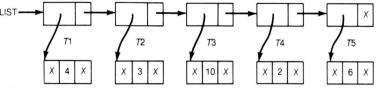

WEIGHT 25

(a) List of Five Records Pointing to Five Initial Trees of the Huffman Algorithm

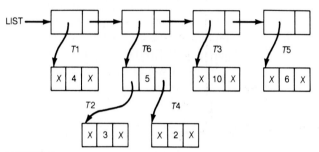

WEIGHT 30

(b) List after Combining Two Trees with Smallest Values

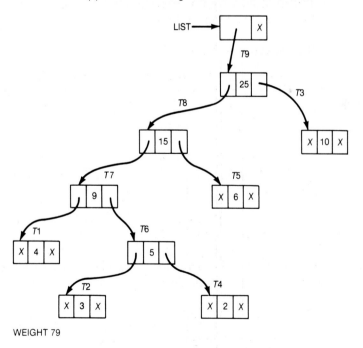

WEIGHT 79

(c) Final List and Huffman Tree after Repeated Combinings of Values

Figure 11.6 A Linked List Representing the Trees Constructed by the Huffman Algorithm

records of the tree might be stored using pointer variables or in arrays. The records have LEFTPTR, INFO, and RIGHTPTR fields, the INFO field containing the value assigned to the record's subtree by the Huffman algorithm. Thus each list record represents a tree. WEIGHT is a variable initially set to the sum of the n weights and incremented by the value attached to each combined tree.

The implementation could proceed by traversing the list to find the trees with the two smallest values and combining these trees as dictated by the algorithm into a new tree whose value would be the sum of their values. The two trees must be deleted from the list, and the new tree added to the list; the result is shown in Figure 11.6(b) after one combination has taken place.

Every time two trees are combined, the length of the list decreases by 1. The final list would contain one record; its information field would point to the root of the generated Huffman tree. WEIGHT would contain its weighted path length. For this example, the resultant list would be as shown in Figure 11.6(c).

The list traversal required to find the two smallest value trees results in a worst-case time proportional to the length of the list for each traversal. Since the tree must be traversed $n - 1$ times, the worst-case time is $O(n^2)$. We can do better.

To improve the implementation it is necessary to find the two smallest values quickly, without traversing the entire list. Recall that a heap, in this case a *min heap*, always has its smallest record at its root. Suppose the records of the binary tree are kept in a heap, or better, suppose the pointers are kept in the heap. Each pointer points to a corresponding record of the binary tree. The initial heap is shown in Figure 11.7.

To find the two smallest values simply remove the top heap pointer $T4$, reheap, and again remove the top pointer, $T2$. The records corresponding to the two smallest values can be combined. The new pointer to the combined record can then be placed at the top of the heap (which was left vacant), and the heap reheaped. Figure 11.7(b) shows the heap obtained by removing $T4$, reheaping, and removing $T2$. The two trees removed are combined and reheaping is done to obtain the heap shown in Figure 11.7(c).

With this implementation the computer time consumed in finding the two smallest values, combining their corresponding records, and reheaping is $O(\lg n)$. Since the entire process is repeated $(n - 1)$ times, the total time will be $O(n \lg n)$. It was the proper choice of data structure that made this improvement possible!

11.3.4 A Proof

For those readers who would like a proof of the Huffman construction, the following is an interesting example of the use of mathematical induction applied to trees. It can easily be adopted to prove that a recursive program for the Huffman algorithm is correct.

Assume the weights are $w_1, w_2, \ldots, w_n$ and are indexed so $w_1 \leq w_2 \leq \ldots \leq w_n$. An optimal tree can always be found since the number of trees with n nodes is finite. It is clear that the Huffman construction yields optimal trees for $n = 1$ and 2. This is the basis for the induction, which will be on the number of weights or terminal nodes, n. The induction hypothesis is that the Huffman construction yields optimal trees for any $n - 1$ weights. We must show that as a result, it must generate optimal trees for n weights.

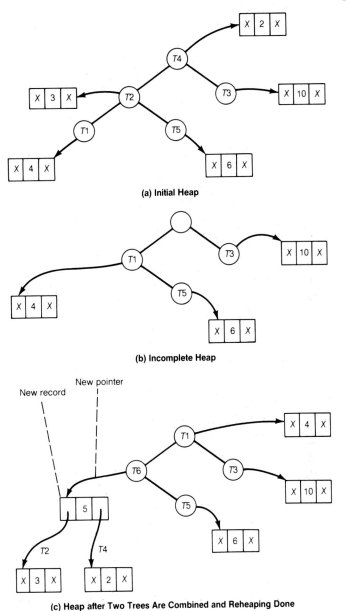

(a) Initial Heap

(b) Incomplete Heap

(c) Heap after Two Trees Are Combined and Reheaping Done

Figure 11.7   Heap of Pointers of the Fibonacci Tree

Given any tree with n terminal nodes, T_n, in which Figure 11.8(a) appears as a subtree, let T'_{n-1} be the tree with $n-1$ terminal nodes obtained from T_n by replacing this subtree by the terminal node shown in Figure 11.8(b). Then the weighted path length of T_n equals the weighted path length of $T'_{n-1} + (w_1 + w_2)$.

Given T'_{n-1}, inversely, T_n can be obtained from it. Therefore, T_n must be optimal with respect to weights $w_1, w_2, \ldots, w_n$, if and only if T'_{n-1} is optimal with respect to weights $(w_1 + w_2), w_3, \ldots, w_n$. This is because if only one tree were not

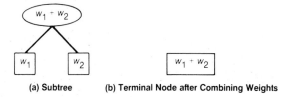

(a) Subtree   (b) Terminal Node after Combining Weights

Figure 11.8   Subtree Replacement

optimal, it could be replaced by an optimal tree, thus improving the weighted path length of the corresponding version of the other.

By the induction hypothesis, the Huffman construction yields a tree, T'_{n-1}, with $n-1$ terminal nodes that is optimal with respect to weights $(w_1 + w_2), w_3, \ldots, w_n$. The corresponding tree, T_n, with n terminal nodes is just the tree given by the Huffman construction for weights $w_1, w_2, \ldots, w_n$. Since T'_{n-1} is optimal so is T_n. This completes the proof.

11.4 Optimal Binary Search Trees

So far we have been considering binary trees with nonzero weights assigned only to terminal nodes, and with attention focused on terminal nodes. We now consider **extended binary search trees**, which have keys stored at their internal nodes.

Suppose n keys, $K_1, K_2, \ldots, K_n$, are stored at the internal nodes of a binary search tree. It is assumed that the keys are given in *sorted* order, so that $K_1 < K_2 < \ldots < K_n$. An extended binary search tree is obtained from the binary search tree by adding successor nodes to each of its terminal nodes as indicated in Figure 11.9 by □'s.

Although the programming goal in this chapter is to find optimal binary search trees, extended binary search trees are used along the way. In the extended tree, the □'s represent terminal nodes, while the other nodes are internal nodes. These terminal nodes represent unsuccessful searches of the tree for key values. The searches did not end successfully, that is, because they represent key values that are not actually stored in the tree.

In general, the terminal node in the extended tree that is the left successor K_1 can be interpreted as representing all key values that are not stored and are *less than* K_1. Similarly, the terminal node in the extended tree that is the right successor of K_n represents all key values not stored in the tree that *are greater* than K_n. The terminal node that is accessed between K_i and K_{i+1} in an inorder traversal represents all key values not stored that lie *between* K_i and K_{i+1}. For example, in the extended tree in Figure 11.9(b), if the possible key values are $0, 1, 2, 3, \ldots, 100$ then the terminal node labeled 0 represents the missing key values 0, 1, and 2 if K_1 is 3. The terminal node labeled 3 represents the key values between K_3 and K_4. If K_3 is 17 and K_4 is 21, then the terminal node labeled 3 represents the missing key values 18, 19, and 20. If K_6 is 90, then terminal node 6 represents the missing key values 91 through 100.

Assuming that the relative frequency with which each key value is accessed is known, weights can be assigned to each node of the extended tree. They represent the relative frequencies of searches terminating at each node. The weighted path

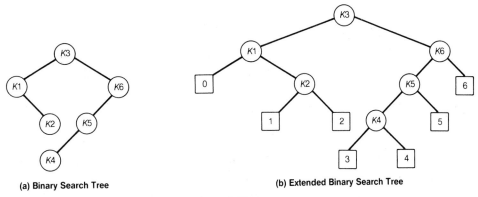

(a) Binary Search Tree   (b) Extended Binary Search Tree

Figure 11.9 Extension of a Binary Search Tree

length of the extended tree is then a natural measure for the average time to search the binary search tree for a key.

Example 11.2   Find the extended binary search tree that has the minimal weighted path length. The optimal binary search tree is obtained from this tree simply by omitting the extended nodes. □

If the weights attached to the internal nodes of the extended binary search tree are zero, this problem is similar to the Huffman coding problem. The difference is that the task is to find the binary *search* tree with minimal weighted path length, whereas the Huffman algorithm finds the binary tree with minimal weighted path length. Since the binary search trees are only a subset of all binary trees, the Huffman tree will yield a value of the minimal weighted path length that is never larger than that of the optimal binary search tree. The Huffman algorithm will not solve the current problem unless, by chance, the tree that it constructs is a binary search tree or can be converted to one with no increase in the weighted path length. An algorithm, the Hu–Tucker algorithm, has been developed for this special case, and requires, as does the Huffman algorithm, time $O(n \lg n)$ and $O(n)$ storage. Initially, its time was thought to be $O(n^2)$, but Knuth showed how to reduce this time by selecting the appropriate data structure.

11.4.1 Finding Optimal Binary Search Trees

An obvious way to find an optimal binary search tree is to generate each possible binary search tree for the keys, calculate its weighted path length, and keep that tree with the smallest weighted path length. This search through all possible solutions is not feasible except for small n, since the number of such trees grows exponentially with n. A feasible alternative would be a recursive algorithm based on the structure inherent in optimal binary search trees. Such an algorithm can be developed in a way similar to that used for the construction of Fibonacci trees in Chapter 6.

How do we decompose the optimal search tree problem in Example 11.2 into components with the same structure? Consider the characteristics of any optimal tree. Of course it has a root and two subtrees. A moment's reflection should convince you that both subtrees must themselves be optimal binary search trees with respect to their keys and weights. First, any subtree of any binary search tree must be a binary search tree. Second, the subtrees must also be optimal. Otherwise, they could be replaced by optimal subtrees with smaller weighted path lengths, which would imply that the original tree could not have been optimal.

Since there are n possible keys as candidates for the root of the optimal tree, the recursive solution must try them all. For each candidate key as root, all keys less than that key must appear in its left subtree while all keys greater than it must appear in its right subtree. To state the recursive algorithm based on these observations requires some notation.

Denote the weights assigned to the n stored keys by β's and the weights assigned to the terminal nodes by α's. The weight assigned to K_i is β_i for $i = 1, 2, \ldots, n$, and that assigned to the external nodes labeled i is α_i for $i = 0, 1, 2, \ldots, n$. Let OBST(i, j) denote the optimal binary search tree containing keys $K_i, \ldots, K_j$, and let $W(i, j)$ denote its weighted path length. OBST(i, j) will involve weights α_{i-1}, $\beta_i, \ldots, \beta_j, \alpha_j$.

The optimal tree with root constrained to be K_k and containing keys $K_i, \ldots, K_k, \ldots, K_j$ must then have OBST$(i, k - 1)$ as its left subtree and OBST$(k + 1, \ldots, j)$ as its right subtree. Its weighted path length, $W(i, j)$, is given by $SW(i, j) + W(i, k - 1) + W(k + 1, j)$, where $SW(i, j)$ is the sum of the weights $\alpha_{i-1}, \beta_i, \ldots, \beta_j, \alpha_j$. $SW(i, j)$ is the value assigned to the root of OBST(i, j), the sum of its weights.

Finally the algorithm can be stated.

For each K_k as root, $k = 1, 2, \ldots, n$
   find OBST$(1, k - 1)$ and OBST$(k + 1, n)$.

Find a k that minimizes $[W(1, k - 1) + W(k + 1, n)]$ over $k = 1, 2, \ldots, n$.

OBST$(1, n)$ is given by the tree with root K_k, OBST$(1, k - 1)$ as its left subtree, and OBST$(k + 1, n)$ as its right subtree.

The weighted path length of OBST$(1, n)$ is $W(1, n)$. $W(1, n) = SW(1, n) + W(1, k - 1) + W(k + 1, n)$.

The execution tree for OBST$(1, 4)$ is given in Figure 11.10. Apparently this algorithm exhibits the same proliferation of recursive calls for identical component problems as did the algorithm for the Fibonacci tree construction in Chapter 6. These are summarized in Table 11.1. This inefficiency can be avoided by using a bottom-up construction, just as was done before for Fibonacci trees. To do this requires a clear understanding of exactly which optimal subtrees must be retained for later reference.

All possible optimal subtrees are not required. Those that are consist of sequences of keys that are immediate successors of the smallest key in the subtree, successors in the sorted order for the keys. The final solution tree contains all n keys. There will be two with $n - 1$ keys, three with $n - 2$ keys, four with $n - 3$ keys, and in general $k + 1$ with $n - k$ keys, for $k = 0, 1, 2, \ldots, n$. Consequently there are a total of $(n + 1) \times (n + 2)/2$ optimal subtrees to be retained. Notice that to determine OBST(i, j) requires knowing the optimal smaller subtrees involving weights:

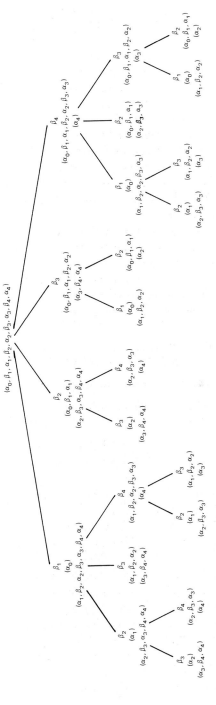

Figure 11.10 The Execution Tree for $n = 4$

(α_{i-1}) and $(\alpha_i, \beta_{i+1}, \ldots, \beta_j, \alpha_j)$ i.e., OBST$(i, i-1)$ and OBST$(i+1, j)$

$(\alpha_{i-1}, \beta_i, \alpha_i)$ and $(\alpha_{i+1}, \beta_{i+2}, \ldots, \beta_j, \alpha_j)$ i.e., OBST(i, j) and OBST$(i+2, j)$

$$\vdots$$

$(\alpha_{i-1}, \beta_i, \ldots, \beta_{j-1}, \alpha_{j-1})$ and (α_j) i.e., OBST$(i, j-1)$ and OBST$(j+1, j)$.

The bottom-up approach generates all smallest required optimal subtrees first, then all next smallest, and so on until the final solution involving all the weights is found. Since the algorithm requires access to each subtree's weighted path length, these weighted path lengths must also be retained to avoid their recalculation. Finally, the root of each subtree must also be stored for reference.

This algorithm requires $O(n^3)$ execution time and $O(n^2)$ storage. Knuth, who developed this solution, noticed an important fact that reduces the execution time to $O(n^2)$. He was able to show that the minimization need not be over all k from 1 to n. Instead, the minimization may be taken only over all k between $r(i, j-1)$ and $r(i+1, j)$, where $r(i, j)$ denotes the root of OBST(i, j). See Knuth [1973b].

Intuitively this is plausible because OBST$(i, j-1)$ is the optimal binary search tree containing keys $K_i, \ldots, K_{r(i, j-1)}, \ldots, k_{j-1}$. Thus taking $K_{r(i, j-1)}$ as its root gives the tree just the "balance" it needs to be optimal, distributing keys to its left and right subtrees in the optimal way. OBST(i, j) includes K_j as well. If its root is also $K_{r(i, j-1)}$, then K_j will appear in the right subtree of this optimal tree adding more weight to its right subtree. Think of the optimal tree as "balanced"; its root should not be a predecessor of $K_{r(i, j-1)}$, since this would cause even more weight to appear in its right subtree. Reasoning this way, it is not unreasonable to expect the root of OBST(i, j) to be $K_{r(i, j-1)}$ or one of its *successors*. Thus looking only at k where $r(i, j-1) \leq k$ should suffice. A symmetric argument should make it equally reasonable that looking only at k, $k \geq r(i+1, j)$ should suffice. The actual proof is complex and adds little insight, and hence is omitted here.

The bottom-up algorithm, incorporating the new minimization limits, may now be written.

Table 11.1 Components Replicated by
Recursive Calls

Replicated Component	Occurrences
$(\alpha_2, \beta_3, \alpha_3, \beta_4, \alpha_4)$	2
$(\alpha_0, \beta_1, \alpha_1, \beta_2, \alpha_2)$	2
$(\alpha_1, \beta_2, \alpha_2, \beta_3, \alpha_3)$	2
$(\alpha_0, \beta_1, \alpha_1)$	4
$(\alpha_1, \beta_2, \alpha_2)$	5
$(\alpha_2, \beta_3, \alpha_3)$	5
$(\alpha_3, \beta_4, \alpha_4)$	4
(α_0)	4
(α_1)	3
(α_2)	4
(α_3)	3
(α_4)	4

1. For i from 0 to n
   a. Set $W(i + 1, i)$ to 0 and $SW(i + 1, i)$ to α_i
   b. For j from $i + 1$ to n
      Set $SW(i + 1, j)$ to $SW(i + 1, j - 1) + \beta_j + \alpha_j$

2. For j from 1 to n
   a. Set $W(j, j)$ to $SW(j, j)$ and $r(j, j)$ to j.
      (This initializes all OBST's containing 0 keys and 1 key.)

3. For L from 2 to n
   a. For j from L to n,
      i. set i to $j - L + 1$;
      ii. set $W(i, j)$ to $SW(i, j) + \text{minimum}[W(i, k - 1) + W(k + 1, j)]$, the minimum to be over k satisfying $r(i, j - 1) \le k \le r(i + 1, j)$ and set $r(i, j)$ to a value of k corresponding to the minimum.

Actually, the $W(i, j)$'s will differ from the weighted path length of OBST(i, j) by the sum of $\alpha_{i-1}, \dots, \alpha_i, \dots, \alpha_j$. This does not affect the final tree but means that to obtain the true weighted path length, $(\alpha_0 + \alpha_1 + \dots + \alpha_n)$ must be added to $W(1, n)$.

Arrays for W, WS, and r seem to be a natural choice for implementing this algorithm and provide rapid access to the information required for the processing involved.

Example 11.3 Find the optimal binary search tree for $n = 6$ and weights $\beta_1 = 10$, $\beta_2 = 3$, $\beta_3 = 9$, $\beta_4 = 2$, $\beta_5 = 0$, $\beta_6 = 10$, $\alpha_0 = 5$, $\alpha_1 = 6$, $\alpha_2 = 4$, $\alpha_3 = 4$, $\alpha_4 = 3$, $\alpha_5 = 8$, and $\alpha_6 = 0$. $\square$

Figure 11.11(a) shows the arrays as they would appear after the initialization, and 11.11(b) gives their final disposition. The actual optimal tree is shown in Figure 11.12; it has a weighted path length of 188.

Since this algorithm requires $O(n^2)$ time and $O(n^2)$ storage, as n increases it will run out of storage even before it runs out of time. The storage needed can be reduced by almost half, at the expense of a slight increase in time, by implementing the two-dimensional arrays as one-dimensional arrays using the technique of Chapter 2. Using one-dimensional arrays may enable problems to be solved that otherwise will abort because of insufficient storage. In any case, the algorithm is feasible only for moderate values of n.

In order to understand exactly how the algorithm creates the optimal tree, you should simulate the algorithm to reproduce the arrays of Figure 11.11.

11.5 Nearly Optimal Binary Search Trees

To date, no one knows how to construct the *optimal* binary search tree using less time or storage in the general case of nonzero α's and β's. For this reason it is important to develop algorithms that produce good, but not necessarily optimal, solutions with less time and storage being required. Algorithms have been found that construct *nearly optimal binary search trees*. The weighted path lengths of such trees cannot differ by more than a constant factor from the optimal value.

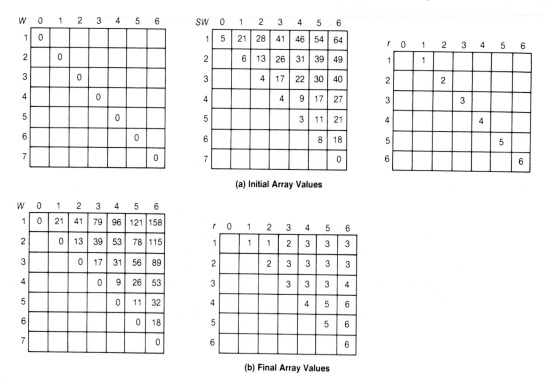

Figure 11.11   Arrays Used to Implement the Bottom-up Recursive Algorithm for Finding Optimal Binary Search Trees

11.5.1 Greedy Binary Search Trees

One such algorithm produces *greedy binary search trees*. These trees are constructed by an algorithm using the greedy method. Unlike the Huffman algorithm, which is also based on the greedy method, they are not guaranteed to be optimal, but *are* guaranteed to be nearly optimal. Other distinct nearly optimal tree constructions are found in Mehlhorn [1975, 1977] and in Horibe and Nemetz [1979]. A comparison of all these and other algorithms for the generation of nearly optimal binary search trees appears in Korsh [1982]. The proof that the following greedy method yields nearly optimal trees is in Korsh [1981].

In constructing a nearly optimal binary search tree by the greedy method, the programmer must ensure that the solution *is* a binary search tree. Looking at the optimal tree (Figure 11.12) found by the preceding section's algorithm will provide the idea behind the greedy tree construction. Think of the tree being generated by creating the subtrees shown in Figure 11.13, one after another, starting with the subtree with K_4 at its root and ending with the final optimal tree. Each subtree has its value, the sum of its weights, associated with it.

Each subtree is formed by taking for its root a key that has not yet appeared, and adjoining a left and right subtree. These subtrees may correspond to an extended node (with weight some α_i) or to an already produced subtree. The value of the subtree formed is given by the β_i of its key plus the value of its left and right subtrees.

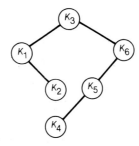

Figure 11.12 The Optimal Binary Search Tree Found by Means of the Bottom-up Recursive Algorithm

These subtrees must be selected in a constrained fashion, or the resultant tree will not be a binary *search* tree. These constraints will appear shortly, but for now, the main point is that the weighted path of the optimal tree is the sum of the values of each of these subtrees. The greedy trees are built by always selecting the next subtree to generate as the one with smallest value from among all those satisfying the constraints. This is exactly how the Huffman construction works, except there are no constraints on the choice of subtrees since the resultant tree need not be a binary *search* tree.

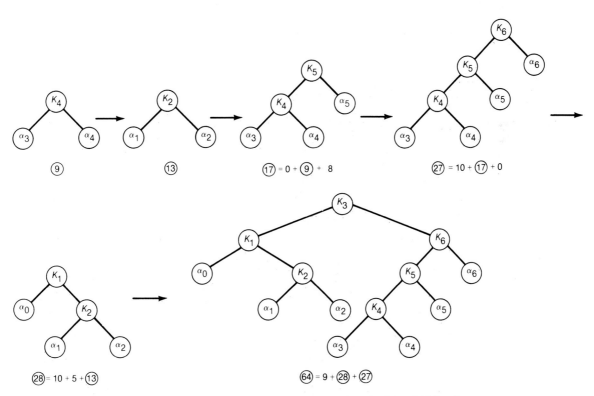

Figure 11.13 Trees Created from Subtrees (Circled Numbers Are the Trees' Values)

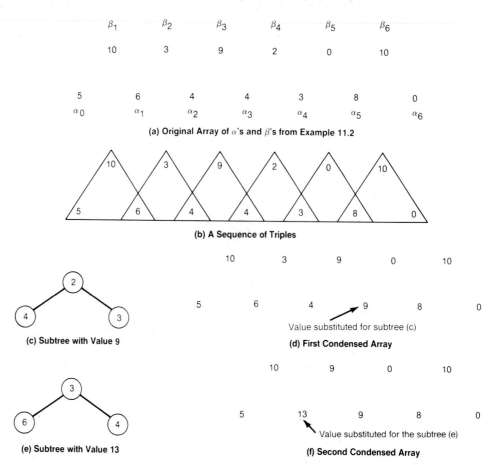

(a) Original Array of α's and β's from Example 11.2

(b) A Sequence of Triples

(c) Subtree with Value 9

(d) First Condensed Array

Value substituted for subtree (c)

(e) Subtree with Value 13

(f) Second Condensed Array

Value substituted for the subtree (e)

Figure 11.14 Construction of Greedy Binary Search Tree

11.5.2 Greedy Construction

To start the development, we use the α's and β's of Example 11.3 and array them as shown in Figure 11.14(a). In an inorder traversal of *any* binary search tree with the six keys, the weights assigned to the accessed nodes would occur in the order $\alpha_0\ \beta_1\ \alpha_1\ \beta_2\ \alpha_2\ \beta_3$ and so on. This sequence looks like *triples;* see Figure 11.14(b). A value can be associated with each triple by summing up its weights. Thus the triples just shown have values 21, 13, 17, 9, 11, and 18, respectively. A greedy tree is constructed by always finding an allowed triple with minimal value and generating its corresponding subtree next. The weighted path length of the resultant tree is the sum of the weights of the $(n-1)$ triples thus created.

The greedy construction procedure is as follows. The allowable triples shown in the array have values 21, 13, 17, 9, 11, and 18. The triple with the lowest value (9) is

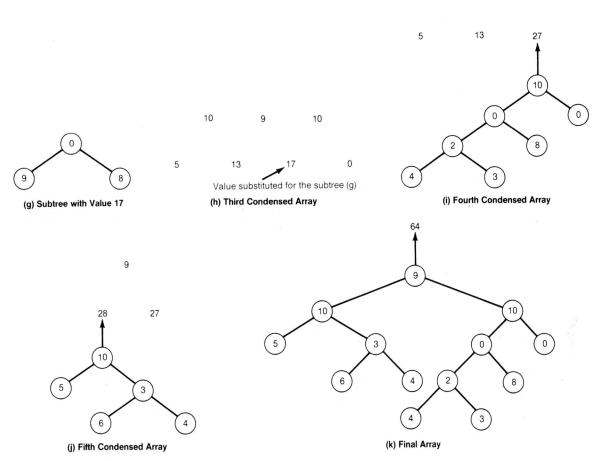

(g) Subtree with Value 17

(h) Third Condensed Array

(i) Fourth Condensed Array

(j) Fifth Condensed Array

(k) Final Array

Figure 11.14   *(continued)*

Combining the corresponding key and terminal nodes yields the subtree shown in Figure 11.14(c). Its assigned value is the triple value 9. Delete that triple from the array, and replace it by a terminal node value of 9 as shown in Figure 11.14(d).

Now repeat this process. The next minimal value is 13, corresponding to the triple

$$3$$
$$6 \qquad 4$$

This gives the subtree shown in Figure 11.14(e). The condensed array is shown in Figure 11.14(f). Repeating the process finds the minimal triple whose value is 17; the corresponding subtree is Figure 11.14(g). The new array is shown in Figure 11.14(h). Continuing in this fashion produces the arrays shown in Figure 11.14(i), (j), and (k).

The greedy tree thus constructed by always taking the minimal triple is shown in Figure 11.15. Its weighted path length can be found by keeping an accumulated

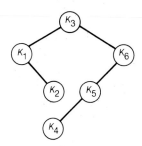

Figure 11.15   Greedy Binary Search Tree Constructed as Illustrated in Figure 11.14

sum as in the Huffman algorithm. In this case the greedy algorithm actually yields the optimal tree.

11.5.3 Implementation

Just as in the Huffman tree construction, if we are not careful we will end up with an $O(n^2)$ time implementation. Instead, a heap can be used similar to that for the Huffman construction, to obtain an $O(n \lg n)$ time requirement and $O(n)$ storage. However, we can do even better.

This method would lead to a sequence of $n - 1$ combined triples with values ν_1, $\nu_2, \ldots, \nu_{n-1}$. In this sequence, $\nu_1 \le \nu_2 \le \ldots \le \nu_{n-1}$. That is, the triples are generated in order, from smallest to highest value. The algorithm introduced now also generates a sequence of $n - 1$ combined triples, but their values will not necessarily be the same as $\nu_1, \nu_2, \ldots, \nu_{n-1}$, nor will they necessarily be generated in order by size, smallest to largest. The algorithm, however, will produce that greedy tree that would have been obtained had they been combined in order by size when it is unique. A unique tree exists when there is exactly one smallest triple at each step. In general, the resultant tree will be greedy, but will not necessarily be the same greedy tree generated by $\nu_1, \nu_2, \ldots, \nu_{n-1}$, nor will it necessarily have the same weighted path length.

We start with a list-structure illustrated in Figure 11.16. Each record represents a potential triple to be combined in the construction of a greedy tree. Traverse the list starting at the left and search for a *locally* minimal triple, that is, a triple whose value does not exceed the value of its successor triple. No triple to the left of this locally minimal triple can be combined before it in any greedy tree construction. In addition, any future combining of locally minimal triples to its right cannot cause the resultant tree to fail to be greedy. In other words, combining the minimal triple always allows a greedy tree to be constructed with the combined minimal triple as a subtree. So, combine the locally minimal triple (say it is the *i*th), and obtain the new list-structure shown in Figure 11.16(b).

Here α'_{i-1} and α'_i were both set to the value of the combined triple $\alpha_{i-1} + \beta_i + \alpha_i$, the *i*th record was deleted, and the pointers changed as shown. The left to right traversal is continued, starting now at the $(i - 2)$th record, combining as before for each locally minimal triple encountered. Details involving the ends of the list-structure can be handled by special checking or by introducing artificial records with large weights at the ends. This results in the construction of a greedy tree. This procedure is reminiscent of the evaluation of an infix expression of Chapter 10. That algorithm is greedy in the sense that we look for the highest local priority operator to evaluate first in a left to right scan, evaluate it, and continue from that point. Applying this algorithm to Example 11.3, the starting list-structure is as shown in Figure 11.16(c).

The first locally minimal triple found is 6 3 4; the list-structure resulting from combining it is shown in Figure 11.16(d). Starting again at the first record, 4 2 3 is the next minimal triple, yielding the list shown in Figure 11.16(e). Starting again, the first record here is found to be the locally minimal triple to obtain the list shown in Figure 11.16(f).

Starting again at the next first record, 9 0 8 is the next locally minimal triple, and gives the list shown in Figure 11.16(g). Again, we start at the first record; the next locally minimal triple is 17 10 0. The result is shown in Figure 11.16(h). Finally, the triple 28 9 27 is combined to obtain the result shown in Figure 11.16(i).

We have constructed the same tree as before (in Figures 11.14 and 11.15). Again, this need not always occur. Even when it does however, as here, the order in which the subtrees were formed need not be the same. We generated subtrees here with values 13, 9, 28, 17, 27, and finally 64, rather than in order from smallest to largest as in the other method. Both trees in this example have the same weighted path length of 188.

This implementation takes time and storage only $O(n)$! This was made possible by the new method coupled with the proper choice of data structure.

11.5.4 Alphabetic Codes

Consider the twenty-seven characters of the alphabet with relative frequencies given in Section 11.3 as weights. Order them as $\Delta < A < B < C < \ldots < Z$. Suppose we want to construct an extended binary *search* tree with these characters associated with the terminal nodes. We take the weights given there as the α's of this problem, and take the β's to be zero. The extended binary search tree will then generate what is called an *alphabetic code*. The optimal binary search tree will have weighted path length 5,200, and the greedy binary search tree will have weighted path length 5,307. Recall that the Huffman tree had weighted path length 5,124. Requiring use of a binary search tree rather than a binary tree results in an increase relative to 5,124 of only $(5,200 - 5,124)/5,124$ or 1.5 percent. The greedy construction yields an increase relative to 5,200 of $(5,307 - 5,200)/5,200$ or 2%.

11.6 Conclusion

Binary trees are useful data structures for encoding and decoding information. The Huffman algorithm generates optimal binary trees for this purpose and can do so efficiently. Binary search trees are useful data structures for storing information that is to be searched; they also produce good codes.

Greedy binary search trees, which are nearly optimal, can be generated very efficiently. The greedy method of algorithm design does not yield optimal solutions but may still yield very good solutions. Again, it was demonstrated that careful selection of data structures can significantly change the time requirements of an algorithm.

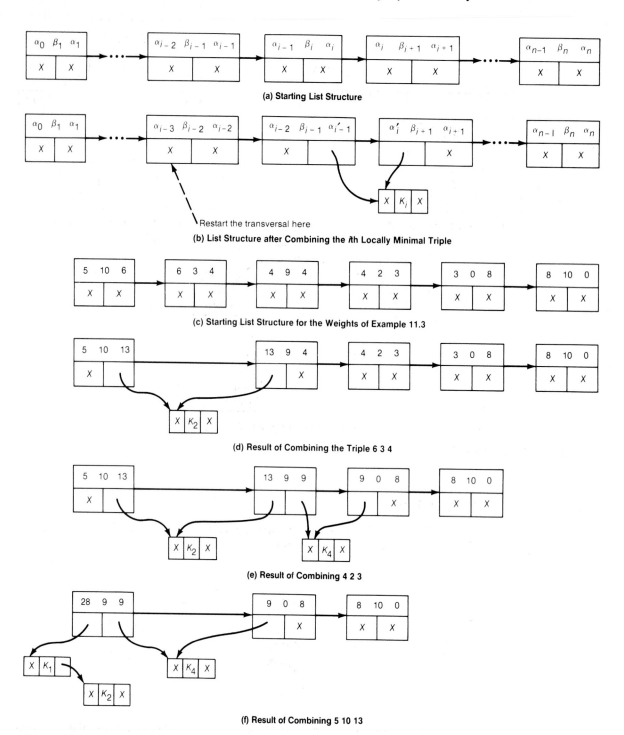

Figure 11.16   Implementation of the Greedy Algorithm

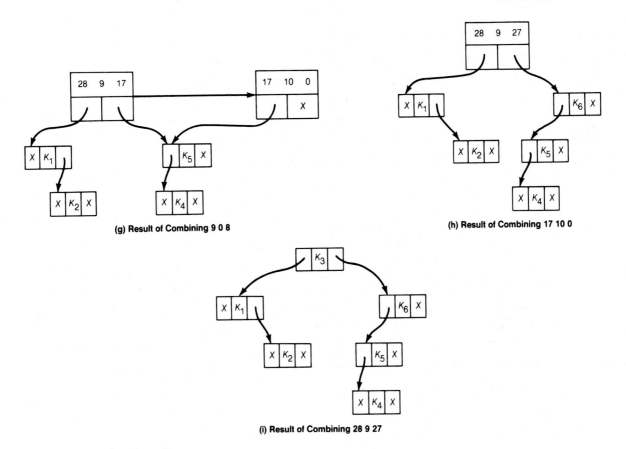

(g) Result of Combining 9 0 8

(h) Result of Combining 17 10 0

(i) Result of Combining 28 9 27

Figure 11.16 *(continued)*

□ **Exercises**

1. **a.** Using the definition, calculate the weighted path length of the following tree. The weight of a node appears at the node.

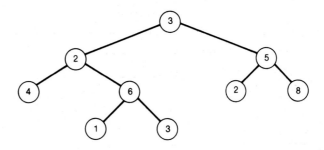

b. Calculate the weighted path length of the tree using the other method of assigning a "value" to each node and adding up all the "values."

c. Calculate the weighted path length of the same tree by adding the sum of all its weights to the weighted path length of its left subtree plus the weighted path length of its right subtree.

2. Write a PROCESS routine to turn a postorder traversal into a procedure for determining the weighted path length of a binary tree T based on the method of Exercise 1b.

3. Determine the Huffman code (tree) for weights 1, 2, 3, 4, 5.

4. Determine the weighted path length for your solution to Exercise 3.

5. The Huffman tree for n weights will always have $(n - 1)$ internal nodes and n terminal nodes. This is because it is a *full* binary tree. That is, every internal node has exactly 0 or exactly two successors. Prove, by induction on the total number of nodes of a full binary tree, that this is true.

6. Write a nonrecursive procedure, HUFFMAN, with parameters N, WEIGHTS, TREE, and CODE. WEIGHTS is an array containing N WEIGHTS, CODE is an array returned containing the N codes (sequences of 0's and 1's) assigned to each weight by the Huffman code, and TREE points to the root of the corresponding Huffman tree upon return. Your procedure should take $O(n \lg n)$ time.

7. Write a recursive version of the procedure of Exercise 6.

8. Simulate the proof by induction on n, that the Huffman tree yields a binary tree with minimal weighted path length for n weights for Exercise 3.

9. Write a procedure DECODE with parameters N, ALPHA, and TREE. ALPHA is a sequence of N 0's and 1's, and TREE points to a Huffman tree for the twenty-seven characters of Section 11.3 (determined by their weights). DECODE is to decode the sequence of N 0's and 1's into the corresponding characters. The sequence represents a coded version of a message composed of the characters.

10. Suppose you know the Huffman tree for the twenty-seven characters of Section 11.3 (determined by their weights). Write a procedure ENCODE to encode a message composed of the characters into the Huffman code. To do this you might consider the use of the following data structures:

a. The Huffman tree

b. An array with twenty-seven records kept in sorted order by character, each record containing a character and its corresponding Huffman code

c. A hash table of records, each record consisting of a character and its Huffman code — the key is the character

Discuss the relative advantages and disadvantages for each of these in the procedure ENCODE.

11. Write a procedure ENCODE to encode a message in a Huffman code.

12. Let $\alpha_0 = 10$, $\alpha_1 = 6$, $\alpha_2 = 8$, $\alpha_3 = 4$, $\alpha_4 = 2$, $\beta_1 = 2$, $\beta_2 = 5$, $\beta_3 = 7$, and $\beta_4 = 6$. Determine the optimal binary search tree by generating all possible binary search trees storing the three keys with weights 2, 5, and 7, and calculating their weighted path lengths.

13. The recursive approach of Section 11.4.1 is based on the idea that an optimal binary search tree must have an optimal left and an optimal right subtree. Can you use this idea to show that some of the trees you considered in Exercise 12 could have been ignored in searching for the optimal tree?

14. Simulate the bottom-up algorithm of Section 11.4.1 to reproduce the arrays of Figure 11.11.

15. Why do we want to find nearly optimal binary search trees rather than optimal search trees for large numbers of keys?

16. Find the greedy binary search tree for the weights of Exercise 12 using the definition of a greedy tree, and determine the relative difference between its weighted path length and the optimal value.

17. Find the greedy binary search tree for the weights of Exercise 12 using the implementation of the greedy tree construction. Is its weighted path length the same as the greedy tree of Exercise 16?

18. Write a nonrecursive procedure GREEDY to implement the greedy tree construction of Section 11.5.3.

19. Give a recursive definition of a greedy binary search tree.

20. Write a recursive procedure GREEDY to implement the greedy tree construction of Section 11.5.3.

21. Another method of constructing a nearly optimal binary search tree is to select the key to be placed at the root to be a key that minimizes the difference between the weights of its left and right subtrees. Having obtained the root, apply this procedure recursively to construct its left and right subtrees. This is a top-down construction as opposed to the greedy tree construction, which is bottom-up. What tree does it generate for the weights of Exercise 12 and for the example of Section 11.5.2?

22. Write a recursive procedure for the construction method of Exercise 21. How much time does your procedure require?

23. Can you find a way to implement the procedure of Exercise 21 in $O(n)$ time, where n is the number of internal keys to be stored?

24. What will a greedy tree look like if the n β's are zero and the $n + 1$ α's are given by the first $n + 1$ Fibonacci numbers? Give two answers — one when the greedy tree definition is used, and one when the $O(n)$ implementation is used.

☐ Suggested Assignment

a. Write programs to find and output optimal and greedy trees and their weighted path lengths.

b. Explain why the greedy tree implementation with the list structure is linear in time. (*Hint:* When the next locally minimal triple is to be found, only list-structure records not previously accessed will be considered, as well as two records that were previously accessed.)

Some Pointers on Storage Management

12.1 The Need for Storage Management

In languages such as COBOL, FORTRAN, and Pascal, arrays are *static* data structures: they do not change size or shape during execution of a program. Chains, however, do change size though they don't change shape. They are *dynamic*. List-structures, more complex lists, and binary and general trees can change both size and shape and thus are also dynamic data structures. The basic distinction between *static* and *dynamic* data structures relates to whether a fixed amount of memory can be allocated in advance of program execution. Static structures can have a fixed amount of memory allocated for their sole use prior to program execution. For dynamic structures, the amount of required memory is not known in advance and thus cannot be allocated in this way.

In FORTRAN and COBOL, the total amount of storage needed by the variables of a program is known by the compiler and can be set aside before program execution. This means that a fixed amount of storage is allocated to static variables for the entire execution of the program. Although the same technique could be used in Pascal, the language is designed so that, instead, static storage is allocated when needed, and is used for other purposes when not needed. This requires storage management *during* program execution. Dynamic structures such as lists and trees need even more complex storage management during program execution.

Consider a program that maintains a data base of stock portfolios for the clients of a brokerage house. Suppose each client's stocks are kept in a binary search tree ordered by stock name, with each node of the tree represented as a record containing information about the stock. It is not possible to predict in advance how much storage is needed since how many stocks each client will buy is not known. Experience may show that all clients' stocks will never number more than 2,000, but the distribution of these stocks among the clients varies throughout the year. Thus it will be necessary to have storage available for 2,000 records. At a given moment this storage will be distributed among the clients' binary search trees. Whenever a stock is sold for one client, its storage must be deleted from that client's tree. It may be needed later to store the record of a stock just bought for another client. This allocation and reclaiming of record storage during program execution requires dynamic storage management. Some languages, such as Pascal, may provide the needed storage management. FORTRAN does not; thus the FORTRAN programmer must provide it.

This chapter discusses the fundamentals of storage management techniques. It offers insight into how programming languages manage storage and provides a better appreciation of the pitfalls that lie below the surface features of a language. Such insight is especially important when the programmer employs complex data structures that share storage.

You have already seen how the simple case of fixed-length records with no sharing might be handled (Chapter 3). Problems arise when these limitations are removed. The remedies involve the creation and processing of data structures tailored to these needs. Some sophisticated traversal algorithms have been developed to conserve storage. They are introduced here for three reasons. First, they are essential for the implementation of those data structures. Second, they are interesting and elegant in themselves. And third, they serve as a good example of the use of data abstraction.

Although storage management is viewed here from the perspective of a program's needs, these same techniques are employed by operating systems to deal with the allocation and reclamation of storage for individual programs. In this case the amount of an individual storage request is significantly larger than that made by individual programs as they execute.

In some programming, an upper bound on the problem size is not known in advance. One way to deal with this situation is to pick a reasonably large size and declare static data structures of this size. If the problem exceeds this size, an error message may be printed. When the number of available memory elements is fixed, there will always be some problem size for which programs fail. However, it is possible that the program uses several data structures. During execution, when one data structure is large, the others may be small, so that the *total* amount of storage required for all the structures may actually be available at all times. With static data structures, where memory is allocated and remains dedicated to a particular structure, storage must be allocated to accommodate the worst case. If, instead, the available memory can be used for the data structure that currently requires it and reclaimed for later use when that structure no longer needs it, then larger problems can be solved. This point is illustrated in the following examples.

Example 12.1   The LISTS array used to store successor records for the topological sort of Chapter 9 allows all successor lists to share storage. No storage is dedicated to any individual list. As long as the *total* number of successors on all lists does not exceed the length of LISTS, the program will execute correctly. This contrasts with the alternate collection of N arrays discussed in Section 9.6. With this approach, storage is dedicated to each list, and although twice as many total successors may be accommodated, no list can contain more than its dedicated amount. □

Example
12.2

Suppose five stacks are each implemented, as in Chapter 4, using static array data structures, each requiring a maximum size of 5,000 elements. This requires 25,000 total memory locations. However, if the number of entries in all the stacks, at any one time, never exceeds 10,000, then proper sharing of storage may allow a reduction of up to 15,000 in the amount of storage needed. ☐

Example
12.3

A program can store, in linked representation, a number of binary trees that must be traversed using stacks. If the trees must be stored and traversed simultaneously, it is possible that available storage for the records of the tree nodes and for the entries of the stacks is not sufficient for the worst case. However, if the available storage can be shared, so that it is used for tree records or for stack entries when needed, then the program might execute correctly. ☐

In Example 12.1, the records sharing storage all have the same size. In Example 12.2, the five stacks can all store records of the same size, *or* they can store records of different lengths. Example 12.3 requires records, which may or may not be of the same length for each binary tree, and stack entries to share storage. Normally, the record lengths would be significantly greater than that of the stack entries. One fundamental distinction between storage management techniques involves whether or not the storage allocated will all be the same size. When dealing with the fixed-size case, it is convenient to use the techniques for storage allocation and storage reclamation, discussed in Chapter 3, which involve a list of available space. When dealing with more general data structures or with the variable-size case, additional complications arise.

12.2   The Heap

As one or more programs execute they may require storage for the creation of records, records that typically are to be inserted into dynamic data structures. How can a given amount of storage that is made available for the creation of these records be managed efficiently? This is the problem to be addressed.

The records, or more generally, the components of dynamic data structures, are referred to as **nodes**. The region of memory consisting of contiguous elements that is dedicated to the storage of these nodes is called the **heap**. It is a generalization of the heap considered in Chapter 3 in which all nodes need not be the same length and nodes may appear as part of more than one data structure. Associated with each node is a length field, indicating the size of the node (that is, the number of memory elements it uses). If all nodes were the same size, there would be no need to store size information within each node. All dynamic data structures reside in the heap. At all times, the heap may contain three kinds of nodes:

- ☐ Nodes that are *in use* because they appear on dynamic data structures
- ☐ Nodes that are *not in use* and appear in no dynamic data structure but are on the current list of available space
- ☐ Nodes that are *not in use* because they are in no dynamic data structure but are *not* on the list of available space

Nodes on the list of available space are said to be **known**. Nodes that are available but not on the list of available space are called **garbage**. All **heads** (names) of dynamic data structures, which point to their first records, are outside the heap and are kept track of in some way. This means that at all times the program knows what dynamic data structures are in existence, since their names are known.

Example 12.4   Suppose AV, L, and T are, respectively, the heads of the available space list, a list, and a binary tree. A heap containing these dynamic data structures may be visualized as in Figure 12.1. Each node has been labeled to indicate its current status:

> 1—in use since the node appears on L or T
> 2—not in use but on the available space list
> 3—not in use and not on the available space list, hence garbage

☐

Storage allocation now involves three tasks:

1. Decide which node on the list of available space will be made available when a request for creation of a node is made.
2. Delete that node from the list of available space.
3. Set a pointer value to point to the node.

An AVAIL-like function will do these three tasks (see Chapter 3).

12.3 The List of Available Space for Variable-Length Records

When dealing with variable-size records, which is the usual situation, storage management is complex because of **fragmentation**. The fragmentation problem is as follows. When all records being allocated dynamically are the same size, then, as long as unused storage finds its way to the list of available space, it can be reused. However, it is possible, with variable-size records, that storage for a large record is needed yet is not immediately in existence. Suppose each available block of *consecutive* elements of storage is kept on the list of available space as an individual record, with a field of each record used to store its length. It is possible for records of length 10, 15, 3, 20, and 45 to appear on the list when a record of length 65 must be created, but no individual record is large enough to be allocated for it. However, a total of ninety-three elements is unused. This is the **external fragmentation** problem: enough storage is unused to satisfy the need, but no record currently on the list of available space can be used. It may be resolved by invoking a **compaction** procedure, which moves the field values in used nodes to contiguous elements of memory at one end of the heap. All unused elements then also become contiguous and can represent a node large enough so that the needed storage can be taken.

Example 12.5   Suppose the compaction procedure is applied to the heap of Example 12.4, which was illustrated in Figure 12.1. The result may be visualized as in Figure 12.2. ☐

Compaction is an extraordinary procedure. Like garbage collection, it is a time-consuming process that the programmer or computer system should only invoke

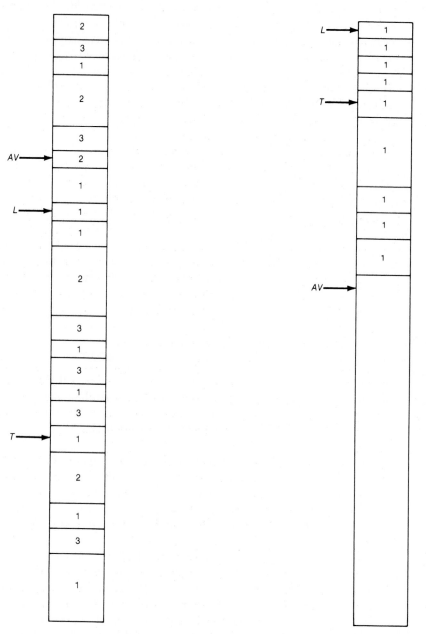

Figure 12.1 A Heap Containing the Available Space List (AV), a List (L), and a Binary Tree (T) and Nodes Labeled 1, 2, or 3 to Show Status

Figure 12.2 The Heap of Example 12.4 (Figure 12.1) after Compaction

infrequently. When variable-size nodes are being managed, it is possible to organize the list of available space in an attempt to minimize fragmentation and thus the need for compaction. However, in limiting fragmentation, the program should not spend too much computer time determining which node to allocate each time a request is made. Organizing the list of available space and using a reasonable policy in selecting the node to be allocated helps to reduce fragmentation. Additional time, however, is required to search the list to select the node to be allocated and to place a reclaimed node in proper position on the list. *Coalescing*, the creating of larger nodes by joining adjacent unused nodes, can cut down on fragmentation. These policies and organizations must be addressed by designers of compilers or operating systems and by programmers when they must create storage management schemes for their own use.

Recall that the more structured or organized the data, the faster the access to required information. At the same time a price must be paid to maintain the organization. The primary considerations for a storage management scheme are the time to satisfy a request for a new node, the time to insert a node on the list of available space, the storage utilization, and the likelihood of satisfying a request. How well these characteristics turn out for a particular storage management scheme depends on the sequence of requests and returns. Mathematical analysis is generally not possible and simulation must be used to evaluate different schemes. To provide some idea of the trade-offs and possibilities, three fundamental organizations for the available space list and appropriate allocation and reclamation policies are presented next.

12.3.1 Two-Way Circular Lists

The simplest organization for the list of available space is a two-way circular list, with nodes kept in arbitrary order, in order by size, or in order by actual memory address. Two-way lists are convenient for making insertions and deletions. Circular lists allow the list to be traversed starting from any list record, and in either direction. A request for a node of size L then requires a traversal of the list, starting from some initial node.

Two simple policies for selection of the list node to be deleted to satisfy a request are *first-fit* and *best-fit*. *First-fit* selects the first node encountered whose size is sufficient. *Best-fit* does a complete traversal and selects that node of smallest size sufficient to satisfy the request. Of course, if an exact fit is found, the traversal need not continue. For both policies, any leftover storage is retained as a node on the list.

When a node is returned to the list, its neighbors (in terms of storage addresses) are coalesced with it if free, and the resultant node properly inserted on the list. All nodes require tag and size fields, with the list nodes also needing backward and forward link fields. The tag field distinguishes nodes in use from those not in use, depending on which of two values it contains.

Allowing the starting node to circulate around the list, always being set to the successor of the deleted (or truncated) node, typically improves performance. This circulation provides time for the smaller nodes left behind it to coalesce so that, by the next time around, larger nodes have been formed.

Intuitively, spending more time fitting the size of the selected node to the size of the requested node should cut down on fragmentation effects. Surprisingly, this need not always happen, but it is the normal situation.

12.3.2 The Buddy System

Faster request and return time response may be achieved by the buddy system. This scheme assumes the heap is of length 2^m for some integer m, and occupies addresses 0 to $2^m - 1$. Over time, the heap is split into nodes of varying lengths. These lengths are constrained to be powers of 2 and nodes are kept on separate lists, each list containing nodes of a specific length. An array A of length m contains the heads of these lists, so $A[k]$ points to the first node on the list corresponding to length 2^k. Initially, $A[m]$ points to the first address of the heap and all other array entries are null, since all other lists are empty.

To satisfy a request for a node of length n, k is set to $\lceil \lg 2^n \rceil$. If $A[k]$ is not null, a node is deleted from its list to satisfy the request. Otherwise, the next nonnull list is found. Its nodes will be of length 2^r, where $r > k$. A node is deleted from that list and split into two nodes, each of length 2^{r-1}. The node with the greater address is placed on the appropriate list; the other is used to satisfy the request if $r - 1 = k$. Otherwise, it is split and processed in the same way. Eventually a node of length k will be generated to satisfy the request.

During this iterated splitting process, each time a node is split, it is split into two special nodes called **buddies**. Buddies bear a unique relation to each other: only buddies are allowed to coalesce. Although this can result in unused nodes being contiguous but not coalescing because they are not buddies, it is a rare occurrence. This restriction allows very fast coalescing of buddies, as will be shown.

When a node is to be returned to the list of available space (a misnomer now), its buddy is first checked to see if it is not in use and, if it is not, the buddies are coalesced. This node is, in turn, coalesced with its buddy when possible, and so on, until no further coalescing is possible. This coalescing process is the reverse of the splitting process that created the buddies in the first place.

At this point you must be wondering how a node's buddy is found. The scheme ensures that it may be done quickly because a node of size 2^k with starting address

$$b \ldots b \; \underline{0} \; \underbrace{00 \ldots 0}_{k}$$

has as its buddy a node of size 2^k with starting address

$$b \ldots b \; \underline{1} \; \underbrace{00 \ldots 0}_{k}$$

In general, given the address of a node of size 2^k to be returned, its $(k + 1)$th bit (addresses are expressed in binary notation) is changed from 1 to 0 or 0 to 1, and the result is the address of its buddy. A tag field is used to indicate whether or not a node is in use.

Example 12.6 How does the buddy system respond when m is 6 and a sequence of requests is made for nodes of size 8, 16, 4, and 6? □

The sequence of memory configurations is as shown in Figure 12.3(a). If the node of length 16 is now returned, the configuration becomes as shown in Figure 12.3(b).

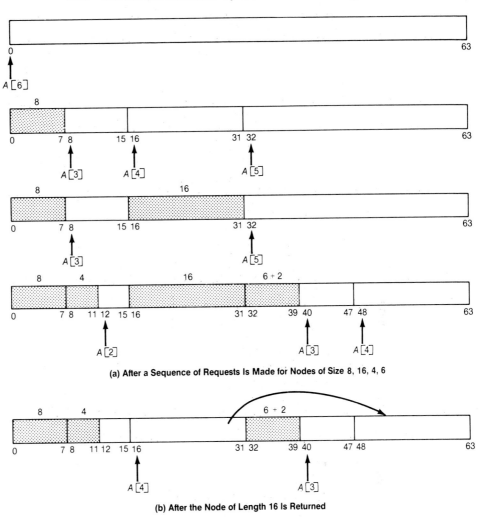

(a) After a Sequence of Requests Is Made for Nodes of Size 8, 16, 4, 6

(b) After the Node of Length 16 Is Returned

Figure 12.3   Sequence of Memory Configurations for Example 12.6

A[4] is now the head of a list with two nodes, each of length 16. The released node of length 16 starting at address 16 (10000 in binary) has the node of length 16 starting at address 0 (00000 in binary) as its buddy. Since it is not free, it cannot coalesce with it. Neither can it coalesce with the node of length 4 starting at address 12, since that node is not its buddy.

The distribution of nodes can be mirrored by a binary tree. This tree is a kind of derivation tree for nodes currently in existence and expands and contracts as nodes are split and coalesced. The tree shown in Figure 12.4 reflects the configuration for Example 12.6 before the node of length 16 is returned.

Buddies appear as successors of the same parent. Thus [12, 15] and [16, 31], although contiguous in memory, are not buddies and so may not be coalesced.

With the buddy system, lists are never actually traversed to find storage to allocate, although time is spent finding the proper list from which to take the storage.

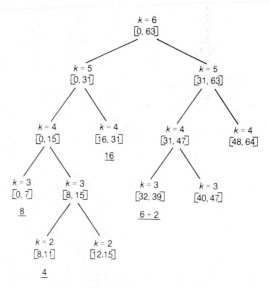

Figure 12.4   Binary Tree Reflecting the Memory Configuration for Example 12.6 Just before Return of Node of Length 16

The result is quick response to requests and returns. However, in contrast to two-way lists, this scheme produces significant *internal* fragmentation. ***Internal fragmentation*** occurs when allocated nodes are larger than requested, resulting in wasted storage residing within a node. This is one of the drawbacks of the buddy system. Similar schemes have been studied which allow a greater variety of node sizes to appear. They also tend to be fast, and to reduce storage loss due to internal fragmentation.

12.3.3 Indexing Methods

The best-fit method utilizes storage very efficiently, causing little internal fragmentation. Buddy systems produce significant internal fragmentation but offer fast allocation by narrowly restricting the search for a proper size node. It is possible to achieve good storage utilization and allocation time by combining their features. This is done by using appropriate structures. The ***indexing*** approach breaks up the list of available space into collections of two-way circular lists. Each of these circular lists contains nodes of just one size. Each node on the circular list represents a block of consecutive memory locations available for the storage of a record of the size of the node. Assuming that requests for nodes of sizes, say 1 to 4, are very frequent, an array A contains pointers to each of the four lists corresponding to these sizes. The last array entry contains a pointer to an AVL tree. The nodes of this tree are circular lists, each list corresponding to specific size nodes which are requested much less frequently. Thus $A[2]$ contains a pointer to a circular list containing four blocks or nodes, each of size 2. In the AVL tree pointed to by $A[5]$, the root node is a circular list containing three blocks of size 10. The tree is ordered on the basis of node sizes. A typical configuration might be as shown in Figure 12.5.

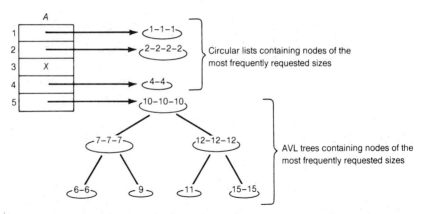

Figure 12.5   An Indexing Array Containing Pointers to Circular Lists and an AVL Tree Storing Circular Lists

In this way, a specific request for a node of length less than 5 can be quickly satisfied if the exact matching list is not empty. If it is empty, the next nonempty greater size list can be used, with one of its nodes being truncated to satisfy the request. Any leftover is inserted on the appropriate list. For instance, with the situation of Figure 12.5, a request for a node of size 3 will be satisfied by deleting a node of size 4 from the list pointed to by $A[4]$. This node will be split into a node of size 3 to satisfy the request and the leftover node of size 1 inserted on the list pointed to by $A[1]$. In the infrequent case when the requested node size is 5 or greater, the AVL tree must be searched similarly. It is clear that this scheme can cause internal fragmentation, but the search times should be fast on the average.

Choosing the appropriate scheme of storage management is obviously a difficult task. It requires insight into the kind of request and return distribution involved in a given application. In the worst case all schemes may fail miserably. Intuitively, good performance should result when the distribution of node sizes on the list of available space reflects the distribution of requests and returns. In turn, this distribution should be reflected in the distribution of node sizes actually in use. This is analogous to the situation mentioned in Chapter 11 for the distribution of letters in printer's boxes. The distribution of letter requests is reflected in actual text, and the printer's ordering policy for letters should have caused the contents of the letter boxes to reflect this distribution also, in the olden days of monotype typesetting.

The three techniques considered in this section, and other techniques, are compared extensively in Knuth [1973a] and Standish [1980]. Also see Tremblay and Sorenson [1984].

12.4 Shared Storage

When components of data structures are identical and require significant amounts of storage, it is only natural to attempt to avoid component replication. This means that identical components will all share the same storage, so references to each will always be to the same place. As an example, consider Figure 12.6. The two list-

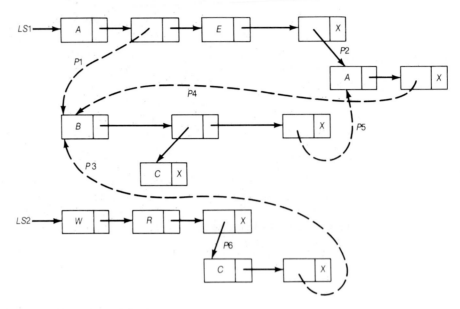

Figure 12.6   A Shared Sublist

structures $LS1$ and $LS2$ share a common sublist. As a result $P1$, $P3$, and $P4$ point to
the shared sublist.

As usual, what we gain in one area we pay for in another. Here, storage is saved,
but the price is paid in more complex processing. In particular, suppose the sublist
pointed to by $P3$ is to be deleted from $LS2$ by setting $P3$ to null. Since $P1$ and $P4$ still
point to it, it is not valid to return its records' storage to the list of available space,
as would be the case with no sharing. Deciding when and how to reclaim deleted
records or sublists by insertion on the list of available space requires more sophisticated reclamation algorithms than those of Chapter 3.

12.5   Storage Reclamation Techniques

What is meant by saying that a node or component of a data structure is to be
reclaimed for use is that the storage used for its records is to become known to the
AVAIL module. That is, the storage no longer needed by its records is to be inserted
on the list of available space. There are two basic methods of reclaiming released
nodes, *garbage collection* and *reference counters*. Other methods are essentially
combinations of these. These methods are the two extremes with respect to the time
at which storage is reclaimed. Garbage collection does not make storage available for
reuse until it is needed; reference counters make storage available for reuse as soon
as it actually becomes reclaimable.

12.5.1   Garbage Collection

Garbage collection is a reclamation method that is used when the available space list
is empty or when the amount of storage that is known to AVAIL becomes less than

some given amount. Until that time, whenever a sublist is to be deleted from a data structure, the deletion is accomplished by updating appropriate pointers, but the storage vacated by the sublist's deletion is not made known. Initially, all records are assumed to be unmarked. The garbage collection routine works by traversing each data structure that is in use, and "marking" each one of its records as being in use.

To accomplish this properly, the garbage collector program must know the names of all data structures in use. We have assumed that these are accessible through variables outside the heap. After marking, every record of the heap that is *not* marked will be made known (that is, placed on the available space list). Every record that is marked will be reset to unmarked so the garbage collector will work properly on its next call. The marking phase of the garbage collector works by traversing all data structures in use. Thus marking routines generally take execution time proportional to the number of records in use and hence are slow. Similarly, the collection routine, which inserts the unmarked records on the list of available space, takes time proportional to the heap size.

Example 12.7

Apply garbage collection to the heap of Example 12.4. □

In the marking phase, the garbage collection would traverse L and T, marking all their nodes. The collection phase would then traverse the heap and collect all unmarked nodes on the available space list. Assuming the garbage collector recognizes when two unmarked nodes are adjacent and combines them into a larger node, the resultant heap would appear as shown in Figure 12.7. A better approach may be to both garbage collect and compact together, thus producing an available list consisting of one large block (reducing fragmentation).

12.5.2 The Reference Counter Method

The *reference counter method* assumes that the first record of every sublist in use has information giving the number of pointers that point to it. This number is called the *reference count* of the sublist. The pointers can be stored in the name variables or in sublist fields of complex records. A "smart" header record may be used for this purpose. It is assumed here that only sublists may be shared. Each time a new pointer refers to a sublist, the reference count of the sublist must be increased by 1. Each time a pointer that refers to a sublist is changed so it no longer points to that sublist, the reference count of the sublist must be decreased by 1. After a decrease that leaves the reference count at zero the storage for records of the sublist may be made known. Again, a data structure traversal may be used to determine which storage elements are to be made known. No traversal algorithm has been given in this text for data structures that allow sublist sharing. Such algorithms differ from the list-structure traversal algorithm because of the possibility of looping or revisiting records. As an exercise you should modify the list-structure traversals of Chapter 5 to work for this more general case. The idea is to mark each accessed record and make sure that marked records are not revisited.

Deletion of a sublist whose reference count has become zero is similar to the traversal of successor lists for an object that has been removed from the bag in the topological sort algorithm. The sublist must be traversed and, in addition to

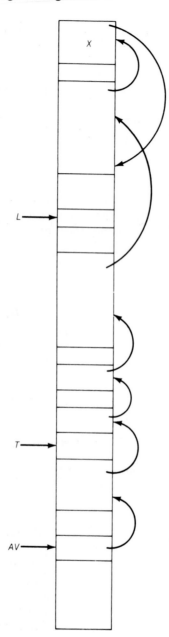

Figure 12.7 Heap from Example 12.4 after Garbage Collection

the storage for all records being inserted on the list of available space, each sublist pointed to by a record must have its reference count decremented by 1.

Example
12.8   Associate reference counts with the first record of each of the sublists of Figure 12.6. The list-structures with associated reference counts would appear as shown in Figure 12.8. □

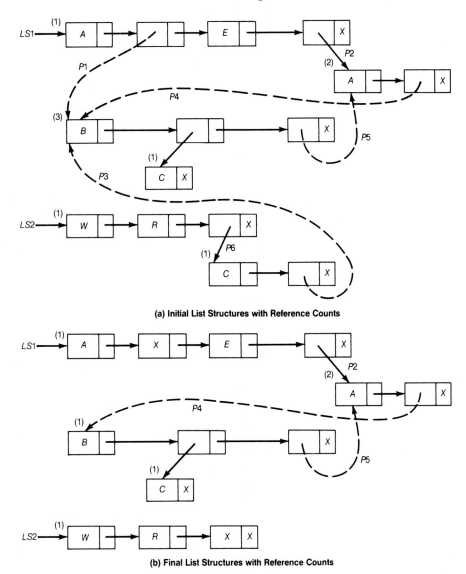

(a) Initial List Structures with Reference Counts

(b) Final List Structures with Reference Counts

Figure 12.8 List-structures of Figure 12.6 with Associated Reference Counts

Suppose $P1$ is set to null. The reference count of its sublist would be reduced to 2. Since it has not gone to zero, no storage is available for reclamation. If $P6$ is then set to null, the reference count of its sublist would be reduced to 0. Its storage could be reclaimed. This would require that $P3$'s sublist have its reference count reduced by 1. The result would be as shown in Figure 12.8(b).

A problem can occur with the reference counter method whenever loops appear, as demonstrated in the following example.

Example 12.9   Consider the loop in LSI of Figure 12.9. What happens when $P1$, $P2$, and $P3$ of Figure 12.6 no longer reference the sublist? Then this sublist has no variables refer-

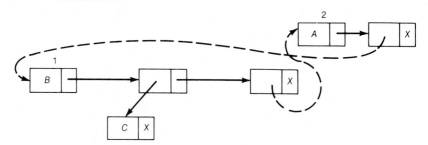

Figure 12.9   A Lost Loop

encing it. It cannot be accessed since we do not know where it is. It is serving no useful purpose; yet its storage was not reclaimed since the reference count of records 1 and 2 never went to zero. This problem is analogous to the existence of loops in the input for a topological sort. Such unused storage, or garbage, can accumulate and clog the memory. □

It is possible to share individual records, as well as sublists. In this case, garbage collection will still work, as will the reference counter method. Now, however, the individual records, not just sublists, must have reference counters associated with them, requiring additional storage and updating overhead. Loops may cause the same problems for shared records as for shared sublists.

Again, three basic techniques — garbage collection, reference counters, or programmer controlled reclamation, or a combination of these — may be used for storage reclamation. Garbage collection represents one extreme: nodes that are no longer needed in a dynamic data structure are deleted from the structure, thus becoming garbage. They are not returned at that time to the list of available space even though they are then reusable. Reference counters, at the other extreme, return such unused nodes to the list of available space as soon as possible, when their reference counters become zero. Programmer control allows the programmer to use commands signaling that nodes are no longer needed by a dynamic data structure. The nodes may then be returned to the list of available space directly, or, if reference counters are used, their reference counts will be decremented and tested for possible return to the list of available space. Later in the chapter some examples of this use of reference counters are given. Also illustrated are some problems that storage reclamation may cause — garbage creation and dangling references.

A number of trade-offs are possible. For example, reference counters require additional storage and additional time to increment, decrement, or test when insertions and deletions occur. However, they do not always work. The reason is that garbage can accumulate when loops are present in the dynamic data structures (as in Example 12.9). If the amount of garbage generated in this way is significant, it can limit the size of the problem that can be solved. Still, reference counters allow the reclamation process to be spread over time. Garbage collection, in contrast, occasionally requires a relatively large block of time. Garbage collection is a more complex technique involving more sophisticated algorithms. Recall that when garbage collection is invoked, even though many available nodes may exist, they are not known. It is not possible simply to look at a node of the heap to determine if it is in use.

To summarize, garbage collection works in two phases. The first phase, or marking phase, requires the traversal of all dynamic data structures in existence. Recall that the heads of such structures are assumed to be known. Initially, whether in use or not, every node has a field which is marked "unused." As each node of a dynamic data structure is accessed in the traversal, it is marked "used." When the marking phase is completed, the heap then consists of nodes that are marked "unused" and nodes that are marked "used." Consequently, it is now possible to look at a node and determine its status. The second phase, or collection phase, involves a traversal through the nodes of the heap. Each node marked "unused" is inserted on the list of available space. Each node marked "used" is merely marked "unused" so that the garbage collector will work correctly the next time it is invoked.

The marking algorithms known are quite elegant. The traversal of the dynamic data structures cannot simply use a stack, since no nodes are known in which to implement the stack. Instead, these algorithms allow the traversals to be accomplished by using tag fields (usually one bit) associated with each node. It is even possible to do the traversals with no tag fields, and with a *fixed* amount of additional storage required. Of course, if we had an infinite amount of storage available, no reclamation would be necessary. Storage management would be trivial! The next section features three traversal algorithms for use in phase I of the garbage collector, or in other applications where storage is at a premium. See Pratt [1975] for more on storage management. The algorithms to be discussed next and generalizations are also given in Standish [1980].

12.6 Stackless Traversals

Garbage collection routines require the traversal of dynamic data structures that are more general than binary trees, such as list-structures and more complex lists. Algorithms for their traversal are generalizations of those we consider. For increased clarity, we will restrict our discussion to binary tree traversals, and present three techniques that do not use extra storage for a stack.

These algorithms may be written assuming a particular binary tree implementation, such as arrays or pointer variables. Instead, to emphasize data abstraction and modularity, the following procedure has been chosen. The procedure is a preorder traversal saving the path from the root on the stack.

```
procedure PREORDER(var T : binarytree);
var
    NULL, P, LPTR, RPTR : binarytree;
    S : stack;
begin
    SETNULL(NULL);
    P := T;
    SETSTACK(S);
    while (P <> NULL) do
        begin
            PROCESS(T, P);
            LPTR := LEFT(P);
            if LPTR <> NULL then
```

```
                              begin
                                 PUSH(P, S);
                                 P := LPTR
                              end
                          else
                              begin
                                 RPTR := RIGHT(P);
                                 if RPTR <> NULL then
                                     begin
                                        PUSH(P, S);
                                        P := RPTR
                                     end
                                 else
                                     P := NEXTSUBTREE(S, P)
                              end
                     end
              end;
```

For each traversal, the basic concept is described. Then the appropriate implementation for the routines of the procedure is described.

Consider the binary tree of Figure 12.10, and suppose NODE.P has just been
processed during the traversal using the PREORDER procedure. The stack will
contain pointers $P1$, $P2$, $P3$, $P4$, $P5$, $P6$, and $P7$. At this point, the traversal of the left
subtree of NODE.$P4$ has been completed. The purpose of the NEXTSUBTREE(S, P)
module in the preorder traversal algorithm is to find NODE.$P4$, to allow the traversal
to pick up at its right subtree. In general, whenever the stack is not empty, a null P
value signifies the completion of the traversal of the left subtree of some node. The
traversal must then pick up at that node's right subtree. There may be more than one
such node; it is the most recent that must be found. The stack allows this node, and

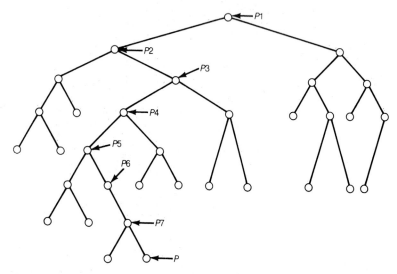

Figure 12.10 A Binary Tree T

its right subtree, to be found conveniently. NEXTSUBTREE(S, P) is called after the terminal node pointed to by P has been processed. It finds the nonnull right subtree that must be traversed next, returns a pointer to it, and updates the stack to reflect the path from that subtree's root to the root of the tree. If no such nonnull right subtree exists, then it returns a null value. Each of the three traversals we now consider actually uses stack information, but this stack information is, in effect, stored in the tree, eliminating the requirement for *additional* stack storage. The PRE-ORDER procedure treats the tree as a data abstraction, so it is independent of the tree implementation.

12.6.1 Threaded Trees

A *threaded tree* implementation of the PREORDER traversal procedure is shown in Figure 12.11. It resulted from the replacement of the null left and right pointer field values of each node of T by a pointer to the predecessor, and to the successor, respectively, of that node in an inorder traversal of T. These pointers are called *threads*. The "leftmost" node of T does not have a predecessor, and the "rightmost" node of T does not have a successor. Their left and right null pointers, respectively, are left unchanged, and are not considered threads. We assume that a field is associated with each node to indicate whether the node contains threads in its left link field, its right link field, in both, or in neither.

To preorder traverse threaded trees, proceed as before, but whenever a node with threads is reached, follow its right pointer. This pointer leads directly to the node whose right subtree must then be preorder traversed. Notice, for example, that the right thread of NODE.P points to NODE.P4. The traversal is complete when a null right thread is encountered. Threaded trees may also be easily inorder and postorder traversed.

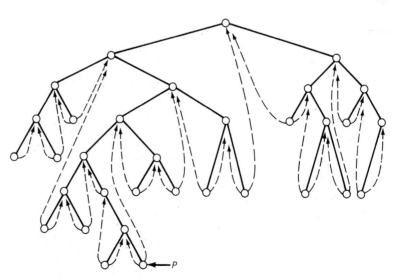

Figure 12.11 A Threaded Implementation of the Binary Tree *T*

Procedure PREORDER may be used for the traversal of a threaded tree, with STACK declared to be of type binarytree, by implementing its routines as follows:

Routine	Task
SETNULL	determined by the implementation (array or pointer variables)
SETSTACK(S)	sets S to null
PUSH(P, S)	sets S to P
LEFT(P)	returns a copy of LEFTPTR.P if it is not a thread, a null value otherwise
RIGHT(P)	similar to LEFT(P)
NEXTSUBTREE(S, P)	set S to P while (RIGHTPTR.S is a thread), set S to RIGHTPTR.S Return a copy of RIGHTPTR.S

12.6.2 Link Inversion

Now consider the tree of Figure 12.12. It represents the binary tree T of Figure 12.10 during a *link-inversion traversal* after NODE.P has been processed. Notice that a path exists in the tree from PREDP back to the root. Each node has a tag field associated with it, and all tag values are initially zero. PREDP always points to the predecessor of P in T, and every node on the path from PREDP to the root has its right pointer field pointing to its predecessor if its tag field is 1, and its left pointer field pointing to its predecessor if its tag field is 0. The root of the subtree whose left subtree traversal is complete after the processing of P may be found by following the backward links from PREDP until a tag value of 0 is encountered. As the path back

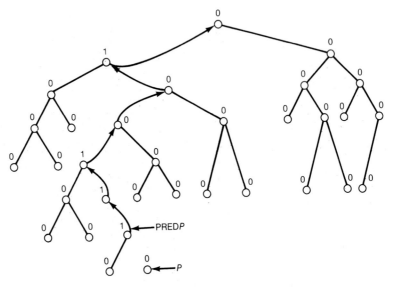

Figure 12.12 A Link-inverted Binary Tree T

is followed, a tag of 1 at a predecessor node means we are coming from the node's right subtree. A tag of 0 means we are coming from the left subtree. Again, for NODE.P this leads to NODE.$P4$.

Using the backward links with appropriate tag values to preserve the path to the root is the essential concept of a link-inversion traversal. During the traversal, the creation of appropriate links must be handled. For example, as the path to NODE.$P4$ is traversed, after P has been processed, the nodes with TAG values of 1 must have their correct right pointer values restored, and when NODE.$P4$ is found (TAG = 0), its correct left pointer value must be restored, its tag field set to 1, its right pointer field set to its predecessor, and PREDP and P correctly updated before NODE.$P4$'s right subtree is traversed. The traversal is complete when the backtracking leads to a null PREDP value. Figure 12.13 shows the state of the tree just before NODE.$P4$'s right subtree is traversed. NODE.P must now be processed, then its left pointer field must be set to its predecessor, PREDP updated to P, and P updated to the left pointer value of NODE.P. The traversal then continues with the left subtree of P. Initially, P must be set to T and PREDP to null.

Procedure PREORDER may be used for the link-inversion traversal, if STACK is declared to be of type binarytree, and its routines are implemented as follows.

Routine	Task
SETNULL(NULL)	determined by the implementation
SETSTACK(S)	set S to null
PUSH(P, S)	if LEFTPTR.P is not null, then
	set LEFTPTR.P to S and S to P
	else
	SET TAG(P) to 1, set RIGHTPTR.P to S and S to P
LEFT(P)	returns a copy of LEFTPTR.P
RIGHT(P)	returns a copy of RIGHTPTR.P
NEXTSUBTREE(S, P)	set FOUND to false
	while ((not FOUND) and ($S <>$ null))
	if TAG(S) = 1 then
	set PRED to S
	set TAG(S) to 0, S to RIGHTPTR.S,
	RIGHTPTR.PRED to P, and P to PRED
	else
	set PRED to LEFTPTR.S and LEFTPTR.S to P
	if RIGHTPTR.$S <>$ null then
	set FOUND to true, TAG(S) to 1, return
	RIGHTPTR.S, and set RIGHTPTR.S to PRED
	else
	set P to S
	set S to PRED
	if S = null then
	return null.

In this implementation S plays the role of PREDP.

In a stack traversal, the storage required for the stack is proportional to the depth of the traversed tree. In the threaded-tree and link-inversion traversals, stor-

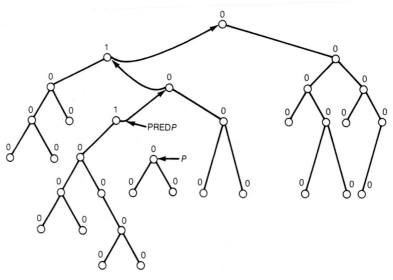

Figure 12.13   New State before Subtree Pointed to by *P* Is Traversed in Binary Tree *T*

age is not required for the stack, but is required for the tag fields. This storage may actually be available, but unused, because of the implementation of the tree records. In this case, using it for the tag fields costs nothing. Otherwise, the additional storage is proportional to the number of nodes in the traversed tree. For the stack traversal, the constant of proportionality is given by the length of the pointer fields, while in the threaded-tree and link-inversion traversals, it is given by the length of the tag fields.

The threaded-tree traversal is simpler than the link-inversion traversal and does not disturb the tree itself during the traversal. This allows more than one program concurrently to access the tree. However, the insertion and deletion of nodes in a threaded tree is more complex and time consuming. Inorder and postorder traversals may also be done using link inversion.

12.6.3 Robson Traversal

It is remarkable that an algorithm has been found which does not require a stack or even tag fields. This is the *Robson traversal,* and is the final stackless traversal we consider. Again, we give a preorder version, although it may be used for inorder and postorder traversals as well.

Consider the tree of Figure 12.14. In the link-inversion traversal, for every descent to the left from NODE.*P* (that is, every traversal of the left subtree of NODE.*P*), the left pointer field of NODE.*P* was set to point to NODE.*P*'s predecessor. For every descent to the right (to traverse the right subtree of NODE.*P*), the leftpointer of NODE.*P* was restored to its original value, the TAG of NODE.*P* was set to 1, and the right pointer field of NODE.*P* was set to point to NODE.*P*'s predecessor. Consequently, when at completion of the traversal of the left subtree of some node *Q*, it was possible to follow the backward pointing pointers to *Q*. *Q* was the first node encountered with a tag value of 0, on the path back.

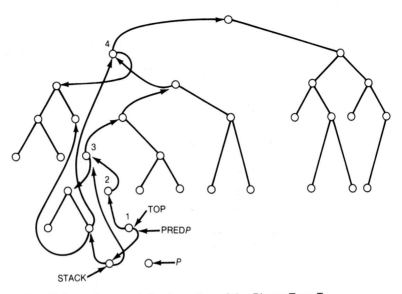

Figure 12.14 Robson Traversal Configuration of the Binary Tree *T*

The Robson traversal does not have tag fields available for this purpose. Instead, a stack is kept in the tree itself, which will allow node *Q* to be found. *Q* is the root of the *most recent* subtree, whose nonnull left subtree has already been traversed and whose nonnull right subtree is in the process of being traversed. A variable TOP is used, and kept updated, to point to the current node *Q*. A variable STACK is used, and kept updated, to point to an entry for the *next most recent* subtree whose nonnull left subtree was traversed and whose nonnull right subtree is in the process of being traversed. Variables *P* and PRED*P* are used, as in link inversion, to point, respectively, to the node currently being processed and to its predecessor. Each stack entry, except the current top entry, is kept in the "rightmost" terminal node of one of the subtrees whose nonnull left subtree has been completely traversed, and whose nonnull right subtree is in the process of being traversed. In Figure 12.14, when NODE.*P* is being processed, there are four subtrees whose left subtrees have already been traversed and whose right subtrees are currently being traversed. Their roots are labeled 1 to 4 in Figure 12.14. Nodes, 1, 3, and 4 have nonnull left subtrees. Each of these nodes has its left pointer field pointing to its predecessor, and its right pointer pointing to the root of its left subtree. Node 2, which has a null left subtree, has its original null value, and its right pointer field is pointing to its predecessor. Nodes 1, 3, and 4 are thus the roots that must have stack entries. TOP points to the most recent, node 1. STACK points to the stack entry corresponding to the next most recent root, node 3. This stack entry is kept in the rightmost terminal node of node 1's left subtree. This rightmost node has its left pointer field pointing to the node that contains the next stack entry, and its right pointer field pointing to its corresponding root (node 3 in this case). All stack entries (except the first, pointed to by TOP) have this same format. In Figure 12.14, the last stack entry points to node 4.

Notice that a path back to the root always exists from NODE.PRED*P*. In Figure 12.14, after NODE.*P* is processed, the traversal of node 1's right subtree has

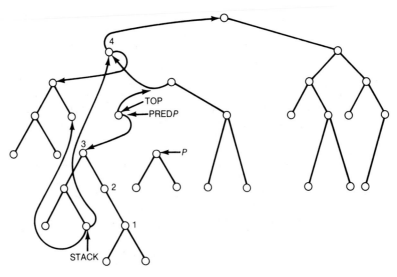

Figure 12.15   Robson Traversal before *P* Is Processed in the Binary Tree *T*

been completed. This also completes the traversal of the right subtrees of nodes 2 and 3, and the left subtree of node 3's predecessor. The Robson traversal now proceeds by following the backward path, restoring appropriate left or right subtrees along the way, until the predecessor of node 3 is encountered. At this point, its right subtree must be traversed. Figure 12.15 shows the situation just before that traversal. During the traversal of the backward path, if NODE.PRED*P* has a null right subtree, or TOP ≠ PRED*P*, then we are coming from the left subtree of NODE.PRED*P*, otherwise from the right subtree. Thus the stack entries allow node *Q* to be found even though no tag fields are used.

During the backtracking, the stack is popped, and TOP is updated as necessary. TOP and STACK are initialized to null, PRED*P* to null, and *P* to *T*. An additional variable AVAIL is used, and updated, to point to a terminal node every time one is encountered, so that its pointer fields are available if a new stack entry must be created. In this case, the available node must retain a pointer to NODE.TOP in its right pointer field and a pointer to the current entry to which STACK points in its left pointer field, STACK must be updated to point to the new entry, and TOP must be updated to point to the new top root. At all times, the path from PRED*P* back to the root is stored in the tree, as well as the stack of entries pointing to roots of subtrees (with nonnull left subtrees), whose left subtree traversals have completed, and whose right subtrees are being traversed. Each node along the path from PRED*P* to the root is in one of the following states:

> If the node's left subtree is being traversed, then
> > its left pointer is pointing to its predecessor, and its
> > right pointer is undisturbed.
>
> If the node's right subtree is being traversed, then
> > if the node has a null left subtree, then
> > > its right pointer is pointing to its predecessor

else

its left pointer is pointing to its predecessor, and its
right pointer is pointing to the root of the node's
left subtree.

The following routines are to be used with the preorder traversal so that it implements the Robson traversal. STACK is declared to be of the same type as binarytree, and S plays the role of PREDP.

Routine	Task
SETNULL(NULL)	determined by the implementation
SETSTACK(S)	sets TOP and STACK to null and S to T
PUSH(P, S)	if LEFTPTR.P is not null then
	set LEFTPTR.P to S and S to P
	else
	set RIGHTPTR.P to S and S to P
LEFT(P)	returns a copy of LEFTPTR.P
RIGHT(P)	returns a copy of RIGHTPTR.P
NEXTSUBTREE(S, P)	set AVAIL to P
	set FOUND to false
	while ((not FOUND) and ($P <> T$))
	if TOP = S then
	save STACK in HOLD, pop the stack by setting TOP to RIGHTPTR. STACK, STACK to LEFTPTR.STACK, and LEFTPTR.HOLD and RIGHTPTR.HOLD to null. Save LEFTPTR.S in PRED, restore LEFTPTR.S by setting it to RIGHTPTR.S, restore RIGHTPTR.S by setting it to P, set P to S, and S to PRED
	else
	if LEFTPTR.S = null then
	save RIGHTPTR.S in PRED, restore RIGHTPTR.S by setting it to P, set P to S, and S to PRED
	else
	if RIGHTPTR.S <> null, then
	push an entry for S onto the stack by setting LEFTPTR.AVAIL to STACK, RIGHTPTR.AVAIL to TOP, STACK to AVAIL, and TOP to S. Return the value of RIGHTPTR.S, set RIGHTPTR.S to P, and set FOUND to true
	else
	save LEFTPTR.S in PRED, restore LEFTPTR.S by setting it to P, set P to S, and S to PRED.
	if $P = T$ then
	return null.

12.7 Pitfalls: Garbage Generation and Dangling References

This chapter has shown how a list of available space can be maintained to keep track of storage known to be currently unused. Storage may be allocated dynamically, during program execution, by deleting appropriate elements from this list when needed. NEW, in Pascal, relieves the programmer of managing this list.

The need and means for storage reclamation have also been discussed. Garbage collection and reference counter techniques (or some combination) may be used for this purpose. When a node of a binary tree, or list, or other dynamic data structure, is not needed, the programmer frequently knows at what point this occurs. Some high-level languages allow commands to be used by the programmer to signal this occurrence. For example, some Pascal compilers provide a procedure DISPOSE. Like NEW, its parameter will be a pointer type variable. When P points to a node that the programmer knows is no longer needed, DISPOSE(P) may be invoked. This signals that the storage pointed to by P may be relinquished and reclaimed for use for another dynamically allocated data structure. Exactly how DISPOSE uses this information is determined by the compiler.

High-level languages are usually designed with particular storage management schemes in mind. However, the language specifications, or standards, do not normally specify that these schemes must be used. In Pascal, it is possible for a compiler to use garbage collection or reference counters, to leave the reclamation entirely to the programmer, or to use some combination. If necessary programmers may even write their own programs to manage storage. We will not discuss these problems further except to illustrate two potential dangers.

Consider the following disaster segment as illustration.

```
(1)   P := Q;
(2)   NEW(R);
(3)   R↑.LEFTPTR := TREE;
(4)   DISPOSE(TREE);
(5)   PROCESS(S);
(6)   S↑.LEFTPTR := LEFTTREE;
```

Suppose P, Q, R, S, LEFTTREE, and TREE are all pointer variables pointing to nodes of the same type. Before the segment is executed, the situation might be as shown in Figure 12.16(a). Statement (1), when executed, results in the situation sketched in Figure 12.16(b).

The tree, pointed to by P originally, now has no pointer pointing to it. Hence there is no way the program can access any of its nodes. Also, the storage allocated to this tree, while no longer in use, has not been returned to the list of available space. Unless the storage management technique uses garbage collection, or reference counters, that storage is lost. It cannot be accessed and will never be returned to the list of available space; it has become *garbage*. If DISPOSE(P) had been invoked before statement (1), then this might have been avoided, depending on whether DISPOSE recognizes that the other nodes of the tree may also be returned. If DISPOSE merely returns the storage for the node to which P points, then this could have been avoided only by the programmer traversing the tree pointed to by P, and "disposing" each of its nodes.

Suppose, instead, that DISPOSE uses reference counters, and, recognizing that the tree pointed to by P has no other references, returns its storage to the list of available space. Now, statement (2) is executed. The result is shown in Figure 12.16(c).

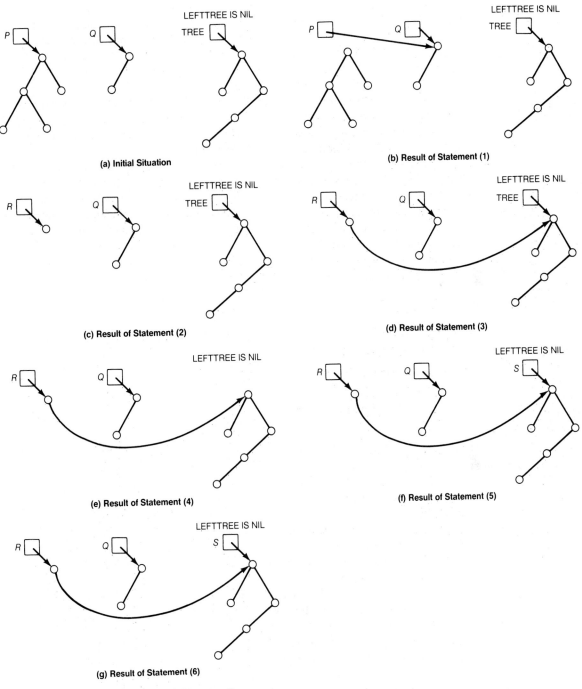

Figure 12.16   Simulation of the Disaster Segment

After statement (4) is executed, assuming that DISPOSE simply returns the storage allocated to the node pointed to by TREE to the list of available space, we get Figure 12.16(e). However, the node pointed to by $R\uparrow$.LEFTPTR is now on the list of available space. $R\uparrow$.LEFTPTR is called a *dangling reference* because it points to a node that is on the list of available space. When PROCESS is invoked in statement (5), it is possible that it invokes NEW(S), so storage is allocated to S. Then we have the situation shown in Figure 12.16(f).

Statement (6) produces Figure 12.16(g). The binary tree that R now points to has been changed, because of the dangling reference. The programmer, unaware that this has occurred, may find the program's output incorrect and be unable to determine what went wrong. This is especially difficult to discover, since the next time the program executes, PROCESS may not need to invoke NEW(S). Even if it does, the storage allocated by NEW to S might not cause this problem. Still, the programmer may not realize that an error has occurred.

Of the two problems, garbage generation and dangling reference generation, the latter is more serious. Garbage generation may cause longer execution time, or, at worst, program failure. Dangling references, however, may cause serious errors undetected by the programmer.

12.8   Conclusion

Dynamic data structures require dynamic storage allocation and reclamation. This may be accomplished by the programmer or may be done implicitly by a high-level language. It is important to understand the fundamentals of storage management because these techniques have significant impact on the behavior of programs. The basic idea is to keep a pool of memory elements that may be used to store components of dynamic data structures when needed.

Allocated storage may be returned to the pool when no longer needed. In this way, it may be used and reused. This contrasts sharply with static allocation, in which storage is dedicated for the use of static data structures. It cannot then be reclaimed for other uses, even when not needed for the static data structures. As a result, dynamic allocation makes it possible to solve larger problems that might otherwise be storage-limited.

Garbage collection, reference counters, and explicit programmer control are three techniques for implementing storage management. Combinations of these techniques may also be designed. Potential pitfalls of these techniques are garbage generation, dangling references, and fragmentation.

High-level languages may take most of the burden for storage management from the programmer. The concept of pointers or pointer variables underlies the use of these facilities, and complex algorithms are required for their implementation.

While this material should have managed to capture your attention, it may now be reclaimed for use.

☐ Exercises

1. a. Consider the suggested assignment of Chapter 9. Suppose only two hundred memory elements are available for LISTS to store successors. Give an example of a problem with fewer than twenty objects for which the implementation of (a) will work but the implementation of (b) will fail. Assume COUNT and SUCC have length 20, the LISTS array of (a) has length 200, and the list array of (b) is 20 × 10.

 b. Can you find such an example for which (b) works but (a) fails?

 2. a. Consider two implementations. First, a total of 50 memory elements in an array are to be dynamically allocated and reclaimed so that a binary tree, in linked representation, as well as a stack, may be stored in the array. Second, an array of length 35 is to hold the binary tree, and another array of length 15 is to implement the stack. Each array is dynamically managed. The binary tree is to be preorder traversed using the stack. Give an example of a binary tree, with fewer than 35 nodes, that may be successfully traversed with the first implementation but not the second.

 b. Suppose that after a node is accessed and processed, its storage may be reclaimed. Give an example of a binary tree, with fewer than thirty-five nodes, that may be successfully traversed with the first implementation but not the second.

 3. In Exercise 1, the LISTS array of (a) functioned as a heap. Why was its storage management so simple?

 4. In Exercise 2, the arrays functioned as heaps. Why was the first implementation able to do traversals that the second could not do?

 5. In the first implementation of Exercise 2b suppose that, after a node is accessed and processed, it is simply put onto the available space list.

 a. Is the head of the tree a dangling reference?

 b. Are fixed-size or variable-size nodes being dealt with?

 c. After your answer to Exercise 2b is traversed, what will be garbage, and what will be on the list of available space?

 6. This is the same as Exercise 5, except that, after a node is accessed and processed, it is *not* put onto the available space list. After the binary tree has been traversed, the head of the tree is set to null.

 7. Why is compaction not necessary with fixed-size nodes?

 8. Suppose Example 12.3 deals with three binary trees. Each node has an integer valued INFO, LEFTPTR, and RIGHTPTR field. The stack needs elements that are also integer valued. An integer array of length L is used as a heap in which nodes of the binary trees and the stack are stored. Assume one additional field is used for each node to indicate its length. Design a storage allocation scheme and write an appropriate AVAIL function.

 9. a. Suppose in Exercise 8, when a node of a binary tree is deleted, its predecessor node will be changed to point to the left successor of the deleted node. Write a procedure DELETE that carries out this deletion and also returns the storage used by the deleted node to a list of available space.

 b. How would the DELETE procedure change if reference counters were used as a reclamation scheme?

 10. Write AVAIL for the two-way circular list implementation for

 a. randomly ordered list entries

 b. list entries in order by size

 c. list entries in order by address

 11. Write AVAIL for the buddy system implementation.

 12. Write a RECLAIM procedure for the buddy system.

 13. Why will garbage collection take a longer time when many nodes are in use and a shorter time when few nodes are in use?

 14. What are the disadvantages of reference counters compared to garbage collection?

 15. Write a procedure to traverse a list-structure with shared sublists to reclaim storage of a sublist whose reference count has gone to zero.

 16. Write a procedure to insert a node in a threaded binary tree T. The node is to be inserted as the node accessed next in an inorder traversal of T after NODE.PRED is accessed.

17. Write a procedure to delete a node in a threaded binary tree T. The deleted node is to be NODE.P.

18. Write a procedure to return a pointer to the predecessor of NODE.P in a threaded binary tree T.

19. Write a procedure to read information into the INFO fields of a binary tree T, implemented using pointer variables. The INFO fields will contain character strings of up to twenty characters. The input is given in the order that the INFO fields would be accessed in a preorder traversal of T.

20. How will your solution to Exercise 19 change if the binary tree T is implemented as a threaded tree?

21. Implement the transformation of Section 6.6.1 using a list implementation for the stack. The binary tree is implemented using pointer variables as a threaded tree. Assume the general tree is given by a two-dimensional array of size 50×50. If the $[I, J]$ entry of the array is 1, then NODE J is a successor of NODE I; if the $[I, J]$ entry is 0, then NODE J is not a successor of NODE I.

22. This is the same as Exercise 21 except the general tree will be given by a list of successors for each node. These lists should be pointed to by pointer variables, one for each node of the general tree. The binary tree should be a link-inversion tree.

23. Suppose input, representing a general tree, is given as a sequence of pairs. A pair I, J implies that NODE J is a successor of NODE I. A sentinel pair has its I, J values equal. For example, the general tree of Figure 6.13 might be input as B,F A,C D,J I,K I,L C,H B,E I,M A,D D,I A,B B,G X,X. Write a procedure that will create the successor lists of Exercise 22.

24. Simulate the preorder traversal implementation for the link-inversion traversal of the binary tree of Figure 12.10.

25. Simulate the preorder traversal implementation for the Robson traversal of the binary tree of Figure 12.10.

26. Why will there always be enough storage in the binary tree, during a Robson traversal, for the stack of root nodes whose left subtrees are nonnull, whose traversal has been completed, and whose right subtrees are being traversed?

27. What purpose does the stack of Exercise 26 serve in the Robson traversal?

28. Write a procedure to do an inorder traversal of a threaded binary tree T.

29. Write a procedure to do a link-inversion traversal of a binary tree T assuming the tree is implemented using pointer variables.

30. Write a procedure to do a Robson traversal of a binary tree T assuming the tree is implemented using pointer variables.

☐ Suggested Assignment

a. Write and run a procedure to copy a list-structure with shared sublists. Use pointer variables.

b. Explain how storage may be reclaimed if all nodes of the copied list-structure that have nonnull sublists are deleted.

c. Why would we not write recursive versions of the three stackless traversals?

d. Simulate the different implementations for the list of available space of Section 12.3 choosing a number of request and return distributions.

Bibliography

Adelson-Velskii, G. M., and Landis, Y. M. [1962]. "An Algorithm for the Organization of Information." *Doklady Akademia Nauk*. 146(2), 263–266; *Soviet Mathematics*. 3, 1259–1263.

Aho, A. V., Hopcroft, J. E., and Ullman, J. D. [1983]. *Data Structures and Algorithms*. Reading, Mass.: Addison-Wesley.

Aho, A. V., and Ullman, J. D. [1972]. *The Theory of Parsing, Translation, and Compiling*, Vol. 1. Englewood Cliffs, N.J.: Prentice-Hall.

Aho, A. V., and Ullman, J. D. [1977]. *Principles of Compiler Design*. Reading, Mass.: Addison-Wesley.

Amble, O., and Knuth, D. E. [1974]. "Ordered Hash Tables." *Computer Journal* 17(2): 135–142.

Austing, R. H., et al., eds. [1979]. "Curriculum '78: Recommendations for the Undergraduate Program in Computer Science — A Report of the ACM Curriculum Committee on Computer Science." *Communications of the Association for Computing Machinery* 22(3): 147–166.

Baase, S. [1978]. *Computer Algorithms: Introduction to Design and Analysis*. Reading, Mass.: Addison-Wesley.

Barnes, J. G. P. [1982]. *Programming in Ada*. Reading, Mass.: Addison-Wesley.

Barron, D. W. [1968]. *Recursive Techniques in Programming*. New York: American-Elsevier.

Bayer, R., and McCreight, E. M. [1972]. "Organization and Maintenance of Large Ordered Indices." *Acta Informatica* 1(3):173–189.

Bays, C. [1977]. "A Comparison of Next-Fit, First-Fit, and Best-Fit." *Communications of the Association for Computing Machinery* 20(3):191–192.

Bell, D. A., and Deen, S. M. [1984]. "Hash Trees Versus B-Trees." *Computer Journal* 27(3): 218–224.

Bell, J. R. [1970]. "The Quadratic Quotient Method: A Hash Code Eliminating Secondary Clustering." *Communications of the Association for Computing Machinery* 13(2): 107–109.

Ben-Ari, M. [1982]. *Principles of Concurrent Programming*. London: Prentice-Hall International.

Bentley, J. L. [1982]. *Writing Efficient Programs*. Englewood Cliffs, N.J.: Prentice-Hall.

Bird, R. S. [1977a]. "Improving Programs by the Introduction of Recursion." *Communications of the Association for Computing Machinery* 20(11):856–863.

Bird, R. S. [1977b]. "Notes on Recursion Elimination." *Communications of the Association for Computing Machinery* 20(6):434–439.

Bitner, J. R., and Reingold, E. M. [1975]. "Backtrack Programming Techniques." *Communications of the Association for Computing Machinery* 18:651–656.

Bowles, K. L. [1980]. *Beginner's Guide for the UCSD Pascal System*. New York: McGraw-Hill.

Brooks, F. P. [1974]. *The Mythical Man Month*. Reading, Mass.: Addison-Wesley.

Bunneman, P., and Levy, L. [1980]. "The Towers of Hanoi Problem." *Information Processing Letters 10*:243–244.

Comer, D. [1979]. "The Ubiquitous B-Tree." *Computing Surveys 11*:121–137.

Crane, C. A. [1972]. Linear Lists and Priority Queues as Balanced Binary Trees. Unpublished Ph.D. Dissertation. Stanford University, Stanford, Calif.

Dahl, O.-J., Dijkstra, E. W., and Hoare, C. A. R. [1972]. *Structured Programming*. New York: Academic Press.

Dijkstra, E. W. [1972]. *Notes on Structured Programming*. London: Academic Press.

Dobosiewicz, W. [1978]. "Sorting by Distributive Partitioning." *Information Processing Letters 7*(1):1–6.

Earley, J. [1970]. "An Efficient Context-Free Parsing Algorithm." *Communications of the Association for Computing Machinery 13*(2):94–102.

Elson, M. [1975]. *Data Structures*. Chicago, Ill.: Science Research Associates.

Fagin, R., Nievergelt, J., Pippenger, N., and Strong. R. H. [1978]. *Extendible Hashing—A Fast Access Method for Dynamic Files*. Research Rept. RJ2305. IBM Research Division, Yorktown Heights, N.Y.

Feller, W. [1975]. *An Introduction to Probability Theory and Its Applications*. 2nd ed. New York: Wiley.

Findlay, W., and Watt, D. A. [1981]. *Pascal: An Introduction to Methodical Programming*. 2nd ed. Rockville, Md.: Computer Science Press.

Floyd, R. W. [1964]. "Algorithm 245: Treesort3." *Communications of the Association for Computing Machinery 7*(12):701.

Floyd, R. W. [1979]. "The Paradigms of Programming," *Communications of the Association for Computing Machinery 22*(8):455–460.

Fredkin, E. H. [1960]. "Trio Memory." *Communications of the Association for Computing Machinery 3*(9):490–500.

Garwick, J. V. [1964]. "Data Storage in Compilers." *BIT 4*:137–140.

Golomb, S. W., and Baumert, L. D. [1965]. "Backtrack Programming." *Journal of the Association for Computing Machinery 12*(4):516–524.

Greene, D. H., and Knuth, D. E. [1981]. *Mathematics for the Analysis of Algorithms*. Cambridge, Mass.: Birkhauser, Boston.

Grogono, P. [1980]. *Programming in Pascal*. Rev. ed. Reading, Mass.: Addison-Wesley.

Hirschberg, D. S. [1973]. "A Class of Dynamic Memory Allocation Algorithms." *Communications of the Association for Computing Machinery 16*(10):615–618.

Hoare, C. A. R. [1962]. "Quicksort." *Computer Journal 5*(1):10–15.

Horbibe, Y., and Nemetz, T. [1979]. "On the Max-Entropy Rule for a Binary Search Tree." *Acta Informatica 12*:63–72.

Horowitz, E. [1983]. *Programming Languages: A Grand Tour*. Rockville, Md.: Computer Science Press.

Horowitz, E., and Sahni, S. [1976]. *Fundamentals of Data Structures*. Woodland Hills, Calif.: Computer Science Press.

Horowitz, E., and Sahni, S. [1978]. *Fundamentals of Computer Algorithms*. Potomac, Md.: Computer Science Press.

Hu, T. C., and Tucker, A. C. [1971]. "Optimal Computer Search Trees and Variable-Length Alphabetic Codes." *SIAM Journal of Applied Mathematics 21*(4):514–532.

Huffman, D. A. [1952]. "A Method for the Construction of Minimum-Redundancy Codes." *Proceedings of the Institute of Radio Engineers 40*:1098–1101.

Hull, M. E. C. [1984]. "A Parallel View of Stable Marriages." *Information Processing Letters 18*:63–66.

Jensen, K., and Wirth, N. [1978]. *Pascal User Manual and Report*. 2nd ed. New York: Springer-Verlag.

Johnson, D. B. [1975]. "Priority Queues with Update and Finding Minimum Spanning Trees." *Information Processing Letters* 4(3):53–57.

Jones, W. B. [1982]. *Programming Concepts: A Second Course*. Englewood Cliffs, N.J.: Prentice-Hall.

Keller, A. [1982]. *A First Course in Computer Programming*. New York: McGraw-Hill.

Kernighan, B. W., and Plauger, P. J. [1978]. *The Elements of Programming Style*. 2nd ed. New York: McGraw-Hill.

Kernighan, B. W., and Plauger, P. J. [1981]. *Software Tools in Pascal*. Reading, Mass.: Addison-Wesley.

Knuth, D. E. [1971]. "Optimum Binary Search Trees." *Acta Informatica* 1(1):14–25.

Knuth, D. E. [1973a]. *The Art of Computer Programming. Vol. 1: Fundamental Algorithms*. Reading, Mass.: Addison-Wesley.

Knuth, D. E. [1973b]. *The Art of Computer Programming. Vol. 3: Searching and Sorting*. Reading, Mass.: Addison-Wesley.

Koffman, E. B. [1985]. *Problem Solving and Structured Programming in Pascal*. Reading, Mass.: Addison-Wesley.

Koffman, E. B., Stemple, D., and Wardle, C. E. [1985]. "Recommended Curriculum for CSE, 1984." *Communications of the Association for Computing Machinery* 28(8):815–818.

Korsh, J. F. [1981]. "Greedy Binary Search Trees Are Nearly Optimal." *Information Processing Letters* 13(1):16–19.

Korsh, J. F. [1982]. "Growing Nearly Optimal Binary Search Trees." *Information Processing Letters* 14(3):139–143.

Korsh, J. F., and Laison, G. [1983]. "A Multiple-Stack Manipulation Procedure." *Communications of the Association for Computing Machinery* 26(11):921–923.

Kruse, R. L. [1984]. *Data Structures and Program Design*. Englewood Cliffs, N.J.: Prentice-Hall.

Larson, P. [1978]. "Dynamic Hashing." BIT 18(2):184–201.

Lin, S., and Kernighan, B. W. [1973]. "A Heuristic Algorithm for the Traveling Salesman Problem." *Operations Research* 21:498–516.

Linger, R. C., Mills, H. D., and Witt, B. I. [1979]. *Structured Programming Theory and Practice*. Reading, Mass.: Addison-Wesley.

Litwin, W. [1980]. "Linear Hashing: A New Tool for File and Table Addressing." *Proceedings of the Sixth International Conference on Very Large Data Bases*. Montreal, pp. 212–223.

Martin, W. A. [1971]. "Sorting." *Computing Surveys* 3:148–174.

Maurer, H. A., and Williams, M. R. [1972]. *A Collection of Programming Problems and Techniques*. Englewood Cliffs, N.J.: Prentice-Hall.

Maurer, W. D. [1968]. "An Improved Hash Code for Scatter Storage." *Communications of the Association for Computing Machinery* 11(1):35–37.

Maurer, W. D., and Lewis, T. G. [1975]. "Hash Table Methods." *Computing Surveys* 7(1): 5–20.

Mehlhorn, K. [1975]. "Nearly Optimal Binary Search Trees." *Acta Informatica* 5:287–295.

Mehlhorn, K. [1977]. "A Best Possible Bound for the Weighted Path Length of Binary Search Trees." *Society of Industrial and Applied Mathematics, Journal of Computers* 6(2): 235–239.

Morris, R. [1968]. "Scatter Storage Techniques." *Communications of the Association for Computing Machinery* 11(1):35–44.

Naur, P. (ed.). [1963]. "Revised Report on the Algorithmic Language ALGOL60," *Communications of the Association for Computing Machinery* 6:1–17.

Nievergelt, J. [1974]. "Binary Search Trees and File Organization." *Computing Surveys* 6(3): 195–207.

Peterson, J. L. [1980]. *Design of a Spelling Program: An Experiment in Program Design*. Lecture Notes in Computer Science. New York: Springer-Verlag.

Peterson, J. L., and Norman, T. A. [1977]. "Buddy Systems." *Communications of the Association for Computing Machinery* 20(6):431–435.

Pratt, T. W. [1975]. *Programming Languages: Design and Implementation*. Englewood Cliffs, N.J.: Prentice-Hall.

Reingold, E. M., and Hansen, W. J. [1983]. Boston, Mass.: Little, Brown.

Robson, J. M. [1973]. "An Improved Algorithm for Traversing Binary Trees without Auxiliary Stack." *Information Processing Letters* 2:12–14.

Robson, J. M. [1977]. "A Bounded Storage Algorithm for Copying Cyclic Structures." *Communications of the Association for Computing Machinery* 20(6):431–433.

Robson, J. M. [1979]. "The Height of Binary Search Trees." *Austrian Computer Journal* 11(4): 151–153.

Schorr, H., and Waite, W. M. [1967]. "An Efficient Machine-Independent Procedure for Garbage Collection in Various List Structures." *Communications of the Association for Computing Machinery* 10(8):501–506.

Sedgewick, R. [1977]. "Permutation Generation Methods." *Computing Surveys* 9:137–164.

Sedgewick, R. [1983]. *Algorithms*. Reading, Mass.: Addison-Wesley.

Shell, D. L. [1959]. "A High-Speed Sorting Procedure." *Communications of the Association for Computing Machinery* 2:30–32.

Skvarcius, R. [1984]. *Problem Solving Using Pascal Algorithm Development and Programming Concepts*. Boston, Mass.: PWS Publishers.

Standish, T. A. [1980]. *Data Structure Techniques*. Reading, Mass.: Addison-Wesley.

Stanfel, G. L. [1970]. "Tree Structures for Optimal Searching." *Journal of the Association for Computing Machinery* 19(3):508–517.

Stone, H. S. [1971]. "Parallel Processing with the Perfect Shuffle." *IEEE Transactions on Computers* C-20:153–161.

Stone, H. S. [1972]. *Introduction to Computer Organization and Data Structures*. New York: McGraw-Hill.

Stone, H. S. [1980]. *Introduction to Computer Architecture*. 2nd ed. Chicago, Ill.: Science Research Associates.

Sussenguth, E. H. Jr. [1963]. "Use of Tree Structures for Processing Files." *Communications of the Association for Computing Machinery* 6(5):272–279.

Tenenbaum, A. M., and Augenstein, M. J. [1981]. *Data Structures Using Pascal*. Englewood Cliffs, N.J.: Prentice-Hall.

Tremblay, J. P., and Sorenson, P. G. [1984]. *An Introduction to Data Structures with Applications*. 2nd ed. New York: McGraw-Hill.

Ullman, J. D. [1982]. *Principles of Database Systems*. Rockville, Md.: Computer Science Press.

Van Wijngaarden, A., et al. [1975]. "Revised Report on the Algorithmic Language ALGOL 68." *Acta Informatica* 5:1–236.

Walsh, T. R. [1982]. "The Towers of Hanoi Revisited: Moving the Rings by Counting the Moves." *Information Processing Letters* 15(2):64–67.

Weinberg, G. M. [1971]. *The Psychology of Computer Programming*. New York: Van Nostrand.

Welsh, J., and Elder, J. [1982]. *Introduction to Pascal*. 2nd ed. Englewood Cliffs, N.J.: Prentice-Hall.

Wexelblat, R. L. [1981]. *History of Programming Languages*. New York: Academic Press.

Williams, J. W. J. [1964]. "Algorithm 232: Heapsort." *Communications of the Association for Computing Machinery* 7(6):347–348.

Wirth, N. [1971a]. "The Programming Language Pascal." *Acta Informatica 1*:35–36.

Wirth, N. [1971b]. "The Design of a Pascal Compiler." *Software-Practice 1*:309–333.

Wirth, N. [1973]. *Systematic Programming: An Introduction.* Englewood Cliffs, N.J.: Prentice-Hall.

Wirth, N. [1976]. *Algorithms + Data Structures = Programs.* Englewood Cliffs, N.J.: Prentice-Hall.

Index